P9-ARZ-799

COMPUTERS, AUTOMATION, AND SOCIETY

THE IRWIN SERIES IN INFORMATION
AND
DECISION SCIENCES

Consulting Editors
Robert B. Fetter *Yale University*
Claude McMillan *University of Colorado*

COMPUTERS, AUTOMATION, AND SOCIETY

EDWARD J. LAURIE
San José State University

1979 **RICHARD D. IRWIN, INC.** Homewood, Illinois 60430
Irwin-Dorsey Limited Georgetown, Ontario L7G 4B3

ISBN 0-256-02139-2
Library of Congress Catalog Card No. 78–61193

Printed in the United States of America

1 2 3 4 5 6 7 8 9 0 ML 6 5 4 3 2 1 0 9

PROLOGUE

This is not a book about how to operate computers or one in praise of current computer applications. Rather, I wish to explore with you certain basic qualities which make the computer the rare and special device it really is. In doing so, I must, of course, present a number of ideas—different views of our current world. These views are intended to sum up a long experience in the computer field, trigger discussion, create some reasonable debate and thought. Only thus can we (you and I) examine the paths we have tread so far in putting to work one of the most complex devices in the long history of the human race.

We, together, will have a look at some of the major institutions and organizations which, united, make up what we call our American culture, society, and civilization. We will look at them from a somewhat different view than is ordinary. We will question whether or not the computer has turned out in quite the way we all expected. This must be done because we must seek thought rather than salvation through the machine. What is important is to examine, question, talk, and think. Machines can, after all, dominate only fools. Wise people will always wish to ponder and to ask questions.

In the early part of the book the approach to matters is historical, not to get them out of the way, but because that is how events actually occurred—one at a time, over time. We will interpret, where we can, some of these events and where they have led.

Some of what is explored is simple, some complex, some downright scary—it has been that kind of a century. In some ways the computer could actually work to change the values and the systems by which we live and by which we work. We ought to try to understand how all may come about.

Peter Drucker of management fame and gentle cynicism, says computer people are ignorant, arrogant, and too enchanted with their own tools. He does not regard computer experts as dangerous except as management neglects to manage them. In this he well might be correct. To the degree management loses control to computer people because what they say seems mysterious, management has aided arrogance and compounded ignorance. A tool is a useful tool only to the degree it is handled with skill and knowledge and a keen sense of its limits. This principle holds true for the general public as well. We all must know something about computers, how they work, how they can be misused, how they can affect our lives and our attitudes. What we know can never mislead us.

Each of the tools of the human race seem, in themselves, to be something of an extension of the abilities of the human being. In the computer we have our first full-fledged attempt to mechanize some of the functions of the human brain. Such a device, complex and powerful, is dangerous if misused—but, couldn't we say that about any of the major tools that really count?

I am much in debt to H. H. Sayani of the University of Maryland; Patricia Vacca of California State University, Dominiquez Hills; William Keys of Long Beach City College, California; and Edward Rategan of the College of San Mateo for careful reading and much constructive criticism of the manuscript in its original form.

I am even deeper in debt to Grace Hertlein of the California State University at Chico for the most thorough review of a manuscript I have ever read and for so many excellent suggestions that I could not fit them all in. My promise to her is that I have saved the criticisms and intend to use those I couldn't use this time, at any future time I have the opportunity.

A very helpful senior secretary who works within hailing distance of my own typewriter said the other day that I ought to identify this book as, "words by Edward Laurie, spelling by Lillian Travis." She is correct. I should, and here I have done so.

Naturally, I alone must carry the responsibility for any errors or omissions which have crept into the manuscript. The good people listed above did the very best they could with me—the only material they had immediately at hand.

December 1978 EDWARD J. LAURIE

CONTENTS

CHAPTER 1

THE PROBLEM

PURPOSE OF THE CHAPTER

In this chapter we are interested in stating the problem which is to be the heart of the book. That done, we will explore a single example of technology and how it grew beyond our wildest dreams. Then we will try to define, in the easiest way possible, a number of terms which we will be using all through the text.

At the end of the chapter we will provide a short summary of all that has gone before. We will introduce a number of highlight questions which will call your attention to the important matters discussed. And finally, we will recommend a few readings for those of you interested in learning more about the material in this chapter.

TERMS AND CONCEPTS

We will, in this chapter, give definitions to the following terms and concepts:

society	civilization
culture	bureaucracy
management	mechanization
physical power	intellectual power
high technology	automation
American civilization	computers
institutions of civilization	

It is not vital that you agree with the definitions. It is important that you understand them so what is said in the book makes some sense.

THE PROBLEM

Of all the many creatures that live upon the earth, it is the human animal who has reached the top in technological development and, perhaps, self-deceit. We like to congratulate ourselves upon our achievements and we like to deny that we have lost control over some of them. If we have so erred, we cannot begin to regain control until, like Frankenstein, we are willing to admit we have created a real monster or two. Once such a beast has been uncovered, and its virtues and its failings defined, we can put it under careful rule and thus make sure it remains our servant and never becomes our untamed master. Such controls as we might wish to forge should be based on knowledge and not prejudice or fear, or we deny to our own creations the power to do us good as surely as we deny to them the ability to do us evil.

One of the possible wayward devices of which we speak is the modern electronic computer. In just three decades it has moved from a mysterious electronic marvel, hidden here and there in mathematical laboratories, to a workaday machine which simply cannot be avoided by anyone having even the most casual contact with the major institutions of our society.

The computer is credited with the depersonalization of our lives, with the role of disemployer, and is blamed for nearly every printing and arithmetic error we can find. The device, rightly or wrongly, carries the credit for the growth of business into multinational giants, for certain kinds of lies and deceits in politics and government, for the mishandlings in our mail and telephone systems, and just about any other social problem you care to run across and name.

Are any of these claims true? Yes, some of them are. The only way we are going to know for certain, though, is to understand what a computer can and cannot do, what the major institutions of our own society are, and how the computer is integrated into these operating social systems. Then we can begin to make sane judgments about what curbs should be put on the device, or what freedoms should be extended to it.

The computer is an achievement of high technology. As with other technological creations, the computer has many side effects. Some of these were expected and others were not. There are certainly more to come, if for no other reason than the computer is going to continue to be applied to more and more intellectual tasks in more and more of our institutions.

We want to know just what effect we can expect from the use of high technology in the American society. Will the American civilization take on new and unexpected features as automation and computing develop further? Will the American family survive social change? Will the society be able to keep its democratic form in the face of the need for long-term planning and predictability? Will control of information bring the private enterprise system further into the hands of ever fewer and more powerful people? Can the government or any of its agencies misuse information to gain dictatorial control over the lives of its citizens? Will the American desire for continued privacy be ended by huge electronic files of information called data banks?

We will have occasion to see what effect the computer might have on the organizational structure of the bureaucracy as it applies to government, to the institutionalized religions (churches), and to enterprises. We are interested in finding out whether or not automation and the computer will affect the value systems of the society as a whole.

THE METHOD

We are going to have to know a reasonable amount of information about the computer if we are to understand both its advantages and its limitations. To make the job as interesting as possible we are going to follow the computer through some of the more famous aspects of its historical development. We will try to understand how a computer is fed information, how it stores such material, how it can operate (calculate and do logic). We will try to understand, not the details of programming, but the concepts. We will discuss the different levels of language which computers can handle. And in Appendix A we will introduce BASIC, one of the simpler and frequently used computer programming languages. A knowledge of a computer language is not vital to understanding this book, but it will make many points clearer. Since Appendix A is self-contained, you can study it at any point on your way through the text.

When we have sufficient knowledge to be able to understand the abilities and limitations of these "intellectual map followers" (for that is what computers do); we will attempt to see what possible effects they can have on our various social institutions. We are going to be concerned about exciting potentials in the future: data bases, management techniques, computers as utilities, intellectual symbiosis (the working together of people and computers to solve problems), automation, the office in the home, credit and money, and possible fourth-generation computers.

Most important of all, we want to break way from enchantment with the latest computer gadgets. That is, we want to be able to understand what is basic to computer operation and application. We must see the forest even though, from time to time, we will be interested in individual trees. We also are going to give some serious attention to the triumphs and failings of the host of bright young people who have made the computer world their way of life.

There are very serious dangers in enchantment with machinery and systems. There are even deadlier sins to be committed when the language spoken by a group of experts is not easily understood by those who ought to be in control of their own destiny. Naturally, everyone takes pride in a knowledge of a specialized field and in the achievements this can bring about. But if one hides behind a special screen of formal language in order to hide one's limitations and weaknesses from others, and to attempt to prevent a genuine and realistic examination of what one can and cannot do, it is to society's interest to deprive such persons of such power as effectively and quickly as possible. The weapon to use is knowledge.

Let us explore an earlier example of applied technology and see what some of the unexpected and unusual side effects have been. This will give us an idea of the range and depth of changes we might expect.

THE WHEEL CULTURE

Once upon a time, in the senior schools, one could hear a particularly interesting and revealing question: "Do you have wheels for the weekend?" Wheels meant automobile. The auto meant freedom, mobility, and certain rights of independent judgment. The lucky person with a car could go almost anywhere, be quite comfortable doing it, and along with some 50,000 fellow Americans a year, die as a bloody pulp on a concrete ribbon that wanders the nation in search of scenery or cities.

If you go to your local drugstore and browse through the magazine racks, you will note a rather large collection of magazines about the automobile. Each of these magazines deals with some different kind of car or some different aspect of cars. From hot rods to limousines, the magazines are specialized. The trunk of the tree is the car, but the tree has many different branches.

Let us do a little thought experiment. Let us imagine that 40 years ago you flew over the city of Los Angeles and made note of its highways and roads. Maybe you even had a chance to take a picture of the city from very high up.

Now, 40 years later, let us assume you flew at the same height and took a picture of the same area. Compare the two pictures in terms of the number of roads and freeways and the number of cars upon those roads and freeways. The difference should be almost overwhelming. Clearly, roads and cars have multiplied amazingly. Clearly, the air is dirtier and more of the land is taken up with roads at the cost of lovely farms and green hillsides and pleasant streams.

When Henry Ford and others put the automobile into mass production they did not foresee the spreading concrete cancer near our cities, nor did they foresee the fact that the automobile in the mass would spew poisons into the air and quite possibly kill us by the millions. They thought they would provide a means by which the farmer could get to town and do the shopping. They thought they had provided a mechanical horse which would not befoul the streets of the city with manure and draw flies and disease. In fact, they thought they had discovered a cheap means of transportation which would be cleaner and healthier than the horse and buggy. Well, for a while, they did. But they did not predict the side effects of such massive spreading of a good idea:

1. Cars would multiply until their numbers became so dense they would represent a public problem and a general danger to health.
2. The roads required for swift automobile movement would eat up a large proportion of the cultivable land of the United States.
3. The automobile would choke the inner cities to death.
4. The city would move to the country, inventing what we now call suburbia.
5. The motel, the drive-in movie, the drive-in restaurant, and the drive-in bank would isolate many human beings from their fellows and prevent conversation among them while they transacted the ordinary business of living.
6. The housewife in suburbia would have to face a special form of solitude and isolation unless she, too, had a car and she, too, could leave home of a morning for the day.
7. The demand for gasoline and other oil by-products would reach

such proportions as to make the United States of America dependent on imports and hence vulnerable to economic blackmail.

8. Wars could and would be fought over the location of oil pipelines. The right of one nation to demand, by force, the resources of another would be thought acceptable in certain cases.
9. The automobile would kill more Americans than all our wars combined. Automobile accidents would become so common as to hardly command a major headline in the newspapers.
10. The automobile would change the cultural habits and the morals of a nation. When you can drive far away from home you are, in fact, a free stranger.
11. The automobile can give even the frailest driver an awful sense of power. People who would never be rude or aggressive on foot can become so in a car. A ton or two of active machinery in the hands of the emotionally unstable is, regrettably, a lethal weapon.

Surely, given these grim facts, we will junk our cars and go about our business and our living in other ways. We most certainly will not! We have learned the value of mobility and the joy of freedom.

Also, we have increased the length of our lives by the amount of time we have abolished in the process of getting from here to there. This increase in activity time is more important to us than the risk of death and dismemberment. Let us not bypass the increase in activity life-length too casually. We will mention it again later in the text—it is one of the benefits of technological achievement.

What has all this about cars to do with computers? It is a warning—that and only that. What happened to us with the automobile could very well happen to us with the computer. We do not know what the computer will do to our private lives, our thinking ability, our flexibility. We can surely expect to be as surprised in the case of the mass use of the computer as we were with the result of the mass use of the automobile. We didn't do too much thinking, early on, about the possible dangers of the car. It would pay us to learn from our oversight and do some very hard thinking about the possible dangers of the mass use of computers. In this book we will try to do just that.

We must now turn our attention to a number of general definitions so that in the remainder of this book we will know what we are talking about. We need to define society, culture, civilization, bureaucracy, management, and mechanization in some simple and useful way.

We want to discuss, however briefly, the meaning of physical power, on the one hand, and the meaning of intellectual power, on the other. And we are going to explore the terms *high technology, automation,* and the *computer.* We can then turn our attention to the institutions of civilization in general and the form those institutions have taken in America in particular.

Oddly enough, it is not important whether the definitions of terms used in this book are true. What is important is that you understand the definitions so you can follow the logic. Doing so, you can think independently and be as critical as you please. Definitions, after all, are never true or false. As Humpty Dumpty put it in *Through the Looking-Glass:*

> "When I use a word," Humpty Dumpty said in a rather scornful tone, "it means just what I choose it to mean—neither more nor less."
>
> "The question is," said Alice, "whether you can make words mean so many different things."
>
> "The question is," said Humpty Dumpty, "which is to be the master,—that's all."

SOCIETY

Societies are collections of people who have banded together to achieve some common ends. Usually the ends are economic and definitive. A social group wishes to continue to exist both as a collection of individuals and as a defined unit. If the individuals in the set are fed, clothed, and warmed by their activities (the economic goals), they will survive as individuals. The definitive goal of the group is to provide individuals within it with an identity. Samples would be: "I am an American." "I am a human being." "I am one of this nation's elite."

The members of the society wish to know who they are, how they relate to other members of the group, how the group in turn relates to the world at large, how they are to behave, and what the goals of existence are.

We believe, but we do not *know,* societies probably began when one or more families, who were related, got together for mutual protection and mutual work to survive. Such a group is usually called a clan.

CULTURE

Any society will have a culture. Culture includes at least a collection of traditions (though the reason for them may long have been forgotten), a set of survival techniques and artifacts, a collection of artistic artifacts, a collection of mores—that is, methods of behavior which are defined as acceptable or unacceptable, which contain a defined set of interrelationships among its members, which hold a cosmic view: how the society fits into the world at large.

Societies will, sometimes almost by accident, develop a technology. The problem is that the technology can often have hidden effects on the culture and hence upon the society that developed it. If the society cannot recognize the influence of the technology upon its own culture, it cannot predict the kind of future it will have. If the future cannot be predicted, the element of total surprise could be fatal to the particular society as a society.

All societies have cultures. But not all societies are civilized. We need to turn our attention to that somewhat difficult matter.

CIVILIZATION

During the ninth century, England, which had the beginnings of a civilization, also had a prayer: "O Lord, protect us from the wrath of the Northmen." The Northmen were the Vikings. The Vikings had a fascinating, complex, and long-established culture. But of them, we can surely say they were *not* civilized. For civilization involves a certain elegance of the spirit that permits the differences of others to exist unattacked, yes even admired, for their very strangeness. In short, what we call civilization is very much concerned with the matter of preservation and tolerance. Cultures are more narrowly concerned with survival and identity.

Technology is one of the main support systems of civilization. Almost all cultures have some form of technology, usually primitive. But if a culture is to turn into a civilization, it requires a sophisticated technology. The Egyptians had it. The Greeks had it. The Romans had it. The English had it. The Americans, at least the thoughtful ones, aren't sure whether they have it yet or not. They don't want to claim the best technology in the world because, historically minded, they have seen that all those who claim the highest civilization and the highest technology soon die as nations and as empires. Perhaps humility is the road to salvation—perhaps not. We can at least admit, though, that we have a very high-powered technology which can put men on the moon, send exploration vehicles to Mars, and think about a closer examination of the planet Saturn. If we are not yet totally civilized, we are perhaps off to a good running start.

Our technology needs to bring about a division of tasks such as will permit the existence of a rather large group of individuals devoted to problems of the mind. Who are we? How did we get here? Where are we going? What's it all about, Alfy? In sum, a civilization has come to birth when the witch doctor has turned into a philosopher, and not before. Civilization is born when art is recognized as art. Civilization exists when we can meet someone and say of him or her, "This is a kind, gentle, knowledgeable, understanding person who shows a touch of elegance."

Or, and this may be the most important point of all, perhaps civilization exists when one can pause in the headlong technological run and ask serious questions about whether our mechanical achievements are leading us to humanity, to comfort, and to pleasure. If the benefits are doubtful or debatable, what then the use of the polished chrome and the purring machine? This is a good question for the civilized being to ask—a nasty thought, however, for the pure technologist.

We stop. We have explored dangerous waters in a rather crude way. We will have to leave to lengthier books the problem of a clearer definition of society, culture, and civilization. We have said enough for our own narrow purposes. We hope these definitions are somewhere close to reality, but it is not worth our time to nit-pick.

BUREAUCRACY

Bureaucracy, as we use the term in this text, has to do with the formal organization through which the government, the church, or the enterprise achieves its goals. A bureaucratic-type organization involves defined tasks which can be filled by any individual able to perform them. The slots in the hierarchy depend upon ability, not upon blood relationships. The various positions in the administrative structure of a bureaucracy are carefully defined as to duties, responsibilities, and salary. A family could not constitute a bureaucracy, by definition, because the relative powers of its members are determined by sex, age, and family connection. A bureaucratic family would be a flat contradiction of terms.

Bureaucracy has earned itself a rather bad name of late. In part, this is due to the assumption that size and bureaucracy are synonymous, and that size means indifference. We might do well to *paraphrase* Sir Winston Churchill: "A bureaucracy is the worst possible form of organization unless you consider the alternatives." Sir Winston was speaking of democracy, not bureaucracy, but we do not stretch the truth that much with the substitution of terms in the statement. We do not seem to have any genuine alternatives at the present time.

MANAGEMENT

A manager is an individual holding a defined bureaucratic position who functions as a leader. It is the combination of defined power *and* leadership which makes a manager a manager and not an administrator. Since leadership is a relation between an individual and a group, it cannot be a set of qualities possessed by an individual. Hence, it is possible for a manager to fail with one group of individuals and to succeed with another using exactly the same techniques of administration.

When a bureaucracy is *administered* it well deserves all the unhappy adjectives attached to the operation. When a bureaucracy is *managed,* it quite likely attains the goals it was designed to achieve. It may even be efficient!

Management, then, is nothing more or less than the directional activities of a manager. The manager leads people in the enterprise to the acceptance of certain mutually beneficial goals. That done, the manager designs the operational techniques by which the goals will be pursued, and then establishes a system of measurable activities so such movements as do take place can be determined to be either goal-directed or antigoal.

Great difficulties have been created when administrators, who by definition do not know how to function as leaders, identify themselves as managers. When such people make use of computers to administer the activities of an enterprise, they can be credited with all the unhappy adjectives and grim predictions made for a computerized world in the public press. We will be much concerned with this dangerous application of computers in later parts of the text.

MECHANIZATION

Mechanization has to do with the application of physical devices to productive tasks. In the main, these devices make use of other power forms than animal or human muscle. The devices, though active, are not made of living tissue but rather of various metals, plastics, and alloys. The machines to which we refer may be as simple as a cigarette lighter or as complex as a petroleum cracking plant. They are based primarily on the application of the powers of the wheel and the lever.

Mechanical devices require an energy source. Primitive early machines usually involved either human or animal energy. The sled is a transportation machine which required either people or oxen to pull it. Modern machines attempt to avoid animal and human muscle power and make use of other more powerful energy forms—steam, gasoline, electricity, oil, and the atom. Falling water (to drive mills) was probably one of the earliest applications of other-than-muscle energy. In fact, it is still much used to generate another form of power—electricity. Waterfalls are hard to move. But the electricity generated by waterfalls can be moved thousands of miles.

Let us now turn our attention to the matter of power itself. We want to discuss physical power by which work is actually done, and intellectual power by which the work to be done is organized. They can be treated separately. We must, however, constantly remember they are interrelated—one type of power seldom shows up without the other.

PHYSICAL POWER

Technology has brought a number of new forms of physical power to humanity. It began, probably, with the discovery of fire. With fire came steam. Steam drove machinery, though often such machinery was massive and awkward. Then the gasoline engine arrived and with it power in a more compact form. About the same time, the turbine and the electric motor were invented. Here we achieved greater strength in even more compact form than the gasoline engine could provide. Then, as a result of the scientific work conducted during the late 1930s and World War II, came the atom.

Fire can burn. Steam and gasoline can explode. The electric motor can burn or shock. The atom can explode or burn in a slow and deadly way.

Each of our achievements in gaining physical power has been increasingly dangerous when carelessly managed. The danger is in direct proportion to the amount of power achieved. Fire can burn only so long as fuel is provided. Steam can explode or burn only so long as heat is available. Electric motors and other such devices can shock only as long as there is power in the lines of the system. Each of these physical powers will quickly die when neglected. And each of these power sources usually can do only limited and local damage to populations when it has escaped control. But the atom? Ah, that is a horsepower of quite another color. The atom can provide almost unbelievable energy. It can also, out of control, wipe out a city, sink an island, end a civilization with a most effective bang. And neglected, or carelessly treated, it can linger for thousands upon thousands of years poisoning all the life around it. Well, some bacteria are adaptable and very tough. The raging atom cannot end all life, but it can end all the life we find interesting.

The human race and its many societies have learned to live with fire, with steam, with the gasoline engine, and with electrical power. The race is now very much in the process of testing whether or not it can live peacefully with the atom as a power source. Many species, but not all, of living things will surely vanish if we miscalculate. Infinite power brings infinite risk.

We must, however, pause and think a moment. We have been so concerned with physical power in our everyday lives, politics, and aspirations that we have quite neglected the development of another form of power—unseen, like the family ghost, but ever-present. We mean intellectual power.

INTELLECTUAL POWER

Intellectual power—that is, the ability to investigate, to understand, to quantify, to predict, and to simulate—has always been present in one form or another in the long history of humanity. Verbal and symbolic communication will do as two early examples of the human race's developing intellectual power. For if we can signal and if we can talk, we can find common purpose with others of our species. More important, we can pass along what we know and want. And we can receive what others know and want. We can, then, form societies whose complexity and scope are directly related to our ability to communicate.

It is interesting to note that humanity has always helped its own intellectual efforts with mechanical devices, ranging from the simple abacus to the most modern giant computer. In our next chapter we will begin a historical exploration of some of these developments. Here we are concerned to note this second and often misunderstood form of genuine power. Information is the vehicle of organization. Organization is the means to the effective use and spread of power.

Technology, then, has taken two major forms. In the first case, technology has been applied to the development and uses of physical energy through machines to do work, or shorten distance, or extend the day. It also has been used by some people to gain mastery over others—to dominate. A tank is such a device. In the second case, technology has been applied to the development of useful means of communication and calculation. It also has provided the method by

which we deceive and lie to others. Physical power is required by societies to achieve economic survival. Intellectual power is required by societies for organizational survival. These two power forms cannot be separated. We separate them here and discuss them as entities only for purposes of better understanding.

The Industrial Revolution (actually an evolution involving hundreds of years) represents the agonies and joys of human adjustment to the mass mechanization of physical work. The Informational Revolution (which is taking far less time than the Industrial Revolution to come about) represents the ongoing agonies and joys of human adjustment to the mass mechanization of intellectual work. The marriage of physical working machines to intellectual working machines has brought us to what we call "high technology." This marriage is also called "automation."

HIGH TECHNOLOGY

During her adventure in the woods, Goldilocks met three bears—a papa bear, a mama bear, and a baby bear. We know Papa Bear was bigger than Mama Bear and Mama Bear larger than Baby Bear. How big was Baby Bear? Well, he must have been about the size of Goldilocks since she fitted his chair and his bed. Well, how big was Goldilocks? Just about the size of Baby Bear! We have run into something of a circle. We know the relationships between the bears and that's about all. Definitions involving the differences between *ordinary technology* and *high technology* leave us in the same condition. But we will struggle on, anyway.

High technology is closely involved with the processes of microminiaturization of electrical circuits, the development of computers, the generation of refined power forms, and the automation of many repetitive physical and mental tasks. More important, high technology is of such complexity that the creation and design of its equipment often require years of consistent application of effort. The moon shot is a good example—ten years from start to finish. This means planning must take place early in the process and must be followed carefully over an extended time. It also means once you have started this long, expensive process it is going to be very difficult to stop.

Perhaps we can define high technology in terms of the complexity of the task being attempted and the length of time necessary to accomplish the task. Building an ordinary automobile is pretty much an example of ordinary technology. The construction of the car can take place in a single day. The planning for the construction should not require much more than a year or two. If it does, we have an example of poor management and poor planning, not difficult technology. For our own, the American automobile, we must ask hard questions: why our manfacturers cannot effectively raise gas mileage without difficulty, and why our cars require catalytic converters, when many European manufacturers have already raised gasoline mileage and do not require catalytic converters to meet pollution standards. Since Europe and Japan have managed the task (their existing machines prove it), perhaps the problem really is poor management and poor planning. Or maybe earlier planning has been difficult to change. Claiming that something can't be done when it has been done is strange logic.

Building an ecological system to be housed in a rocket to transport astronauts to the moon is an example of the application of high technology. The planning for such an activity must begin about a decade before the expected accomplishment of the task. Vast resources are required and large numbers of intelligent individuals must be brought together. New techniques must be developed, new metals manufactured, new computers designed. The line between simple technology and high technology is certainly fuzzy. But fear not—today's high technology will be tomorrow's simple technology, since we all suffer from the ego of our time.

The planning and time required for the development and use of high technology brings about some of the rigidities and difficulties we want to discuss later in the book. For when one is committed to a ten-year project, one finds it very difficult to stop the process in midstream. By then the investment of money and time and intellectual effort has been so great that the admission of an ill-chosen goal becomes unthinkable. There is serious danger here—let us not treat it lightly nor forget it.

AUTOMATION

Automation is the achievement of self-directing productive activity as a result of the combination of mechanization and computation. That is, a machine is automatic if it is so designed as to be able to follow a specific set of defined operations, without human intervention, which result in an expected product or service. Built into the process is the ability to recognize and correct errors in the process itself. To date there are few if any totally automated manufacturing plants, though a petroleum cracking plant could be said to come passably close to the goal.

Automation requires some interesting rigidities if it is to function in an economically acceptable manner. It is generally understood that an automated plant has to run at 60 percent or more of its maximum capacity in order to repay the investment in physical equipment. More important, the product manufactured during such a capacity run must have a *guaranteed* market in order to make the process worthwhile at all. Further, since the process is by definition automatic, there is no direct connection between productivity and human labor. Maintenance crews might be necessary, as would a few supervisory personnel. These people would be on salary. The salary would have no necessary relationship to the amount of the product produced—whether the plant runs at 60 percent of capacity or at 90 percent. If you think a moment about the matter, you can see we are going to develop a very strange society indeed if we are fully automated: guaranteed markets, fixed wages, minimum amounts of acceptable production, guaranteed sources of raw materials, and very few individuals who do actual physical work upon the product itself.

We are going to be very much concerned with any productive system that has *inherent* rigidities. Bears don't fly and automation doesn't allow certain kinds of flexibilities to the human race.

COMPUTERS

There have been many definitions of computers—some of them rot and rubbish. A computer is an electronic device capable of following an intellectual map. We call the map a program. The computer, by following the program, can do arithmetic and it can do logic. It is not a calculator solely; it is an information machine. It makes use of a simple two-state (binary) number system to accomplish predefined intellectual tasks of potentially great complexity. Given a correct set of procedures and a correct intellectual map to follow, the computer is capable of decision making. It is also capable of what we have previously labeled as intellectual activity. The computer cannot think if we define thinking as what human beings do. The computer can think if we define thinking as problem solving based on a set of carefully defined procedures.

We can write the intellectual map which a computer is to follow in such a way as to include, in the map itself, *methods* of modifying the map! The map can only be modified to the degree of foresight we have had in designing the map to provide the computer with rules of operation. Since the computer can work very rapidly and can explore *all* of the possible pathways designed into the map, it is possible for the computer to discover map-links which, though we designed them, we did not notice. Is this creative thinking? Who knows! The element discovered was inherent in the map (computer program) which was designed—else the element could not have been discovered.

The individual steps by which a computer sniffs its way through a program are so simple, limited, and narrow as to dispel any notion of black magic or "thinking" on the part of the machine. Leave out a single step, with no provision in the program for such a possibility, and the most exquisite and expensive computer comes to a useless halt and twiddles its electronic thumbs until someone with a brain comes along to bail it out.

It is electricity and speed that give the computer its air of magic. Only by understanding the nature of computers and computer operations can we treat the machine with any genuine sense of reality as to its abilities and its limits. We will, during the early chapters of this book, explore the computer just enough to accomplish this proper amount of know-how. We need never fear any device we can understand, and, in the understanding, unplug if necessary.

Let us now turn our attention to some of the institutions of civilization which will make use of both automation and computing to achieve their several ends.

THE INSTITUTIONS OF CIVILIZATION

Civilizations may be said to be supported by four interacting human institutions:

1. The family.
2. The government.
3. Institutionalized religion (churches).
4. The enterprise.

These basic institutions may take many different forms. In one civilization the family includes a father, a mother, and probably children. In another society it may include one husband, many wives, and many children. In yet another, one wife, many husbands, and possibly children may define a family. Around this central core may cluster all manner of relations—grandparents, uncles, aunts, cousins, and so on.

At one time in the history of the human race, the family was the basic economic unit. This may not necessarily be true anymore. The family, however, is still the most common elementary unit in societies. It is often held together by legal, blood, and emotional ties.

The family's economic fate has often hinged on technology, and with this dependency we find its self-view changing dramatically from time to time. The possible effect of the computer on the family's definition of itself is one of the most interesting problems we face during our explorations in this book.

The government is the legal management of the civilization. It may consist of a hereditary elite, a political elite, or an intellectual elite. Or sometimes the civilized government may consist of all of these elements. The important thing about a government is that it is the *recognized* legal entity of rule and has, among other powers, the control of life and death and taxes over its citizens. Less obvious is the fact that the government has the power to decide who its citizens are!

Nearly all civilizations have had religions of one form or another. The church, as here used, is the organizational representation of the religion. The church could be said to constitute the spiritual guide and the spiritual definition of a people. Churches, formal or informal, usually are most concerned with what is good and what is bad, what is the purpose of life, and what happens if anything, after life. Sometimes the government sponsors a single church, to the disadvantage of others. Our own government is founded on the principle of separation of church and state.

The enterprise is a broad and difficult term. We use it here to mean the particular economic institutions used by the civilization to fill its material needs and wants. Again, it is possible for the enterprise system and the governmental system to be intertwined as they are in certain Communist countries. Or in a theocracy, the government, the church, and the enterprise system may all be of a single interrelated form.

The government could be said to be concerned primarily with legal goals. The church could be said to be concerned primarily with spiritual goals. The enterprise could be said to be involved primarily with economic goals. While this is broadly true, we should remember to be careful to recognize the frequent chances for overlapping as in the case of a military/industrial complex—defense industry.

Some details. The family can serve three primary functions as an operating unit: definitive, regulative, and economic. The definitive function of the family consists of assisting each indivdual member to determine both her or his place and identity. The regulative function of the family is basically training in what is acceptable conduct and how one relates to other human beings inside and outside the family unit. In agricultural lands the economic function of the family is both clear and obvious—children represent available labor power as soon as they are old enough to contribute. Of course, these days, it is a good deal harder to define just what are the economic functions of individual family members. There is usually, however, a major breadwinner and sometimes supplementary ones.

Government functions usually include the military, educational, and regulative. The military function of government is most often the defense of the borders of the nation as self-defined, and the maintenance of international status. The educational function of the government is to sponsor schools (though these may vary in purpose from the truly analytic to the truly propagandistic, or anywhere between). The regulative function of the government usually has to do with the body of law adopted for the state and the powers (most often police) that are put into play to be certain the laws are obeyed—hence we have officers of the law, of the courts, and of the jails within the regulatory powers of government, whether the government unit be national, state, regional, or local. Of course, in many lands the military takes over the internal regulatory powers and such law as exists internally is the law of force.

The church, as a formal institution or set of institutions, deals with special education, with charities, and with rituals. The church educational enterprises may be very narrow, as in the case of special "Sunday schools," or be very broad, as in operating full-fledged schools which are a protest against those established by the governments. The charitable functions of the church are usually concerned with the support of its poor and with its missionary work in other "deprived" lands. The ritualistic functions of the church have to do with spiritual definition and the development of habits of attendance and support.

The enterprise system has to do with the extraction of materials from the environment, their conversion into production goods, and the availability of useful services (often interpreted as salable services). The enterprise could be operated by the government, the church-government, or by the private enterprise system. Or it can represent a host of combinations of these forms.

THE AMERICAN CIVILIZATION

Let us flatter ourselves a little and admit America to the role of a civilized nation. As a civilization, America makes use of the family as one of its primary units. Commonly, the family is said to consist of two adults of opposite sexes, and sometimes one or more children. The family is permitted, in America, certain definitive, regulative, and economic roles.

The American government handles the military on both a national and state level. It involves itself in education at the national, state, and the local levels.

In the main, the American civilization leaves the matter of economic productivity of goods and services to the private business enterprise system. Mostly, the American enterprise system defines its success in terms of long life (corporate existence), growth (the size of the enterprise and its direction of change over time), and profit (the amount of money to be divided among owners after taxes and other obligations).

The American civilization has some interesting characteristics that we ought to consider:

1. A belief in the democratic form of government. Governmental power is derived from the common population and is entrusted in individuals through the processes of election and appointment. The power is subject to recall through petition or election.
2. A belief in the motive power of the free enterprise system. The free enterprise system is defined as the most productive system in the world due, mainly, to the persuasive power of the search for profit.

3. A belief in the demonstration of success through economic power and large-scale consumption. Large salaries, high corporate, church, or governmental hierarchical positions, and the ability to spend large sums of money all represent achievement and success.
4. A firm belief in the economic power and hence the usefulness of high technology—primarily demonstrated in a variety of complex machines of various kinds.
5. A belief that education improves a human being both in terms of potential economic usefulness and spiritual or moral worth.
6. A belief in the economic pursuit of happiness. The notion is that the more goods and services an individual pursues and possesses, the more likely the individual is to find satisfaction in life.

There are other characteristics, but these will do for our purposes. All are called "American traits," but these are certainly open to challenge.

IMPLICATIONS

Even from this introductory and somewhat broadly definitive chapter we can draw a few implications.

First, we want to notice that technological achievements have *unexpected* side effects. We used the automobile as an example of ordinary technology (one which is now both common and familiar) to show how what was planned is not necessarily what happened. Certainly, then, we can learn to at least look more carefully at the computer—an example of very high and rapidly expanding technology. Some of the results we get will be equally unexpected and may have an even greater impact on our lives than the automobile. Don't say that this is obvious, for if it were, we would be much *more* careful about what we are doing.

Second, we might have noted that *we* develop and describe our cultures and our civilizations. And the technologies we apply and use either directly or indirectly guide our perceptions and hence our definitions of ourselves. In fact, we might go so far as to say that a human being is the strangest of all the animals—a self-defining being. This is why the artifacts of the race are so important—they are extenions of the individual and hence part of the definition.

Third, we noted that definitions are neither true or false but merely conveniences to help us in the matter of understanding. Since they are conveniences, they can and they will be changed from time to time as the human being, that self-defining animal, moves to new perceptions by and through technology. None of what we say or explore, then, in this text, can be said to be a final truth. None of the computer uses we explore are necessarily fixed or permanent unless we insist that this be so. The machines will develop. The systems that use the machines will grow. The people who use the machines will develop, too. All our todays will become yesterdays, and all our current certainties, fiction, not because we are strange but because we are yet developing.

Fourth, we implied a certain basic discontent with our current achievements. Part of this discontent is due to the fact that we sometimes confuse the term *standard of living* with the term *standard of life*. The former refers to all the economic artifacts which make life easier to live—food, clothing, and shelter. Standard of life, on the other hand, has to do with what we are getting out of our existence in terms of spiritual pleasure, comfort, and hope. It is probably true that one cannot aspire to a high standard of life until one has achieved a satisfactory standard of living. But we must always remain wary and not suppose that a high standard of living guarantees a high standard of life. It doesn't.

Finally, the implication of this chapter is that the computer does not exist in some kind of holy vacuum. To study the computer without understanding where, how, and why it is used is to learn a high skill and then surround the skill with arrogance and ignorance. This is the grave danger in all technological civilizations, and it is the ignoring of that danger which has sent all the previous civilizations to their respective graves.

SUMMARY

In this introductory chapter we have looked at one example of our society's technology, the automobile. We did this in order to explore some of the unusual and quite unexpected side effects that inventions have had upon our society. We then turned our attention to some working definitions for society, culture, civilization, bureaucracy, management, and mechanization.

We have discussed, briefly, the two forms power can take, physical and intellectual, and we have, hopefully, noted they are intertwined, the one always enhancing the other. We also have attempted to understand the difference between simple technology and high technology, although we have recognized the difference is one of degree rather than kind. We also have attempted a reasonably simple definition of automation and of the computer.

The broad institutions which operate in support of what we call civilization, family, government, church, and enterprise also have been mentioned. That done, we have attempted to see what particular forms these support systems have taken in the American civilization.

All of that was to keep to the main business of the chapter—the attempt to define the central problem which appeared early in the chapter—the influence of the computer on all of our operating institutions. Of course, the thorough definition of the problem will be *this book itself*. Solutions will arise as we explore and understand.

HIGHLIGHT QUESTIONS

1. What is a side effect? Why should we be interested in the side effects of technology?
2. What is the difference between a culture and a civilization?
3. What is the relationship between "society" on the one hand, and "culture," on the other?
4. Give a definition of bureaucracy. What are the two advantages of bureaucracy over other forms of organization you can think of?
5. Define management.
6. Define leadership.
7. Define administration.
8. What are two types of power? How do they differ? Which is the more important?
9. What is a machine? How is it different from a living entity?
10. How do we distinguish, in general, between low technology and high technology?
11. Give a definition of automation. How is automation different from mechanization?
12. Give a short definition of a computer. How is a computer different from a calculator?
13. What is an intellectual map? What is a computer program?
14. Name three support institutions of what we call civilization. Which do you think is the more important?
15. Why would a person who is not going to be either an engineer or a computer programmer want to know anything about computers?

READINGS

Clark, Kenneth. *Civilisation: A Personal View*. New York: Harper & Row, 1969.

Both a pleasant series on television and an excellent book. Sir Kenneth attempts to explain what civilization is and ought to be. And, of course, one can learn a great deal about Western cultures.

Mott, Paul E. *The Organization of Society*. Englewood Cliffs, N.J.: Prentice-Hall, 1965.

A brief and not unpleasant explanation of the fundamentals of sociology. The book is done in propositional form with a convenient summary at both sets of end pages.

Toffler, Alvin. *Future Shock*. New York: Random House, 1970.

Highly speculative. Certainly very interesting. Touches upon information and computers. The solutions to the problems presented are thin and not well thought out. But it is a good explanation of the problems faced by American civilization and culture.

CHAPTER 2

FOUNDATIONS

PURPOSE OF THE CHAPTER

Any living creature processes data. Cues are received from the environment, are evaluated, and are responded to. It is this three-way activity which we call *data processing*. So, you might ask, what is all the current excitement about? Two important elements: the data are being processed at speeds never before attained by any living thing, and the data are being processed by electronic machines.

The great pressures of World War II for accurate information and analysis mark the time when data processing came to general public attention and began to interest the ordinary citizen. During the war electronics came of age and found application, among other areas, in the processing of data.

Of course, throughout earlier eras, there were men and women of genius who found the concept of information and its handling of enormous interest. Many of them are unknown to us by anything other than the mathematical tools and inventions they left behind. Others we know by both achievement and name. It is the purpose of this chapter to consider a few such people, their intellectual or mechanical creations, and how they led to the computing world we now know.

After we have explored some of these achievements we will consider their implications.

TERMS AND CONCEPTS

In this chapter we will define and explore the following terms and general concepts:

sticks and stones as binary counters
one-to-one correspondence
abacus
mechanical accumulation
intellectual mechanization
difference tables
instruction modification
card sorter
ENIAC
IBM 650
program loop
digits
calculus
zero
program
difference engine
conditional transfer
program modification
punched cards
UNIVAC I
symbolic programming

THE STICK AND THE STONE

We know that somewhere some long time ago a primitive genius decided he or she could make nicks on a stick of wood or a piece of antler and that these nicks would represent people or objects. We have come so far since then that we might just curl a lip and sneer and say something like, "Mickey Mouse—obvious." But it wasn't so obvious then. And if you ponder the matter at length you'll find we haven't come all that far. Those single nicks (or their absence) are an example of binary (two-state) representation. Not only was the antler or the stick a representation of something else, it was both brief and portable. We are still spending a lot of our time and our ingenuity in trying to make records and files both brief and portable.

So let us give our ancient genius his or her due and move on. We can move on just because he or she did that little trick.

The next clever person decided that pebbles would do as well as nicks. The pebbles have a further advantage, they can be manipulated —that is, you can add pebbles to a pile or take them away. This is a sort of primitive form of calculator and a rather clever one at that. You can't knock this kind of system for cost since there are so many pebbles around. Again, each pebble can represent something else and we call the system *one-to-one correspondence*.

All our complexities come from putting together, in various combinations, a large number of very simple principles. The glittering generality, which on the surface seems too clever and so complex, when understood is as simple and straightforward as the nicks on the antler or the pebbles in the hand. If this were not true we would all have to bow to despair, and learning would be no fun at all.

We know other creatures have a primitive number sense. If two

African farmers with guns enter an orchard, foraging baboons in the area will leave and seek safety in the bush. If only one farmer returns to the house the baboons are not fooled and will remain in hiding. If both farmers return the baboons will promptly reinvade the orchard for their supper. This also is true in the case of three farmers entering and only one or two returning. The able baboon loses count at four farmers entering the orchard and three returning, and as a result is apt to get killed.

Our one-to-one correspondence ability is more sophisticated than the general and limited number sense of other animals, and it has led over time to far greater achievements. Sticks and stones can do much more than break bones—they may be used in matching games. You might say they represented the coding of things into sticks or stones. And coding is very important in the computing field.

THE HAND

Some later genius, and no one knows how much later, must have substituted the genuine counting process for the simpler one-to-one correspondence activity. The genius may have decided to match fingers to people. Later, names may have been given to fingers, and finally names to the people in groups when they matched the finger groups. Doing this was a great leap forward. It compares with the discovery of fire.

We have long suspected the source of our decimal system—a number system to the base ten—was the human hand. Here, readily available, are ten digits which can be used for various forms of counting. Children who are learning numbers use their hands a good deal. And even a few great mathematicians have from time to time been caught at this activity.

We refer to our fingers and thumbs as digits. We can do simple whole number arithmetic with these digits. When we talk about a digital calculator or a digital computer, we mean simply that it counts in this discrete way. We mark divisions on the wheels of old-fashioned adding machines—usually labeled zero through nine. We do not, of course, mark fractions. If we want to do fractions with adding machines, we use decimal points to achieve what we call decimal fractions. And in computers we use imaginary decimal points wherever and whenever we need them.

Human hands have obvious limitations. When one wants to keep track of numbers greater than ten, one is inclined to have to do complicated things with memory, or gather a large group of cooperative friends. Other forms of digital calculation had to be invented for larger numbers, so people invented them.

SAND AND PEBBLES

One of the ways ancient folk handled the job of extending digital counting beyond the hand was to draw a set of grooves in the sand and use pebbles to represent digits. The individual pebble was called a *calculus,* and from this we get some of our modern mathematical terms.

Let us imagine we have two grooves in the sand. Suppose also we have six calculi (pebbles) in one hand and five calculi in the other. We also have worked out the rule that as soon as we fill the rightmost groove with nine pebbles and wish to add another, we will empty that groove and carry the next additional pebble into the groove to the left. Each pebble in the left groove will represent ten pebbles to the right. Each pebble in the rightmost group will stand for itself only—one pebble. We stack the first handful of six pebbles in the rightmost groove thus:

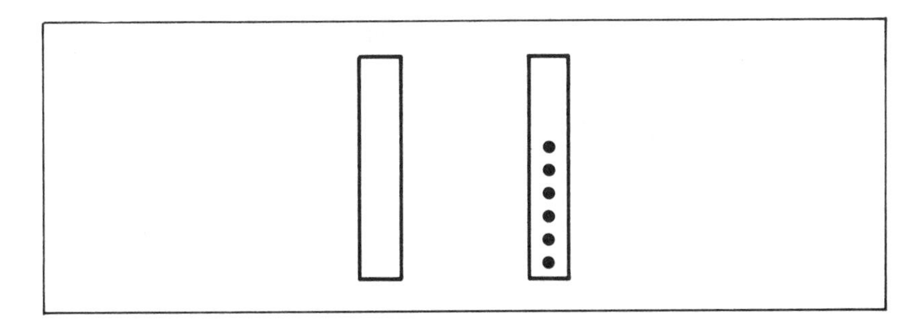

Then we stack as many more from our other pile (five) of pebbles in the groove as are required to fill it up:

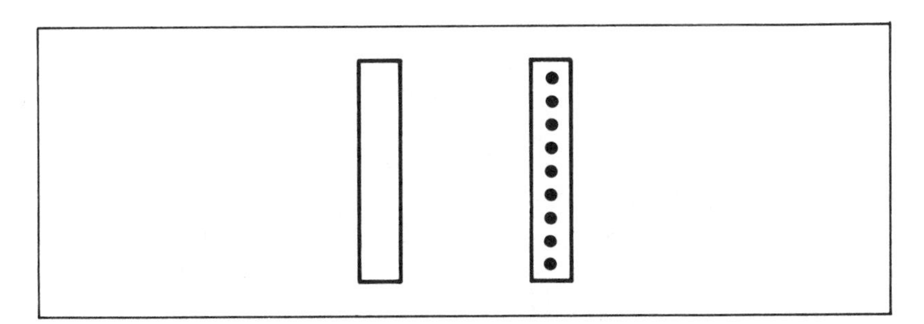

The rightmost groove is full and we still have two pebbles in one hand. We take one of the pebbles from one hand, and since it has no place to go, we put it in the second groove; such a move *also* means we brush out all the pebbles in the column to the right.

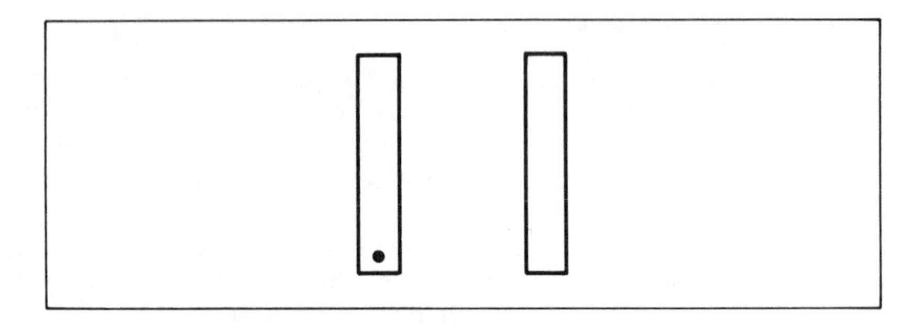

Finally, we put our last pebble in the right-hand groove, now empty, and we have done our simple addition problem to our satisfaction—more important, we have done it mechanically. The single pebble in the left-hand groove represents ten pebbles and the one pebble on the right stands for itself. Ten and one equal eleven. We have the answer to our problem of summing the five pebbles that we had in one hand and the six that we had in the other. The final tally is shown below.

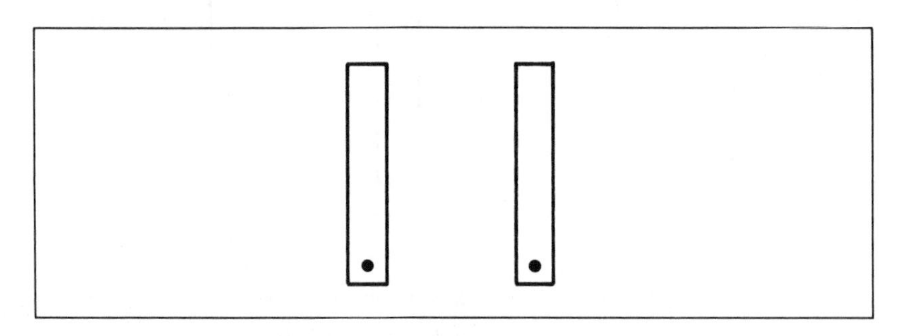

We could, clearly, use more grooves to the left, making each one stand for ten of the pebbles in the groove to its immediate right. With this simple technique we can add into the thousands, hundreds of thousands, or higher.

Ancient people did not handle the matter in quite this manner, but the procedure does show us how to build a rather excellent mechanical adder out of simple pebbles and sand and a few rules. We have, as they say, mechanized an arithmetic task and taken a considerable strain off the mind and memory.

THE ABACUS

The abacus is nothing more than the conversion of sand grooves to wires and of pebbles to beads, all on a single frame. A few other artful improvements have been made, but the function is much the same.

The abacus in one form or another is still the fundamental arithmetic machine in the world at large. In China the abacus would be called a *suan-pan,* in Japan a *soroban,* and in Russia the *s'choty.*

One of the many forms the abacus might take is shown in Figure 2–1.

FIGURE 2–1. An abacus

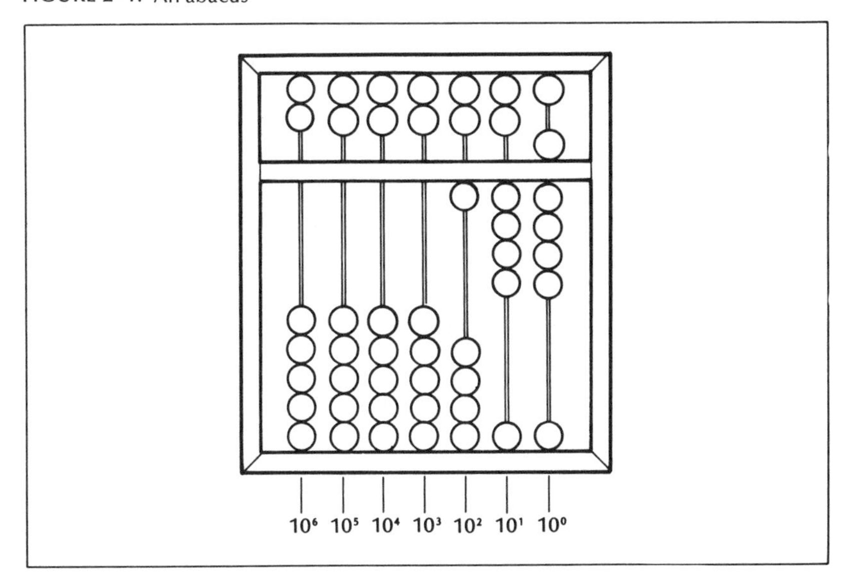

Notice in the illustration that the main frame of the abacus is divided into two sections. One section contains two beads per wire, and the larger section contains five beads per wire. When the two beads in the small section are fully against the outer frame, and the five beads are fully against the outer frame in the opposite direction, we have the quantity zero for that particular position. In the illustration, this is the case for the first four wires starting from the left.

A number "1" is represented by moving a single bead from the larger set toward the center dividing board of the abacus. The numbers "2," "3," and "4" follow a similar pattern. But "5" is represented by a movement of one of the pair of beads from the outer frame edge to the dividing board, and the lower set of five beads is moved downward again. We have here an example of what is called the bi-quinary code. It takes two signals (or absences) to encode a single number. The number recorded in the illustration, reading from the left would be 0 0 0 0 1 4 9.

Back in November 1946, the U.S. Army newspaper, *Stars and Stripes,* sponsored a contest between an expert on an adding machine,

Private Thomas N. Wood, and an expert abacus operator, Mr. Kiyoshi Matsuzaki. The *Nippon Times* described the result: "Civilization, on the threshold of the atomic age, tottered Monday afternoon as the 2,000-year-old abacus beat the electric calculating machine in adding, subtracting, dividing, and a problem including all three with multiplication thrown in, according to the UP. Only in multiplication alone did the machine triumph."

It was not until the invention of the electronic computer that the abacus was required to take a back seat. And since the abacus is quite economical compared to modern computers, it is not likely to lose its championship spot as the most common and most used calculating device in the world. If the abacus does have a rival it is the small hand-held electronic calculator we are all so familiar with today. But in those areas where batteries are scarce, the abacus will surely carry on.

THE IMPORTANCE OF ZERO

At one time or another, someone wanted to write down the result of some calculations that had been made with the help of a sand table or an abacus. When this early clerk tried to do so, a fundamental problem came up—how to record any empty columns? If there is a three on one wire, followed by two empty columns, and then a five, how could one note this without drawing a picture?

Today we would say this was simple and would simply copy the number down as 3005. But zero is a concept of such subtle nature it took humanity some four or five thousand years to define its meaning. A genius in India invented a word, *sunya,* meaning empty column. With a symbol to stand for *sunya,* copying became relatively simple. It took a number of centuries for *sunya* to come to the West and for the West to develop the concept of zero as we now use it. It was not until around 1500 that zero became a common arithmetic symbol.

Zero is one of civilization's great achievements because it has made it possible for ordinary people to calculate. Until the 1500s those who could do arithmetic were rare creatures indeed.

Let us use zero and see how important it really is in giving us the power to deal with large numbers. Since ours is the decimal system, we say we work our arithmetic to the base ten. What we really mean is each shift of a number to the left one position means the value of that number is the number times some power of ten. If we write 123 and try to read it as a number we mean $1 \times 100 + 2 \times 10 + 3 \times 1$. Putting it another way, we mean $1 \times 10^2 + 2 \times 10^1 + 3 \times 10^0$. Each shift to the left, as we can see, means a larger power of ten is used. We could do the job in table form if we desired:

10^3	10^2	10^1	10^0
	1	2	3

All we have to do is take the value of our marker for each position and multiply it by the appropriate power of ten. And we should note that 10^0 (or any other number X^0) is defined as having a value of 1. If we don't do this, our arithmetic systems break down—consistency at any price, even at the price of invention.

What we have explored so far seems obvious. The jaded student might wonder why we waste time. We should understand what marks genius is that when such a person has pointed out a new method of thinking to us we always say, "But, of course, that's obvious." Such a genius is entitled to the rejoinder, "If it is so obvious, why did you not see it before?" To such a remark there is seldom an adequate response.

Let us leap some miscellaneous centuries now and consider some of the contributions of geniuses we know.

BLAISE PASCAL (1623–1662)

Blaise Pascal was both a scientist who used advanced mathematics and a prober into religious areas. We are interested in him because somewhere between 1642 and 1645 he designed an arithmetic machine to help his mathematician father. What is even more important, he built the device and it worked—see Figure 2–2.

The machine, as we can see, included a number of wheels carrying number positions from zero to nine (somewhat like dials on a child's typewriter). When a wheel on the right had reached the count of ten, it moved the wheel to its immediate left forward a notch by means of a special ratchet system. This type of activity is called "mechanical accumulation," and accumulation is no more and no less than addition.

Notice the wheel positions carry discrete numbers. Notice, too, the register up above carries discrete numbers. All wheels move in units of one. Clearly we have a digital calculator.

Answers in the register positions at the top of the machine can be reset to zero (for the next calculation) by the small dials located immediately above the numbers—tedious to be sure, but accurate and effective.

FIGURE 2–2. Pascal's calculator

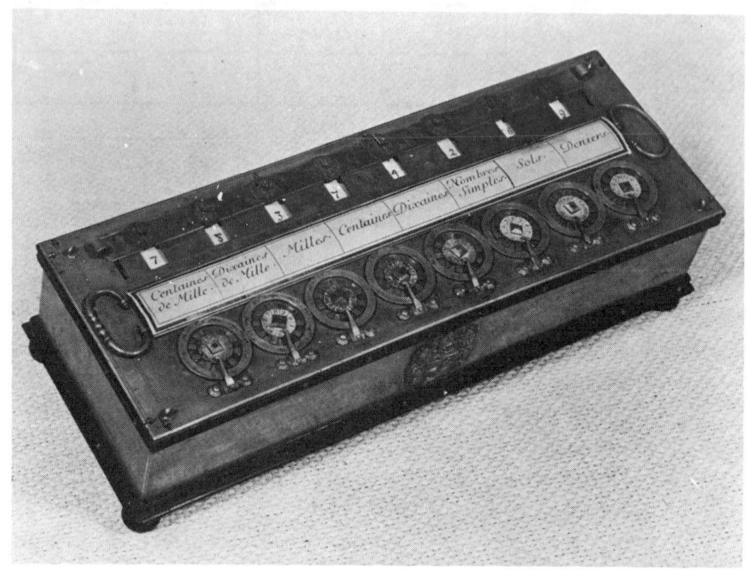

Courtesy of International Business Machines Corporation

GOTTFRIED WILHELM LEIBNIZ (1646–1716)

Leibniz, a mathematician and a philosopher, took the next logical step forward in working with calculating machines. He designed a machine to multiply and to divide in a direct fashion. And even more interesting, he wanted to mechanize the calculations for astronomical tables in order to free good minds for more important work.

What we have now, so far, is a brilliant mathematician with a touch of the lazy in his soul who built an adding machine for his father. Then we have another genius, a great philosopher, who takes the matter an additonal step to multiplication and division. Both Pascal and Leibniz saw the mechanization of intellectual labor as relief from tedium. And it is so, once one learns the art of adding, subtracting, multiplying, and dividing: the performing of such necessary tasks is a dreary business. More fun to turn a crank or push a lever and dream of more interesting things.

JOSEPH MARIE JACQUARD (1752–1834)

It was not Jacquard's intention to contribute directly to data processing. He was interested in developing looms for weaving. In order to allow less talented weavers to produce complex designs, he developed a set of metallic punched cards which would control the raising and lowering of threads in the loom and hence the fabric design itself. He could, then, design a set of cards which, when fed sequentially through the loom, would produce designs as complex as his own enormous artistic talent would permit. Some of his cloth products from these card-run looms were so fine and so complex they were comparable to first-rate engravings.

What we have here, of course, is the first example of information contained in punched cards. In a general sense, we have an example of a complete series of operations, one per card, which when combined, would be called a weaving *program*. The program is the pack of cards. Since we are dealing with processes rather than computations, we can credit Jacquard with an early success in the field of automation.

It must be admitted that Jacquard's contribution to data processing was inadvertent, but it was very important nonetheless.

CHARLES BABBAGE (1792–1871)

The creator of modern mechanical drawing, believer in operations research, Lucasian Professor of Mathematics at Cambridge, submarine inventor, astronomer, archaeologist, Charles Babbage receives the much deserved credit for fathering *all* of the major concepts of the modern computer. This incredibly talented and wonderfully evil-tempered man had an abiding interest in automatic calculation, and he developed his first machine—the difference engine—as a result of an interesting mathematical phenomenon which occurs in difference tables and which is of importance to the development of navigation and actuarial tables.

We must first realize that during Babbage's time the arithmetic processes did not seem as simple and as straightforward to the average person as they do today. The number of people who could multiply large numbers with speed and accuracy was few. It was difficult to get trained people to work out tables of numbers which represented the sum of the squares and the cubes of numbers ($x^2 + x^3 = ?$).

It is easy enough to say the square of 2 is 4 and the cube of 2 is 8 and the total those two make is 12. But when one is dealing with the square and cube of 122 plus their summing, things get complex and the opportunity for error grows. Babbage developed a method of doing these calculations automatically.

Table 2–1 will serve to explain how Babbage came to call his invention a difference engine.

If we assume a partial list of the sum of the squares and cubes of the natural numbers, and in the second column of each such list compute the differences between each successive number of the first column (the sums of the squares and cubes), we get a list of first-order differences (2, 10, 24, 44, 70). In the next column we compute the differences between the numbers in the previous column and get a

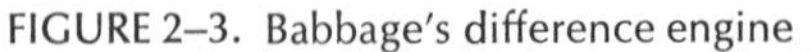

FIGURE 2–3. Babbage's difference engine

Courtesy of International Business Machines Corporation

list of second-order differences (8, 14, 20, 26). In the final column we compute the differences between the numbers in the third and find they are constant. Our third-order differences are always 6.

It then becomes clear it is possible to arrive at the figures in column one, the sums of squares and cubes, by going the other way. Assume the next item in column four will remain a constant 6 (it will!). Add 6 to 26 in column two for a sum of 32. Add 32 to the last item in column one for a total of 102. Add the 102 to the 150 in column zero to calculate the next figure in that column, 252. By simple addition it is possible to calculate the sums of the square (36) and cube (216) of 6 to get 252. With numbers larger than ten the savings in mathematical effort becomes impressive.

TABLE 2–1.

		1	*2*	*3*
$0^2 + 0^3 =$	0			
		2		
$1^2 + 1^3 =$	2		8	
		10		6
$2^2 + 2^3 =$	12		14	
		24		6
$3^2 + 3^3 =$	36		20	
		44		6
$4^2 + 4^3 =$	80		26	
		70		
$5^2 + 5^3 =$	150			
$6^2 + 6^3 =$	???			

Babbage simply wanted to do this mechanical type of computation by means of a machine which would itself be an expression of the rules we have just explored, hence the name *difference* engine.

Before he had completed and demonstrated a working model of the difference engine (which he never actually did complete), Babbage expressed an intention of making a still larger device, an analytical engine, capable of doing all of the mathematical operations. This device was intended to make use of punched-card input, internal storage of numbers and programs, an arithmetic and logic unit, and appropriate output—all of the functional elements of a modern computer.

More important, from a modern point of view, he wanted to make the machine capable of comparing two quantities and to jump to other instructions (out of the normal sequence) if certain results of the comparison were to come about (the first number smaller than the second, for example). We call such an operation a *conditional transfer.* And more important still, he wanted to give the machine the capability of changing the instructions stored inside itself based on measurements of previous calculations. Today we call such an operation *instruction modification* or *program modification.* Putting it another way, the computer instructs itself based on the results of its own work.

Babbage's devices were ahead of their time. The British tool and machine industry was not up to the kind of work Babbage would demand of it. And, of course, he did not have the electronics industry available, either. Ordinary mortals would have surrendered, but Charles Babbage, no ordinary mortal, took the British machine tool industry by the scruff of its unwilling neck and hurled it 50 years into the future—all this while conducting a lifelong vendetta against London organ grinders (and presumably any monkeys they might have had) whom he hated.

One gets a wonderful mental image (however untrue it might in fact have been) of the London organ grinders joyfully passing under Babbage's window of a morning and the aggravated old man hurling invective at them from his balcony. Thus fired up with vitriol he could go about the business, in the proper mood, of shaping up the British machine industry. It wasn't enough! Eventually even the patient British government tired of Babbage and of lending him money for his work.

A model of the difference engine was eventually built by someone else and actually was used for insurance calculations around 1863. It is always good to remember that Babbage's difference engine was mechanical (wheels and gears) and it performed all the major functions which computers perform today. This is one way of controlling the unfortunate assignment of magical powers to our modern electronic devices. They do what they do in a swifter and more silent fashion, but they can do no more than Babbage's hand-cranked devices would have done.

HERMAN HOLLERITH (1860–1929)

Herman Hollerith worked in the U.S. Census Bureau and, sometime prior to 1890, found himself with a problem. By the methods current at the time he would not be able to tally all the census returns of the 1890 census prior to 1900 (the population had grown by 25 percent between 1880 and 1890 and showed no signs of slowing). In the meantime, he would be faced with the necessity of taking the 1900 census, which probably could not be hand-tallied until well past 1910. Another census was needed in 1910, of course.

Hollerith could either persuade people to stop having children until he caught up, or he could develop some advanced method of tallying the census returns. He chose the latter alternative and developed a card punch and an electromechanical card-sorter/tallying machine.

Undoubtedly Herman Hollerith, who was a well-read man, knew about Jacquard and his looms. It also is quite probable that he knew something about Charles Babbage. Whatever the case, he invented punched cards, which were of card stock rather than metal, and developed machines to punch these cards and to sort them into piles based on some characteristic or other, and to tally while sorting. The result was a happy one. He was able to produce the results of each census prior to the necessity of taking another. Perhaps survival is, after all, the real mother of invention.

An early version of the sorter is shown in Figure 2–4. Notice the cards are to be stacked vertically, after sorting, in the center of the machine. A card-sorter operator could presumably stay very thin and nimble, given the form of exercise required to pick up the cards. Too, cards had to be picked up carefully, in order, or the job remained to be done all over again. Still, it was an improvement in terms of human efficiency if not in comfort.

What we called the IBM 80-column punched card code some years ago is now more generally called the Hollerith card code in honor of the man who invented the card punch and sorter and put Jacquard's and Babbage's ideas to a practical data processing use. And we often call the 80-column card itself a Hollerith card.

FIGURE 2–4. Hollerith sorter

Courtesy of International Business Machines Corporation

Figure 2–5 shows one of the earliest IBM card punches (the 010). Notice only numbers and spaces can be handled by the simple machine. The card itself appears to the left as it exits from the punch.

FIGURE 2–5. IBM 010 card punch

Courtesy of International Business Machines Corporation

MARK I

Howard Aiken, a Harvard professor, worked with International Business Machines Corporation from about 1937 to develop an electronic computer that used paper tape as input and worked with electronic relays. The computer was called Mark I and was perhaps the first successful electromechanical digital computer.

Mark I was operational in 1944 and had a long and happy life, working until 1959. Here we might call attention to a simple reality—a machine is not obsolete as long as it can do what it was designed to do and we do not shift our expectations.

We can see the Mark I in Figure 2–6. More important, review the size and length of its system, compared to the modern IBM System/32 shown in Figure 2–7, and recognize the small S/32 has well over 1,000 times the speed and capacity of the older device.

The differences in speed and capacity between the two machines are due in large part to the movement from electromechanical elements to purely electronic elements. And yet, for all the enormous differences in cost, in size, and in power, only 30 years separate the two devices.

A year before Aiken and IBM designed and built Mark I a most remarkable English mathematician named Alan Turing proved it would be possible to build a machine which, using only the symbols *X, 0,* and *1,* can imitate any machine, in terms of behavior, that can be described on the tape using the three symbols. We cannot exaggerate the brilliance of the conception nor can we go into much detail in

FIGURE 2–6. Mark I

Courtesy of International Business Machines Corporation

FIGURE 2–7. IBM System/32

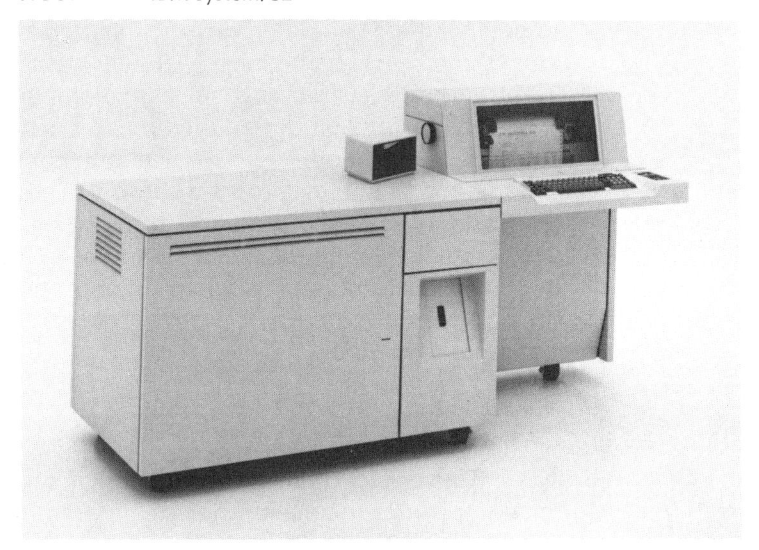

Courtesy of International Business Machines Corporation

this short work. But we can note that Turing provided the theoretical framework upon which high-speed electronic computer designs were based.

For its moment (1937), though, Aiken's machine was both a public wonder and the most powerful "calculator" around.

At about this same time, George Stibitz, working with Bell Telephone Laboratories, was developing a very similar type of computer. It was demonstrated at the 1940 meeting of the American Mathematical Society. The time was ripe, and ideas of a similar nature were afoot in several fields.

ENIAC

The first truly electronic (as versus electromechanical) computer was built at the University of Pennsylvania. It was designed by John Mauchly and J. Presper Eckert. Thousands of electron tubes were used in ENIAC (Electronic Numerical Integrator and Calculator) and gave calculating speeds thousands of times faster than the earlier electromechanical devices.

Then came other more advanced machines with strange-sounding names—EDVAC and EDSAC et al. Some of these provided internally stored programs (series of instructions to the computer which could be interpreted electronically and followed) and the ability to execute several thousand instructions without any human intervention. These changes marked the end of the computer adolescent period. About this same time Dr. John von Neumann, a brilliant mathematician, pointed out that if the computer's instructions were stored inside the computer, these very instructions could be treated arithmetically (altered) by yet other instructions, since a computer can only tell an instruction is an instruction during the time it is actually executing it —otherwise it is just another group of numbers in storage. An instruction late in a computer program can be an instruction to alter an earlier instruction in the program. Then, when the computer is sent back to the beginning of the program by a final instruction it will, in effect, be executing a program different from the first one. This sort of thing can go on and on. We call such a slightly altered sequence a *program loop*.

UNIVAC I

Univac I (Universal Automatic Computer), marketed by Sperry Rand, marks the first entrance of the computer into the commercial world. In the early 1950s it was possible for a business firm to acquire an electronic computer. There were, however, many difficulties, since most firms that did purchase such computers found they did not know how to utilize them properly, and they did not, in fact, have personnel capable of making the required programs and alterations in company records systems.

These were times of grand experiments, great failures, and several startling successes. Sylvania and the Franklin Life Insurance Company managed to use Univacs successfully and, in the process, set a pattern for many future computer users to follow, from the initial investigation of feasibility to the final day of installation and successful operation.

THE IBM 650

Henry Ford put the American public on the road with the invention of that wonderfully simple and straightforward machine, the Model T. It did exactly what it was supposed to do, and no more. It got you from here to there. It was relatively easy to operate and maintain, and the discomfort of its use was bearable. It was not a charming machine—coming only in black—but it was capable and it was strong.

The IBM 650 was not unlike the Model T. It was manufactured and distributed in relatively large numbers (over 1,800). It did what it was supposed to do, with a fairly good record of operating versus repair time. With its internal magnetic drum memory and its happily clacking card input and output devices, it had its limitations in regard to speed and capacity; but it brought computing into American industry in a big way. It dispelled any sense of magic, too—the magnetic storage drum rotated at 12,500 rpms, with a singular happy whine—the chatter of the card output punch could drown anyone's conversation —work was being done!

Probably more important, the IBM Corporation, with its long experience in office services and business records development, could provide the novice users with a backup team of computer experts. Also, the IBM training schools accepted customers as students and ground out a constant stream of competent computer programmers, coders, librarians, operators, and systems analysts. These people, in their turn, set up in-company training programs for company employees, and the world of computers graduated into a respectable part of the workaday business world.

Figure 2–8 shows the IBM 650. The power unit is to the extreme left. In the middle we can see the computer console, which also housed the central processing unit. To the right, and connected to the system by a large cable, is the card reader and punch. The cards, when produced by the computer, had to be taken to a special printer before the information could be read directly by human beings.

All we have so far described could be lumped under the title of "first-generation activities." Computers up to this point depended on vacuum tubes for their life flow. Tubes, of course, generate heat and heat creates reliability problems. The next move, what we call the

FIGURE 2–8. IBM 650

Courtesy of International Business Machines Corporation

"second generation," was toward transistors and diodes, which allowed for smaller computer packages and eliminated many of the heat and maintenance problems, and also provided computers with a new degree of reliability.

We must not think the improvements in the physical components alone were responsible for the dividing line between first- and second-generation computers. A good deal of valuable experience was gained in matters of feeding information into the systems and in organizing information produced by the systems.

Since many computer operations were repetitive from one program to another, clever people were designing simple program subunits which could produce reports for any program written if they were incorporated into that program. These standardized elements were to continue to develop and to become what we now call subroutine libraries available to most computer people everywhere. The willingness to share information from one computer group to another has been one of the very powerful forces in the rapid developments during the last three decades.

The second generation of computers is marked by what we call *symbolic programming.* It was Dr. Grace Hopper of Sperry Rand who put the idea forward most clearly. In the early days a computer programmer wrote numbers to be fed into the computer. One or two digits would represent the particular instruction (add, subtract, multiply, and so forth) the machine was to execute. Other collections of numbers represented particular locations inside the computer memory where the factors for the problem could be found. Symbolic programming permits the use of such words as ADD, SUB, MULT, instead of the numbers representing those operations. Also, symbolic programming permits the programmer to give alphabetic names to locations in storage. This makes the writing of a computer program a much simpler and less error-prone process. But it is necessary to feed the program itself through the computer for translation before it can be executed by the system. There must already be, inside, a program to do the translating. We have programs for turning alphabetic programs into numeric programs.

Putting it another way, the computer accepts a symbolic program, translates the symbolisms into a numerical program, then turns to that numeric program to actually follow the commands in dealing with the data. Rather clever, really. We ask the computer to do much of the work of programming itself. But naturally we previously must have put together a program for the computer to follow in designing the program in its own language. We have, in short, programs for programming programs.

IMPLICATIONS

In our short segment about making marks on antlers and sticks, we referred to some ancient genius who let one thing represent another. And this same genius developed a record, and a counter, which could be transported with ease. Nicks could be matched to things, pebbles could be matched to people. The count of the symbol could be used to represent the actual count of the "real" objects they represented.

Today, in that splendid wonder we call the computer, we let little magnetic spots (or their absence) represent things or people, or both. Our technology has made monumental strides, but our intellectual development is not all that far from those ancient folk who fought the weather, other animals, and themselves to stay alive and to assemble the first primitive families and to build the first primitive cultures. The lesson here is that you do not need a very complex kind of arithmetic to keep track of information. It is not a matter of the quantity and variety of symbols you use, but rather a matter of careful planning.

In our short essay on the human hand we uncovered the fact that the decimal system which we use probably came about not so much by design but by virtue of the existence of five digits on each of the two human hands. This should remind us that we are influenced mightily by our environment. And we can include the tools we build as part of that influential environment, too.

Sand tables and the abacus are, quite clearly, early attempts to mechanize the simpler processes of arithmetic. The idea of mechanization of number handling is the single great idea that would ultimately lead through a long slow path to the modern electronic computer.

It can be safely said the human race ran away from the concept of zero for a very long time. It is an important discovery, nonetheless, because it gives us the power to use truly effective positional notation, and because it simplifies many mathematical processes. Try and imagine a roman-numeral computer and how such a device might have to work! It could probably be done, but it certainly would be an expensive and awkward creation.

Positional notation and the concept of zero made the building of simple arithmetic machines possible. So, we paid brief deference to Blaise Pascal and Gottfried Wilhelm Leibniz. But it was Jacquard's idea of the programmed weaving card that is the most critical achievement. From this brilliant stroke it was possible for Charles Babbage to move to the card as input to a computing machine. We must not underrate the enormous achievement of Babbage—his machines would have contained most, if not all, of the features of the modern computer. His problem was the friction created by mechanical parts. His work had to wait upon the arrival of electrical mechanisms. But the implications for the future were clearly there.

Herman Hollerith made the input cards of cardboard stock, and he designed a sorter. The basic implication of this activity was that it would be possible to build other special-purpose machines to handle cards containing alphabetic or arithmetic information. The processes were established and it now remained merely for the push of events—the need for computation.

The movement from Aiken's Mark I through the lusty IBM 650 did not take very long. The true computer had arrived and had become a relatively common artifact of the race.

Of course, the primary implication of all that has been contained in this chapter is that inventions do not appear out of vacuums, however great the genius. The important lesson is that a series of ideas lead down a long slow path to the arrival of a great and useful artifact. While we must not disrespect individual inventive genuises, we must always realize the great things of today rest step by step on the achievements of the past—anything else would be to frighten our young out of attempting what appears to them to be a full-flown invention.

SUMMARY

We have had a very brief look at some of the ideas behind computer operations, and at some of the men and women who put them into action. We have learned data processing is an activity common to all living things and is as old as life itself. What is new is the speed with which we can operate, and the mechanisms through which we work. We have encountered the abacus and the importance of zero as a place holder. We have met Joseph Marie Jacquard, who first used punched cards, and Charles Babbage, who first developed all the elements of the modern computer (though in simple mechanical form).

Herman Hollerith came to our attention because he made use of the punched card and the card sorter to handle volumes of data. And we have been introduced to Howard Aiken, Mauchly, and Eckert—early builders of computers.

The first electronic computer was ENIAC. The machine that put computing on the road to rapid success was the IBM 650. It was Grace Hopper who conceived, most clearly, of the benefits of symbolic programming.

We have learned that a collection, or set, of instructions is called a program. We have learned that computers can alter their own instructions by means of other instructions, thus building variety into a series of instructions. We have mentioned that a computer can translate a pseudo-English program into a numeric program which it can accept and use to operate on internally stored data.

In the next chapter we will turn our attention to a simplified computer. It could represent one of the computers of the "second generation" or one of the newer, cheaper, more powerful, small computers of the current "third generation" of machines and systems.

Small computers may often be used on a problem or departmental basis rather than as part of an integral corporate-wide communication system. The concept of a totally integrated business-wide communication system has been more difficult to achieve than at first had been anticipated. Part of the difficulty has been simple mismanagement, part has been due to certain technical failings of the computer systems themselves, and part has been due to the one-sided or limited training acquired by the computer people upon whose heads has fallen the task of large-scale system design. The managers, the engineers, the computer programmers must all share some of the blame. Their principal problem has been a lack of true intercommunication. We will be devoting considerable attention to the matter later in this work.

HIGHLIGHT QUESTIONS

1. Give a definition of data processing. What are the three major elements involved?
2. At about what time did data processing really come to the attention of the general public?
3. Give a description and an example of the one-to-one correspondence principle.
4. What type of computer is the human hand?

5. Explain briefly how you would add 7, 8, and 11 using grooves and pebbles.
6. How would the number 23 be recorded on an abacus?
7. Show how the number 324 could be interpreted using a base of ten.
8. For what type of invention was Joseph Jacquard known?
9. Who is credited with the title, "the father of the computer?"
10. What was the purpose of the difference engine?
11. How was the analytical engine better than the difference engine in concept?
12. What computer system really put computing into the business world on a large scale?
13. What is symbolic programming?
14. Given a symbolic program and a translator program, which would require to be in the computer first?
15. What is the result of the translating activity, a program, or data answers to problems?

READINGS

Newman, James R., ed. *The World of Mathematics,* vol. 1, part 3. New York: Simon & Schuster, 1956.

A delightful set of mathematical essays by famous mathematicians and others. Part 3, "Arithmetic, Numbers and the Art of Counting" provides a pleasant historical view of some of the material covered in this chapter.

Newman, James R., ed. *The World of Mathematics,* vol. 3, part 19. New York: Simon & Schuster, 1956.

In this part, entitled, "Mathematical Machines: Can a Machine Think?" three famous theorists deal with the problem in a pleasant way. The Turing essay should be studied with care.

Stibitz, George R., and Jules A. Larrivee. *Mathematics and Computers.* New York: McGraw-Hill, 1957.

The machines discussed in this book are long out of date. But chapter 4 gives a brief history of computers to 1957 which might be of interest to the serious student. The chapter (5) on numerical analysis is also useful and the mathematical principles are, naturally, not out of date.

PAMPHLET

The World of Information Recording. International Business Machines Corporation. San Jose, Cal.: I.B.M.

A brief little history of information recording from 5500 B.C. to modern times. Shouldn't take more than 30 minutes to read. A copy of this pamphlet can be acquired by writing I.B.M., GPD Laboratory Communications, 5600 Cottle Road, San Jose, Cal. 95193.

CHAPTER 3

AN ELEMENTARY COMPUTER

PURPOSE OF THE CHAPTER

In this chapter we are going to have to plunge right into computer waters and paddle around a good bit. This is the type of chapter which should be read carefully—and more than once. There are a number of standard computer terms to be explored and roughly defined. We will accomplish this with both explanation and contextual usage. We will try to understand in a *general way* how a computer actually works. To go into refined detail would take a book at least the length of this one—which is not our purpose.

At the end of the chapter a few excellent introductory works, which largely confine themselves to the contents of this chapter, but in greater detail, will be listed.

Most of the terms introduced in this chapter will be dealt with in more detail, as required, in subsequent chapters. Here we are trying for familiarity rather than detailed comprehension.

TERMS AND CONCEPTS

All of the terms listed below will be used in this chapter. Watch for them as the material is read.

stand-alone computers	system
MIS	main storage (central storage)
data bank	arithmetic unit
digit	logic unit
interfacing	CPU
IBM System/32	input unit
hardware	auxiliary storage
software	output unit
diskette	byte
online	register
offline	destructive read-in
instruction	nondestructive read-out
online mass storage	floppy disks
master program	disk pack
supervisory programs	cylinder
addresses	program loop
word	

As much as possible the concepts and terms listed above are worked into the general context of the chapter to create a smooth flow and to link the different concepts in a continuous way.

THE THIRD GENERATION

Most second-generation computers were what we call "the stand alone" variety. That is, the computer was thought of as an isolated computing unit. It was capable, to be sure, of a great deal of activity; but one might find two or three small computers in a business, each installation performing somewhat isolated tasks for individual departments. Partly, this was true because many of the computers were brought into the company at first to do scientific or mathematical jobs for engineering or chemical problems. Business applications came along to fill in idle computer time, and on an experimental basis.

Very soon people began to realize the business uses of computers might be every bit as productive as the scientific uses. And a series of business-oriented computers were designed and built. They could do scientific work, too, but their primary purpose was the handling of quantities of business data. The IBM 1401 system shown in Figure 3–1 is rather typical of the breed.

Early third-generation computers were giants—the kind of devices

FIGURE 3–1. An IBM 1401 computer system

Courtesy of International Business Machines Corporation

required to effect full-scale management information systems (MIS). For the moment let us define a management information system as an attempt to create a vast electronic store of information necessary to conduct a business and which can be called upon by various electronic information stations to provide information to any legitimate caller. Such a caller could ask for the information in an unusual format, and the computer system (an inherent part of the MIS) should be able to provide all the necessary information, recalculated for special purposes, and presented in a format which would be readily readable.

Ideally, any business activity would cause information relative to that activity to be generated in electronic form, be stored in an appropriate electronic data bank, and be classified and reclassified in storage so it would be in the proper places for all the pertinent and proper uses.

Great things were expected of such a full and complex management information system. But, as one would expect with such a grand ideal, there were unexpected problems.

None of these total systems worked out as well as dedicated boosters predicted. A total system means just that—everything in the way of information properly classified, stored, indexed, and available. Sometimes, the difficulty was due to lack of sufficiently sophisticated equipment or of large enough electronic computer memories—the data bank—where the term *data bank* means a large-scale organized electronic filing system of information basic to the operation of the business unit or firm as a whole. Sometimes, the trouble was due to computer people who, however expert in their own areas—and they were expert—did not understand management as a practical day-to-day art. And quite often the human element entered in. People did not want to be numbered and calculated and centralized. People felt the need to defend their territories and their privileges. So progress in the direction of a total management information system has been slow and frustrating. People had, in many ways, always been numbered, and calculated, and centralized; but there was something magical about the speed of electronics—something rather frightening, when results could be achieved in fractions of a second without much obvious human scurry, search, and sweat.

No small amount of credit for the general failure of MIS must go to the blind faith of computer experts who genuinely felt they and their machines could replace competent management. They based their hopes on the accumulation and analysis of information fed into a total electronic system. From this the course of human events and management direction was assumed to be clear and obvious. Of course, it wasn't, and it isn't, and it never will be. The experts said they could build models of the business world, then all that would be required would be the feeding of new data into the model, and the proper course of action would surely follow. The models were often based on very shaky assumptions. And naturally, they simply could not encompass all that needed to be known—models, after all, must remain reasonably simple. Model building is going on all the time. But it has turned out to be a very difficult art. Progress will come, but it will come slowly.

The third-generation computers grew massive and powerful. Their storage capacities could reach trillions of digits. They ate punched cards at the rate of thousands per minute. They could produce reports at the rate of pages per minute. Figure 3–2 shows a large-scale, third-generation computer system.

We may now be entering the fourth generation of computers. Oddly enough, we may be coming full circle. Microminiaturization has brought the power of the large computer into much smaller

FIGURE 3–2. IBM S/370 computer, model 165

Courtesy of International Business Machines Corporation

packages. A stand-alone system—one which is small and operates without connection to a larger central computer—can now be just about as powerful as a third-generation medium-scale or large computer system. The simple typewriter now has a memory capable of containing from 50 to 100 pages of information which can be reproduced or electronically altered and then reproduced on demand. Hobby shops now carry small computers to which one can attach a typewriter/printer or a cathode ray tube display (something like a small television screen), or both. Such small-scale systems may be purchased for a few thousand dollars. And such small systems can have memories up to 2 million digits or more. A digit, of course, is a number, or a letter, or any of the special signs we use, such as the $ sign or the *.

Perhaps of even greater importance, the small computers can now, more and more, make use of standardized parts. These can be connected one to the other (called *interfacing*) in such a way that a person can actually hand-build a complex computer system to suit his or her private needs. Junior high school youngsters are busy here and there in the land putting together a computer for classroom use, probing the complexities of a computer language or two, and studying the rigors of logic in the process.

There will be people who say we have not yet reached the fourth generation of computers. It doesn't really matter. Whether this be the end of the third generation or the beginning of the fourth, we are moving toward a decentralization of many computing activities. It is not so much a matter of planning as it is an availability of small and powerful equipment.

THE IBM SYSTEM/32

In this chapter we are going to explore a small computer, the IBM System/32. In Figure 3–3 we have marked and labeled the several major hardware components. *Hardware* is the term we use to describe the physical elements of a computer system. *Software* is the term we use to describe the programs which make the computer work as a data processing system. Because in this chapter we are going to talk about hardware and how it works, we are speaking of an elementary computer. When we add the software features to our discussion in the next chapter, we will be speaking of an elementary *system*. The difference is important, as we shall soon enough see.

Because the modern small systems are so very complete, we can use them to describe just about all the elements and operations we would expect to find in a large-scale computer system. This is one of the phenomena making it seem possible that the fourth generation of computers is at hand.

FIGURE 3–3. The IBM S/32 computer hardware

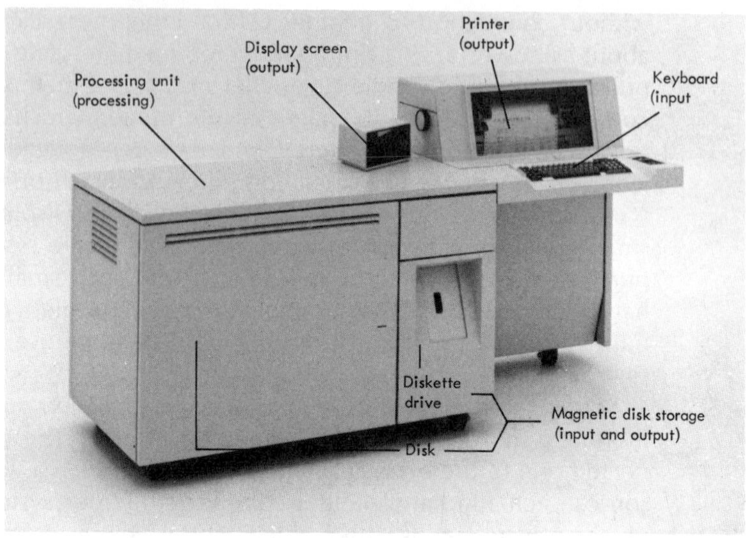

Courtesy of International Business Machines Corporation

Let us approach our understanding of computer hardware and some of the functions by using simple logical diagrams. Figure 3–4 shows a schematic drawing of the major elements of a stand-alone computer.

FIGURE 3–4. An elementary computer

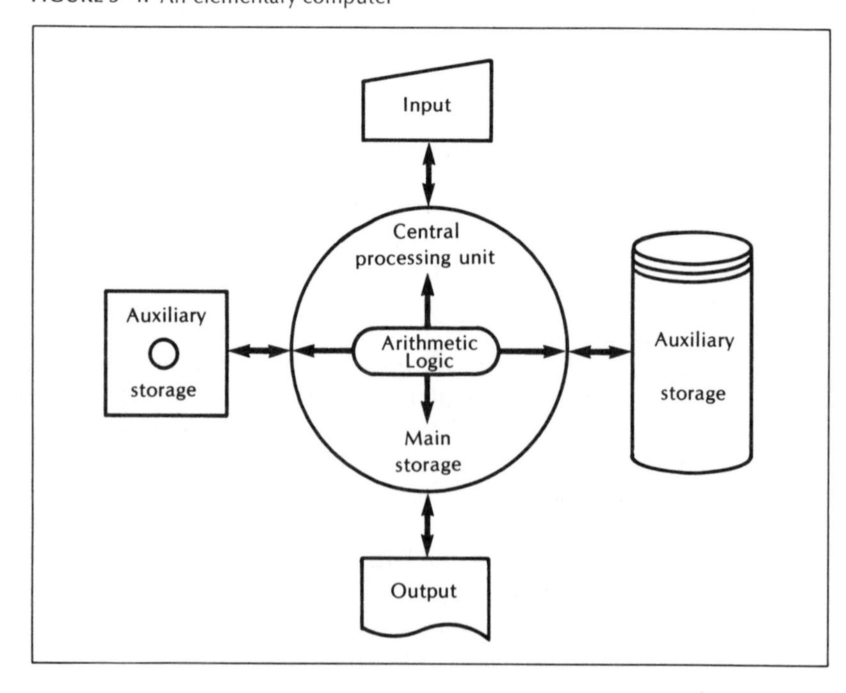

Main storage, the arithmetic unit, the logic units, and major system controls are all located, functionally, in the large center circle. This circle represents what is commonly called the "central processing unit"; often the letters *CPU* are used by computer people as an expressive shortcut.

The primary input unit in our diagram is marked with the symbol which can represent a keyboard device. The output is shown with an outline suggesting a printed report, and hence represents some kind of a printer.

We have put two types of auxiliary storage to the left and right of the central processing unit. To the right is the symbolic representation of a mass disk storage unit. To the left is a symbol representing what we call a *diskette.* The diskette is much like those small 45 rpm phonograph records with which the last generation of students was so familiar. These will be explored in detail as soon as we understand something of the movement of data within our computer hardware collection.

We can say, therefore, that our small stand-alone computer consists of an internal memory called *central storage,* some kind of keyboard device called an *input unit,* some kind of printer called an *output unit,* some kind of special internal registers, which do arithmetic and are called the *arithmetic/logic unit,* automatic control devices called *internal control,* and some additional storage facilities connected to the computer are called *auxiliary storage.* The internal memory, the computer console (lights and switches), and the arithmetic/logic and other internal registers (temporary storage bins for numbers) are sometimes housed in a single cabinet and are often called the central processing unit. Since we are dealing with a very small computer, just about everything is housed in the single desk-sized cabinet.

ONLINE, OFFLINE

When a device such as a typewriter keyboard, or a printer, or a disk drive is directly connected to a computer so messages may be sent between the central processing unit and the device, we say it is "online." The diskette to which we referred a moment ago is only online when it is put onto the machine built to read it. When the diskette has been taken off the diskette drive, placed in its envelope, and stored on a handy shelf, that diskette is "offline." The computer itself can read and write any data placed in an online device. Human intervention is required to bring offline data to the computer.

The arrows in Figure 3–4 show the communication pathways in the computer. Normally, input data is read into storage, then moved to the arithmetic unit for calculations or logical operations when required, then moved back to storage, and finally written out on the output unit when enough information has been accumulated.

We might also choose to read information in from a diskette in which case the diskette is classed as input. If we choose not to write a report but rather record on a diskette, the diskette is classed as output. The same holds true for the larger mass storage disk unit.

Control of these input/output devices may be automatic—that is, under computer program control—or it may be handled through messages sent into the computer via the attached typewriter keyboard.

The console of a computer is simply the "dashboard" of the unit—the lights and knobs and switches required to start, stop, and operate the mechanism. The console typewriter (which we have called input) is one of the means by which the computer operator may contact the computer with special instruction or signals, and it also permits output messages to come from the computer to the console typewriter. In a well-worked out program the computer can actually dictate to the computer operator just exactly what is to be done and when it is to be done.

Reading into the computer and writing out from the computer may be done using the auxiliary storage devices, such as magnetic disk packs, magnetic diskettes, magnetic tapes, and magnetic drums.

In Figure 3–5 we are looking at the same logical situation, but this time we refer to specific types of devices which make up the S/32 computer. We have:

FIGURE 3–5. S/32 logical organization

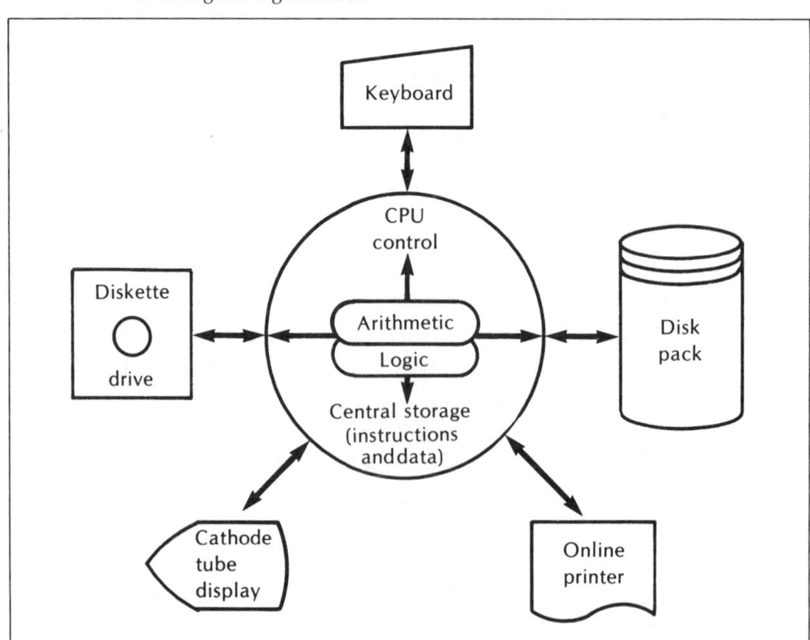

1. A typewriter keyboard (input).
2. A diskette unit (auxiliary storage and input/output).
3. A disk pack (auxiliary storage and input/output).
4. A cathode ray display tube (output).
5. A printer (output).

We also have certain logical elements:

1. Internal storage (main memory).
2. Arithmetic unit (calculating registers).
3. Logic unit (the calculating registers and some special purpose ones).
4. Automatic controls (internal engineered monitoring systems).

The logical elements, once again, make up the central processing unit of the computer. The typewriter, diskette drive, disk pack, cathode ray display tube, and printer are all online devices available to the computer for input functions or output functions, or both, and, in some cases, for storage functions.

Notice in Figure 3–5 we have indicated that both the computer instructions and the problem data which the instructions will work on have been stored in the central storage (main memory). It is the ability of the computer to follow internally stored instructions without interruption which makes it an instrument so much more powerful than a simple calculator.

INFORMATION PATHWAYS

Let us explore some of the possible general information-flow paths inside the computer:

Input to central storage to output.

Input to central storage to arithmetic unit to central storage to output.

Input to central storage to auxiliary storage.

Input to central storage to auxiliary storage to output.

In most cases information must be in central storage before it is transmitted to the arithmetic or logic registers of a computer; and in most cases information must be put back in central storage from arithmetic registers and logic registers before it can be further treated. The central storage, then, is the working "chalkboard" of the computer. We do not expect to store instructions and data there for any length of time. But it is the worksheet of the computer. We will put instructions there and data there when we are working on a particular problem. When these instructions and relevant data are not in the working area of the computer, we would expect to find them stored on the disk pack, or on diskettes. In the case of the disk pack we would then have online mass storage. In the case of the diskette removed from the diskette drive and stored on shelves with a host of other diskettes, we have an example of offline mass storage.

Let us explore some specific information flows using the names of the actual devices attached to the computer:

Keyboard to central storage to online printer. This might be a simple case of converting information to a printed report. We can type the material directly into the computer and ask for a written report. Here the input unit and the computer serve to operate as a typewriter. We can go one step further, however; we can type the information into the central storage in one manner and then, with suitable further instructions, ask the computer to produce the report in another format.

Keyboard to central storage to arithmetic unit to central storage to online printer. Here we are feeding basic information into the computer, asking for certain intermediate calculations, and then producing a written report. This is a basic operation which could find a myriad of applications. Note we are talking about data flow in general, not about specific applications to billing or to accounts receivable and the like. We will come to these specifics in due course.

Keyboard to central storage to diskette. What we are doing in this instance is keying information into the computer to be written on a diskette for future use. We are effecting a special kind of storage. Given the enormous capacities of a diskette (compared to written reports) we are not only putting information into computable form, we are microminiaturizing stored information. In this day of need for great volumes of information, we are making economical storage possible. This function of certain types of computer operation is often overlooked by novice and professional alike.

Diskette to central storage to disk pack. In this instance we have decided that some information on the diskette is worth storing in a permanent file online to the computer. Here an important value judgment is being made as to the nature and necessity of future information. In most instances the value judgment is based on the frequency with which the information is required. Here we might just note that human handling of data is the most expensive possible choice. If we can put information on an online device we can materially reduce the cost of seeking, finding, and using such data.

We have explored as many data-flow paths as we need for explanation. We hope the concepts are reasonably clear to you. The computer does a good deal more than compute—this is the important lesson.

CENTRAL STORAGE ORGANIZATION

Central storage is made up of a number of addressable "cells." Each cell can hold the equivalent of a digit. A digit, we recall, can be a letter, a number, or a special symbol. Actually, the representation of a digit inside the computer is in a form called binary code, but these facts need not cause us any alarm. We will think in terms already familiar to us. Now, each of these cells has an "address"—a unique number which indicates the particular box in which a digit of information is stored (much like the house number of any particular house in any particular city). For the sake of uniformity, the cells will be numbered 00000 to 65535 in a 64K computer (K = 1024). This keeps the length of the address uniform throughout the system. We could think of the addresses as extending in a single line:

			$										...						A					
0	0	0	0	0	0	0	0	0	0	0	0	0		6	6	6	6	6	6	6	6	6	6	6
0	0	0	0	0	0	0	0	0	0	0	0	0		5	5	5	5	5	5	5	5	5	5	5
0	0	0	0	0	0	0	0	0	0	0	0	0		5	5	5	5	5	5	5	5	5	5	5
0	0	0	0	0	0	0	0	0	0	1	1	1		2	2	2	2	2	3	3	3	3	3	3
0	1	2	3	4	5	6	7	8	9	0	1	2		5	6	7	8	9	0	1	2	3	4	5

Notice we have a $ sign stored at address 00003 and an *A* stored at address 65530.

We don't normally need to address each and every digit in storage. Usually, the computer is so constructed it is possible to merely give the first address of a group of digits (leftmost storage location) and an entire set of data items can be moved. A computer word is usually defined, for the particular computer, as the amount of information which can be contained in a typical register of that computer. *Register* is a term used to describe both the arithmetic and logic units which will be used in the calculations (think of them as you would the display section of a hand calculator—where numbers can be temporarily held). Sometimes, then, the computer will pick up the number of digits required to fill a basic register and the number of digits so selected will receive the defined "word." In other cases, one can specify in the instruction itself how many digits are to be handled. There are many mechanical ways of reducing the number of addresses one must give the computer. The main point is to remember that we can find anything we want in central storage, and we can move it anywhere we want it to go by means of properly stated addresses.

We have been using the term *digit* to describe an arabic numeral, a letter of the alphabet, or a special sign ($, %, and so on). Actually, an address refers not to a digit in that form in the computer but to its binary representation. The contents of a single addressable computer cell often carry the label "byte." A byte is made up of eight (ignoring some sophisticated details) binary digits (symbols *1*, or *0*, which represent the recording of binary numbers in the computer). The shortcut term for binary digit is "bit." So, a byte is made up of eight bits which express in binary code the digits (numbers, letters, signs) with which we are more familiar.

So, if you hear about the byte as the basic storage unit in a computer, you will remember that a byte usually can contain a digit as we are here using the term. A word, in turn, is defined as being made up of so many bytes—in many cases four—the capacity of a register in a particular computer system.

ARITHMETIC UNITS

All computers are intended to do arithmetic. And all computers will have some kind of arithmetic unit to handle such problems. In some cases, these "registers" are merely locations in storage where the computer can do its work. In others, they are separate number-collection units. Most registers, when they are used, have some kind of "word" size. The word size can be stated in terms of "bits" (binary digits—numbers made up of the two elementary signs "0" and "1") or in terms of bytes.

For our purposes we merely need to know that the registers or other arithmetic units participate in such operations as add, subtract, multiply, and divide. They can examine a number to determine whether it is negative, positive, or zero. And they can compare one number in one register with another number in another register to see which is the larger or the smaller. These latter operations are called logic operations since no final arithmetic result takes place—both numbers will still be whole and well in the arithmetic unit when the comparison is complete.

How many registers or units in a computer? As many as you please. Usually, the larger the computer system and the more complicated the tasks planned for it, the more "registers" there are likely to be available for use.

Because registers are usually of a finite size, four bytes, or eight bytes, we tend to want to form our information in workable units of a similar nature. Such manipulation of data may be represented by the reduction of a very long name to a shorter format, or the ignoring of certain low digits in numbers of some complexity and size. Though it is often made light of, this is not an uncommon practice in the computer field, particularly in the area of data processing as versus mathematics.

One may wish to be rid of names entirely. Why not replace them with numbers? There is, you see, a constant pressure on the computer people to handle items more efficiently, more "cleanly," and without a lot of fuss and bother. And there is an equal eternal pressure to fit the problem to the limitations of the particular machine with which one must work. Even though computers are general-purpose machines and hence theoretically can deal with any problem, there is always this push in the direction of molding the problem to fit the devices used for the solution. We measure what we can and then we say what we measured is important because we have measured it. In the computer we fit what we can and then we claim what we have fitted best represents the outside reality. It may, and it may not.

Groups of digits used for special purposes, such as social security number, payroll number, or invoice number, are called "fields." Computer people prefer standardized fields when recording information. And since one does not wish to waste a lot of leading zeros, one often sets a field size which is going to be satisfactory in not all but a majority of cases. Perhaps you've had the experience of seeing your name shortened on an address mailer prepared by a computer. It did not hurt much, that lopping off, but you did lose something of your identity in the process. A very large number of these computer shortcuts can lead one a dangerous way from the real complexities of life and the world. Hence, many computer models which claim to represent the world of economics, or the world of mechanics, represent only what can be understood and digitalized by programmers. The answers received from such models are as artificial as the models themselves.

DESTRUCTIVE READ-IN, NONDESTRUCTIVE READ-OUT

All computers make use of a very basic principle of recording. Information read into the computer storage destroys whatever information was there prior to the reading. But reading out from storage does not damage in any way the material being read out. The situation is very much like that of a common tape recorder. When one records on the magnetic tape, one destroys whatever music or conversation was there before. But one can play the magnetic tape as often as one pleases without harming either the conversation or the music.

This principle of destructive read-in permits one to pick a spot in storage and read information into the location. Then certain basic arithmetic functions can be performed on that information when it is read into the arithmetic registers. The results of the calculations then can be stored somewhere else in storage and subsequently printed or displayed. A second read-in operation can then take place. The new information erases the old. But, and this is very important, the same instructions now may be performed on the new data that were performed on the old. The new items may be calculated in the registers in exactly the same way, read from there to the output section of storage (erasing the earlier information there), and then printed or displayed. One can go round and round with this type of procedure. We can see, then, the principle of destructive read-in and nondestructive read-out will be very useful for a series of well-defined and repeated operations.

The principle may be cleared if we use an illustration (Figure 3–6). We have labeled each of the boxes from *A* to *F* so we can discuss them readily. *A* marks the keyboard entry device of the computer. We would type out a datum on it along with the location in storage *B* where the datum is to go. This is the first transfer of information, from keyboard to central storage.

We will assume at this point a program in storage takes over the rest of the operations. We can, you see, store the instructions to be followed in storage just as well as we can the datum we are working on. So the instructions in storage cause the datum to move from *B*

FIGURE 3–6. Schematic movement of data

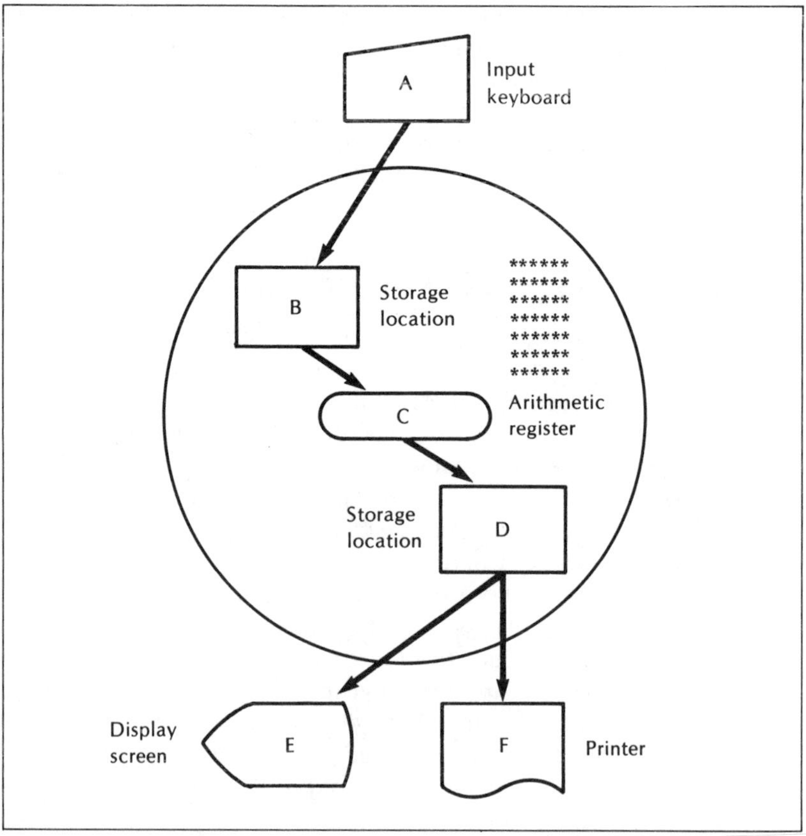

to *C* (the arithmetic registers) for certain mathematical operations to be performed. That done, the answer is moved from *C* to *D,* which is another location in storage. A further instruction causes the datum at *D* to be displayed at *E* and then to be printed out on a report via the printer *F*. Notice the information has been read out of *D* twice, once to the display screen *E* and once to the printer *F*. Nondestructive readout can be useful.

Now then, if we type in another datum and use exactly the same instructions we had in storage (indicated by the series of stars in the illustration), then exactly the same process will be repeated for that second datum. Where it goes it erases the old datum. Where it leaves it does no harm to itself. Perhaps human behavior is something like that. We can do little harm by leaving an area but quite a bit of harm by arriving at another one.

COMPUTER CYCLES

Every computer cycles. The computer goes through an instruction cycle, a data cycle, an instruction cycle, a data cycle, and so on. This is necessary since the computer must "know" when the numbers it is dealing with are really instructions and when the numbers are really data. Both, you recall, will be in storage and available to the machine.

During an instruction cycle the computer goes to some appropriate location in storage, finds the series of numbers which constitute the instruction, places them in an instruction register, and then decodes the instruction to learn what is to be done and where.

INSTRUCTIONS

Let us assume the simplest of possible situations. We are going to type a series of instructions into a particular storage location (and subsequent locations as needed to hold them). We will not worry for the moment precisely how the computer knows that we are typing instructions and not data. We use a little technique called "bootstrapping." That is, the first instruction we type is basically an instruction to tell the computer to accept instructions. That is enough information for now. We will type something like this:

"Begin storing these instructions at location 1000. Now,

1. Activate the keyboard.
2. Accept a datum and store at location 5000.
3. Move the datum at 5000 to the arithmetic register.
4. Square the datum in the arithmetic register.
5. Store the datum in the arithmetic register at location 6000.
6. Display the datum at 6000 on the display screen.

7. Print the datum at 6000 on the line printer.
8. Go back to instruction 1."

Of course, computers don't normally accept long, wordy English-language instructions. Our actual instructions might be in a pseudo-English code like this:

1. REC KBD (receive from keyboard).
2. ST 5000 (store what is typed at 5000).
3. MV 5000 TO R1 (move contents of location 5000 to arithmetic register #1).
4. R1 × R1 (multiply contents of arithmetic register #1 by itself).
5. MO R1 6000 (move contents of register #1 to storage location 6000).
6. DIS 6000 (display contents of location 6000 on cathode tube).
7. PRT 6000 (print contents of location 6000 on the printer).
8. BR 1000 (branch to instruction located at 1000).

We will assume we loaded this little "program" in binary symbols into location 1000 and into all subsequent storage locations as were necessary to hold the information. These short alphabetic and numeric combinations are very similar to the kinds of instructions one can give the computer in what is called symbolic language.

It is time to turn our attention to the hardware attached to the computer and explore, in general terms, the function and capacity of each.

KEYBOARD UNIT

A basic computer keyboard input unit looks much like an ordinary typewriter keyboard. Sometimes the numbers are arranged to the right of the alphabetic part of the keyboard so they may be operated exactly as a ten-key adding machine. Figure 3–7 shows the IBM S/32 keyboard input configuration.

FIGURE 3–7. IBM S/32 keyboard unit

Courtesy of International Business Machines Corporation

You might be able to notice in the illustration that the configuration of numbers is to the right of the typewriter keyboard, and also note there are numbers in the normal typing position. And naturally there are a number of additional keys and a light panel to permit the computer to work effectively with the unit.

This type of unit, then, combines the common features of a typewriter keyboard, with which most of us are familiar, with the peculiar needs and demands of a proper communication with the computer itself.

DISPLAY SCREEN

The display screen (Figure 3–8) attached to the IBM S/32 can display the information that is keyed into the keyboard, permitting operator verification of what has been typed. The unit, in cooperation with the computer, can also advise the operator when keying errors have been made. Or, the computer can request specific additional information as needed.

FIGURE 3–8. IBM S/32 Cathode display screen

Courtesy of International Business Machines Corporation

The cathode ray tube has a capacity of six lines of forty characters each, for a total capacity of 240 characters.

In other computer systems the cathode display screen is combined with a keyboard. When this configuration is used we often call it a "terminal." In such cases the terminal may be quite some distance away from the computer proper. We also can have typewriter terminals which combine both the input and output function. In the case of the S/32, the keyboard constitutes input alone, and the cathode ray tube constitutes output alone.

DISKETTE AND DRIVE

The small computer we are considering is equipped with a diskette drive that can receive and perform both reading and writing functions on small plastic disks. Because these disks are flexible they are called "floppy" disks. Figure 3–9 will give you some idea of the approximate size of the disks and how they may be handled and filed.

The diskettes can each contain about 242K digits (K = 1024), give or take a few thousand depending upon the systems on which we intend to use the disks. The S/32 diskette can contain from 246,272 bytes of data up to 303,104 bytes. A byte, again, is the basic recording unit for most computers. We will not explore it further at this point but again mention that a byte can contain, usually, one digit of information. So, as we have said before, storage capacities are frequently given in bytes.

Early computer designers bragged mightily about computer capacities of 20,000 digits. Compare this, then, to the contents of one diskette and realize, if you please, you may have as many diskettes as you wish. Of course, all but the one on the drive will be offline.

The diskette drive itself is at the front of the cabinet which contains the S/32 computer. (See Figure 3–3.)

Figure 3–9 not only shows the diskettes but shows that the machine

FIGURE 3–9. Handling diskettes

Courtesy of International Business Machines Corporation

on which they are resting is an input/output device for a larger computer system. In this way the output of a small S/32 can be used as input for a large central data processing system. We are all familiar, probably, with punched cards. The Hollerith punched card could contain 80 digits of information and was read by high-speed card readers into the computer system. And, of course, the computer could produce punched cards as a result—often in the form of payroll checks and the like. Now the diskette with its 240,000 digits can be read and written in a way quite similar to punched cards. But note the enormous difference in the capacity of the diskette, compared with the old-fashioned punched card. We still have the advantage of what is called "a unit record," but we have a unit record of 3,000 times the capacity. It should not be hard to conclude that the speed of input/output operations is enhanced enormously by the reduction of the number of physical records which have to be handled to attain any particular level of digit input or output.

DISK PACK

The term *disk pack* is used to describe a set of magnetic disks (somewhat like metal phonograph records), permanently mounted on a large spindle, with a comblike structure which can read the contents of the disks. Figure 3–10 shows a disk pack with the read/write heads in position between the disks. Now, it works out that when the entire read/write comb structure is in a position to read

FIGURE 3–10. IBM disk pack and read/write heads

Courtesy of International Business Machines Corporation

track 1 of disk 1, it also is in a position to read the contents of track 1, disk 2, track 1, disk 3, and so on. Track 1, disk 1, by the way, is the outer track on the underside of the top disk of the pack. We do not use the top of the top disk or the bottom of the bottom disk in any disk pack (due to potential for damage to those exposed surfaces). Disk tracks are counted from the outside edge of the disk in toward the spindle. Tracks are rings in the computer world unlike the continuous inward spiral of the common phonograph record. So our data storage actually would take the form of an imaginary cylinder from the top to the bottom of any given set of disk tracks. Using your imagination, if you remove the outer track from each of the disk surfaces used for recording, and place them in a mental stack, you have what we call a recording cylinder. It is really no more complex than that.

Figure 3–11 shows the concept of the cylinder of information rather nicely for a large pack of disks with about 203 tracks on each disk.

FIGURE 3–11. Information cylinder

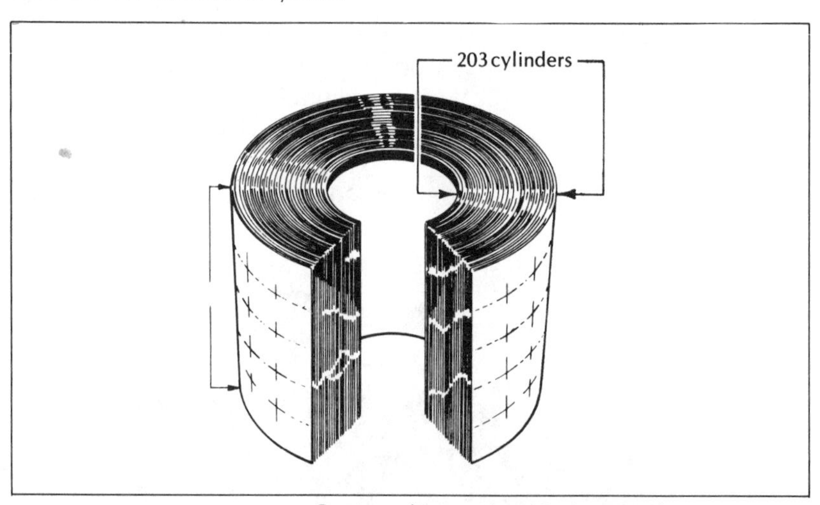

Courtesy of International Business Machines Corporation

And Figure 3–12 gives us a clear schematic illustration of the positions of read/write heads in relation to the set of disks on the spindle. Notice that the top surface of the top disk and the bottom surface of the bottom disk are not used.

Some disk packs are removable and may be, in terms of the pack itself, online or offline depending upon whether they are stored on shelves or mounted in the disk drive. In the case of the little S/32 system, the disk pack is a permanent feature which cannot be re-

FIGURE 3–12. Schematic of disk pack

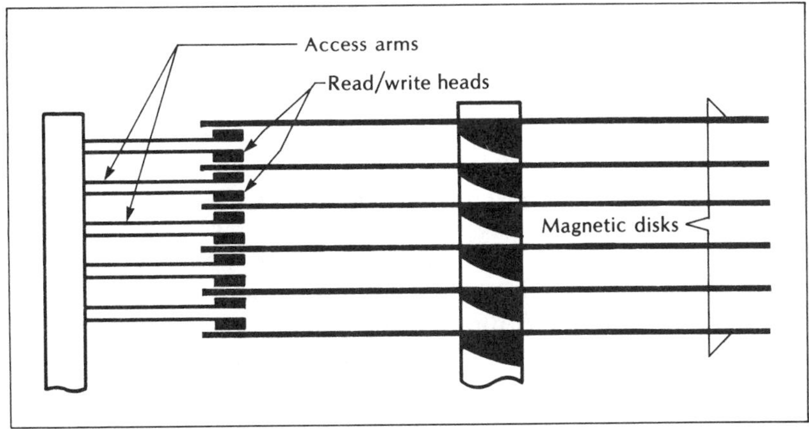

Courtesy of International Business Machines Corporation

moved. Depending upon the model of S/32 selected, the capacity of the disk in terms of bytes (remember, a byte can store a digit of information) is from about 5 million to 9 million. Here, indeed, we are talking about "mass" storage.

ONLINE PRINTER

Online printers are usually of either the serial or the line type. That is, the serial printer works something on the order of a typewriter producing one character at a time across the page. The line printer works a line at a time. For the S/32 the serial printer can work at about 40 to 80 characters a second, depending on the choice of equipment. Line printers can work at speeds of from 50 to 150 lines per minute.

Assuming a standard word of five digits, the line printer can work at something near 480 words per minute—sufficient production speed for the smaller installation. A line printer can achieve a speed nearly ten times the minimum serial printer rate.

The computer and the online printer can interact in such a way as to generate just about any format one might desire. The rearrangement of information in central storage can take place at enormous speed. So it is possible to bring data out of central storage onto an online printer in any particular arrangement one desires. And naturally, this ability to arrange stored data in a variety of ways holds equally true for the diskette and the mass disk storage unit as well. One of the enormous advantages of the computer is this ability, once it has the basic data, to present just about any type of report (and all the necessary arithmetic involved) we might desire.

CENTRAL STORAGE

The capacity of the central storage unit of the S/32 can range from 16,384 characters to 32,768, depending on the model of the particular machine one selects. Remember, the central storage is to be thought of as the working blackboard of the system. Usually, only those instructions and data necessary to accomplish tasks will be resident in storage at any given time. The mass of data would be on the disk pack or the diskettes. Again, the central storage unit, the arithmetic/logic units, and the automatic control sections of the computer make up what we call the central processing unit.

Automatic control merely refers to all of those electronic marvels inside the computer devoted to keeping messages flowing where they are supposed to flow, monitoring the transmission of information to be certain nothing is lost, and keeping tabs on the effective working of all the interrelated computer elements. These systems are so sophisticated these days that we can credit the computer with fail rates (mechanical) from one in a hundred thousand up to one in a million. When we realize human beings make mistakes at a rate of about one in ten, we can get a fair grasp of the improvement of accuracy in data handling which a well-designed computer can achieve. More important, most computers these days notify the operators when any type of error has been detected. Some experts estimate only one error in a billion might slip through undetected.

VIRTUAL MEMORY

Some computers make very effective use of a combination of a small central storage and a large fixed-disk unit. The transmission of data and programs is so well worked out one can think of a "virtual memory" as large as that of the disk unit itself—usually several millions of characters. One achieves virtually the advantages one would have if one had on the computer a central memory of millions of digits; but since disk units are cheaper than central computer memories, the overall cost is very low.

The central storage of most computers is so designed that it is possible for the computer to get to any location (address) in storage as fast as it could to any other. We can see that this would not be true of the disk drive or the diskette since they are arranged in tracks, and naturally it would take time for the comb structure of read/write heads to move from one disk track to another. By using the cylinder storage concept of data storage one can avoid unnecessary movements; but in the final analysis, the information on each track is in serial order and it will take time to find the correct datum. On the average, half the words stored on a data track would have to be searched before a particular datum would be found. The bigger the track in capacity the slower the search. No such disadvantage accrues to the central storage unit, which uses a matrix principle to search out items. But these matrixes are very expensive to build and the storage cost per datum is higher than any other medium. So computer designers prefer to keep central storage down and trade on the advantages of "virtual memory."

CHANNELS

On larger computer systems the input/output units are linked to the computer through channels. These channels are not only transmission lines, but have some abilities to control the formats and the like of the data being transmitted. The combination of channels, input/output devices, and large-scale memories permits computers to share information in three different ways, each one faster than the other. First, a computer may share an input/output unit with another computer. In such an instance the input/output unit has a connection to a channel leading to computer "A" and a connection to a channel leading to computer "B." Second, a computer can share a channel with another computer. The channel, of course, can handle a number of different input/output units, which means the data transmission possibilities are much larger. Third, two computers can share a memory. This is the most expensive form of sharing and the most powerful. Each computer can make use of the "chalkboard" they mutually share. Thus, whole blocks of data can be moved in and out of the shared storage at enormous speeds.

ALTERING INSTRUCTIONS

We mentioned earlier in the chapter that computers had to work in cycles in order to be able to distinguish data from instructions, since both could be stored in the computer in digit form. And in this simple statement lies the root of one of the most interesting and powerful of the computer abilities. For if the computer picks up an instruction which directs it to do some arithmetic on another instruction (stored in binary form), the computer will treat that latter instruction as it would any other datum on which it is to work. Hence, the computer has the power to use arithmetic to alter instructions. Then, in due course, the computer can retravel the program to the altered instruction and do something "new."

Perhaps the procedure will be clearer if we consult Figure 3–13. Here the instruction cycles are marked out on the left and the data

FIGURE 3–13. Computer instruction and data cycles

	Instruction cycle	Data cycle
1.	Analyze numbers in instruction register	Perform the instruction on the data
2.	Analyze numbers in instruction register	Perform the instruction on the data
3.	Analyze numbers in instruction register	Perform the instruction on the data
4.	Analyze numbers in instruction register	Perform the instruction on the data (an instruction in storage)
5.	Analyze numbers in instruction register (the former altered instruction in storage)	Perform the instruction (as modified) on the data in storage

cycles on the right. The computer begins with block one in the instruction cycle and then moves back and forth—instruction cycle, data cycle, instruction cycle, data cycle, and so on.

Let us try a further explanation by means of a mock program. We should set up some simple rules:

1. In our imaginary computer all instructions are ten digits in length when stored in the computer.
2. Each datum we might wish to work with in storage is also in ten-digit form. (The number 400 would be expressed 0000000400.)
3. The computer program itself will be stored at locations beginning with address 1000.

4. The data with which we want to deal will be stored at locations beginning with 5000.

So, while we know a ten-digit instruction is stored in the central memory thus:

x	x	x	x	x	x	x	x	x	x			. . . x's = the ten-digit instruction
1	1	1	1	1	1	1	1	1	1	1	1	
0	0	0	0	0	0	0	0	0	0	0	0	
1	1	1	1	1	1	1	1	1	1	2	2	addresses of the "x" containers
0	1	2	3	4	5	6	7	8	9	0	1	

we will require only to specify 1010 (the address of the first digit of the instruction) to call it up from storage. And let us imagine, anytime we wish to move data into a register, this same ten-digit transfer takes place automatically because the rule in the computer is to fill the register with the addressed digit and all subsequent digits required to fill it.

Instructions are in storage as ten-digit numbers. Data are in storage as ten-digit numbers. The computer works in cycles. Let us invent a problem, write some instructions, and see what develops.

Imagine we have several thousand ten-digit numbers in storage. All we wish to do is move them from storage to the online printer. A simple task, this. But do we require to write several thousand instructions to accomplish this? No, we don't. We require only to write a short little program—but include in that program the means by which the computer can alter instructions. Suppose our data are stored at addresses 5000, 5010, 5020, and so on. We might try writing a program:

```
PRINT 5000
PRINT 5010
PRINT 5020
PRINT 5030
      .
      .
      .
```

It would certainly make up in monotony what it lacked in adventure were we to have to write out these instructions for several thousand items. So let us remember our instructions are in storage, too, at certain addresses. We will show, at the left, the location of the instruction in storage (remember, it will take up ten storage digits). Then we will show the instruction itself.

Our first instruction, located at 1000 through 1009, would be:

```
1000 PRINT 5000
```

So much for our first instruction. What would our next one be? Why, to change 5000 to 5010 (the location of our second datum). So we write:

```
1000 PRINT 5000
1010 ADD 0000000010 TO 1000
```

What is at location 1000 (and the nine following locations)? Why, PRINT 5000. What happens when 0000000010 is added to that instruction? Why, it appears, then, as PRINT 5010. And that is exactly what we need to be able to do our next PRINT.

We need yet a third instruction to complete our instruction "loop."

```
1000 PRINT 5000
1010 ADD 0000000010 TO 1000
1020 BRANCH 1000
```

The branch instruction has sent our computer back to location 1000 for its next instruction. But the 1000 instruction contains PRINT 5010, which the computer executes. Then it moves to the ADD command again and adds 0000000010 to location 1000, which converts the instruction to PRINT 5020. Then the computer follows the branch and goes back to 1000 again to execute the new instruction.

Of course, if you are quick-witted, you have noticed we have no way to get out of the loop. The computer will go in eternal circles. But we have clever little ways to take care of that matter, too.

We have written out our instructions in something close to English. You should note that before such instructions are placed in storage they would be converted into ten-digit numbers and ultimately into binary inside the computer. But this unusual form will do for explanations.

Let us imagine we have 500 different items to handle in our little program. As long as we are going to be working on any datum which is not the five-hundredth, we want to go back to the beginning of the program and keep going. Therefore, we must devise some kind of *test* so the computer can tell how many times it has been through the loop. With 500 items we would expect the first address to be 5000 and the last address to be 9990. So when we get to 10,000 we do not need to go back to the beginning of the program. Our test number, then, will be 10000. So we might write our program:

```
1000 PRINT 5000
1010 ADD ØØØØØØØØ1Ø to 1000
1020 SUB 1000 FROM 1ØØØØ
1030 IF + GO TO 1000
1040 STOP PROGRAM
```

We have fudged a little to keep our program simple. That is, the numeric code which represents the command PRINT would be stored in some of the locations at 1000–1009. But we could fix our constant (that's what the 10000 test figure is called) to take note of this. If the actual instruction at location 1000 were 4900005000 (where 49 would be the signal for PRINT), then our test constant would be constructed 49ØØØ1ØØØØ.

We used slashed 0's (Ø) in our little program to show the difference between an address or location (such as 5000 and 1000) and and an actual figure which was to be used (such as 1ØØØØ). We did not wish you to confuse a location of a number with the number itself.

LOOPS

We are now prepared to define a programmed "loop" as a series of instructions which will be repeated in slightly altered form until some "exit" condition is met. If you have followed the previous little program carefully, you will understand some of the enormous power we can give the computer by means of altered instructions and test constants. We must remember, however, to keep a few items straight:

1. Computer instructions are in central storage and hence can be addressed (treated as data).
2. Instructions may be altered and then reused to achieve a series of activities on data.
3. Constants are not the same as addresses. In the former case, the number is the number to be used in the calculations. In the latter case, the number is the location of some other number (an instruction or a datum).

IMPLICATIONS

In terms of computer hardware, we are moving in something of a circle—from small stand-alone computers to centralized giants to small integrated computers. Of course, the new small computers are almost as powerful as the third-generation giants. And the new small computers need not really stand alone—they are most likely to be an integral part of a company-wide computer communication net.

This newer use of computers has such wide possibilities we will devote a whole chapter to what will be called "distributed data processing." This new formal use of computers should gradually return control to management and should be, over all, less frightening since more people will be in intimate contact with the smaller systems.

In exploring the IBM System/32 we have tried to lay the groundwork for a general understanding of how information flows inside the computer. We want the implication of rather rigid patterns and flows to sink in at an early point in the text. There clearly are ways in which information may be moved around, and there are ways in which it cannot. So a certain orderliness, not itself a necessary evil, is forced upon anyone who would deal intimately with computers and use them to accomplish intellectual work.

With diskettes and disks and the like we are more and more involved in the business of microminiaturizing information itself. That is, we can store more and more information in less and less space. And while we are storing the information in this modern form we are reducing the storage costs and, hopefully, the retrieval costs. This will mean more information will be available to more people in the future. Whether this is good or bad depends upon what people will do with the information.

We explored the concepts of "bit" and "digit." The important implication is that we can talk about the computer and what happens to it in *representational* terms. We can speak of storing digits even though we know full well that the actual storage is in "byte" form. This will not affect the knowledge we require for understanding. For instance, when we talk about reading a digit into storage, we could more accurately say we push a digit key on a keyboard which is then automatically converted into appropriate binary representation, which is then converted to appropriate pulses and then reconstructed inside the computer in some other representation mode for storage (electronic pulses into magnetic bubbles, and the like). All this, of course, would be tedious reading no matter how exact. And it simply isn't necessary. But yet another implication: Each step we take away from the actual reality of which we speak could be hazardous. Someone somewhere must actually know what is going on. And someone somewhere must ultimately be responsible for the determination of the accuracy and authenticity of what is said to be stored.

Destructive read-in means certain elementary precautions must be taken with records to be sure no inadvertent destruction takes place. When there are no original paper documents involved—when the actual recording is itself magnetic and alterations can be made in fractions of a second to hundreds of thousands of records, we must be very careful. If it is possible to make cheap and massive records in a short time in the first instance, it is equally possible to alter such records for private purposes. Each step in the chain of progress uncovers additional dangers and misuses.

The ability of the computer to alter its own instructions and to then perform those altered instructions has wonderful implications for ever more complex programs. These will bring the visual computer performance to ever better imitations of human methods of work and response. The implication is that we could begin to credit the computer with the kind of intellectual power we have, not on the basis of actuality but on the basis of appearance. And this, too, is a special kind of hazard.

Now that we have explored the capacities of a small computer system, and a relatively cheap one, we can see that the future may well hold computing facilities for the very small business and for the home. These computers, in turn, can be linked to information networks (the telephone system is an example) and further integrate each citizen into the national computer information system. As in the case of power companies, a complete net of this type has hazards in the way of massive breakdowns. If, as families, as small businesses, as social organizations, we have come to depend upon integration into a national net to perform our daily functions we could, in the case of a massive power failure, find our culture and our civilization effectively brought to a halt.

Programming, if it becomes a common activity, has its own implications. It is, after all, an orderly way of thinking about problems and their solutions. It is not, however, the *only* way to think about them. Each culture tends to define for its members what constitutes correct thinking. We know some cultures treat *progress* and *time* in ways quite different from our own. We know, too, there is no right or wrong in such matters. We can say, because we are Western, it is wrong to interfere with progress as we define it. But there are cultures which think otherwise. So there may be many unexpected effects on thought and thinking when our computer world has grown and worked its way into daily lives to an even greater extent than it has to date.

SUMMARY

We have come a fair distance in this chapter. We have looked at the logical structure of a simple stand-alone computer. And we have explored the actual hardware attached to an existing small computer. We have learned the meaning of the terms central processing unit, output, input, printer, disk drive, diskette, online, offline, central storage, arithmetic unit, logic unit, auxiliary storage, and internal control.

We have seen that a diskette can be offline or online depending upon whether it rests on a shelf or is mounted on the diskette drive. We have learned something of the flow of data through a simple computer. And we have learned something of the usefulness of destructive read-in and nondestructive read-out.

We have noted that every cell location in storage is addressable. We have explored computer cycles and seen how useful the cycle principle can be when we wish to alter instructions by means of other instructions.

And we have played a little at constructing small programs. Admittedly, these have been in an imaginary language—part number and part alphabetic. But there are such languages. A program, then, is nothing more or less than a series of computer instructions to complete a given task.

In our look at the physical elements of the S/32 computer we could see a device with several possible input/output configurations and a rather healthy amount of storage. Such a machine during the second computer generation would have been called a giant—but today it is a small and elementary system.

We explored, briefly, the concept of virtual memory. It is a method by which a limited central memory can take advantage of the capacities of a disk drive to behave as though a large central memory were available.

Toward the end of the chapter we applied what we had learned about computer cycles and the alterability of computer instructions to construct a simple programmed loop—one of the most powerful features of the modern computer. We now are ready to move on from a simple computer to a simple computer *system* that can make use of a number of previously prepared special programs to make itself into a very powerful system—really an information machine.

HIGHLIGHT QUESTIONS

1. Define "MIS."
2. What might mark the "fourth generation" of computers from the "third generation?"
3. List three input units connected with the IBM S/32 computer.
4. List three output units connected with the IBM S/32 computer.
5. What is a diskette?
6. What does the term *online* mean when it is used in conjunction with input/output units?
7. Give a simple example of data flow through a small computer using the arithmetic unit.
8. What can a single cell of storage contain?
9. Give an example of the uses of destructive read-in.
10. In what way does the computer cycle?
11. What is a computer program?
12. What is a constant?
13. Define the term *address.*
14. What is a computer channel?
15. Give a verbal description of a programmed "loop."

READINGS

Awad, Elias M. *Introduction to Computers in Business.* Englewood Cliffs, N.J.: Prentice-Hall, 1977.

An up-to-date presentation of the basics of computing from the business point of view. Well organized and easy to read. The chapter on program-planning tools and procedures is particularly recommended.

Colbert, Douglas A. *Computers and Management for Business.* New York: Petrocelli Books, 1974.

A fairly detailed book with chapters on computer history, the details of computer numbering systems, and a good treatment of management and the computer.

Gruenberger, Fred. *Computing: An Introduction.* New York: Harcourt, Brace & World, 1969.

This book is more mathematically oriented than the others listed above and is more thorough about the fundamentals of computer logic. In general an excellent intellectual trip for students with natural abilities in logic and structure.

CHAPTER 4

AN ELEMENTARY SYSTEM

PURPOSE OF THE CHAPTER

We are now going to explore the concept of the computer as a system. Basically, a system is the effective combination of computer hardware (the physical facilities) and computer software (the various types of programs available to run the machine or to communicate, or both, with programmers and operators). The combinations of hardware and software give the computer the ability to deal with a variety of problems at very high speed. And the special kinds of software most recently developed allow programmers and operators to communicate with the system in something very close to ordinary language.

There is really no way to avoid some detail in this chapter. We want you to be aware of the various types of programs which make the modern computer system useful. At the end of the chapter we will list several books which contain greater detail about particularly useful computer languages and programs. Here we will only do what we believe to be the minimum for reasonable understanding.

TERMS AND CONCEPTS

There are a number of terms in this chapter which we will attempt to define by use, and where we must, in some detail. Again, we are not seeking flawless definitions, but rather a general understanding of the meaning of the term as it is used by computer people in their conversations with one another.

operating system
supervisory root
assemblers
executive program
problem data
overlay area
nondestructive read-out
housekeeping routines
compiler-language program
mnemonic aids
error messages
FORTRAN
BASIC
user data
private library
tasks
command statements
job control statement
batch processing
multiprogramming
computer library
supervisory program
compilers
problem programs
protected storage
destructive read-in
utility programs
assembler-language program
operation codes
machine address
macro instruction
COBOL
user programs
standard programs
jobs
long-term storage
procedure
application programs
real-time processing

THE OPERATING SYSTEM

When we receive a computer from the manufacturer these days, we are getting much more than the simple hardware we explored in the previous chapter. We also get a large number of computer-company-provided programs which, when combined with the computer hardware, make up what we call the computer system. Again, the hardware would be all the physical devices we need. The software would be all the master programming elements needed to make the computer operate as an intelligent system. These programming elements, when combined, are called the *operating system.*

Even computers as small as the IBM System/32, which we have explored in the last chapter, are provided with operating programs that make it possible for us to treat the system as though it were an intelligent unit.

Let us list a few of the major elements of an operating system and explain each in turn. All of these elements are stored in the computer library. But the computer library can contain many other things. So, while the operating system contains many elements which are stored in the library, the library contains many things which are not part of the operating system. Now to our list:

1. The supervisory root.
2. The supervisory program.
3. Assemblers and compilers.

Figure 4–1 illustrates what we have just said. The large circle in the illustration is the library. Within the library we find our supervisory root, the rest of the supervisory program, and some assemblers and compilers. We will, in due course, find there is much more contained in the library.

FIGURE 4–1. The computer library

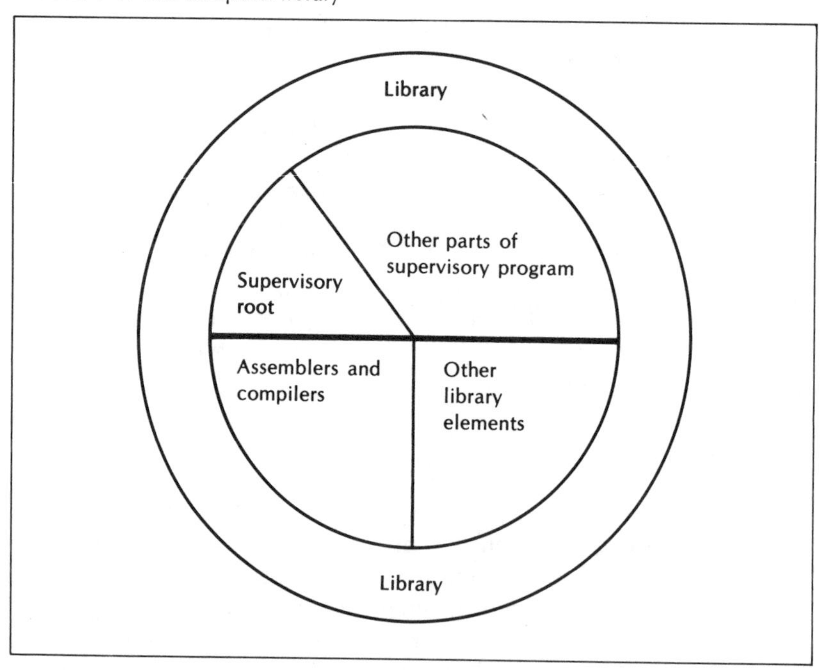

SUPERVISORY ROOT

The supervisory root is something of a *special* executive program. This root resides in a small reserved section of computer storage and can call in other parts of the supervisory program as needed by the system. We could, one supposes, put the whole supervisory program (that part of the operating system which actually runs the computer for us) into storage. But since only one part of this program could be used at any given time, it might be more economical of space to bring parts in only as needed. So the supervisory root stays in storage throughout the operation and calls in other parts of the total supervisory program as they are needed. The remainder of internal storage can be used for storage of problem programs and problem data.

Let us use a little analogy to make clear what we have said. The supervisory root is the *senior* manager. The senior manager calls in any of the junior managers (the other parts of the supervisory program) to handle specific tasks the computer has to do. These junior managers can use any workers (other parts of the operating system) to accomplish the tasks they are to perform.

The supervisory root is automatically loaded during any of the "ready" routines that computer operators use to get things started of a morning. The full supervisory program is usually on a diskette or disk pack of some kind "on call" to the computer at any time. Or if the system is small, the supervisory program is read from a diskette into the main disk storage and will then stay on call.

When the supervisory root enters the computer it goes into a "protected" area—one that cannot be erased accidentally. The rest of the supervisory program comes in, a bit at a time as needed, to an "overlay" area. Let us not make this more complex than it need be. Remember destructive read-in and nondestructive read-out? Well, an overlay area is merely an area in storage where each new part of the supervisory program erases the part that was there before. So it is a rapid one-way system of reading out of disk storage into the central storage. What is read in is still on the disks (nondestructive read-out) but erases what is in the overlay area (destructive read-in).

SUPERVISORY PROGRAM

As we said, the supervisory program as a whole usually resides in a reserved section of the main disk unit or in units attached to a computer. By "reserved" we mean not available to programmers for their own programs and data.

The supervisory program is broken up into segments concerned with different tasks to be performed. We will divide these tasks into two types:

1. Internal computer operations.
2. Utility programs.

We will not deal with computer internal operations save to say that the supervisory root sometimes needs other parts of the supervisory program in order to be able to handle the internal operation of the computer with efficiency and dispatch. Or again using our little analogy, the senior manager can call the junior managers into play to perform certain internal functions that make it possible for the junior managers to make the best use of the workers. We'll let it go at that.

Utility programs are another part of the supervisory program. They have less to do with internal operations than they have to do with specific chores in relation to the operating system as a whole. Remember, the operating system is a broad term that includes the supervisory program and *other* matters which we will take up in due course.

Let us pause, at this point, and review Figure 4–2. We will see that we have refined our picture just a touch.

FIGURE 4–2. The computer library

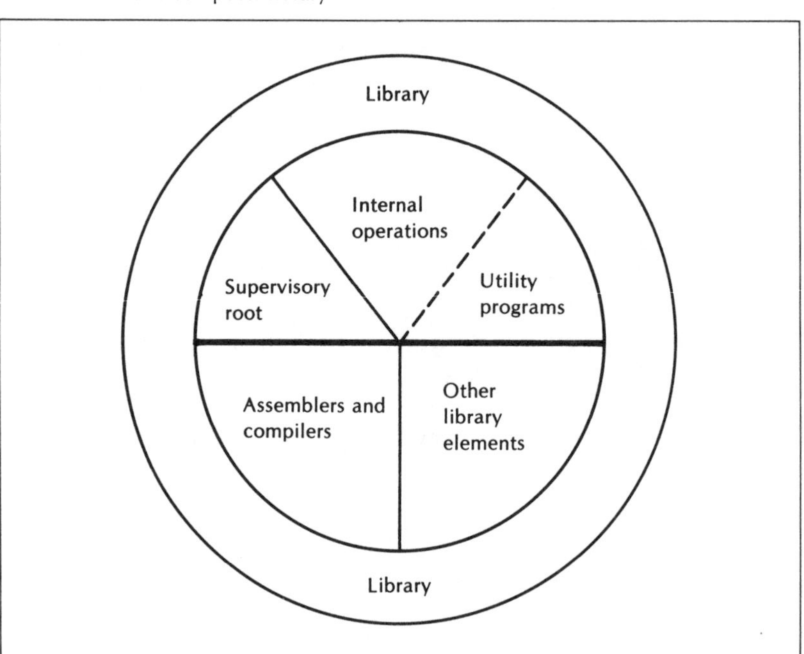

UTILITY PROGRAMS

Utility programs are pretty much what they seem to be—housekeeping routines for keeping up the overall successful operation of the computer. For example, there are library routines for keeping the full computer library of company programs and programmer programs in good order. There also will be whole routines for keeping careful track of programmer data as it will be stored in the system.

Again, don't make this more complex than need be just because it is high-speed and electronic work we are doing. These utility programs are of the same general types we would have to do to keep an ordinary library in good order, or to keep a file room neatly handled so we can find what we need when we need it.

The library routines will keep appropriate lists of all the programs and data online to the computer system to get the work done. The various file routines will keep the files in some orderly ascending sequence or descending sequence, according to the name of the file and the subnames which designate different parts of the files. From time to time the file routines will be called into play to clean out, clear up, and reorganize whatever files the system contains.

So far, then, we have seen that an operating system contains a supervisory root and the rest of the supervisory program. We have learned that the supervisory program is made up of various utility routines (or programs, if you will). Is that all there is to an operating system? No. We have more steps to go to complete the picture.

TRANSLATION PROGRAMS

Programmers write their programs, these days, in pseudo-English languages, such as assemblers or compilers. We will take each of these two types of general language programs in order and deal with them in some detail. But first we must be sure we understand that assembler programs and compiler programs (as these terms are here used) refer to the *function* of translation. That is, they have the task of converting the programmer's general language into the specific (binary language) which the computer can actually deal with. That is why these "assemblers" and "compilers" are thought of as part of the operating system itself. So our list grows a little when we describe the operating system of a computer:

1. Supervisory root.
2. Supervisory program.
   a. Internal operations.
   b. Utility routines.
3. Translating programs (assemblers and compilers).

There now, that's not quite as complex as it seemed in the beginning!

ASSEMBLERS

Early programs were written in decimal equivalents of the binary code, then punched into cards, one instruction per card, by keypunch operators using keypunch machines. The keypunch keyboard had numbers and letters on it. When these keys were struck, the appropriate alphabetic or numeric information was "coded" into the cards. When the cards were read by the computer card reader, the codes were converted, automatically, into the appropriate binary code for internal storage in the computer. Or if the information was fed into the computer directly, by means of the computer typewriter console, exactly the same kind of translation automatically took place.

This translation process was certainly better than trying to write in binary code. But it still meant a programmer had to memorize half-a-hundred different two-digit numbers which were the operation codes of the computer (directions to the computer on what functions, such as add, subtract, and so on, it was to perform), and had to remember the various locations in storage where instructions and data would be placed (usually five- or six-digit numbers). The programmer also had to keep very close track of the internal layout of the computer memory. What had been stored, and where? Would it not be better to be able to speak to the computer in an alphabetic language? The programmer could then remember details much better if the language spoken to the computer closely resembled the language spoken regularly to others. So, what we call *assemblers* were designed and built.

An assembler is a generalized program, in storage, which takes upon itself the task of translating an alphabetic set of instructions, one at a time, into their proper number form for computer execution. Notice, now, something very important: The computer is not executing the program the programmer has written. That is, it is not going to be dealing with any data to solve a problem. What it will do is take the programmer's work, which is written in *assembler language,* and translate it, one instruction at a time, into a program the computer can later understand—one in the appropriate binary code. Only when the translation has been completed for the whole assembler-language program does the computer go to that particular translation to see what it is to do with the data. It is, you see, a two-step process.

In the early days it was the computer operator/programmer who had the job of telling the computer it had an assembler-language program needing to be translated. And it was the operator/programmer who had to tell the computer that it was done with the translation and now could turn its attention to the execution of the freshly translated program. And it was the operator/programmer who had to be certain the data for the program got loaded at the proper time in the two-step process.

Why not, someone inquired, have the supervisory program of the computer turn its attention from time to time from the maintenance of libraries to the proper handling of translating processes? No sooner are such questions asked than bright programmers roll up their respective sleeves and go to work.

Let us detail the steps necessary to achieve a translation of an assembler-language program into a machine-language program in the pioneer days:

1. Write a program in the assembler language.
2. Have the assembler-language program keypunched on cards, one instruction per card.
3. Load the assembler translator itself on the card reader.
4. Place the programmer-written assembler-language program behind the assembler translator in the card reader.
5. Issue the command to the computer to begin the loading operation.
6. When the assembler itself had been loaded, a signal card, sandwiched between the two decks of cards, would tell the assembler it was time to go to work on the assembler-language program and do the translating.
7. The computer output on the card-punch machine would be a translated deck of program cards.
8. The programmer would load the translated program back into the card reader, put a proper signal card immediately after, and set the data deck behind that.
9. The computer would load the program, turn control over to it, and would go to work on the data.
10. The end result punched out on the card-punch machine (or the printer, if there was one directly online to the computer) would be the end of the problem.

Now, then, let us detail the steps necessary (assuming we happen to be using card decks) if the assembler itself is part of the resident programs inside the computer, and if the computer is under the control of a supervisory program:

1. Write a program in assembler language.
2. Load the program you have just written with an interleaving card between it and your data deck. (Data deck also is loaded at this time.)
3. Turn control over to the supervisory program.
4. Accept the punched-card (or online printer) result. This is your finished problem.

All those nasty little intervening steps have been taken care of by the computer supervisory program. It is the supervisory program which determines what kind of translation is to take place, moves the translator from disk storage to internal memory, feeds in both the assembler-language program and the data, stores each in an appropriate memory area, proceeds with the translation, saves the translated program, turns control over to the translated program and tells it where to find the data to work on, and then, finally, sees to the appropriate output of the finished results of the problem.

It may seem to the programmer that the computer speaks the assembler language, because one sees only the loading of an assembler-

FIGURE 4–3. The old-fashioned way

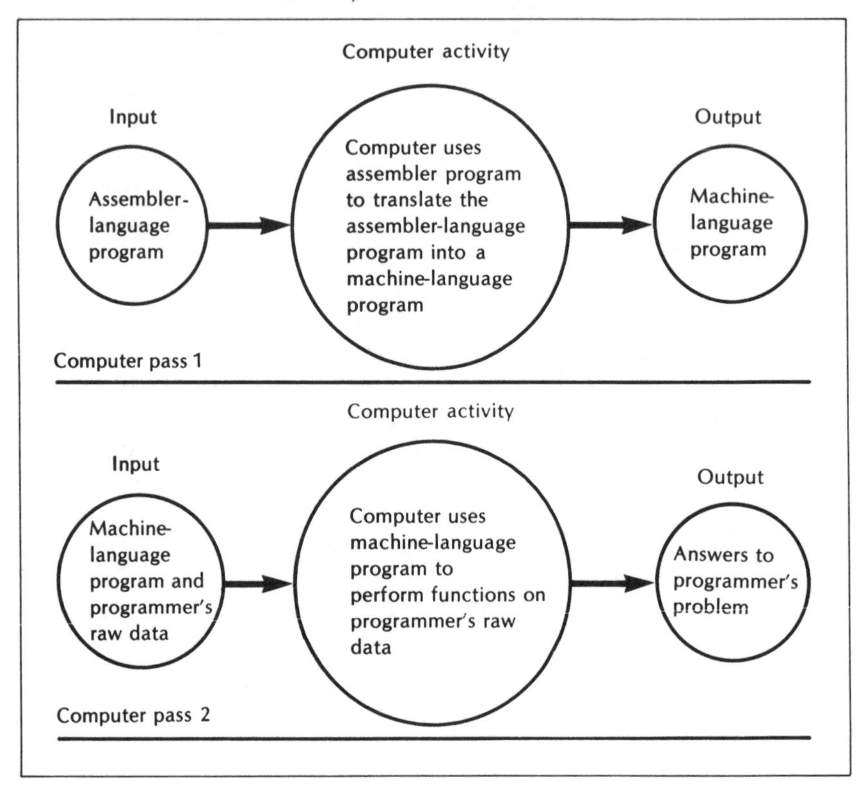

language program which has been written and then, shortly thereafter sees the results in the form of the answers to the problem. But all of these intermediate steps just outlined had to take place before that result could occur. The computer, though, instead of the computer programmer or operator, does the dirty work.

Figure 4–3 illustrates the old-fashioned method of translation that required two passes through the computer system. Figure 4–4 illustrates the more modern way—steps and time are saved.

Who wrote the assembler itself (the program which does the translating of the assembler-language program written by the programmer)? Usually, such programs may be written by the experts at the company producing the particular computer that one rents or purchases. Who writes the assembler-language program? It's the programmer who has a problem to solve.

Certainly assembly programming was a blessing. One could now use mnemonic aids, such as "ADD" to represent the instruction for addition, "SUB" for the instruction for subtraction, and so on. The assembler encountering these mnemonics would convert them into the proper binary command for the computer by simply looking

FIGURE 4–4. The modern way

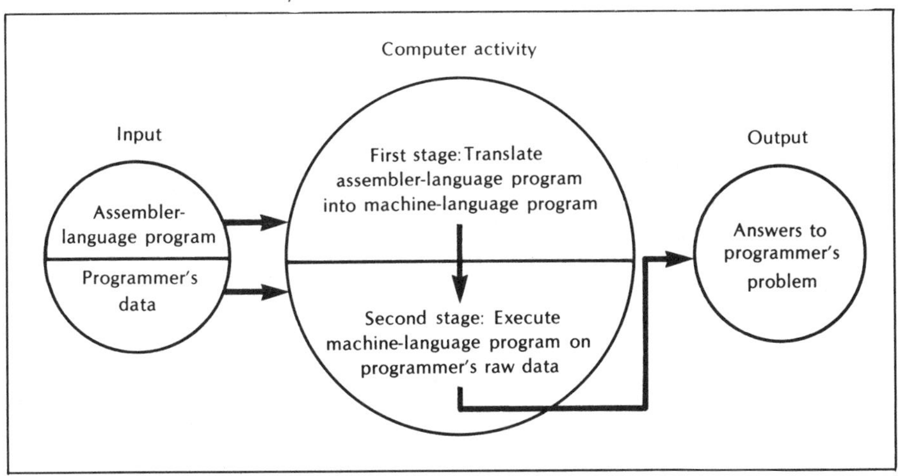

up the proper relationship stored in its memory. Again, notice that this conversion has nothing to do with solving the programmed problem, or with the use of raw data. The program has to do with the business of translating from one kind of language into another. More important, by ingenious assembler programming we could leave the problem of storage locations to the computer itself. That is, we could name places, such as SSOC or PAYROLL, and let the computer decide where those addresses would really be in storage. In our program we would refer only to those mnemonic storage names. The computer, during the translation process, would convert such references to actual addresses in storage and remember them by constructing an appropriate reference table. And as the assembler moved through the program, translating, it would always put the correct, actual machine-address location in the place of the mnemonic whenever it encountered one of the alphabetic addresses the programmer had made up.

Typically, one might write a program which said:

```
START  RCD  PAYROLL
GO     MV   PAYROLL+7, JELL
       ADD  PAYROLL+15, JELL
            .
            .
            .
```

Each of these pseudo-English instructions would be punched on a punched card, in the old days, or typed directly into the computer on a terminal, in modern times. The assembler program would be inside the computer and would translate each instruction as received, one after other, either storing the translated instruction away in memory, until the complete program had been put together, or punching out translated instructions one card at a time. The assembler would turn each instruction into its numeric equivalent—the kind of language the computer could understand. The translated program might have the form:

```
01000 16 17000 00010
01012 18 17007 18007
01024 19 17015 18007
           .
           .
           .
```

Notice, again, no actual calculating has yet been done on any raw data. It is necessary to turn control over to this program in storage and feed the data into the computer. We have said all that earlier, but it is wise to repeat the matter to be sure the process is understood.

Assemblers were a blessing. But they were rather tedious in performance: At least a couple of passes through the smaller computers were necessary before one could get the results of the program. And, of course, even the assembler language required a good deal of knowledge about the specific workings of the particular computer one happened to have. Still, there were virtues, too. The computer seldom made mistakes about its assignment of actual storage addresses to the programmer's alphabetic names for locations. Nor did the assembler program confuse one operation code with another and put down the wrong one, as programmers often did. More wonderful yet, the assembler program doing the translating "knew" all the rules of the assembler-programming language; and when the program writer of an assembly-language program made a mistake or violated any of the rules of the language, the computer could pick it up during the translation process and issue special error messages either on the console typewriter or the online printer. All this meant programming was easier, faster, and more efficient.

Because many of the steps a computer must take to solve problems are pretty much standard, macro instructions were the next invention. A macro instruction is an assembler-language instruction that calls up a series of other instructions which represent a series of standard operations the computer would be expected to do. When you ask someone to please empty the garbage pail you are giving a macro instruction. You don't want to go into detail about how to cross the kitchen floor, open the cabinet under the sink, reach down and seize the bag, close the cabinet door, walk across the kitchen floor, exit through the garage to the storage area near the drive, drop the garbage in the pail, and close the lid. Each of these steps would be individual instructions.

An assembler-language macro instruction, then, called up a series of regular instructions which performed something of a routine nature the computer would have to do. Many complex problems are made up of these standard little sets of basic operations. Much programming effort and time was saved.

COMPILERS

The next step? Invent an even more elegant pseudo-mathematical or pseudo-English language for programming. Fix things so a single pseudo-English statement might generate many machine-language instructions instead of merely one. Fix the language so formulas of various kinds could be written just as they would be (or nearly so) in the hands of a competent mathematician. Or fix things so a business type of person could write out a program in pseudo-English that could be read and understood by other business types not only as a program but as a business document. Call this new program translator a "compiler." And so, we got FORTRAN (Formula Translator) for the mathematical folk and we got COBOL (Common Business Oriented Language) for the business folk. Both of these higher-level languages are called "compiler languages." Both can be used by programmers to describe jobs to be done by the computer. Both of these languages require translation by the computer before they can be executed by the computer. So we have the FORTRAN language (for programming) and we have the FORTRAN compiler (for translating). We have the COBOL language (for writing programs) and we have the COBOL compiler (for translating the programs).

Since compilers can create more than one instruction for each of the statements being made in the programs written in such languages, a certain amount of actual programmer control is sacrificed. The computer will do the standard thing in the process of translation. The compiler has to include a set of rules which will always result in the same kind of program step or steps from the same kind of program-language instruction. But, blessings be on the compiler! One does not need to know very much about one's particular computer. The languages are fairly standard for use on one machine or another. Only those master programmers who create the COBOL or FORTRAN compilers for their own particular computer systems have to know all the details. The average programmer escapes much work and much study. One then can concentrate on the problems one wants to solve, and not so much on the computer that is to solve them. A simple FORTRAN statement, like $A = B + C - D$, can generate as many machine-language instructions as are necessary to do the job. Or a COBOL statement, such as MULTIPLY HOURS BY RATE GIVING GR-PAY, also will result in several machine-language instructions.

When the terminals (typewriterlike devices connected to the computer at a distance) came into common use, FORTRAN was modified into a simplified language called BASIC or SUPER BASIC. And COBOL also was adapted for use on the terminals. Engineers, students, business folk (who knew little about the computer) could contact it via the terminals, issue a number of statements in an appropriate language, followed by data, and get results. To the programmer, the computer seemed to speak the new compiler language. It couldn't, of course. It had to accept these pseudo-English or pseudomathematical statements, translate them, and then and only then execute them with the given data. But since computers now work in millionths or billionths of a second, it would seem to each individual using a terminal that the computer was giving its undivided attention, and that the computer spoke the language of the programmer. There is a danger here, if one is simpleminded. One can get the foolish notion that the computer understands what one is saying. We must not do this. A clock does not understand time even though it keeps time well enough. A calculator does not understand a problem even though it is monumentally useful in the solution. A computer, sophisticated device though it be, understands absolutely nothing—or, at least, that is true of all the computers in the world today. There are, though, those who would give the computer added features and greater dimensions. And when, one day, a computer is in another room and you can conduct a conversation with it for an hour or more on any subject of your own choosing, and you cannot detect anything wrong with the answers, compared with a conversation with a human being, then maybe we can credit the computer with thought. We can, as yet, construct only what we can understand—and we do not understand the human brain.

We are now able to repeat our short list in a slightly more detailed fashion. These, then, are the elements of the operating system:

1. Supervisory root.
2. Supervisory program.
   a. Internal operations segment.
   b. Utility programs.
3. Translating programs.
   a. Assemblers.
   b. Compilers.

All the programming and organizational efforts mentioned so far are designed to help problem programmers with the work to be done. In order to do this we have to provide programmers with room for their own programs and their own data in the library of the system. It is time, then, to turn our attention the computer system library and its major elements.

ONLINE LIBRARIES

What are some of the elements we would find in a complete computer library of today? Let us make a list:

1. The supervisory root.
2. The supervisory program.
   a. Internal operations segment.
   b. Utility programs.
3. Translating programs.
   a. Assemblers.
   b. Compilers.
4. User programs.
5. User data storage files.

The last two elements, user programs and user data storage files, are our current concern.

USER PROGRAMS

User programs can be divided into two main categories—those programs which are standard (that is, commonly available to solve ordinary problems which will occur frequently), and those which are programmer generated on an individual basis. Standard programs came about because in the early days of computing those who understood the required computer languages were few and the problems they faced were many. Quite naturally these people tended to communicate with one another a good deal. And more important, they began to exchange programs. If one person had prepared a good general and workable payroll routine, it could be exchanged with another person at another similar computer installation who had worked out an effective inventory program. Soon clubs of various kinds were formed. They published bulletins advising one another of the various special or generalized programs they had available for common use. The computer manufacturers soon joined these organizations and made many of their general programs available.

People who use a computer these days usually work through a terminal—some kind of typewriter device with or without a cathode ray display tube. Programs will be created by the user right at the keyboard while working with the computer. One may then ask the computer to store one's program in a private library (one which no other programmer can enter). Different parts, or whole programs, that are to be stored may be given names and dates. The computer will put them away in the programmer's library. They may be called on demand, by name. One also may specify the length of time the program or program part is to be kept, and the computer supervisory routine can see to cleaning up the files on a periodic basis.

USER DATA STORAGE

Not only do some of the larger computers provide the individual programmer or user with a private library for programs, but for data as well. When a programmer is using a good deal of information, it may be entered through a terminal once and once only, and will subsequently be available for call-up with a simple name reference.

Since the supervisory routine is equipped to keep up data banks as well as program banks, the programmer can actually alter data by giving instructions to the supervisory routine and then turn the matter of updating and alteration over to it. Again, a very few of the signals put in through the terminal keyboard can send the computer off on a host of correctional or updating activities. Also, we should note, the kinds of tasks performed by the computer are generally standardized. That is, most files require certain kinds of basic cleaning up and arranging. Some items have to be withdrawn in an orderly way and new items have to be inserted. Usually, sequencing is either in ascending or descending order. And usually, the data in the data bank are made up of standard-length units to make matters simple and straightforward. In the larger computers this need not be the case. But most procedures for handling data banks are standard. A genuinely unusual data bank would require the programmer using the

FIGURE 4–5. A complete library

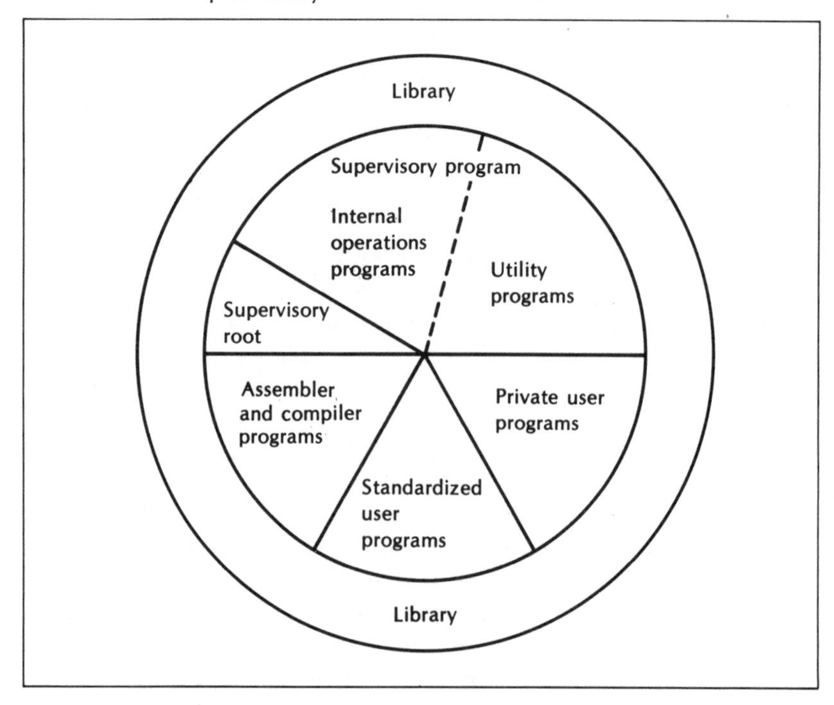

material to plan out special maintenance programs for the data file. Of course, the computer would duly put this program away in the user program file and it could be called up on demand.

A good installation, then, would soon have a library of well-worked-out programs which could be used to solve any number of standard problems faced not by one business alone but by many. Most of the program exchanges were arranged on the basis of type of computer. Those programmers working with the old IBM 650 would join a club made up of IBM 650 programmers. Those working with one of the Control Data systems would do much the same.

The next step in the process was to design a method of knitting one or two programs together to form a broader program that could handle a variety of problems. And happily, just about this time the computer manufacturers were developing very large computer memories. The high-speed inner memory of the computer grew much larger, though at some expense, and the auxiliary memories were improved in capacity by the invention and use of the magnetic disk. Now it was possible to not only collect a number of standardized programs but to arrange them in a library on the disk—in such a way they could be read into internal memory on demand without the intervention of card-deck preparation and loading. This is largely the source of the term *online library*.

JOB CONTROL

The assemblers and the compilers and the libraries on disks gave great help to programmers in getting on with their work. But, along with these developments, computer hardware grew increasingly sophisticated. Computer memories went up by a factor of ten and then by an additional factor of ten. Computer speeds moved from thousandths of a second to millionths of a second to billionths of a second. This speed and memory size posed very special problems for handling the movement of the data inside the computer itself. If the internal operations of the computer remained under programmer or operator control, most of the calculating time would be wasted. So the master supervisory programs we referred to earlier were written. They would reside inside the computer and could deal with the different types of tasks to be done. For example, a FORTRAN program might require translation and then a COBOL program might also need to be translated. As soon as these tasks were done, the calculations on the COBOL program were needed, perhaps one or two other waiting jobs had to be accomplished, and finally, the FORTRAN program was to be run.

The operator or programmer, or both, must learn a set of special instructions in a special language to be able to talk directly to the supervisory routine itself. This language is commonly called "job control language." Each special instruction to be given to the supervisory routine is called a "job control statement." Don't complicate! All we are doing here is speaking directly to the supervisory program in a simple special language.

Job control statements could be typed into the computer via the computer console typewriter, or they could be placed on cards which preceded the deck of cards each programmer wished to feed into the computer.

JOBS VERSUS TASKS

A job is usually the term used to describe the entire particular activity that a programmer might want done. For instance, one might write a program in the FORTRAN language and prepare a number of data cards for the program (when translated) to work on. The entire process is the programmer's *job*. But, from the point of view of the computer, the job could be said to be made up of separate *tasks*. The first task would be the translation of the program, and the second task would be the running of the translated program. But the computer might wish to use its time more wisely than the individual programmer would. For example, five FORTRAN programs may be ready for translation. The computer would find it more economical to load the compiler (from disk to internal memory), to translate all of the FORTRAN language programs at once, and then and only then, to turn its attention to actually executing the translated programs, one after the other, with the required data (also available, say on diskettes).

Things would be happening inside the computer so fast that the matter would not be of concern to the individual programmers. They would, from their point of view, get the results just as rapidly in one way as another. But the computer would have exercised a series of decisions based on the supervisory program resident in its memory. It would be dealing with tasks, not jobs. The programmers would be dealing with whole jobs, not separate tasks. The computer, by means of tasks, would be maximizing the use of its internal time, and the programmer would be maximizing the use of external time. In the end, both purposes are served and all is well.

OVERLAY AREAS

The storage overlay areas are very active places. Data are regularly brought to these areas, automatically erasing whatever was there before. We mentioned the overlay area of the supervisory program.

This is generally a reserved section for the supervisory program's exclusive use. But all the rest of the internal computer memory is really an overlay area as well. Think of the available section of internal memory as a common blackboard on which each program writes the information needed, brings in the data needed, and then departs. New programs and new data will come into this area moment by moment to replace whatever was there before. With the exception of the supervisory root and the supervisory overlay area, the rest of the main internal memory is dynamically available to the supervisory program to deal with any user problems. Long-term storage (a day or more) will have to be on disk drives, diskettes, or other auxiliary memory devices connected to the computer.

Figure 4–6 will give you some idea, graphically, of what we have been talking about.

FIGURE 4–6. Storage assignments

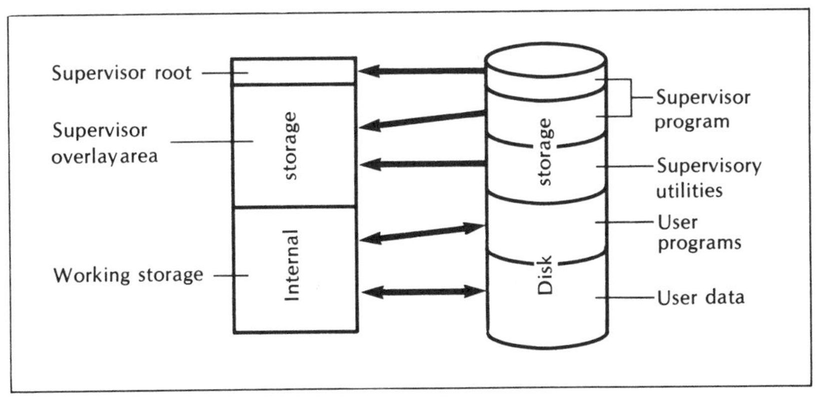

Most of the time our supervisory program (including the root) resides in the disk storage. Seldom would this be interfered with, except accidentally. At the beginning of computer operations for the day the supervisory root would be sent into internal storage. Then control would be turned over to the supervisory root to deal with the day's management problems in terms of data to come and go out of the internal memory. The arrows from disk storage to internal storage often are only one way, thanks to destructive read-in. There is never any information to retrieve from storage as far as the supervisor program, supervisory utilities, and some user programs are concerned. Nondestructive read-out means that what is read out of the disk remains on the disk. Of course, if one is altering one's own special programs, the arrow is a two-way one, because new information can be sent back to the disk to overlay what was there before. And the same holds true for user data. If users don't alter their programs, however, they can remain as unsullied and sacred as the supervisory program and utilities themselves.

PROCEDURES

Earlier we mentioned conversations with the computer about what is to be done using the operating system via a series of statements called job control statements. It would be tiresome if we had to write and rewrite these statements every time we wanted a familiar job to be done. So the next logical step was to group statements together which would describe a complete and familiar task.

The collection of job statements is called a *procedure*. Each procedure has a name. It is, then, only necessary to call up the procedure by mentioning its name to the computer supervisory system. In this way the computer calls up the whole procedure and then turns its attention to executing the procedure, one job control statement at a time. The job control statements, of course, tell the computer what to do about the particular job at hand. For instance, the job control statements might require the computer to load the FORTRAN compiler into the computer, translate a program which it reads in from a diskette in the FORTRAN language, then temporarily store that program so it could go on with other FORTRAN language programs read in from the same disk. Eventually, the procedure job control statements might inform the computer that it had completed the task of translation and now could go about reading in data for the first of the translated programs from some other identifiable diskette, which it would call for via the computer console printer or the computer cathode ray display tube. A programmer would then, under the instruction of the computer, go and get the proper disk referred to by the computer, load it on the diskette drive, and inform the computer that all was ready for the computer to go to work. Notice here that the computer is controlling the computer room personnel by making certain basic demands of them. Before you get the notion the computer operators are the helpless slaves of the machine, you must remember that all this planned activity is to make the job of the operators more straightforward and less prone to error. There still are emergencies and still a number of intellectual tasks which operators must do that are beyond even the most magnificently endowed computer. We let the computer do all the standard thinking, and thus reserve ourselves for what we do best—emergency thinking in novel situations. This the computer cannot do well if it can do it at all. In fact, the computer can only deal with problems which have been thought out in advance. Or in a more sophisticated world, it can only deal with new problems if the technique of dealing with new problems has been completely described to it and it is given the means to recognize a new problem when one comes by.

COMMAND STATEMENTS

Procedures are called up by command statements. Command statements are usually very brief, partial sentences. They point to the procedure which is needed. The procedure called up is a collection of job control statements. The collection of job control statements tells the computer exactly what it is to do to accomplish some task or group of tasks assigned to it.

Command statements usually contain nothing more than the name of the procedure and the source of the procedure—that is, in which diskette or in which part of a disk drive it can be found. Command statements are deliberately constructed to resemble normal human forms of communication. They usually are short, to the point, and easy to remember. But do not forget, they merely refer to a series of job control statements.

Figure 4–7 might help to make the series of events clearer. But the wonder of it all is that much ordinary work can be done by simply issuing a command statement. If the work is routine, all the other elements have pretty well been worked out. And how this sort of thing happens with the IBM System/32 we will now bring into focus.

FIGURE 4–7. Command statements, procedures, jobs, and tasks

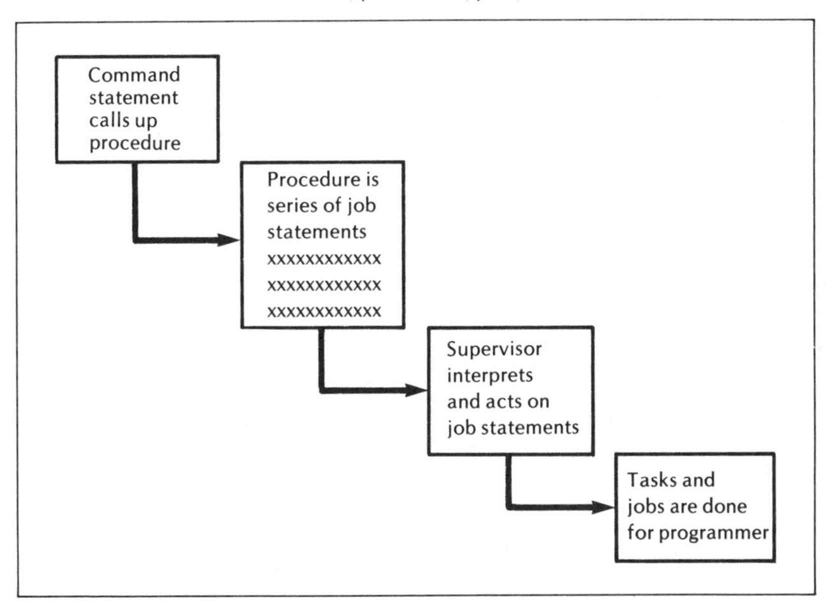

SYSTEM/32

Now, with our preliminary work done, we can take a look at the IBM System/32 as a computer system and see some of the programming features that are provided with that small computer.

The System/32 is equipped with a number of special programs which permit the programmer to deal directly with the system. The supervisory routine of the computer is called a system control program—no matter, it is the good old supervisory routine with which we are familiar, on a somewhat smaller scale. Communication between the computer operator and the system is handled by what is called an operating system command language—exactly what we meant when we used the terms job control and referred to groups of job control statements.

In the case of standardized operations, the communication with the system is by means of the command statement. Remember, a command statement calls up a particular procedure. And the procedure, as we recall, is nothing more or less than a collection of job control statements telling the computer system exactly what we want done.

Since most billing operations are rather straightforward for most business organizations of the size using a computer similar to the System/32, the system is provided with a simple procedure for handling such matters. The word BILLING typed on the typewriter keyboard will call up the billing procedure. So, when the computer user wants to perform a billing operation, he or she merely has to type the word BILLING, push the appropriate key on the typewriter keyboard, and the entire process will be performed, including the production of a printed report. Of course, the operator must be certain to have the correct diskette on the diskette drive and the blank paper in the printer. And one must previously, in another routine, have told the computer the name assigned to the data to be used in the billing operation. The information would then have been included in the job statements which make up the billing procedure itself. Usually, such matters are handled by a SAVE command statement. When this statement is given, one expects to give the data file to be saved a name. It is this name which will be incorporated into the billing procedure automatically. And naturally, one usually will have to give some kind of diskette identification if one wants to be certain to have the computer automatically check to make sure the right diskette is on the drive with the right information at the right time. Usually, such key numbers appear at the very beginning of a file. And the computer has a comparable number in its job statement routine to effect such a check. If all is not well, the computer operator is notified that the wrong diskette has been placed on the file. No magic here, just good forward planning.

Words like BILLING or SAVE, and many others, are the actual command statements for the IBM System/32. These command statements call up procedures (as we have said earlier). The procedures are made up of a series of job control statements which guide the computer through a standard set of operations.

Let us now summarize some of the things we have discussed. The System/32 will come complete with a supervisory program. We can speak to this "control" program through the command statements, if we are doing standardized operations, and through the command language, if we are doing something special of our own design.

When we are typing command statements we are dealing with one of the so-called high-level languages. Immediately beneath it is the procedure which is also a set of high-level language statements in the sense that we understand how to write such statements and use them. But underneath all this the procedure which is executed by the computer is in machine language—binary code of one kind or another.

If one knows very little about computing and the computer, one can nonetheless quickly make use of its standard facilities by carefully selecting the command statements which will trigger the kind of operation one desires. If one has been around the computer and learned the various usable statements in the command (job) language, one can design and name one's own procedures. Once the procedure has been designed and debugged (made free of error) and given an appropriate command name, one can use that name to call up the procedure. One has written one's own command statements for the system.

Here then, we have two levels of computer use—simple and sophisticated. The more sophisticated we are in our knowledge of the various languages handled by the computer system, the more individualized and complex our use of the system can be.

CONTROL (SUPERVISORY) PROGRAM FACILITIES

Let us now talk a bit more about the control program concept and what it can do to make the computer into a true computer system. The control system can be contacted through command statements typed on the keyboard of the System/32 typewriter. Some of the special keys on the typewriter keyboard also work as command statements. The cathode ray tube will display the command statements which are typed or keyed and will also provide messages to the operator from the control program when any number of standard errors are made. One typical error might be the misspelling of a procedure name (command statement). The computer control program would scan a list of acceptable command statements or procedure names in its basic file and report to the operator if the command statement called for does not exist in its file.

Let us put the matter even more simply. The operator talks to the computer through the keyboard of the typewriter. The computer talks to the operator through the cathode ray tube display system by flashing messages, or through the output printer by printing messages. The person and the computer work together to accomplish tasks to be done, provided those tasks have been carefully described (programmed) for the system either by the computer manufacturer or by the computer user.

The System/32 has control program facilities that include methods of maintaining the data files—those files which might be on either the diskettes or the main disk unit of the system. Such programs are called *utility programs* and will see to the basic and orderly housekeeping of the System/32 memory files. New procedures can be devised, and the utilities will see these are properly filed along with their names, which constitute the command statements appropriate to call up any particular procedure.

APPLICATION PROGRAMS

Manufacturers of small sophisticated computer systems like the System/32 have gone an additional step during recent years. It is now possible to buy, along with the computer system, a number of standardized, well-designed programs which apply to a particular *type* of business or industry. These special-purpose programs are called *application programs*. Some are suited to the construction business, others to the small retailing operation, still others to the wholesale food distribution industry. There are many more.

Again, we must note something special which will concern us in detail later in this book. When one buys an application program or set of programs for the computer system, one is accepting a standardized definition of one's needs and the steps which will be followed to satisfy them. Applications programs can be tailor-made only for the very large computer systems, as all programming is expensive and here we are talking about programming facilities as merchandise —they must be sold for profit. For the smaller computer installations the programming facilities are standardized. One computer user's application programs will be very much like those sold to any other similar computer user. A certain kind of industry-wide uniformity is bound to result from a large number of such programs in common distribution.

Even more important, we might want to note that the standardized programs have been designed by people outside the field. We do not mean to say programmers in the computer company have not consulted with experts in the field. What we mean is that the programs are ultimately designed by people who could not possibly be as familiar with the day-to-day operations of a particular type of company as could that company's own personnel.

Programmers, however well intended, tend to take the easiest steps they can in the solution of a problem. By this we mean some procedural steps are simpler than others for the programmer to write and to test. The programmer is usually more concerned with self-convenience than with the convenience of the ultimate user of the program. Try as one might, any programmer will have only limited success in imagining the needs of the personnel of the user company. And he or she will always be a step further removed from a knowledge of the satisfactions or disappointments of the user company's customers.

However, for many small businesses this type of standardized application programming, representing as it does the best efforts of a number of business and programming experts, is a distinct improvement over what the small businessman might be able to design or purchase. So we can expect a general improvement in the performance level of a small business making use of standardized programs and computer facilities. But we can also expect something of a loss in the way of creation of new solutions to basic industry problems. A standardized program may raise the level of a poorly run small business. It may enhance the profit picture for an ordinarily well-managed small firm. But by its very nature, it cannot trigger a totally new solution to any problem which falls under its jurisdiction.

REAL-TIME PROGRAMMING

We want to go one step further in understanding modern computer systems. When we were talking, earlier, about decks of cards being read into the computer to be worked on, we were talking about what is called *batch processing*. That is, a number of similar types of activities or jobs are grouped together so the computer can work on them all together. Or more typically, all the sales receipts for the day are collected and then converted to some kind of computer input form, cards, or computer scannable sheets of paper, and then they are all run through the computer during the night hours. This means one computer program can deal with a great chunk of data which is already fairly well organized.

Real-time data processing means nothing more or less than the computer has the ability to deal with each transaction as it occurs, regardless of its type. We are interested in real-time data processing from the point of view of the individual who uses a terminal to contact a computer. Certainly, it must be clear that a millionth or billionth-of-a-second computer can hardly waste valuable time chatting back and forth with a single individual at a single terminal. This would be a monstrous ineconomy. No, the computer works so very fast it can actually talk to dozens or hundreds of terminal operators at a time. What it does is collect the information coming in from the terminal a character at a time. It builds up the different messages in different parts of storage so in the end it has a complete message received from each terminal. Inside storage, then, are dozens or hundreds of individual messages. The computer acts on each of these as they are completed.

Imagine a hundred people sitting at a hundred terminals. Each time one of them is typing in a message at the terminal keyboard (at the fastest possible rate), that programmer thinks the computer is answering directly, since the response on the computer's part seems to be instantaneous. But the computer has been cycling through a circle of 100 terminals, picking up a character at a time from each terminal. It moves so fast none of the terminal operators will note the matter. Some messages will be shorter than others, and each will have some special signal marking its end. As it moves along the computer gets these end signals and then goes about the business of executing the commands or statements or sorting the data it is receiving in an appropriate area assigned on contact with that terminal. As time permits, the computer interrupts the cycling process (it moves so fast no one will notice), and actually runs the programs concerned in its "spare" time.

Multiprogramming—the idea that the computer can plan the tasks it is to do rather than handle single jobs—and the enormous speeds of modern computers add up to the ability to do "real-time" data processing (computer responses are so rapid no intervening time seems to have gone by to accomplish the actual calculations). Since the computer may be putting together a hundred different messages from a hundred different terminals and the data the terminal operators are also sending in, we can see the need for very large high-speed internal storage. And since the movement of data is in terms of millions of digits per second internally, and the calculations may be at the same rate, we can see the need to turn the internal control of computer over to a resident supervisory program. No human being could handle such a complexity at such a speed.

We need only to note, in conclusion, computers are that fast—and they do have that huge capacity and are run by supervisory programs of great sophistication. As a result, you and I can sit at a terminal and contact a computer with our problems and our data and live under the happy illusion we have had its undivided attention. We haven't, of course, but we don't care since the result is exactly the same.

AN APPLICATION

Let us now consider, as briefly as we can, a rather simple application of the System/32, making use of one of the typical application programs provided by the manufacturer of the device. We will be dealing with a Construction Management Accounting System. This particular system could be used by any contractor who has between 10 and 250 employees.

Typically, a construction company will have a president, a project manager, one or more field supervisors, an office manager, and one or more clerks. The jobs to be done will demand estimates, the construction plan itself, and field supervision and control.

Job estimates are essential as major input to any bidding which has to be done, and also as the first step in the construction plan itself should the bid be successful. Once a bid has been accepted the full construction plan must be developed in regard to labor, equipment, subcontracts, and materials. When construction has begun, the job of careful field control is essential to monitor material and labor usage, to avoid waste, and to deal with all the normal billing operations and payrolls.

The primary documents from which accounting and control operations will develop are labor time sheets, various invoices that record purchases of supplies and materials, and salaries of "exempt" employees. (Exempt usually means exempt from hour wage rates—straight-salaried personnel—clerks, accountants, and so on).

What standard results can the IBM System/32 produce from such basic computer input? The computer can generate, from the labor time sheets, an appropriate weekly payroll. Such a payroll production would include the FICA, local, state, and federal taxes, and would produce the appropriate paychecks, payroll reports, and union reports as required. The standard federal W-2 reports also would be prepared automatically from the basic input information.

From basic invoice information an accounts payable record would be automatically prepared and the normal record keeping functions performed. Included in such an accounting system would be all subcontract accounting work.

The computer also can prepare a general ledger and provide job costing reports so the contractor and staff can keep careful track of job costs—such information is very important for future bidding.

Two benefits accrue from the System/32 and the IBM Construction Management Accounting System (which can come with the system). First, the computer performs the basic functions of several bookkeepers or office staff people in a continuing, consistent, and economical fashion. More important, the computer can produce a host of special and revealing management reports. It is these reports which will tell the executive staff how things are really going—and, as a result of proper basic entries in the Construction Management Accounting System, they can be automatically generated.

Suppose, as president of such a firm, you are wondering what the total profitability of your firm is at the moment. Upon request, the computer system can produce a Statement of Income as shown in Figure 4–8.

FIGURE 4–8. Contractor's statement of income

STATEMENT OF INCOME

BYB CONTRACTORS COMPANY
NEW YORK, NEW YORK

S T A T E M E N T O F I N C O M E — PREPARED 9/25/74

FOR MONTH OF JAN. TO JAN. — REPORT INCLUDES MONTH 01

	----- C U R R E N T -----		PCT	--- L A S T Y E A R ---		PCT
CONSTRUCTION INCOME		46,000.00	100.00		45,000.00	100.00
LESS: DIRECT CONSTRCT COSTS:						
COST OF CONSTRUCTION - MATERIAL	5,000.00		10.86	1,000.00		2.22
COST OF CONSTRUCTION - DIRECT LABOR	10,150.00		22.06	1,000.00		2.22
COST OF CONSTRUCTION - SUBCONTRACTS	1,000.00		2.17	1,000.00		2.22
COST OF CONSTRUCTION - EQUIPMENT	.00		.00	1,000.00		2.22
COST OF CONSTRUCTION - GENERAL EXPENSES	600.00		1.30	1,000.00		2.22
TOTAL DIRECT CONTRACT COST		16,750.00	36.41		5,000.00	11.11

Courtesy of International Business Machines Corporation

A manager, scanning such a Statement of Income, can quickly and easily determine the current percentage direct labor is of construction income, make comparisons with the previous year, and the like.

Or suppose the contractor wishes to get a view of all costs and all revenues from all the current jobs in progress. The computer can, with the proper command statements, produce a Job Cash Flow Analysis similar to the one shown in Figure 4–9.

Certainly, in reading the Job Cash Flow Analysis, the contractor would be very interested in any projected losses in the far right-hand

FIGURE 4–9. Job Cash Flow Analysis

JOB CASH FLOW ANALYSIS

BYB CONTRACTORS CO. NO. 01 ×××× SUMMARIZED JOB CASH FLOW ANALYSIS ×××× DATE 9/25/74 PAGE 1 JC190

			----- C O S T -----				----- B I L L I N G -----			
JOB NUMBER	JOB NAME	% COMP	TOTAL ESTIMATED	EST. COST COMPLETED	ACTUAL COST COMPLETED	PROJ. COST REMAINING	CONTRACT AMOUNT	TO-DATE	REMAINING	PROJECTED PROFIT OR LOSS
326	POLICE HEADQTRS	33	832,175	274,617	270,057	548,297	950,000	215,000	735,000	131,646
327	MEDICAL BLDG.	92	800,000	736,000	730,113	63,488	750,000	750,000		43,601-LOSS
328	MINING COMPANY	86	750,000	645,000	645,095	105,015	850,000	660,000	190,000	99,890
329	WASHINGTON CO.	78	535,000	417,300	417,404	117,729				

Courtesy of International Business Machines Corporation

column. The earlier the contractor is advised of any such problems the quicker remedial action can be taken. In most cases, continued losses can at least be cut down and, in some cases, they can be compensated for by more efficient methods on other jobs—this is often accomplished by the skilled reassignment of key personnel.

When the contractor wishes to know more about specific costs for any particular job, he or she can have the computer system produce a Job Cost Analysis Report similar to the one illustrated in Figure 4–10. Such a report will reveal any direct labor costs which are projected to exceed the amounts budgeted. These are good management warnings.

FIGURE 4–10. Job Cost Analysis Report

JOB COST ANALYSIS REPORT

BYB CONTRACTORS CO. NO. 1 **** JOB COST ANALYSIS BY QTY/PERCENT REPORTED **** DATE 9/25/74 PAGE 1 JC110

326 POLICE HEADQTRS

COST CODE	COST TYPE	COST DESCRIPTION	ESTIMATED QUANTITY	QUANTITY TO DATE	QTY THIS WEEK	% COMPLETE	BUDGETED COST	TO-DATE COST	SHOULD BE	PROJECTED COST
002110	S	DEMOLITION					1,300			1,300
010000		GENERAL REQUIREMENTS				65	8,000	5,474	5,200	8,422**
		GENERAL REQUIREMENTS					2,000	25	25	2,000
	E	GENERAL REQUIREMENTS				75	3,000	2,554	2,250	3,406**
	M	GENERAL REQUIREMENTS				100	2,000	2,307	2,000	2,307**
	S	GENERAL REQUIREMENTS				65	16,545	10,575	10,754	16,269
021200		EXCAVATION				75	1,000	1,234	750	1,645**
	S	EXCAVATION				75	19,375	16,258	14,531	21,677**
026000	S	PAVING AND SURFACING					11,300			11,300
031000		CONCRETE FORMWORK	60,000	48,500		85	69,565	55,250	59,130	65,001
	E	CONCRETE FORMWORK				75	40,865	29,601	30,649	39,468
	M	CONCRETE FORMWORK				80	10,230	11,100	8,184	13,875**
032000		CONCRETE REINFORCMNT	100	65		65	24,320	17,118	15,808	26,336**
	E	CONCRETE REINFORCMNT				80	1,000	800	800	1,000
	M	CONCRETE REINFORCMNT		15,000	[illegible]	[illegible]	[illegible]	35,050	34,003	[illegible]

Courtesy of International Business Machines Corporation

Suppose you, as the contractor, want to know about the productivity of your labor force (labor cost is an extremely important part of the construction business). You can ask your computer and its related application programs for a Labor Productivity Report. Such a report is shown in Figure 4–11.

Now, with this sketchy application, let us sum up what we have here. We have a small-scale but powerful computer with its related programming systems. By also purchasing appropriate application programs (from the manufacturer) for our system, we can go about the business of mechanizing our record keeping. We require fewer people to do the job and we have better control over the records of the firm. We can frequently produce the major paperwork (payrolls and the like) quickly and automatically if we have established our basic record-entry system as recommended.

Most important, we can get automatically generated management reports of various kinds to help us do the job better.

Admittedly, these are standard programs. But, well-managed; standard programs and standard reports can mean the difference be-

FIGURE 4–11. Labor productivity report

LABOR PRODUCTIVITY REPORT

BYB CONTRACTORS CO. NO. 1 **** LABOR PRODUCTIVITY REPORT **** DATE 9/25/74 PAGE 1 PR.[illegible]

COST CODE	COST DESCRIPTION	QUANTITY EST.	QUANTITY TO DATE	UNIT COST EST.	UNIT COST TO DATE	TO DATE OVER ** OR UNDER	THIS WEEK QTY.	THIS WEEK UNIT CST	NET CHG. UNIT COST	PROJECTED OVER ** OR UNDER
326	POLICE HEADQTRS									
031000	CONCRETE FORMWORK	60,000	48,500	1.16	1.14	970				1,200
032000	CONCRETE REINFORCMNT	100	65	243.20	263.36	1,310**				2,016**
033000	CAST-IN-PLACE CONCRT	1,600	960	6.00	6.37	355**				592**
033600	SLAB-ON-GRADE CONCRT	15,400	10,640	.36	.39	319**				462**
	** JOB					1,014**				1,870**

Courtesy of International Business Machines Corporation

tween a profitable firm and one that is going under. And, of course, the system also has the flexibility that we can prepare our own special reports and use the command language and the job control statements we wish to generate for ourselves. We might begin with the application programs of a standard type and end with a uniquely designed and productive information system of our own.

So the small computer with its operating system and appropriate applications programs can be used in the wholesale food distribution business, the construction business, hospitals (for financial management), for retail stores of various kinds, for office equipment manufacturers and suppliers—for just about any small retail, wholesale, or manufacturing concern you care to name.

In the larger organizations, systems like the System/32 may be used on a departmental or a regional basis to handle domestic issues and then submit reports to a centralized management elsewhere. The possibilities are as endless as the ingenuity of the manufacturer of the computer and the user of the computer will permit.

It has been said that a business can survive almost any tragedy except the destruction of its records. We can put this another way—those businesses which do survive will survive because they have found out how to keep accurate records and how to use the information these provide to make judgments.

IMPLICATIONS

The implications of what we have discussed in this chapter are enormous. For instance, our historical review of the changes in computing indicates an acceleration in the capacities of computers beyond almost any other type of invention. Memory capacities go up ten times over, and then ten times over again. The cost of storage drops with equal drama. The field of microminiaturization and micromanufacture continually add new developments which reduce costs, increase capacities, generate newer and better forms of auxiliary storage, decrease the size of the computer as a physical entity, and constantly decrease the amount of time to accomplish any given task.

Even more important is what this means for software. The computer can now store ever larger and more sophisticated supervisory programs without reducing dramatically the amount of storage available for problem programs and problem data. This means the sophisticated software can imitate human intellectual behavior with greater and greater precision. It also means we can intercommunicate with the computer more and more as though it (the machine system) were another intellectual being. The languages approach our own natural languages and develop greater flexibility. The computer programs are so designed as to anticipate many types of standard behavioral patterns. The user needs to know less and less as the computer learns more and more.

This also means the computer can be used with increasing result in certain types of language analysis, art work, musical score analysis, and perhaps ultimately, the development of several remarkably different art forms themselves. Put another way, as the computer grows in sophistication, it can be given ever more complex tasks which previously had been thought to be the exclusive property of the better-educated or better-endowed members of the human race.

Ultimately, we would wish to have one general computer language which could embody in its operation both the mathematical requirements of the scientist and the linguistic requirements of the business people. If the language is broad enough and general enough it could, without too many internal adjustments, perhaps embody the whole scope of human linguistic activity.

There are dangers to be considered, too. In moving from the fundamental binary code to the higher-level languages we leave behind some of the reality of dealing with the computer. When we can call up job statements with simple commands, and each of these job statements can call up a series of instructions, and each of these instructional series represent a standard way of doing something, we have begged off invention and made the development of a new routine somewhat more difficult. If the performance in the first instance is reasonably satisfactory, we are not quite so apt to pursue greater perfection, greater economy, or greater efficiency.

The particular method of solving a problem, because it has been solved in the peculiar way of the computer, may well be adapted as a cultural norm. Other types of solutions could be looked on with suspicion. And naturally, the more we have invested in the particular solution technique the more reluctant we are to consider alternatives. Anyone who has read even a little bit of history is aware of these cultural traps: The earth is flat! The sun rotates around the earth! Women are more emotionally unstable than men!—and any amount of other rubbish which the race has long had great difficulty shaking off. We should not think, because we have made some small progress in shaking off old nonsense, that we are any less vulnerable to the new forms that nonsense may take.

We can get rid of the obvious errors. But we sometimes forget that many cultural traditions were useful in their time. The difficulty we face is how to determine when that time is past and how to accommodate ourselves to change. The computer can have greater influence in cultural affairs than almost any other device, since it is both mechanical and intellectual—it can do physical tasks for us and it can do "thinking" tasks for us. Here then is a compound tool.

Samuel Johnson put together the first broadly used dictionary. It helped to standardize spelling and took away that wonderful freedom which people had—to spell words the way they thought the words *ought* to be spelled. Is it possible that in developing refined languages to deal ever more accurately with the computer we would restructure our own native forms of expression? Would some of our wonderfully vague terms, which permit people to agree when there is no ground for agreement, vanish and leave us in naked conflict? It is certainly one kind of development which could occur.

If we can develop computers able to deal with vocal input, we certainly are going to have to settle on something close to phonetic spelling, or give ourselves over to very complex programs and great expense. Perhaps, after all, that would be an improvement. Think of the joy of the first grader who learns to spell cat "kat" (which he or she always thought was the right way to do it, anyway), or knee "ne."

SUMMARY

The concepts of supervisory programs are not necessarily simple, and the beginner might do well with a repetition of basic principles cast in slightly different contexts, touched on again, and then again.

We have seen the giant appetite of the modern computer and something of the ways we have to deal with that appetite. In the beginning, the computer was fed by keypunch operators and programmers working around the clock. For all of that effort, most of the time the computer sat idle since the speed of its internal structure was astronomically ahead of the speed of the mechanical devices trying to keep it fed.

With the development of supervisory programs, much of the work formerly done by programmers and computer operators could be turned over to the computer itself. At that point, the computer ceased to be a collection of very sophisticated hardware and became a sophisticated system.

Early programmers solved some of their problems by forming software clubs and exchanging programs with one another and with the computer companies who manufactured the machines. This process still continues. Such collections of programs resulted in libraries. The libraries demanded ever-increasing storage facilities. Happily, the auxiliary storage devices increased dramatically in capacity, as did the high-speed internal memories of computers.

Early programmers solved some of the language problems with the development of assemblers and compilers. These higher-level languages required translation before they could be used on data. But since the speed of the computer had increased a hundredfold, such repetitions did not cause any problem. Both assemblers and compilers have the advantage of simplicity from the programming point of view and the advantage of familiarity from the language point of view. Also, assemblers and compilers had a far better accuracy record in programming than the programmers themselves.

Job control statements are a handy high-language-level method of constructing procedures—those common routines which the computer operator or programmer might want done relatively frequently. Furthermore, since procedures can be given a name, and supervisory programs can deal with these names as pointers to the procedures, the job of contacting and working with the computer can be simplified.

The ability of the supervisory program to break the computer operation into tasks rather than entire jobs has led to multiprogramming, which has led to the ability of the computer to do real-time data processing. The common use of computer terminals has been one development of this process.

We have looked at some of the software facilities which come with even small computer systems: supervisory programs, assemblers, compilers, utility programs, application programs.

We have explored, very briefly and very simply, some of the internal data movement of a modern computer. We have described and discussed overlay areas as a natural outgrowth of the principle of destructive read-in and nondestructive read-out.

We have, then, enough information to understand some of the future hazards that computing will bring, some of the potential rigidities the very nature of the computer system demands, and some of the uniformities that may creep into our business world whether we like them or not.

HIGHLIGHT QUESTIONS

1. Define the term *computer hardware.*
2. Define the term *computer software.*
3. Tell how a computer is less than a computer system.
4. Distinguish between an assembler program and an assembler-language program as the terms have been used in this chapter.
5. Name some of the ways a compiler differs from an assembler.
6. Name some of the ways a compiler language differs from an assembler language.
7. What is a mnemonic?
8. Name two compiler languages and describe, briefly, their different purposes.
9. Does the System/32 have a compiler facility? What is its name?
10. Define a job control statement.
11. Define a procedure.
12. Define a command statement.
13. Write a single paragraph which puts job control statements, procedures, and command statements into proper perspective.
14. What is the difference, from the computer operational view, between a task and a job.
15. In your own words, in a paragraph or two, see if you can give a description of how 20 terminals would be contacted by the computer and how it handles the information it receives from each of the terminals.
16. List some of the things you might expect to find in a fairly large computer library.
17. What is the difference between a utility program and a user program?
18. Relate the term *overlay area* to destructive read-in and nondestructive read-out.
19. What is the meaning of the term *working storage?*
20. What are some of the advantages of application programs for a small business? What are some of the disadvantages of such programs?

READINGS

Couger, J. Daniel, and McFadden, Fred R. *Introduction to Computer Based Information Systems.* New York: John Wiley & Sons, 1975.

This book will take you step by step through the many concepts involved in understanding, developing, and using a computer based information system. The questions can be answered directly in the book—space is provided.

Hare, Van Court, Jr. *Introduction to Programming: A BASIC Approach.* New York: Harcourt, Brace & World, 1970.

This book has something on the history of computing. It also introduces the BASIC language, which would be particularly useful to students who have a computer terminal nearby. Overall, a good introduction to most major programming concepts.

Lynch, Robert E., and Rice, John R. *Computers: Their Impact and Use.* New York: Holt, Rinehart and Winston, 1977.

This fine text will take you step by step through many of the topics of covered in *Computers, Automation, and Society,* and then lead you into the rigors of the FORTRAN language in a most pleasant manner.

Seeds, Harice L. *FORTRAN IV for Business and General Applications.* New York: John Wiley & Sons, 1975.

Another very good book on the FORTRAN language. A paperback with plenty of examples. A very good section on programming preliminaries—flowcharts, printer spacing cards, and card layout forms is included.

CHAPTER 5

INTERCHANGES WITH THE COMPUTER

PURPOSE OF THE CHAPTER

In this chapter we are going to explore a few of the most frequently used methods of contacting the computer and receiving information from it. We are speaking about person-to-computer contact, on the one hand, and computer-to-person contact, on the other. We want to learn enough to be able to recognize many of the devices when we see them, and we want to know enough about how they operate to clear up any mystery with a little knowledge.

We also should observe that the person-to-computer-to-person types of devices are undergoing a dramatic development and change. Today's method of handling the intercommunication between human being and machine will be tomorrow's quaint and historic novelty.

TERMS AND CONCEPTS

We will attempt to give sufficient information about the terms and concepts which follow to make it possible for you to use them in reasonably well constructed and meaningful sentences. Such a goal will bring some reality to our conversations.

Hollerith card
zone punch
coding matrix
halfword
double word
modem
cathode ray tube
magnetic characters
special symbols
data collection system
common-carrier lines
product code readers
wand
optical character recognition
range limitation
smart terminals
digital plotter
audio-response
mark sensing
96-column card
digit punch
byte
word
telephone terminal
light pen
inquiry/display station
check scanners
check sorter
transmission terminal
voice-grade line
bar codes
scanners
special type fonts
second-level planning
time sharing
portable terminals
voice input
central position fallacy

THE HOLLERITH CARD

Short of hiding in a dark cave somewhere in the very backwaters of the United States during the last three decades, you simply could not have avoided encountering punched cards. They are fading away now—there are newer and easier ways to contact the modern computer. Yet you will see enough of them still in use to warrant at least a brief look at two major types.

Herman Hollerith devised the early punched-card forms and his name has been attached to the most common of these. Figure 5–1 shows the coding for numbers, alphabet, and special characters.

We do not wish to go into very much detail about the coding. Notice there are printed rows, from 0 to 9. A punch in a particular column in any of those printed rows (from 0 to 9) would represent that particular digit. For the alphabet a combination of punches would be used—12 and 1 for A, 11 for 1 for J, and 0 and 2 for S. A 12 punch and 2 punch in the same column would represent a B, a 12 and a 3 a C, and so on. The 11 and 2 would represent a K, an 11 and 3 an L, and so on. Sometimes three punches are used in the same col-

FIGURE 5–1. The Hollerith punched card

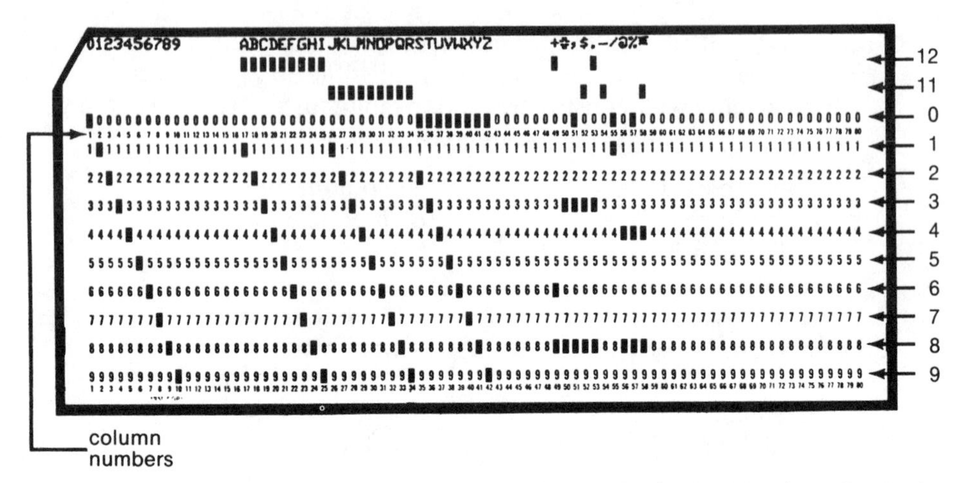

Courtesy of International Business Machines Corporation

umn to represent a special character. These codes are not, however, the binary code. When they are read by machines it is one of the functions of the reading machinery to change these card codes into the particular form of binary code used by the particular computer.

Again, examine the illustration. A digit punch alone (0 through 9) represents a number. A combination of one zone punch and one digit punch represents an alphabetic character. A combination of one zone punch and two or more digit punches represents a special character ($, *, #, and the like). Notice in the illustration that the 12 and the 11 zones are not printed on the card, though we have used numbers on the right of the illustration to show their relative card positions. Notice that the horizational zero position is used as a zone when combined with some digit punch, and as a digit punch indicator when it stands alone.

IBM 96-COLUMN CARD

For use with many of its smaller computers, the International Business Machines Corporation has developed a smaller card with greater capacity than the old Hollerith card. The card provides three sections in which a character may be recorded. In other words, there are three recording bands across the card rather than only one. Of course, in the smaller IBM card each section width is only 32 positions, instead of the Hollerith 80. But three such bands give 96 recording positions, rather than 80 in a card about one third as large as the Hollerith card—see Figure 5–2.

FIGURE 5–2. The IBM 96-column card

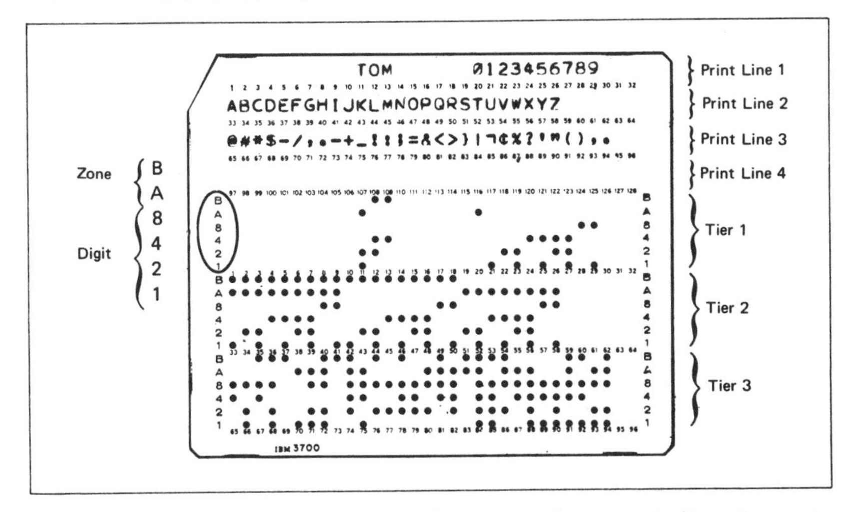

Courtesy of International Business Machines Corporation

Notice in the illustration that the coding is done by small circular punches in B A 8 4 2 1 positions. The B and A positions are zones, and the 8 4 2 1 positions are for recording digits. The number three, for instance, would be represented by a punch in the 2 position *and* a punch in the 1 position of the same column of one of the three bands (a 2 and a 1 are a 3). The B and A zones individually represent the equivalent of the 11 and 0 zones, respectively. The 12 zone of the old Hollerith card is represented by both a B and an A zone punch. So we can work out an equivalency to the old Hollerith card by proper coding in the new 96-column card.

EBCDI CODE

In Figure 5–3 we have a matrix for the Extended Binary-Coded Decimal Interchange Code—one of the common codes in IBM computers and abbreviated EBCDIC.

It is not difficult to read the matrix. Let us find A. We look up to the top of the chart, above the A and find bits 0 and 1 are to be 11. Bits 2 and 3 are to be 00. So we assemble these and we have 1100. Then we look to the left of the row in which the A appears and we get the code for bits 4, 5, 6, 7. These are 0001. The complete code for the letter A inside the computer is, therefore, 1100 0001. Now it just happens these eight binary digits make up what we call a "byte"—the basic storage unit in many modern computers. Two bytes make up a halfword. Four bytes make a word. Two words make a double word. Figure 5–4 shows the combinations.

FIGURE 5–3. The EBCDIC coding matrix

Bits 0-1	00				01				10				11			
Bits 4,5,6,7 / Bits 2-3	00	01	10	11	00	01	10	11	00	01	10	11	00	01	10	11
0000					SP	&	-									0
0001							/		a	j			A	J		1
0010									b	k	s		B	K	S	2
0011									c	l	t		C	L	T	3
0100									d	m	u		D	M	U	4
0101		NL							e	n	v		E	N	V	5
0110									f	o	w		F	O	W	6
0111									g	p	x		G	P	X	7
1000									h	q	y		H	Q	Y	8
1001									i	r	z		I	R	Z	9
1010					¢	!		:								
1011					.	$	,	#								
1100					<	*	%	@								
1101					(	)	_	'								
1110					+	;	>	=								
1111					|	¬	?	"								

Courtesy of International Business Machines Corporation

FIGURE 5–4. Bytes and words

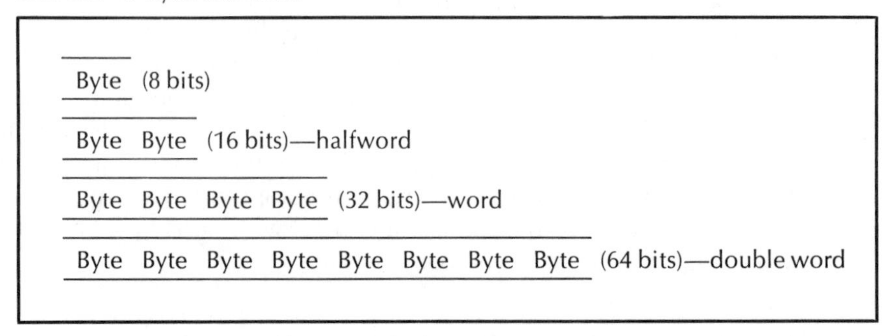

A byte is made up of eight bits (binary digits). Since a bit is either zero or one, on or off, light or no light, we can see how the expression of numbers can be mechanized in the computer. When we strike a key on a typewriter connected to the computer, or feed in a punched card, or feed in a sheet which can be read by the computer scanners, this information is converted to the appropriate form of binary code which the machine can handle and store.

What we have explored is sufficient information, for our purposes, about the way the computer receives and stores information. We are much more interested in the types of devices we might run across when we wish to communicate directly with the system. We need not concern ourselves overmuch about the exact form the information takes when it reaches the inside of the computer. If we strike the correct key or prepare our scannable forms correctly, the information will be duly converted and properly recorded.

TELEPHONE TERMINALS

A terminal is nothing more than the end of the line. Or in the case of computer work, it might be more appropriate to say the beginning of the line—that point at which information for the computer originates.

One very straightforward method of contacting a modern computer is via the telephone. A form of the touch telephone called a Transaction Telephone[1] is coupled with a special display device, such as VuSet.[2] One simply calls the computer using the telephone. A special recognition tone is returned to the caller, which tells him the computer is on the line and ready to receive data. Then the user pushes appropriate buttons on the telephone to enter the data. The screen, if required, will display the information as it is entered. When the computer responds, it will respond with printed information on the display unit. The caller can then disconnect and the information will remain on the viewing screen until such time as it is no longer needed and is cleared by the viewer.

Figure 5–5 shows the Transaction Telephone and the VuSet display screen. Four lines of information regarding a Mr. A. B. Smith are shown on the screen.

Figure 5–6 illustrates the communication links—telephone to central telephone office to 'VuSet modem to the computer.' A modem, or "data set" as it is sometimes called, has to do with changing direct current signals to the kind that can be handled by telephone transmis-

---

[1] The Touch-Tone Transaction Telephone is a registered trademark of AT&T Co.

[2] VuSet is a product of the Plantronics Company.

FIGURE 5–5. Transaction Telephone and VuSet display

Courtesy of AT&T Co. and of Plantronics Company

sion circuits. When a direct current signal is changed (from computer equipment to transmission form) we call the process "modulation." When we are going the other way, we call the process "demodulation." The equipment handling these twin tasks goes by the term *modem* or by the term *data set*. The term modem is preferred, since data set can refer to clusters of information stored in the computer itself. The computer then sends the return message to a VuSet modem and from there it goes to the central office and finally to the VuSet display.

Another form of the Transaction Telephone is shown in Figure 5–7. The primary uses of this type of device would be for credit authorization or check verification. The system can collect and store information about transactions while the contract with the computer is being established. When the connection is completed, the telephone will automatically transmit all the stored data. Special features, such

FIGURE 5–6. Telephone and VuSet communication links to the computer

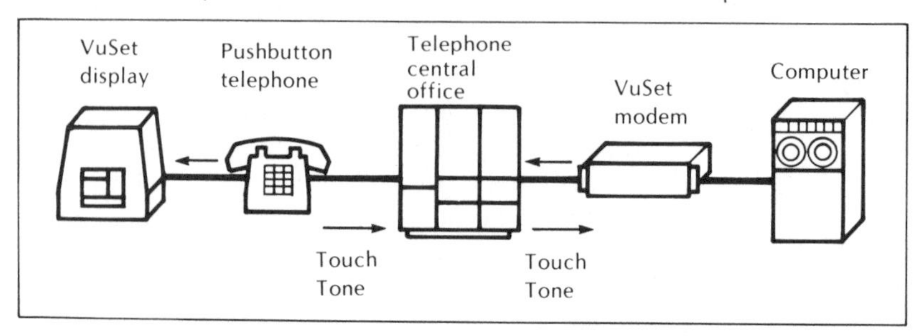

FIGURE 5–7. Transaction Telephone

Courtesy of AT&T Co.

as automatic dialing and magnetic card reading, can be added to the basic system.

THE LIGHT PEN

The light pen is used in conjunction with a cathode ray tube (CRT). Or putting it another way, we can use a pen instrument which beams a light at a television screen to write on the screen. The message is read by the computer from the screen and put into internal storage just as a message coming in by any other method is handled. Figure 5–8 shows a young terminal operator drawing (or correcting the drawing of) a house projected on a cathode ray tube by the computer. The computer can record the drawing corrections, place them in storage, and then flash the corrected drawing on the screen for further examination and correction.

The amount of information fed into the computer by the light pen is deceptive. All information in the computer is ultimately in the form of binary coded numbers explored earlier. The simple lines on the cathode ray tube are so converted. This means the actual amount of numeric information stored may be very large, even though only a line or two had been rather quickly drawn by the young woman. In a complex geometric form a single stroke of the light pen might generate thousands of special formulas in the computer memory. The light pen, then, can be a very rapid method for getting a specific type of information into the computer. We must not be deceived by apparent

FIGURE 5–8. The IBM 2250 display unit and light pen in use

Courtesy of International Business Machines Corporation

simplicity. Nor should we overlook the important interaction taking place between the computer and the woman. She is giving the computer information and she is receiving information in return. She may draw a slightly wobbly line—the computer will correct it. She may ask the computer for information regarding specifications for the building of what is pictured and will receive a detailed answer. The young woman also may ask the computer to rotate the image on the screen to provide a different perspective. Once given that new perspective, she may wish to alter the image and then have the computer compare the new configuration with an old one previously drawn. The computer can highlight the differences in both terms of basic design and in terms of possible cost. In more complex programs the computer could even make recommendations for further changes.

INQUIRY/DISPLAY STATIONS

Usually an inquiry/display station is located a considerable distance from the actual computer or computer room. Often it may be a simple device at a desk somewhere within the organization which is directly connected to the computer. Typically, you might find such a device in the office of an engineering executive. This will permit directly asking the alerted computer for a certain kind of report or drawing on the cathode ray tube, and also permit the entering of specific information into the computer without having to leave the office or the desk. Figure 5–9 shows such an inquiry/display station that makes use of a typewriter keyboard and a cathode ray tube. Of course, an inquiry station could simply be a typewriter connected directly to the computer. The computer would receive inquiries from the typewriter and answer back via the typewriter. Sometimes, though, a picture really is worth a thousand words, and the comprehension is greater than would be the case with words or numerals alone.

A display station can usually show from 50 to 60 lines of copy. Usually a line is about 75 characters in length. The information can be

FIGURE 5–9. IBM 2260 inquiry/display station

Courtesy of International Business Machines Corporation

generated so fast on the screen by the computer that the entire printing surface may appear in an instant. The computer also can draw a picture on some display screens and revolve the picture on command, giving the different views required. Of course, the more flexible the picture making and the writing ability of the cathode tube, the more expensive the inquiry/response station is likely to be. We should not purchase more information generating ability than we actually need for any given case in point. But we should remember our needs and demands are likely to expand in the future as we get used to having the kind of information we need when we want it.

In most cases a simple inquiry station made up of a typewriter which can receive information and type information received would be a good deal cheaper than an inquiry/display station made up of the input keyboard and the output cathode ray tube. The addition of a light pen would require greater complexity and hence greater cost than the simple inquiry/display station.

CHECK SCANNERS

If you have a checking account you are probably familiar with the strange figures written across the bottom of the check. They are constructed in such a way that a scanner can place them over a matrix and "read" the actual digits and the special code signals which precede or follow them. Figure 5–10 shows a check with such figures across the bottom.

Figure 5–11 shows an enlargement of the magnetic characters against a matrix. These characters are so designed that even if they are out of position, or partly obscured in the matrix, they will still present

FIGURE 5–10. Check with magnetic ink characters

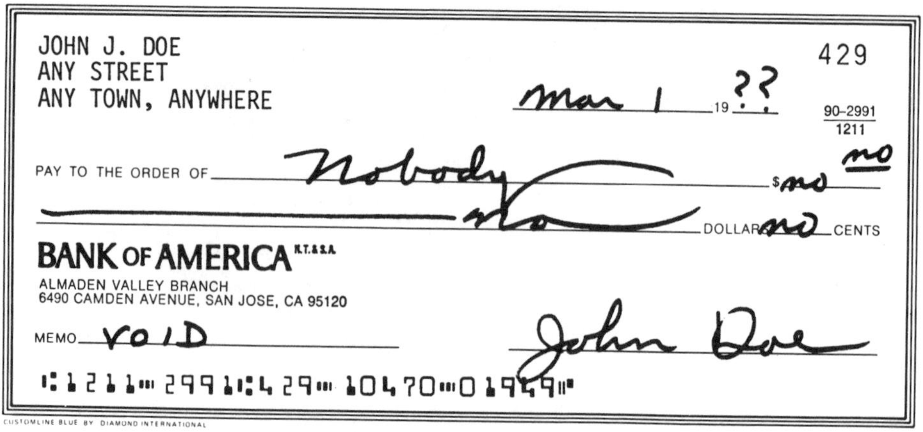

JOHN J. DOE
ANY STREET
ANY TOWN, ANYWHERE

429

Mar 1 19 ??

90-2991
1211

PAY TO THE ORDER OF Nobody $ no no

No DOLLARS no CENTS

BANK OF AMERICA N.T.&S.A.
ALMADEN VALLEY BRANCH
6490 CAMDEN AVENUE, SAN JOSE, CA 95120

MEMO VOID

John Doe

1211 2991 429 10470 01949

CUSTOMLINE BLUE BY DIAMOND INTERNATIONAL

FIGURE 5–11. Characters in a matrix

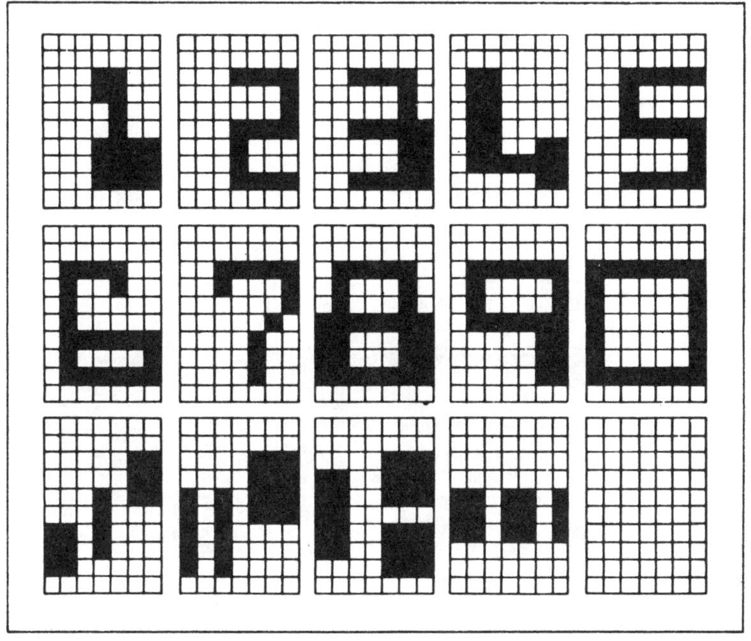

Courtesy of International Business Machines Corporation

a unique configuration which the scanner can recognize. You can doubtless read the numbers themselves plainly enough.

Filgure 5–12 gives the meanings of the different special symbols. No amount symbol appears at the bottom of the particular check illustrated, because the amount of the check has not yet been keyed

FIGURE 5–12. Special check symbols

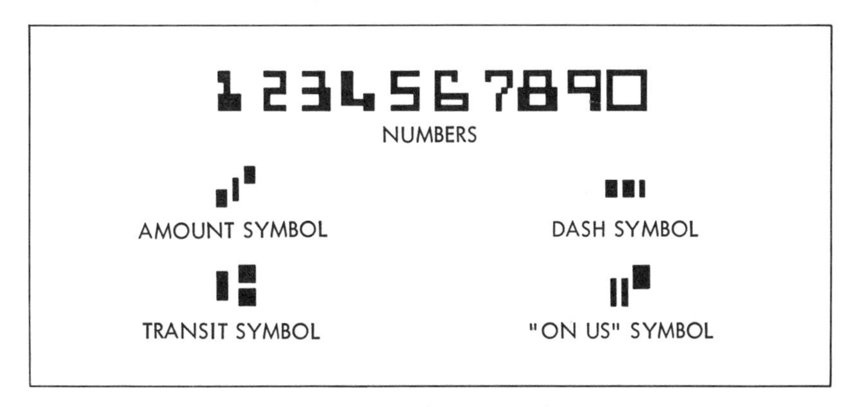

Courtesy of International Business Machines Corporation

in by the operator who prepares the checks for the scanner. When the amount is added to the bottom of the check, it would appear to the right and would be preceded and followed by the amount symbol.

Figure 5–12 illustrates the special symbols for amount, transit, dash, and "on us."

Finally, we ought to have a look at a typical high-speed check-sorting machine, such as the IBM 1412 Magnetic Character Reader. The device is shown in Figure 5–13. It is by means of such devices that

FIGURE 5–13. IBM 1412 Magnetic Character Reader

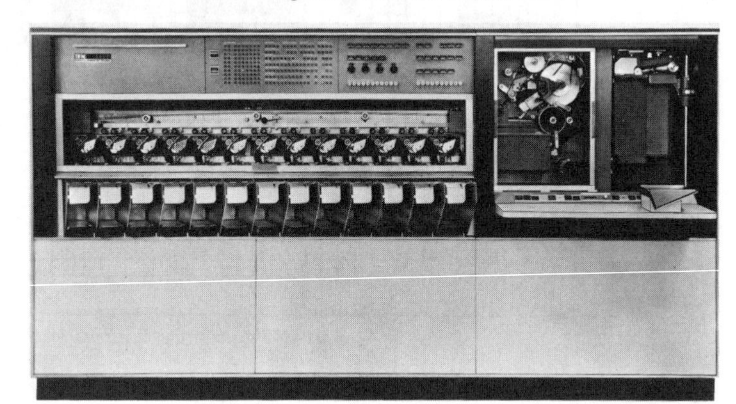

Courtesy of International Business Machines Corporation

banks are able to sort and handle billions of checks a year and, in most cases, properly debit and credit the right accounts in the right banks at the right time for the right amount. Without such high-speed devices the cost of handling checks would soon grow prohibitive. As in manufacturing plants, mass production brings a reduction of cost per item.

DATA COLLECTION SYSTEMS

Data collection systems are most likely to be found on the floors of production plants some distance away from the actual computer system. They provide the computer with up-to-the-minute information about manufacturing operations. Also, the computer can respond to inquiries from plant operation managers on printers attached to the collection devices. Collection devices can often accept time-punched work cards, special keyed-in information, special inventory cards, worker plastic identification badges, and the like. This can mean the computer is up to date on how many hours each worker has worked to that moment, what particular jobs are worked on, and what remains to be done. In turn, this information can be arranged into the proper accounting structures to show an inquiring corporate manager what the current costs of manufacture are on any given set of products in terms of materials, labor, and overhead. Figure 5–14*A* shows an input station of a data collection system. Figure 5–14*B* shows the printer of the same system.

The IBM 1031 input station can transmit about 60 characters per second to a distant computer, and the IBM 1033 printer can operate at reasonably comparable rates.

The point to remember, though, is not the speed of any individual data collection system but rather that a large number of such stations can be linked to a computer and can all operate in a "simultaneous" manner. A typical data collection system can deal efficiently and at high speed, with punched-time cards, employee identification badges, inventory cards, and other typical shop information. No shop clerk can match this type of information production and transfer.

FIGURE 5–14A. IBM 1030 data collection system
(1031 input station 5–14A)

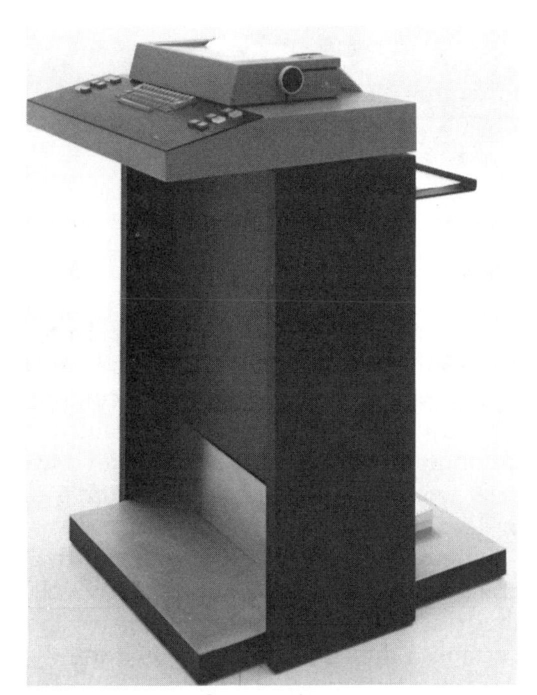

Courtesy of International Business Machines Corporation

FIGURE 5–14B. IBM 1030 data collection system (1033 Printer)

Courtesy of International Business Machines Corporation

TRANSMISSION TERMINALS

Transmission terminals are very similar to inquiry stations. But here we are thinking of receiving information from terminals not a few hundred or thousand feet from the computer but perhaps hundreds or thousands of miles away. This means the terminal is connected to the computer via telephone or telegraph wire networks—"common-carrier lines," as they are called. Figure 5–15 shows a data transmission terminal.

In the case of the IBM 1001 unit shown in Figure 5–15, we are discussing a system able to transmit at 12 characters per second over either leased or public common-carrier lines. The telephone is used to establish the connection in much the way you and I use the telephone to establish contact with a friend in a distant city or in the neighborhood. The data-handling segment of the unit makes use of a simple keyboard (to the extreme right in the illustration), or a punched-card reader (in the center of the illustration). Because the information is transmitted over voice-grade lines, the speed of the transmission is somewhat more limited than it can be over special direct computer cables. But since the connection is making use of already existing communication nets on a sporadic basis, the results are satisfactory and the price is reasonable.

FIGURE 5–15. IBM 1001 data transmission terminal

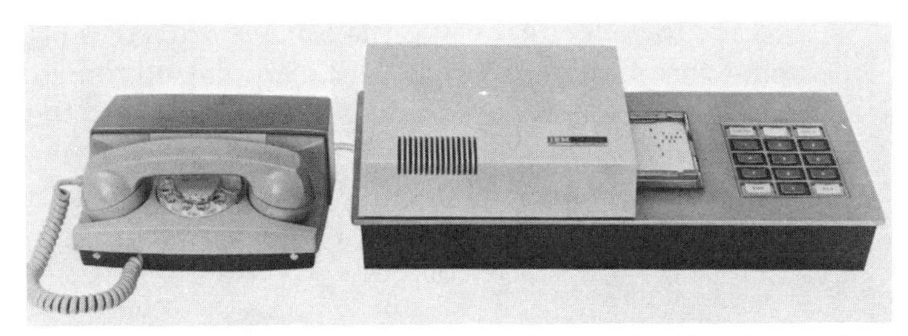

Courtesy of International Business Machines Corporation

UNIVERSAL PRODUCT CODE READERS

Technically, universal product code readers are not as direct as a person using a light pen to change a design because, the person cannot read the information in the product code. He or she must rely upon the numbers appearing below the bars, and these numbers, in turn, may be special codes which will trigger a host of other information stored in a computer. Figure 5–16 shows a typical universal product code strip.

FIGURE 5–16. Universal product code symbols

The codes are often item inventory numbers. The number is looked up in a computer inventory array, which reveals the price per item and other pertinent information. The computer is capable of compiling a total for all such items read into it and can then produce through a cash register, which is an integral part of the system, an appropriate total and also a sales slip. At the same time the computer can update the records of the organization in terms of item turnover, possible reorder points, and similar accounting records. Or the light pen and slot scanning device can be connected to simpler mechanisms, which can merely produce appropriate amount totals from an appropriate cross-indexed list of bar codes and prices.

In Figure 5–17A we see a typical light pen, or wand, and 5–17B the IBM 3666 checkout scanner. An item carrying a stick-on bar code label merely has to be passed over the reading slot in the top of the scanner to generate the information needed. For bulky or odd-shaped items the scanning pen is best. For flat-bottomed or rectangular packaged products the scanning slot can be faster. The idea, of course, is to leave the recognition of codes to machinery that is constructed to make far fewer errors than a clerk reading prices would make.

FIGURE 5–17A. Optical light pen

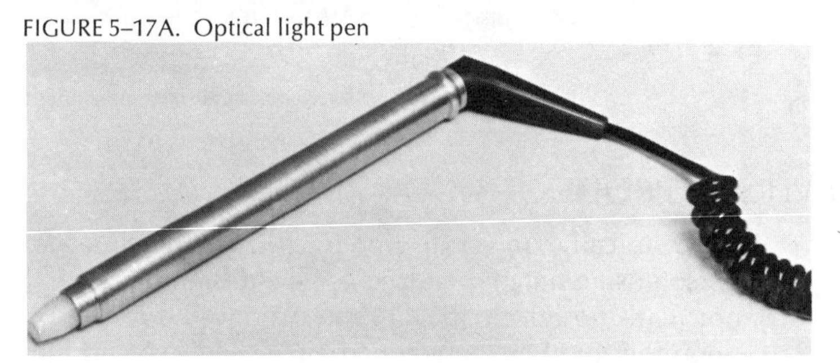

Courtesy of International Business Machines Corporation

FIGURE 5–17B. The IBM 3666 checkout scanner

Courtesy of International Business Machines Corporation

There has been some public resistance to the use of bar codes on merchandise in retail stores. Actually, the use of such codes and code-reading systems can materially improve not only the accuracy of calculations but the speed with which clerks can handle checkout lines. The worry about "hidden" prices may be relieved by including clearly readable price stamps on the merchandise along with the universal product code symbols. At least this would seem wise for a few years until the public becomes comfortable with the reliability of the bar codes themselves. In the long run, however, the goal is to have the bar codes printed right on the merchandise labels and to eliminate the necessity for clerks to affix prices to each and every item on the display shelves. The shelves, of course, could carry the prices for public view.

Whether public resistance will continue for a long time or whether some less expensive solution to the problem can be reached, we cannot say. Accuracy and speed are once again pitted against the more basic needs of human beings. In the past, efficiency and speed have almost always been triumphant. Still, if the cash register can produce a detailed list of products purchased with both produce name and pertinent size and price information, the suspicious customer may be satisfied. In the meantime, both bar code and arabic-numeral price information seem to be an acceptable combination—not quite as speedy as computer people wanted, not quite as bad as the ordinary customer expected. Too, we must remember the deep resentment and resistance of customers when the telephone company moved away from the combination of letters and numbers that gave us such lovely combinations as REgency 2-2000 and CHerry 4-7000 to such dullards as 732-2000 and 244-7000. The latter lack glamour and are harder to remember. But habit takes over and we are all more or less used to seven-digit local numbers and to ten-digit national phone numbers. We grumble, but we adapt—the story of the human race.

SCANNERS

Scanners, as we will here use the term, can be of two types—those capable of reading magnetic ink characters (which we have discussed earlier in the chapter) and those capable of reading special characters or marks printed on paper. This latter process is called optical character recognition (versus magnetic character recognition). Figure 5–18 shows a modern optical page reader which can handle documents ranging from 3 by 1.6 inches all the way up to documents measuring 9 by 14 inches—a pretty fair range.

It is a little difficult to pin down the exact reading speed of an opti-

FIGURE 5–18. IBM 1288 optical page reader

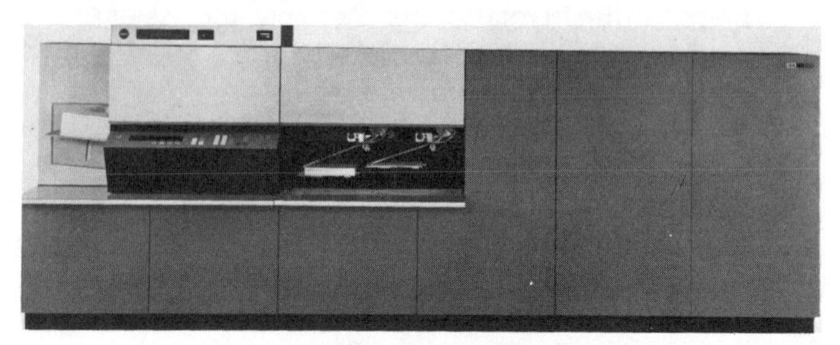

Courtesy of International Business Machines Corporation

cal page reader, because a good deal depends upon the size of the document being fed through the machine and upon the number of lines on a page and the number of words to a line. But we can calculate a range of about 7,872 characters per minute for the reading of punched cards (the printing on the card is read, not the holes) to 45,500 characters per minute for a standard 8½-by-11-inch sheet of paper being fed through the machine at the rate of 14 pages per minute.

SPECIAL TYPE FONTS ARE USED FOR WRITING THESE RECOGNIZABLE PAGES VERY SIMILAR TO THE TYPE IN WHICH THIS PARTICULAR SENTENCE IS BEING PRODUCED. A TYPICAL SET OF SCANNABLE CHARACTERS WOULD BE 1234567890, ABCDEFGHIJKLMNOPQRSTUVWXYZ, AND ⑂⑀⑁$%|&*{}—+ǂ":?., =⑄'/.

Scanners hold a great deal of promise for the future. During the last decade they have become a good deal more reliable and have been designed to read an ever greater variety of print symbols, special marks on papers, careful hand printing, and photographic materials. Ultimately, the goal would be to eliminate many of the intermediate data preparation forms, like card keypunches, and be able to feed ordinary human-prepared daily documents directly into the machines, convert this information to electronic pulses, and feed the information directly into the computer.

Perhaps a more familiar form of the scannable document would be the gasoline charge slip. Figure 5–19 is a mock-up of such a card.

The customer is issued a plastic credit card by the company; it contains an identification number, the name (and address) of the customer, the date when such cards were first issued to the customer, and the expiration date of the current credit card itself. When a

FIGURE 5–19. Gasoline credit charge slip

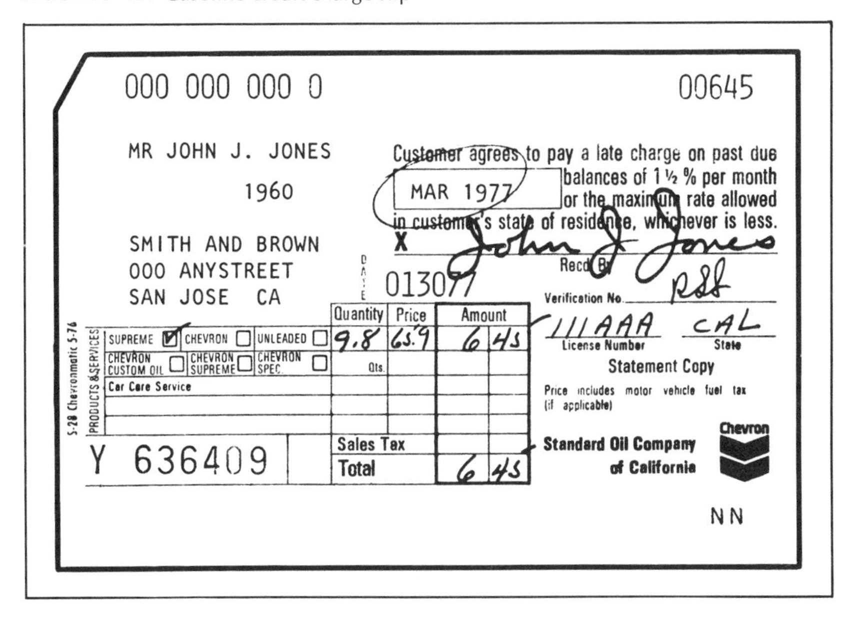

000 000 000 0 00645

MR JOHN J. JONES
1960

SMITH AND BROWN
000 ANYSTREET
SAN JOSE CA

Customer agrees to pay a late charge on past due balances of 1½ % per month or the maximum rate allowed in customer's state of residence, whichever is less.

MAR 1977

X John J Jones

DATE 013077

Rec'd By

Verification No. R88

PRODUCTS & SERVICES			Quantity	Price	Amount
SUPREME ☑	CHEVRON ☐	UNLEADED ☐	9.8	65.9	6 45
CHEVRON CUSTOM OIL ☐	CHEVRON SUPREME ☐	CHEVRON SPEC. ☐	Qts.		
Car Care Service					
Y 636409			Sales Tax		
			Total		6 45

S-28 Chevronmatic 5-76

111AAA CAL
License Number State

Statement Copy

Price includes motor vehicle fuel tax (if applicable)

Standard Oil Company of California

Chevron

NN

gasoline purchase is made at the station the card is handed to the pump attendant, who places the card along with a blank charge slip in a small machine near the pumps. Then the attendant sets a series of levers that record the amount of the purchase along a vertical scale. The lever at the top of the machine is then shoved across the card-holding machine. This causes the customer's number, name, first date of joining the company, and card expiration date to be imprinted on the credit slips. The name of the service station, its address, and the amount of the purchase would be recorded at the same time.

In Figure 5–19 the characters in the upper left-hand corner of the card (the customer's number—000 000 000 0), and the characters in the right-hand corner (00645—the amount of purchase) can be read by a scanner connected to the computer at the gasoline company office. The customer's name, date of joining the company, date of card expiration, and date of purchase of the gasoline also can be read by machinery. So, too, can the name and any special identification number of the service station itself.

Since we are interested in data processing and its potential for accuracy, you might notice in the illustration certain built-in error checks. The service station attendant has circled the expiration date (March 1977) to indicate he or she has checked it to be certain the card is not out of date. Also, the attendant has been required to write the amount of the sale in handwriting. This can be compared to the keyed-in amount of the sale (6.45). Also, the attendant may be required to initial the card as a further control check. All these activities serve to reduce the errors which can occur between person and machine.

We should see a good deal more of this initiation of computer usable information at the point of sale in the future. The more work individuals do at the point of sale, the less there is to be done at the computer center. And since the salesperson is obviously more intimately acquainted with what happened at the point of sale, the more information obtained from him or her the better.

MARK SENSING

Perhaps in the process of registering in a class, or of taking an examination, you have been required to fill in little printed bubbles with marks from an ordinary pencil. Whenever and wherever you have done this, you have been preparing a special form which can be "mark sensed" or scanned. A number of machines have been devised to recognize the presence or absence of such a mark and to construe either one as information to be fed into a computer. Such devices are considerably less expensive than those designed for reading print and can be made to handle the mark-sensing chores quickly and easily.

From time to time when you buy an electric mixer, razor, iron, or other device, you are given a "guarantee" card and asked to make marks in little boxes on the card which are "yes," "no," "don't know" responses to specific questions. These cards serve two purposes—to register the fact of purchase for purposes of guarantees, and to provide marketing information to the company selling the product. The cards, if they are properly filled out by the customer, can be read rapidly by special scanning devices and the information can be fed directly into the computer. This type of scanning is cheaper to handle than letter or numeral reading. The bubbles are in predetermined positions. The recognition device built into the scanner has only to record the presence or the absence of a black mark within the bubble.

COMPUTING INQUIRY STATIONS

We have discussed the simpler inquiry stations earlier in the chapter. Here we are going to be concerned with more recent and sophisticated inquiry stations using cathode ray tubes for graphic output as well as printers for permanent records. Even though an inquiry station, shown in Figure 5–20, is made up of an input device (typewriter-like keyboard) and an output device (cathode ray tube) only, this type of inquiry station can be equipped to have a considerable computing power of its own, becoming a "smart terminal." This is one of the more recent developments that increases the power of what we call "remote terminals." It is now possible with such devices to do a good deal of the basic organization of data which is to be fed into the computer. And if the problem is relatively simple, the smart terminal can solve the problem without the necessity of contacting the

FIGURE 5–20. Remote terminal

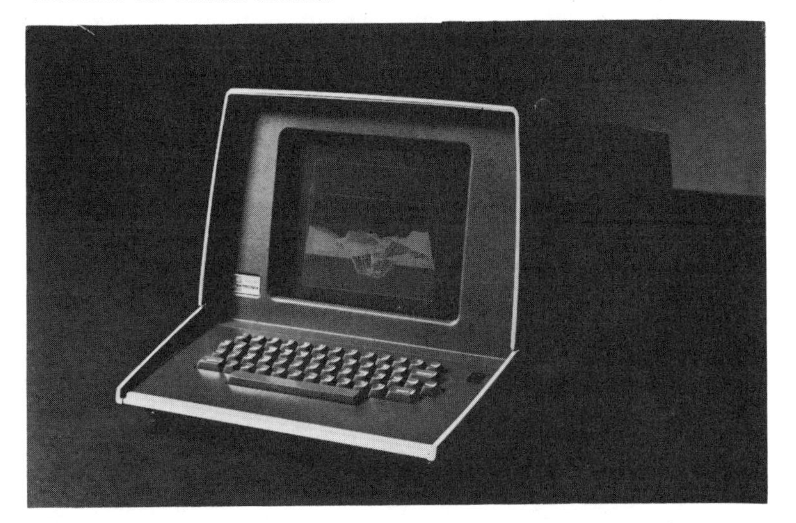

Courtesy of Tektronix, Inc.

computer. We have, then, both an inquiry/response terminal and a small computer at our disposal.

Let us again introduce the concept of time sharing. What we mean by the term is that hundreds of different remote terminals may share the capacities of a single large computer—this due to the enormous speed of the computer and the slowness of ordinary human response. Time sharing, because of its "ring-around-the-rosy" nature, permits what we call real-time data processing. If most of the problems are simple and can be handled by the remote terminal, with only occasional recourse to contacting the computer, more of these units can be hooked into the system and more individuals can contact the computer as required. We are, then, combining the abilities of a remote terminal with the abilities of a small computer to be able to load the large computer with a maximum of possible contact points. All this is due largely to the microminiaturization of computer parts and to the advanced methods of computer circuit design. The terminal, basically a small unit, will gain increasing computing power over the years.

Many of these newer terminals not only can present complex graphic displays on the cathode ray screen but can, at the same time, produce a hard copy of the information and record the information by means of a type recorder so it can be reproduced again later. Such a combination of elements is shown in Figure 5–21 to the left of the young people considering a graphic problem. The tape unit is to the extreme left in the installation. In the middle we can see the remote terminal itself. To the right is a hard-copy graphics reproducer. Here what is shown on the cathode ray tube is drawn out on paper for leisurely consideration, storage, or mailing. If these facilities are not required often, only one such unit may be required. In the illustration, we see three of the simpler devices in the background staffed by three young women.

FIGURE 5–21. Cathode ray tube display with hard copy device and magnetic tape recorder.

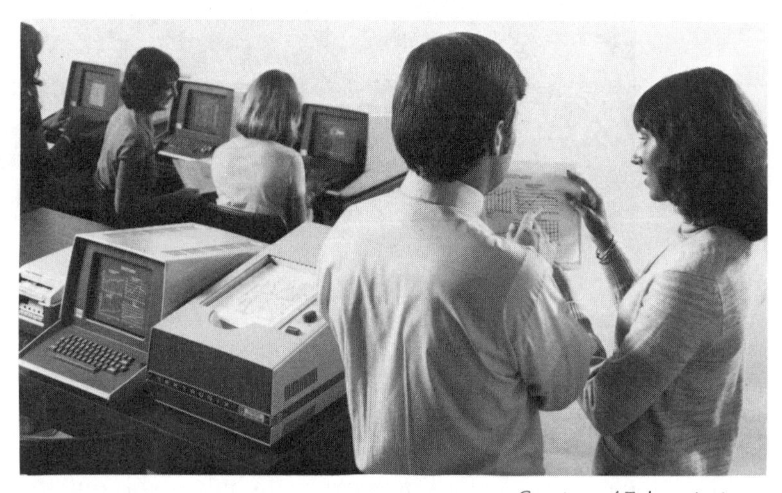

Courtesy of Tektronix, Inc.

DIGITAL PLOTTERS

It might be that we do not need an inquiry/station to produce the kind of information we want. Our wants may be simpler. What we might require would be merely graphic output from the computer. A clear diagram can take the place of hundreds of paragraphs of complicated explanation, particularly in the fields of mathematics and engineering. There is an increasing use of digital plotters directly connected to the modern computer system—even the smaller computers. Such plotters can produce graphs, charts, drawings, and other line displays. Figure 5–22 shows such a plotter in action producing a complex geometric figure which, in formula form, could not otherwise convey nearly so neatly so much valuable information. Some managers, bound to the concept that all documentation must be words, have sometimes neglected the economic value of this kind of presentation.

FIGURE 5–22. Complot DP–3 digital plotter producing a graphic display

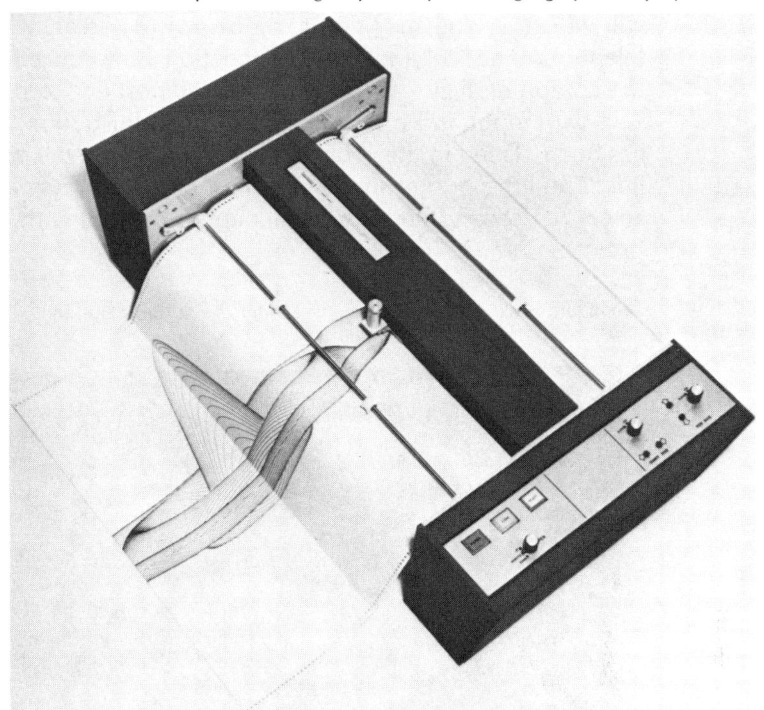

Courtesy of Houston Instrument, Inc.

Why the term *digital plotter?* Because computers work in units (chunks) rather than continuous condition. That is, numbers are expressed as wholes or as decimal equivalents of fractions. A digital plotter, then, is a device which converts these chunks into a continuum so that straight and curved lines may be drawn. We've all done something very similar when we mark out a few points along a curve and then try to draw a continuous line to touch all of those points. The same kind of translation, or "interpretive" process, takes place whenever a visual display screen shows something other than the actual digits or letters or the actual special symbols. These graphic displays are not really facts, then, but inferences from a number of points. This does not mean we shouldn't have faith in what the screen produces; but it does mean we ought to be aware that what we see is the result of a number of adjustments between points and inferred connecting lines. Naturally, the closer the points being followed by the inferred line, the less guesswork is involved.

PORTABLE TERMINALS

Today it is possible to carry your own computer terminal with you wherever you may go. It can be put to use anywhere there is a telephone line to handle the connection between the terminal and the computer. Figure 5–23 shows a small portable terminal with both keyboard input and printer output. In the illustration, the telephone has been placed in the proper position to handle the communication link. The little printer in the illustration can produce about 30 characters per second on the special paper provided with the system.

FIGURE 5–23. Texas Instruments Model 745 portable terminal

Courtesy of Texas Instruments, Inc.

This type of device is just another aspect of the power of time sharing. It depends, of course, on computers capable of gathering information a character at a time from hundreds of different terminals, assembling those characters into individual messages, analyzing the messages, doing what they call for in program execution, and then returning hundreds of answers piecemeal to different terminals so the end result is a complete and particular message for each of the terminals. Modern computers can do this easily. All depends, of course, on sophisticated programming, which we do not wish to probe at length in this text. It is sufficient for our purposes that we know there are such programs and that they will work reasonably well.

AUDIO-RESPONSE UNITS

While voice input to computers is in the distant future, voice output from computers is not. There are basically two ways vocal output can be generated by a computer. There can be a collection of prerecorded messages held inside the computer, which can be selected for response on the basis of some code number or set of code numbers. This would not be unlike being able to call up a number of simple records on a juke box. Another type of response system would be the assembly of words by the computer from a prerecorded vocabulary. This technique, though, does not produce a very human-sounding message, since each individual word is recorded without any possible voice inflections pertinent to the message as a whole. We all know you can say "Good morning" in many different ways. If the entire message is recorded, we can add much meaning by the inflections. But if each word is separately recorded and then computer assembled, the tonal inflections giving subtleties of meaning are lost. What price mechanization?

Figure 5–24 shows an audio-response unit which makes use of a special prerecorded vocabulary on a large magnetic drum. Typically, one might call the computer with a special series of numbers dialed on the telephone, which will trigger either a full message prerecorded or will cause a special message to be assembled from the normal vocabulary of the machine.

In the early days, computers could respond via console lights, console typewriters, card punches, or online printers. We have come a long way with portable terminals, cathode ray tubes, and audio-response units. There will be many more inventions of this type to come. But do not think the computer can only "talk" to you as a result of some inquiry you have triggered. With modern technology, the computer can detect a problem in your program, "dial" your telephone number and, when you have answered your phone, construct an appropriate audio-response message to explain to you what needs to be done to correct the problem. This is all currently possible with the equipment on hand.

FIGURE 5–24. IBM 7770 audio-response message unit

Courtesy of International Business Machines Corporation

VOICE INPUT

Whatever you may have heard to the contrary, we are a long way from an accurate and acceptable method of talking directly to the computer in our several languages and our hundreds of accents. In fact, the natural languages (English, French, and so on) are sufficiently inconsistent, redundant, and expansive to indicate we are not likely to ever create a computer with such a capability—nor would we necessarily want to, for the expense might far exceed the benefits. But if the problem of recognizing root sounds—in spite of distortions of accent and tone—can be solved, it certainly would be possible to dictate numbers, several commands, and similar formal language elements to a computer and receive direct responses. Ideally, it might be possible to develop a rigorous formal language with which we could speak directly to a computer. The formal languages are those with a limited vocabulary and a fixed syntax, and worked out for the specific purpose of communicating to the computer. COBOL and FORTRAN, of which we have heard, are examples of formal computer languages. At the moment they cannot be orally delivered to the computer. But if any likely form of direct talk to the computer is possible, this is the type of language which will first be spoken.

IMPLICATIONS

In ancient days, one needed to be very certain that information was of some importance before it was transcribed or sent to others. The process of writing things down and making extra copies and the cost of storing things that were written down was considerable. There was, then, a natural restraint upon the amount of information floating about, and a certain pressure to be sure any information transmitted and recorded was of some genuine importance. With the new devices which link people and computers that we have been exploring in this chapter, the problems of limited communication and the pressures for limited communication begin to disappear. The question naturally arises whether all this information recorded in computers is of any real importance. It is said that this is the best-informed generation that has ever lived. Perhaps it would be better to say this is the *most* informed generation that ever lived—where *most* means quantity and not quality. Because of the computer and because of the new devices which conveniently link people and computers, we have achieved something that we call cheap information. We are going to have to be very careful, though, to be sure that the cheap information also has not been cheapened—by that we mean we may be telling a lot of people a great deal more than they want to know or need to know.

The terminals of various kinds which permit us to communicate quickly and personally with the computer also generate a unique kind of symbiosis—a relationship between person and machine. We are not yet certain what that may mean in terms of the human behavior and alterations which might take place in that behavior from our past performances. But, as surely as the automobile has brought us both freedom and grief, we expect the computer to do the same. Artifacts—and the computer for all of its complexity is an artifact—tend to appear in our cultural traditions and to set expectations. Because they are tools and hence extensions of ourselves, we tend to integrate them into our perception of the world. For instance, while the automobile has given us a sense of individual mobility far beyond anything from the past, the computer has given us an enormous life extension. The extension is not in terms of years of life but in terms of problems which can be solved in any given year. So our problem-solving ability has jumped from the normal three score and ten to something over 300 or more years. The computer has compacted the time necessary to solve problems. Compaction is one way of extending the power of years. And, of course, the computer has reduced the cost of solving problems. We now, as a normal part of our culture, expect very complicated mathematical and logical problems to be solved in the blink of an eye. Without the computer such an expectation would be thought to be the first sign of serious insanity. The solution, quickly and cheaply, of complex problems in a society also builds up a special kind of dependency. We are familiar with the close interrelationship between the automobile and oil. We have faced near disaster due to enormously increasing oil prices. A similar dependency may develop in terms of the problems which we currently can solve. Our society has grown complex to the degree we can actually handle the complexity. If our machines are taken away from us, much of our current organization will probably collapse. Sentiment notwithstanding, we are not likely to be able to gracefully return to the farm once we have tasted life in the computerized civilization of the city. More important, our productivity is linked with our complex organizations. The larger farms, and many of the larger organizations, are efficient because they can mass-produce. The amount of production per acre or per man will fall, with a retreat to simplicity. Many will die if such a retreat is forced on us by virtue of the failure of the new integrated information systems we have built.

THE COMPUTER AS GO-BETWEEN

Another serious implication we can draw from the information so far presented in this chapter is the meaning of the computer as an intermediary. Here we mean the nature of the communication nets that we are establishing sets up a person-to-*computer*-to-person system in which we cannot work easily person-to-person. We have grown dependent upon the storage and interpretive quality of the computer to clarify and to develop the message from one human being to another. There is a potential for loss here. Could we some day in some way meet the kind of situation where we simply could not properly communicate from one soul to another without the trusty computer to consolidate, diagram, and interpret? Let us not be so foolish as to say such a situation could not in fact develop. There are people living today who claim they can communicate good or bad news much better over the telephone than they can person-to-person. This is no trivial or idle signal. There is, then, a peculiar type of isolation that can develop when we are using a mechanical system as an intermediary and when we build in a dependency on that system for the interpretation of human actions, desires, and hopes. There is bound to be, by the nature of the mechanisms, a certain kind of uniformity in such communication systems. This may force a decline in what we call genuinely creative communication—the kind of situation where one person triggers something unusual and new in the very process of trying to be understood or appreciated.

It is said that television has crippled the art of conversation. Certainly, we must admit that the six to seven hours a day people spend watching TV is not open to deep intellectual conversation. We do not, glued to the one-eyed monster, spend as much time knowing each other as we might. Similarly, the computer could create a similar distortion and interference in the business enterprise, and ultimately add to the effect of TV in the home. The computer, after all, can only accept information which has been designed to be accepted by the computer in the particular type of information net we have set up. A truly creative and unusual communication in such a circumstance would not be acceptable by *definition*. Here, then, lies the greatest danger—if the humanity which we all admire is in fact admirable! We would do well to recall that to be human is to communicate and to communicate in a human way—this includes what we call emotional overtone. To date, no computer has been capable of communicating with adroit emotional overtones. Something is lost in the process of mechanizing the mind and the thought.

ON PRIVACY

Such terminals, and other telephone-type links as we currently have designed for use with the computer, quite obviously point to the integration of the home and the office—the home and the work to be done—the home and the school—and the home and the government. Something is going to be lost in the process—possibly both the possibility and the desire for privacy. The home may lose one of its great values, the blessing of refuge. Of course, the computer can add materially to the skillful management of the home and of the office—but the price may be something we do not quite expect and certainly claim not to desire.

And finally, if the computers are more and more given the capability of pictorial (versus verbal) presentation, we may become less and less skilled in conjuring our own mental pictures from the written word. Again, it is said that television has cut into our ability to understand what we read. The same effect may be somewhat multiplied when the computer is fully capable of presenting information in picture or diagrammatic form. We gain in efficiency what we may well lose in ability. Several times, the average members of the human race have lost their ability to read and write. The recovery has always been slow and the price has been poverty. If our computer systems break down we might find an enormous dependency of what we were not truly aware. We may, by then, have become functionally illiterate—unable to deal with each other except with the aid of mechanisms. This surely would toss us swiftly back into what we call the "dark ages of man." We will not stop the television programs, we will not sledgehammer the computers on that account. But we must decide, if we are not to be exposed to serious dangers, to continue to keep and husband those personal reading and writing skills which we required before the advent of the television and the computer. To do other-

wise is to become peculiarly vulnerable to energy shortages—and this could be a kind of energy shortage far more serious than the one with which we currently must deal.

ON PLANNING

How the information is to be recorded must be carefully planned *before* the event to be recorded occurs. This means someone somewhere has to imagine, as well as can be done, what information is required from the event. And human imagination is notorious in its ability not to know precisely what will happen in the future and not to know what information will be needed to solve a future problem. For every event we formalize by planning ahead, we lose the opportunity to record genuinely new and unexpected information. This is a most dangerous rigidity.

Of equal importance is the fact that we simply cannot often plan to ask for all the information we will need in the future. So our problem is not one of rigidity, directly, in this case, but rather one of omission. How many times have you had to backtrack on some job or other because you forgot to ask the things you needed to know to complete the job when you had the chance? Actually, you should not feel too guilty. If we could predict the future with accuracy, we would all be very rich and the stock market would not be a gamble at all.

The problem is that we assume, before the fact, we can actually determine all the information we need, design appropriate means to record it, feed the information into the computer, and really end up with what we want to know to make judgments. It is the *assumption* and not the planning that can become dangerous. If we could admit with ease the error of our ways, things would not be too bad. But for every step along the road to the computer, there is a natural and grave reluctance to admit we have not gathered enough information—and an even more severe resistance to going back to collect further data. The result is that many decisions, allegedly based on collected information, are based on dreams and hopes and little else.

TWO-STATE CHOICES

Still another problem is the yes/no nature of the computer. Long handwritten answers of the essay type just don't fit themselves readily to computer input. What is desired is check marks. And check marks are best used to answer *yes, no, don't know* questions. Perhaps the problem will become clearer if we deal with an old and loaded question: "Have you stopped beating your wife?" If you say yes, the presumption is you used to beat her and now have stopped. If you say no, the assumption is you are still beating her. There is no room in this type of question to say indignantly, "I have never beaten my wife and I do not intend to do so in the future!" We cannot directly blame the computer for this problem. People, after all, do design the forms and the questions and the mode of the answer. But the problem is very real and it is very dangerous.

FORCING CHOICES

Let us take another case in point. Computers handle numbers with greater speed and greater ease than they handle alphabetic characters —which demand a rather special form of coding. Thus, many computer people have forced identification numbers on people as a matter of convenience. Convenience for the computer and convenience for the program, not convenience for the customer—there lies the rub and the error. People do not like to be dehumanized—computers really don't care.

And let us also speak of the matter of range limitation. Perhaps you have run into questions designed to determine your age, wherein you were asked to make a check on a line where the group of questions covered a rather broad range:

0 through 5 years of age ______
6 through 10 years of age ______
11 through 15 years of age ______
16 through 20 years of age ______
20 through 25 years of age ______
Over 25 years of age ______

If you happen to fit into one of the five-year gaps you are probably not too unhappy. But your author usually finds himself in the "Over ______ years of age" category and he deeply resents it. One does not like to be an afterthought. One does not like to merely round out a distribution. One is, after all, a person and has pride in one's specific age, and perhaps takes pleasure in having survived so long without major wear and tear.

Of more importance, a narrower refinement of the range in many cases would give significantly different distributions—and this is even more important than wounded pride.

All of these rigidities are common to mechanized information systems and are worthy of a listing:

1. Failure to correctly imagine a future event.
2. Omission of important information.
3. Forced choices.
4. Inaccurate ranges.

By planning ahead and getting event-point cooperation in data preparation for computer input, we have solved the problem of data preparation from a mechanical point of view. But in so doing we have opened ourselves up to at least four serious types of error, which can provide ready but inaccurate information on which to base judgments. Each solution generates new problems. Some of the new problems generated may themselves be more dangerous than the old ones.

THE FALLACY OF CENTRAL POSITION

We have explored a number of the more modern ways of interchanging information with a computer. The variety of devices able to perform this basic function is great. We might make the error of becoming so enchanted with the mechanisms that we fall into the *fallacy of central position*. What we mean by this term is the illusion that, because what one does is interesting or complex or demanding, what one does is the most important thing in the universe. Since the computer demands a great deal of attention, and since many of its rituals are rigid and fixed, there is a tendency for computer people to demand that business folk and others using the devices fit into those patterns the computer people feel they can handle with ease and convenience. This is not as it should be. The business people or others using the computer should be certain that their demands are made to serve the business or other human purposes, and not those of either the computer or the computer room personnel. Computer people are important. Computers are important. But they exist to serve human demands made to solve human problems. It is the challenging task of computer people to so devise their programs and their systems that they can meet the problems presented to them in the form in which they are presented, that they can solve them in reasonably quick time, and that they can present them in clear, concise, and easily understood terms. To the degree that computers and computer personnel cannot accomplish these tasks, they are a clear and patent failure. But we make progress. The remote terminal is a more personal form of communication than the old-fashioned punched-card reader. Graphic output is clearly more understandable than long columns of numbers. There is hope for a more pleasant communicative future between human and machine.

SUMMARY

In this chapter we have had a look at many devices which we use to communicate with the computer, and at many of those devices by means of which the computer communicates with us. We have tried to confine ourselves to those devices which seem more intimate, because human beings can, by means of them, deal directly with the computer. We must remember, though, we have by no means covered all of the ways it is possible to contact a computer, either directly or indirectly.

The punched card first came to our attention in the chapter because it is still being used a good deal, and possibly because, old form that it is, it is entitled to both honor and recognition before it goes off to permanent and final retirement. By means of the EBCDIC coding matrix we could see how the card codes are translated into a binary coded form more acceptable to the modern computer. We learned a byte is made up of eight binary digits, and that four bytes make a computer word. Two bytes make a halfword and eight bytes make a double word. Many computers make use of this "word" format.

Those chores accomplished, we moved on in the chapter to consider telephone terminals. These will be important when, in Chapter 7, we talk about the computer as a potential public utility. Certainly, telephone terminals make it easy to contact the computer—since there are so many of them and they are in so many places. The light pen and the display units that are capable of receiving messages from the light pen can be of great assistance to those involved in engineering and design. The kind of interaction between the computer and the operator is swift and intimate. Actually, by means of such interaction the intelligence and abilities of the operator are enlarged and enhanced. Such symbiotic relationships between people and machines are usually given the name "intellectual enhancement."

We explored inquiry/response stations of a simpler form in this chapter—those with a typewriter keyboard and a display screen or printing facility, or both. There are so many different models we can pretty well choose exactly what we want for any given computer installation or for any particular task. Our guiding principle should be to never buy or rent more equipment than we need, but to always to be sure to look ahead and see how our requirements might grow.

Check scanners have made it possible for banks to survive in spite of the avalanche of checks which have struck them in the last decade. Had high-speed magnetic ink check readers not been invented it is likely we could not find enough man or woman power to handle the job of sorting. It is said the old-fashioned telephone switchboard, had it survived, would require the hands of over half of the population of the United States between the ages of 8 and 80 to handle the current load. Fortunately, automatic switching was developed. Similarly, it is likely the number of people required to help the banks sort checks would grow to somewhere near equal proportions were it not for the invention of the magnetic scanners currently in use.

Data collection systems of the type described in this chapter will find ever-growing use on manufacturing plant floors. The sooner the information is relayed to the computer the sooner it can calculate and manipulate the data to give management the kind of information it needs to intelligently run the plant, adapt to changing jobs, and consider the problems of the future.

Universal product code readers and universal product codes are finding their way into stores where there are vast numbers of items in the inventory. Grocery stores and hardware stores and variety stores come to mind. Here the problem is to develop a speedy and accurate way by which prices can be read into cash registers, and computers, to tally the cost of a sale; but more important yet, a way to keep up the inventories and also the information management needs.

Scanners capable of reading whole pages of print also were discussed in the chapter. Many scanners require very special type fonts, or very careful printing, before they can accurately handle information. Other types of scanners, the "mark sense" type, usually can only handle pencil marks made in appropriately placed balloons. These, naturally, can accept less information but are simpler to construct and maintain. We noticed the uses of scanner preparation in service stations—a method of gathering the kind of information required to constitute complete and ready computer input. This brought forward the concept of the *event-point*. This, the actual place and time of the sale, or other recordable happening, is the place and time to gather the information needed for the computer. But we had to make note of the natural difficulties in trying to predict future needs based on past experiences. We require some method of monitoring the process as it goes along, and we must learn not to be reluctant to attempt to get more accurate information along the line if we need it. Pride not only goeth before a fall, it goes often before financial disaster. We would like to get all the information we need at the event-point—but we must have it no matter *how* and *when* we gather it, if we are to be effective.

We discussed, in the chapter, some of the rigidities and errors which the limitations of computers force upon us. Errors of omission, prediction, forced choice, and inaccurate range determination were discussed briefly.

We also had a little time to explore computing inquiry stations—those devices which go beyond simple inquiry and response, and which have the potential to operate as a self-contained mini computer when faced with limited problems. We discovered that the more the terminal itself can do the less it needs to demand of the computer, and the more that such devices the computer can therefore handle. We found that digital plotters record inferences as well as facts. And we saw that some terminals are truly portable. They can be carried easily and can be linked to the computer wherever there is a telephone available.

We explored audio-response units, which exist. And voice-receiving units, which do not. We defined mark sensing, and concluded with the "fallacy of central position."

HIGHLIGHT QUESTIONS

1. The Hollerith card has both columns and rows. How many columns does the card have? How many rows does it have? How many numbers, or letters, or characters, could one get on such a card?
2. What is the purpose of the EBCDIC coding matrix?
3. What is a byte? How does it relate to a computer word?
4. With what device would we most likely use a light pen? What kind of communication with the computer does it make possible?
5. What would be the main elements of an inquiry/display station? What kind of information can be displayed?
6. How are modern checks handled by banks?
7. Where would you most likely find a data collection system? What types of information can such a system gather?
8. Give a brief general explanation of a "universal product code." Where would we most likely find such codes?
9. What is a checkout scanner? How would a light pen be used with such a device?
10. Discuss some of the problems which can occur when we plan ahead to collect information from an event-point.
11. List a few of the rigidities which can occur when we mechanize information collection systems.
12. What is a computing inquiry station? How does it differ from an inquiry/response station? How do these two systems relate to what we call "remote terminals?"
13. What is the difference between a natural language and a formal language?
14. What are some of the limitations of digital plotters in terms of trying to convey accurate information?
15. What are the two types of messages which current models of audio-response units can handle? What are the advantages and disadvantages of each?

READINGS

Davis, Gordon B. *Introduction to Computers.* 3d ed. New York: McGraw-Hill, 1977.

A recent publication with two chapters of particular interest. Chapter 2 contains a good discussion of the uses of computers, and chapter 8 is an up-to-date treatment of data preparation, input, output, and data communications. The treatment illustrations are recent and should be of interest.

Spencer, Donald D. *Introduction to Information Processing*. 2d ed. Columbus, O.: Charles E. Merrill, 1977.

Chapter 8 is an up-to-date treatment of input and output devices, and chapter 20 is a good discussion of information processing methods. Again, the illustrations in the text are of recent vintage.

Vazsonyi, Andrew. *Introduction to Electronic Data Processing*. Rev. ed. Homewood, Ill.: Richard D. Irwin, 1977.

The book contains a first chapter with a pleasant treatment of the social implications of the computer. Also, the book contains a good chapter on computer-based information systems.

Magazine

Datamation. Technical Publishing Company, 1301 South Grove Ave., Barrington, Ill. 60010.

The magazine is an excellent way to keep up to date in the computer field. There are feature and news sections, and several departments, including one on recent publications. Both hardware and software and services have a section. Also, the advertisements are a good method for keeping up to date on the development of new terminal devices.

CHAPTER 6

FIRST RECAPITULATION

PURPOSE OF THE CHAPTER We have covered a rather significant amount of material in the first five chapters of this text. It is time for a recapitulation of what we have learned so far. First we will take each of the questions for discussion from each of the earlier five chapters and provide an answer for them. That done, we will present a test on the subject matter material which has gone before. And finally, we will provide the answers to the test so you may check your own knowledge retention.

HIGHLIGHT QUESTIONS, CHAPTER 1

1. What is a side effect? Why should we be interested in the side effects of technology?

A "side effect" is basically an expected or unexpected secondary result of some action. When one takes a special drug to cure a particular disease, one might suffer nausea or headache—unfortunate side effects.

We are interested in side effects of technology because they may often be both unexpected and unfortunate, such as the case of smog related to the automobile and certain types of industrial activity.

More important, we would like to be on the watch for any unexpected and dangerous side effects that might arise through the large-scale application of computers to the many problems of our society. We cannot predict exactly what the side effects will be, though we know there will be some, but we want to be watchful enough to begin to take remedial action early enough to be able to adjust or achieve a cure.

2. What is the difference between a culture and a civilization?

A culture includes, usually, a collection of traditions, a set of survival techniques and artifacts, a collection of artistic artifacts of various kinds, and a set of mores—methods of behavior which are approved.

A civilization is something more than a culture. We said, in the text, that the Northmen were cultured, or at least had a culture, but they were not civilized. Civilization includes a certain elegance of life view, a natural reluctance to destroy that which is not understood, a deep concern with the betterment of life. A civilization, while more than a culture, must rest on cultural achievements.

In our own vocabularies and usages of language we must be a little bit careful. Commonly in this country we say that someone is "cultured" when we really mean that she or he is "civilized."

3. What is the relationship between "society," on the one hand, and "culture," on the other?

In the text we defined a society as a collection of people banded together to achieve some common ends—usually survival as a group. Once a society has developed, it must rest on ideas and understandings held in common—it is out of the commonly held ideas and understandings that culture, as we have defined it, develops.

An artifact might develop as a useful tool to assist a society in the search for growth and survival. When the artifact is commonly accepted and is handed down as a traditional tool or mode of task accomplishment, we have developed a cultural artifact. Cultures, of course, serve as starting points for civilizations and, more important, often define the thought patterns and the intellectual limits which the civilization may achieve.

4. **Give a definition of bureaucracy? What are the two advantages of bureaucracy over other forms of organization you can think of?**

A bureaucracy is a mode of formal organization which defines tasks to be accomplished, sets the standards for any particular job which is to be involved in the performance of a task or tasks, and which sets up the methods for personnel selection for jobs. And, too, a bureaucracy will define the interrelationships of all the jobs and tasks under its jurisdiction.

One advantage of the bureaucratic structure is that the jobs to be done are clearly defined and related to the organization as a whole.

Another advantage of the bureaucratic structure is that the occupants of jobs are selected not in terms of blood relationships or other irrelevant factors but upon the recognized ability to perform the task at hand.

Bureaucracies have grown in number and in size because they are better alternatives to organizations put together by royal or dictatorial decree, and because they attempt to recognize ability and pay salaries commensurate with both ability and achievement in the job.

5. **Define management.**

In the text we stated that management was nothing more or less than the directional activities of a manager. We defined a manager as an individual holding a defined bureaucratic position who functioned as a leader. Leadership means more than simply performing defined duties—it involves a constant reevaluation of the goals of an enterprise, the structure of an enterprise, and the relationships of the people to one another. The bureaucrat merely performs. The leader thinks about what he or she is doing and sets directions.

Management, then, is the process of directing activities to achieve established goals, and the process of goal examination and redirection itself. A manager occupies a bureaucratic position but he or she *leads* from that position.

6. Define leadership.

Leadership is a function, not a set of qualities. A leader can only lead in relationship to a group. It is the ability of an individual to direct a group successfully which we call leadership. Since leadership is a function, certain behavioral patterns required to establish leadership over a group can be learned. But, since leader and group can vary in time and circumstance, a successful leader of one group is not guaranteed the successful leadership of some other group.

Some people are more successful than others in developing the behaviors necessary to persuade a group to perform well. These people are often called leaders. Leaders without formal positions are frequently called "natural" or "informal" leaders. Leaders with defined positions and the ability to develop successful group relationships are often called "recognized" or "formal" leaders.

7. Define administration.

Administration, as we have used the term in the text, has to do with the performance of a set of defined responsibilities and duties. To administer only is to immediately set limits to what can be done, since nothing which has not already been defined and described can be handled. Hence, we use the term *administer* differently from the term *manager.* Management envisions a dynamics which goes beyond the simple performance of defined tasks to the exploration of new relationships and new possibilities.

In the text we have said that an administered bureaucracy is as dull as it is stagnant, whereas a managed bureaucracy has a good chance of succeeding in performing the tasks it has been assigned and yet has sufficient flexibility to deal with new tasks and new goals.

8. What are two types of power? How do they differ? Which is the more important?

We can, if we wish, divide power into two types—physical and intellectual. Physical power refers to those devices which have been designed to replace human muscle. Originally, such burdens were passed on to animals of various sorts. Of recent centuries, the task has fallen upon a number of cleverly designed machines making use of coal, steam, or electrical energy.

Intellectual power, as we have defined it, is the ability to investigate, to understand, to quantify, to predict, and to simulate. Of late we have been able to pass on some of these tasks, if carefully outlined and defined, to mechanisms depending upon electrical energy—the computers and their near cousins, the calculators.

Of the two, we might suspect intellectual power to ultimately be the more important, since it involves perception, purpose, and guidance. Mechanical machines would be relatively useless without such governance.

9. What is a machine? How is it different from a living entity?

It will not do to say that the difference between a machine and a living entity is obvious. Consider, if you will, the tobacco virus. In general, we define a machine as a structure made up of a framework and having both fixed and moving parts designed to do some specific kind of work. A living entity is usually defined as having the capacity of accepting food, being capable of growth, and ending activity in death.

In the future we may find it difficult to tell the difference between a living organism and a machine. In the case of a mechanical heart transplant we remain clear in mind. But, and notice this, our confidence is based on quantity and not kind. That is, add many additional parts to your "human" mechanism and at what point does the human being become "machine?"

The lesson here may *seem* simple, but we should pay attention to it. Nothing is so misdirecting as the simple-minded assumption that once something has been "defined" it is understood. Be wary, in the computer field, of those who sneer because you do not see the obvious.

10. How do we distinguish, in general, between "low technology" and "high technology?"

High technology is generally very complex and requires considerable and careful planning. Careful planning takes time and skill to achieve. *Low technology,* as the term is used, generally means less complex devices which can be assembled quickly. There is not, of course, a clear line between the ordinary technologies with which we are familiar and the high technologies currently under development. Today's high technology (as history shows) is likely to become tomorrow's low technology.

The automobile might be classed as ordinary technology in the United States and many Western nations, and high technology in some of the third world countries. A good example of low technology might be the hammer.

All of this might lead us to believe that the matter of whether a technology is high, ordinary, or low might merely involve the degree to which an understanding of the technology is common.

11. Give a definition of automation. How is automation different from mechanization?

Automation, as we have defined it, is the achievement of self-directing productive activity as a result of the combination of mechanization and computation. Actually, we have in a mind a device which can measure its own output, compare this output with some preset standard, and then adjust its own operations to eliminate, as much as possible, any output variations from the norm.

Automation is different from mechanization to just the degree the device is able to determine its own conduct in terms of variation from some norm.

Again, as our mechanisms grow more complex, the fine line defining the difference between automation and mechanization grows fuzzy. Our main task is to try to distinguish as best we can when we are mechanizing a process and when we are automating it.

12. Give a short definition of a computer. How is a computer different from a calculator?

A computer is an intellectual map follower.

A computer used to be easily distinguished from a calculator by virtue of a greater degree of flexibility, evinced by the fact that the program for the computer's operation could be stored internally. A computer was thought to be a more general mechanism than a calculator. The latter usually had to have a good deal of human intervention to perform its task.

Again, with the advent of the small electronic calculator, the line between calculator and computer grows fuzzy. Many of our new hand-held calculators are capable of storing both data and short programs, and can execute these on the basis of a single push of a button. This used to be exactly what we said about computers.

In the main, though, computers are still more general than calculators, being capable of both logic and arithmetic. And they usually have greater capacities for data and programs. And, at the moment, they are more expensive.

13. What is an intellectual map? What is a computer program?

An intellectual map could also go under the name of "algorithm." An algorithm is any special method of solving certain kinds of problems. We expect an algorithm to lay out all the steps necessary to solve a particular problem, and to be complete and consistent. We would make the same demands when we use the term intellectual map. A computer program, in the main, is nothing more or less than a series of instructions which also must be complete and consistent. These instructions, executed in some given order, should result in a solution to the problem.

Since many computer programs involve choice points—that is, the computer will execute one set of instructions if a certain condition is met, and will execute a different set of instructions if the condition is not met—the term *map* naturally comes to mind. When we instruct someone to come to our house (marked with an *X*) and give him or her a map, we do not know exactly which combination of streets will be chosen. We do know, if the person duly arrives, that some correct path was followed, and we may normally assume the streets followed were on the map. When the computer is following a carefully planned set of instructions, we can say without serious contradiction that the computer is following an intellectual map.

14. Name three support institutions of what we call civilization. Which do you think is the more important?

Three support institutions of what we call "civilization" would be the family, the government, institutionalized religion. A fourth would be the enterprise.

In terms of the long history of human survival, the family would seem to be the most important, since it is the most basic of the support institutions. Developments of late might bring us to wonder if this will long continue to be true. Perhaps we should hedge and say the family is the most traditional of the support systems of civilization.

There would be good grounds for admitting that the government might be even more fundamental than the family. The survival of the family might, for a civilization to exist, depend upon order and protection, both of which are supposed to be provided by government. Those who speak out for law and order know that at least some minimum of both is necessary for the stability and survival of any civilization or, for that matter, any culture.

Would we stretch the point to say that all four of the support institutions are necessary for a civilization, although they may take many different forms?

15. Why would a person who is not going to be either an engineer or a computer programmer want to know anything about computers?

We might well quote another question asked in the early 1900s: Why would a person who is a horse lover and who needs horses want to know anything about automobiles? Well, because they are going to be as common as dirt in no time at all. The same is quite likely to hold true for computers. When men and women have invented tools and found them useful, they tend to let them multiply. Early hammers must have been very scarce—but not for long—they were too useful in the production of other tools and artifacts. Computers relieve us of many tiresome old intellectual burdens and intellectual processes, and we are likely to constantly increase their use. And as these devices are mass produced, the price falls dramatically. Ultimately, we have found a way to do cheap logic and cheap arithmetic, and we will not dismiss easily or lightly such a wonderful relief to the tedium of doing standard arithmetic and logical tasks. Human beings (bless them all) are usually as lazy intellectually as they are physically. The latter weakness has brought many wonderful tools and machines. The former weakness has broken through to a new frontier.

HIGHLIGHT QUESTIONS, CHAPTER 2

1. Give a definition of data processing. What are the three major elements involved?

A general definition of data processing wc ld be: receiving cues from the environment (external and internal), evaluating the cues received, and responding to the cues. The three major elements involved make up the definition.

Any living creature is involved in data processing, in one way or another, from the simplest amoeba to the most brilliant human being. If fact, we might well define death as the ceasing of the function of data processing in organic systems. It is as good a definition as any of that final and mysterious process.

2. At about what time did data processing really come to the attention of the general public?

Data processing began to be mentioned frequently in the public press at the conclusion of World War II. Data processing development came about because millions of men and women were under military control during World War II, and military establishments require enormous amounts of information. The record-filing job of the army, navy, and air force almost staggers the imagination.

Many of the technologies developed during the war were further developed and put into the civilian market from 1946 to 1956—the computer was no exception.

3. **Give a description and an example of the one-to-one correspondence principle.**

Basically the one-to-one correspondence principle is merely a matter of matching one form of representation with another. For each object in set *A* there is a symbolic or actual representative in set *B*. We could use pebbles to represent people. And because of this link between the people and the pebbles we could use the number of pebbles to represent the number of people. In a somewhat primitive way, this is a form of coding.

4. **What type of computer is the human hand?**

The human hand would be classified as a digital computer. Each digit on the hand (four fingers and one thumb) is a discrete and entire unit. We give the name "digits" to fingers and toes just because they are discrete units. Analog computers, on the other hand, would use something of a continuous (on a gross level) nature, like electrical current—theoretically, there would be many possible current readings between one volt and two.

5. **Explain briefly how you would add 7, 8, and 11, using grooves and pebbles.**

Imagine two grooves—a right groove and a left groove. The first seven pebbles would be placed in the right groove. We would remember the rule that the maximum capacity of a groove is nine pebbles. When we reach ten pebbles in any groove, we would be required to sweep the groove clean and put a single pebble to the left. So, with our next eight pebbles, we begin to add to the first (right) groove. One makes eight, one more makes nine, one more makes ten (leaving us five). So we sweep the right groove clean at this point and put a single pebble in the left groove. We now put the remaining five pebbles in the right groove. Then we take our eleven (the last set) pebbles and begin adding into the right groove. When we have added in five of the eleven pebbles we are required to sweep the groove clean and put another pebble in the left group (where we now have two). Then we place the remaining six pebbles in the right groove. We now have two pebbles in the left groove and six pebbles in the right groove representing 26, the total of 7, 8, and 11. The important element here is that we have mechanized the adding process by knowing a few simple little rules of carry and clean sweeping.

The groove system, or groove table (sometimes called a sand table), would be an example of a digital computer since we do not have fractional units, only whole pebbles. If we knew some sort of a decimal systems, of course, we could use decimals and pebbles to represent decimal fractions.

6. How would the number 23 be recorded on an abacus?

Assuming an abacus of the type illustrated in the text, the number 23 would be recorded by pushing three beads of the lower frame of the rightmost wire toward the dividing bar of the abacus. The number two of 23 would be recorded by pushing two of the beads of the lower frame of the second to rightmost wire toward the dividing bar of the abacus. All other beads on the device would be pushed to the bottom or the top of the abacus, depending upon whether they are in the upper frame or the lower frame of the device. The number to be read off the abacus would then be 0000023.

7. Show how the number 324 would be interpreted using a base of ten.

The number 324 would be interpreted using a base of ten to be: $3 \times 10^2 + 2 \times 10^1 + 4 \times 10^0 = 3 \times 100 + 2 \times 10 + 4 \times 1 = 300 + 20 + 4 = 324$.

Ten is the base of the system (or "radix," as it is called) and each shift to the left represents a single increase in the power of the base. The rightmost position power is always zero, and any number to the zero power (or more correctly, here, any base number) is defined as equal to one.

8. For what type of invention was Joseph Jacquard known?

Joseph Marie Jacquard is noted for his contributions to the weaving industry and, more particularly, for his design and use of semiautomatic looms. He designed machines which would follow prepunched patterns set up in metal cards. We use Jacquard as an illustration of the ability to encode a "program" of sequential operations in coded form in a stable medium (the metal cards).

9. Who is credited with the title, "the father of the computer?"

It is customary to credit the wonderfully short-tempered, aggressive, and brilliant Charles Babbage with the title. He envisioned all of the major elements of the modern computer in mechanical rather than electronic form. If his ambition to build an automatic computer failed, it was because he was born before his time. In a later century, with electricity well known, he might have been able to devise a machine which would operate successfully. During his own time his major enemies were the friction involved in ordinary mechanical devices and the slap-dash quality of machine tools of his time. He did much to improve the quality of the production of the latter devices.

10. What was the purpose of the difference engine?

The difference engine was a device designed to automate (as much as possible) the calculation sum of the squares and cubes of whole numbers. The sums of the squares and cubes of the whole numbers were used for navigational computations—a very important matter in those early days of Charles Babbage.

11. How was the analytical engine better than the difference engine in concept?

The difference engine was what we might call a "special purpose" computer designed to handle the creation of the sums of the squares and cubes of whole numbers. The analytical engine, a considerably more ambitious enterprise, was to be a general-purpose computer which could handle addition, subtraction, multiplication, division, and a few fundamental logical operations.

12. What computer system really put computing into the business world on a large scale?

The IBM 650 would have to be given the credit of putting computers in large numbers into business. There were several reasons for this: The system was relatively simple and had a fairly good operational record; IBM had previously developed a national distribution network for its other office machines; and IBM was willing to train customers in the use of the machines.

13. What is symbolic programming?

Originally, computer programs were written in numerical equivalents of the binary code. Symbolic programming is the next stage. A number of mnemonic (the first *m* is silent) devices could be used—combinations of letters, such as ADD to represent the code for addition, SUB for subtraction, and so on. And storage locations (usually numbered addresses of items in storage, where the term address means the identifier of the physical location in storage of the datum) could be given alphabetic/numeric representations which might remind one of the nature of what was stored, such as SSEC for social security data. The computer, then, would read in the symbolic program, translate that into its equivalent in the computer's "native" language, and then turn its attention to executing the program in its native language. More simply put, a symbolic program must be translated into a machine-language program before it can be executed.

Purists might say that unless a program is actually written in binary code it is, in fact, symbolic. But traditionally, we have assumed any program written only in arabic numerals was in "machine language," even though this was known not to be true. It was the introduction of mnemonic aids which brought about the common use of the term *symbolic programming*.

14. Given a symbolic program and a translator program, which would require to be in the computer first?

Since it is the function of the translator program to work on the symbolic program to create a machine-language program, the translator program would have to be first in the computer to receive the symbolic program.

In modern machines, with large-scale memories, the translator and the symbolic program could be loaded at the same time, and then control would be turned over to the translator, with instructions as to the location of the program to be translated.

15. What is the result of the translating activity—a program or data answers to problems?

The translating activity will result in a computer executable program in the appropriate machine language of the computer concerned. Again, translation is the first step, execution the second.

HIGHLIGHT QUESTIONS, CHAPTER 3

1. Define "MIS"

The letters *MIS* represent the terms *M*anagement *I*nformation *S*ystem. More recently, the term *IMIS* is used. This term is the abbreviation of *I*ntegrated *M*anagement *I*nformation *S*ystem.

Hugo Berlet, in chapter 2 of the Diebold Group's *Automatic Data Processing Handbook* (New York: McGraw-Hill, 1977), gives the following definition of IMIS: "IMIS is an information system making use of all available resources to provide managers at all levels and in all functions with the information from relevant sources necessary to enable them to make timely and effectively decisions for planning, directing, and controlling the activities for which they are responsible."

The definition was formulated by the Diebold Research Program, Europe, in 1965, and still finds common acceptance.

Our own textual definition was: "A management information system is an attempt to create a vast electronic store of information necessary to conduct a business which can be called upon by various electronic information stations to provide information to any legitimate caller."

2. What might mark the "fourth generation" of computers from the "third generation?"

The third generation of computers, in the main, could be said to be large-scale centralized systems. The fourth generation of computers will be smaller—but equally powerful, decentralized, and with the power to be integrated as a system but operate independently of the system when required.

We suspect the fourth generation of computers will mark something of a "battle" between those who support the notion of a highly integrated, powerful, centralized system, and those who believe in a thoroughly distributed computer net, staffed by powerful small computers, which have the option of independent action and data bases—or integration with and dependency upon a massive central system organized around a large-scale data bank.

The telling feature as to whether or not one type of system concept will triumph over the other rests upon whether or not management finds control easier in one case than the other.

3. List three input units connected with the IBM S/32 computer.

1. A console typewriter keyboard.
2. A magnetic disk storage system.
3. A magnetic diskette storage system.

4. List three output units connected with the IBM S/32 computer.

1. A cathode tube display screen.
2. A printer.
3. A diskette storage unit.

   Also,

4. A magnetic disk storage system.

5. What is a diskette?

The diskette is much like those small 45 rpm phonograph records with which the last generation was familiar. Each diskette can contain about 242K digits (where K = 1024). In this definition, each byte is assumed to be able to carry one digit—alphabetic, numeric, or symbol representation. The disks are flexible and sometimes carry the term "floppy disks." Diskettes can be thought of as unit records in the sense that it is possible to take the disk off the disk drive, slip it into an appropriate storage envelope, and file the disk away. In this sense, we can have an unlimited set of disks available to the computer system. We would, of course, require some kind of orderly library or filing system for keeping track of such records when they are not mounted on the disk drive.

6. What does the term "online" mean when it is used in conjunction with input/output units.

Online, as the term is used in the text, simply means that the computer can call up the data from one of the auxiliary devices, or write out data on one of the auxiliary devices on the basis of instructions in storage *without* actual human intervention. The proper data on a diskette already mounted on the disk drive would be online to the computer. A diskette not mounted on the disk drive, but on a shelf in the library, would not be online to the computer, because a specific action has to be taken to move the disk and make its contents available to the machine—in this latter case, human intervention.

7. Give a simple example of data flow through a small computer, using the arithmetic unit.

One simple example would be the acceptance of input from the computer typewriter. This data would move into storage. From there the data might be called up by instructions to have arithmetic operations performed in the arithmetic unit. The information might then be moved from the arithmetic unit to storage and from there be written on one of the floppy disks.

8. What can a single cell of storage contain?

As we use *cell* in this text, a single cell can contain a digit. We have defined a digit as a letter, a number, or a special symbol.

Actually, the representation of a digit inside the computer is in the form of binary code. We often call the storage cell of the computer a byte. In most cases (but not all), the computer byte will hold a single number, letter, or special symbol.

Each of the bytes in storage has an address (a location number which is unique). But we normally do not address every digit in storage (where the term *address* means "call-for"). We make use of the address at the front of the "string" (collections of digits) we want.

In other machines we can call up "words." Words, as we have

explained, are just what they sound like—collections of digits of defined length.

9. Give an example of the uses of destructive read-in.

Destructive read-in permits us to use the same instructions operating on the same data locations in storage to handle different data elements. The first data element read-in would be manipulated in a particular way. The second data element read-in would eliminate the first. The computer could then repeat the original manipulations, using the original data locations; but because of the destructive read-in, the first datum would be replaced by the second, and the results of the calculations would be different. This system could go around and around as often as it pleased the programmer in seeking the solution to the set of problems involved.

10. In what way does the computer cycle?

Most computers have an instruction cycle, wherein the particular instruction to be executed is selected from storage, placed in an instruction register and analyzed, and then executed. The execution is the second half of the computer cycle called the data cycle. So computers move from instruction to data cycle, instruction to data cycle, just as surely as the clock goes from tick to tock. It is the cycle itself which tells the computer whether it is dealing with an instruction qua instruction or a datum. The repetition goes ID,ID,ID,ID,ID. . . . "I" represents instruction cycle, "D" represents data cycle.

11. What is a computer program?

A computer program is a series of computer instructions which the computer will follow to execute the solution to some particular problem.

Or we could call a computer program a step-by-step intellectual map which a computer is to follow. Each step of the intellectual map would represent a computer instruction to be executed, including such instructions or instruction groups which would cause the computer to take a divergent path. The program, as an entity, must contain all paths which the computer would be required to follow in any given case. A complete program is one which leads to the solution of the problem as prescribed by the programmer.

12. What is a constant?

A constant is some unchanging quantity (arithmetic or symbolic) that the computer might find useful on more than one occasion in the execution of a program or a group of interrelated programs. For example, in testing inventory items to determine whether or not reordering should take place, the computer might be given the figure 100 as a constant below which inventory items must not fall in number.

Or the computer might be given a combination of letters and symbols to be compared with the combination of letters and symbols attached to a client name. Any time a dead match is found between the combination of letters and symbols held by the computer (the constant), a special action is to be taken by the computer for that client. This would be an example of a symbolic constant.

13. Define the term "address."

The term *address* as used in the computer field is a "label" of a particular area in storage—much like the house numbers are locators of buildings in a town or city. Notice that the numeric address of a data cell or group of cells has nothing to do with the content of the cells, anymore than the size of a house number has anything to do with the number of actual residents in the house. Addresses may also be symbolic. That is, in certain types of programs, addresses may be words or symbols which hint at the content of the data cells being addressed. But ultimately, the address is a numeric representation—a locator, if you will. Symbolic addresses are used in assembler or compiler programs, but must ultimately be converted to actual machine addresses before the computer can engage in the actual search for a datum.

14. What is a computer channel?

Channels are the means by which many input/output units are linked to the computer. The channels are not only transmission lines but have some abilities to control the formats, and the like, of the data being transmitted. In one sense, at least, they could be thought of as limited-purpose input/output computers. One of the functions of a channel is to compensate between the enormous speed of the computer itself and the relatively lower data-handling speeds of the input/output units.

15. Give a verbal description of a programmed "loop."

A programmed loop is a series of instructions designed to be repeated until some special exit condition occurs, at which time the computer moves out of the loop and continues in the normal sequence of instructions.

For instance, one may wish to repeat a series of mathematical approximations until the result of the last approximation has reached a certain preset criteria of precision, at which time the repetition would cease.

Or in a very simple loop, one might decide to repeat the series of instructions 20 times. A counter box would be set up to accumulate the number of trips through the loop. When the counter box contained a 20 which met the constant value 20 previously set aside as a test value, the computer would cease to repeat the instruction loop.

HIGHLIGHT QUESTIONS, CHAPTER 4

1. Define the term "computer hardware."

When we use the term *hardware,* we are referring to the various physical mechanisms which make up the computer system itself. This would include the central processing unit, various input and output devices, auxiliary memories, and the like.

Of hardware we can say that we can put our hands on real objects—feel, see, sometimes listen to items occupying three-dimensional space.

2. Define the term "computer software."

When we use the term *software,* we are referring to the many programs which make the computer work as a data processing system. Such programs can be on several levels—those that are an integral part of the day-to-day computer operation (supervisory programs), those that serve special functions (translators of various kinds), those that actually work on data input (machine language programs). A good software system is one which is fully integrated with the physical hardware of the system to maximize the effectiveness of the system as a unit.

3. Tell how a computer is less than a computer system.

Basically, a computer alone is to be thought of as hardware. It is the addition of software which makes the computer act in what we call a "system" fashion. While computer hardware, alone, could be operated by a skilled individual, that individual would be playing the relentless roll of the software programs. This would limit the computer to the time frame of the individual and materially destroy one of the computer's great advantages —speed. Software turns most of the computer operations over to the computer itself, and it is this self-direction which permits maximization of the speedy and thorough nature of the computer itself.

4. **Distinguish between an "assembler program" and an "assembler-language program" as the terms have been used in this chapter.**

   The assembler program is a translator. That is, it is the purpose of the assembler program to work on a symbolic program and convert that symbolic program into machine language so the computer can actually execute the program.

   An assembler-language program is a program written in symbolic language which must be translated *by* the assembler program before it can be executed by the computer system.

   So the *assembler program* is the translator. The *assembler-language program* is that which is to be translated. The result of the translation is a machine-executable program in machine language.

5. **Name some of the ways a compiler differs from an assembler.**

   Assemblers normally work on a one-to-one basis. That is, every machine-executable instruction will be represented, before translation, by a symbolic instruction in the assembler language. This is not strictly true, but close enough to the truth to be useful in a general text. A compiler, though, may generate a number of machine-language instructions from a single compiler statement.

   The assembler, then, is more closely related to the abilities of a particular computer—at least this is true of the assembler language. To write a program in assembler language, the programmer must know many details about the particular computer. Since the compiler language is more general, it is less closely related to the computer system—at least this is so as far as the programmer is concerned.

   The generality of the compiler language, compared to an assembler language, permits a greater commonality between programmers. In spite of the fact that two programmers work on entirely different machines, they may discuss the finer points of a compiler language quite readily.

6. **Name some of the ways a compiler language differs from an assembler language.**

   Assembler-language statements must closely mimic, in symbolic fashion, the machine-language instructions of a particular computer. A compiler-language statement, generally, is more problem oriented—that is, a very long compiler-language statement may be written which will generate many machine-language instructions that do not appear to have a direct relationship to the compiler statement itself.

Assembler-language programs usually use symbolic representation of machine-language instructions, such as ADD or SUB, for the action specified by the machine-language instruction itself. The compiler may use operators, such as "*" to represent multiplication, or "+" to represent addition. Many compilers can make use of a greater range of macro instructions than can assemblers. A macro instruction is a symbolic instruction which will bring up some standard set of machine-language instructions to perform a particular task. The compiler often permits a statement to be written as a very close approximation to a mathematical statement or a typical business expression. Assembler languages are more limited than this and cannot really be cast in what appears to be human-amenable language.

Because they are more general and less machine-oriented than assembler languages, compiler languages are usually easier to learn, and what is learned can be applied to actual problems more quickly. And, of course, a compiler-language program may have broader application over a greater range of computers. All these elements are advantages for the learner and the programmer.

7. What is a mnemonic?

Basically, a mnemonic is nothing more than a memory aid. In an assembler language we might use the word ADD as a representation of the computer code for addition. The computer code might be 24, or some such number. Assembler-language programs are often written in such a way that terms (SSEC is one) are used to indicate the storage location of a social security quantity. The name of the storage location becomes a memory aid to the programmer about what is contained in that particular part of storage.

In the old poem, "Columbus sailed the ocean blue in fourteen hundred ninety-two," the word *blue* is the mnemonic aid.

8. Name two compiler languages and describe, briefly, their different purposes.

Probably the two most famous of the compiler languages are FORTRAN and COBOL. FORTRAN is a formula translator principally designed to be of help to people with mathematical or scientific problems. COBOL has been designed to be a commonly oriented business language, documentary in nature. Theoretically, any mathematically oriented person familiar with the operators (+, −, *, and so on) in FORTRAN could determine something about the task to be performed. And COBOL is supposed to be clearly enough written to serve as an explanatory and documentary language which can be read by any competent business person.

Ultimately, one would want to have a language closely approximating English (though probably quite limited in vocabulary) which could be used for both mathematical and business problems, and which would be close enough to the natural language to be readable to anyone of ordinary intelligence. We still have a fair way to go on that matter.

9. Does the System/32 have a compiler facility? What is its name?

The System/32 has something rather close to a compiler language (though the nature of the equipment limits the possibilities), called "System Command Language."

This system language permits the computer operator to address the computer in system command language by making what are called "command statements." The command statements themselves closely approximate ordinary English language usage to describe the tasks to be performed. Words like BILLING and SAVE have something very close in command language to their general meaning in English.

10. Define a job control statement.

As the term *job control statement* has been defined, we mean something close to what is called a command statement in the System/32. Generally, a job control statement is a command which calls up a series of instructions, the function of which is to perform the steps necessary to solve a particular task or major element in a task. In a way, we could say that a job control statement calls up a computer subroutine, where subroutine has been defined as a series of instructions which can, given a particular datum, treat the datum in a special way—such as taking the square root of a number.

Actually, a group of job control statements could be grouped in such a way (as a subroutine at a higher level) that a higher-level (say JOB^2) statement could call them up. Here we would get into a hierarchical set of translations. The limitations to this kind of activity are the capacities of the computer and the necessary complexity of the translator.

11. Define a procedure.

For our purposes, a procedure is the set of machine-language (ultimately) instructions which a job statement will call up. We can sometimes say that a procedure is a set of compiler statements or a set of assembler-language statements if we clearly understand that these generalized statements cannot themselves be executed by the computer but need to be translated.

Machine-language instructions are the result of translation. Symbolic statements may be grouped to represent procedures. Procedures may be represented by job control statements. A collection of job control statements could be called up by a higher-level job control statement—wheels within wheels within wheels.

12. Define a command statement.

As we have used the term *command statement,* in reference to the IBM System/32, we mean something very similar to the term *job control statement,* as we have defined that term in the chapter.

13. Write a single paragraph which puts job control statements, procedures, and command statements into proper perspective.

Job control statements are the "tag" or identifier of collections of instructions which constitute what we call "procedures." Procedures are merely collections of instructions which, when properly executed, will perform some standard computer-type task. Command statements are synonymous with control statements. With System/32 the programmer uses command statement to perform standardized operations. With other or larger systems the programmer might use job control statements to achieve the same purpose.

14. What is the difference, from the computer operational view, between a task and a job.

From the computer operational view, a job is made up of a series of tasks. The tasks are of such a nature that they each represent a complete type of standard mathematical (or business) operation. The computer is concerned with the execution of tasks and can work on these independently to maximize the effectiveness of the time available. The completed tasks can then be assembled to represent the particular job specified. The programmer might think of the translation of his program from a compiler language to machine language *and* the execution of the machine-language program on provided data as a single job. The computer might break the job into the task of translation, on the one hand, and the task of execution, on the other. It is of no concern to the programmer that this is an "internal" division of duties as long as the end result, from his point of view, is the completion of the job he had in mind.

15. In your own words, in a paragraph or two, give a description of how 20 terminals would be contacted by the computer and how it handles the information it receives from each of the terminals.

The computer would work with the 20 terminals on a ring-around-the-rosy basis. It would contact each of the 20 terminals in turn, receive a single signal from each, collect the signals in 20 different storage areas, wait for a signal that all of the messages from each terminal had been completed, and then commence work on the messages as entities.

Let us assume 20 people are handing us individual messages one letter at a time. We would travel down the length of the group collecting a single letter from each until we had collected all the messages. Then we would begin to act out the messages received. Naturally, we would require 20 different pages (or sections) of our notebooks to collect the messages, and we would need to keep them properly in order. Now, we might wait until we had collected all the messages from all 20 before we acted on any of them; but this would not be wise, as some messages might be shorter, and hence completed more quickly, than others. So a better policy would be to collect until a completed message signal was received and then take care of that message. In the meantime (during dull moments) we would continue to collect individual letters from people who had not yet signaled the completion of their messages.

If you will imagine that we collect one signal from each person every five minutes, you can get some grasp of the spare time we might have in between collections for other duties. Of course, we would also have to imagine that the people from whom we are collecting are so slow in their responses that they don't notice that five minutes has gone by for each letter collection from each of them. Rather insulting to the individuals concerned, but in fact the computer, if it could think, would think of people as being that limited and that slow.

16. List some of the things you might expect to find in a fairly large computer library.

A large-scale computer library would contain all of the compilers and assemblers necessary to translate the compiler-language and assembler-language programs written by the system's programmers. The larger the library the more of these types of translators one might find. The library would probably also contain all of the "housekeeping" programs necessary to keep the library edited and up to date. There also might be a number of special file-maintenance programs which would work to keep the basic system files up to date and also keep up the user files upon request. There would be room in the library for system programs (all programs used by the computer center people in their work with the system), company programs (all those programs having to do with the computing needs of the company personnel), customer programs (those programs generated by permitting clients or customers to use the company's computer to their own ends—usually for rental fees). Again, there might be three or more data libraries: the computer center data library, the company data library, and the customer data library, with appropriate facilities for maintaining and updating these collections. And the library might also contain a number of "industry" programs—that is, programs which have been shared, as being useful, among the members of an industry.

17. What is the difference between a utility program and a user program?

Usually, a utility program is one which has a specific function to perform for the computer center itself—maintaining files, updating library additions, and the like. A user program, though, would be any program written by a user to solve any problem of particular concern to the user. You can see we would likely find a great variety of programs in the latter case, and considerably fewer (more generalized) programs in the former.

Or putting it another way, we might say that utility programs have the purpose of assisting the data processing center in giving service to users, where the user service is the execution, successfully, of the user programs.

18. Relate the term "overlay" area to destructive read-in and nondestructive read-out.

We can think of an overlay area in storage as a reserved area into which we expect to read parts of the supervisory program when they are needed by the computer to accomplish a task. Now, because of destructive read-in—that principle which says that when something is read into storage it destroys (or "overlays") whatever was there before—we do not require any erasures of any type. By only using the part of the supervisory routine that is needed by the computer at any given time, we save a significant amount of space in storage since supervisory routines are rather lengthy and complex.

Nondestructive read-out would permit transmitting any information in the overlay area to some other part of the computer without harming what is in the overlay area. In some complex computer systems it would, then, be possible to move, temporarily, part of a supervisory routine to another reserved section in central storage, overlay another part of the supervisory routine into the overlay area, and then read back into that same area the original part of the supervisory routine when it is again needed. This would, in some instances, save a good deal of computer time since contact with any auxiliary storage device (disk, or drum, or data cell) would not be necessary.

19. What is the meaning of the term "working storage?"

When we use the term *working storage,* we usually have reference to the high-speed central storage unit of the computer, which is used in the same fashion we would use the blackboard. If parts of central storage are reserved for supervisory root programs, we would use the term *working storage* to describe that part of central storage not so encumbered.

20. What are some of the advantages of application programs for small business? What are some of the disadvantages of such programs?

Usually, application programs are industry-oriented programs prepared by the computer manufacturer to accompany the computer and to provide standard solution systems to standard problems normally encountered by that industry. The advantage is, of course, that the industry programmers do not need to create the programs—they are provided as an additional facility of the computer. This might mean that the level of programmer skill in the industry need not be as high as that of the personnel of the computer manufacturer, but the benefits would be reaped by the industry.

The disadvantage of such application programs is that they must be generalized and standardized. This means that the types of solutions to problems generated by individual firms in the industry will tend to be alike and as limited as the foresight of the computer manufacturer programmers.

HIGHLIGHT QUESTIONS, CHAPTER 5

1. The Hollerith card has both columns and rows. How many columns does the card have? How many rows does it have? How many numbers, or letters, or characters could one get on such a card?

The Hollerith card has 80 columns. The card actually has 12 rows though the digit printing on the card marks out only 10 of those rows—0–9. The Hollerith code would permit 80 characters on a card—one character (number, letter, or special symbol) per column. Numbers would be made up of a single punch in one column. Letters would require a zone punch and a numerical punch. Special characters could require zone and two digit punches or three digit punches in given column.

2. **What is the purpose of the EBCDIC coding matrix?**

The matrix itself is merely a structured summary form of presentation of the logic of the coding system. The EBCDIC code itself was designed to assist IBM in the matter of integrating its computer systems into national standards of coding. There is a U.S.A. Standard Code for information interchange (known as USASCII–8). It is slightly different than the EBCDIC code. We used EBCDIC because of the prevalence of IBM computers in our world and because the illustration is somewhat simpler.

3. **What is a byte? How does it relate to a computer word?**

A byte is made up of eight bits (binary digits). In most cases the byte is the smallest storage unit (from a linguistic point of view). That is, a byte normally can hold one number, or letter, or character representation. It is possible, under special circumstances, to use the byte to contain two numerals, but we need not go into detail here.

In many IBM computers four bytes make up a word. So two bytes are called a halfword, and eight bytes are called a double word. Many registers in IBM equipment are designed to contain one word (32 bits—four bytes). In the case of large numbers or great degrees of precision, two registers can be linked together to permit the use of double words.

4. **With what device would we most likely use a light pen? What kind of communication with the computer does it make possible?**

The light pen is used in conjunction with the cathode ray tube. We would say that the kind of communication involved would be person-to-computer or computer-to-person (as against machine-to-machine).

In another way, the light pen might be said to make possible "generalized" communication. That is, a single gesture of the light pen might cause the computer to generate an entire series of computing steps to accomplish what is indicated. The indication is general; the result is a series of discrete adjustments or computations.

The "generalized" communication to computer systems shows a great deal of promise.

5. What would be the main elements of an inquiry/display station? What kind of information can be displayed?

The inquiry/display station's main elements would most likely be a typewriter keyboard for input, a cathode ray tube for display, and sometimes a hard-copy printer. In some units the printer is a separate unit, and in others the typewriter keyboard is expanded to the equivalent of a regular typewriter with appropriate output abilities.

6. How are modern checks handled by banks?

Most modern banks make use of "automatic" check sorters. The sorters are high-speed machines capable of reading the specially coded numbers at the bottom of the modern check. The idea, of course, is to make it possible to sort checks very rapidly and to transmit them as quickly as possible to the bank on which they are actually drawn. Billions of checks are handled in this manner each year. Devices capable of reading the magnetic ink characters across the bottom of checks are called "check scanners."

7. Where would you most likely find a data collection system? What types of information can such a system gather?

Data collection systems are designed to operate at the point where the action is—for example, the manufacturing plant floor where daily operations take place. In such a system, the intent would be to gather information about the progress of each manufacturing job and be able to charge the labor, materials, and supplies directly to the appropriate account. At the same time, an attempt is made to keep a correct employee work schedule for each and every employee working on the job.

The fundamental notion behind the placement of this kind of equipment is to disperse the creation of information to the place where the information is generated, and to "farm out" the coding of such information as much as possible so no central coding agency is required.

8. Give a brief general explanation of a "universal product code." Where would we most likely find such codes?

The "universal product code" is basically a bar code system. An 11-digit symbol can be recorded on labels, and the like, in the form of a vertical set of bars of different thicknesses. The code could become an integral part of the printed package or label of canned or bottled goods. We are most likely, currently, to encounter the bar code on grocery products.

It seems likely the bar code (universal product code) will have increasing use, though it may require a double identification—both the code and the price on the package. The time savings involved at check-out counters, however, might still produce economies and the bins, rather than the individual merchandise items, may carry the actual price on display.

9. What is a check-out scanner? How would a light pen be used with such a device?

Basically, a check-out scanner is a unit which can read the universal product code electronically. The scanner is hooked into a computer system, which can then determine the price of the object, post appropriate inventories, and so on, based on the information revealed in the product code. Some devices currently used require the item carrying the bar code to be passed over a light plate on the surface of the device, with the bar code on the surface passing over the plate.

The light pen is sometimes used to scan the bar code; in particular, this system is useful when the product or package carrying the bar code does not present a flat surface which can pass over a scanner plate. As with the scanner plate, the light pen "recognizes" the code and, in symbiosis with a computer, calculates appropriate account and cash register information.

More and more the scanning mechanism, the cash register, and the computer are all linked together into an accurate and rapid recognition and response system.

10. Discuss some of the problems which can occur when we plan ahead to collect information from an event-point.

Plans are, after all, projections into the future. And we can be reasonably sure we cannot think of or account for any number of variables which might intervene between now and the future event-point where we wish to collect information. So the primary difficulty would be that all of the information we plan to collect is not all of the necessary information required by the event itself. And plans often determine equipment, and equipment, in turn, determines the kind and quantity of information that can be recognized and dealt with.

Another problem might be that while we can, during the planning stage, deal with information gathering in a leisurely manner, the event itself may be short, emotional, and dramatic.

There may not be time enough to collect all of the information required, for the event and haste might make such collection incomplete. Also, errors can occur during the collection time.

We must also remember that the relationships between variables that we think exist now might not exist in the future. A variable which we had planned for, at a low value level, might suddenly take on unexpected importance. The plan, then, would break down not because we did not expect the variable but because the variable had a greater importance or impact than we expected. And this impact might reduce the value of other variables that we had determined were the key ones, and hence had planned to collect more information than needed.

11. List a few of the rigidities which can occur when we mechanize information collection systems.

As we have mentioned in another context, the mechanization of an information system requires planning, and planning cannot take care of all the possible variables which might occur in the future. In such events we sometimes find the system is rigid—that is, it cannot take into itself unexpected variables for which no provision has been made.

The capacity of the system also may serve to make rigid what it can contain. If, for example, planning has not included proper methods for the expansion of the basic recording element (word, or whatever) when such an expansion is needed, then the whole system would have to be revised to accommodate the change. This might prove to be prohibitively expensive.

Some types of information do not lend themselves readily to either-or situations, or to quantification. Unfortunately, there will be a tendency in any mechanized system to eliminate those items which do not readily fit the mold or the machinery. In this way, certain types of information would be lost. Conversation is sometimes more useful than a written memo because conversation is accompanied by gestures and changes in tone, which a memo cannot traditionally show. Hence, the mechanization of the communication from personal exchange to memo causes a loss of information content.

In preparing information for a computer system or information collection system, we tend to categorize or "model." That is, we tend to need simple structures—abstractions of reality. We must be wary when we use such models—and remember they really are abstractions and not the reality itself. Oversimplification can be as much a rigidity as too much red tape can be.

And finally, since computer information must be in a form suitable to the types of communication devices and computers we have on hand, there is a tendency to formalize the steps which must be taken to prepare the information for entry. The formal states can become very complex and can make for rigidity. Forms are usually designed to put the information into proper quantities and classifications. Something is almost always lost in such translations.

12. What is a computing inquiry station? How does it differ from an inquiry/response station? How do these two systems relate to what we call "remote terminals?"

An inquiry station is merely a device which permits an individual to contact the computer (as through a typewriter keyboard) to ask some question and receive (through a cathode ray tube or printer) an appropriate response.

An inquiry station would not differ in any particular way from an inquiry/response station, though we might use the latter term to describe a system which permits large quantities of information to be sent to the inquirer, while the former term might be used to describe equipment with rather limited output abilities.

Remote terminals can be thought of as a special case of the broader classification inquiry/response station. The word *remote* tells us that probably the device is a considerable distance from the computer, may make use of telephone equipment, and may actually be portable.

All of these terms, then, are used to almost interchangeably to describe equipment which permits a user to contact the computer and receive some kind of appropriate reply. Smart terminals (those capable of some degree of calculating and logic activity on their own) are actually very sophisticated versions of what we call inquiry/response stations.

13. What is the difference between a natural language and a formal language?

When we use the term *natural language* we are referring to a language such as English or French. The languages are dynamic and open-ended. That is, they change over time through use, and new words and constructs can be added to them as required. The type of English we speak today is far more comprehensive than the English of several centuries ago.

A formal language, though, is one that has been designed, usually, for a specific purpose. The computer languages of FORTRAN and COBOL are formal languages. In formal languages, the vocabulary is usually purposive and limited, changes involve the whole system, and the rules and regulations are more circumscribing than in a natural language.

We might, in some future day, create a computer capable of handling English reasonably well. But we are not really likely to find such a computer to be the most economical way to handle that particular type of communication.

Finally, we might note that formal languages are metaphorical—that is, they are abstracts of our natural languages. Some part of the abstraction is due to an attempt to remove emotionally loaded words from the context of the formal language, so that the logical processes will take dominance. In that sense, mathematics is a formal and metaphorical language.

14. What are some of the limitations of digital plotters in terms of trying to convey accurate information?

Computers work in discrete units of information (chunks). When this "digitalized" information is fed into a digital plotter, whose purpose usually is to make continuous lines, some compromise with the information is required. The plotter must decide or interpolate between points in the process of drawing a curve—such a curve is always an approximation.

Also, to keep costs to some reasonable level, digital plotters actually may work on a coarser matrix than we would prefer. That is, we settle for fewer dot positions per square inch than we would like, leaving to the plotter the task of filling in between the actual dots with lines of one kind or another. The finer the mesh in the fabric of the plotter (the more points per square inch that can be utilized), the more accurate the plotter will be.

Finally, we might want to plot very large diagrams; but again we must surrender to some reasonable size of paper and range of plotter. In this we tend to go for the "average" rather than the extremes.

15. What are the two types of messages which current models of audio-response units can handle? What are the advantages and disadvantages of each?

Currently, audio-response units can play back fully recorded messages where the message is the unit, or they can assemble a message out of individually recorded words. In the first case, the proper intonations can be used since the message is recorded as an entity. In the latter case, each word would be pronounced correctly; but no inflections or unusual tones would be allowed, since each word is going to be assembled into a sentence the meaning of which is unknown to the mechanism doing the assembling—the result is a monotone message, which sounds very mechanical. The information is transmitted, but without normal human expression.

If realism is desired, the fully recorded playback message is the best choice. If accuracy and variety of messages are desired, the unit-assembled message is probably a better choice. But the process of assembling messages is a complex one, and hence we would expect the latter type of system to be more expensive than the former.

We have now completed our task of giving discussion answers to the highlight questions of the first five chapters. And in answering these questions we have tried to tease the bright student into thinking more about the matter, and we have tried to trigger some other ideas not necessarily given full treatment in the chapters themselves. We have, in short, tried to talk to the student as though he or she were present and had asked the question in the context of a conversation. We are, after all, in search of understandings and ideas, not of parroted information.

We have also tried to stretch our vocabularies a little—perhaps to force an occasional trip to the dictionary.

STUDENT SELF-TEST

There are two ways in which the self-test might prove useful. You might wish to take the test without reference to either the chapters in the book or the answers which follow the test. If you achieve a grade of 70 percent or more, you can safely assume you understand most of what you have read. If you take the test as an open-book test (referring, when needed, to the chapters themselves), you would need to achieve a grade of 90 percent or higher to feel confident that you know the material. The search for answers, of course, itself constitutes something of a thorough review of what has gone before.

Take a separate sheet of paper and list the appropriate terms for the blanks below:

1. The computer is an achievement of ________________ technology.
2. Collections of people who have banded together to achieve some common ends are called ________________.
3. ________________ includes at least a collection of traditions, a set of survival techniques and artifacts, a collection of artistic artifacts, a collection of mores, a defined set of interrelationships among its members, and a cosmic view.
4. ________________ involves a certain elegance of spirit which

permits the differences of others to exist unattacked, and is intimately concerned with the matter of preservation and tolerance.

5. A ________________ form of organization involves defined tasks which can be filled by any individual competent to perform them.
6. A ________________ is an individual holding a defined bureaucratic position who functions as a leader.
7. ________________ has to do with the application of physical devices to productive tasks.
8. ________________ power is the ability to investigate, to understand, to quantify, to predict, and to simulate.
9. ________________ is intimately involved with the processes of microminiaturization of electrical circuits, the development of computers, the generation of refined power forms, and the automation of many repetitive physical and intellectual tasks.
10. ________________ is the achievement of self-directing productive activity as a result of the combination of mechanization and computation.
11. A ________________ is an electronic device capable of following an intellectual map.
12. The institutions of civilization are the ________________, the ________________, ________________ and the ________________.
13. The ________________ constitutes the legal management of a civilization.
14. The church could be said to be concerned primarily with ________________ goals.
15. The family can serve three primary functions as an operating unit: ________________, ________________, and ________________.
16. Government functions usually include the military, ________________, and regulative.
17. American enterprise is concerned with production, extraction, and service for a price to attain a ________________.
18. Definitions could be said to be neither ________________ nor ________________, but merely conveniences to help us in the matter of understanding.
19. Sticks and stones could be used as ________________ counters.
20. We have long suspected the source of our decimal system is the human ________________.
21. The decimal system is a number system to the base ________________.
22. When pebbles and grooves were used in calculation, the pebble was called a ________________.
23. The ________________ is nothing more than the conversion of sand grooves to wires and pebbles to beads, all on a single frame.
24. ________________ is a concept of such subtle nature that it took

humanity some four or five thousand years (of the historical period) to define its meaning.

25. The master weaver who developed the punched-card concept for automating his looms was ____________.
26. We call ____________ ____________ "the father of the computer" because of his invention of the difference engine and the analytical engine.
27. When a machine moves out of the normal sequence of its instructions on the basis of a comparison of some kind, we call the action a ____________ ____________.
28. The census taker and inventor of the punched-card sorting machine was ____________ ____________.
29. The first truly electronic (as versus electromechanical) computer was built at the University of Pennsylvania and was called ____________.
30. When the computer is sent back to the beginning of a program segment by an ending instruction to execute a program slightly different from the first execution, we call the slightly altered sequence a ____________ ____________.
31. The computer that became common in the business world, and of which could be said "it was the Model T of the computer world," was the ____________.
32. The second generation of computers is distinguished from the first by what we call ____________ programming.
33. Positional notation and the concept of ____________ made the building of simple arithmetic machines possible.
34. The letters MIS, in the computer field, stand for ____________ ____________ ____________.
35. ____________ is the term we use to describe the physical elements of a computer system.
36. ____________ is the term we use to describe the programs which make the computer work as a data processing system.
37. The letters CPU, in the computer field, stand for ____________ ____________ ____________.
38. Another name for internal memory is ____________ storage.
39. A typewriter (keyboard and printing capabilities) connected to a computer system would be an example of an ____________/ ____________ unit.
40. When a device, such as a typewriter keyboard or a printer, is directly connected to a computer so messages may be sent between the central processing unit and the device, we say it is ____________ ____________.
41. When a diskette has been taken off the diskette drive unit, placed in an envelope, and stored on a shelf, that diskette is said to be ____________ ____________.

42. The ______________ of a computer is simply the "dashboard" of the unit—that is, the lights and knobs and switches required to start, stop, and operate the mechanism.
43. One common information pathway in a computer would be input to ______________ ______________ to output.
44. Central storage is made up of a number of addressable ______________. Each ______________ can hold the equivalent of a digit where a digit can be a letter, a number, or a special symbol as we commonly construe the terms.
45. The unique number which represents a particular location in storage is called an ______________.
46. One name for a block of storage cells is the ______________.
47. ______________ is a term used to describe both the arithmetic and logic units which will be used in the calculations.
48. A computer ______________ is usually defined, for a particular computer, as the amount of information which can be contained in a typical register of that computer.
49. All computers are intended to do both ______________ and logic.
50. Information read into the computer storage destroys whatever information was there prior to the reading. We call this ______________ ______________.
51. Reading out from storage does not damage, in any way, the material being read out. We call this ______________ ______________.
52. A computer goes through cycles. One cycle is called the instruction cycle and the other is called the ______________ cycle.
53. A list of instructions that a computer is to execute is called a ______________.
54. When a cathode ray tube is connected to a computer for output purposes, we sometimes call it a ______________ screen.
55. A diskette is often called a ______________ disk.
56. The term ______________ ______________ is used to describe a set of magnetic disks permanently mounted on a large spindle with a comblike structure which can read the contents of the disks.
57. Online printers may be of either the ______________ or line type.
58. Some computers make use of a combination of a small central storage and a large fixed-disk unit to simulate a larger central storage system. We call such a storage combination ______________ ______________.
59. On larger computer systems the input/output units are linked to the computer through ______________.
60. An instruction which, after a test of some kind, sends the computer out of the "normal" pathway of the instructions is called a ______________ instruction.
61. A series of instructions that will be repeated in slightly altered form

until some exit condition is met is called a ____________________
____________________.

62. A symbolic program which represents computer instructions on a one-to-one basis is called an ____________________ language program.
63. The computer program which translates a symbolic program into a machine-language program (where the symbolic program is a one-to-one representation of a machine-language program) is called an ____________________.
64. Another name for a resident program, or operating program, would be a ____________________ program.
65. An alphabetic representation of a machine-language operation code which is chosen to remind the programmer of the operation to be performed is called a ____________________.
66. An assembler-language instruction that calls up a series of other instructions, which represents a series of standard operations the computer is to perform, would be called a ____________________ instruction.
67. A program written in FORTRAN is a program written in ____________ language.
68. The program, in storage, that translates a FORTRAN program into a machine-language program is called the ____________________.
69. A compiler language specifically tailored for use with computer terminals is ____________________.
70. A set of special instructions which talk directly to the supervisory program within the computer are called ____________ ____________ statements.
71. ____________________ is usually the term used to describe an entire particular activity which a programmer might want done.
72. The computer, using the supervisory routine, breaks down what the programmer wants done into smaller units called ____________________.
73. A collection of job statements is called a ____________________.
74. The supervisory root program is usually automatically loaded during some kind of load or ____________________ routine.
75. The parts of the supervisory routine that are transient are read into an ____________________ area.
76. Housekeeping programs needed to keep the computer library in good trim also go under the name ____________________ programs.
77. The macro statements used by the IBM System/32 for communication with the system are called ____________________ statements.
78. The process of auditing a program to remove any errors the program might contain is called ____________________.
79. Well-designed standard programs which apply to problems of a particular type of business or industry, and which are provided by a computer manufacturer, are often called ____________________ programs.

80. When a number of similar types of activities or jobs are grouped together so the computer can work on them all together, we call this ________________ ________________.
81. ________________ processing means that the computer has the ability to deal with each transaction as it occurs, regardless of its type.
82. When the computer can "plan" the tasks it is to do, rather than handle single jobs only, we use the term ________________ to describe this ability.
83. ________________ ________________ languages require translation before they can be used to operate directly on data.
84. The rather common 80-column, 12-row card, used for computer input purposes, is called the ________________ card.
85. A byte is made up of ________________ bits.
86. ________________ bytes make up a computer word.
87. The light pen is used in conjunction with a ________________ ________________ tube.
88. A device, hooked into the computer system, which can provide the means for input or output, and which can be operated by an individual, is called an ________________/________________ station.
89. Machines capable of reading the magnetic ink printing at the bottom of checks, and which can sort them, are called check ________________.
90. Communication devices linked to the computer via telephone or some other transmission line generally go under the name computer ________________.
91. A bar code, printed on product labels, which can be read by a light pen or a special scanner is called a ________________ ________________ code.
92. A computer terminal capable of performing many basic computer functions on its own is called a ________________ terminal.
93. A device capable of accepting digital computer output and converting this into line drawings of various kinds is called a ________________ ________________.
94. FORTRAN is an example of a ________________ language.
95. English is an example of a ________________ language.
96. A device which can respond, under computer guidance, to a question over the telephone is called an ________________ ________________ unit.
97. The idea that whatever we do is the most important thing going on, because we are serious about doing it, is called the fallacy of ________________ ________________.
98. Computer terminals permit an interrelationship between the person and the machine. Such an interrelationship could be called ________________.
99. The smaller IBM card, a replacement for the Hollerith card with smaller computer systems, has ________________ columns split into three rows.

100. The place where we most want to collect information, and which is the site of the action about which we want information, is called an ________________ ________________.

Tests ought to have purposes. This test was put together to give you an opportunity to see how well you had been able to remember and understand the meaning of a number of terms which were introduced in the first five chapters.

ANSWERS TO TEST QUESTIONS

When you check to see whether or not you had the correct term in your answer, you may also give yourself credit if you picked an equally descriptive alternative.

---

1. high
2. societies
3. culture
4. civilization
5. bureaucratic
6. manager
7. mechanization
8. intellectual
9. high technology
10. automation
11. computer
12. the family, the government, institutionalized religion, enterprise
13. government
14. spiritual
15. definitive, regulative, economic
16. educational
17. profit
18. true, false
19. binary
20. hand
21. ten
22. calculus
23. abacus
24. zero
25. Jacquard
26. Charles Babbage
27. conditional transfer
28. Herman Hollerith
29. ENIAC
30. program loop
31. IBM 650
32. symbolic
33. zero
34. management information system
35. hardware
36. software
37. central processing unit
38. central
39. input/output
40. online
41. offline
42. console
43. central storage
44. cells, cell
45. address
46. page
47. register
48. word
49. arithmetic
50. destructive read-in
51. nondestructive read-out
52. data
53. program
54. display
55. floppy
56. disk pack
57. serial
58. virtual memory
59. channels

60. branch
61. programmed loop
62. assembler
63. assembler
64. supervisory
65. mnemonic
66. macro
67. compiler
68. compiler
69. BASIC
70. job control
71. job
72. tasks
73. procedure
74. ready
75. overlay
76. utility
77. command
78. debugging
79. application
80. batch processing
81. real-time
82. multiprogramming
83. high-level
84. Hollerith
85. eight
86. four
87. cathode ray tube
88. inquiry/display
89. scanners
90. terminals
91. universal product
92. smart
93. digital plotter
94. formal
95. natural
96. audio-response
97. central position
98. symbiosis
99. ninety-six
100. event-point

CHAPTER 7

COMPUTERS AS UTILITIES

PURPOSE OF THE CHAPTER This chapter trades on much that we have learned before. We are going to take some of the terms, like *utility, data bank,* and so on, and think of them in new ways. We are going to wonder why predictions of public computer utilities have not come true as quickly as we supposed they would. And we are going to explore some of the disadvantages of the public utility over the private utility, and vice versa.

Most important, we want to peer into the possible future that either public or private computer utilities might bring. We want to think about the possible advantages and the possible dangers such conveniences might bring. And since a utility is primarily a social service, we want to see what effect utilities might have on some of our social norms and ideals.

TERMS AND CONCEPTS

Some of the terms listed below should, by now, be familiar. We will use them in a different way—broaden them a little. Other terms that will be used in this chapter are somewhat new. In many cases the context will give the meaning. Where this is not possible, they will be defined for you.

national network
information depository
household terminal
ratio of average use
community facilities
regional facilities
high-density transmission
communication satellites
average transmission load
shared programs
royalty programs
semi-utilities
standard billing programs
IBM 5100
BASIC
national computers
large-scale indexes
block diagramming
approved response
government regulation
information utility
open programs
terminal identification
leased telephone lines
APL
regional computers
local utility
self-protective mechanisms
peak loads
unit service costs
utility overlapping
common carriers
overlapping operations
information turnover
exchange speed
closed-circuit television
computer overloads
user programs
security systems
EFT
minicomputers
intelligent terminal
lease-line fees
burst mode
domestic language
common response
dangers of centralization
household calculating power
conversation mode
proprietory programs
customer billing
auxiliary tape unit
security measures
ground laser stations
preferred response
information as a commodity

AN ERRONEOUS PREDICTION

For over a decade now, one could read in most computer publications, and often in the public press, about the oncoming age of the computer utility. Various experts predicted that by 1975 many many homes would be equipped with a computer terminal, and this device would have access to a giant computer. Each of the giant computers, in turn, would be linked to one another to form a national network of information depositories. The householder could rely upon the computer to construct the weekly menus according to the best rules of nutrition. The computer would also take care of calculating the household bills and would, through a contact with the bank computer, see to their prompt and efficient payment. The children in the household would be in touch, through the household terminal, with several of the local libraries, and could use those computers to help them with their writing, calculating, and research.

It is well past 1975—and no such computer miracles have occurred. To be sure, a few clever engineers have computer terminals in their studies. And their mates do use the computer to help them construct the family menus. The engineer also may have written a program to take care of the calculations of the monthly bills. But there is no link to the bank and there is no direct link to the library.

Computers eventually can become utilities, both public and private. We will have to look at some of the features of each of these two primary types of utilities to see which will come first, and how they differ the one from the other.

PUBLIC UTILITIES

A public utility, as we know it, is most often a private or quasi-private corporation which is, in fact, a monopoly for a given type of service, and is, therefore, regulated by the state and federal governments. The typical utility would be the local power company, the local telephone company, or the local water company.

Most public utilities are privately owned, to be sure. But since they are the only firms in the area providing the needed service, and since competition in these areas is not encouraged, some careful regulation is required. The organization that can shut off your water supply, when you do not have a quick and reasonable alternative, is an organization which could wield a dangerous amount of power, and is an organization which could charge very high prices for the services it offers. But to have two firms running water lines, or power lines, to all the local homes, and to indulge in raw competition with one another, is to duplicate a needed service and to waste money for all. So economy demands monopoly, and the monopoly requires regulation.

If computer service to home and business is to take on the aspects of a public utility, then there are cautions which must be exercised. Many of the regulations which are applied to the power company, the telephone company, and the local water company will be applied to the computer company as well. And of course, if the telephone company is to become a central part of the computer utility (as is likely), then many of the current regulations will apply automatically. Equally, all those aspects of the public utility which are currently unsatisfactory to many people would automatically now extend themselves to the computer utility as well.

In actual fact, the private computer utility is much more likely to develop first, since initial costs are high and large amounts of data would have to be regularly transmitted to make such a system economical. And there are certain fixed traits of the public utility that can be altered or resolved more easily with the private utility.

A public utility requires an enormous initial capital investment. The fixed capital of the enterprise is a large part of the total cost of delivering the service to customers. The amount of labor relative to the amount of capital investment is small. The utility must be able to offer service to most of the people in the geographic area it dominates. It cannot, as in the past, add a few new customers a month as it expands its facilities. It must be prepared to serve the majority of the people in any community almost from the start. For average-size communities, then, we are talking about the initial investments of tens or hundreds of millions of dollars.

A public utility must build and provide facilities which can handle peak loads of activity, in spite of the fact that quite often this capacity will not be needed and will not be used. It must, however, have the capacity available should it be called upon to provide excessive service. Any public utility must be able to guarantee the service it is supposed to provide. We would not long tolerate an electric company that had to shut down supplies of electricity to homes from time to time due to an overloaded demand.[1] We certainly would not want a telephone network that would not permit us to make telephone calls, when and where we wished most, if not all, of the time. We want to call the fire department when we have a fire—not when the telephone company has made occasional service available to us.

Typically, a public utility is centralized. That is, for a large geographic area there is only the one supplier of the service. Mostly, this monopolistic arrangement has originated because competition would be wasteful. And, of course, the large initial investment requirements would also tend to weed out casual or trivial competition.

Finally, the bigger the public utility, and the greater the use of its services, the less each unit of service will cost. Until the recent energy shortages, most of our public utilities spent a good deal of time and a great deal of advertising money trying to persuade us to increase our uses of their services. And quite frequently, the rate per unit of service cost to the customer dropped as the total usage increased. It paid to have and to use many electrical appliances.[2] It paid to use

---

[1] Given the energy shortage and its problems, this statement has to be taken with a grain of salt.

[2] See note 1.

many extra cubic feet of gas. All this would reduce the per unit cost and maximize convenience in the home. Lately, that is not a very popular concept.

THE PRIVATE UTILITY

The private utility (here defined as one which is privately owned and which is not under obligation to provide services to the general public) does not have quite the same problems the public utility has.

The private utility does have an enormous capital investment to make. But it can be put together by business partnerships, or by combinations of the type we will soon discuss. This will spread the initial capital cost over a broader range and will not severely cripple any single company's financial structure.

But where the public utility is required to build facilities to handle peak loads of demand, even if the normal day-to-day use of the utility is below such peaks, the private utility can plan more carefully and can actually regulate the use of the utility so as to reduce the total amount of carrying capacity and to spread the load evenly. One can tell one's employees when they can and cannot use a transmission system, and how much their use shall be. One cannot so easily handle the general public in this manner. Nor can one predict accurately any changes in usages which might come about. The public utility has a vast number of single small users who could blend their demands for service into strange combinations at any time. The private utility can dictate the usage as it sees fit. There may indeed be many users, but they are under direct management control. So the original investment in a private utility may be more carefully planned, and may be somewhat smaller in scale and cost, than an equivalent public utility.

The private utility will also be centralized—at least as far as the owning company or company partnership is concerned. But there could be many such private utilities overlapping one another geographically. There might be several communication nets owned by several businesses, all competing with each other in a single geographic area. The business with the best and cheapest communication net would be the business with the distinct competitive advantage.

Where the public utility will often have a low ratio of average use to the total capacity of the system, the private utility, by careful planning, can see to it that the ratio of average use is very close to the maximum capacity of the system—hour after hour, day after day, week after week. The less is the idle communication time, the more economical the system.

Given these differences between the public and the private utility, we can see why we will have a host of private computer utilities before we get around to the matter of building public computer utilities.

Private versus public utilities

TYPES OF UTILITIES

Utilities have been classifiable, in the past, into four general headings. We have those utilities which we call common carriers—the airlines, the canals, the railroads. We have utilities which we customarily call power utilities—those providing electricity and gas to homes and businesses. We have certain kinds of community or regional facilities—sewage disposal systems and water systems of various kinds. And we have the so-called communications facilities. These would include the television and radio networks, the telegraph companies, and the telephone companies. The computer utility most likely would fall into this latter category—communication. Certainly, we all recognize that the computer can make use of some of the standard communication facilities already provided—telegraph and telephone lines.

THE ELEMENTS OF THE COMPUTER UTILITY

Before the idea of a computer utility—the piping of computer abilities to offices and homes—could be given serious consideration, a number of developments had to take place in the computer field.

First, the internal memories of computers had to expand enormously. (These are the high-speed chalkboards we mentioned earlier in the text.) The computer needed the ability to store dozens of computer programs in its internal high-speed memory, as well as a large amount of raw data. Of course, the computer could only execute one program at a time; but the others had to be available on demand—there would be no time for scanning large disk storage units, or drums, or other auxiliary storage devices. When several programs are available in internal storage, ready to be executed, we call the function "multiprogramming." Before multiprogramming developed, the opportunity for a true computer utility was nonexistent. When the computer needs additional data for a program it is executing and has to wait, it can immediately shift to another program in central storage and work on that while it awaits the signal that the information needed for the first program is internally available.

Second, supervisory programs—or management or operating programs, as they are sometimes called—had to reach a sufficient degree of sophistication to be able to kick back and forth at will among these several internally stored programs. And even more important, these supervisory programs needed the ability to keep all the different data elements coming in from all the different sources in separate recognizable areas. Programs and data had to match accurately. Of course, as the sophistication of the supervisory or operating programs grew, they occupied more and more space in the internal memory. Ways had to be devised to keep usage of this space to a minimum. We talked about one way to solve the problem—overlay areas—in an earlier chapter.

Third, the cost of internal storage had to be reduced considerably. This was done in two ways. First, the cost of each physical item inside the computer was reduced, and second, the speed of the computer was improved. Microminiaturization helped in both cases. The greater the turnover of information inside the computer, the less the cost per calculation and per datum. In the early computer days, a single digit in internal storage cost $1.00. Later this cost was reduced to $0.10. A few years later the cost dropped to $0.01. Then it moved to $0.001 (1 mill). With the modern systems, we have internal storage costs of less than a hundredth of a cent per datum—and the cost is still dropping.

Fourth, the exchange speed of information from auxiliary storage to internal storage had be be increased enormously. Great chunks of data had to move in and out of the computer from these auxiliary devices, under control of the operating system, at rates of millions of bits per second. This meant the seek-and-find techniques for auxiliary mass storage had to be improved. Overlapping operations had to be devised here. While the channel looked up information on one set of disks, information had to be traveling through the channel from other sets of disks. The computer had to be able to notify the channel to go to work, and then had to have the ability to cut off communication with the channel and go about other work until a special interrupt signal was received. Then, and only then, would the computer interrupt its internal efforts to see about the matter of data transmission.

Think of it as a simple management delegation of authority. The computer (the boss), told a channel (the underling) to go and get appropriate data. Then the computer went about other business, having delegated the job. When the problem had been handled, the underling merely notified the boss that all was ready for the internal work to continue. Conceptually, the matter is easy. Mechanically, the matter required the development of very sophisticated equipment. But it is here and it is working.

Fifth, computer terminals had to be reduced in cost and increased in ability and sophistication. These devices had to be genuinely usable with a multitude of abilities that could suit a variety of individual needs of computer utility consumers. We have seen something of the great variety of terminals available in an earlier chapter. Different combinations of cathode ray tube, typewriter keyboard, printer, and light pen have been made available to suit a variety of tastes and needs. The most important recent development is the intelligent terminal—one with some computing capacity of its own. This development maximizes the computing power of the individual user and minimizes the amount of contact necessary with the larger computers in the system.

Sixth, if there were to be large banks of data stored at the computer site, methods had to be worked out to keep this information reasonably secure. Programmers using the utility had to have some assurance that the information they put into the computer could not be used by others not authorized to do so. We will deal with these problems in greater detail in the next chapter, when we take up the topic of data banks.

Seventh, all the operating techniques we usually associate with a well-managed public library had to be developed and applied to mass data banks. It would do the programmers using the utility little good if they could not call up their programs on demand, and if they could not be firmly convinced that the data they put in last week was the data they got out this week.

Eighth, all these elements we have mentioned had to be tied together in a tight communication network, online, ready to go on demand. The network had to be available, economical, accurate, and reliable.

These several important elements all had to be under reasonable control before serious talk about computer utilities could move—

from fantasy to fact, from hope to happening, from planning to performance. The job is by no means yet done, but it is on the way.

VOICE-GRADE TRANSMISSION

The ordinary telephone lines, so familiar in the United States, were not originally designed for high-density transmission of information. Rather, they were built to transmit a reasonable facsimile of the human voice. We call such lines "voice-grade." But you cannot crowd an ordinary telephone line by attempting to transmit millions of bits of information per second—it simply isn't up to the job. For the ordinary individual with rather limited computer input and output expectations, the voice-grade line is generally adequate. It is not as accurate as we would like, nor as fast as we would like, but it will do the simpler jobs. Businesses, on the other hand, have massive computer usage requirements. They must transmit millions upon millions of bits of information at very high speed to keep their larger computer installations productive and busy. This means there is a pressing need for some kind of high-grade data transmission system. Many such systems are now under construction or being planned for construction. But the lack of them in the last decade and a half, and their cost, has slowed down the true establishment of the computer utility as it had been envisioned.

EXAMPLE OF A PRIVATE DEVELOPING UTILITY

Recent newspaper items have informed the world that three large companies are setting up an informational transmission system that will run into the millions of dollars. International Business Machines Corporation, Aetna Life and Casualty Insurance, and COMSAT General have formed a partnership to start this new communication venture. The partnership, Satellite Business Systems, will see, eventually, to the launching of special-purpose communication satellites. Large amounts of data can be transmitted by these satellites (millions of digits a second or more) to any part of the continental United States from any other section. IBM, for example, will be able to transmit great masses of data at high speed between the IBM plant on Hicks Road in San Jose, California, and the IBM plant in Poughkeepsie, New York.

While Satellite Business Systems goes about the complex matter of launching its own satellites, the partnership will lease the use of those satellites already in outer space. IBM will test the transmission facilities by communicating between San Jose and Poughkeepsie. When this initial system has been checked out, IBM will add four or five more of its plants to the network. Eventually, Satellite Business Systems will put two of its own satellites in orbit, with the approval of the Federal Communications Commission. When the system is reasonably complete, the three companies in the partnership will have about 400 earth stations in communication with the satellites. The stations will be able to transmit voice messages, digital data, and copies of important documents or drawings. More interesting, video conferences—electronic executive meetings—will be possible. If this becomes a reality it will no longer be necessary for company executives to catch airplanes and flit hither and yon around the country. Closed-circuit television will permit company executive meetings on very short notice, with a fraction of the expense usually involved in air travel. The amount of time saved in transit will also be considerable.

Estimates are that by 1986 Satellite Business Systems will have invested over $400 million in the creation of this private utility. But we should note the early entrance of the FCC into the negotiations. Private utilities are themselves not immune from regulation by the federal government.

The complex radar dishes located at each station in the system will be able to transmit millions of digits of information per second—getting around the limitations of the ordinary voice-grade communication lines. At the moment the companies will lease some facilities from extant public utilities, but it is clear they are going in the direction of a self-contained system.

From a corporate point of view, the advantages of owning one's own communication and computer utility are obvious:

1. Information transmitted can be carefully controlled in such a way as to enhance the security of the transmission.
2. The system can be designed to handle the average transmission load, and the amount of use can be carefully controlled.
3. Executive conferences will remove the necessity for executive trips and eliminate that not inconsiderable expense in terms of both time and money.
4. Excess capacity could be leased by the corporations to other businesses so idle capacity need not be wasted.
5. Control can be tightly centralized while the actual corporation facilities are widely scattered.
6. Information available to corporate management can be instantly made available to any plant or other facility managers on demand.
7. Computer overloads at one location can be spread to other locations throughout the continental United States.
8. Customer contacts and services will clearly be improved. The facilities of the largest and best part of the company can be instantly available to any part of the company, however small, and however isolated.

While the public utility has large capital investments to face, geographic domination of a specific area, the necessity of the economies of scale, the need for a large reserve capacity to meet unstable service demands, the private utility has large investment, can be more geographically spread out and not alone in the area, faces the economies of scale, but need not have a large reserve capacity since the use of the system can be controlled to keep demand from becoming unstable. Further, the private utility can grow a bit at a time, testing each element in its network, and then move on with improvements. Public utilities are required to have their services available to all people and groups in the area upon demand. This precludes a slow and cautious development.

UTILITY PROGRAMS

Let us assume, for the moment, that we actually managed to put together a computer utility of the public type. Let us assume, further, voice-grade lines are sufficient for the handling of a standard type of computer terminal, and that the utility rate is low enough so a reasonable number of users would avail themselves of the service. What types of programs would be handled?

First, we would expect the computer public utility to provide a number of standard programs to perform normal mathematical functions, certain types of household chores, and the general accounting requirements of families. These standard programs would be available to any user. The person at the contact end of the network (the terminal) would merely request a particular type of program by name. The computer would respond through the terminal, informing the user that the program had been placed into internal storage and was ready for contact. We would expect the less-sophisticated terminal user to be able to speak to the computer in a general command language. For instance, "INCOME TAX, LONG FORM" should make a program available which contained all the routines and information necessary for the computer to carry on a two-way conversation with the terminal operator to effect a complete income tax return. In this "conversation mode," the computer would ask for the types of information required by the income tax form. We would expect such statements from the computer as: "AMOUNT OF INTEREST INCOME PLEASE BY NAME OF PAYEE AND BY AMOUNT." The terminal operator would then simply key in the name of the bank or other loan agency paying the interest and give the yearly amount. The computer would store this away and then perhaps request: "AMOUNT OF DIVIDEND INCOME PLEASE BY NAME OF ORGANIZATION PAYING AND BY AMOUNT." And so it would go.

Or in a more sophisticated situation, the computer could, when

"INCOME TAX, LONG FORM" had been requested, print out a whole series of questions which the person at the terminal could answer at leisure. When all the questions had been answered, the householder would contact the computer with a statement like: "INCOME TAX, LONG FORM, INFORMATION READY." The computer could then request the amounts needed, item by item, from the terminal operator. This done, the computer would then print out the income statement in its entirety. The name of the accounting firm designing the computer income tax system might also be typed at the bottom to indicate the chance of a well-worked out and accurate tax return. Of course, all would depend upon the honesty of the terminal operator in giving the correct amounts. But since the income tax people generally require some support statements, the problem would likely be no worse than it is today. Certainly the general calculations and the logic of the income tax forms would be better than in the past.

The householder might be charged a small fee for the use of the computer and another small fee for the use of this standardized income tax program. In effect, one would still be using a tax consultant, but would be using the consultant one step removed—the computer being the intermediary. We can imagine the tax consultant receiving some kind of royalty for every use of the successful tax program. We could also expect an audit could be made of the program rather quickly and easily by the income tax people themselves. If they were assured of the accuracy and legality of the income tax program in the computer, and they were assured (by support documents) of the accuracy of the amounts typed in by the householder, they could be fairly certain (and rather cheaply, too) of the accuracy of the tax return itself. It might even pay the federal and state governments to design the appropriate computer utility programs themselves.

We could go yet a step further. Certain proportions (e.g., the amount of cash contributions which can be deducted for charity) could be built into the computer program. If an individual is claiming too much in the way of cash charity contributions, as compared to the gross income, the computer could warn the householder during the preparation process itself.

One might get these statements: "MEDICAL DEDUCTIONS ARE IN EXCESS OF THE AMOUNTS ALLOWED FOR YOUR GROSS INCOME BRACKET." Or one might receive a statement such as: "THE ITEMS YOU SPECIFY DO NOT QUALIFY AS LONG-TERM CAPITAL GAINS."

So much for standard programs. We have explained enough for one to understand the type they might well be. Shared programs would be another category. Here we refer to programs designed by other computer terminal operators who are willing to let the programs become available to anyone who wishes to use them. A bright young mathematical student may have invented a rather simple method for handling chi-square or some other statistical formula. The student might declare the program to be "OPEN." This would mean the computer could store the program in its general program area. From time to time the computer center would print a list of user-designed programs which are available to anyone on request. And, of course, the computer center would most likely have to print some kind of a disclaimer along with the program list: "This company is not responsible for the accuracy or usefulness of the user-generated general programs in this list."

Another type of shared program might be the "royalty program." A user may have written a program which might seem so useful and so handy that other terminal users might be willing to pay a small fee for the use of the program. The computer utility could print a list of these types of programs, give a brief description of their qualities, and then collect a small royalty for the terminal user who designed them. Again, there would have to be some kind of legal disclaimer by the computer utility, and quite probably some kind of legal responsibility on the part of the designer of the program. These are matters which will most surely come up in any society making use of a general computer utility system. The courts, we might guess, will have much work to do in the future to handle all these interesting matters.

Finally, the computer utility would have in its files what we call "proprietory programs." They are programs designed by the terminal user for a specific and confidential purpose. They are private property and are not to be loaned out to anyone on request under any circumstances. Here the computer utility is responsible for some kind of security system for proprietory information. There must be no means by which another terminal user could intentionally or inadventently tap into this material and make use of it.

Security systems need to include some method of identifying the terminal user, to be sure the right person is asking for the right information. Special code identifiers are usually given out. When the user contacts the computer utility, the identifier code must be used. If one can give the proper code (which only the user is supposed to know) the information in the proprietory files will be made available promptly. Or the computer user might have a special plastic badge—something like a credit card—which could slip into the terminal slot to clear the way to the special programs. These types of security are not very difficult to break, however. Best of all would be some method by which the individual could be identified by fingerprints or other peculiarly individualistic means. Recent attempts have been made to analyze the motions an individual makes when writing a full signature. Apparently each person makes a series of measurable motions which are personally unique and which cannot be duplicated by a forger. The question is whether or not the kind of equipment to detect these types of particular motions can be built cheaply, and can be generally distributed among computer terminal users. For the moment, special identification codes are the most commonly used methods of keeping proprietory information out of the hands of those not entitled to use such material.

SEMI-UTILITIES

Certain types of computer services are made available these days which could be said to border on the utility concept. For example, many banks have very large computers, and these banks have instituted basic computer programs and services to help bank customers in special ways. Some banks will handle the matter of billing customers for a client. The client has a terminal at the place of business and may transmit information about charges made by customers to the bank. The bank, with its large computer facilities, can see to billing the client's customers, the receipt of checks sent in by customers, and the preparation of certain basic business documents. Thus, we find banks entering into general billing services—one of the areas thought to be particularly important to the computer utility.

Ultimately, such a banking service would be expected to grow to the point where the exchange of checks might not be necessary. A customer's expenditures could be sent directly to the bank by computer. The bank would see to increasing the accounts of those individuals to whom the customer is paying money. And the bank could see to increasing the customer's account as other computer terminal users notify the bank to deposit money in that account. What we have here is an exchange of funds electronically. Such an exchange goes by the title "EFT"—electronic funds transfer. We can expect this kind of transfer to grow during the coming years. In a major instance, banks would like to be able to clear all checks with other banks by this means and save some of the problems of check transfer and mailing. It might be possible, in the not too distant future, for the banks to transmit images of checks held rather than the real thing. This would materially cut down on the cost of handling checks and might bring bank customers a considerable saving in both time, money, and lost checks.

Many small computer installations earn a living by handling the data processing needs of small businesses. In particular, these installations take care of billing the business customers, collecting the amounts due, and creating the basic business records and statements. This means much information must be transferred between the small business and the computer installation. In the past this transfer has been taken care of by mail or by courier. Usually, the business prepared punched cards to reflect customer charges. When enough of these cards had been assembled, they were sent by courier to the computer installation. A number of standard billing programs were then thrown into action, and the bills for the small business were prepared and sent out. When the business received payments from customers, these payments were also recorded on punched cards, and when sufficient numbers had been gathered they were shipped off to the computer installation for updating the business accounts. The computer installation played the role of electronic bookkeeper for the firm and for many other similar firms as well.

Now, of course, the idea would be for the small computer installation to be hooked directly to its clients by means of computer terminals. As information relative to its day's receipts and expenditures is gathered by the small business, these facts could be sent directly to the computer installation over leased telephone lines. This materially speeds up the operation and reduces the chance of lost documents. Equally, the completed business statements could be transmitted to the small business, and on its own terminal the information would appear in proper form.

We can see, then, a developing competition between the bank and the computer installation itself. Each one is gradually impinging on the territory of the other. Each is involved in the electronic transfer of information and each is approaching the electronic transfer of funds.

A SMALL BLACK CLOUD

Many years ago a very great physicist mentioned that Newton had solved basic physics problems for all time, and that there were only two small clouds on the horizon remaining to be incorporated into the Newtonian system of physics. The planet Mercury was guilty of some very strange behavior unaccountable in the Newtonian scheme of things, and electrons did not behave precisely as Newtonian physics would have them do. Unfortunately for that particular physicist, the two little black clouds turned into massive storms and Einsteinian physics took over, leaving Mr. Newton's work not as a summation of all physical knowledge but as a good first approximation.

Today there is a small black cloud on the horizon of the computer utility—it is the minicomputer. These very small computer systems are dropping fast in price, and are increasing enormously in ability and storage capacity. Some of the small devices are capable of storing three million or more digits on small floppy disks. These disk storage systems, combined with the principles of virtual memory, have made the small computer something to reckon with. The prices of these systems are well under $10,000 and dropping almost as rapidly, relatively speaking, as the prices of electronic calculators. The question will come up: Why should one pay out for computer utility service when one can own a small but very powerful computer privately?

The IBM 5100 Portable Computer, shown in Figure 7–1, is a good example of this type of device. The small system can hold up to 64K (K=1024) bytes of storage. Programs can be created and stored on auxiliary magnetic tape units. The system can write on these tapes at 950 characters per second, and read from the tape into internal storage at 2850 characters per second. Many engineers, and others who would normally have a computer utility terminal at home, would find these capacities and speeds quite to their liking. Once they had paid the price of the system they would no longer face rental charges for utility service.

The IBM 5100 has two keyboards. One is very similar to a typewriter keyboard, but with a number of extra characters. Since capital letters are used in the system, the shift key can provide different symbols for every letter position. Also, the little computer has an adding machine type of keyboard to the right of the typewriter keyboard. Numbers can be entered through the typewriter keyboard or, much faster, if one is familiar with handling the normal number key configuration of a ten-key adding machine. The 5100 also is equipped with a small cathode ray tube for displaying information. A separate online printed can be attached to the system, and so can an auxiliary tape unit. And if it is required, the IBM 5100 can be hooked into larger computer systems and serve the function of an intelligent data termi-

FIGURE 7–1. The IBM 5100 Portable Computer

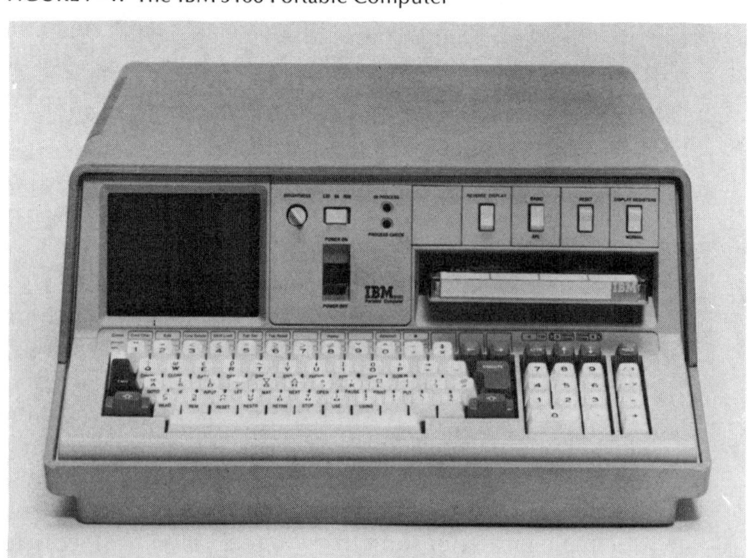

Courtesy of International Business Machines Corporation

nal. The 5100 can speak either APL (a high-level mathematical language) or BASIC (one of the more common computer languages which have been used on terminals and which is in the form of simple statements, such as GET, PRINT, SAVE, LOAD, and so on).

Other small computers of this type can be purchased with one or two floppy disk sets so that the actual computer memory on hand could range from three to six million digits. This is more than enough basic capacity to satisfy many individuals who would otherwise require the services of a computer utility.

The private computer has some advantages. It is usually a one-time cost item, though a repair contract would probably be wise with such a complex system, however small it might be in appearance. The personal computer does not require extensive security measures, since only the person who purchased the machine need have access to its memory. The private computer does not require transmission lines, either voice-grade or otherwise, so no lease-line fees would have to be paid. The private computer is available now but still has the ability to be hooked into larger computer systems when and if the computer utility truly becomes available.

So there is a new and unexpected form of competition here. The end result may be a happy marriage—or the dominance of one system or another. We cannot yet tell.

THE UTILITY NET

Let us assume technology continues apace and that we begin, in a decade or less, to acquire genuine computer utilities. What kind of computer utility net can we expect?

First, we will require a number of very large computers scattered throughout the nation on a regional basis. Let us assume a computer facility for every 10 million inhabitants of the United States. This would mean something on the order of 22 major computer centers. They probably would not be distributed around the country on a geographic basis, but rather on a population basis. California would have more computer facilities than Nevada, Idaho, Utah, New Mexico, and Arizona combined. Each of these regional computers would have radar-dish facilities for communication with a number of satellites hovering in fixed and appropriate orbits over the continental United States. Information could be transferred from one regional computer center to another at enormous speed by making use of these fixed satellites. When we transmit millions or tens of millions of digits per second we are working in what is called "burst mode." All this really means is that we are sending information very rapidly in large globs from one point to another in space.

A number of smaller satellite computer installations (local centers, we might call them) could be linked to the larger installations by means of ground laser stations or microwave stations. Here the messages are not sent into outer space, but merely sent from one radar-like dish to another in a visual line at near-ground level. Such transmission lines already are used by the telephone and telegraph companies. These small stations also could work in burst mode, receiving and sending information to the regional center. If information is to travel cross-country, such information would be sent from one regional station to another via satellite.

Each of the smaller computer installations would be directly connected by better-than-voice-grade lines to individual businesses or, by simple voice-grade lines, to individual homes in the general geographic jurisdiction of the smaller computer installations. Here, then, we would have built a national network. Anyone with a data terminal in the home or in a business could reach any other terminal in a home or in a business wherever it might be in the United States.

The regional data processing utilities would be massive information storage centers. They would require data banks which could contain trillions upon trillions of digits of information online, ready to be searched out and called up into the high-speed internal memory of the system. The local data processing utilities would have much smaller storage facilities, and these would be used primarily for locally needed information of the common sort; they also would contain large-scale indexes of all the different information held by all the different regional utilities in the country. This look-up and reference system would be essential if such a national utility were to be workable.

Use of certain standardized programming languages would probably be required by all terminal users. We could expect a business language, a mathematical language, and quite probably a "domestic" language. The domestic language would be of the command type covered in an earlier chapter. The terminal user would probably have to learn something close to a basic form of English. He or she would have a vocabulary of one or two thousand words which could be put together into simple sentences. These pseudo-English sentences could then be interpreted by the local center. Actually, they would call up a number of job control statements, which in turn would call up a number of standardized procedures that the computer could execute. All through this system would run the thread of standardized language, standardized procedures for problem solution, and a standardized form of result. Just as the television set in each home is gradually erasing the wonderful dialects of an earlier and more local United States, the computer net would gradually erase the unusual solution to a common problem. Here we might uncover the first serious danger—a kind of creative ossification. If the problem is not a fairly standard one, or if it cannot be stated accurately in the limited language facility available, the problem would be said to be unsolvable—or at least unworthy of the attention of a busy national utility.

Of course, the more sophisticated programmer who knew either the business language or the mathematical language could state the problem in much more exact terms and could, at least, get something akin to the unique solution to a unique problem. But we should note these languages, too, of necessity, must be limited. The computer is not guilty of imagination or creative construction. It will do what it is told to do, no more and no less. It will do only what it can find a program for. If we have not thought in advance of the method of solving the new problem, we are not likely to get much help from the computer. The computer, for instance, is not likely to notice a peculiar and unexpected relationship between two items if it is not executing a program instructing it to look for just such "unexpected" relationships. The computer does not sit back, twiddle its mind idly, and then suddenly say, "Aha." Human beings do that without knowing quite how it is done. Until we do know what underlies those wonderful moments of "aha" when rare geniuses reach up and catch a star, we cannot program it. In fact, the kind of mind required to construct excellent, complete, and logical computer programs is not necessarily the kind of idle dreaming mind that comes up with a rare but valuable "aha!"

Computers, like accountants, are very orderly. Artists and other creative folk are not noted for order or method. Computer programmers like to think in boxes, wherein each box represents a procedure made up of several computer statements. Each of these boxes is linked one to the other with directional arrows. One is supposed to move from this procedure to that one in an orderly and routine way. We call this process "block diagramming." It is wonderful for computer people and lousy for predicting human behavior.

IMPLICATIONS

There are several major implications of what we have considered in this chapter. And since they are major, we will dignify them with several titles, such as cultural uniformity, the sin of civilization, and so on. Let us realize, then, that all of what follows could be put under the single title, "implications," but we choose not to do so for the sake of attention and the sake of emphasis.

CULTURAL UNIFORMITY

The computer utility will add pressure to a developing phenomenon called cultural uniformity. A mass communication net, and we have one in national television, can turn the individual regional areas of the United States into a dreary similarity. So, too, can a computer utility. Perhaps the utility is the more dangerous since it, by design and by nature, is intended to deal with the business of solving problems. At least the primary function of the television is entertainment, not education.

Cultural uniformity is very dangerous since it can turn the common response into the preferred response, and the preferred response into the only approved response. One who dares to be different is classed as heretic and, we might note, heretics have short and unhappy lives. If the cultural uniformity happens to get the blessing of religious orders, what is common can well become sacred. To violate sacred edicts is to court sudden death or cruel punishment. We would like to think that in this, our own enlightened age, such things cannot happen. But they do and they have, as recently as the Vietnam war.

The physicist Robert Oppenheimer once said Albert Einstein leaped mentally from mathematical mountaintop to mountaintop while lesser lights (like himself) spent many weeks and months patiently treading the lower hills and valleys until they could arrive at one of the good Dr. Einstein's peaks. Can you imagine what might have happened to that genius's intuitions if he had been forced to tediously spell out every step to a computer before he could solve the problem he had in mind? The computer, you see, has no place and no use for intuition. It cannot skip a single minute step. This we must remember.

Cultural uniformity in the matters of morals, dress, and deportment is dreary but survivable. Cultural uniformity in the matter of thinking is narrow and dangerous to the survival of the culture. If it is true that the world changes without consulting us, then it is true we must be able to change with it if we are to survive. The bones of dead cultures that could not survive the unique, cover the planet from end to end.

THE DANGERS OF CENTRALIZATION

Centralization of business, of government, of churches, and of entertainment has all taken place in the last few centuries. No one can deny that there are many benefits to be obtained from centralization —uniform control, the benefits of large scale, better chance for survival, the ability to buy and maintain high management talent, certain kinds of efficiency, reduced costs, the advantages of mass production of products and services, and so on.

Centralization carries a very serious hidden danger, however, one that should never be ignored: That which is centralized is easily *seiz-*

able. If there are ten or twenty national networks, a revolutionary group would be relatively hard put to take over all the networks at the same time. One or two they might get before the alarm could be sounded. But 20? Not likely.

During World War II, just before the rescue of the city of Paris by the allied armies, a great battle took place in the city. The Free French underground and the Communist underground both tried to seize the Paris telephone system. Why? Because one who could control that vital and centralized communication system could control the city. The Free French underground won the battle, but not until it had played a hard game and paid with blood and terror. What is true for the Paris telephone system is more poignantly true for a national centralized computer utility system. If the system is under heavy government regulation, and if the system is made up of a rigid bureaucratic hierarchy, then whoever seizes the center of control has successfully seized and dominated the system. Today's computer specialist's dream could well become tomorrow's vehicle of inordinate tyranny. Our dreams have a habit of turning sour.

AVOIDING THE DANGER

Can the dangers of bureaucracy and of centralization of something as vital as a national computer utility be avoided? Yes, it can indeed. We must be very certain to permit the development and growth of a number of private utilities. The utilities must be permitted to compete directly with the public utility in offering comparable services. And more important, while these private utilities must be regulated in a general way, they should be regulated in a manner distinctly different from the public utility.

Currently, we have several national television and radio networks. They compete with one another. They are privately owned but governmentally regulated. Also, we have public service television, which purports to offer what the privately owned networks cannot. There is precedent, then, for competing utility nets. We would hope the private utilities would be more creative, more adaptive, and more adventurous than the public utility, but this need not be the case—witnesseth the dreary uniformity of the private television networks and the sometimes unique and daring adventuring of the public television system.

How much government regulation should be applied to the private computer utilities? As *little as is necessary* to keep them doing what they have received license to do—no more, no less. In short, it should be the job of the government to keep the utilities competitive and to keep them honest.

OF RHYME AND REASON

Anyone who has studied the development of public utilities has studied a certain kind of indeterminant confusion. Why is it that gas companies have become utilities but coal distributors did not? Is it because gas lines had to be strung into each and every home? Was it because the customer became dependent upon the system for heat and salvation? Well, what about the person who delivered the coal by truck to the owner of a coal stove? Was not the coal stove owner pretty well hooked into a system from which there was no exit without serious expense? Did not one depend on the coal company and its drivers for one's heat and well-being? Yes, one did, but not enough for a utility to be born.

Why is it that the water company became a utility and the iceman of yesteryear did not? Before the days of the refrigerator the householder was very much dependent upon the deliveries made by the iceman to keep food from spoiling. Yet the ice companies and the icemen (we cannot say "persons" for they were all men in those prelibeRation times) did not become public utilities. Was it because water demanded a hookup and ice delivery did not? Well, then, what about the television or the radio network—both are regulated to a fair-theewell, and they do not require hookups to the houses of the land. No, we are dealing with a sort of catch-as-can-can system of things. One dependency seems to demand government regulation of the close utility-oriented type, and another, dependency does not. We should remember this particularly interesting hodge-podge when we discuss the regulation of the computer utility. If there is indeed rhyme and reason, then trucking companies as well as railroads are to be classed as public utilities. Certainly there ought to be a number of competing garbage collectors in our cities—by no strange quirk of government regulation should a single garbage company be given a city-wide franchise. They are, of course.

If we are forced into a single public computer utility, it probably will be because of limitations in the number of satellites which can be projected into space, or because of the limitations on radar communication networks, or because only a few large industries can dare to enter such an expensive field with such a huge initial capital investment. But a single utility will not be healthy. It will put culture and civilization into peril. It will make seizable what ought not to be.

REALITIES

We have enjoyed some speculation—hopefully, speculation based on the realities of modern technology, and speculation based on early developments in selected areas. The computer utility or utilities will come, but it or they will come slowly. Why? Because some laws of economics are immutable. We will make use of such services as we need and as we can afford them. Right now there is serious question as to how much calculating power the average American householder might need. We do not here doubt the enormous need for arithmetic power on the part of the business folk, or the engineers, or the scientists. But we need to remind ourselves that most people are not given to these occupations. Most people most of the time do not do that kind of calculating and that kind of mental work. There is an old slogan which we might well ponder: "Five percent of the people in the world think. Five percent more of the people in the world think they think. Ninety percent of the people in the world would quite frankly rather die than think." Maybe it is true, maybe not. For a certainty, we can say that home demands for vast computer services will have to be generated, probably by advertising, probably by argument of great power at little expense. The original computer inroads will be made where they are needed, by government, by industry, by science, by education. The rest of us may be content to twiddle on the sidelines until the advantages are proven and until the advantages of computer utilities to others competitively hurt us. Then, and only then, will we see about establishing utilities of this nature in our homes.

Well, will such pressures ever occur? We know, in the first instance, that more and more jobs in this nation—nearly half—have to do with information rather than physical production of goods or the physical delivery of services. If this is so, then we are going to make use of an information utility. If IBM is planning to set up a system whereby its own executives no longer need to travel to confer and to communicate effectively, then it will not be long before other executives in other businesses want, indeed must, do the same. What is sauce for the goose is also sauce for the goslings.

If information is a commodity, and it is, and if information will one day constitute the work of the most of our working people, and it will, then why not eliminate by means of a computer utility the necessity for all of us to travel to and fro to offices and homes? Why not leave the home in the office? Why not clear the freeways and the byways of traffic and smog? Think, if you will, of the saving of energy! Think of the decrease in smog! . . . Think of the lovely loss of traffic jams and frustration. Think of the pure air. Think, too, of the isolation, the loss of contact of an intimate nature with one's fellows. Think, if you will, of the tiresome monotony of one's own household day after day after day. Think of the awful inertia of informational transfer without physical movement on the part of the transferee.

All of our intellectual axes have double edges—they cut both ways. We trade one discomfort for another. For all of that, though, the computer utility will come. Businesses will start the ball rolling down life's competitive hill. Government will surely follow. The average person, otherwise left out, will add the computer to the household and, with a sigh, hope for the best of all possible worlds. Wise folk and heretics will meow in dark corners and invent ways around the system. Do not denigrate them, for they may well be our future salvation.

OTHER OBSERVATIONS

We might wish to ask ourselves some other questions. How efficient are public utilities? We ask the question in two ways. First, we worry about the ordinary mechanical efficiency. How responsive is the utility system to our information needs? Can it send the messages quickly and cheaply? Does the answer come in enough time to be of value? The second way of asking such a question has to do with the matter of quality of transmission. Does the TV picture, with its audio component, really transmit the same kind and the same amount of information as the personal conference? Is there any virtue in conferences where people actually attend? And, of course, we might ask if it is wise not to travel? Is it not said that travel broadens a person's horizons. Is there not some virtue in moving from here to there beyond that would normally occur because the trip is business? Is any trip, anywhere, merely business?

We have not explored the consequences of a failure of a major public communication utility. We are now familiar with blackouts in major cities. We know something of the trauma they create and the perversities they bring out in rather ordinary people. What, then, if we are linked into a complex public communication utility and a breakdown occurs? What kinds of rages and frustrations must such a failure bring down upon our heads? It will not do to say such things *cannot* occur. They have! They do! And we all know better.

Is it a good thing that a person need not figure out his or her income tax? Is it wise in a democracy to pass the intellectual task to a mechanism which uses a standard set of procedures, responses, and formats to deal with the problem? Is this not a peculiar form of intellectual tyranny which might well put the ordinary citizen out of the practice of handling, however poorly, his or her affairs? It is unwise to put too much of one's personal affairs in the hands of others—something of the person is lost in the process, and certainly, something of liberty as well.

Also, we must ask ourselves about either public or private utilities and their fees. What will be the fees? Will they become a standard part of the household budget, as is the case for electricity, gas, oil, water? How far do we wish to tie into utility nets and thus remove ourselves from the ability to operate independently of them? Thomas

Jefferson believed in the small independent farmer. Alexander Hamilton believed in large industry and commerce. Hamilton had the better foresight. But we might wonder whether or not Thomas Jefferson saw the greatest danger.

Finally, in any semi-utility of the bank-service type there is bound to be a loss of what we call human concern. In olden days the local doctor would know which patients could afford to pay and which patients could not. And he or she just might skip billing certain customers as an act of understanding and humanity. What of the billing service now working for the doctor? Will it do the same? It will not! The billing service has a different function entirely. It is not within the scope of the duties of the billing service to weigh the human values of concern to the doctor. The man or woman who works in the billing agency does not come from quite the same background as the physician. How much of the human element are we willing to sacrifice in the name of efficiency? It is a hard question. Somewhere there must be a stopping point.

SUMMARY

In the beginning, we noted that the prediction of the nation-wide computer utility in the mid-1970s did not come true! The primary reason is quite likely the cost of such a utility to both businesses and individuals. Still, there are signs the utility will arrive in its own good time, for it is, after all, a competitive advantage to those moneyed and skillful enough to develop it. We explored the general meaning of a public utility and noted the monopolistic nature of such an organization, and the necessity of regulation by state and federal agencies. We then gave consideration to the private utility and discovered, among other things, the private utility might be able to develop first—primarily because of certain uniformities and cost savings it could effect.

We then noted there are at least four different types of utilities, and that the computer utility might come under the class called "communication utilities." We discovered several different developments had to occur in the computer field before the utility concept could become a reality. Memories had to expand. Supervisory programs had to be improved. Internal storage costs had to be reduced. The exchange speed of information between auxiliary memory and internal memory had to be enhanced. Computer terminals had to be reduced in cost and increased in versatility. And, of course, security steps had to be taken to protect utility information.

We learned voice-grade lines have limited message-carrying capacity. On this account alone, if not for other reasons, the private utility might be able to develop first, since it has the financial capability of stringing private high-burst lines. The Satellite Business System complex was explored briefly as an example of a newly developed private utility.

The three primary types of computer utility programs—standard, shared, and private—were discussed. Identification problems of terminal operators were given brief consideration, and we found that security might not be all that secure.

An example or two of developing semi-utilities received brief consideration in order to highlight certain areas of future competition. And the mini computer was given some hard thought as a possible serious competitor to the public or private computer utility. Mini computers will quite probably continue to develop in sophistication and to drop in price.

Toward the end of this chapter we considered a potential computer utility net. That done, we looked at some of the consequences—cultural uniformity and the seizability of centrally organized entities. These dangers considered, we gave some thought to methods for avoiding the danger.

Those matters put aside, we explored how utilities came to be, and we failed to find any real clear-cut reason for the existence of one type of utility and the nonexistence of another.

HIGHLIGHT QUESTIONS

1. Give one or two reasons why the predictions of full computer utility nets in the mid-1970s did not come true.
2. Give some characteristics of public utilities.
3. Give several characteristics of private utilities.
4. What are several ways in which a private utility differs from a public utility?
5. Generally describe the four major types of utilities with which we are familiar.
6. List four major computer developments which helped make the possibility of a computer utility move from dream to reality.
7. What is the primary difference between a "voice-grade" transmission line and a "burst-mode" transmission line.
8. What are a few of the economic advantages a private computer utility might have over a public computer utility?
9. Name and describe three different types of programs we might expect to find in a public computer utility.
10. Of terminal users, who would find a command language most useful, and who would find BASIC language most useful?
11. Name two typical methods of data bank access security and tell why each one is not particularly effective.

12. Why does it seem that developments in the mini computer field might interfere with the development of public computer utilities?
13. Would the mini computer interfere in any particular way with the development of private computer utilities?
14. What are some of the features we might expect in a public computer utility net?
15. How can it be said a public computer utility might cause cultural uniformity?

READINGS

Head, Robert V. *Manager's Guide to Management Information Systems.* Englewood Cliffs, N.J.: Prentice-Hall, 1972.

Chapters 5, 6, and 7 are of particular interest as references to this chapter of our text, although the book is also very useful reading for any consideration of data bases (the subject of a later chapter of this text). It is a pleasantly short book, some 176 pages in all.

Parkhill, D. F. *The Challenge of the Computer Utility.* Reading, Mass.: Addison-Wesley, 1966.

Although this little book is now somewhat out of date, it does deal directly and in detail with the difficulties and possibilities of setting up computer utilities. The book is slightly over 200 pages in length and is well worth the reading. There are several chapters devoted to particular utilitylike applications which should be given special attention.

Squire, Enid. *The Computer: An Everyday Machine.* 2d ed. Menlo Park, Calif.: Addison-Wesley (Canada) Ltd., 1977.

This is a straightforward paperback about the computer. It should be read if you are still having some trouble sorting out the details of all that has gone before in this text. Probes some language details which should be of interest.

CHAPTER 8

DATA BASES

PURPOSE OF THE CHAPTER

We have, in earlier chapters, had occasion to consider auxiliary storage devices as they related to the systems under discussion at the time. Now we turn our attention not only to those mass storage devices as mechanical entities but to what they mean in the construction of data bases. Some of the material we will consider is, therefore, repetitious—but that is a good way to learn. Also, it is good to learn about the same thing in different contexts—this gives us some clear idea of the generality of the device, and helps us in the matter of projecting intellectually what else might come up.

Data bases are being developed privately—the corporate world is never one to surrender the advantages brought by size and economic power. Bureaus of the government also are busy developing data bases. Our main question is whether or not we wish to establish nation-wide or regional data bases, and what such establishments would mean to our way of life and culture. So let us begin.

TERMS AND CONCEPTS

In this chapter we will run into some new terms. Sometimes they will be given specific definitions, and sometimes we will depend upon their contextual presentation to do the defining for us. And we are going to run into many terms we have met before—but in a slightly different set of circumstances.

random storage
magnetic disk
serial reading
data transfer rate
channel linking
honeycomb
data set label
high-density tape
grandfather, father, son principle
read-only tape
frequency chart
file duplication
cross-indexing and files
elective information commitment
magnetic tape
linear reading
overlap
spool
staging
volume format
real-time processing
read/write head
frequency organization of files
identification
field
intracompany data bases
address
tracks
disk storage units
access time
tape band
destaging
megabyte
file protection
transaction tape
overflow tracks
authorization signal
national index
national information net
intercompany data bases
electronic switching
data blocks
data cartridge
ports
information cylinder
batch processing
character mode
control block
time-bound material
file loan
internuncial memory pools
data base auditing

WHAT IS A DATA BASE?

Quite a number of years ago, a particularly amusing Broadway play called the *Desk Set* was made into a motion picture starring Katherine Hepburn and Spencer Tracy. The gist of the film concerned the attempt of a computer expert, Spencer Tracy, to provide a newspaper library with a computer data base. Unfortunately for Mr. Tracy, the librarian, in the person of Miss Hepburn, had a memory far superior to and far more flexible than that of the computer. You can still see this delightful film on television if you have a passion for late hours. All worked out well, after many complications, when the computer expert was finally able to demonstrate his intention was not to replace the librarians but rather to assist them. This, then, is the first requirement of a sound data basis—to assist and not to replace those who, after long lives of experience, know every minute detail of the enterprise.

We must make a very important second caution. Data bases can become, of themselves, so complex and enchanting we forget, in our enthusiasm, why they are established and what their ultimate purpose is to be—the convenience of those who require a fully detailed and accurate memory of the activities of the enterprise over time.

What, exactly, is a data base? It is nothing more or less than an electronic file, usually on disks or tapes, which contains all the information we would ordinarily expect to find in the old-fashioned file cabinets of an enterprise. It is, in short, the *organized* memory of the business. In such an electronic file we expect to find what we have done in the past, just exactly what we are currently doing, and what we have agreed to do in the future.

STORAGE AND SEARCH

Those who construct data bases have three great ambitions, and face the agony that, so far, these ambitions conflict with one another. First, we have the desire to build the biggest possible data bases. Second, we must know that we can find information stored there very quickly, hopefully in minute fractions of a second. Third, we want to make the storage as cheap as possible.

Random storage, a type which makes up most internal computer memories (the chalkboard we have talked about earlier), has the quality that any datum stored therein can be found very very quickly. In fact, you can get to any spot in random storage as fast as any other. But, of course, random storage is very expensive to construct. We need this random search ability in the central processing unit of the computer; so we have it there in spite of the expense. Auxiliary storage, though, represents a clear compromise between random searching ability and mass storage and cost.

In random storage, a datum stored in a storage unit can be called up at an instant. Each storage unit has an address, and one can call up information from any address without any type of inline search. But is it not clear that this cannot be true of a reel of magnetic tape? The datum we might be seeking on the tape may be the very last item. A minute or two could be lost winding the tape from the beginning to end to find the item. On the average, a half a length of the tape must be traveled for any ordinary search for a single datum. Well, you might point out, a minute or two isn't all that long. It is when you consider the computer works in billionths of a second, the slower computers in millionths of a second. It is a shocking waste to have a computer idling its abilities for 99 percent of its available operating time. So we develop compromises of various sorts. We arrange information on tracks around a magnetic disk. We make a stack of these disks. We then put read and write (read/write) heads on each and every disk. We can, by electronic switching, get to any one disk as fast as any other. We can then jump from one track to another. This does require time, but less time than it would take to get through the full track reading in a serial way. Once we find the track, however, we are going to have to read serially exactly as we do with a magnetic tape reel. Again, on the average, we can find a datum in the time it would take to cover one half the length of the track.

We have lost some time, though not as much as we would with tapes. We have increased the expense, though not as much as we would with magnetic random storage. We have compromised where it was necessary, though we bemoan the necessity. And the nature of tapes and disks is such that we can store millions upon millions of digits in a very small space.

And, of course, we have worked out other compromises which are fairly effective. We don't read in single items or in small groups of items from the disks and tapes. We try to read reasonably large blocks of data into the computer random memory where we can then go about our work in a random way. Also, we do multiprogramming. We allow the computer to be working on one block of data while another block of data is being read into another area of internal memory and while another block of data is being read out of another store area. We overlap our operations wherever and whenever we can. In spite of this effort, a good deal of the computer's valuable time is wasted. There is plenty of room for improvement.

MODERN MASS STORAGE DEVICES

Disk banks. One of the better achievements of the last decade has been the development of large-scale disk units to achieve mass online storage and, at the same time, provide for an almost infinite capacity of offline storage in a mode that could quickly be loaded on the disk drives. Figure 8–1 shows the IBM 3330 disk storage units (four of them) and their related control devices (above each pair of disks and to the extreme right of the entire set).

Each basic disk unit consists of a control panel and two disk drives. Each disk pack has a capacity of 100,000,000 (100 million) bytes. A byte, we recall, can store a letter, a number, or a character. This means that for each of the double disk units we can achieve at least 200 million bytes of storage. And, of course, when four such units are connected, as they are in Figure 8–1, we are talking about a minimum of

FIGURE 8–1. IBM 3330 disk storage and control

Courtesy of International Business Machines Corporation

800 million digits. What is more imporant is the flexibility of "seek and find," which disk units naturally provide. It is possible to get to any individual track in the system very quickly and then to any datum on the track. A single datum can be dug out of the system in somethings like forty thousandths of a second.

Normally, though, we would transmit large blocks of data in and out of the disk units to the central processing unit memory. In such an event we can speak of data transfer rates of 800 thousand or more bytes per second. Further efficiency can be achieved because we can send out orders to the disks independently for seek-and-find operations, and this means it is possible to overlap many of the search-and-transmission activities—cutting down considerably on the access time to any datum or block of data.

Let us sum up. We can have 800,000,000 (800 million) bytes of storage online with the IBM 3330 storage facility. We can double the amount of storage if we are storing only numbers and not symbols or characters—a peculiarity of the byte structure. We can expand the capacity by virtue of being able to pull out the disk drawers and replace any disk with another one kept on hand. So it is possible to build up an active file of trillions of digits if required—all we need to do is plan carefully to be certain we have the right disk packs in the right drawers at the time when the computer program calls for them.

We need a little perspective about these capacities. An ordinary novel has about 400 pages. Usually, there are about 38 lines per page. And the average line is made up of 70 characters. So for our book we have about one million characters. The IBM 3330 storage facility, then, could store the contents of 800 complete books. This is actually a fairly formidable amount of information. And we have not considered any number of reserve disks which could quickly be loaded on the system. Nor have we considered linking, through channels, three or four of these IBM 3330 disk storage units. With the larger computer systems this can easily be done.

Data cartridges. Data cartridges, when they are combined into a mass storage facility, provide an enormous increase in storage over the typical magnetic drum or disk pack. Each data cartridge is about two inches in diameter and about four inches in length. A magnetic tape band is wrapped around the data cartridge. The tape band has the equivalent of 677 inches of tape on which records may be written. A single cartridge can hold slightly over 50 million bytes of information. The tape, which is wrapped around the drum, is considerably longer than the drum, so we get what is called a "spool" effect. Two of these data cartridges can hold as much information as an entire large disk pack.

The device which holds all these cartridges in a sort of honeycomb arrangement is called a 3850 mass storage facility. The system has special "ports" where one can insert or remove cartridges at will—though this should not be a common function, because the basic idea is to get mass online storage available without the necessity of a lot of human intervention (as would be the case with magnetic tape units).

Figure 8–2 shows a drawing of the cabinet structure of the 3850 (specific models might have such numbers as 3851 and so on, depending upon capacities).

Figure 8–3 gives us a close-up view of the cartridges in the honeycomb structure of the storage device, and also shows a view of the access equipment whose function it is to search out and identify a particular cartridge.

FIGURE 8–2. IBM 3850 mass storage facility

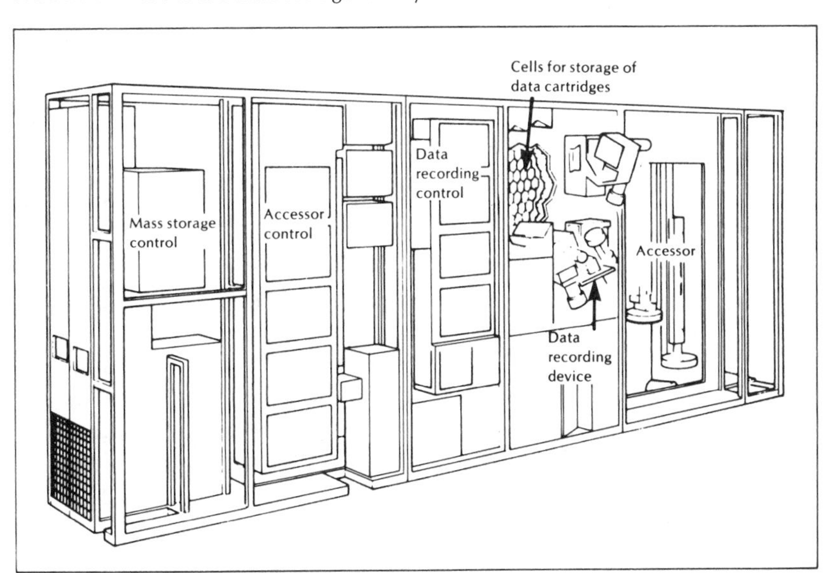

Courtesy of International Business Machines Corporation

FIGURE 8–3. Inner structure of the 3850 mass storage facility

Courtesy of International Business Machines Corporation

The IBM 3851 (a specific model of 3850) mass storage facility can hold up to 235 billion bytes of data. However, it does not work in isolation. The information on cartridge tapes is "staged" into the main computer memory. By that we simply mean that the contents of two cartridges can be read to an intermediary—an IBM 3336 disk pack (100 million bytes of capacity). From the disk pack it is, in due course and as needed, bounced into the main computer random storage (central memory). The staging (going in) and destaging (going out, from memory back to cartridges) permits an appropriate adjustment for the speed variances of the different devices and allows certain overlap operations which do not require the central computer to waste time waiting for searches to be completed.

Remember the concept (chapter 3) of cylinders of information stored on disks? Well, it is possible to think of information stored on cartridges as being stored in cylinders, too. A complete set of cylinders (using all the available tracks on a disk pack) makes up what we call a "volume."

Volumes are nothing more than gross storage units. Usually, for example, a tape reel can be thought of as a volume. In the volume we store all the data sets (collections of information, in byte form, that have a special label or name and can be searched for via that label or name). The use of data sets and volumes permits the identification of large data units, even though we are bouncing them around from cartridges to disks to memory, and even if we ultimately store them on some other and different memory device.

By the way, magnetic disks and magnetic data cartridges are of that class of storage devices called *d*irect *a*ccess *s*torage *d*evices (DASD). All it really means is that the information is on call from the computer without human intervention. To be sure, we can take cartridges out of the honeycomb or put others in, but we won't need to do that very often. With tape units, however, it ought to be clear that we would require a lot of human intervention since tape reels have to be taken off of drives and put away or mounted on drives *before* the computer calls for the information.

So, in the cartridge structure and the honeycomb arrangement, we have the advantages of enormous capacity online, the volume format so useful to large-scale storage devices, a very rapid actual transfer rate of blocks of information through the staging system, and cheap storage per megabyte (millions of bytes).

Tapes and drives. The earliest form of online mass storage was the magnetic tape reel with its associated drive unit. In fact, many installations today still use a number of tapes drives since this is a very economical mass storage form. Figure 8–4 shows a typical magnetic tape drive unit. The tapes, of course, can be taken off the drive and replaced by other tapes.

A magnetic tape can contain around 800 bytes per inch. A typical magnetic tape is 2,400 feet long per reel. So, we are talking about 28,800 inches, each of which can contain 800 bytes of information. When we multiply this, we find the typical magnetic tape can contain about 23,000,000 (23 million) bytes. Since we can take the reels from the drive and interchange them at will from a tape library, we will have a very large storage capacity indeed! But we also have lost some advantages—someone must be in attendance to put the correct reel of magnetic tape on the correct tape drive at the correct time. And a whole system of library procedures is going to be required to see to the proper storage and cataloging of hundreds or thousands of tape reels.

Some tape units permit 1,600 bytes per inch (high-density tape), and this means a typical reel can contain some 46 million bytes of information.

Dozens of tape drives can be connected to the computer, however, so we can put quite a bit of information online at any one time. We are still required to do some careful planning. We cannot simply update a single file at will without wasting a great deal of time and

FIGURE 8–4. IBM 2401 magnetic tape drive

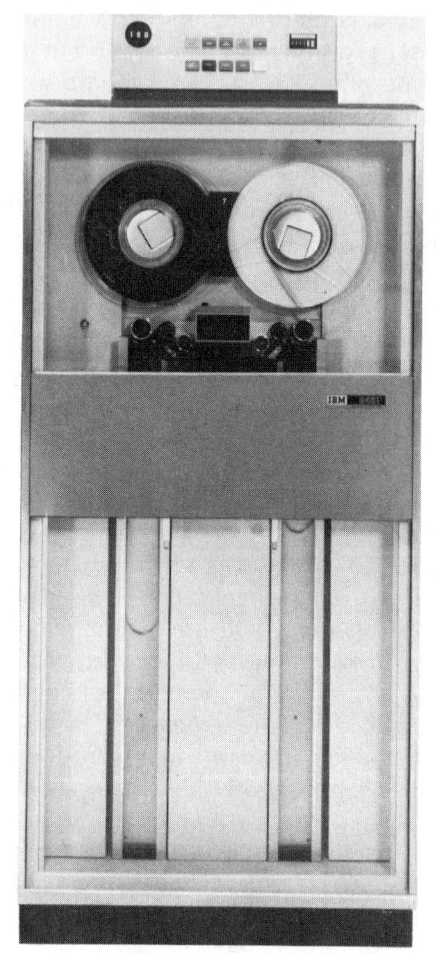

Courtesy of International Business Machines Corporation

money in the search. What we must do is group together all the like items that will be needed to update serially a single magnetic tape as we move along. This method of handling data is called *batch processing*. Clearly, we lose something—there is a time lag between the moment when the data are on hand and the moment when they can be properly posted to the records, usually 24 hours.

Disks, on the other hand, allow us to seek out any single datum on the disk and immediately update the information. Or we can call at will for any single item from the disk units and have that information almost immediately available and displayed. Tapes are more economical but provide serial restrictions.

How fast can we read from or write on tapes? It varies somewhat from drive to drive, but a normal range is 15,000 to 30,000 bytes of information per second serially. The rates tend to be controlled by the density of the writing on the tape.

One solution to the tape problem is to have our main data library on magnetic tape. Then information can be read at very high speed from the tape into the disk units available to the computer (staging). Once this burst transfer of information is done, the searching, writing, and updating can be done on the disks. Then the data can be sent at high speed back on the tape for further storage, until needed at some later time. This system works very well in situations where we have weekly or monthly activities requiring no intervening alterations. Daily activities should probably be done on magnetic disks. And if we are in a position to require very current information throughout the day, based on outside inquiries, we ought to use a mass-disk file of some kind. This type of work we call "real-time processing."

Protection of files can be a problem. Many tape units have safety rings on them that prevent writing on the tape. The tape then becomes a read-only tape and no one can accidentally or deliberately alter the record. Another method of dealing with the problem of protection of files is the grandfather, father, son principle. That is, we save the day-before-yesterday's main tape and the updating information on another "transaction" tape, and we save yesterday's main tape and its transaction tape, and finally we have on hand today's main tape and its updating information tape. So if, unhappily, we do make an error and erase today's tape, we can immediately update the situation by using yesterday's record and yesterday's updating information. Or we can back up yet another day by taking advantage of the grandfather units of storage. These latter activities are called "organizational protections," as against the "mechanical protections" of the tape guard rings and the like.

Disk packs. Figure 8–5 illustrates a typical disk pack drive unit. A disk pack is a collection of disks, usually five or six, in a single transportable housing, with handle, which can be inserted in the disk drive unit at will. What of the capacity of a single disk pack? Well, we are talking about 50 million-plus bytes of storage in the full character mode, and double that if we are talking about storing only numbers. Quite a lot of capacity for each of the portable disk packs. Advantages? An enormous offline storage capacity similar to that achieved with tapes. But unlike the tape unit, once the disk pack is loaded it is possible to have random search and random posting of information.

With the graphic illustration (Figure 8–6) we can see the access

FIGURE 8–5. IBM 3350 disk storage drive

Courtesy of International Business Machines Corporation

FIGURE 8–6. Graphic representation of disk unit

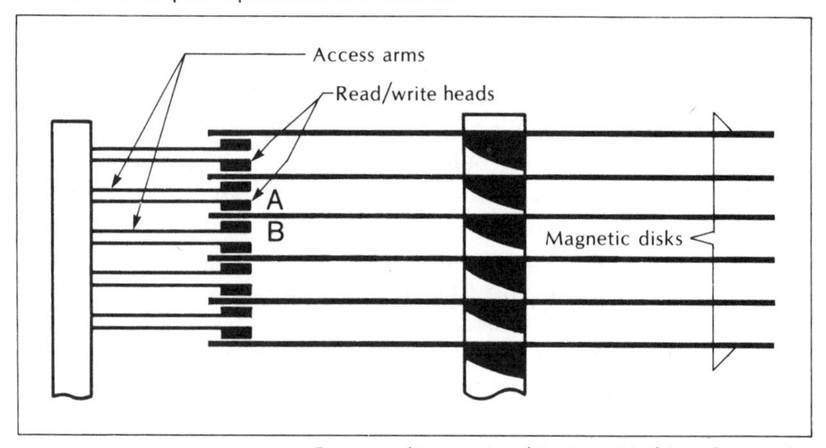

Courtesy of International Business Machines Corporation

arms that scoot over the disks for proper reading placement, the read/write heads, which actually note the information contained in the disks, and the central drive shaft of the unit. Each read/write head travels from track to track to find the proper reading area (to or from the direction of the main shaft). Since there is a read/write head for each and every disk surface (excepting the very top and very bottom surfaces) the hunting job is confined to seeking out the proper disk track. Each track, of course, contains a collection of information in bytes. Typically, each disk or collection of disks is a specialized file. The program for dealing with that file is first loaded into the computer and then the proper disk with data is placed on the disk drive for treatment.

When all the access arms carrying the read/write heads move, they move together. This means that when the access arms move, any track in a similar vertical position for any read/write head is equally accessible with no further movement of the access arms. We covered that concept of a "cylinder of information" in chapter 3.

With the disk packs we are currently discussing, each cylinder of information would be made up of 19 tracks (the number of read/write heads on the access arms). Typically, a disk pack will have 404 tracks on each disk, with seven reserve tracks in case of material damage to those regularly used. So, we will expect to have 404 cylinders of information. We would store track by track in each cylinder, and then cylinder by cylinder from the outside, in order to minimize the amount of movement of the access arms necessary for the storage or retrieval of large amounts of information. Each disk track can hold 13,030 bytes. For a typical disk pack capacity, we would multiply the 404 cylinders times the 19 tracks times the 13,030 bytes. We can, however, have as many disk packs to use with one or more disk drives as we choose. In the case of both, the diskette (mentioned in chapter 3) and the disk packs, we have a large online storage capacity and an almost unlimited offline one.

FILE ORGANIZATION

The most common methods for arranging files are ascending sequence or descending sequence. In the former case, we go from *A* to *Z*, or from a smaller key number to a larger one. Think of the contents of an entire disk unit as a volume—much like a book. This volume will have a label. If more than one disk drive is connected to the computer, the first job for the computer is to find the proper volume. Once this is done, the volume label will lead the computer to the table of contents of that volume. Scanning the table of contents of the volume (much as we do the index of a textbook) the computer finds what is called a "data set control block," which, by means of a data set label, points to the location of the data set on the proper track. The hunt is very straightforward. Find the volume by means of its label. Read the table of contents of the volume until you find the data set control block for the data. Read the data set control block to find the location of the data. Move to the proper data track. We do that very activity when we do our own searches. First we find the book we want by title (volume label). Then we look in the index (volume table of contents). Then we turn to the page we want (data set control block). And finally, we find the proper paragraph we want to read (the data set itself).

Overflow tracks at the end of each disk usually are used to store additional information until such time as the entire file can be reorganized by using one of the computer's housekeeping routines. In other words, when we go to add data into a data set we don't necessarily have to rearrange the whole set at that time. The item is merely added to an overflow area. When the computer does its data hunting, a scan of the original track also will lead it to the overflow track to find what is needed. Later, when there is time, the housekeeping routines will put everything into its proper place on the main track and clear the overflow tracks.

Some very well-worked out storage systems make use of what we call "frequency organization of files." All this means is that we keep the most frequently needed materials readily available. We have a routine by which the computer monitors the frequency of calls for particular data sets. Based on this frequency chart, the computer locates those materials where they are easily read in and out of main storage. Well, we do that sort of thing ourselves, don't we? We keep things that are called for frequently—like telephone numbers of our immediate friends—right on the desk where available. For infrequent calls we are content to refer to the telephone directory. There is, then, nothing peculiar or strange about the "frequency organization of files." People do it all the time. Why not, then, computers?

Earlier we mentioned the use of both disks and tapes to provide flexibility and still reduce costs. We mean simply that the main storage of a system could be tapes. At the beginning of the day, material that is to be used frequently could be read in batch processing mode onto the appropriate disks. Then, all day long, the disks could be used for active read-out and posting of records. At the end of the day, the disk contents could be put back on the tape, thus updating it until the next time the information is needed. Some disks would always contain the same information, read from and added to hourly. Other material is time-bound. That is, the material is only updated and read from at some fixed period during the week or month. Here is an example of a need to read onto a disk a batch of material from a tape, update everything as required, and then read the material back from the disk to the tape and put it away in storage for safekeeping.

Again, we have need to mention that part of our data organization has been purely mechanical—dictated by the nature of the medium on which the storage takes place. Another part has been organizational—we make up our minds how the data are ultimately to be stored and how many different modes of storage, or shifts of storage modes, we might need to fulfill the several purposes of our enterprise. It is the skillful combination of the two which makes an excellent and workable data base, and the sloppy combination of the two which brings about the data disasters we hear about from time to time when customers' accounts are hopelessly fuddled or lost or destroyed altogether.

SECURITY NEEDS

The computer is a machine. It has no conscience and little skill in evaluating human beings. If anyone has access to the computer, he or she can, regardless of character, get information out of the system. All one needs is knowledge, not character. But trying to get knowledge out of another human being usually requires something more. The individual you ask for information is going to make a quick examination of you, ask for identification, make value judgments about your appearance, your nature, and whether you ought to be askng the question at all. Often these judgments are made intuitively and very rapidly. If you have no business in the file room, the file clerk will probably quickly note that fact and refuse you access to the materials.

We need security methods for computer information. In fact, since so much information is stored and is so readily available to persons with the proper keys, we have to be doubly careful. In most cases, the person making an inquiry of the computer must have some proper type of identification—a special badge, a key code number, a physical key to a physical inquiry station. These methods are by no means foolproof. It is said that a clever Harvard freshman can break any code anywhere any time if he or she has been challenged by a colleague. This has been done just often enough to give us pause. Security is much more an illusion than a fact.

If it is true that individual voice recordings are as unique as fingerprints, and if it is true that fingerprints can be recognized in full detail by heat sensors, then it is likely that these two techniques could be the best file protection possible. Before one could get information into or out of a computer, one would have to provide one or the other means of identification. Certainly these would be more reliable than plastic badges, since such badges can be stolen or imitated rather easily.

Probably the best security currently available is organizational. Banks and credit agencies have long had to deal with the problem of security and, all things considered, they have done fairly well. A centralized computer system, at least, can be protected in the normal way. But a number of special problems come up when we speak of the home computer terminal making use of telephone lines. Here the security problem is more severe. We need some kind of recognition or authorization signal which is reliable and which will permit immediate access to data banks to those who have the right and authority to use them. This is a social problem which is going to grow, and we will discuss the matter in fuller detail toward the end of the chapter.

SHARING DATA BASES

The number of computers in the United States passed the hundred thousand mark some years ago and continues to grow. This means there are thousands upon thousands of data bases around the country of various degrees of completion and sophistication. Why not link these together for mutual benefit? This can be done in several different ways when business security and competition are not at stake.

One method of linking two computers, and hence the data bases connected to them, would be called device sharing. In this type of arrangement, two different channels from two different computers connect to a single input/output device. The input/output device can then receive information from and input information to both computers as required.

Another method of sharing is called channel sharing. In this arrangement two different computers can share the same channel. The channel, in turn, can be connected to a dozen or more different input/output units. Here we get much more data turnaround and a more complete type of sharing. Inquiries to either computer, and hence to either data bank, can be made from several different devices at each location.

Primary memory sharing is the ultimate in data base sharing. Here either computer can make use of the other's core memory. This means any information entered in either computer from the auxiliary storage devices can be used by the other. In effect, both computers act as one.

Another common method of data base sharing is the actual duplication of files. That is, one computer center can prepare duplicate tapes of all the information at its disposal. These tapes then can be given or loaned to the other data center. Reciprocal arrangements of this kind permit any data center in a net of data centers to have the same information available to any other. When new data are accumulated in any computer center, copies can be made and shipped to the other centers.

Finally, one center can, upon request, loan certain of its files to another data center. Mailing lists are typical of this kind of information loan from one data center to another—usually such loans are intrafirm rather than external, however. More commonly these days, a computer center that has compiled a fine mailing list may lease or sell such a list to another center on request. In some states, the department of motor vehicles sells the current lists of new car owners to private industry. Whether or not this is an acceptable activity of a government agency is currently under heated debate. For the moment, however, it is not an uncommon practice.

THE NATIONAL DATA BASE

Computer experts have dreamed for a decade or more of having a national data base—a collection of information on every citizen in the country available, on request, to any data center in the country. There are various versions of such a plan. The bravest of these would have a single national data base in a giant computer center in Washington or some other city. The information contained in such a single center could be tapped into by any authorized user anywhere in the country via the common-carrier communication lines—telephone or telegraph. Or in some instances, large-scale users of the national center could be directly connected to it via cables or satellite communication centers.

A more modest plan is to have from five to ten regional data centers in the country. Communication between the centers would be via satellite and cable. Great blocks of information could be transmitted between the centers, on need, by burst mode.

A still more modest plan would be to provide a number of large data centers with a list or national index of data available. Such information would be shared among computer users. The national data center would maintain the index and the index only. When the national center received a request for data it would advise the inquiring agency of the location of the information. Negotiations for the data would take place between the centers. The center desiring the data might have to pay the center with the data on file some kind of modest user fee to pay for problems of maintenance and transmission. There are several regional credit centers in the United States which work in this fashion.

AN INTEGRATED DATA BASE

Some United States counties have a somewhat different dream. They wish to have a map of the county which contains every residence in the area. The computer would maintain the map and a complete informational file on all those living at a given address.

Should one, for instance, be perking along the highways and byways in excess of the legal speed limit and run across one of the local police officers, the latter could, by an inquiry to the county data center, learn all he or she needed to know about the citizen currently under scrutiny. If the individual had ever been arrested before, such information would come out. If he or she had neglected to pay debts or had skipped payment of a parking ticket, this, too, would be revealed. In short, there would be no denying past infringements on the part of the arrested individual. All would be revealed upon inquiry. The social security number or the driver's license number would be the officer's key to the information about any citizen.

IMPLICATIONS

Again, we have several major implications, with all their offshoots, so we had better break our discussion into several major headings—beginning with "the dangers" we see in the immediate future.

THE DANGERS

Suppose, now, we did indeed have a national data base. And suppose further, that data base contained just about all the information possible on any individual in the United States based on his social security number. Suppose further, every individual had to have a social security number and a file, beginning the day of birth. What kind of a world would it be? Let us answer that by telling a short tale of yesteryear.

In the good old days—the period prior to World War II and its mass registration of individuals—people could, when they had gone broke in a business, or gotten themselves fired from a job, move to another state in another part of the nation and begin again, sure in the knowledge that it would be a rare day indeed when their past errors and past sins caught up with them. There is something hopeful about such an escape. One could always look to the future with hope and aspiration. One would know his past skeletons would be kept snugly in their respective closets. There would be no curse to haunt and follow one. Errors could be forgotten. New beginnings could be made. Tomorrow will be better!

But given a national data base, and some system of identification of every citizen in the nation, is it not clear there could be no escape? Justice would always triumph. One could not get a driver's license, a job, a credit rating, without this national check. If one had made earlier errors, they would follow him or her all the rest of the lifespan. This is justice, to be sure. But as one gets older one is not so certain justice is what one wants for oneself or one's fellows. Rather, one begins to believe in mercy. We can suppose that is because there have been so many small errors in the past. And as we grow older, each of us would rather forget any number of indiscretions. It would be a grim world indeed where each of us must so behave as though every single act would follow us through eternity. Some religions had such a notion and, if anything, such religions were grim, killed off adventure, created timidity and terror, kept aspirations at a minimum. We have been many centuries escaping those curses—we ought to think twice before beginning them again. The spirit of the average human being is a fragile thing, to be cultivated and nurtured and often offered freedom. To analyze, record, and quantify the spirit is to kill it.

Another great danger in the national data base is the curse of widespread error. Again, if you have received, however incorrectly, a bad credit rating, it would be pleasant to believe it could either be edited out of the record or at least escaped. But a national data base is a giant enterprise. Should errors be made they are going to be very hard to correct or even to find out about. Have you tried to drop membership in a book club lately? No small enterprise that! It takes severe purpose and tenacity and much time to manage the job of disconnection. Multiply that by ten and you will know something about the difficulty of getting a correction made on your record in a national data base. Currently, the newspapers are full of the terrible punishments and injustices which have fallen on some of our fellows when they received a poor credit rating, just or unjust.

We mentioned earlier that data bases had a basic unit—field. The question naturally arises: How large should the basic unit of storage be? Are all of us so much alike that a single unit fits all the cases that might come up? Will not something important, some qualifier, be left out? Would this not, in itself, constitute misinformation? Who will make the decision about the size of the storage word? Who will make the decision about which information is pertinent and which information is just plain nosy? Who will determine the size of the file kept on each human being? Shall they all be uniform? Will important people have a larger file than lesser folk? How will status be determined? Is one's employment and one's income relevant information to be spread about at will? How far up in the political and social processes will these vital and important judgments be made?

Well, let us tell you this much about many public and private data bases as they exist today. The decisions about the size of the record, the size of the data word, the contents of the file, are often made by the lowliest programmer in the establishment. More often than not the programmer, while an expert at the trade, doesn't know much about the business. The decisions are made under pressure because no one else has made them and because top management thinks it has other more important concerns. The collection of data for its own sake can often become the function of the data center. Management seldom if ever worries about what is stored, as long as management gets the information it wants when it wants it. And, of course, quite often the information that management gets is out of date or wrong. Often this is due to the very simple fact that the management did not decide early on what kind of information it wanted. And so the data center is nothing more than a patch job. Bits of information are collected and filed, item by item, as they appear to be needed. The entire enterprise can lack plan, purpose, and integration. And this is far more common today than you would suppose. We need not, then, expect a national or regional center to be much of an improvement in this respect. If human behavior is anything, it is notorious for the persistence of its common errors and common assumptions.

Cross-indexing has always presented something of a problem in the management of data bases, either local or management. If someone says something to you, like "sled," "Christmas," and "mother," a whole set of memories otherwise long forgotten can be triggered. The mind can generate image after image—seemingly out of the past as far back as one would care to know. How are these linkages made? How is it those few words can generate mental picture after mental picture—generate memories of long-lost conversations—produce emotional tones long suppressed and generally forgotten? We simply don't know. We think it may have something to do with sympathetic harmonics, but we haven't the slightest idea just how these things get triggered. When one violin string is played, the others twang faintly in sympathy—they pick up the vibrations. Does something like that happen in the human mind? Are there a myriad of little gates that will open the floodgates of memory when some kind of similarity takes place, or when some peculiar conjunction of words comes up? Does a word like "past," when referring to Christmas, manage to link up "past" with a whole set of internuncial memory pools? Of course it does, or we wouldn't be able to remember a thing. Just how this is accomplished is a long way from discovery.

The national or regional data base would love such an index system as is so casually given by the human mind. But such an index is not possible. We need, therefore, a number of files and cross-files, indexes and cross-indexes. We need all the tricks of the librarian. And like the librarian, we can surely lose an occasional link and thus lose an occasional book. The librarian can make a full and personal inventory of a section of the library at will. Lost books can be discovered when compared with the library indexes and files. Similar activities will have to be worked out for the regional or national data center. The difficulty here is that we are not, in such an electronic memory, dealing with physical objects whose absence can be detected (as is the case with books or magazines). No, we are dealing with information in electromagnetic form. Should it be inadvertently erased, and no other records handy for comparison, the information is gone.

Who is to be the final judge of misinformation? Can the individual merely deny it? Is he or she more the authority than the machine? What legal processes are to be available for clearing erroneous records? Court procedures cost money. Can the average citizen afford such an expense? Probably not.

Currently, under law, it is possible for an individual to ask for the file kept on him or her in a data base. But not everyone knows such a file is being kept. And not everyone knows where such a file is being kept, if it indeed is in existence. How is one to find out these things? And, of course, it costs a good deal of money for a data center to prepare a complete printout of an individual's record and to arrange for mailing the information. Who is to pay for these costs? Surely it is important that every person have access to any file being kept which can affect that person's future. There must, then, be some published record of all the individuals on file in a given installation. These lists must be made available in the public presses. There must be some kind of annual audits to be sure the lists are accurate and up to date.

There also must be some kind of accuracy audit procedures created for any data base anywhere. We are all familiar with the situation wherein a long-dead individual is found on advertising lists. Or we are all familiar with the case where we receive from two to five brochures from the same company at about the same time. We got them because our names had been written down in several different forms —first name and initial and last name; first name, middle name, and last name; first initial, middle initial, last name—and so it goes. There is obvious waste here, but that is one of the hazards of business. There is obvious duplication here and, in terms of persons and files being kept for serious purposes, that is a more dangerous matter.

POWER

Information is power. One of the characteristics of a democracy is a certain slippage in the performance of public duties. In most cases, this is due to the fact that the public, a wandering herd, is difficult to define and locate. There is a certain guarantee of freedom in the inability of the government to track us down at every whim. There is a certain democratic power in the right of privacy—which ought to be firmly defended. How much right does the government have to information about the individual citizen? To what purpose will such information be put? Let us look at a dangerous example.

In the name of affirmative action, any number of races, creeds, and sexes have been required to identify themselves on various forms and records—this to the end that minorities would be given a better break in life than they had had in the past. Liberal groups, shouldering the moral burden of the Civil War and the slaver, have fought mightily to see that minority people are identified as such, categorized as such, and given such exceptional benefits as those liberal individuals feel is just. But there is a most dangerous assumption underlying all of this activity, however good in purpose and just in achievement it may be—we assume this information will always be under the care of benign individuals. And who is to say that this is certain and that this is true?

In Holland during World War II, the German occupation government asked people to come into public buildings and identify their history—particularly whether or not there was any Jewish ancestry in the background. The purpose was alleged to be social. The actual purpose, as we now know, was a study in genocide. One old Dutch gentleman, who innocently reported on himself and his neighbors as required by "law," described the horror of walking down to the railroad station every day to see the Jewish families being shipped off to an unknown fate. He described the personal horror he felt at his own accidental cooperation in such an enterprise. He claims to carry still, after all these intervening decades, the full burden of guilt and anguish.

Let us then remember that information about individuals is often the power to use and manipulate them in one way or the other. They can be boosted or hounded by the one who holds such information in hand. Until we know precisely how data bases are to be used, and until we have a fully created set of legal recourses at our disposal, and cheaply, too, we had better be very careful about our enthusiasms for centralized information. What is that old biblical saying? "Beware of false prophets, which come to you in sheep's clothing, but inwardly they are ravening wolves." It could be so with information. It could be so with national or regional data bases.

SYSTEM MEMBERSHIP

A national data base is nothing more or less than an element in a national information system. Systems, as we know, determine the behavior of the elements within the system. Let us take a simple case in point.

When you purchase an automobile, you are not so much making a single purchase as entering into a complex transportation system. This system will involve you in a host of future problems and future purchases. You will be required to purchase gasoline, oil, and lubrication jobs from time to time. You will face, on occasion, the need for repairs to your automobile. You also will be required, like it or not, to pay a number of taxes connected with the matter of keeping up the roads, the gutters, bridges, and the like. Many of these things you will pay for whether or not you own a car. If you don't, those who do have automobiles will benefit from the contribution you are required to make. If you do, you at least will share in some of the benefits, to say nothing of the expenses.

A national data base is going to enter you, willy-nilly, into a vast information system. This system will be tied in to matters of housing, jobs, credit, family, and the like. By diligence, you might avoid initial membership in the system. You will, in such a case, avoid all the possible benefits from such a system—such as a ready credit rating, should you wish to make a time purchase or to borrow money. And in the system or no, you are going to have to carry some of the financial burden of that system, either through the money spent on purchases, which include such costs, or through taxes.

But let us suppose you have had an unfortunate past record in matters of finance. You have failed to pay a number of bills over time, and you are given a poor credit rating. In a national information net this information will tag you wherever you are and whatever you do. You will very effectively be cut out of a large segment of American life. More important, you will not readily have the chance to escape the record and establish a newer and better one. If you were ever bankrupt you will find it difficult to borrow money to start into business again. If you are trying to avoid certain family responsibilities by running away, you will either be a total outcast or you will be caught the first time you try to enter the informational net. Whatever your purpose, your total record will be available to those who would do commerce with you. Your only alternative is an almost total isolation from all the normalities of life in the United States.

Worse yet, the system itself will set the parameters of your way of life. You must pay your bills on time when "on time" is decided by credit agencies. You must live according to your means for your means will be well known. You cannot take a foolish fling since salespersons everywhere can check to see whether or not such a purchase is within your means, as prudent business folk have defined those means. Freedom, you know, is the right to fall flat on your nose if you choose to be careless. A national information net would have, among its many purposes, the one of keeping you in line as a responsible and sober citizen who knows the limits and follows them. This may be good business. It well may be good government. But it surely isn't freedom. And therein lies the rub.

SOME SOLUTIONS

First and foremost, we should not try to rush headlong into a national or regional data base. We ought to have both the economy and the wit to allow individual enterprises to design, place into action, and amend data systems until a "body of knowledge" about their creation and use becomes common property. One can benefit by the errors of others and prevent much future misery. The establishment of private data bases is going on all the time. There is much being learned and much yet to learn. So let us not rush into the midnight of a national data base until we have seen the quiet evenings of early adventures in the area.

Second, we ought to allow a good deal of legal work to take place in the definition of information and what constitutes a record. We need a good deal more work on the definition of "privacy" as it applies to individual citizens and as it applies to business enterprises. Much of this type of definitive development will have to take place in courtrooms. Currently, such matters relate to business and credit records. Fine. This is the area to do the painful labor. Rather a few unhappy folk than a national mass dismay.

Third, some method of elective information commitment might have to develop. That is, before a national data base or even regional data bases should be established, the citizenry of the country ought to have a chance, at the ballot box, to determine the kind of information that ought to be stored therein. Matters of relevancy are going to be difficult to decide, at best.

Fourth, some standard technique for auditing and clearing out files will have to be developed—something which can be applied on a national and regional basis. And decisions ought to be made about how long a bad record should remain in the data base. Is there to be no forgiveness? How long should an unfortunate record be maintained? Should one's children be saddled with the sins of the parents? Should the parents be saddled with the sins of the children? What does clearing the record really mean? If it is a shortage of credit, are there remedies beyond finance? Is a court action necessary? Or might the record automatically be discarded after a reasonable length of time? What is a reasonable length of time?

What is the relationship between a regional or national data base and the Federal Communications Commission? What about the Federal Trade Commission? Who will have jurisdiction over the national airwaves? Over the satellites which transmit the information?

Fifth, someone or some agency is going to have to determine what is valid information for a data base. By that we mean the quality and the kind of information. Can pornographic materials be stored? What is the length of information which is required for a given type of data? Are there to be physical limits to what can be recorded?

You protest, do you not? These are not solutions—merely questions and problems! But, of course. Solutions come out of the right questions. We are already familiar, or at least have commented upon, the dangers of forming conclusions before we have any facts. If we have trouble trying to determine what kinds of information we need in the future so that we can collect data now, imagine the difficulties we are going to have in trying to think through all the ramifications of a national or regional data base. No, it is better to let things work out as follows:

1. Allow private enterprises and local state agencies to use computers and establish their individual and peculiar data bases.
2. Allow individual citizens to take these businesses and agencies to court when they impinge upon their rights.

3. Allow the establishment of intracompany and intercompany data bases under the regulation of the Federal Communications Commission and the Federal Trade Commission. Let these agencies wrestle with the early problems.
4. Allow manufacturers to continue to compete with one another in the business of establishing communication nets. Insist that the competition between the computer companies and the public utilities continue in the matter of using satellites and stringing communication nets.
5. Allow accounting firms and accounting fraternities to continue the development of appropriate computer data base auditing procedures.
6. Explore where possible the difficulties and the benefits created by data bases, and also communication nets.
7. Elect public officials who are aware of the potential of the problems in this new development, and who at least promise to make appropriate studies of possible solutions.
8. Insist on the right to examine and vote upon such solutions as are worked out in the public's name.

In short, the solution is to allow the democratic processes of a democratic country full cry and sway. And the solution is to allow private enterprises to battle matters out between themselves whenever possible. Competition is the heady stuff of unique solution to unique problems. And the solution is to allow the state agencies to develop their own centers and their own bases in competition with the private sector of the economy.

Great power and great prosperity attach themselves to any possibility of data bases and instant information flow. Great consequences of an unsuspected variety also will follow. The automobile has brought us personal freedom of movement—a command of space and time never before permitted to man. The automobile also has brought smog, traffic jams, and the suicide of the central cities. We can solve many of these problems now that we know what they are. Similarly, the national or regional data base will bring great benefits and great problems. As Samuel Johnson said, "Eternal vigilance is the price of liberty." And so it remains.

A FUTURE APPLICATION

Let us combine what we have learned about the computer as a potential utility and what we have discovered about data bases into an imaginery application of the future.

Mr. Arthur Smith is an author of mathematical and computer books. He works in his study in the suburbs in the neighborhood of San Francisco, California. He produces textbooks for colleges and universities and he also writes general popularizations of these two fields for the general public.

The COMPUT (Computer Utility) Company of San Francisco for several years has been laying high-grade telephone lines, with the cooperation of the telephone company, to several well-to-do San Francisco suburbs where it was discovered there was a reasonably large market for in-the-home computer utility services.

Mr. Smith has a computer terminal in his study that consists of a typewriter/printer and a large-capacity cathode ray tube. The terminal system he uses can also do a number of calculations and has a small memory of its own. Accordingly, the terminal is equipped with a casette input/output system. That is, the work that Mr. Smith does can be recorded on casette tapes—at the same time it appears on the cathode ray tube and is typed directly into a central computer in San Francisco. While this is a somewhat more expensive and sophisticated system than the ordinary, Mr. Smith feels it is ideal for the type of calculating and writing work he must do for a living.

Mr. Smith can contact the central computer in San Francisco by simply throwing a switch on his telephone (which is an integral part of the computer terminal), and dialing a special San Francisco telephone number. When the computer in San Francisco is ready to deal with Mr. Smith, the word READY appears on the cathode ray tube and is also simultaneously typed out on the typewriter/printer.

This week Mr. Smith is working on chapter 4 of his second major computer book. He has stored all of the material developed so far in the data base in the computer in San Francisco. Whenever he wants to review any part of the work he has done to date, he merely types RECALL on the typewriter and then specifies what he wants. For example, the particular book in question is identified as BKC2 (book, computer, number two). Chapter 4 is identified as C4.

If Mr. Smith wishes to have a look at paragraph 2 of page 37 of chapter 4 of his second computer book, he types "BKC2 C4 P37 PA2." Then he types the word GO on his typewriter and the material appears on the cathode ray tube. If he types GOTY, the material is produced on the cathode ray tube and at the same time is typed out on the typewriter/printer. If he types GOTYRCD, the material is produced on the cathode ray tube, typed out on the printer, and also written on a blank casette in the casette input/output unit attached to his terminal. In short, Mr. Smith has a three-way recording system at his disposal.

Most of the time Mr. Smith merely calls up, on the cathode ray tube, the material he is working on and simultaneously records the material on the casette. This means that he can disconnect from the central computer and work on his own for a while without paying computer-line-rate charges. Since his own terminal has some calculating and memory capabilities, it is his habit to recall as much as a chapter from the central computer, display the parts he is working on with the cathode ray tube, and then modify this material independently. Later, when he has the material in a full form that he likes, he reconnects to the central computer and properly stores the material in his private library in the data base.

When the programs Mr. Smith uses as illustrations in his book are simple, he can use his own terminal exclusively. When, however, he is demonstrating a large and complex program, he takes full advantage of the enormous calculating power and memory of the centralized computer utility.

Mr. Smith, we can see, has the best of both possible worlds. He has, in effect, a small independent computer at home which he purchased for $10,000. He is charged a minute-by-minute rate for the time he uses at the central computer utility. On the average, Mr. Smith's computer utility bills run about $250 per month. Given the enormous boost in his productivity as a result of the central facility, Mr. Smith feels the charges are reasonable. With the computer utility and his own terminal, he can produce a book in an average time of one and a half years, as against the three years such work normally took when he did the work unaided and alone on the ordinary electric typewriter in his study.

There is a further advantage which we should mention. When Mr. Smith has completed his book he can, by appropriate telephone activity, notify the computer center that he wishes the material transmitted directly (via national computer utility net, of which COMPUT Company is a member) to the publishing company's data base in Chicago. When the publishing company has been notified that the material is on hand, its editorial staff, using their own more complex company terminals and computing equipment, can immediately go to work on the material. What is more, part of the Chicago service is photographic typesetting. That is, when the publishing company editors have finished their work, they send the typesetting specifications to their computer utility and the author's material is typeset immediately.

The Chicago computing utility transmits the finished material directly to a large printing house, used by the publisher, which is also tied in to the Chicago computer utility and is also a member of the national computer utility net.

The net result of this very rapid and complete communication system is that the production of a textbook or general book on the part of the publishing firm can require from 40 to 90 days as against a previous time of approximately 6 months. In the case of some of the smaller and less complex books, the publishing company reports it has been able to put the book on the market in as little as 35 days from the time of receipt of the material.

The San Francisco computer utility has recently developed an additional facility which Mr. Smith finds remarkably useful. The COMPUT Company is now tied in with the San Francisco Public Library. This means that whatever books and other materials in the library are on microfilm (and the library estimates that 90 percent of its holdings are now in that form) can be transmitted to the COMPUT utility and in turn be transmitted to any of the company's customers.

Mr. Smith has merely to sit in his study and call up pages of books on his cathode ray tube—any books or articles in the SF library. He can, when he wishes, record these materials on his own tape casette unit for later reference. He also can store material he wishes to quote in the private library at the SF utility, and all the appropriate bibliographic references are immediately and correctly attached to the quotations. Mr. Smith finds this extremely useful when he is constructing bibliographies and making direct quotes in his manuscripts.

Mr. Smith also can do topical searches of any material available in the San Francisco library when he is doing the research necessary to support an idea or opinion about which he is writing. There is a small charge for these services made by the library to the computer utility and the computer utility in turn to the terminal user. But again, Mr. Smith finds this kind of facility such a time-saver and help that he does not begrudge a single penny. He estimates he now can do from five to six times the amount of research, without leaving his home, that he could do before. And in calculating his savings, he includes the wear and tear on his automobile, the gasoline consumed, and the time that would be lost had he been forced, in the old-fashioned way, to leave his home and do his own visitations to libraries in the area.

SUMMARY

In this chapter we have attempted to determine the primary purpose of a data base—assistance to those who know their jobs. We have explored the concept of an organized business or social memory. We have explored the complex problems brought about by the contest between the storage of masses of data and the need to search such masses for immediate information.

We have had a look at mass disk data banks, at data cells, at tapes and tape drives, and at disk packs. And we have again encountered batch data processing as against random search and updating techniques.

We have explored some of the fundamental methods of file organization, and considered some of the basic problems of data security. We have talked about the three major methods of sharing data bases among computer centers and also about some loan and leasing techniques.

This all done, we gave some thought to national and regional data bases, and particularly, to some of the problems they might bring about. We took a look at the concept of the integrated data base from a county point of view. We found some serious difficulties for recalcitrant citizens in the existence of such a base.

There are many dangers inherent in a national data base, and toward the end of the chapter we gave consideration to a few of these. In particular, we were concerned with errors and what they might do to individual careers. We also thought a bit about the problems of cross-indexing files, and found the human mind far more sophisticated in this matter than any known mechanical technique currently at our disposal.

We explored the concept that information is power and that power can be abused, no matter what our individual intentions. We learned something about the difficulties of system membership. System membership involves us in future commitments, many of which can be narrow and difficult. And we concerned ourselves with some possible general solutions, but found that these solutions were mostly made up of unanswered questions—but that is the way with solutions. First the question of the right kind—and then the answer. The answer leads to other questions and the other questions to yet other answers. So it goes. In the main, we think it best to let the normal democratic processes and conflicts go to work on the probem. The immediate solutions are never ideal, but they damage fewer people than grandiose attempts on a national scale.

Time and conflict. These are the most reliable methods of solution. In the meantime, the minor development of data bases continues in a local way.

HIGHLIGHT QUESTIONS

1. What is a data base?
2. What, generally speaking, would we expect to find in a proper data base?
3. Data bases involve us in three basic conflicts. What are they?
4. Briefly describe data disk banks.
5. What is a data cartridge? What does it contain? What is the smallest recording medium in a data cartridge?
6. What are the advantages of magnetic tapes? What are the disadvantages?
7. What do we mean by the term *batch processing?*
8. How can tapes be used in conjunction with disks to achieve some random searching?
9. Describe a portable disk pack.

10. Give the best description you can of a cylinder of information. Relate such a concept to the disk track.
11. What are the two most common forms of file organization?
12. What purpose does an overflow track serve?
13. List as many security needs of a data base as you can.
14. What are three forms of data base sharing?
15. What would be the advantages of an integrated data base? What would the disadvantages be?
16. List some important dangers which would apply to a national data base.
17. How does a data base index system function?
18. What kinds of power might accrue to one who controlled a data base?
19. What are some of the implications of a data base system? What would this mean to an individual who was not a member of the system?
20. What types of federal controls would you expect to be exercised over a national data base system?

READINGS

CODASYL Systems Committee. *A Survey of Generalized Data Base Management Systems.* New York: Association for Computing Machinery, 1969.

This is perhaps a bit too technical for the beginner, but it represents a very thorough treatment of some fundamental matters in data bases and their proper management. Several systems are described in detail.

Head, Robert V. *Manager's Guide to Management Information Systems.* Englewood Cliffs, N.J.: Prentice-Hall, 1972.

A short book, but a good one. Has a very nice bibliography. Chapters 2 and 3 are specifically involved in dealing with data bases and are well worth the time of the interested student.

Orlicky, Joseph. *The Successful Computer System.* New York: McGraw-Hill, 1969.

Here's a nice book from the management point of view. It is written in a straightforward manner. You will find a consideration of computer selection, feasibility studies, system operation, and the like, directed toward the manager faced with the problems of understanding what is going on around him.

CHAPTER 9

DISTRIBUTED DATA PROCESSING

PURPOSE OF THE CHAPTER

In this chapter we are going to look at a new way of handling data processing problems that is currently, as a result of technological developments, lurking just beyond the horizon. We refer, of course, to the concept of distributed data processing, and it is a concept first and machinery second. Whether or not it will materially change both our approach to computer installations and the activities in management as they relate to computers and computer centers is not yet clear.

We will explore some of the ramifications of smart terminals, mini computers, and the kinds of communication nets we can string together when we relate such items. We will learn what this means to the type of data base we might wish to keep in the firm.

And we will have to have a look at some of the conflicts, both in methods and in personnel, that such changes might bring about.

Before we turn our attention to the broader implications of this type of thinking and this type of machinery, we will want to see a few of the more domestic (business) implications of distributed data processing from the point of view of the managers of the enterprise.

TERMS AND CONCEPTS

Some old familiar terms are going to come back to haunt us in this chapter and, of course, we will introduce one or two new ones in their proper place in the discussion.

- operating personnel
- inner operations
- on-site data handling
- lag time
- network pattern
- cost of memory
- act of classification
- decentralization argument
- focus of the enterprise
- updating active files
- physical indexing
- mapped organization
- tapping a data base
- tailored terminals
- file protection procedures
- double transmission
- line capacity
- exception data
- POS contact
- informational workers
- spare-time updating
- computer mapping
- security practices
- data record abstracts
- functional slaves
- computer-set deadlines
- in-process personnel
- common-call data
- star configuration
- step-star linkage
- information overlap
- defensive documentation
- blanket data base
- freedom of information acts
- resonant data base
- interfacing
- badges
- cost-of-achievement ratios
- distributed minis
- reality value
- activity nodes
- ring configuration
- ring-star system
- identifiers
- mental indexing
- contingency planning
- keys
- downstream loading

LIMITS OF TECHNOLOGY

Technology both rules and limits us, though we frequently prefer to pretend otherwise. No matter what the presidential drive and energy, it took ten full years to prepare for the trip to the moon—a technical triumph, of course, but also a very clear statement of the domination of the current technology and its logical limits. The rapid development of large-scale computers during the late 1950s and early 1960s forced certain centralized management patterns upon business enterprises wishing to make full use of the computers. And until three recent developments in computing made alternatives possible, management was largely trapped in the centralized mode. But dramatic decreases in the cost of computer memories, the development of terminals with computing power of their own, and the growth of the communication lines have made a return of management control both possible and probable.

OPERATING VERSUS COMPUTER PERSONNEL

The development of the large-scale centralized computer installation in the business firm brought a related development—a layered hierarchy of skilled computer personnel who often worked in direct competition with the regular operating personnel of the business. That is, the sales people, the clerks, the production people, the supervisors, and the lower-level managers all had a tendency to surrender their rights of judgment to the computer expert who told them what the computer could and could not do for them. They, the operating personnel, needed information and needed it badly. They also were aware of the limitations of their own perspectives in regard to the enterprise as a whole. So they frequently gave up on special requests for information, rather than spend the long and often fruitless hours documenting their needs, trying to understand the alien tongue of the computer expert, and justifying to others what they knew, themselves, to be obvious.

Even worse, the computer has a huge capacity—a constant appetite for data. Operating personnel were frequently asked to contribute information to the building of the central data base—so much so, the operating personnel were often sent stacks of computer printouts to update, amend, and edit. This reversed the purpose of the computer. Instead of providing operating personnel with information so they could turn their full attention to the tasks for which they were hired, the personnel found themselves constantly feeding information to the computer, as though this act itself was the primary function which they were required to perform. The operating staff became the functional slaves to the computer and to the computer personnel, instead of the other way round. What is even deadlier, the computer personnel often made decisions about what information was important—decisions which they were not entitled to make, either by training or experience. The result of all this, naturally, is an enterprise which spends far too much time inspecting itself and not enough time dealing with products and customers and services.

The processes here described have three deadly effects on the future of an enterprise. First, the operating personnel feel very vulnerable. They know they require up-to-date information to operate, and they do not wish to offend the computer people and hence be cut off from information sources on which their jobs depend. Second, the computer personnel can grow arrogant and self-centered. That is, they can concern themselves so much with their own inner operations that they forget they are really satellite to the success of the enterprise. The planet forgets it is a reflector and thinks itself a sun! Third, a deadly time lag sets in between the time information is needed for effective dealing with customers and the time the information can be provided conveniently by the computer center. The computer center begins to set the deadlines and determine the timeliness of the information. The customer becomes the outsider—frustrated and dependent. Business losses are generally the result.

SMART TERMINALS AND MINI COMPUTERS

In an earlier chapter we discovered computer terminals could, themselves, do a good deal of processing. More and more they have been equipped with sufficient memory and sufficient command structure to handle symbolic languages, to process data, and to store the result in their own internal storages. The primary boost to this development has come because of the microminiaturization of memory components and their subsequent dramatic drop in cost. So we are reaching a point where the smartest of the smart terminals are very nearly mini computers themselves. And, of course, the mini computers also have grown in terms of language capabilities and memory capacity.

Many firms have invested millions of dollars in large-scale centralized computer systems and have not been entirely satisfied with the results. The conflicts, earlier mentioned, between operating personnel and the computer staffs have become clear. The rigidities and lag times created by complex centralized systems also have become evident. Therefore, many new additions of computer equipment have been in the form of mini computers located near the problem point itself. And there has been a development which places more reliance on terminals as communications devices, in lieu of punched cards, tapes, and diskettes.

Once you begin to place computer terminals or small computers at the point of maximum use in a business, you have entered into distributed data processing. You now face a philosophic conflict between centralization and decentralization. You also will have to decide how much data handling is to be done "on site" and how much is to be communicated to the central computer system. These are not decisions which should be taken lightly. There are a number of problems and implications which we now must explore. These will affect the business organization, its efficiency, its philosophy, and its security.

THE 80/20 DATA PROCESSING RULE

There is a sometime rule in the computer field in regard to the use of mini computers or smart terminals. This rule of thumb simply states that it is wise to make use of a smart terminal or a mini computer at a particular work site when 80 percent of the computing needed to be done is used right there at the site. When only 20 percent of the work needs to be transmitted to the centralized data processing unit, you can save both money and time with distributed data processing concepts.

The potential savings comes from the fact that communication links and their operating costs have not come down as dramatically as have terminal and mini computer costs. It is cheaper to do the calculating right on site than it is to do the double transmission required to contact a large data center and then receive the answers to your questions.

More important than the cost saving is the simple truth that the operating personnel dealing with a problem have a greater interest in getting the right answers quickly than do the people at a distance in the computer center. These people are "in process" with the customers and can exchange information more readily and more realistically. And since they are in direct contact with the customers, they are under a natural pressure to give maximum service. The smart terminal or the mini computer, in such a situation, retains its normal place as nothing more than tool to serve a specific purpose. It does not, under such a situation, tend to become an end in itself.

There is another powerful force at work at the point of customer contact. This is called "reality value." By this we mean that the employee working with a customer has a full connection to the value of any datum in terms of completing the transaction on which he or she is currently working. Computer people, at a distance, do not have the experience or the contact to give any particular value to any specific datum. To the computer people at the center, one item is no more valuable than another. To the employee working with the customer, experience will have given him or her a hierarchy of importances. The employee can get out the most important information first and fastest and can determine what is critical and what is mere detail or icing on the cake. In short, operating personnel are trained to make just the kind of judgments they need to make to complete transactions with customers—computer personnel, as such are not.

A final powerful argument in favor of distributed data processing from the operational point of view is the disappearance of "lag time." Lag time is the amount of time it normally would take to get an item online to the computer center, get it processed, and get the answer returned. In theory, at least, computers are supposed to be so fast that the operator at the terminal no sooner moves fingers from the keys than the answer is pouring out. In fact, this is often not the case. In many cases, the kinds of information required at the terminal point are not "online" at the computer center. This can involve delays up to several minutes. And we are assuming in many cases that the line capacity of the computer is large enough that busy signals do not occur very often. Again, the reality of the situation and the eternal busy signals belie the dream.

PROCESSING NETWORKS AND NODES

Distributed data processing takes a network view of the enterprise. That is, we want to seek out the so-called activity nodes of the enterprise—those places where the action actually takes place—where customers are contacted, where sales are closed, where information is generated, and where information is needed. We want to link all of these nodes together but, more important, we want to provide each of these activity nodes with the computational power to handle at least the 80 percent of the needs that would commonly arise without necessary recourse to a centralized computer installation.

If the activity nodes have considerable computing power of their own, it may not be necessary to link them to the central computer with communications lines. Magnetic tape casettes or magnetic diskettes might be just the vehicle for the transmission of information when required. This could be handled either by the interoffice mail system or by special messenger. Transmission could take place either hourly, daily, or weekly, depending upon the nature of the data and the degree of independence achieved by the smart terminal or mini computer at the activity node site. Since mini computers and many of the smart terminals have memory capacities into the millions or tens of millions of digits, we could expect the vital information to be distributed throughout the activity net. Each activity node would have on file what we call "common call data"—data which is necessary to perform the daily tasks. "Exception data"—the unusual material infrequently needed—could be stored at a central location. The important question for centrally stored data is: How important is the information in terms of time and in terms of money? If the infrequent datum is needed at once and involves very large sales or other money-heavy activities, a communications link directly to the computer center might be advisable. If smaller amounts are involved and time is not essential, then the diskettes and casettes might be quite sufficient for the purposes at hand. Here, as in any sensible business enterprise, we must pit cost against earnings. There is no other really valid way to judge the matter.

Could the central computer installation be eliminated entirely? This is a good question, one which distributed data processing may force more and more. Actually, it would depend on what we call the "network pattern" that a firm prefers to develop. There are two primary forms, the ring and the star. And there are sophisticated combinations of these which we might wish to consider.

THE RING

In the ring pattern of distributed data processing, we do not have a centralized computer system but rather have a series of fairly sophisticated mini computers linked to one another, as shown in Figure 9–1.

In the ring configuration shown, we may assume we have four mini computers of some decent power. They are all linked together in a communication ring. The data base of the firm is therefore spread out into four major segments. But, of course, each computer can call for information from the others and make use of that segment of data base housed by the other computers. In the ring plan there is no highly centralized computer unit which feeds the others. Each of the

FIGURE 9–1. Ring configuration of computers

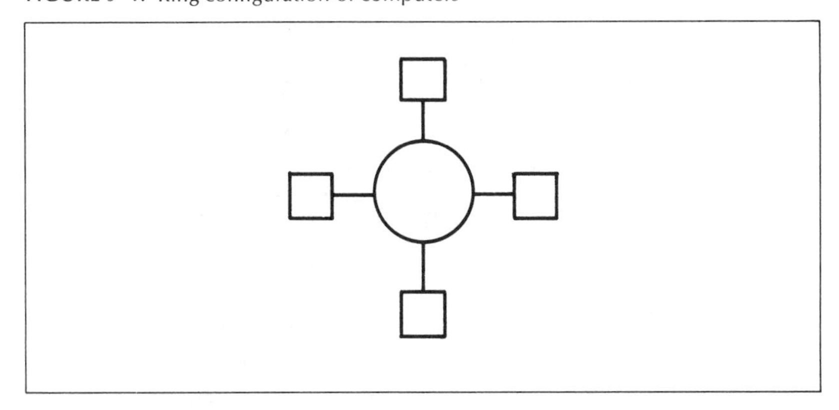

ring members is as important as any other and as important as the functions it performs. Rings could, of course, contain as many mini computers as one might wish to link together. In a large organization a ring might be made up of from ten to twenty such computers, with the data base spread out accordingly.

And again, we might note the online communication link would only be essential if the nature of the business required constant and heavy intercommunication between the computers. If the intercommunication were less pressing, the transfer of casettes or diskettes might be sufficient.

Few of the ring configurations are in existence today. But they are being considered by a number of firms. With continued progress in the increased memory of mini computers and with the growing development of ever smarter terminals, we can expect considerable experimentation with the ring form in the future.

THE STAR

In the star configuration of data processing, we are apt to find a central computer hooked directly to a series of simple or smart terminals. The sketch in Figure 9–2 illustrates the concept.

The star concept currently is more common than the ring. Typically, we would meet the star configuration in the airline reservation system, or in a retail store where the cash registers are hooked directly into the computer system. In these cases, we are talking about point-of-sale (POS) contact with the main computer via terminals.

In the star configuration, we may have a single massive data base. All POS contacts must rely on the central computer for the basic information needed. With smart terminals the traffic could be cut down considerably. If the terminal is capable of basic computing functions, and if about 70 to 80 percent of the work is of that simple nature, the use of direct communication lines would be minimal. But, of course, in the case of a complex reservation system where we do want the in-

FIGURE 9–2. The star configuration

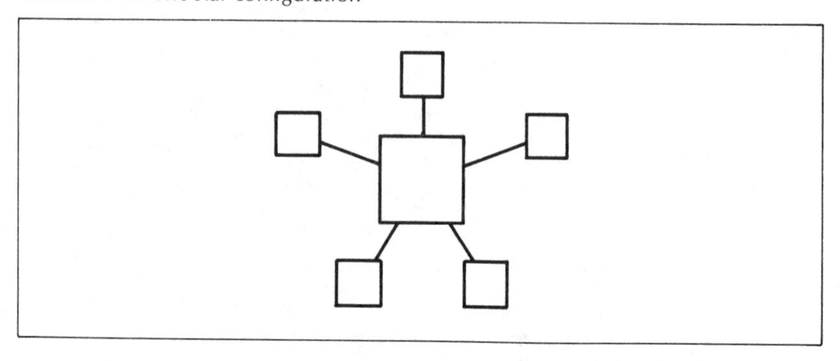

formation centralized, the simpler terminals will do nicely. In the case of the department store point-of-sale machines, we need to ponder whether immediate contact with the central computer is essential. Might it not be enough to be able to do the basic calculating, prepare the bill of sale, keep appropriate inventory records on casettes on a smart terminal, and then at the end of the day transmit the tapes to the central computer installation for updating of store records? How often is it necessary to make purchases? How important is the inventory count? These are the types of questions we must answer to make proper judgments about the capacity of the connection to a central computer unit. And we once again should remember the cost of calculation and the cost of memory is still considerably below that of the cost of transmission of information.

COMPLEX CONFIGURATIONS

The ring and the star are extremely simple computer nets. There is no reason why we could not have a star system in which a central large-scale computer was linked directly to a number of mini computers. These mini computers, in turn, might be star-linked to a number of simple or smart terminals. Figure 9–3 illustrates the possibility.

Let us be aware of something important. While these step-star and ring-star diagrams are more complex than the simpler earlier diagrams, they are *simplifications!* The actual programs which would have to be written to handle these more complicated information exchanges are large and difficult.

FIGURE 9–3. Step-star linkage

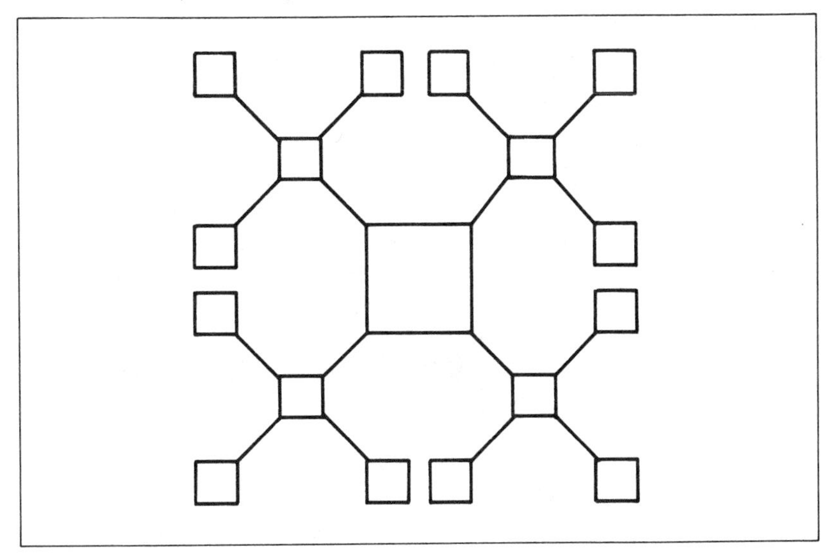

When one is working with very complicated programs, it is wise to have a simplified diagram in front of one to keep perspective. The terms *ring, star, step-star,* and *ring-star* are not yet commonly used—but they will be in time.

In the step-star linkage one can see a large-scale central computer connected, in the illustration, to four mini computers, each of which is in turn connected to three smart terminals. Here we have an example of twelve simple data bases (those held by the smart terminals), four intermediate data bases (those held by the four mini computers), and one large central data base.

If the data bases were properly organized, the 12 simple data bases would contain all the essential information for at least 80 percent of the calculations required to handle the details of point-of-sale or point-of-contact activities without recourse to the mini computers. The mini computers, in turn (all four of them), should contain data base information sufficient to handle about 80 percent of all inquiries coming to them from the terminals. These data bases would probably require to be larger and more sophisticated, since they would be dealing with a number of exceptional problems which the smart terminals could not handle on their own.

And the large-scale central computer ought to have contact with the mini computers only for that 20 percent of their activity which would be beyond the abilities and informational capabilities of the mini computers. All this means that the main computer receives only about 4 percent of the workload from the terminals and only 20 percent of the workload from the mini computers.

Does this situation seem too complex to be realizable? It shouldn't. Businesses had to organize files in this manner for decades prior to the arrival of the computer. It was exceptional material which found its way from the local offices to the regional offices, and from the regional offices to the central headquarters of a company. Summaries were sent and not details. The problem lay in careful planning and in clear jurisdictional definitions, not in the transmission of information—and it still does.

What we have to watch out for is the passion for centralization and the passion to know. Both of these diseases strike the central computer center once it is installed. It is a natural disease, but a dangerous one. We automatically assume the central computer center must have all of the detailed information in the enterprise in order to be able to operate. But this simply isn't so. What has happened is that since the central computer installation can demand and receive all the detailed information of the enterprise, and since it can, however badly, store all that information, the details take on an attraction and a value which they simply do not inherently have. We are always prone to measure, and since we have measured, to decide that what we have measured so carefully is valuable. The act of measurement gives an importance of an artificial kind. Equally, the act of translation into computer language, and the act of classification and storage, can give a datum a sanctity which it could never maintain were it placed on a piece of scratch paper and stored in a file drawer.

Another somewhat complex configuration would be the ring-star system shown in Figure 9–4.

FIGURE 9–4. The ring-star configuration

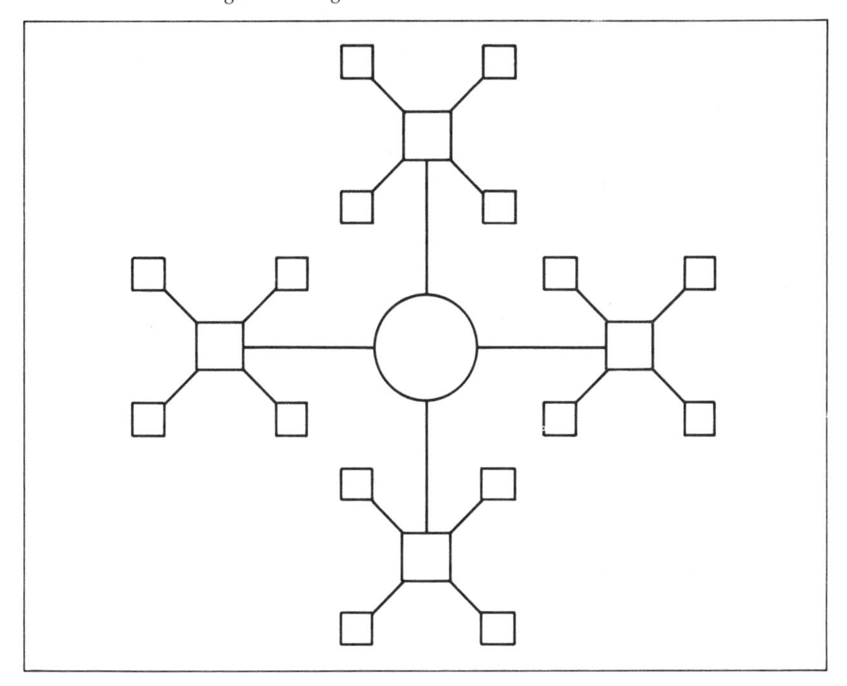

In the ring-star configuration we have four mini computers, each with its own data base. Each of the minis can communicate with any other mini (indicated by the circle connection). And each of the minis is hooked via the star system to four smart terminals. Now we have twelve secondary data bases and four primary data bases to deal with. The principles of division would be functional in this case. What are the functions of the terminals connected to each mini computer? Are they handling different types of information? What would be the degree of information overlap required of the four mini computer data bases? How often would they have to communicate with one another?

If the functions of the four minis are different in serious ways, it might again be sufficient to have the linkage between them be casettes or diskettes that could be shipped through the intracompany mails. Careful planning of the data bases in the first instance might make this a very economical method of handling a dispersed data base. But, of course, if a great deal of exchange is required, the four minis could be connected with communication lines.

CENTRALIZATION VERSUS DECENTRALIZATION

The development of smart terminals, mini processors, and communication networks has thrown management back into control of the data processing systems. Once again management can face up to the old philosophic debate about centralized activity versus decentralized activity.

In the early computer days it was imagined that a highly centralized computer system would eliminate middle management. What we would have would be a few top policy makers in the organization along with their top operational counterparts. All the rest of the people in the organization would be workers. Most middle management decisions, it was said, were routine, and the computer, given the proper criteria, could surely take that job itself and perform more consistently and more rapidly and more economically.

It did not happen. Middle management grew apace. Computer personnel took on all the levels and all the functions of the many-layered enterprise. Computer centers had high managers and middle managers and low managers. The enterprise developed yet further high, low, and middle managers to do business with the computer hierarchy—and so it went. What went wrong? Computer languages are complex and computer reports are complex. It took a number of middle management people to try to interpret the computer printouts and derive decisions from them and convert those decisions into operating policies. The situation simply grew more complex. And because the higher corporate personnel could get information at an increasing rate, they decided to take over more and more of the decision processes themselves and demanded increasing documentation. So the regular middle and lower management personnel found themselves busier than ever. To be sure, they were not making decisions—they were busy filling out computer reports of all kinds. Decisions were replaced by clerking and by documentation and the several levels of the enterprise. And naturally, the rigidities and timidities grew in scope.

Now, with the exception of certain military operations, one can only generate real interest in an activity to the degree one has control of that activity. This should be the most compelling argument for decentralization. Economy should be another. It should not be neces-

"YOU ONLY KNOW WHAT IS HAPPENING IF YOU ARE IN THE MIDDLE!"

sary for the experienced point-of-action individual to rely heavily on documentation and proof—his or her experience and immediate knowledge of the environment should be sufficient for intelligent action. Oh, to be sure, each will need the assistance of information from past records from time to time. But his or her knowledge is immediate and their action pressing. The higher one moves the decision in the normal hierarchy, the more substantiation any point of view must have, and this means the more paper and reports there are that must back it up. So we get into a repetitive cycle. Each level, being further removed from reality, demands greater paper records to learn enough to make a judgment. Enormous staffs of experts are required to study and prepare these reports. Other experts are required to summarize them for quick executive action. Hundred upon hundreds of people are not involved in any direct activity related to production or sales, but rather are involved in the activity of documenting the activity of others and justifying that activity. It is a dangerous and vicious system—the paper becomes the reality and the goal, the enterprise loses touch, and the enterprise founders.

Computers, properly distributed throughout the firm, properly supported by data bases no larger than they need to be, ought to be able to reduce this enormous cross-talk, which is one of the great expenses of modern business. It is claimed that two out of every three workers in the nation are informational workers. So it may be; but one wonders why this has always been viewed as a blessing, and why serious questions about the necessity of the information have not been asked.

If distributed data processing becomes a reality in the enterprise, and if the data bases are themselves distributed to those points where they are needed, then it ought to be possible for computer programs from central computers to abstract from the distributed memories such information as is needed for the summary reports to management. The data bases themselves, and their activity records, would constitute the documentation support needed. Perhaps this in itself would reduce the function of "defensive documentation," which occupies the time of so many lower and middle managers these days.

POWER STRUCTURE CONFLICTS

Distributed data processing is apt to be slowed down considerably by its natural conflict with already well-established central processing configurations. People do not like to give up the perquisites of power no matter how compelling the argument for surrender might be. Central-unit data processing managers are not likely to want to see their installations dismantled and spread around the organization, since this would generate lower-level computer managers and eliminate the central jobs.

And, of course, distributed data processing would force the operating personnel itself to learn more and more about computing. This would mean the magical phrases, used defensively by computer people to hold others at bay, would break down. The operating personnel would want to know why certain things could not be done for their convenience, rather than for the convenience of the computer or its personnel. These might often be hard questions to answer. The focus of the enterprise would not then be on record keeping, as such but rather on the activities taking place at the point-of-sale or the point-of-contact.

In firms with already well-established central processing units, additions might be made of mini computers at selected points in the enterprise. Many large installations are nearly taxed to their current limits and cannot expand much further without a major investment. Shrewd managers may prefer to add the minis and the smart terminals a few at a time, where they are needed, and gradually decrease the importance of the central unit. This sets up, of course, the kind of conflict of which we speak. There would be an inherent and perfectly natural rivalry between the professional computer personnel and the new operating personnel who know and understand the computer—as a tool and not as an occupation.

THE BLANKET DATA BASE

During the mid-1950s, when it became apparent the cost of storing data would drop dramatically in the near future, computer people began to dream of, and design, blanket corporate data bases. It was their intention to have and store *all* the records of a firm, no matter how large the organization might be, in a single accessible location. On the surface it appeared to be a sound, though possibly expensive, future achievement.

As local data bases began to grow in size, however, it soon became apparent there were some inherent hazards. First, the larger the data base, the more difficult the business of cross-indexing. Many items in business, invoices for example, may need to be filed by customer name, by geographic area, by street address, by product, and so on. In a computer base, each of these items will require storage space, and very complex cross-indexes must be built. Second, there seemed to be a shortage of the type of personnel who had both expertise and experience in the business of cross-indexing itself. Third, different areas of the corporation called different items by names of their own invention. A human being can respond to a request for information in

Expanding data bases

very general terms. A computer can only do so if all of the possible combinations, strange identifiers, and generalities can be filed in the index. The computer normally cannot puzzle its way through a blank. Nor can it hunt on the basis of the gist, rather than the substance, of a request. Finally, all of the information which goes into a computer data base has to be prepared, one way or the other, by human action —either at the point of creation or by experts at the center. The difficulty with entries from the point of action is that the people there have more realistic and pressing concerns than the matter of indexing correctly. And the experts in indexing at the center may or may not know of all the possible types of identifiers that a single item might generate. So the job turned out to be more difficult and more expensive than had been anticipated. And the dream began to fade to more realistic achievements.

The law of the land is dynamic. What this means to computer people is that the contents of a data base may or may not suit the legal information requirements at any given moment. This, in turn, means some techniques must be developed to update or clear the data processing files from time to time. For a small data base, this is no particularly difficult task. During spare moments computer people can do the revising piecemeal. But for a massive or central data base we are talking about expenses in the hundreds of thousands of dollars. And we are talking about updating massive but active files over time. Sometimes the process itself of updating can interfere with programs and their effective use. Here we probably need not be reminded that each new item attached to an indexing identifier means a program revision. How many programs? As many as would possibly use any element in the index system.

We have not explored the difficulties encountered with data bases and the various "freedom of information acts" which have been passed or may be passed in the near future. Some information in the files will be true public property, and no restriction can be put on its use. Other elements in a file may be of the type which it is quite clearly illegal to release willy-nilly. Again, the indexes in a massive data base must carry these classifiers to meet the rigors of modern law. Again, the revisions to put an old data base in modern condition may be excessively expensive and complex.

The dream of the national, or even regional, blanket data base has foundered on cost, complexity, the overrating of the computer, and the underrating of the human animal.

Distributed data processing will create special problems in matters of security and in the protection of distributed files. But it obviously will offer enormous advantages in allowing the tailoring of data bases to specific needs. And since the number of programs used at a particular small data base should be fewer than the number of programs required at a centralized data base, modifications should be a lesser chore. Certainly, the possibilities of spare-time updating would be greater in several small data bases than at a single large one. Also, the local data base would have the advantage of requiring less physical indexing. The operating personnel, at the point of action, would likely know all of the possible permutations a given item might require. Since they, themselves, may be operationally competent at the computer, they could often do their own mental cross-indexing—an obvious time and space saver.

The large regional or national data base is not likely to arrive for quite some time, if it does at all. Distributive data processing and the return of control of events to management may well do it in. But here we might be a little cautious. The genius of man is not to be taken lightly. One day, somewhere, somehow, some genius will develop a resonant data base. That is, she or he will construct a computer with memory pools of such a nature that a single word will trigger, through a resonance system, other words which, because of the experience of the computer, have been associated one way or the other with the word in question. It sounds a little complex because it is—as is the human brain which does exactly that by processes and means we have yet to determine. Should our future genius succeed in the development here described, the national base could be a reality, without the inconveniences we have considered early. But then we ask ourselves a fundamental question: What is the capacity of such a mechanical brain before the mechanical equivalent of madness sets in? We do not know. But let no man or woman claim the future might be dull!

PLANNING AND TRAINING

Distributed data processing will come somewhat slowly in spite of the ready development of mini computers, smart terminals, and the continuing decrease in the costs of storage. This is so because there will be a large degree of training required if operating personnel are to work intimately, as they should, with either the smart terminals or the mini computers. And, of course, the more distributed the data processing—that is, the more data bases, the more mini computers, and the more smart terminals there are spread throughout the organization to all the points of sale or points of contact—the more people will require to be trained. The earlier fears of people and the earlier reluctances for fresh problems and complex training will be multiplied manyfold. The rewards are great, however. And the trainers will have one most powerful tool of motivation. There is always a great appeal to people to seize control of their own activities. If those who must train can make clear to the operating personnel of the enterprise that they can learn how to handle computers, terminals, and data bases, and that the reward will be more intimate control over their own performances and their own destinies, the motivation will be there in full force.

The training should be somewhat simplified with the use of control languages for both the terminals and the mini computers. This implies rather large memories, but as we noted, these are coming cheaply and soon. In an earlier chapter we explored the command language for a small computer with a limited memory. The same type of language could be used with a smart terminal, and certainly could be used with any one of the modern minis.

An effective training program requires careful planning. In the case of distributed data processing, there are two major planning programs which will have to be developed. First, the organization qua organization must be well-mapped, else it will not be possible to overmap the mini computer systems onto the enterprise to locate them properly at the points of action. A full-flown analysis of a large organization can take several years. Often, though, the primary ad-

Mapping the enterprise

vantage of such an activity comes not from the installation of the computers but from the analysis and self-examination itself. In the old days, there was a hoary joke that about 60 percent of the benefit to be gained from installing a computer came from a company's preliminary self-analysis. The additional 40 percent of benefit came when the computer was installed and effectively running. Many companies would have benefited from planning for a computer whether or not they ever got around to actually installing one. The same general rule holds true for distributed data processing in an even more important way. Many firms are not totally aware of either the actual location or the real importance of the points-of-customer contact. There always is a tendency in large organizations for many of the legions of support personnel to forget the major purpose of the business, which is successful customer contact. An organizational reexamination often can bring to everyone's attention the great importance of those who do the actual dealing with the public. Perhaps it also will call attention to the genuine achievements of such people.

Once the computer-mapping on top of the extant organization has taken place, the business must turn its attention to the preliminary training of those who will be handling the computer equipment, writing the programs, designing the data bases, and redesigning the forms to acceptable computer format. All this work has to be accomplished while the normal work-a-day world continues at its regular pace. The cost in terms of man and woman hours will be enormous in any organization of more than moderate size. This extreme cost is another reason why distributed data processing will come slowly. But distributed data processing has the advantage that it can be brought into the organization piecemeal. Links, either telecommunications or casette/diskette, can be maintained with the central computer installation while the distributed minis and terminals are coming in. Plans could be made to divide the central data base and distribute it as the new physical equipment arrives.

Finally, the field of smart terminal and mini computer development is dynamic. Contingency planning has to be a way of life. One must speculate to some degree about the future abilities of future equipment. This has to be done with caution, since one cannot always depend upon the hopes and dreams of the computer manufacturers. Many planned developments in the computer field have gone by the wayside, before fruition, because of unexpected technological developments or because the market for the particular invention simply did not exist as anticipated. Contigency planning, then, must be anchored carefully on hard future plans of the computer designers and engineers, and not upon their wilder speculations. This is no easy task. But here again, any distributed activity represents less of a commitment than a total centralized computer system. With careful interfacing, it should be possible to move in the terminals and the minis a few at a time and still keep pace with the newer developments.

So—it would seem that all the arguments for the slower arrival of the distributed data processing system also are the arguments for its certain, albeit, careful arrival.

The planning, both organizational and technical, will take place because the advantages of putting the computer power where it is needed in the organization is overwhelming and clear.

SECURITY AND CONTROL

One of the arguments often given against distributed data processing as a concept is that the matter of security and the matter of control would be made more complex than would be the case with a highly centralized single computer center. The argument is spurious. Security and control are management problems—not peculiar computer problems. Management would face no more difficult a task in handling distributed data processing than it faced in the matter of distributed cash receipts or of distributed product delivery. It is the nature of a data base to be more secure than a file drawer or a set of files. To successfully tap a data base takes a degree of skill beyond that to snoop through a system of files. Computer security can at least be as effective as a lock on a file room door. And if reasonably done, it can offer a greater security than one would suppose.

Distributed data bases are more secure just because they are distributed. The more separate data bases there are in an organization, the less chance for any single individual or small group of individuals to be able to tap and gather all the information. To be sure, it will be necessary to put certain standard security practices around the business of transmitting information from one data base to another. But again, these are problems rather standard to most businesses. If cassettes and diskettes are the transferred items, the normal security rules for any valuable object would apply to the handling and the transfer. Management has dealt with this mundane matter not for years but for centuries. And we might note, the losses are newsworthy just because they are rare.

If the distributed data bases are linked by communications lines, more complex security measures must be taken. But again, these have been developed in the past. Security badges or simple keys are still fairly useful. And because the operating personnel, themselves, are concerned with the information, and because they will perforce be using the data bases and the minis and the terminals to a fuller degree than they would use a centralized computer unit, they would be reasonably certain to stumble across any irregularities the quicker.

Finally, we might note that the job of auditing distributed data bases is somewhat simpler than the job of auditing a single massive data base. For one thing, the audits need not occur all at the same time. Since they would be briefer, they could occur more often. Since they do not tie up a single centralized unit, on which the fortunes of the enterprise depend, they can also be more thorough and represent less inconvenience to the enterprise. And we need not forget that the ability to keep secrets (including embezzlement) is inversely related to the number of people involved. We would logically expect a greater number of people to be involved in distributed data centers than we would in a single complex center.

Security will not be an easy job for distributed data processing; but then security never has been an easy task. Management, however, will be in greater control of the distributed centers than it has ever been of the single large center—and this bodes well for the enterprise.

Control problems refer more to the simple tasks: of being certain that the kind of information at the several data bases is the kind of information that ought to be there. Control also involves monitoring the effectiveness in terms of duty performance of both terminals and mini computers. Again, if it is true that operating personnel will be intimately involved in the use of the terminals and the mini computers, then it follows that the productivity of these individuals will be a good deal easier to measure than has been the case of the computer experts gathered in the single data center. Not all managers (in fact, very few) know enough about the fine details of computing to know for certain whether a computer center has performed well or not.

Many managers have come to the reluctant (and unprovable) conclusion that the central data processing center is far more expensive than they ever expected, both in terms of day-to-day operating costs versus operational benefits and, more particularly, in terms of complex communication requirements and manufactured rigidities. They have been intimidated by the size of the computer center and by the strange and holy language of the experts. But with distributed data processing, they will be able to talk to operating personnel who, because of their day-to-day experience with the computers, should be able to translate for the manager into operating terms—these the managers understand full well.

We can expect, then, as distributed data processing arrives, that managers will take a deeper interest in computing. They will be less intimidated by small installations than by larger ones. They will have less difficulty communicating because they often will be talking to their own experienced operating personnel. They will be able to measure the benefits, or losses, more accurately and more readily. In short, the managers will have regained the control of the enterprise.

TAILORED TERMINALS

Distributed data processing also will present management with the opportunity to tailor the computer terminals and the minis, with which they may be connected, to the particular tasks at hand. We would not expect the terminal in the hands of the bank teller to be exactly the same as the terminal in the hands of a cashier at a grocery store. We would not expect the mini computer, receiving the information from a host of bank tellers, to be exactly like the mini computer receiving the sales information from the grocery store cashiers. The art of interfacing (linking the terminals, computers, and special equipment) has grown mightily in the last decade. Even the mini computers can have tailor-made results when a number of components are assembled as required.

While it is equally true that the centralized data operation can itself be tailor-made to suit the particular needs of the enterprise, the results are often standardized just because it is the function of the central computer unit to so design its work that it serves the entire organization. This usually results in the forced standardization of form, a series of general compromises in regard to the size of the basic storage datum, and the development of standardized forms of various kinds. While these are well designed, they cannot serve all groups in the organization equally well. It is their standardization itself which makes them less than adequate for many if not most of the point-of-sale or point-of-action activities.

If the distributed data processing net is made up of mini computers and smart terminals reporting to individual mini computers, we can

expect a great deal of tailoring to be possible. If 80 percent of the work is done at the terminals and only 20 percent at the minis, then it would be possible to tailor the activities for every terminal. The 20 percent of the information which needs to be reported to the minis could be put in some standard form. In the case of the complex step-star system, only 4 percent of the information would require to be standardized, since it is that 4 percent which would finally reside in the central computer data base. Abstracts of data records can be standardized without the need to standardize the materials from which the abstracts are made.

Tailored terminals also offer the advantages of direct cost-to-achievement ratios. That is, we do not need to put complicated smart terminals at those points with simple data processing needs. We do not require uniformity throughout the enterprise. The same might hold for mini computers in the net. Several of the mini computers could well be more limited than others. Again, the nature of the job to be done, and the importance of the information, would dictate the amount of equipment investment to be made, item by item. This kind of cost-to-achievement is not directly possible when we are talking about a large-scale centralized computer system with a standardized method of performance.

IMPORTANT MANAGEMENT QUESTIONS

Before managers can plunge into the business of establishing a distributed data processing system, they are going to have to develop reasonable answers to some very difficult questions. Who is to have final responsibility for the computer and smart terminal net? Who is to do the actual programming of the mini computers in the enterprise? Who is to measure the success of the individual terminals and the individual mini computers? If these can be measured, how will the total success of the net qua net be measured? What specific file protection procedures will need to be established? Should they be standardized throughout the net? How many files will it be necessary to maintain?

What we need to answer these questions is a combination of knowledges. We naturally would have to have some computer expertise involved. And we surely would have to see that operating personnel were concerned intimately with the early decisions. There is no way that management can avoid intimate contact with the problems of both the technicians and the operating personnel. But this, in itself, is a very good thing. Too often, in the past, top management has tended to ignore the centralized computer center just because, once the investment has been made and the personnel have been hired, the center could be effectively ignored. Some time would pass, in many instances, before management would realize it had actually, by ignorance, lost control of the enterprise and its day-to-day functioning.

The distributed data processing net's greatest virtue may be in the forcing of the participation of the three major elements in the net—the experts, the operating personnel, and the management.

THE LANGUAGE PROBLEM

COBOL (a common business-oriented language) currently is used more in business nets (such as currently exist) than is any of the other formal computer languages. But it was not specifically tailored for use in the kinds of distributed data processing systems that we have been discussing.

While it is quite possible that smart terminals one day may have sufficient memory to be able to use command languages, this capacity may be delayed for a few more years. In the meantime, the net must make use of what we call "downstream loading." That is, either the minis or the central computer system must take care of a good deal of the translating of command languages used by terminals into actual computer actions. Earlier in the book we noted that command languages pull into use what we call job control statements of various kinds, and that these statements, in turn, call up procedures which are themselves made up of collections of individual computer instructions. A good deal of memory capacity and a fairly large operating system in storage is required for this kind of activity. The solution is to make use of communication lines and have either the minis or the central computer carry the translation load and the subsequent memory load on their own—communicating with the terminals as need be.

Suppose, though, we use some kind of star-ring system. At the center of the star would be a fairly complex mini computer with some considerable storage capacity. Four percent of the work of the organization would be stored in this mini, because of its general nature and because this standard information has been bucked up through the system. The remaining capacity of the mini would be reserved for the storage of a high-power operating system with the language-translation features currently found in large computer systems. It would be the job of this "central" mini computer to handle the receipt and translation of the command statements from the various terminals, and to send back to those terminals the appropriate machine-language programs. The central mini could relay the information through the distributed minis which deal with the terminals—leaving those intervening minis with the job of data analysis and storage, but not with the additional burden of operating systems sufficiently complex to handle command languages, control statements, and translation. Can such a system be put together? Yes, from a technical point of view. But whether management is, or wishes to be, up to the organizational task is yet another matter. We always must remember that none of these changes comes free—they occupy the time of operating and management personnel at all levels, and that time costs a great deal of money when attention is taken away from the operational duties normal to the enterprise. Would the result be worth the cost? Yes, if it works. Is there any guarantee that such a system would really work? No, there is not—no more so than there is a guarantee that a centralized data processing center will solve all the problems it is supposed to be able to solve.

What will occur, then? The mini computers and their related terminals will come into the enterprise on tiptoe, probably not in the dark of night but gingerly. The results of early localized experiments will determine whether the final plunge will be made. And this, after all, is probably the wisest way to go about making dramatic changes in the enterprise.

Information is said to be the heart of the enterprise. But this is not strictly true. Useful or applicable information is the heart of the enterprise. Too often these qualifying adjectives are forgotten, and information is admired whether it is useful or not. This is not a new problem nor is it peculiar to distributed data processing concepts. It is as old, at least, as the Roman roads.

IMPLICATIONS

We have explored a few of the in-house implications for the business enterprise interested in distributed data processing. Let us now turn our attention to a few of the implications for the broader society at large.

The typewriter presents us with a few clues. Originally, typewriters were used in businesses and pretty much businesses only. Then, bit by bit, they moved into the public schools in typing courses, which were designed to be useful in vocational training. This meant a large number of students learned to type whether or not they would ultimately wind up as typists or secretaries in the business enterprises. Eventually, portable typewriters were invented (rather early, actually—in the 1920s) and young people were encouraged to use these smaller machines at home for a host of useful purposes. Then, the electric typewriter moved into the business world, the schools, and, ultimately, we got the electric portable.

This succession might well go with the smart terminals or the very mini computers. They could become, via distributed data processing, very familiar to many types of workers. The need for training on these devices could move to the lower schools. Then a few interested people might buy their own systems (by then the prices might well be down considerably) for their own homes. This is one of the more likely ways in which the computer would enter the home as a useful device. Now then, if the smart terminal is reasonably priced and can be linked into a general computer system via the telephone lines, so much the better—and so much the quicker the computer will enter the home.

Distributed data processing, then, more than any other current development, may be the means of making the computer a commonly understood tool. The mystery will vanish (as it currently is doing with most of the simpler calculators) and computers truly will become an ordinary extension (tool) of mankind.

The line between the sophisticated smart computer terminal or mini computer and the complex electronic calculator will grow even fuzzier. Students, their parents, hobbyists, and others, will all come to use these devices without trauma. The devices will enter the psychic realm of the household as just another useful appliance. This, of course, may bring a special kind of dependency. We will expect to be able to perform complex calculations with a mere flip of a switch. Hopefully, we will understand what we need to do with these complex calculations. Hopefully, we will not become so dependent that we cannot do what we are used to doing without them. But there is always a danger of this.

The nature of the new tool, though, should not be overlooked—it is an intellectual device, not a physical assistant. That is, a special kind of symbiosis will exist between the calculator, the computer, and the person. Properly used, this interrelationship between person and computer should do much to enhance the intellectual abilities of masses of people. We should, in short, be able to produce a generation of extremely capable people who can daily handle problems currently far too complex to be dealt with by what we call "ordinary folk." But those who cannot afford the devices, even if these become relatively cheap, are much more severely cut out of the mainstream of life than one might suppose. Those people with too little intelligence to easily handle this new symbiosis will find the gap between them and their brighter sisters and brothers deeper, sharper, and more poignant. This may not bode well for social serenity and domestic peace. And almost without saying, the gap between the third world (have-not nations) and the industrial states will grow wider.

Since information is power and power is productive, we could expect a country occupied by skilled computer people to develop a standard of life very much higher than one without. And the penalties for ignorance would grow both economically and psychologically more severe. This does not bode well for a world which should peacefully get along with itself.

If the smart terminal is properly linked into the mainstream of a society, and all that society's members are expected to avail themselves of its use (as they currently do of the telephone), then we have done something rather drastic in changing our definitions of ourselves. We want to remember that the human being is a self-defining animal, and that the tools he or she uses are part of the definition.

Suppose we have smart terminals in our homes. What of our libraries? Why, they would most likely be not so much libraries of books but giant data banks that could be tapped at will. Suppose mini computers are in our homes. What of our libraries? Why, they might become libraries of programs. One would take out casettes and disks, not books.

SUMMARY

In this chapter we made, at the beginning, a distinction between operating personnel and computer personnel. In particular, we were concerned with the problem of the surrender of control by the operating personnel, in part because they could not understand the language or the purposes of the computer people, and in part because the central computer was too far away and too exotic for serious consideration. We noted that the contact with the computer people by the operating staffs often required complex formal documents and the act of surrender of their own intimate control of events. There is, then, a natural antagonism between operating personnel and computer personnel. In the past, this has presented special problems to management and often resulted in inefficiencies and rigidities. We noticed, also, in this chapter, a tendency for computer experts to become arrogant and isolated from the primary purposes of the organization.

Smart terminals and mini computers now present the business organization with the ability to construct a new kind of data processing net which more closely reflects the normal organization of the business. The emphasis would be, in such a configuration, on point-of-sale or point-of-action data use and data gathering.

We explored the meaning of the 80/20 data processing rule, and this led us to examine the possible network and information-node constructions that distributed data processing may allow. The ring configuration does not require a central computer unit; the star configuration does. But in either case, we assume the ability to make use of smart terminals reporting to mini computers. In the star system, the minis might be reporting directly to a central computer. We also took a look at two more complex configurations, the step-star linkage and the ring-star formation.

We dealt in this chapter with the possible return of control to management, and the need, once again, to deal with the age-old question of centralization versus decentralization. Here we noted it is the management philosophy itself that will influence the kind of distributed data processing net which would be constructed.

Certain power structure conflicts are bound to arise in an organization with a large-scale centralized computer system, when distributed data processing arrives on the scene. We noted that people in power seldom are willing to surrender their rights and privileges—even if this is, in the long run, good for the enterprise as a whole.

We gave some attention to the concept of the "blanket data base." We questioned its value, in this chapter, and explored some alternative layouts which might be more effective. Also, we made note of the fact that legal matters make dealing with large data bases very difficult. The size of the data base and the press of business at the data processing center make wholesale revisions of bases considerably more difficult than might be expected. Too, we noted that the larger the data base the more complex that the matter of cross-indexing items could become. And we saw that the operating personnel would probably be more aware of cross-indexing needs and uses than the computer personnel, isolated as they often are, in the main data center.

One of the elements which may seriously delay the arrival of distributed data processing is the necessity of careful planning and of enterprise-wide training that such a system would require. We noted the rewards might be very great and the motivation to succeed be very high. But without careful management, the rewards might not come and the motivation of personnel might not develop. In fact, we noted that one of the primary benefits of distributed data processing might be the shotgun wedding of operating personnel, computer personnel, and management—to the betterment of the business.

In this chapter, we took the view that security and control matters are no more difficult with distributed data processing than they are with centralized data processing—or with any complex distribution of function, whether it be cash registers or inventory. If control is returned to management, the problems of security become a standard management matter. And we noted, management had been dealing with that particular problem, one way or the other, for centuries. We do not wish to make myths of difficulties which might not exist. We also pointed out that the job of auditing distributed data bases actually might be more convenient than auditing a highly centralized and excessively busy central data unit. And because audits could be better distributed in time, the chance exists for even closer control.

We noted that the possibility of carefully tailored terminals and mini computers exists for distributed data processing in a way not truly possible for the centralized computer unit.

We noted several serious important questions for management, though we could not, in fact, answer any of them. The answers will come with experimentation and experience.

Finally, we dealt briefly with the language problem for smart terminals and minis and explored, tersely, the concept of "downstream loading."

HIGHLIGHT QUESTIONS

1. Distinguish between *operating personnel* and *computer personnel,* as those terms are used in this chapter.
2. What would be one or two possible areas of conflict between operating personnel and computer personnel?
3. What is a smart computer terminal?
4. Name a few of the advantages of decentralized activity.
5. Name some of the advantages of centralized activity.
6. Explain the 80/20 data processing rule.
7. What is a network node?
8. Distinguish between the simple computer ring configuration and the simple star computer configuration.
9. Would downstream loading be easier with the ring computer configuration or with the star computer configuration?
10. What would be some of the power conflicts which might occur during a changeover from centralized computer structure to distributed data processing?
11. What do we mean by the term *blanket data base?*
12. In a smart terminal to mini computer to central computer configuration, what would be the percentage of load on the central computer if the 80/20 data processing rule works out perfectly?
13. Describe some of the security problems which you think might be unique to distributed data processing configurations?
14. Distinguish between problems of security and problems of control as they relate to distributed data processing.
15. What do we mean by *tailored terminals?*

READINGS

Burck, Gilbert. *The Computer Age.* New York: Harper & Row, 1965.

In this small book one might wish to browse through the section on artificial intelligence, since it involves what we have called "symbiosis" and what is often called "intellectual enhancement." It is a book written primarily for the layman.

Magazine

DATAMATION. Technical Publishing Company, 1301 South Grove Ave., Barrington, Ill. 60010.

You should refer to recent copies of *Datamation* if you want to keep up with the discussions in regard to distributed data processing. Currently, there are no textbooks per se in this area. But the discussions in *Datamation* are well written and up to date, and you can enjoy the debate itself.

Weizenbaum, Joseph. *Computer Power and Human Reason*. San Francisco, Cal.: W. H. Freeman, 1976.

Here is a truly brilliant and delightful book. It isn't about data bases, but it has an interesting chapter on tools and artificial intelligence. It may have difficult places, but any small struggle is worth the effort. We will refer to this book again in later chapters.

CHAPTER 10

AUTOMATION

PURPOSE OF THE CHAPTER In the earlier chapters in this book we examined something of the history of the computer, elementary computers, and computer systems, learned something of the methods of contacting the computer, took a look at the computer as a utility, explored some of the problems inherent in setting up data bases, and considered the possibilities for distributed data processing. We now turn our attention to a closely linked and parallel development, that of automation.

In this chapter we will *not* try to explore automation in all of its possible dimensions—that would take a book twice the size of this one. Rather, we are going to look at the fundamental notion that underlies the process and attempt, where we can, to distinguish between mechanization and automation. And we are interested in just *how the computer links into this broad area*—what it can do to enhance or deter automation. We also must give some thought to our current and possibly enduring energy problems, since these will have some serious effect on the progress of automation.

TERMS AND CONCEPTS

There are a number of special terms used in connection with automation studies. We will want to use them in the proper context and define them where we must. Again, we are not attempting to define the terms or concepts in pedantic and rigorous ways, but rather in the way they are currently used in the culture.

automatization
transfer table
feedback
fly-ball governor
servomechanism
class A servomechanisms
process industry
capital investment
by-products
appearance of difference
rough terrain
flow monitor
mechanization
second industrial revolution
office automation
self-directing calculator
service industries
franchised businesses
energy
standard of life
energy-net problem
right to employment
control positions
automation
Industrial Revolution
negative feedback
output
counter
intellectual slavery
redundant facilities
guaranteed market
standardized product
job-order production
job-order shop
automated conveyors
production techniques
craft industry
intellectual mechanization
word processing machine
mechanization process
personal-service tasks
people-intensive industries
standard of living
moonlighter
product life
product centers

THE TERM

Three decades ago, Del Harder of the Ford Motor Company used the term *automatization* to describe the mechanical handling of automobile parts between some of the assembly processes at the Ford manufacturing plant. Mercifully, the term now has been shortened to *automation*. Since then, unfortunately, the word has been used to describe a second industrial revolution, to predict economic disaster for the ordinary working person who uses hands more than head, to describe any process which appears to be mysteriously routine, and to explain any unemployment which has occurred due to the vagaries in economic relations between countries and hemispheres.

What was going on at the Ford plant, three decades ago, to create all this excitement? Well, an engine block is a rather massive piece of metal—very difficult to move around accurately and easily. The block requires any number of special holes to be bored at selected points by various drill presses before it can be turned into a useful object—the engine of an automobile. For the holes to appear at the right places, the block has to be moved, turned, and very accurately positioned for the next set of drill operations. In early days, this meant a lot of people had to do a lot of careful and dangerous hauling and tugging and checking to be certain the block was in the right position at the right time. The "transfer table," as the automated mechanism was called, took care of most of these problems with ease, with accuracy, and without danger to Ford personnel. It also eliminated, after a fashion, all those tugging and hauling tasks and the people who performed them.

But had not this kind of replacement of people by machines been going on for hundreds of years? Yes, it had. The original Industrial Revolution has been nothing less than a long series of decades, each one of which saw some machinery take over some of the previous muscle jobs performed by either animals or human beings. We call it a revolution because we are looking back over a span of years. It is our long perspective which permits the term. And the term is incorrect. Actually, to all those millions of people over those hundreds of years, it was an industrial evolution. They were, as people are today, concerned with their own few decades of life and work and pleasure. For some, the "revolution" was a dreadful inconvenience. For others, it represented golden opportunity. Any number of people missed the whole thing—that is, they didn't know there was an evolution taking place, let alone a revolution. They just worked and lived and died and gave no thought at all to how we moderns would feel about their era.

All this is not to deny that change is more rapid these days than it used to be. At least this statement is true, if we confine our remarks to the matter of technology and its application. If, on the other hand, we apply change to what we call basic human behavior, there would be good arguments available that no serious changes had taken place since the early Greeks first taught us how to question and how to think.

There was, however, in the transfer table at Ford Motor Company, an addition called "feedback." It will be our task to explore the concept before we can really get down to the business of defining automation itself and making a sharp distinction, if such is possible, between industrialization and automation.

FEEDBACK

For any work we do there is usually some standard of performance. We know what we want to achieve, and we know when we have not succeeded. *Negative feedback* (the term is more accurate than that of feedback alone) is simply information which is fed back into a work process so we can adjust, while working, to better meet the standard we have set. It is called negative feedback because the information returning to the system is a measure of the error in achieving the performance we wanted.

When you reach for a pencil lying on a desk, your intention is clear enough. You wish the hand to travel directly to the immediate area of the pencil in one precise motion. You wish your fingers to close about the pencil in a particular way developed by past habit. You do not wish to miss the object by an inch or two, either way. As you are reaching for the pencil you receive two types of negative feedback. First, your eyes are scanning the immediate area and you can see if your reach is going in the right direction, and you can see any general error. You are, in fact, watching the progress of your own arm and hand while you are keeping a casual eye on the location of the pencil on the surface of the desk. At the same time, the muscles in your arm are feeding back information about the movement of the arm and the hand. Which is more important, the eyes or the muscles and nerves in the hand and arm? Since blind people can play the piano and do any number of other remarkable things, we suspect the muscles and nerves are more important in providing feedback information to the body.

We also know that when people suffer from certain diseases of the brain or the muscles they cannot easily reach and seize a pencil. In one type of disease, the information fed back from the muscles and nerves comes too late and the hand will fluctuate wildly back and forth. In another type of disease, the individual has to concentrate very hard to control the oscillations of the hand. The tremor never totally goes away, but the pencil can be seized and can be used. In these cases, there is something clearly interfering with appropriate negative feedback.

Possibly the oldest and the simplest example of negative feedback is the fly-ball governor attached to a steam engine. Figure 10–1 shows a schematic of such a device. James Watt invented the fly-ball governor in 1788—perhaps a more important invention than the steam engine itself. The central shaft in the picture is connected to the engine output by the gear at the bottom. This causes the shaft to spin. As it spins, centrifugal force causes the two metal balls to fly up and away from the central shaft. Such an action, because of the scissor construction of the arms attached to the balls, will make the throttle lever at the top come down a little, cutting off steam input to the engine. Of course, as the engine begins to slow down too much, the balls will fall inward toward the center of the shaft, and this will

FIGURE 10–1. The fly-ball governor

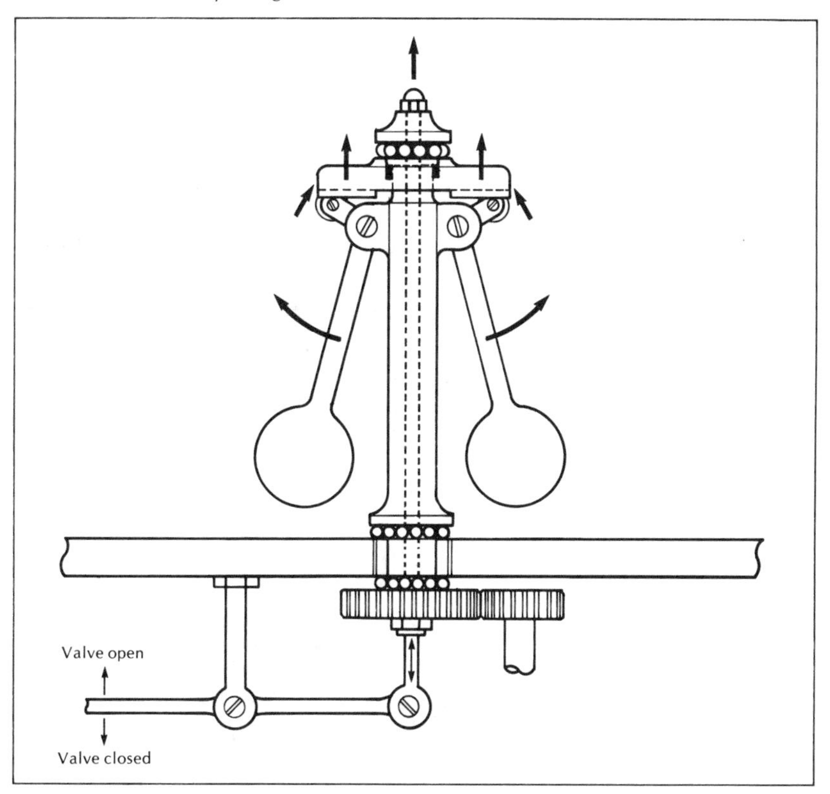

cause the control at the top to rise—feeding more steam into the engine. Without this simple but powerful control, the steam engine would continue to increase in speed or to oscillate wildly around the original throttle setting. With the fly-ball governor, there will be original variations, but things should steady up at the original throttle setting very rapidly. The important point is that the speed of the engine causes the shaft to rotate, which in turn causes the fly-ball governor to do what it does. The output of the machine is part and parcel of the regulation of the machine. This is the most important idea in automation.

Another good example of negative feedback would be the furnace thermostat. Perhaps we set the temperature in the house for 68°. When the temperature drops to 66° the furnace comes on. When the temperature reaches 70° the furnace shuts off. Notice we only achieve the 68° mark in passing. If our controls were too refined, the furnace would operate almost constantly. So what we get is a gentle oscillation around the 68° mark. For heating homes this is quite all right. For very accurate manufacturing processes it is not. The point here is that the variation from 68° is what drives the furnace on or off—negative feedback—variation from a preset standard.

SERVOMECHANISMS

Steel rolling mills turn bars of steel into thin sheets of the metal, useful for making tin cans and the like. The steel is flattened from bar form to sheet form by a series of giant rollers. In days of yore, it was necessary from time to time to shut down the rolling mill, measure the output, and then either tighten the pressure of the rollers or set up a pull between the last two sets of rollers to achieve the proper thicknesses. Figure 10–2 is a schematic of this last part of the rolling process.

FIGURE 10–2. Roller sets

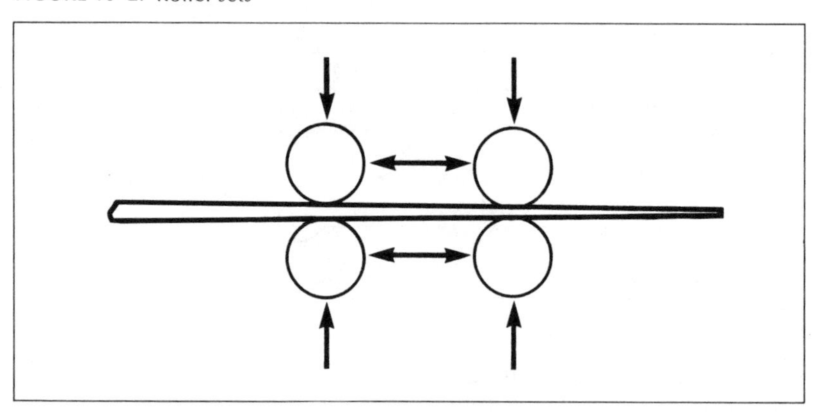

If we could measure, very accurately, any small variations in the thickness of the steel coming out of the rolling mill (and we can), and if we had large and powerful electrical motors attached to the rollers (and we do) that could increase roller pressure or, as when we pull taffy to make it thin, increase the pull between two sets of rollers, we would not need to stop the rolling mill and make periodic adjustments. And since rolling mills can run at 40 miles per hour or better (in terms of rotational speed), we could enormously increase the output.

How do we accomplish these things? Well, first of all, we would make use of a radiation emitter, which would be underneath and reach clear across the sheets of steel as they came out of the rolling mill. Above the steel sheet and the emitter we would have a radiation counter. This counter would measure the thickness of the steel, and any variations thereof, far better than any person could with a set of micrometers. Furthermore, the measuring could take place clear across the sheets of steel as the mill was running. Now, when the radiation counter found the amount of radiation was dropping (due to an increase in the thickness of the steel), it could send electrical signals to large electric motors connected to the steel rolling mill. These motors, called "servomechanisms," would increase the adjustments of the roller pressure and thus get thinner steel. Or they could cause the rollers to ease up on the pressure slightly and thus get thicker steel. Or they could combine this function with the creation of a greater or lesser tug between the two sets of rollers at the end of the process. These combinations of activities would give a uniformity to the steel—without the intervention of gangs of workers to make adjustments. And here we have a primary argument for automation. It would be possible to increase the output of the steel mill from four to ten times over. It would be possible to reduce the number of personnel required to run the mill. We would be able to produce better steel, cheaper.

CLASS A SERVOMECHANISMS

Often servomechanisms are classified according to their abilities. A class A servomechanism would be one that could direct the adjustments to steel rolling mills and the like by doing its own measuring, setting its own criteria, making its own comparisons and adjustments. In short, a good example of a class A servomechanism is an intelligent human being. This is why, of course, men and women have been attached to machinery in production lines ever since the beginning of the Industrial Revolution. It has been a form of intellectual slavery to the machine.

With the advent of the electrical motor, the radiation counter, the understanding of negative feedback, the development of computers, we ought to be able, at long last, to free millions of people from the chore of intellectual machine tending.

We now are ready to consider the necessary elements of automation. First, we need some standard or criteria of performance. Then we require some measuring device which can record any deviation from the preset standard. That done, we require a negative feedback mechanism which can tell the servomechanisms what adjustments are necessary to put the main processing machine back on course. The larger the feedback, the larger the necessary correction. And we must be certain that our corrections reach the machine in time and do not overcorrect, or we would be setting up a series of destructive oscillations in the mechanism. We can see that automated machinery is not only going to be rather complex, it is going to be very expensive. This, in part, explains why the "second industrial revolution" has been slow in coming.

PROCESS INDUSTRIES

The continuous process industries, such as the petroleum cracking plant, or chemical plants, have been the first to put automation to work. There are two good reasons for this early application. First, the industries are dangerous and corrections in process must be made very quickly. Second, the plant itself is a single complex system of pipes, valves, and monitoring system—ideal for the first application of the techniques of automation.

If the continuous process plant is properly constructed, there need be no direct labor involved. That is, the material to be worked on flows into the plant from pipelines or appropriate conveyors. Once the material is in the grip of the plant, the entire processing is automatic and is monitored in some central station. The station would require the supervision of one or two engineers per shift. And, of course, certain basic types of maintenance personnel also should be on hand on a regular basis.

Often the maintenance people should have little to do. Normally, the automated processing plant would be able to note if any valves are malfunctioning, and should be able to reroute materials through alternate routes. This means, of course, that the plant would have had to be constructed with certain redundant facilities—another reason for the enormous capital investment required to achieve true automation. The maintenance crew would receive notification from the central control room of the plant about what lines were needed to be cleaned or what valves were to be replaced.

Now then, if the supervisory engineers are working on a salaried basis and the maintenance people also are required to be on hand and are salaried, we can see the automated processing plant requires no direct labor of any kind. It then would be cheaper for the plant to run as close to maximum production as possible. Also, the more gallons or feet of material flowing through the plant, the less is the capital cost which needs to be attached to each item and the less the cost of the item to the public.

For any plant to run close to maximum production, the product of the plant must have some sort of guaranteed market. Many of the automated plants simply could not afford to run at anything less than 70 percent of full production. Just how one goes about developing guaranteed markets is not quite clear in a capitalistic economy.

And finally, we should note that a totally automated plant is in itself a relatively rigid structure. If the plant has been built for the cracking of petroleum into various products, it would indeed be a very expensive matter to shut the plant down and turn it to the production of certain kinds of chemical cleaners. The plant, after all, is a total system dedicated to one or two primary products, and to one or two by-products. The plant would require to run at near maximum for a certain number of years, making about the same product, before the capital investment could be said to be written off in full.

How much money are we thinking about, when we speak of a petroleum cracking plant or some other equally complex automatic factory? We are speaking of a capital investment of between $100 million and $250 million at the outset—no small amount. And we also are speaking of one or two years of construction prior to the issuance of the first salable products. Any such investment is going to require long study and very careful planning to avoid enormous and shattering losses. Perhaps here, too, we can see why the automated factory is somewhat slow in coming.

We have learned a great deal about process industries in the last several decades. We have learned how to plan the flow of materials very carefully. More important, we have learned to derive salable by-products from the very processes used to produce the major product. All these have been major steps toward reduction of manufacturing waste and, in the long run, toward reduction of costs to the consumer. If the processing plants can indeed be automated, as we have here described, and if, and only if, they can be made to operate at near maximum production capacity, we can expect enormous further reductions in the cost of many standardized manufactured goods.

But let us here consider something important. In the early stages of automation, many process plants *must* make a standardized product. And if there are by-products from the manufacturing process these, too, will need to be standardized. In one sense this means a narrowness of consumer choice. The products will be cheaper and more plentiful, but they also may be very boringly alike. Later, when more complex plants are built, it might be possible to build certain kinds of fortuitous procedures into the plants. The alternatives would be computer monitored so we could, in fact, assemble a variety of products. Again, there must be a caution. It would not be possible, necessarily, to build a genuinely different product. What we would get would be the appearance of difference achieved by the addition or removal of certain standard "trim" items. Is this sufficient variation for a people? Perhaps, perhaps not. We may have to resolve the question of whether "plenty" is our goal or "variety."

JOB-ORDER PRODUCTION

A job-order plant is basically a collection of general purpose machines which can produce small lots of product on order. We may be extruding aluminum window frames on one job, making small aluminum engine blocks on another, and producing certain kinds of finished aluminum cases on still another order. Small lots, a good deal of movement around the factory, and a series of general-purpose machines which will require setups from time to time as the tasks change, these are the factors in job-order production. Can such a plant be automated? Not easily, and not without the intervention, full scale, of the computer.

Individual machines (for example, a complex milling machine) can be programmed to deal with material in three dimensions—and a variety of material at that. To accomplish this task, the machine must be able to respond to digital information (the presence or absence of holes in a paper tape, or the presence or absence of magnetic spots on a magnetic tape). Or the complex milling machine could be equipped with a small memory which is, in turn, hooked into a general-purpose computer. The computer would project to the machine memory sufficient information to accomplish a particular task, repetitively, on a particular product. The instructions we are speaking about here are very complicated to construct. We are, after all, asking a machine to shift and measure in three dimensions. But some very interesting new methods of recording information have made this a distinct possibility. A master machine, run by a master machinist, can be hooked into a computer. As the master machine under the skilled guidance of the expert, goes through the process of making the first item, the information is copied into the computer. It is this copy information which is then fed back into other similar machines, which can be set up to produce what the master machine has produced in the first instance.

Of course, we cannot rig conveyors to handle all the possible different paths between different machines in the general job-order shop. Here the class A servomechanism (human) is at its best. Here there is what we call "rough terrain" to travel, and human beings are peculiarly adapted for rough terrain.

What to do then? Well, first of all, the individual machines can be equipped with tape memories of one kind or another so they can follow complex patterns to produce particular parts. These tapes, and not the machine, can be made to vary from job to job. And in some instances, movement between one or two machines, if there is frequent and common movement, can be mechanized. But the most important task is to turn over to the computer the job of scheduling the different jobs in the job-order shop. It will be the computer and not people who will determine which machines are idle, which jobs are yet to be done, and the particular route through the shop which is the most economical to produce the maximum number of products from the minimum number of machines. This is a task peculiarly suited to computer solution. The computer can determine the shortest path through the shop for any job order. It can, with proper equations, determine the best combination of machines to produce the product, taking into consideration such matters as retaping the machines and set-up times. Properly programmed, the computer can weigh all of the important and relevant factors for all of the jobs and make the best possible combinations of movement, given the fact that no combination will be perfect for every product moving through the shop. The cost and importance of each of the product batches would be an important factor in achieving some near-ideal arrangement of schedule. All this information could be combined with known product-delivery deadlines.

We can see that the number of factors to be considered in a well-ordered job shop could very well overwhelm the average foreman. The computer, though, is peculiarly suited to handling a host of variables and running these variables through a veritable sea of permutations. In short, the computer simulates the job shop as a working entity. Various combinations of product and paths can be tested by the machine. Cost figures can be attached to each of the possible arrangements and the most economical pattern can be selected.

So if it is true, and it is, that computers can monitor the flow of liquids in a process industry, then it is equally true that the computer can monitor the general movement of individual orders through a job-order shop. In the former case, the movement of liquids (or easily transported dry particles) is under the direct control of the computer via its servomechanisms, which can arrange flow through pipes, turn valves on or off, alter pressure in the lines. In the latter case, that of the job-order shop, the movers are still people, but the pattern of the movement through the shop is carefully planned and carefully monitored by the never-tiring, ever-watchful computer. The signals for movement of materials are specific orders produced by the computer to be followed by particular individuals working in the shop.

At first blush this may seem a terrible thing to do to the human animal—to put her or him under the intellectual dictation of a machine. But in fact it is not. There are many people in the world, of limited intelligence, who seek and require some kind of productive work. They could not, of themselves, follow the complex interrelationships a job-order shop can generate; but they can, of themselves, move materials at the bidding of the computer. We have, in America, long spoken of the bottom 15 percent of the population who are constantly unemployed because they cannot read or write readily, and because they cannot think their way through complex problems. It does no disservice to such people to give them employment, to pay them weekly for jobs well done, to help them off the welfare rolls of the several states.

Sometimes, in our haste to automate, we forget that a job, however dull it may seem to us, is better than enforced idleness and the general indignity of welfare or unemployment. We forget that many people will accept work on simpler jobs. What they desire is the knowledge that they make some valuable contribution by their work. Oddly enough, the movement of materials between machines in the job-order shop is a very valuable service indeed. The salaries required by people who do this task would be less than the enormous cost of building conveyors between machines that could generate the myriad peculiar combinations of movement through a job-order shop required by a dozen different jobs with a dozen different specifications. It is the scheduling which lends itself to automation, not the movement of materials.

Of course, this cannot be said of the automobile plant or any other large-scale enterprise which makes hundreds of thousands of similar products. In this latter case, the movement of material from one machine to another can indeed be made automatic. Model changes may be made from year to year, but from that point on, the plant operates full tilt to produce similar items. Even more important, in that kind of continuous manufacturing operation, the computer can join with the automated conveyors to produce a variety of final product mixes. The task here is to bring to the point of assembly a number of different items based on an estimate of the different types of end products expected, or of items based on customer orders for different types of products. But we are not speaking of the frame of a car or of the two or three different engines. We are referring to the miscellaneous differences which can occur—colors of body paint, colors and selection of fabric, presence or absence of automatic shifts, or power brakes and power steering. This surface mix can be automated without interfering very much with the basic assembly task.

MECHANIZATION AND AUTOMATION

If you have been reading the newspapers of late, you have doubtless run across articles decrying the automation of farm production and the automation of service industries (such as the fast food service restaurant chains). The newspapers are wrong, of course. What is being talked about is not automation but merely mechanization. All that has happened to the fast food service is that the everyday normal production techniques used in any modern factory have been brought to bear on the matter of creating a hamburger, a milkshake, fried chicken, or what have you.

And let us not be in error—the "automatic" tomato picking machine is merely a mechanism which, under the guidance of a human being, has taken over, with mechanical fingers, the job formerly held by hosts of stooping workers. The process is not automation, it is mechanization. Or let us simply say of the fast food chains and of the farms that they have come under the Industrial Revolution, not the "Second Industrial Revolution." Can you have two different "revolutions" going on at the same time? Yes, you can. In different sections of an economy, this is quite normal. We would like to believe our economies are tightly integrated, but they are not. So, that long-time, misnamed Industrial Revolution continues its evolutionary path. In the meantime, automation is getting off the ground so expensively and so slowly it is better construed to be an evolutionary process.

Further, we must not confuse the process of automation with the simpler process of centralization. It is true, indeed, our farms are turning more and more into giant agribusinesses. But this is the normal centralization which can take place when we are mechanizing a "craft" industry. This is as old as the Industrial Revolution itself. Did not the "revolution" take place when the cottage industries of England were gathered under one roof to take advantage of the application of steam engines to drive machinery? Did the chicken lay the egg or did the chicken hatch out of the egg. Which came first? Neither. The one is a concomitant part of the other. You cannot have the one without the other. Each is the other side of the single coin of which we speak.

OFFICE AUTOMATION

The term *office automation* is frequently and erroneously used to describe the interjection of the computer into the paper-handling activities of modern business offices. A more correct descriptive phrase would be *intellectual mechanization*. It is possible, of course, to build a certain amount of negative feedback into office procedures. We could so program the computer that it could advise appropriate office people of deviations from expected norms in the matter of overdue accounts, items needing inventory replacement, and the like. Or we could, if we had the equipment, go a step further in the process. The computer could contain, within its program store, the addresses of vendors, individuals with overdue accounts, and so on, and could, if proper mailing equipment is directly attached, proceed with the entire task. Here we face the same types of questions we faced in regard to the job-order shop. Is the kind of complex and expensive equipment that could handle items produced by the computer and turn them into mailable copies worth the money? Given the typical office salaries, probably not. The only cases where such mighty investments would be warranted would be where the mailings are in enormous volume and frequent throughout the year. So we might expect the larger oil companies, with their millions of customers, to do everything in their power to automate the normal billing procedures and to automate (as far as they can) the money-receiving procedures. But the smaller office with only a few people would hardly be able to achieve anything bordering on truly automated procedures. For the immediate future we will not expect to see a truly automated office.

But the computer itself is changing. Where once it was a self-directing calculator it is now more and more a word processing machine. It is the word processing capability combined with distributed data processing which will change the office format with which we are all so familiar.

Some of the changes in the future of the modern office and some of the forces which will resist such changes are sufficiently important to warrant a full chapter later in the book.

SERVICE INDUSTRIES

Major changes have been taking place in service industries during the last decade or two. Originally, it was expected that while manufacturing industries automated, the service industries would accept the displaced personnel. But something quite different has been taking place. The service industries, particularly food service, dry cleaners, and the like, have been applying standard manufacturing techniques to their operations, with the express purpose of either raising the productivity level of service employees or getting along with fewer of them.

Again, the application of modern manufacturing techniques to service industries is much more a matter of mechanization than it is automation. And like any effective mechanization process, certain fundamental changes have been made:

1. Tools have been specifically designed to perform specific service tasks. For example, mustard and mayonnaise dispensers have been designed specifically to allocate so much and only so much of that type of garnish to the common hamburger.
2. The layout of a fast food service kitchen has been designed on a work-flow basis to meet specifically the several tasks involved in the preparation of certain foodstuffs. Additions to the menu involve a reordering and often reconstruction of the kitchen facility and the subsequent development of additional special-purpose tools.
3. The design of major kitchen equipment has been made to facili-

tate the use of the specific tools designed for the various food preparation jobs.

4. A standardized physical plant has been prepared which is both an appropriate "plant" for the food production but simultaneously a standard advertisement in itself (e.g., the golden arches of McDonald's).
5. Redecoration and modernization procedures are an intimate part of the total design. Reviews of product sales and effectiveness are an ongoing function of the enterprise.

These, then, are some of the standard mechanization techniques which have been so enormously successful in bringing the Industrial Revolution to fruition and in changing the face of the Western world. And there is much more here than merely the design of tools and machines. What is equally important is the relationship between the individual using the tools and the machines to the equipment itself and to the general operational plan of the enterprise.

We are all familiar with the old-fashioned hamburger stands of yesteryear run by, as we recall, a type of person who was content with a slower and simpler life and who seemed, at least from the point of view of physical appearance, to have indulged in more of the food products personally than were finally sold. Compare such individuals to the sleeker, more rapidly moving, more adventurously courteous species we find in the modern fast food restaurant. Something of a major attitudinal change has taken place along with the tools, the equipment, and the architecture. And it is this psychological change which may, in the long run, be the more important. Service has moved from a necessity to a high art. The challenge is speed and flexibility, not a method to fill an idle day. In fact, Western man, proud and goaded by his own achievement of the Industrial Revolution, finds himself often at odds with the slower paced and much less aggressive remainder of the world. Future wars and contests may occur because of this deepening rift.

Small businesses are disappearing and small franchised businesses are taking their place at what seems to be an increasing rate. With this means of operation, one can gain the advantages of a large organization and the concomitant management expertise while also enjoying the advantages inherent in the small business enterprise. Such a happy combination is likely to continue to encourage growth and development. And, of course, if the franchise organization itself is doing the basic purchasing of materials and equipment for these small businesses, enormous savings can take place because of the size of any given single purchase. And of equal importance, highly skilled purchasing agents can be used—men and women who know where the real bargains are.

This much we can say with reasonable certainty. Small business will continue to mechanize. The franchise units will mechanize because it is good management practice to do so. Their independent small business competitors must equally do so if they are to survive the pressures. But it is not likely that we will see a truly automated small business in the near future. If we do, it would have to be something like an "automatic" dispenser (candy bars, cigarettes, soft drinks) blown large. And such a dispenser-store likely would require the services of a built-in computer system, or at least a regular supervisor and a few maintenance people.

The social problem is that those people displaced by large-scale automating industries will not necessarily be able to find refuge and jobs in the smaller business enterprises. At the moment the only recourse of such displaced persons would be welfare, unemployment insurance, or government-created jobs. As these three alternatives are currently constructed, they are far from satisfactory. Probably what will eventually develop will be a host of new types of personal-service jobs.

What types of jobs could these new personal-service tasks be? Suppose city and county governments could hire bright young college folk with athletic backgrounds to provide full-time playground supervision for schools, neighborhoods, and parks? Is this not an honorable task? Could it not be comparable to any number of other county and city jobs? Of course it could. Suppose, further, that in each city residential block one house constituted a "childhood refuge"—a place where youngsters could go for a meal, counseling, a bed—should some unfortunate event occur to a team of working parents. Or suppose it was the kind of place any youngster could adjourn to after school, if parents and home were not immediately available. Is this not an honorable vocation for a woman with several children of her own who would otherwise be on welfare? Could not the city or the county government maintain the home for her since she would be providing a valuable service to the neighborhood?

Or go yet a step further. We are all familiar with the ice cream man who peddles around the neighborhood on one of those three-wheeled ice cream carts. Could not there be a "storyteller" who did the same—a young man or woman who had, instead of ice cream, a container full of children's stories—whose duty it would be to sit at curbside and tell or read stories to preschool youngsters who would otherwise be idling on the streets. And should any child, preschool or no, decide to learn to read, could not this willing storyteller introduce the child to the task and provide him or her free the book or books of interest. There is no psychological law that states learning has to take place in the formal location and atmosphere of the classroom. There is no psychological law that states the streets and what they teach must always be bad for children and their elders.

Could not each city, each county, each school district hire and maintain a resident sculptor whose job it was to cover the landscape with charming creations? Is this less a service than can be provided by a clerk in a store, a county maintenance person, or a host of other standard jobs of this day and age? All materials would be purchased for the sculptor. Also, a regular and reasonable salary would be provided by the governmental institution hiring the individual. The only ringer would be that the sculptor must conduct informal classes on sculpting for any group of youngsters who would ask and seek to learn. Somehow one concludes this sort of service work might provide us all with a better world and a better environment.

We claim our current crop of college graduates are overeducated and not able to find employment. There can never be too much education for anyone, anytime, anyplace. What is wrong is our silly and narrow view of what constitutes an acceptable job and what constitutes service. In these areas the reformation should not be with the young but with their elders involved in government.

To not receive an education is sad. To waste an education is criminal!

THE COMPUTER *IN* AUTOMATION

We have looked at some of the simpler and broader aspects of automation. This we did for a purpose. Particularly, we wanted to develop the concept of negative feedback, because it is in the feedback loop itself that the computer will combine with automation to make shattering changes in our futures.

In our discussion of the fly-ball governor and the radiation counter, we were looking at simple mechanisms of the feedback type. But imagine, if you will, the enormous degree of refined control we can get when we put not a simple measurer or counter into the feedback loop, but rather a sophisticated high-speed digital computer.

We have examples, already, of the application of simpler computers in our automobiles. Such devices monitor the behavior of the engine and modify the timing and the like to achieve greater efficiency and smoother operation.

Perhaps, after all, this is the most important chapter in the book—particularly for those students gifted with imagination—for in the combination of the computer in the feedback loop and the general principles of automation we get a glimpse of the enormous potentials ahead.

Again, a negative feedback is nothing more than the variation of the machinery from some present criteria. The feedback is used to drive servomechanisms to adjust the primary machines to achieve better output. With the computer in the loop, thousands of variables may be considered and large numbers of servomechanisms may be used. More important, the computer can reset the original criteria anytime such adjustment is necessary. Here we have dynamic control —a replacement of the intellectual tasks of machine tenders of the past.

The computer in the feedback loop

ENERGY AND AUTOMATION

While it can realistically be said that automation will actually require less energy per item manufactured, this may not be quite the problem we face in the future. For it can also be said that automation requires enormous amounts of energy to be *concentrated* at particular locations for particular periods. This concentration of energy applied to manufacture will be competing with other possible energy uses in the society generally. If it is true that the items could be manufactured by work forces which would use a certain minimum of energy in any event for the mere task of living, could it not be said that by *not* automating we would save a certain overall amount of energy as far as the society was concerned? And could it not also be said we would be creating jobs for people who needed them? It is true we might be settling for fewer manufactured items of a particular sort. It is true the manufacturing process might, in fact, be slower. But it would be equally true we would be using less energy and quite probably fewer natural resources in the process of creating jobs by not automating. Our standard of living (the consumption of goods) might be a little lower, but this does not mean our standard of life (value systems, appreciation of life and art) would be any the lower. It is quite true that if a standard of living drops too near the poverty level, it can tragically interfere with a standard of life. But full employment of persons might just exactly prevent such a disastrous drop for a good segment of the population. Also, we do not need to believe a continuing expansion of the desire for artifacts necessarily guarantees an improved standard of life for society as a whole or for any of the particular individuals therein.

Current shortages in oil, gas, and their related by-products (such as fertilizers) are a warning that we may be attempting to consume too much too fast. We use too many intensive energy industries, perhaps, and not enough people-intensive industries. We also must be wary of committed energy nets. By this we mean that one type of manufacturing can require support from several other types of manufacturing. And if this top artifact is energy-intensive, and if the supplementary parts manufacture also is energy-intensive, we have trapped ourselves in an expanding consumption net from which there appears to be no immediate redemption as long as the top industry is going at breakneck pace to make objects which may or may not really be needed. Is a massive marketing activity necessary to sell the product? Then perhaps we ought to review our commitments and determine whether or not the product is really needed and is in any way related to what we call a decent standard of living and what we might choose to call a high standard of life.

The Aswan Dam in Egypt is a classic picture of the energy-net problem. The Egyptian government, faced with uncontrollable floods and an increasing need for agricultural land to feed an expanding population, has built with foreign help a magnificent dam to control the floods. As the dam was built the population of Egypt rose to the point where additional land irrigated by the new dam and flood-control system has managed only to hold the standard of living (admittedly for more people) at the same level as before the dam was built. But because the mighty Nile no longer floods the land and brings fresh soil each season, the Egyptian government is committed to fertilizers of an artificial kind to keep production up. The fertilizers, in turn, depend upon oil, and oil is much in demand these days, and the demand has raised the price mightily. So we find a government in a trap from which there is certainly no easy withdrawal. And should oil continue to rise in price, or grow scarce in the Middle East, the government of Egypt faces a singular tragedy of its own ambition and its own making. But before we condemn their acts, we must resolve the moral question of whether a piecemeal starvation of people over a period of years is worse than or better than the massive starvation of people in greater numbers at a later date. People and governments put off until tomorrow whatever is too uncomfortable to do today. Is life its own justification, no matter how miserly? Or is it better to be unborn?

We can see, from the Egyptian classic, the kinds of problems and traps energy-intensive nets can set for a nation. And we can see that the price of withdrawal can be painful if not fatal for a society. About all that can be said is that we ought to be very careful indeed before we commit ourselves to many more of these energy webs, as the spider of tragedy may be sitting quietly in the middle—waiting.

IMPLICATIONS

Again, we have a few major implications of what has gone before, and we will treat them under the headings of moral issues, guaranteed markets, and control positions. The moral issues, of course, are an intimate part of our culture. As our culture changes, so do our morals. As our morals change, so do we get yet further changes in the culture. The guaranteed markets may do very serious things to what we consider the normal economic functions of a capitalistic democracy. Certainly, we should be interested in projecting what we can as accurately as we can. Control positions may influence the distribution of the population in the nation and several other demographic matters—we ought to give some thought to the matter.

MORAL ISSUES

It has been said that everything which was a sin during the medieval period became a virtue during the Renaissance, and vice versa. Such dramatic changes in our values and philosophies usually take place when we move from one great age to another. If we are about to face the age of automation, we ought to be seeing some of these dramatic changes in moral points of view. Indeed we are. Some thirty years ago any young man or woman who held not one but two jobs was an object of admiration to be pointed out to one's lazy children as a paragon of industry and virtue. Today, we use the term *moonlighter* to describe such ambition—and there is a faint tinge of the disrespectful in our voices. This is, in a way, a complete turnabout of values. In part we might expect the scorn because he or she who holds two jobs has deprived another of one—in times of broad unemployment such concepts can occur. But no, it is more than that. So much has been said about automation and the unemployment it

"MOONLIGHTER!"

is supposed to cause that a whole culture has become wary of anyone who might, out of energy and ambition, possibly deprive others, now or in the future, of the "right" to employment. Notice the choice between "right" and "opportunity." In earlier days people sought the opportunity of employment. Now these people seek the right of employment. This, too, is a change in moral values. And let us not forget the act of leisure has achieved a legitimacy in the last two decades it has never truly enjoyed before, save for those very few lucky people of past ages who carried the title "aristocrat."

Today we speak of the possibility of the four-day week or the thirty-hour week. We have several instances on the calendar when three-day weekends are created by national holidays. And so it will probably go. In part this is to help relieve a general case of unemployment in certain industries and sections of the country. In part this is due to the new legitimacy of leisure. In part this is due to the fear of automation and subsequent massive unemployment, however far away that may actually be. Humanity is prone to act more on ideas than on events. Often the bridges we would burn behind us have yet to be crossed.

The general public's disappointment with both the results and the increasing financial burdens of welfare programs also have had an impact on the psychology of work. It is less popular today to indulge in conspicuous consumption than it used to be. We are now aware about the possibility of depleted resources in a keener way than ever before, and he or she who consumes too much seems somehow greedy and thoughtless. The general feeling seems to be that one job and one income ought to be sufficient for any individual. Families, of course, are permitted to have more than one breadwinner (at the moment) without too much umbrage being taken. This, in part, is because women are fighting for certain basic rights and, in part, because there is a general recognition of the penalties now and in the future of inflation.

In our first chapter we observed that moral values change with technological achievements—the train was used as a case in point. Here a much broader technological possibility sends certain changes as a harbinger of what is yet to come. The odd thing is that the expectation of arrival of a new technology has just about as much impact on values as the actual arrival of a new technology. The human animal is an anticipatory creature.

GUARANTEED MARKETS

Assume a truly automated plant is built. Such an establishment may have three "managers," who each take an eight-hour supervisory shift. It may also have, say, a crew of 12 maintenance personnel on a full-time salaried basis. What are some of the consequences of such an organization and such a material creation?

First, the automated plant, having involved hundreds of millions of dollars of investment, must operate at least 70 percent of its built-in capacity. And let us assume we wish to run the plant around the clock for a full set of three eight-hour shifts. We must feed the beast constantly. Supplies and raw materials must arrive at the plant site in advance, or exactly on schedule, so the operating level will not drop. To achieve such a goal, guaranteed schedules must be arranged. Suppliers must be able to deliver the supplies and materials steadily and without fail. There can be no slipups. We require to have, then, guaranteed procurement.

Second, at the other end of the plant we are going to see the spewing out of a myriad of product units. These units must be sold to provide the wherewithal to purchase the supplies and raw materials to keep the plant running. A serious drop in sales would be a major disaster. Therefore, the plant must have a guaranteed market which is as steady and reliable as the procurement. The closer the plant runs to 100 percent capacity the less money each unit of production will cost. But this means something akin to market saturation in a hurry unless the market is growing. A market can grow dramatically for a few years when an item is new. But what of later years? What of those years between the time the novelty has worn off the product and the plant has been paid for? Clearly, new markets must be achieved one way or the other. Export is one method. Product replacement is another. Competition with similar products is yet another. A constantly increasing population is another possibility. A product that conveniently disintegrates at an appropriate replacement date is the fifth possibility.

Export has its limits. Product replacement is likely to be at a low level, though it may be steady. Competition with other products will be answered by more severe competition from those products—they cannot afford to lose markets, either. We have, of late, in most advanced Western countries, opted for a steady birthrate or something close to it. Limited product life might work out reasonably well until an outraged public caught on to the act. No, none of the alternatives seem satisfactory unless the plant is constructed to produce goods at just the exactly right rate to keep on going. Such exact planning is an admirable goal. Nowhere in recorded history has such an achievement been recorded for any reasonable length of time. Automation could create more problems than it solves.

Suppose, though, automation were achieved in three vital American industries—food, clothing, and shelter. Suppose it would be possible to estimate, through the Census Bureau and similar agencies, just the amount of automation required to deal with a steady-state population in all of these areas. The costs of these three great life-essentials might drop dramatically. And if we could agree to some common level requirement for each of the three, we might be able to put a set of mighty controls on our energy consumption. In fact, if the government, in order to control these matters, taxed individuals with the purpose of redistributing the money by providing the three basic sets of goods "free," a high degree of stability might be reached.

We expect government agencies to build our roads, our airports, our post offices, our sidewalks. We expect to be able to use these without major charges. We pay few tolls to move about over these privately created but publicly financed facilities. Why not food, clothing, and shelter? One supposes it might be because a sidewalk is a sidewalk is a sidewalk but a "man's house is his castle." People show an enormous amount of variation in what they eat, what they choose to wear, and in what style they would live. The oldest of man's economic goods are his (or her) method of expression. We are rather indifferent about roads as long as they are reasonably wide and well kept.

But automation can provide variety, can it not? Yes, on the surface.

The question is: Will such surface variation really be sufficient so people can maintain independent identities? It is a poser for the future—not really answerable now.

CONTROL POSITIONS

Both mechanization and such automation as we currently have result in what we might call "product centers." Product centers may be highly centralized areas of production geographically, or they may represent a single enterprise with enormous capacity. Or, as in the case of the northeastern United States, both.

Large-scale product centers become control centers. By this we mean that the enormous concentration of money and manufacturing power inevitably result in political power of various kinds. The combination of money and political power results in a centralization of control. Powerful control centers tend to set standards, values, and tastes for a given culture or society. In the case of the northeastern United States, they may set the standards and norms for a whole civilization.

Much control can be inadvertent. When men and women see the same skylines, meet in the same clubs, live in the same kinds of neighborhood, they tend to define the world in their own terms. If these common agreements on values and standards are combined with economic and political power, they tend to become the "approved" norms for the society. And since financial success depends upon an intimate integration and involvement with the control centers, the variability of the culture or the civilization will tend to narrow to this accepted norm.

Automation, requiring large investment, steady production, and guaranteed markets, carries the process of centralization and control yet further than mechanization. Some forms of mechanization still can be done on a small scale. A totally automated plant, as we have observed earlier, requires such massive investment to get started, leans so heavily on long-term planning, and depends on such a concentration of skilled personnel, we are safe in assuming only the incumbent control centers can muster the wherewithal to oversee the process. This means the automated plants will be an even sharper focus of current norms and values.

If we would stare into the future with any semblance of reality, we must delineate the characteristics which would make an automated plant, or collection of such plants, work most efficiently. They are:

1. The availability and concentration of highly trained personnel.
2. A certain guarantee of sameness of product (standardization).
3. A certain guarantee of stable markets.

"I DEMAND: INVESTMENT, STEADY PRODUCTION, AND GUARANTEED MARKETS."

The demands of automation

4. A common agreement on standards of value (economic worth of products).
5. A common agreement on standards of taste.

All of these are currently very important to our large-scale manufacturing industries. They are, in many ways, the very seat of the "prosperity" of the middle and working class of the nation. Where the standards or tastes vary from these expected norms, those in control positions can and may muster enormous campaigns of persuasion. We call these activities national advertising. The persuasive activities would have to be on an even greater scale for true automation to be effective.

We should expect, then, an automated society to be a more uniform society than we are currently experiencing. We are not speaking about people's desires but rather about the inevitable result of certain industrial judgments. If there is to be some kind of salvation of variability, it must rest on the unique ability of the computer to bring about the appearance of change or variability without actually trying to force such variability upon the basic manufacturing process itself. The automobile industry has been reasonably successful in this attempt. But the automobile industry in the United States has also been notoriously rigid. Such major changes in product design and size as have taken place have apparently been forced upon Detroit by the importation of small and unusual cars from Europe and Japan. If automation should join with the international corporation to make the centralization of economic and taste control truly international, from whence would these pressures for change come? It is a worrisome question.

All of the discussion above may explain, in some rough way, why automation has not been universally hailed as the salvation of the race, and also why it has been somewhat slower in coming than had earlier been predicted. The human animal becomes bored in steady climes and perhaps prefers the adventure of bad weather and the unexpected. People may be resisting automation not so much out of blindness as out of a sense of the universality of the commitment in narrowing their economic freedoms and their artistic tastes.

A prosperous but narrow and dreary automated society might well wake up one day and find (as is alleged of the Mayan cities) that everyone just got up and went away, out of sheer boredom, to the neighboring hills to sluff off the comforts and the uniformities of civilizations. Such an act is a form of rebellion and a form of adventure. The human race has always been a bad weather animal—it is usually such a set of circumstances which cause its improvement—or so we are told by various experts on the subject of evolution.

SUMMARY

In this chapter we have been introduced to the origination and meaning of the word *automation,* which is bandied about rather loosely these days. If there is a definitive difference between mechanization and automation, it has to do with negative feedback—the ability of the machine or machine system to govern its own behavior by measuring deviations from previously set norms, and having the ability to modify the behavior to meet the criteria established. Human beings are not completely removed from the automated plant, because of the need for supervisory and maintenance personnel; but in the perfected automatic plant there would be no human beings involved intimately in the manufacturing process itself.

We learned, too, the feedback principle is rather old, going all the way back to certain types of controls on the Watt steam engines. We might say that what is new about feedback is its broader application, its electrification, and its ability to absorb the computer as part of the governing process. These changes could result in a qualitatively different set of processes.

We found servomechanisms of one kind or another to be essential in the automated plant, since they are the mechanical means by which a system can correct itself. The steel rolling mill was our case in point.

And for mischief's sake, we classified man as a class A servomechanism—this to show he or she might not so easily be eliminated from the processes of which we speak.

We explored the most likely site for the achievement of automation—the continuous process industry. And we made note of some of the difficulties inherent in any attempt to automate the job-order shop. But here the computer can come to the rescue. We can automate the scheduling involved in the job-order shop, if not the shop itself. The question then becomes a moral one. Should people become an inherent part of any automated process? Was not that the objection to mechanized processes?

We noted any automated establishment would have certain built-in rigidities of scale. These would tend to make serious changes in products difficult—until such time as the investment had been recovered at a profit. We faced the reality of standardized products and guaranteed markets, to say nothing of the need for guaranteed raw materials to keep automated equipment running apace.

We took some pains to distinguish between mere mechanization ("mere" only relatively speaking) and true automation. We noted a continuation of the Industrial Revolution in both agriculture and the small business under franchise. It is important to understand these differences, since we want to know where to put the blame if things go wrong and where to land our praise when things go right.

We gave the idea of office automation a rather cursory treatment, since we intend to explore the idea at greater depth in a later chapter.

We made note that the dream of putting industrial workers displaced by automation into service industries might well "come a cropper," since the service industries are in the midst of the process of mechanization with stunning success and no loss of the quality of service.

We concerned ourselves with the slightly slippery business of determining whether the amount of energy applied to any unit of production is really the primary concern, or whether the very intensity of energy application in itself is the problem. The fact that each product unit is cheap will not help us if we produce so many as to bankrupt our total energy sources in the process. Sometimes the sum of the parts does result in something different.

We explored, briefly, the concept of the energy-intensive net and some of the possible consequences which can occur when we bind ourselves too firmly into such a complex. We used the Aswan Dam in Egypt as an example of just such a dilemma.

We touched a bit, in this chapter, on some of the moral issues which automation might bring upon us. And we noticed there are some signs of the changes which might occur already. Yesterday's industriousness might become today's public sin.

We noted guaranteed markets might be hard to come by. And we noted such markets have dangerous rigidities, of which we ought to at least be aware. We noted also the intimate connection between the guaranteed market and the guaranteed raw material supply—they cannot be separated. We had occasion to look at the problem of market saturation, the current but ineffective cures, and the problems of uniformity. To none of these questions and problems have we been able to give clever and satisfactory solutions.

Finally, we touched upon the notion of control positions and what this might mean for the future, if the source of our automated industries is our current highly mechanized industrial complex. This connection, we found, is almost inevitable. The result would be a greater focusing of trends which are already in process. We notice, too, that the personnel and educational requirements of mechanized industries are pretty much the same, though junior, to the kinds of requirements a fully automated culture might face. That done, we concluded the chapter on a not too cheerful note. Perhaps it is better to be a bit of a pessimist and be pleasantly surprised than to be too much the optimist and be seriously disappointed.

HIGHLIGHT QUESTIONS

1. Explain the difference between mechanization and automation.
2. What is negative feedback? How does it relate to automated devices?
3. What is a servomechanism? How does it tie into automation?
4. Explain how the fly-ball governor on a steam engine works and why it is, in fact, an example of negative feedback.
5. Why will continuous process industries be more likely to automate than job-order shops?
6. How can the computer help the job-order shop to automate, at least in part?
7. List a few of the fundamental changes in techniques and tools which come about because of mechanization.
8. What types of tool techniques and uses would come about, because of automation, that are different from simple mechanization?
9. Why is it that automation must necessarily be energy-intensive?
10. What are some of the inherent rigidities we can expect to accompany automation?
11. Describe an energy-intensive net and give at least one example of your own making.
12. See if you can think of several moral issues connected with automation that were not discussed in the text.
13. Work out, for yourself, as many consequences of the need for a guaranteed market as you can. Do you think these will result in profound social changes?

14. Describe supply, automated manufacture, and guaranteed markets as an input/output system.
15. What basically is a control position?

READINGS

Bagrit, Sir Leon. *The Age of Automation.* New York: New American Library, 1965.

The British view of automation circa 1965. Part 1 talks about automation as an extension of man, which is one of the themes of this particular text you are reading. Also, there is a good section on industrial and economic consequences. The ideas expressed are *not* as old as the publication date might indicate.

Bell, Daniel, ed. *Toward the Year 2000: Work in Progress.* Boston: Beacon Press, 1968.

It is rather fun to read an older book that has made predictions about the future, since part of that future is now. Pay particular attention to the articles on information, rationality, and free choice, and the one on communication.

Burck, Gilbert, and the Editors of *Fortune.* *The Computer Age and its Potential for Management.* New York: Harper & Row, 1965.

Another pleasant and general work, easy to read. Chapter 5, about management never being the same again, is good. The whole book is short and enjoyable. While it is over ten years old, the major concepts presented by the book have not changed very much. Some of the predictions have come true.

Diebold, John. *Beyond Automation.* New York: McGraw-Hill, 1964.

It just isn't possible to talk intelligently about automation without referring to something or other written by John Diebold. As usual, Mr. Diebold is more concerned with the future than the present, though he derives his predictions from the realities he meets now. It is a thoughtful book, well worth reading—pleasantly brief and to the point.

Scientific American, eds. *Automatic Control.* New York: Simon & Schuster, 1955.

This is an old classic. Feedback, the second industrial revolution, information as a control language, and machines and men are discussed in a series of intelligent articles from *Scientific American* magazine. This book is a good introduction to the concepts of automation. It is, in its way, timeless.

Scott, Ellis L. and Bolz, Roger W., eds. *Automation and Society.* Athens, Ga.: Center for the Study of Automation and Society, 1969.

The results of the First Annual Symposium on Automation and Society. Has a number of pioneering treatments of automation and its influence on education, organized society, business, and economics. There are more recent publications than this, but here the basic ideas are set forth.

Silberman, Charles E. *The Myths of Automation.* New York: Harper & Row, 1966.

Time to look at some of the myths of automation and debunk them. Another of the good publications of *Fortune* magazine. Pay particular attention to "The Real News About Automation," and "Is Technology Taking Over?" These articles will give you much food for thought and a good bit of material for discussion.

Simon, Herbert A. *The Shape of Automation for Men and Management.* New York: Harper & Row, 1965.

Herbert Simon is another one of the great names in the study of automation. In this little book we have a very good section on the executive as a decision maker and an excellent chapter on man-machine systems for decision making.

Wall Street Journal Staff. *Here Comes Tomorrow.* Princeton, N.J.: Dow-Jones Books, 1967.

Here we go into the future again (from the immediate past). Good articles on computers, communications, automobiles, the home, and education in an automated world. Once more it is fun to see how many of the 1967 predictions have actually come to pass and whether or not we are still going in that direction. It is an easy book to understand and is quite well written.

Weeks, Robert P., ed. *Machines and the Man: A Sourcebook on Automation.* New York: Appleton-Century-Crofts, 1961.

Another oldie but goodie. Has good sections which define automation, deal with feedback, talk about the second industrial revolution, deal with automation in the office (before some of our recent inventions). Has a good chapter (part 7) which looks to the future.

Wiener, Norbert. *The Human Use of Human Beings: Cybernetics and Society.* New York: Doubleday, 1954.

Cybernetics is the study of the relationships between man and machine. Norbert Wiener could be said to be the genius who started the whole pot boiling. You can understand and enjoy this book. It is an already admitted classic. No student of automation or computers should admit in public that he or she has not read it.

CHAPTER 11

MANAGEMENT PROBLEMS

PURPOSE OF THE CHAPTER

In this chapter we are going to turn our attention to the problems computers bring to the actual management of the enterprise. We have discussed a few of these problems earlier in the work. Here we intend to develop them more fully.

We will ask some serious questions about who needs solutions to problems and who structures the various jobs in the enterprise. The answers are not quite as obvious as they might first appear. We will worry about whether or not the computer or the management of the firm are masters of what is to be done.

TERMS AND CONCEPTS

circular updating processes
feasibility studies
divided loyalties
ultimate computer test
computer printouts
data accessibility
senior management roles
EDP report
computers as calculators
priorities of use
specialist satisfactions
defensive documentation
operational personnel
mass data problems
structuring the job
data processing committee
computer empire
total data processing system
in-house personnel
record dependency
data-use date
diagrammatic images
feedback loops
agenda construction
phase-out section
computer slaves
training schools and programs
data processing family
data-collection date
report readability
dynamic data presentation
operational alertness
report elimination

EARLY INSTALLATIONS

Before we can deal at length with several of the problems faced by management people who have to deal with computers and computer personnel, we must take a short look at the history of the early installations. The way computers arrived may explain the seat of many of the difficulties.

Originally, the computer was assumed to be a complex scientific instrument primarily for the use of engineers and scientists in the business enterprise. Installations, as we observed in earlier chapters, were small, compact, and devoted to specific scientific or engineering tasks. It was not necessary, in those days, for the manager to understand particularly what a computer did. What he had to know was whether the cost of the equipment, or its rental fees, were truly recovered by the solution to pressing engineering or scientific problems. If the engineer or the scientist could demonstrate that he or she could not solve the problem without the help of the equipment, or that the equipment would find the solution more economically than old-fashioned methods, the manager could and would usually authorize the rental or purchase. Also, this equipment would not impinge directly on any of the firm's normal record keeping and accounting functions. The computer was viewed as a greatly sophisticated version of the ordinary calculator.

It turned out, however, that the computer had more actual power than even the engineers had suspected. Once the programs for the system were well developed the solutions came very quickly. This left the computer with considerable idle time.

An idle computer, as a small child's idle hands, doth the devil's mischief make. Some engineers, familiar with business problems, talked accountants into letting them, the engineers, write simple payroll programs or inventory programs. The engineering and scientific people, by so doing, were able to demonstrate that a week-long problem could be handled in the hours from 1:00 P.M. to 5:00 P.M. on a Friday. What is more, it could be demonstrated that the debugged payroll program had a greater accuracy than payroll clerks. It did not take managers too long to decide the computer had broader uses for the business enterprise. But—and this is the important element—the management people did not know very much about computers. As a result, they were inclined to leave the programming function in the hands of the scientists or the engineers even though these people, skilled though they were in their own areas, could not be said to be at all expert in business matters. In fact, the engineering and science people had a tendency to mentally downgrade the office and record keeping functions as trivial. By the time installations had grown to moderate size and had taken over the record keeping and accounting functions of many businesses, it was too late to change the format. The company was committed to computers. To stop and restructure the computer system and its personnel would be too expensive and too risky. The fat was in the fire.

Computer slaves

The deadly attitude grew—clerks and accountants were to be the computer's slaves. That is, they were expected by the computer people to provide the basic information for the system. The clerks and accountants could be required to wade through computer output, make corrections and additions. The data base was king, the scientific people too superior by nature to be bothered with such editing trivia. The engineers and scientists, a mathematical breed, could demand that the clerks and accountants fit their work to match the needs of the computer. Of course, as you can see, this is the classic case of the wagon attempting to pull the horse. A well-established computer system would be required to provide the operating information to the clerks and the accountants as one of its primary functions. True, a circular updating process would have to exist, but tending the data base is not the primary function of operating business personnel.

THE BUSINESS COMPUTER

In due course the business computer arrived on the scene. First management dilemma: Should one set up two entirely different computer centers, one business and one scientific? No, this did not seem, at the time, to make good management sense. Better to add the computers for business to the already ongoing computer center, toss in a few business programs and all would be well. But, of course, it wasn't! The heads of the computer installations were principally mathematicians or scientists. They did not take kindly to the detailed record keeping work of the business enterprise. Nor did they grant high status to those who were not fully trained in the mathematical arts. No serious attempt was made to view the business enterprise as an operating organism—this in spite of many articles at the time about "total data processing systems." The addition of trained business programmers to the installation held off crises from time to time, but did not solve the basic administrative problem. Was the computer center the heart of the business enterprise or not? If so, then the primary work of the computer center was to keep the ongoing business activity well grounded in fact and record. If not, then scientific endeavors were primary. The problem was not, in those early days, dealt with either openly or honestly. The tendency was to let matters drift. Then came the usual crisis. The solution was to call in outside computer and business experts. These good folk would redesign the system and move on. But while it is relatively easy to design a system from the outside, it is not easy to redesign the attitudes of people from the outside. A good system might possibly fall into bad hands—again, additional crises of various kinds would occur. The outside consultants would come and go, but the problems had a tendency to go on forever.

Let us look at the problems, so far, from the manager's point of view:

1. Computer installations in their early form were primarily problem oriented and scientifically oriented.
2. Early computer personnel, while well-trained scientists, were not experts in business.
3. Early business computers were added to previously established scientific installations and were not very effective in dealing with broad business management problems.
4. Early business programming personnel were added into the scientifically oriented computer centers but were not generally accorded much status.
5. No computer systems were established as a general part of the business enterprise.

Certain further developments were inevitable. The business problems presented at the computer center for solution generally were given lower priorities than the scientific problems. It is the nature of people to regard the areas of their own expertise as more important than any other. This meant many business activities were expensively delayed.

When a professional business manager was put in charge of an entire computer installation, he or she found it difficult to communicate effectively with people who had primarily a scientific attitude. And, of course, if the scientifically oriented computer center manager remained, he or she might not be conversant with business problems, programs, or programmers. And again, the scientist did not think such problems worthy of very serious attention.

FEASIBILITY STUDIES

Managers of companies that did not yet have computers did take note of the difficulties mentioned above. And they resolved to avoid them if possible. Part of the solution was to do an in-depth feasibility study of the enterprise before buying or renting a computer and installing computer personnel. Did the company really need a computer? What kind of computer would best serve the company's interests? What would be the cost effectiveness of such an installation? How long would it take to recover the investment? What would be the future of such an installation? Would it have to expand rapidly? What would be the orderly procedures for expansion? Should the system begin small and grow large gradually, or should an attempt be made to create an entire management information system at the outset?

Most early feasibility studies were done by outside consulting firms that had the wit and the wisdom to hire both mathematical computer people and properly trained accountants and office managers. In the main, the results were better than casual growth or casual installation. But a good and thorough feasibility study could take from six to eighteen months. A number of the company's people had to be sent to special schools to be trained. Contracts had to be signed, early on, for the computer so that it could arrive at just about the right time to take advantage of the completed training of the personnel.

Of course, as businesses grew more experienced with computers, the need for outside consultants declined. Also, universities and colleges were training the business graduates in the gentle art of computing. Companies could do their own in-house studies before moving into the computer installation phase. Sometimes the results were better than could be expected—self-interest is a heavier taskmaster than outside interest. And admittedly, sometimes full-scale disasters came rolling along when the in-house personnel were really not up to the job, or when their knowledge of computers was severely limited. This used to be called the "ignorance is blisters" syndrome.

Managers now had new problems to ponder:

1. What is the cost of an outside feasibility study? Does the firm's position warrant such an expense?
2. Where are efficient and intelligent business computer personnel? Can they be hired and integrated successfully into company operations?
3. Should the company set up training programs for its own personnel? Which in-house personnel are best fitted for the training programs? What is the cost of such training?
4. What should be done with personnel replaced by the computer and the computer people? Retraining? Early retirement?
5. What retraining should take place for those people not directly involved with the computer installation itself, but whose work will be seriously affected by the new computer techniques, programs, and printouts? What is the cost of this program as compared to the benefits to be gained in both the short-run and the long-run?

Probably the most difficult problem that managers faced in the earlier computer days was in trying to determine whether short-run losses (often very major) in the business of installing computers and computer personnel would, in fact, bring about long-term gains. This, by its very nature, is not the kind of problem one can face with ease and confidence. Still, the problem had to be faced and some kind of realistic solution had to be worked out. Primary to the business is its future competitive position. It must know how well it can face the future in direct confrontation with other business firms which have gone ahead with their computer installations and made them work successfully.

THE SPECIALIST

Three decades of experience with computers has presented the world with the computer specialist. This, in itself, is probably a good thing. But the difficulty lies in language. The computer specialist does not speak ordinary English. And while there may be good and sufficient reason for much of the complex vocabulary, it sometimes seems the main task of the specialist's language is to keep the nonexpert confused and at bay.

Over the decade, managers have frequently—in conferences, in speeches, and in articles—complained of an inability to bring the computer specialist to the task of communicating successfully with the hosts of ordinary folk who work in the businesses they run. The result has been fear, confusion, and expensive errors that ought not to have been made in the first place.

The specialist also takes a somewhat more scientific world view than a sociological world view. This is not to say sociology is not scientific, but to infer that people problems are often the most serious concern of sociology and also the most serious concern of businesses. And as we all know, people are the more resistant of all natural forces to proper quantification. People tend to do what people do, whether or no this causes problems for those who would study them. The very detachment required for scientific study is often the heart of the problem in dealing with people. Concern and intimacy may get results in the business enterprise, but they are dangerous activities from the scientific point of view. Specialists, scientifically trained as they are, seek satisfaction in logic and in statistics. To them a problem is often solved when it is identified and certain logical constructs are then sent into play. But the problem which has its own psychological side may resist such straightforward logic. It may continue because the people involved do not have the scientific or world view but a deeply personal and ego view. Most managers know this both from intuition and from experience. Many very well-trained scientific people do not. In fact, they often took the route of scientific training to avoid the kind of incommensurables associated with people. Was it not Dr. Einstein who pointed out, with regard to scientific work, that God was subtle but never mean. Well, people can often be just plain mean. Some-

The computer specialist

times they intend to be, more often they don't. But this makes management problems more complex than we would have them if we could reduce them to simple scientific generalities.

The specialist carries another dimension which can cause the resident manager some problems. Specialists usually are dedicated in two directions. That is, they are members of a scientific association or community of one kind or another to which they may feel they owe first loyalty. Their second loyalty may lie with the organization for which they work. This can mean that, in a choice situation between the business firm and the scientific discipline, the specialist may side with the discipline. Now then, disciplines are general and business firms are specific. That is, there is no written guarantee that a general scientific solution fits a particular business and its operations to the degree the application will bring about a profit or even survival. This complex of loyalties makes the specialist a difficult person to deal with from the point of view of the resident manager. And this difficulty exists whether the specialist is a visiting outside expert or an inhouse scientific employee.

THE DATA PROCESSING FAMILY

It used to be said that certain types of relatives should never be invited to parties since they would never come alone. They would bring all their family members with them. The old saying used to be, "To invite George to dinner is to hold a banquet for his relatives." In a way, precisely the same thing could be said about the senior computer specialist or manager—he or she does not come to the business firm alone but brings a host of near relatives—the computer librarian, two or three different types of programmers, the systems analysts, the terminal and console operators, assistant managers, design programmers, and so on.

The manager faces the problem of a productive and growing family within a family. The computer installation and its staff have exactly the same tendency to grow as does the firm overall. Or it may often grow at the expense of other and perhaps equally necessary groups in the enterprise. The data processing center has a manager, after all, who faces the same pressures to get the job done with more and more personnel as does any other manager. Moreover, since the ordinary manager may not be conversant with all of the staff needs of the installation head, he or she finds decision making with regard to staff very difficult. This is not a new problem to business managers, but it is backed by an enchantment with unusual equipment and a hope for the future which may not be warranted. It takes a number of years before new specialties have been around an organization long enough so that the manager may have at least a reasonable working knowledge of the kind of organization needed, the kind of people required, and the kinds of problems which have to be solved. Ordinary office staffs have been with business firms for many, many decades. Accountants and controllers, too, are familiar folk to the experienced manager. But in the short three decades in which computers have grown from babyhood to monsterhood, the managers barely have had time to probe the language and to deal with the immediate and pressing problems. A few more decades will pass before all managers have lived with computers long enough to feel confident in overruling installation managers about their needs on the basis of both intuition and knowledge. We are not there yet.

So the data processing family may continue to grow. It also will, as families do, tend to branch out into a number of different types of certificates of competency and specialty. Each of the several disciplines within the field can grow so exotic and deep that the operating manager may feel no chance at all to probe and understand without an equivalent number of long years of professional training.

RECORD DEPENDENCY

Record dependency is a rather rare form of disease uncommon to former centuries of man. Or more realistically, record dependency used to be associated primarily with military operations. An army did not move on its stomach, it moved on its paperwork. The efficient computer center is a disease carrier—it can build in managers of all types a virulent need for defensive documentation. Defensive documentation is the gentle art of never making a decision without large quantities of facts and paper to support it.

Record dependency is the broader of the two terms. Defensive documentation has to do with decisions being made, not whether they will be made. But record dependency means that often managers will not consider it necessary to make a decision because the reports they have received are inadequate.

The computer encourages both record dependency and defensive documentation. If it is at all possible to get "facts," no matter how wrong those facts may be, many managers will avoid the use of experience and intuition—which are very difficult to document and which are subject to varied interpretations. The final result may be a peculiar form of inertia, which we more commonly associate with bureaucracy, but which we cannot afford to associate with business qua business. Because the computer has been instrumental in manufacturing paperwork at the greatest rate in the history of man, we can expect the continued spread of this disease. The results may be formalisms instead of thought, and inertia instead of action. Both can be fatal to the ongoing business enterprise.

We have considered a few of the problems facing the manager since the advent of the computer and its arrival on the business scene. Let us now turn our attention to several tests which the manager can apply to determine once and for all whether the computer installation in the organization is performing as it should.

THE ULTIMATE TEST

There is one simple but genuine test of success which can be applied to the computer and its installation to see whether things are going as they should. Is the date, when data must be gathered before decisions are made, moving closer to the day when the decision is made, or in the opposite direction? If movement is in the opposite direction, something is seriously wrong with the operaton of the computer center. The whole point of the computer is that it can work rapidly and efficiently. If data must be gathered at ever earlier dates to satisfy the paper-handling needs of the computer center, it is an abject failure. Figure 11–1 illustrates the grim picture.

The problem, in such an instance, lies with the paper management program of the center itself. This is, or at least ought to be, an internal matter. It is a crystal indication of poor computer center management. A senior manager, in such an instance, is fully justified in making serious inquiries into the skills of the computer center manager. It will not do for the data processing manager to attempt to blame personnel or equipment within the computer center—the

FIGURE 11–1. The fleeing data collection date

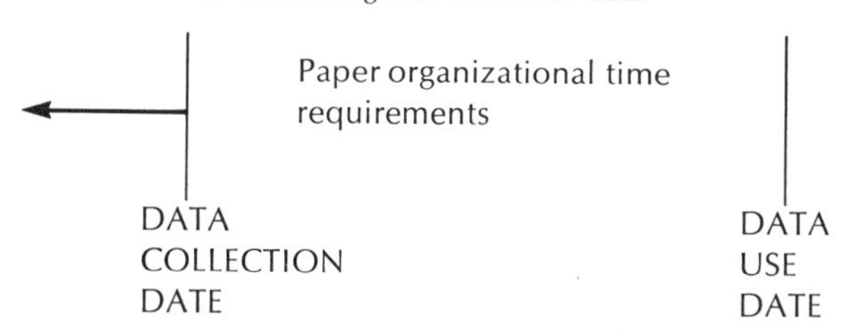

proper selection of both is within his or her jurisdiction. If higher management has ignored requests for better personnel, training programs, or equipment, the data processing manager has some reason to place the blame on higher levels. But if the organization has done the best it could with requests of this nature, then the data processing manager must carry the full responsibility for the failure.

Equally, then, if the data collection date is compressing toward the date when the data for decisions is actually used, the senior manager can feel confident that the external signs from the computer center indicate excellent internal management.

That happy condition is shown diagrammatically in Figure 11–2.

FIGURE 11–2. Compressing data collection date

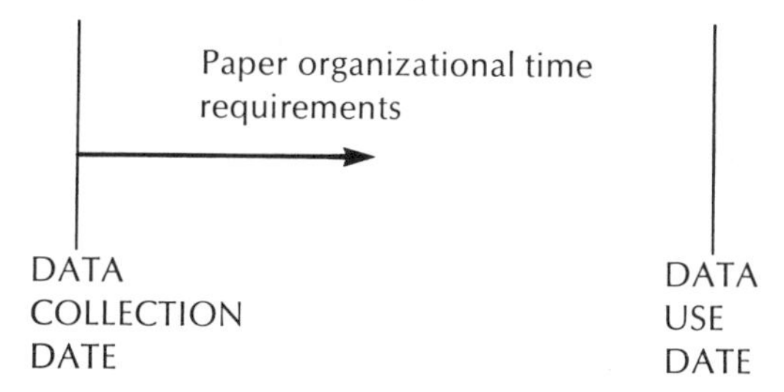

The logic, from the point of view of higher management, is impeccable. The whole rationale for computer installations lies with efficiency and speed and careful planning. Excuses will not erase failures. Special language cannot cover incompetency. Either the computer fulfills the conditions on which it was rented or purchased, or it does not. If it does, this is clearly success. If it does not, this is clearly failure.

Naturally, if the computer center manager has previously advised higher management that equipment is inadequate, or that training programs are derelict and need improvements or that proper incumbents simply cannot be acquired, that is a horse from a different rainbow. Higher management should have been working with the data processing manager to cure these ills, else all the money previously expended has been wasted. In this latter situation, blame must be shared, solutions worked out, and money expended. Mutual recriminations will hardly solve the problem.

OPERATIONAL PERSONNEL SERVING THE DATA BASE

Another very important indication that all is not well in the data processing center is the typical situation where the operational personnel of the enterprise are in a state of abject slavery relative to the computer. That is, we know something is seriously wrong if operating personnel, who ought to be about the operational business of the enterprise, are spending enormous amounts of time decoding information requests from the computer center, editing computer outputs to bring them to some semblance of accuracy, waiting too long for information they need for making decisions, and throwing away much computer output which they judge to be useless. All of these activities indicate a computer center busy serving its own needs and its own ends and ignoring the pressing business of the enterprise itself. Salesmen are supposed to sell, not fill out enormous reports. Clerks are supposed to help customers, not prepare data sheets for the computer center. In fact, another of the basic premises of the computer center is that it will provide just this information to operating personnel automatically and with little expenditure of their own time. A mechanized or automated activity is hardly either, if it requires increasing amounts of personnel time and effort.

So, here again, management has a set of very simple tests it can apply to the question of the effectiveness of the data processing center. There is nothing new here—all of these tests have been applied throughout recorded history to determine whether management junior personnel are performing well. The mysteries of the computer operation and the exotic computer terminology and language should not deter the higher management from the task of analysis and measurement of effectiveness.

REPORT READABILITY

If the reports produced by the computer center for use by the company's operating personnel are not immediately clear and readable, the computer center is failing in one of its major tasks—the communication of accurate information.

Anyone who has read a computer printout of late knows that something else is actually occurring in the workaday world. In fact, some titles and column headings in computer reports are so exotic that the readers actually must refer to a decoding handbook to determine what the titles over the columns really mean. Computer personnel claim this is due to certain inherent limitations in the machinery with which they work. But—and this is important—such an excuse is patent nonsense and should be treated as such. Men and women should not permit themselves to become slaves to a machine. If the machine cannot produce readable reports, junk it. If the programmers cannot program readable headlines, retrain them or junk them, too.

THE MASS DATA PROBLEM

Since the computer is both a logic and an arithmetic machine, there is no reason for great masses of paper printout from the computer. The computer is at least as capable of summary and reduction as is any human being in the business. There ought to be, then, no excuse for 30 or 40 pages of computer printout dumped on the desk of a morning of any manager in the enterprise. It is not this kind of information which is useful for judgment. Computers can diagram. Computers can calculate. Computers can total and summarize. The summary is what management needs, not the great and tedious detail.

So, once again, if the computer center can only produce documents in volume and in great columns and rows, something is wrong with either the programs, the personnel, the manager, or all three.

In part, it is all a matter of the proper attitude and the proper psychology of higher management. The instant an unreadable report of the kind we have been describing arrives on a desk for scrutiny, it should be sent back to the center unless it serves its purpose easily and quickly. Certainly no managers would permit one of their own staff to hand in such a report written out on a typewriter. The top manager would immediately send it back with a few unprintable comments on the margin of the document. Why, then, this strange surrender to the computer and its slavish printers?

A small story may illustrate the problem. Once upon a time there was a testy little Scot who was clearly losing an argument with an Irish friend. As he realized he was indeed losing, the old Scot seized a book, pointed to a supporting point of view in the document, and screamed at his friend, "Why, mon, would ye deny print?" That was supposed to settle the debate once and for all, for there is a magic in the printed word inherited from ancient Egypt. If it is written, they said, so it is true. Well, it may be written but it doesn't necessarily have to be true. Our own daily experience with newspapers proves that. But there is, for many people, something magical and assuring about computer printouts. They look so severe, so formal, so reliable, so impressive. It is hard to deny print. The typewriter, on the other hand? Not so! We all know somebody had to sit down and whip out the message one letter at a time, skilled or otherwise. A letter can be de-

"IF IT COMES OUT OF THE COMPUTER, IT MUST BE TRUE!"

nied its content. Because of electronics and the aura of magic, it seems computer printout cannot. The timidity is in the head of the manager concerned, not in the data on the paper.

More important, it is possible these days to forgo computer printouts entirely by producing appropriate diagrammatic images on cathode ray tubes for terminals in the manager's office. If the manager prefers a hard copy of this material, it can be arranged if the terminal also has printing facilities. Why then should the manager be required to review the data in detail and attempt a painful summation? He or she shouldn't, and that is the major point.

In the near future it might also be a good technique to produce dynamic images on the cathode ray tube. It just happens to be a physiological fact that the right half of the brain is good at analysis and the left-hand side, the speech center, is not. Managers actually might get a clearer message out of some kind of active and geometric presentation on the cathode tube. Cashflow in the enterprise, for example, might best be shown as an ever narrowing or broadening visual river. The profit picture could be shown dynamically on the screen as a moving line traveling through the past to the present. Out of all this the manager might get clearer images of just what is happening in the organization. And naturally, the computer can be asked to produce trend lines into the future to show precisely what a given action might do to the enterprise, all other things being equal. Other things are never equal, of course, but a fair idea of what might happen is better than no idea at all.

DATA ACCESSIBILITY

Another test of the effectiveness of a computer center from the point of view of the general manager is whether the data asked for is received in time in the proper format. These two things, time and format, go very much together. Can the manager ask a few simple questions and expect answers in immediate real-time? Is the data base of the center sufficient to provide the full information requested? If so, the installation would seem to be an adequate one. If not, from the general management point of view, something certainly needs to be done.

There are many computer installations in the country wherein requests for data are delayed longer than they were prior to the installation of the computer. This is a certain sign something has gone wrong with data center planning and management. The excuse of increased complexity will not do. Computers are supposed to be able to deal effectively with complexity. The problem is not in the machine but in the programs and the administration of the center. The general manager who cannot get the needed information is justified in investigating the matter and insisting upon appropriate reform. That not coming, he or she is entitled to seek out new and better personnel for the data center itself.

WHO DEMANDS SOLUTION?

Another interesting little test the general manager can apply, sans knowledge of the detail of computer operations, is the question: Who demands problem solution? Is it the operations management staff or the computer programmers and management staff? Often we find in some installations the demands for solution to problems are coming from the center itself, and the problems demanding solution are related not to the overall operation of the business but to those problems peculiar to the computer center. Again, we can see that this is not appropriate if the computer and the computer personnel are genuinely at the service of the organization and not the other way around. The primary attention of any well-run data center should be focused on those problems called to its attention by the line management. It is they who must act, and it is their action which will most often determine the difference between profit and loss.

Two things can be done. The general manager can make inquiries into the point of origin of problems requiring solution. The results can be put in some diagrammatic form that will clearly permit some kind of statistical comparison to be made. The weight of the requests should be on the operational side. And the manager can inquire into how many of the solutions requested from the center itself are tied to requests for solutions from operations. In most cases, there ought to be a clear and compelling link. It is by these simple tests we can dig out whether the problems taking up the time of operational personnel are clearly related to operations. If this is not the case, the computer center needs an overhaul of one kind or another.

WHO STRUCTURES THE JOB?

In traditional management situations, jobs are defined by some formal process. Usually, a description of the job is prepared by operational management. That done, suitable wage rates are established and suitable people are employed. This is how things ought to be. But there are subtle forces at work when one has let the computer into the nest. The demands from the computer center for information, and the type of printouts sent to different operational personnel by the center, have a tendency , on their own, to define the job that is to be done. This is not a planned or deliberate act. But it is the result of certain types of acts in which nearly all computer centers indulge. One must be wary. Very often the computer center claims not to be able to store, create, or manipulate data in the fashion requested by operational people. The net result is that the operations person needing the information tends to tailor the job to fit the kind of information which it is claimed is available. There is a sort of fatal feedback loop going on here, which can take a firm a long way from its original purposes and a fair distance from reality. It is particularly dangerous because it gives the illusion that genuinely important work is being done and that this work is in some vague way of importance to the firm's success.

Reality means service to customers. Reality means products that consumers want and will buy. Reality means a daily operational alertness to the end goals of the business. If the computer center's requests for information and demands for paperwork, to bolster its data base or make its own problems paramount, occur in great number and detract operational personnel from their more proper concerns, we have a dangerous situation which ought to be stopped the minute operational management is alerted to the problem. The difficulty lies in the last sentence. How can management become alert to this type of problem when by nature and by definition it is a subtle one. There is only one way this can be done. All operational personnel can be asked to keep logs on their own activities. Such logs could be divided into simple categories (the simpler the better), including "duties relative to customers," "duties relative to operational management," "duties relative to computer input or output or other requests," and so on. Again, if the proportions are not in line, operational management can interfere. Do we have any guidelines to follow? Yes, oddly enough we can use the 80/20 rule created by computer people themselves. If more than 20 percent of any operational person's time is spent in intimate communication with the computer center, management may assume it has a problem. This is, of course, merely a rule of thumb. But in lieu of any other better judgmental scale, it will have to do to help management watchdog the business. It may turn out that the firm is primarily one dealing with scientific problems. This being the case, management would know the proportions might be quite different. So let us apply the test as just what it is—a general indicator for ordinary businesses.

We must go one step further. Is the intimate contact made necessary by the nature of the operational job? That is, is it the function of the operational employee to make inquiries of the computer center and relay information to customers and others? The 80/20 rule merely calls attention to the problem. An analysis must follow to determine whether contact above the 20 percent level is justified by the nature of the job. Too, we would want to ask questions about the direction of the flow of the information. Is it from the center to the operational individual, or the other way around? This also may point up special problems. Again, the nature of the job should determine the direction and frequency of information flow. It is largely a traffic analysis problem, not much different from the types of analysis used by city governments to determine whether street lights are required at particular locations.

THE SERVANT

All through recorded history there has existed a peculiar and particular in-house battle between line personnel (those who are directly and legally responsible for action) and staff personnel (those who advise and suggest and study and investigate *for* line personnel). This same natural conflict exists in the matter of the full-scale operating computer center. Is it line or is it staff? Let us resolve that issue at once—it is staff. To be sure, the computer center is a very vital staff function—one without which the enterprise might well founder—but it is staff nonetheless. This means computer personnel are in the role of assistant, aide, or servant to the general good of those line personnel in charge of the successful operation of the enterprise. It is not a question of skill, training, or talent—it is a question of primary function. It is a question of understanding, dedication, and attitude. But we would be remiss if we did not notice that a corporation presidential assistant carries the aura of the office he or she advises. It is a

"I DON'T WORK FOR YOU, YOU ARE SUPPOSED TO HELP ME GET THE JOB DONE!"

foolish individual indeed who does not recognize that aides form hierarchies and that top aides are intimately in contact with line personnel. This is unfortunate since what merely constitutes advice can be construed to be tantamount to an order. And, of course, the higher in the hierarchy the data processing manager, and the more intimate the contact such a person has with the line officers of the corporation, the more wallop that advice and suggestions from that quarter are going to pack. It is difficult under such a circumstance for middle or lower line management to complain and to point out flaws in the function of the data center. But this they must certainly do.

One excellent method for avoiding unwarranted timidity is to have in clear perspective the functions and purpose of the enterprise. When these are being undermined, no matter how inadvertently, there is a certain moral strength in a complaint, no matter what level its origin. It is incumbent, then, upon every member of operating personnel to be certain of his or her duties and of the relationship of these duties to the welfare and purposes of the organization. Such an analysis is beneficial in its own right, of course, but it is also protection against a series of small steps which, carelessly followed, could lead to disaster.

One must never forget that a computer and all its attendant personal are servants of those who must make judgments, contact the public, solve business problems, and lead the business to profit and survival.

THE DATA PROCESSING COMMITTEE

Quite frequently businesses have established, within the organization, a data processing committee. Usually, this committee is made up of people in the middle management area who will have direct concerns about the form and success of the data processing effort. While a great deal of lip service has been paid to having senior management representatives on the data processing committees, this has seldom effectively happened. Or more often, a senior executive sits in on the committee when the original leasing or purchase of equipment is decided (because millions of dollars are at stake) but wanders off to "more serious concerns" as soon as the investment issue is settled.

A data processing committee made up of middle managers can deal effectively with matters of cross-communication and the elimination of problem areas in the business. But such a committee can seldom make a decision of major consequence and then follow through on it within any short time frame. What normally happens is that a representative (or two) of that committee must prepare lengthy and detailed reports and then attempt to persuade top management to join in on the decision.

More often than it ought to occur, the data center manager becomes the chairman or chairwoman of the committee. This happens because the data center manager is very well acquainted with matters technical and can present a number of unassailable arguments for her or his own point of view to the committee. We are not saying that this is some kind of malicious act. The data processing manager has specific problems to solve and, from the computer center point of view, these problems are very real and very important. Outsiders find it difficult to refute arguments couched in a special language and dealing with apparently serious matters that they know they do not understand.

How, then, should data processing committees be constructed? Certainly, at least one top management representative, with the actual power to act, should be present at every meeting. If the meeting is properly structured, that is, if the important matters requiring top management decision are discussed at the early part of the meeting, and the lower level in-house problems delayed until later in the meeting, the top management representative could leave as soon as issues of concern to top management had been dealt with. Oddly enough, a carefully constructed agenda which does not waste executive time is the one way to maintain the top executive interest in matters of importance. What usually drives top management away is a consistent attempt to solve a number of low-level problems while occupying high-salaried administrative time.

A sophisticated way to handle the appropriate agenda construction would be to have at least one short preliminary meeting with the top management representative before any full meeting of the data processing committee. At that time the executive in question could review the agenda quickly with the committee chairman or chairwoman to determine whether attendance is actually required and, specifically, what is the nature of the decision problem to be dealt with. Also, at this time, such important facts as are at hand should be given to the executive in summary form. The better informed the top manager is about the problem before a meeting, the more effective he or she is likely to be in making the decision during the meeting itself. Too often the committee discussions do not lend themselves to immediate decision and a report is required for later thought.

To keep a top executive coming to meetings is not as difficult as it might sound. Actually, what one needs to do is to very carefully work out the implications for the overall business of any major decision which might come up. And if one or two alternate decision paths are worked out, and their consequences, so much the better.

What has been suggested here is merely good management, regardless of the nature of the meeting. This is somewhat more acutely needed in dealing with data processing committees, because data processing managers can tend to get themselves isolated from the major concerns of the enterprise. The data processing center has its siren call for attention, and it is easy to succumb to what is immediate, local, and domestic.

THE MANAGEMENT EDP REPORT

In many businesses the data processing manager is required from time to time to present to higher management a summary of the month's or year's activities. This constitutes what is called "the management EDP report." Again, the primary problem faced by top managers is that the report is often couched in language which is incomprehensible to anyone who has not been trained in the computer field. There is no rational excuse for this. Any competent data processing manager should be able to write a general EDP report in such a way that it could be understood by any ordinary management person.

What are the major items which should appear in an effective EDP report? Naturally, the cost of the operation itself is of importance. How many dollars are spent for what in the computer center? How many dollars of costs are actually assignable to other departments in the enterprise requesting service? What are the communication costs between the center and the people using the information? What are the equipment depreciation and rental schedules? But though these costs are usually attainable, and hence make up the large body of such a report, they are not the most important elements.

The important issue is the matter of genuine service to operational personnel. How is what is being done now better than what has been done in the past? What are the dollar and cent savings to the particular current form of EDP record keeping and communicating? Is there a cheaper method of handling the problem? Are there areas of service which are critically needed and which have been overlooked? Is there general satisfaction with the operation of the computer center, not by those who run it but by those who use it?

What areas of difficulty in the business could be handled or helped by the rigorous application of computer solutions? Now here it should be clear the ideas and the problems cannot originate in the computer center itself—the view is too narrow. What is needed is the development of this part of the EDP management report in close communication (before the fact of the report) with other departmental or area managers of the enterprise. This "potential development" section of any EDP management report should point clear arrows to possible future applications that will enhance either the economic or the competitive position of the enterprise.

A good EDP report also should contain a "phase out section." A phase out section is nothing more or less than an honest evaluation of the parts of the computer operation which were never, or are no longer, of valuable economic or management service to the enterprise. This may be the most difficult section of all for the EDP manager to deal with, because this section requires a genuine recommendation to reduce areas of computer control where they have not faithfully served the primary purposes of the organization. Again, the wise EDP manager would not confine such a report to the knowledge gleaned from inside the computer center, but would rather, or should rather, depend heavily on reports and analyses from other departmental managers in the business. Nothing so pleases an outside manager as the recognition of the problems he or she has faced. Nothing can be so effective as a realistic appraisal of the failure of a service section of the enterprise to an operational area. This is the way credibility for the future is built. This is the one area where a computer center staff can prove the goal of service is really that. This is often an area where money can be saved very quickly. Then, when future applications are developed, the skillful evaluation and savings of the past can be pointed out and leaned upon to bring true validity to arguments given for future expansion.

ELIMINATING SCHEDULED REPORTS

A scheduled report is, for our purposes, a computer report which has a mailing list, which was established some time ago, and which is sent to interested managers or other personnel on a regular basis.

How do we know whether the reports are of value? How do we know if the reports are still required? How do we know if the cost of preparing the reports is recovered by improved performance on the part of those who receive or claim they ought to receive the report? There is a very simple and stunning solution to this problem. Prepare the weekly or monthly (or whatever normal time-span it occupies) report. *But do not send out the report copies.* Hold the reports and await angry calls, heated responses, gentle inquiries. In this way one can quickly tell whether the report is in fact important. Of course, when such calls come in, the report should be quickly sent to the calling individual. But one suspects many calls will never come. Many managers who earlier requested the information may no longer need it. Managers who only feel secure if they collect reports (but who seldom if ever actually read them) may not notice the absence of something they truly don't need. Here lies the truth and here lies the economic revelation.

How can something of this nature occur? Well, in most instances a particular report is requested by one department or one manager, or is even invented inside the computer center itself. Each of us has an idea about what it is we need and want to operate. Sometimes the ideas are not economically justifiable. A series of steps happen which themselves tell the story:

1. Manager A calls in and says certain types of information are required to make decisions—a report ought to be prepared.
2. The computer center studies the question and determines that it can, in fact, prepare such a report.
3. It is determined, however, several managers should receive the report to make its assembly economically justifiable. So other managers in the enterprise are queried as to the value of such a report.
4. Several managers of the organization feel the report might be of genuine value to them and are willing to add their names to requests.
5. A few managers (or maybe many) don't want to indicate ignorance of the area the report covers, or believe at some future time they might find such information valuable, or don't want to admit they really don't need that kind of information (they might look careless or inattentive or slothful). All these may automatically respond in the affirmative when queried about whether or not such a report would be valuable.
6. A broad mailing list for the report is established. The format of the report is settled. The schedule for report publication is made. The computer center is committed to a regular activity.
7. The reports are sent out. From time to time further inquiries will

broaden the mailing list. Eventually, the report may occupy a good deal of computer center time.

8. Many of the operational needs of the business move along and change but the report, an established procedural activity, continues.

For reasons basic to human nature, a simple request of managers about the value of a report does not truly reveal whether the report is useful or not. The certain way is to skip the mailing of the report and tally the result. Here we have what is called hard behavioral evidence. If the report is really used and truly needed, you may rest assured the reaction will be a short time in coming.

It is, naturally, a good deal harder, in lengthy and formal reports, to determine which *parts* are genuinely needed and which parts of the report could wisely be eliminated. Once the usefulness of the report as a whole has been determined, it might be wise to meet with individual managers to determine just *which part* of the report was missed—which part was essential to operational performance. Such an effort could reduce the size of the report very effectively, lessen the cost of its preparation, and increase the value of service for dollars spent. Requests for analysis of a report through the mails are seldom as effective as a personal interview with the manager. Particularly, one ought to take the opportunity to explain that the value of the report qua report is under examination. This may set the right attitude for a realistic evaluation.

Since the preparation and dissemination of reports can become habitual whether or not they are truly needed, the next logical step is to habituate the examination system that determines whether the reports are serving a purpose and that determines whether they are economically worthwhile. Habit can be very efficient if it is properly controlled.

BREAKING UP THE EMPIRE

The third generation of computers were best suited to large-scale centralized operation, as we have noted earlier in this text. The fourth-generation computers need not necessarily be. So, incumbent data processing managers should very soon be about the business of determining whether or not parts of the centralized empire should be distributed to more effective locations. We have discussed this somewhat at length when we considered distributed data processing and the problems inherent in the centralization or distribution of data bases. We come back to the issue here from the management point of view. Which kind of center is most effective in serving the needs of the business? Which kind of operation is more effective economically speaking? Who is best equipped to make the final judgments about centralized data processing versus distributed data processing?

At the outset we are safe in saying that the computer center manager is very much needed in any investigative activity which is to determine the value of the computer center to the business as a whole. And it is certainly in a company data processing committee, attended by at least one high management representative, where such examinations should center. Here and here only can the nature of the business be matched against the implications of the type of computing equipment selected. Only here can the broad policy decisions of the company be made which will guide years of future effort and which will involve the expenditure of considerable sums of money over time. All the expertise of the computer personnel should come to bear on this problem, along with all the known needs of the business from the operational management point of view.

At first glance these decisions may seem frightfully important—that is because they are just that. Still, dealing with just these kinds of problems is what management is all about. Looking to the future and making decisions which will have major impact on future success and future failure is exactly what management as an activity is

"IT IS TIME TO STEP DOWN"

paid for. There is no escaping the need for judgment. And if it comes to the centralized data processing manager that he or she must disassemble the computer center to best serve the needs of the business, so be it. The manager must get on with the job since the survival of the enterprise as a whole is intimately tied up to the survival of any element. A beautiful centralized computer center in a failing enterprise is not unlike riding an UP escalator on the *Titanic*. The illusion of progress is a short-lived one if all sinks.

No effective computer center should ever be torn apart on the grounds of pure speculation, however. If distributed data processing is to be used, it should be used carefully and piecemeal, since it is the nature of distributed data processing that this kind of careful approach can be taken.

IMPLICATIONS

Under each of our major headings in this chapter we have dealt with some of the more specific implications of the computer for each of the management areas of concern. Now, let us turn to somewhat broader considerations.

In earlier days, managers were supposed to be the people who pulled together men, machines, money, and methods to reach a specific industrial goal. This is still a truism, although one that is patently simpleminded. The computer may well reduce the men (or women) employed in particular parts of the enterprise. The machines may become more and more self-directing, or may be linked into centralized computer nets which direct them. The amount of money spent in the processes of manufacture may be less and less on labor and more on capital equipment, including computers. The methods may change to match the new equipment available.

The primary effect of computers on management, initially, was a certain serious loss of control over the affairs of the enterprise. With the advent of more experience with computers, and the development of distributed data processing, there is a good chance managers may take control of the enterprise once more.

It was said, early in the computer years, that middle managers would begin to disappear. The wilder theorists supposed an ultimate enterprise run by a very few men or women at the top and a great mass of workers below, with few if any intervening middle managers or supervisors. What actually happened, of course, was the exact reverse. The term *middle management* has been applied to more and more "experts" in the ranks of the corporate structure. Decision making has been more and more delegated from the top to the middle of the business structure. Partly this has been due to the development of the technostructure (a firm that is dedicated to technology) and partly due to the growth of the enterprise itself—to a point where a few individuals at the top simply could not keep proper track of all of the events. Oddly enough, the computer, properly used, should be able to permit the control of the few over the many. But as we said, it has not.

With the computer becoming more and more the "simple" tool and less and less the "exotic" giant, we should expect managers to tolerate less interference with their several tasks. This will mean the lines of communication will shorten and straighten with concomitant assignments of responsibility along that line.

Computers have not been properly used to do what they do best—calculate and summarize. Managers originally expected to receive more pertinent data. What they have received is more data, period! In fact, they have been almost buried in statistics. Whether this sea of information has made it possible for managers to decide in any improved way is certainly debatable.

But in spite of this, there have been a few broad benefits. The information has not been so much centralized as dispersed. That is, the information is gathered throughout the enterprise and is then dispersed to all of the managers at all of the different levels to the end that they will know almost as much as the senior managers and then can make decisions accordingly. Where this dispersal pattern has been faithfully followed, the enterprise has generally prospered and been more effective. Here, then, is one of the major implications of the computer for management—an information net of sufficient thoroughness that decisions at *any level* can be based on facts, and that the facts upon which judgment will be based will be as good in one part of the enterprise as in another. We call this type of adequate information the *achievement of the facilities to manage*. The young manager, then, has been able to practice the art of decision with the same information which would be available to a senior manager. This means the young manager will have the kind of training to more readily assume the higher responsibilities. Here, then, the computer has a chance to have a genuine intellectual effect, not merely a mechanical one.

Finally, if we use the computers correctly, we will take advantage of their ability to present us with the "dynamic" data mentioned earlier—visual forms to which we can respond rapidly and effectively. This remains one of the highest potentials of the computer and, currently, the least used.

SUMMARY

In this chapter we have by no means looked at all of the management problems concerned with data processing. We have tried, however, to consider some of the areas where the greatest difficulty lies. And we have tried not to solve the problems but rather to bring to them a somewhat different view than can be found in many articles and management journals.

We have explored the nature of early computer installations from the point of view that choices made then still have their effect on what we do now. We needed to know something about how the computer arrived in the business enterprise to see how it is currently used, and about what justifications might have arisen historically for the type of use explored. We noticed the nature of a conflict between the early types of computer personnel and the incumbent operational personnel (particularly managers) of a business.

We observed that the business computer, when developed, moved into the enterprise on the trail of scientific equipment and fell into the hands (quite often) of scientifically trained people. We noted that, however good the interests and intentions of scientifically trained people, they do not always mesh cleanly with the interests and intentions of line managers of a business. In part this is in the nature of the training differences of the two groups, and in part this is due to a difference in the life styles of the two groups.

We explored the use of feasibility studies in the early days and found that they were often expensive, took a long time, and did not always result in the benefits intended. We noticed that the need for feasibility studies presented line managers with problems somewhat different from those they had handled in the past. We noted the arrival of the computer specialist to help line managers with just the kinds of problems feasibility studies presented. Again, there were both advantages and disadvantages to the use of outside experts, and we briefly explored these in this chapter.

We noted the growth of the data processing family within the business unit and found some hazards there. We noted the hazards of the need for specialization within the computer field itself, and we saw the difficulties this presented to operational personnel in the business who need to understand much of this specialization but have not had the true opportunity for adequate training.

We explored the concept of record dependency as a rather modern industrial disease, one that is dependent to a great extent on the development of the computer center and its subsequent ability to provide records and printouts of all sorts to the managers of a firm. Along with record dependency came the art of defensive documentation—another disease that can cost management and the business a good deal of money but return little in the way of real value.

In this chapter we asked ourselves if there was one final and realistic test which could be applied by a general manager to determine whether the computer center was as effective as it was supposed to be. And we found a crude measure which is difficult to deny. Data gathering time should be on a consistent approach path to the date when data are needed. If the indications are a lengthening time between data collection and data use, rather than the reverse, the manager has good reason to make sharp and serious inquiries about the effectiveness of the computer center and the money spent there. We called this the ultimate test because it is.

We explored some of the difficulties faced by operational personnel if they are led into serving the data base maintenance problem instead of the customers of the business. We also had something caustic to say about unreadable computer reports, and we doubted if such reports are valuable.

We saw some of the problems inherent in the ability (and the computer surely has such an ability) to produce great masses of data. We also saw that computer printouts can carry an aura of authenticity and reality which they might not actually have earned. We do not wish to dismiss these problems too lightly, because they can lead the business firm seriously astray. We wondered if the computer, since it has the ability to summarize data in visual form, could not be better used to this end. We doubted the value of too much detail. We also wondered about getting dynamic, as versus static, reports from the computer center.

We also applied a few ancient but still useful management tests to computer data. Does it come on time? Then we asked who demands the solution to problems. The data center itself? The operating personnel? We had the impression such questions could provide very useful information in determining how much of the business effort is concentrated on self-generated problems and how much effort is concentrated on business survival (customer-related) problems.

We wondered who structured the operational job? If the computer center tends to dictate the activities of operation personnel, we defined this as counterproductive. If the operational personnel tended to dictate the activities of the computer center, we felt, in general, that all might be reasonably well.

We asked some hard questions about the attitude toward the enterprise of the computer personnel—servant or master? And we explored something of the problems of the company data processing committee—some of the past sins and some of the ways around them. We wondered about the value of the management EDP report. What should it reveal and to whom?

We looked at the difficult matter of eliminating scheduled reports when they are not truly needed. We found that sometimes the way the reports were generated led to serious questions about their usefulness. We explored some crude but effective methods for finding out whether reports are really useful to those who have asked for them or think them so.

Finally, we gave a bit of thought to the business of breaking up the computer empire (the central installation), and we gave some serious cautions to doing so too hastily and without careful thought. Such decisions can profoundly affect the future of the business, and so such decisions should not be made casually or in moments of enchantment with shaky predictions about the future. It is, after all, the competitive position of the business in relation to other similar businesses that will decide the future—not glamour, not new equipment, not broad sunswept uplands.

All these things briefly considered, we bring the chapter to a close knowing this chapter alone could constitute a book. But if we have opened up some areas where thought will follow, the task has been a good one. If we have created one or two genuine tests of computer effectiveness, so much the better for operational people and so much the better for computer people. Theirs is a symbiotic relationship and neither can probably survive these days without the help of the other.

HIGHLIGHT QUESTIONS

1. What was it about early computer installations which might still affect the way computer personnel deal with operational personnel in the business?
2. Name one or two of the in-house problems faced by operational managers when the business computer arrived on the scene in competition with the scientific computer installation.
3. What is a feasibility study? Why did businesses make use of them in regard to computer installations?
4. Name some of the advantages of making use of an outside computer specialist in the matter of determining whether a business truly needed a computer. What were some of the disadvantages of using such an individual?
5. What is meant by the term *data processing family*? What are some of the new members of that family you might know which are not mentioned in the chapter?
6. What is "record dependency?"
7. What is "defensive documentation?"
8. Just how are record dependency and defensive documentation related? What are some of the dangers involved in these activities for the business?
9. What exactly is the "ultimate test" which a naive manager can apply to determine whether or not a computer center is effective?
10. What is the "mass data problem" from the point of view of the business enterprise?

11. Name a few of the problems involved in data accessibility.
12. Why are we concerned, in this chapter, with who structures the business job?
13. What are some of the problems inherent in a company data processing committee?
14. Name some of the things you believe should be included in any management EDP report.
15. Name at least one method of determining whether or not a consistently prepared business report is really needed.

READINGS

Beer, Stafford. *Cybernetics and Management.* New York: John Wiley & Sons, 1964.

In this small book we discover the meaning and possible uses of cybernetics for management. Also, there are good sections on the theory of automata and intelligent machines. We are given a sketch of a cybernetic factory—one that uses machines and human beings in an interrelated intellectual way.

Bursk, Edward C., and Chapman, John F., eds. *New Decision-Making Tools for Managers.* New York: New American Library, 1963.

In this paperback we are given a view of the application of modern mathematics to business. It is important because it is the computer which will make use of the mathematical tools discussed. This should be a useful book since it is written at the layman level. No great knowledge of mathematics is expected.

Drucker, Peter F. *The Age of Discontinuity.* New York: Harper & Row, 1969.

One can hardly talk about management these days without some reference to Peter Drucker and his writings. In this book he has excellent sections of the knowledge technologies, a society of organizations, and the knowledge society which he feels will develop. A broad book, but worth the reading.

———. *The Effective Executive.* New York: Harper & Row, 1967.

Drucker feels effectiveness can be learned. Chapter 6 in the book is about the elements of decision making, and chapter 7 is about effective decisions. The last two chapters are particularly good reading.

———. *The Future of Industrial Man.* New York: New American Library, 1965.

Drucker again. This time on the future of industrial man. Another broad book. He has a good chapter on the definition of a functioning society. And he has another chapter on the industrial realities of the 20th century which are worth careful attention.

Galbraith, John Kenneth. *The New Industrial State*. Boston: Houghton Mifflin, 1967.

This is now a rather famous book. When we talk about technology and its effect on our society (including computers and all their near cousins), we must be sure to read this volume. Professor Galbraith may not always be right, but he has never been accused of narrowness of thought, dullness, or a failure to provoke others into thought. The chapter on technostructure is a good one. Then, the chapters on the corporation and the entrepreneur and the technostructure should not be skipped. The chapter on the goals of the industrial system should be carefully reviewed.

CHAPTER 12

SECOND RECAPITULATION

PURPOSE OF THE CHAPTER

We have now covered five additional text chapters. It is time, once again, for a recapitulation of what we have studied so far. First we will take each of the questions for discussion from each of the five text chapters and provide an answer to them. Then we will present a test on the subject matter material which has gone before. Finally, we will provide the answers to the test so you may check your own knowledge retention.

Again, we are not going to answer the questions in a cut-and-dried textbook fashion, but rather attempt to give them the true quality of a one-sided discussion —the kind of response you would expect to get were you in conversation with someone.

HIGHLIGHT QUESTIONS, CHAPTER 7

1. **Give one or two reasons why the predictions of full computer utility nets in the mid-1970s did not come true?**

A full computer utility net, of the public type, would require an enormous capital investment. It is the nature of public utilities that they must, in the main, be able to provide both full regular service to customers on demand, and that they must be prepared for peak loads. So, many of the early predictions were derailed simply on the basis of the amount of money to be expended.

The demand for computer services in the home and small business did not grow at the expected pace. While it is true a number of clever people have computers in their homes, the average person is not yet convinced such an expense, however small, is warranted. Most people do not believe they have enough calculation needs to require a computer.

Also, the development of equipment peculiarly and particularly suited to the kind of utility net envisioned is only now beginning to occur. Costs still must decline somewhat, simpler communication languages must be developed, the carrying capacity of telephone and other standard communication lines must be improved, a number of standard libraries and programs must be developed. It will, then, be a while before a public utility net will develop.

2. **Give some characteristics of public utilities.**

A public utility is often a private or quasi-private corporation with a monopoly on a particular service which requires governmental regulation.

A public utility must be able to provide reasonably reliable service and must be able to handle surprise peak loads. The amount of utility use, while often predictable, is sometimes subjected to surprising variations. The ability to handle these must be part of the basic operating ability of the net. In these days of surprise energy shortages, that statement is not, in fact, quite as true as it used to be, and we may have to learn to accommodate a public utility that requires, from time to time, to shut down. But that does not deny what ought to be the nature of the utility.

The public utility normally does not face competition in an area of its jurisdiction from any other similar enterprise. Permission is seldom, if ever, granted to a private, noncontrolled, competitive industry to set up power, water, or sewer lines to homes in direct rivalry to the licensed utility.

The charges visited upon subscribers to a utility are formally reviewed, from time to time, by public agencies. This sometimes means the utility rates are more a political matter than an economic one. At least, this is one of the common complaints of utility managers. A typical case in point would be the recent debates over the price of natural gas when it is shipped across state lines.

The public utility is sometimes prevented from expanding into related service areas when those areas are already being served by another utility originally defined as "different." So, while the telephone utlity might be able to handle certain types of computer load, the telegraph company might protest. These battles are only now taking final shape. The next decade may see their resolution.

3. Give several characteristics of private utilities.

The private utility is privately owned and has no legal responsibilities to provide service to the public.

A private utility does not require enormous initial capital investment since, in effect, it may select the number of "customers" it wishes to serve and is under no obligation to provide for peak loads or the like. The chances are a private utility will be able to "regularize" the amount and kind of service it offers without public interference. That is, the utility may limit the amount of capacity required by spreading the communication load over twenty-four hour periods on a seven-day-a-week basis.

In many cases, we would expect the private utility to be centralized. That is, one company may choose to serve a limited number of customers on a national basis through satellites or the like.

The private utility can establish communication "lines" on the basis of a high rate of average use—that is, it can avoid establishing equal service to all possible customers and can limit itself to full service to a few. The choice remains with the utility, not with the customers.

4. What are several ways in which a private utility differs from a public utility?

A private utility would suffer considerably less governmental (at all levels) regulation than a quasi-public or public utility.

A private utility would be able to plan its growth on the basis of its own managerial judgment rather than on such factors as the number of people moving into a particular geographical area or the number of people "demanding" service. The private utility may extend its services only so long as the service represents a profit.

The private utility may face competition from similar utilities—it will probably not be able to hold a monopoly over a given geographic area or over any particular type of service.

A private utility is most likely to opt for steady and predictable service loads and to maximize its communication net to make the most profit possible.

A private utility may improve and modify the services it offers without review by certain governmental agencies. And, of course, a private utility can choose to go out of business with an ease considerably greater than that of a public utility.

5. Generally describe the four major types of utilities with which we are familiar.

Common carriers—the airlines, the canals, the railroads—are one type of utility with which we are all familiar.

Power utilities—electricity primarily—are another type of utility which we have become accustomed to.

Community and regional facilities, such as water systems and sewer systems, are another familiar form of public utility.

Communication facilities—television, radio, telegraph, and telephone—are the fourth major type of utility with which we are acquainted.

6. List four major computer developments which helped make the possibility of a computer utility move from dream to reality.

One computer development which made the concept of a computer utility possible was the enormous increase in the capacity of computer memories with a concomitant decrease in the cost per unit of storage.

Multiprogramming—the ability of the computer to handle more than one computer program in storage at any given time (moving back and forth between the programs to accomplish similiar types of tasks)—also made the concept of the computer utility less remote.

Sophisticated supervisory programs which could monitor the activities of the computer (avoid slow and bothersome human intervention) make it possible to use the computer as a utility. Also, as the sophistication of the supervisory systems grew, it was possible to simplify the kind of communication language required to get the computer to perform the tasks or jobs desired.

Microminiaturization and other developments enormously increased the speed of the computer. This made it possible for a large number of terminals or other types of contact with the computer to be easily handled without the system overloading or breaking down.

The development of "smart" or "intelligent" computer terminals also enhances the possibility of the computer utility. Much of the calculating burden can be done locally, and then major projects can be passed on to the central computer in the utility system.

7. What is the primary difference between a "voice-grade" transmission line and a "burst-mode" transmission line?

The important difference, from the point of view of this book, between a *voice-grade* transmission line and a *burst-mode* transmission line is the carrying capacity of the line and also the reliability possible. A voice-grade line (typical telephone connection) does not have the capacity to move thousands or millions of bits a second. And the possibilities of "static," which would interfere with the correct bit transmission, are great. The burst-mode line has the capability of carrying millions or billions of bits of information a second, and is of sufficient quality that the static interference and problems of "dropped bits" are minimized and predictable.

8. What are a few of the economic advantages a private computer utility might have over a public computer utility?

A private computer utility may begin in a small way, accept only enough customers to make the operation profitable. It may then expand only as is needed to either increase the service to customers or to add new customers. The utility also may organize its transmissions in such a way that the "lines" are used to capacity. Also, the private utility may form such partnerships and associations as are necessary to increase its financial base, with fewer legal restrictions than we might find placed upon a public utility.

And a private utility may set its own rates, in-house, taking note only of its own competitive situation relative to similar utilities. The private utility can also plan its own expansion in terms of profit, not necessarily in terms of the aggregate of customers arriving in a given area or needing the service.

9. Name and describe three different types of programs we might expect to find in a public computer utility.

First, we might find a number of standardized programs which perform normal mathematical functions or household chores or general accounting requirements.

We might also find proprietory programs—useful ways of doing rather general things but which demand a royalty payment of some kind to the programmer who developed the program.

We might find shared programs in the library—that is, those types of programs which have been developed by others to solve a particular problem but are available on request to other programmers free.

Finally, we might expect to find private programs—those created for and used exclusively by the particular individual who uses the utility. These programs would be subject to security control and would not be for public distribution.

10. Of terminal users, who would find a command language most useful and who would find BASIC language most useful?

Generally, the inexperienced or naive user of a computer utility would use the command language of the system, since this language most nearly approximates normal English. And the command language can offer a number of special programs which can be called up by a single designator or title. The more experienced programmer, used to the system, would probably find it beneficial to construct his or her own programs using one of the standard terminal languages, such as BASIC.

11. Name two typical methods of data-bank access security and tell why each one is not particularly effective.

One "security" method is to require a terminal user to provide the computer with a key code number as an identifier. In another type of situation, the terminal operator has a plastic identity card which must be inserted in the terminal mechanism as an identifier and a clearance signal to the computer. Neither of these methods is very seriously secure, but they do prevent casual use by unauthorized persons.

If a fingerprint identification system could be successfully worked out for identification, this might be the least likely to be misused. Also, voice prints may hold some potential for the future.

12. Why does it seem developments in the minicomputer field might interfere with the development of public computer utilities?

If the mini computers become cheap and if they present reasonably large memories and programming powers, the necessity to hook into a public computer utility would be decreased accordingly. There would still be a need for such a utility for those requiring a great deal of information from various possible data bases. But there is good reason to doubt that the average householder would require such broad information to be available on a continuing basis.

We might, then, divide the householders into those groups who need a little computing power rather infrequently—for them a mini computer in the home (if cheap enough) would solve the problem. For those householders with professional interests related to the computer field, and who could do a good deal of professional work at home, the utility might prove to be the best bet.

But there is no reason to assume that the mini computer cannot be itself hooked into a public computer utility. This would give the serious householder the best of both worlds.

13. Would the mini computer interfere in any particular way with the development of private computer utilities?

It is not likely that the mini computer will seriously interfere with the private computer utility, if that utility is primarily oriented toward the transmission of large blocks of information between intercompany or intracompany computers. But in the sense that a private utility might wish to lease computing time to small users, we can predict that it would.

It is, of course, very dangerous to try to predict the future in the world of computers. Probably no single artifact has been so swiftly, dramatically, and completely changed over time. We can well expect the innovations and improvements to continue apace.

14. What are some of the features we might expect in a public computer utility net?

First we might expect a number of large computers scattered throughout the nation on a regional basis. Communication between these large centers would primarily be in "burst" mode—the transmission of large blocks of information via satellites or through high-grade leased lines.

We might expect a number of smaller installations to be linked into the regional centers. Communication across country would be from small installation to regional center to other regional center to other small installation. The regional centers might act as clearinghouses and contact points.

We might expect the public computer utility net would force the development of a more common computer language—a universal language, if you will. Such a language should be close to natural language form so it could be understood and used by large numbers of uninitiated people.

The public computer utility net would most likely set up a number of standardized operating procedures for customer use. While this has an element of rigidity, it is probably the best way to take advantage of general public services offered. We are all already familiar with the somewhat rigid requirements of the U.S. Postal Service.

And we can expect the computer utility to charge for services rendered on some kind of standard basis, such as the actual computer time consumed or the actual number of digits of information transmitted. These time or unit charges are not much different from the kilowatt or other standard measures used by incumbent utilities today.

15. How can it be said a public computer utility might cause cultural uniformity?

Almost any broad utility will require a number of standard operating procedures to function. The computer utility might wish to confine itself to one or two common programming languages which might, in fact, limit future creativity in these areas. People who wish to contact the utility would most likely have a catalog of standard contact procedures which would be required. While all of these standardized elements are necessary for efficient service and efficient operation, they do force people into a set of common responses which do not account for genius or other creative forms.

Then, of course, the public computer utility is most likely to develop a number of standardized programs for the solution to common problems. The temptation would naturally be to take advantage of those programs already made and not devote long hours to developing different solutions to problems alleged to be already solved. There would, then, be an economic discouragement of fresh approaches to old problems. This could lead, in time, to a general staleness in the ability of the culture to approach old problems in fresh ways or even to ponder entirely new problems. The tendency in this latter case would be to ignore problems for which common solutions had not already been found. We must always remember the majority of mankind thought the world flat for a long long time because thinking that way took care of most of the problems of the day. There is little if any real evidence that we do not continue to err in more subtle areas in exactly the same way today.

HIGHLIGHT QUESTIONS, CHAPTER 8

1. What is a data base?

In brief, what we mean in this text by a data base is the memory of the institution we are talking about. Such a file or memory of the activities of a firm would be, in our case, electronically stored in such a way the information could be readily called out in printed or in cathode ray form.

2. What, generally speaking, would we expect to find in a proper data base?

We can speak, here, in terms of three generalities. We expect to find a record of all that has been done in the past, we expect to find a record of what is currently going on in the organization, and we expect to find a record of what we have agreed to do in the future.

The term *pertinent* must enter into our discussion. We want to store only that information which is pertinent to the development of a full history of the organization in the past. We might not wish to store intermediate results of our efforts, save as those are legally required. In terms of the present situation, we are likely to want to store all the information currently needed and being used. But after the information has been used, there ought to be some kind of weeding process going on before the pertinent information (historically) is put away. And we would expect to find a record of what we agreed to do in the future in a somewhat more limited (though still pertinent) form. Our future plans are not likely to contain a great deal of detail, but rather should represent rather broad outlines, policies, and expectations.

3. Data bases involve us in three basic conflicts. What are they?

First, we wish to have the largest possible memory or storage facility in the computer commensurate with our needs. We also require quick retrieval of any information stored. And we require the cheapest kind of storage possible.

The conflicts are that the larger the memory the more difficult the filing and retrieval are apt to become, and the more the memory is likely to cost.

The quicker the retrieval required the smaller the search area should be, and the more expensive the storage medium is likely to be.

The cheaper the storage the more likely capacity is to be great, but the search and storage techniques restricted, in some linear fashion.

So, in a nutshell, we have *time* of finding against *size* of memory against *cost* of memory. The three things we most need are likely to have to be compromised in some fashion to achieve a balance of our goals. We have size versus speed versus cost.

4. Briefly describe data disk banks.

A data disk bank is made up of a set of disks mounted in a storage, control, and drive unit. In ordinary cases we would have from two to eight disk units contained in a single drive unit. We can get to any disk set as fast as to any other. Once at the disk, though, we need to search out the cylinder of information we want, and this involves a movement of the read/write comb structure from the outermost disk track to the one we want.

In the text we discussed the IBM 3330 disk storage and control unit wherein each disk pack mounted in the unit had a capacity of 100 million bytes.

Though the disks in this large system are not likely to be changed very often, they can be. This means we can have some kind of offline, on-shelf storage of information as well as that actually mounted on the drive units.

5. What is a data cartridge? What does it contain? What is the smallest recording medium in a data cartridge?

A data cartridge is a small drum about four inches long and two inches in diameter. A magnetic band of tape is wrapped around the data cartridge, spool fashion. There are tracks on the tape which we can think of as being organized in cylinder fashion (because of multiple read/write heads which can read the tracks in clusters). A single tape cartridge can hold over 50 million bytes of information.

The smallest actual recording unit in a data cartridge is the byte. The bytes are written out on tracks, and a set of tracks makes up a cylinder. We are likely to call up a cylinder of information at a time as a minimum of information to be transmitted to the intermediary disk unit. The intermediary disk pack can hold the equivalent of two cartridges of information.

6. What are the advantages of magnetic tapes? What are the disadvantages?

Tapes have two primary advantages: (1) they are relatively cheap, and (2) they have a high density of storage—that is, we can get a great deal of information on each inch of tape.

The disadvantages of tapes are that they must be read serially, so on the average we could expect a number of seconds to be involved before we could get to any particular datum on the tape (and this is very slow in computer terms). Hence, we generally read information from a tape in batches.

Also, a single tape reel ties up the capacity of a regular tape drive, and there are only so many tape drives we wish to connect to a computer at any given time. We don't, then, get quite the flexibility we would really like to have. And it takes some time to take a tape reel off a drive unit and replace it with another, and this means more personnel involved in the operation than we would prefer.

7. What do we mean by the term, "batch processing"?

Batch processing merely means the treatment of all similar data items at the same time. For example, we are forced by the nature of the magnetic tape to do batch processing. We would arrange all our accounts payable on a tape in some kind of ascending or descending order (by number or name) and then arrange all posting data in the same way, and then we could run the posting information through the computer and have the accounts payable updated one account at a time in order. We can see that a certain amount of orderly preparation of data is required for such a method of operation. We would have a serial order posting tape and a serial order basic tape record of the accounts. The posting would take place as a sort of a matching procedure (account number), skipping unaffected accounts in the master (accounts payable record) tape. The changes recorded on the altering tape would be called transactions. Hence, we would have a transaction tape and a master tape to deal with.

8. How can tapes be used in conjunction with disks to achieve some random searching?

If we read the contents of a tape reel onto a disk set, then we could take advantage of some of the random features of the disk equipment to update accounts (or other information) on a hunt-and-seek basis. This does require that the tape be so organized that, when the contents are read onto the disks, the information is properly arranged so that the seek-and-find operation will be most effective. But this is not that difficult to arrange.

When all accounts on the disk have been properly updated and arranged, the entire contents can be read back onto a tape reel and the reel subsequently stored offline.

9. Describe a portable disk pack.

A portable disk pack is a packaged unit of disks (usually from six to ten) that can be placed on a disk drive or removed from the disk drive as a single storable unit. Usually, such a pack will have a special cover (for protection of the disk pack and the contents) and an appropriate carrying handle. When the pack (cover, handle, and all) have been properly mounted on the disk drive, the cover and handle are removable. Disk packs can be stored offline in much the same way tape reels are handled.

10. Give the best description you can of a cylinder of information. Relate such a concept to a disk track.

Since disk packs are read onto and written from by a comblike structure which has a read/write head for each disk surface being used, the effect is one of an imaginary perpendicular cylinder of disk tracks starting at the first read/write head on the comb structure and dropping to the bottom read/write head on the comb structure.

Once the comb structure has been placed over a particular track, then all tracks above and below that track (on disk surfaces above and below) are available electronically (as against having to physically move the comb structure). Thus, it pays to arrange information in cylinders—track 1, disk one bottom; track 1, disk two top; track 1, disk two bottom; and so on.

11. What are the two most common forms of file organization?

The most common methods for arranging files are ascending sequence or descending sequence by some key identifier or code number.

We should not, however, fail to note that alphabetic arrangements are also possible and, since the alphabetic material would be expressed in number form inside the computer, the end result in terms of organization could be the same.

12. What purpose does an overflow track serve?

An overflow track provides a means by which items that would normally be filed in a track, in order, can be moved into a nearby area when the track is filled. Links are set up from the track to the item in the overflow track and then back to the track. So the end result is that the item actually appears as though it had been filed in the track in the correct ascending (or descending) order. Later, the track can be updated (all items moved into proper locations from the overflow track) by means of a standard housekeeping program.

13. List as many security needs of a data base as you can.

First and foremost, the computer containing the data base must be able to properly identify those individuals who should have access to the information and those who should not.

Second, the computer handling the data base and the data base itself must be safe from such inadvertent damage as erasure of important records.

Third, the data base must be secure in terms of correct information. That is, the information stored in the data base must be both accurate and up-to-date.

Fourth, the data base must be so organized that authorized individuals cannot accomplish unauthorized tasks with the information. That is, only certain individuals should be licensed to make changes in the records that would affect statements in regard to profits, account values, and the like. And some types of information—those constituting the ultimate record of activities—should not be alterable by anyone at anytime for any reason.

14. What are three forms of data base sharing?

The three forms of data base sharing we have discussed are: device sharing, by means of which two data bases may be contacted by a single input/output unit; channel sharing, by means of which two data bases may be contacted by a number of input/output units using the channels involved; and primary storage sharing, in which the memories of the two computers —which constitute the two data bases—can be used by either computer.

15. What would be the advantages of an integrated data base? What would the disadvantages be?

Let us assume a national integrated data base for purposes of the question. One of the advantages of such a data base would be the availability of a great mass of information from a single central location to anyone authorized to make an inquiry. Very sophisticated methods of updating and clearing of such a file could be developed since only a single massive data base would be involved. Also, it would be possible, in such a single instance, to hire the best talent available in the nation. And a certain amount of economy could be maintained since there would be a large single staff instead of a great variety of staffs.

If we are talking about an integrated data base in terms of regional centers all linked together, we get the same advantages but in a lesser degree. There would be need for more staff members, there would be a need for effective and efficient communication lines between the centers, there would be a need for well-worked-out agreements between the regional staffs. The problem, then, would be to get cooperation at all centers and to keep in mind the primary purpose of the integration.

The disadvantages of a single data base are the need for mass storage beyond certain current abilities, the danger of centralized power in the hands of a few people, the danger to information, generally, should such a single unit fail or be damaged, and the danger that such a single unit could be used for political rather than informational purposes.

Again, in a collection of regional centers the dangers would be decreased, but the complications would increase. Damage to one of the centers would not necessarily cripple the information net of a nation—though it might cause serious problems. It would be harder to get any form of collusion of five or six different groups than would be the case in a single group. Political influence would naturally be dispersed and hard to keep going. But the total effort here is likely to be more expensive.

16. List some important dangers which would apply to a national data base?

Anything which is centralized is subject to seizure. We would not want a political or military threat to a single source of national information.

Anything which is centralized is more easily subject to manipulation than anything which is dispersed broadly over an area.

Errors in a national data base might be very difficult to eradicate or, for that matter, to discover since there might be no other source of comparative information which would dispute what was on file.

An accident at a single data center could destroy decades of careful work and leave a nation without proper records to maintain its status and keep its identity.

17. How does a data base index system function?

Think of the contents of an entire disk unit (or other basic mass storage medium unit) as a volume. This volume will have a label (name). If more than one disk drive (or other basic mass storage unit drive) is connected to the computer, the first job for the computer is to find the proper volume. Once this is done the volume label will lead the computer to the table of contents of that volume. Scanning the table of contents, the computer finds what is called a "data set control block" which, by means of a data set label, points to the location of the data set on the proper track. Let us repeat. Find the volume by means of its label. Read the table of contents of the volume to find the data set control block for the data. Read the data set control block to find the location of the data. Move to the proper data track. Find the item (or collection of items) on the track.

There is yet another type of data base index. In the case of enormous data collections (that is, an enormous number of volumes on file) we might keep a master index volume (a volume of volume names). The first job of the computer would be to scan the volume index to find which volume is needed. Then, from that point on, the inner search goes on as described above. The volume index might be organized in such a fashion that we can look up topical references and find in which volume they would be filed. And this same volume might contain any number of cross-indexed items.

18. What kinds of power might accrue to one who controlled a data base?

One terrible kind of power possible to one who controlled a data base would be the ability to permanently isolate from the mainstream of society anyone who had violated, at one time or another, one of the primary social mores. In the case of a centralized national credit file, the "deadbeat" could not flee to another state or county and begin life anew in the hope that old sins would be forgotten. A truly comprehensive data base and national communication system would prevent this attempt at a new start.

Naturally, a villain in charge of a data base could insert any number of slanders in regard to individuals recorded in the base, and these could cause serious harm. Or such a villain could refuse to permit the cleaning up of files when errors had been made. It is not necessary that the villain in the piece be an individual. The villain might well be the normal inertia and disinterest of an institutional organization. We have had experiences with this type of villainy in the past.

The ability to find anyone, anytime, anywhere is an enormous amount of power. The ability to inform others of the character, past experiences, and misfortunes of another in full detail is the kind of power formerly reserved to God. Of course, on the other side of the coin, detailed information about individuals might lead to helping them. But we should remember the old Quaker's prayer: "Dear Lord, do not protect me from mine enemies for we understand each other and can deal with each other. But do, good Lord, protect me from my friends for, with their many good works on my behalf, they may ultimately do me in." The danger in doing good for others is that the good you do may neither be needed nor wanted. And many a wolf has come knocking at the door wearing the lamb-suit of good intentions.

19. What are some of the implications of a data base system? What would this mean to the individual who was not a member of the system?

Broadly speaking, as we have noted in the previous question a complete data base system means information and information means power. Complete knowledge of an individual could mean the individual is isolated (an outcast) from society if he has been found to have violated the habits, the mores, the customs. Excommunication, as such isolation is called, used to mean in the Middle Ages that one's effectiveness to deal with one's religion and fellows was completely destroyed. It was considered to be the most terrible punishment one could visit upon a man or woman—the ultimate isolation of a social animal.

A national data base system might mean the possibility of total control over every citizen on the part of the government. We do not have enough confidence in the world at large to believe that governments are necessarily benign in their intentions. Those who have information hold power. Those who hold power are always loathe to give it up.

There are those who say that to know an individual fully is to have the power to manipulate and deceive him or her. This kind of possibility should not be taken lightly. We have had some sorry examples of the results of evil genius at work manipulating the ordinary citizen in the past. We might do well to learn from history's lessons.

20. What types of federal controls would you expect to be exercised over a national data base system?

At best there would be a set of federal laws which prescribed what could properly go into a data file, how long that information could be maintained, who should be permitted to receive the information, how errors in information should be corrected, how individual citizens will be permitted to review and protest erroneous information in their files, and some means of economic or moral retribution for those who have been deliberately or negligently mistreated by the system.

Some consistent and regular method of audit should be required by law. Definitions of irrelevancy and harm should be established. That which is irrelevant should be removed. That which is harmful should be subject to some systematic statute of limitations.

None of these things will come easily. Various suits will probably be involved to bring matters to court. But, gradually, a body of law will be built which, hopefully, will contain remedies for the worst of the possible abuses.

HIGHLIGHT QUESTIONS, CHAPTER 9

1. Distinguish between "operating personnel" and "computer personnel," as those terms are used in this chapter.

Operating personnel are those individuals in a firm who perform the regular duties prescribed by the firm. For example, sales people, secretaries, and the like would fall into the class of operating personnel. Most managers would be included in that category for our purposes of discussion.

Computer personnel, on the other hand, are those individuals working in the computer center (or centers). These people have a primary interest in dealing with the electronic system of the enterprise.

The division, of course, is quite arbitrary. But we would expect the operating personnel to be most concerned with accomplishing their own tasks. And we would expect these people to think of the computer as just another tool which they can depend upon to assist them in the task accomplishment.

Computer personnel would think of information and its manipulation as their primary concern. To them, unfortunately, the selling jobs and the like might appear secondary.

2. What would be one or two possible areas of conflict between operating personnel and computer personnel?

One of the primary areas of possible conflict between operating personnel and computer personnel would be the focus of attention. Operating personnel are more likely to focus on the customer of the enterprise than are computer personnel. Operating personnel have a sale to complete, a department to manage, a customer to satisfy. Computer personnel are likely to have a problem to solve, information to gather, programs to write.

Operating personnel and computer personnel are likely to conflict over the matter of what is to be accomplished. Operating personnel could well think of the computer and its problems as relatively unimportant in the accomplishment of their tasks. Computer personnel are likely to think of computer-oriented problems as tasks in themselves unrelated to the "outside" world. The goals of the two groups are likely to be different.

Operating personnel may think of themselves as "line" and of the computer people as "staff," with the clear implication that staff jobs are of lesser importance than line jobs.

Each of the two groups may, because of self-interest, create problems and extra work for the other.

3. **What is a smart computer terminal?**

A smart computer terminal is a terminal with some computing and storage abilities of its own. The ordinary terminal is merely a communication device, connected to a central or mini computer somewhere down the line. The memory and calculating and logic functions would be contained only in the computer. A smart terminal would be capable of doing a reasonable amount of on-sight computing, would have a small but adequate memory, and would refer to the mini or central computer only when its own capacities to handle a problem had been exceeded.

4. **Name a few advantages of decentralized activity.**

The primary advantage of decentralized activity is that the judgments are made intimately at the point of (or near the point of) the problem. This means a greater amount of immediate information is available. It also means those having to solve the problem are immediately involved in the problem and hence have a greater immediate interest in its solution. Also, those nearest the point of the problem are likely to have a greater sense of responsibility.

Decentralized activity is, in most cases, more human. That is, it involves less the feeling of a large and oppressive hierarchy at work. And hopefully, the customer or other person involved can get more immediate action in terms of problem solution. The fewer the levels required to be traveled the quicker the solution is likely to appear.

5. **Name some of the advantages of centralized activity.**

Centralized activity generally has the advantage of greater control over the events—from the point of view of management. Also, procedures can be so standardized throughout the organization that records will be uniform and the actions of the enterprise vis-à-vis the customers more consistent and uniform.

And for complex problems, centralization means the full resources of the firm may be brought to bear to bring about a solution. Centralized activity also permits more specialization than is true of decentralized activities. The expertise involved in dealing with problems can be deeper and generally more carefully considered—away from the stresses and strains of the immediate problem situation. In many cases, this will result in a longer-lasting and more rational solution to the problem.

6. **Explain the 80/20 data processing rule.**

   The 80/20 data processing rule is an experiential rule of thumb —not entirely acceptable to many computer experts. Basically, this rule of thumb implies that it is wise to make use of a smart terminal or a mini computer at a particular work site when 80 percent of the computing needed to be done is used right there at the site.

7. **What is a network node?**

   A network node is a place (in the communication network of an enterprise) where action actually takes place—where customers are contacted, where sales are closed, where information is generated, and where information is needed. Sometimes the places are called "decision points." Since we are speaking of action, we can assume a nodal position is occupied by an individual and that particular individual has the general power to bring events to successful completion or to delay them.

8. **Distinguish between the simple computer ring configuration and the simple star computer configuration.**

   In the simple ring configuration we may assume a number of mini computers linked together in a communication ring. That is, no one of the computers in the ring occupies a dominant position or is the central location of the data base. Each member of the ring carries approximately the same kind of responsibility and holds about an equal share of the data base.

   In the simple star configuration there is a central computer (however large or small) that links to a number of mini computers or smart terminals. We normally would expect the computer in the center of the star to be more dominant than the other members of the configuration and to carry the main part of the shared data base.

9. **Would downstream loading be easier with the ring computer configuration or the star computer configuration?**

   Downstream loading would be easier with the star computer configuration since the term refers to the matter of passing translation (language) loads back to the central computer system. Actually, if we think of the central computer as the top of a hierarchy, "upstream" loading would seem the more natural term. But the term is *downstream* so we are rather stuck with it.

   In a ring system the "downstream" loading would merely be a matter of passing the load from the smart terminal to the mini computer. It could be done, but is more likely when there is a fairly powerful central computer to carry the complex computing and translating load.

10. What would be some of the power conflicts which might occur during a change-over from centralized computer structure to distributed data processing?

We would naturally expect some conflict from those who have a vested interest in a large-scale centralized computer system. There might be a number of specialists in the central computer room who would be loathe to be let go or reduced in power and importance. And, of course, if the operational staff of the firm become familiar with computing (through the use of distributed mini computers or smart terminals), some of the "mystique" of the centralized computer people would vanish.

We also would expect some conflict between the managers (made familiar with computing via the mini computers, terminals, and distributed data processing), and the computer "experts" (who had taken upon themselves many management decisions just because they were large and centralized and no one truly understood what they were doing). As management retakes control of the firm, the conflicts seem nearly inevitable.

11. What do we mean by the term "blanket data base"?

A *blanket data base* is a term used to describe a situation wherein all of the records of a firm, no matter how large the organization might be, are stored in a single accessible location.

12. In a smart terminal to mini computer to central computer configuration, what would be the percentage of load on the central computer if the 80/20 data processing rule works out perfectly?

We would, of course, be very surprised if the 80/20 rule (merely a rule of thumb) worked out perfectly. But if it did, we would expect 20 percent of the work of a terminal to be bucked downstream to the mini computer. Twenty percent of the work of the mini computer would, in turn, be bucked downstream to the central computer. Twenty percent of twenty percent is four percent. The central computer, then, would be carrying only 4 percent of all the calculations and work given to any single smart terminal.

13. Describe some of the security problems which you think might be unique to distributed data processing configurations?

Actually, a distributed data base might make certain security problems easier than a single centralized data base. The individuals working with a smaller set of data bases would have a more intimate knowledge of and a more intimate control over the data base. In a small operation there would be little chance for the stranger to slip in and take advantage of the anonymity of size. And a data base that is spread out is hard to interrogate without alerting someone along the chain.

The centralized activity can control physical access to the equipment itself more rigorously and formally than might be possible with a distributed data processing system. But collusion would be more difficult with the many (distributed data processing) than with the few (centralized data processing).

Distributed data processing would have more areas requiring control, and actually might have more people requiring control. And the abilities of smaller computers to control access might be limited by the cost and type of equipment.

We believe it might be just about a standoff, though we would expect the manager to be somewhat more able to handle the smaller situation than the larger.

14. Distinguish between problems of security and problems of control as they relate to distributed data processing.

When we use the term *security* we tend to have reference to the accessibility of records kept in the data base or bases. When we talk about control, we generally have reference to the ability of the manager or managers to handle the duties and responsibilities of the enterprise itself. Control would naturally, from the management point of view, include the computer as a tool rather than as an end in itself.

We would be remiss if we did not admit that the matter of security and the matter of control are primarily management problems and are not peculiar to the computer field alone. To be sure, the nature of the computer requires special security measures. But the problem is one of proper record care; of being certain that only authorized people see confidential records, of successful auditing, and of seeing that all legal restrictions are properly taken care of.

15. What do we mean by "tailored terminals?"

Tailored terminals are merely computer terminals which have been assembled to handle the special needs of a particular department or other unit of the enterprise. In this day of subcomponents, it is possible to put together just about any device one might need. And there is no economy in adding more features to a terminal than can be properly used by the department or business unit. When a large number of such terminals are to be installed in an enterprise, some careful planning about the features that are needed should pay off in terms of economy and efficiency.

The final test of the tailored terminal is whether it adequately fills the needs of the business unit using it, and whether it is relatively simply to use. The simpler the device is to use, the less prone it is to error.

HIGHLIGHT QUESTIONS, CHAPTER 10

1. Explain the difference between mechanization and automation.

When we apply ordinary production techniques—the application of leverage and power—to a process, we are mechanizing it. Automation involves a good deal more. An automated system would have a means of measuring its own output, testing that output against some established criterion, and adjusting its own processing to meet the accuracy requirements of the output.

The fast food restaurants have been mechanized, not automated. The modern farm is highly mechanized; it is not yet automated.

2. What is negative feedback? How does it relate to automated devices?

Negative feedback is simply information which is fed back into a work process so we can adjust, while working, to better meet the standard we have set. It is called negative feedback because the information returning to the system is a measure of the error in achieving the performance we wanted.

Automated devices are truly automated when the feedback information automatically causes the machinery to adjust to reachieve the norm. The internal adjustments of the machine or system are made by servomechanisms. In a sense, then, the system can act as a cognitive being—it can measure the output, determine the amount of error, adjust for the error, and continue production.

3. What is a servomechanism? How does it tie into automation?

A servomechanism is an energy source (say an electric motor) capable of adjusting a system on the basis of information fed to it. In the case of automated equipment, the servomechanism is the "servant" of the system. When an error is detected, the servomechanism is provided with the means to make corrections. Call such a device a "slave" machine, if you will. Human beings attached to ordinary manufacturing processes in order to correct machine errors are, in that role, acting as servomechanisms.

Servomechanisms are a very necessary part of any automated system, because it is their responsibility to make such physical adjustments as are required by the system to keep to the criteria previously set.

4. **Explain how the fly-ball governor on a steam engine works and why it is, in fact, an example of negative feedback.**

Basically, the fly-ball governor is a scissor mechanism with two control balls at the end. The mechanism is mounted on a shaft so that it rotates with the shaft. As the engine drives the shaft rapidly, the scissor mechanism causes the metal balls to fly outward. This outward movement of the balls pulls down the scissor mechanism to throttle-down the engine. As the speed falls the metal balls tend to drop inward, thus opening the speed valve slightly. The result is a balance of forces which gives the engine a stable speed.

The mechanism is an excellent example of negative feedback because, as the engine goes either too fast or too slow (variations from the throttle setting), the deviation forces an adjustment in the speed toward the norm set.

It is good to learn that feedback, as a concept, may be mechanical as well as electronic, simple as well as complex.

5. **Why will continuous process industries be more likely to automate than job-order shops?**

"Flow" situations are easier to automate than "chunk" situations. This is because valves, pressures, currents, and granular (very small chunk) controls can be handled with ease by electric currents, pipes, and other facilities. Large odd-shaped objects (as would occur in a job-order shop) are much more difficult to handle—hard to get on and off conveyor belts. In the job-order shop the human being is still a very useful servomechanism. In continuous process industries (oil, gasoline, gas, milk, and the like) pipes and valves and flow problems lend themselves to automatic solutions more easily.

6. **How can the computer help the job-order shop to automate, at least in part?**

The computer can assist in a job-order shop in two principal ways. First, the job of keeping track of information about the various jobs can be passed on to the computer. This would lead to the possibility of computer scheduling of the various machines in the job-order shop. Second, the computer actually could be linked to a number of tape-driven machines and could provide them with instructions appropriate to the tasks at hand.

The first application, that of information, is the one most likely to be used currently where possible. The more difficult job of linking the machines to the computer will come more gradually.

7. **List a few of the fundamental changes in techniques and tools which come about because of mechanization.**

The primary purpose of mechanization is to replace human or animal muscle with energy-driven machinery. The primary engines which perform this type of replacement are electric, gasoline, diesel, and steam. Our tools, then, are likely to become less a simple extension of man and grow into complex machines. The tools become more expensive, more complicated, and larger. The capital investment requirements grow accordingly.

When large and expensive tools are used, the techniques for their proper handling also grow more complex, and this means the needed training periods will increase. The job, then, must be planned further in advance, the uses of the machinery must be more carefully and fully developed, and greater management control and evaluation will be required.

Of course, one of the major reasons for mechanization is the increase in productivity per hour of labor (either manual or mechanical). It is this increase in productivity which offsets the increased cost of the machinery. If the former is greater than the latter, we achieve certain kinds of "profits" (or surpluses) which can provide funds for further mechanization and greater increases in productivity. We can get a nation, or a civilization, into a productive upward spiral.

It is the application of science, through technology, to production problems which has given the Western world its enormous productive edge during the last few centuries.

A complex series of educational and economic commitments grow out of the mechanization of productive processes, and these become the "anchor" of the civilization. Without them, the system might quickly break down and collapse.

8. **What types of tool techniques and uses would come about, because of automation, that are different from simple mechanization?**

Just as surely as mechanization is a step up in complexity and cost from simple manual operations, automation is a step up in complexity and cost from mechanization.

We would, in automation, be designing systems rather than just machines, wherein by systems we mean complex assemblages of machines which are automatic in the sense that they are governed by other "intellectual" machines (computers) and servomechanisms.

Since the systems themselves are going to be more complex than the elements (machines) that make them up, we face even greater demands for long-term planning, which will involve greater educational experience, more long-term availability of capital, greater management talent (at high level), and larger production units.

Because of the new developments in electronics and of the need to conserve energy (use of micro currents rather than macro currents) we can expect the types of tools in an automated system to be more electronic in orientation than mechanical. The processes of automation use information as a tool in a very direct fashion. Computers and other electronic devices are peculiarly useful in matters of transmitting and using information. Information, then, becomes one of the primary "tools" to be developed in automated or nearly automated societies.

9. Why is it that automation must necessarily be energy-intensive?

Even though we succeed in reducing many of our electrical demands from macro to micro, it is the nature of automation that we are referring to large-scale operations. This, the large-scale enterprise and the increased production, will naturally lead to greater energy consumption. At least this will be true in the short run (the next 25 to 50 years). In the long run, however, we may so remove the human being from the processes that the temperatures in the plant and the working conditions required for the machines may reduce many of what we think of today as necessary costs. A machine is likely to be indifferent as to whether the plant is cold or warm, lit or unlit. So, while we believe energy requirements will grow in the immediate future, there is no necessity in the notion that in the long run the energy demands will be increased—we may learn many techniques of reducing costs which we now assume are essential.

Automated plants are likely to use very high temperatures (or very low ones), vacuums, and the like in the production processes. All of these achievements are at the cost of energy. And, of course, the automated plants, by their nature, must be large-scale activities. This will tend to concentrate the uses of energy in selected geographical areas. We already are familiar with the fact that an enormous amount of our manufacturing effort takes place in the northeastern United States.

10. What are some of the inherent rigidities we can expect to accompany automation?

Any major automated system is bound to be complex. This means it will require long-term planning. It will not, then, be possible to change manufacturing directions easily. And an enormous amount of money will be invested in the existing automated industries. The pressure would be to continue to manufacture what is being made, since any change in product might involve enormous costs in capital outlay for new plants and new systems.

Since it is efficient to operate an automated plant at something very near maximum capacity, such a steady-state production system requires a steady-state consumption system. There would naturally be pressure for a guaranteed market for products. This, in itself, constitutes a major rigidity.

A truly automated plant would employ no direct labor. There would be supervisory personnel and perhaps repair personnel, and that would be about all. Accordingly, we can see that there would be a tendency for the labor market to turn rigid. The supervisory personnel could become an elite group—unchanging until retirement. The repair crews would tend to form relatively permanent teams since they, too, would probably be on a salaried basis. The result would be a small, relatively stable labor market, with little opportunity for newcomers other than on a replacement basis.

The variety of products also might begin to disappear. It would be even less likely that small manufacturing establishments could compete with large plants than it is today. Therefore, there might be fewer and fewer types of a single product. The temptation would be to say that one type of refrigerator turned out by a few automated plants would be sufficient. Also, product improvements might be slowed down or held off even more than they are today because the automated plant, in all its complexity, might be less easy to change than the ordinary manufacturing plant.

11. Describe an energy-intensive net and give at least one example of your own making.

The most public of the intensive energy nets in America today would be the combination of the automobile, roads, service stations, oil companies, and so on. This complex system, put together to keep the American automobile in motion, consumes a great share of the energy used in America. When we buy an automobile we enter into a complex system which guarantees that we will allocate rather significant amounts of dollars to the use of oil, gasoline, and repair services. So we have the tire manufacturers, the station operators, the road construction crews, the oil companies, the automobile agencies, and the repair shops all consuming energy to keep our machines in motion. There has not been, in the history of the world, so widespread and complex an energy consumption system.

12. See if you can think of several moral issues connected with automation that were not discussed in the text.

If we have automated plants, and if they become very common, we are going to face the very serious question of whether or not it is moral to work. The old Protestant ethic in America is that it is both good and virtuous to work. But if we can, as we have done with farming, use but 5 or 10 percent of our working force to produce all the manufactured goods, what then of the others? Will leisure become a "forced" choice? We know that many retired people suddenly feel that life is no longer worth living. They die early because they have been cut out of what they see as the mainstream of life—the excitement and the daily contacts of the work situation. Could this happen to a large segment of our population?

It may or may not be true that idleness makes mischief. But where large numbers of unemployed youth gather, there does seem to be a greater crime problem. Imagine, then, most of the population unnecessary and unwanted in the work force. What kind of ethical system will we build to keep them from crime and from mischief—to provide them with a life with meaning and a sense of contribution?

Does a human being have a natural right to employment? Does that employment have to be genuinely needed? Is there such a thing as too much leisure too soon? Can we require people to consume what we manufacture whether they want to or not? Can we continue to use up great quantities of the earth's resources and still feel productive and moral in the broader sense? All these are moral issues which automation could bring to the fore.

13. Work out, for yourself, as many consequences of the need for a guaranteed market as you can. Do you think these will result in profound social changes?

A guaranteed market as a goal requires that people have a guaranteed income or you cannot provide purchasing power for the market. To guarantee a market you also have to assure yourself that people will not switch from one product to another too readily or too often. There would be a tendency, then, to cut down on the variety of goods offered, to limit the entrance of new enterprises into the market, to fix the prices at rather rigid levels, and generally try to build as predictable a situation as can be built. All this spells the end of many freedoms for the consumer. In short, we might find ourselves backing into a planned economy, highly centralized, indifferent to human variation and whim.

We can imagine, then, a system of negative income tax payments to make sure that everyone has sufficient purchasing power to keep the automated industries at work. We are likely to find that the type and number of products are being planned years in advance of any public statement of pressing need. We may find our lives worked out, by others, in far greater detail than we consider necessary or healthy.

14. Describe supply, automated manufacture, and guaranteed markets as an input/output system.

The primary inputs to an automated manufacture (once the system has been designed and built) would be materials and energy (not labor). An automated plant, then, will make continuous demands on raw materials somewhere between 70 and 100 percent of the plant's capacity.

The heart of the input/output system (the little black box) is the plant itself—a self-directing, integrated manufacturing complex. The actions taken in the plant bring about the output.

The output of the automated system is the service or the product. In the case of products, we could expect a certain basic uniformity. To be sure, the computer in the system may be able to create a variety of *apparent* differences to satisfy individual tastes; but the basic elements must be, by nature (if efficiency and price are important) pretty much the same. In the case of services in an automated system, we would again expect a certain amount of standardization. Can services be automated? Yes, they can, if the computer is given the intellectual tasks of the system. But again, because of the nature of the computer, only that particular type of service which is anticipated can be provided. Or, more complexly, only that kind of variation in the service which can be anticipated (and hence programmed) can be offered.

The amount of the output of the system would presumably be in balance with the inputs to the system. Again, the result would be a product production of about 70 to 100 percent of the plant capacity. The closer to the 100 percent mark the plant comes, the more efficiently the plant will be used and, assuming no inordinate "rake-offs," the cheaper the resulting product will be.

15. What, basically, is a control position?

A control position is a decision point. More than that, the decision made can, in fact, be executed. That is basically what we mean by control. We mean that once something has been decided it can be done.

When we talk about control positions in relation to automation, we mean to imply that large-scale production centers become control centers. The enormous concentration of money and manufacturing power inevitably will result in political power. Political power means control of the population. With control over the population will come control over tastes, wants, desires, and needs. This could be fatal to a republic or a democracy.

HIGHLIGHT QUESTIONS, CHAPTER 11

1. What was it about early computer installations which might still affect the way computer personnel deal with operational personnel in the business?

Early computer installations primarily were scientifically oriented. What this meant was the manager of the enterprise or business unit did not necessarily need to know precisely what the computer people were doing. A certain type of problem solving or scientific development was expected but, since the computer center was isolated in the enterprise, it could not seriously affect management techniques, though it might well result in the development of new products or new scientific breakthroughs.

Computer personnel, then, were scientists and were used to being somewhat isolated from the mainstream of the business enterprise. To many computer personnel, this isolation and this mystique became an expectation and a way of life. It is in this self-definition that the seeds of dissension between computer personnel and operating personnel were sewn.

2. Name one or two of the in-house problems faced by operational managers when the business computer arrived on the scene in competition with the scientific computer installation.

First of all, it was perfectly natural for the members of the scientific computer installation to expect to be able to dominate the business computer installation and the business personnel. After all, they were there first. Second, having a good scientific background and often a longer training, the scientific people were inclined to look down their noses at the business programmers and other business-oriented computer personnel. This latter group may not have had quite the rigorous mathematical training the scientific people had had.

Operational managers want to have all people in the business working together. So two differently oriented computer groups in the business presented some difficulties in personnel relations and management. This difficulty was compounded by the fact that the manager did not, at the time, have the proper tests of efficiency and accomplishment for computer installations. These are developing, but rather slowly.

No one, in the early days, really knew just how much power the computers actually had. When their enormous true abilities came to the fore, both managers and computer personnel became hard pressed to use the equipment and the programs efficiently. Again, it was a matter of practice and learning and, quite often, simply trial and error. It was not and it is not easy, to determine just how broadly the computer will affect the "normal" operations of the business, and just how much rigidity it will insert in the system in the name of planning, uniformity, and control.

Finally, the computer, by its nature, made input and output demands—both in terms of the amount of information handled and the form the information had to take. Managers tended to abdicate control because they did not understand the system. Often, then, operational personnel became the slaves to the informational demands of the computer, instead of the other way round. Only gradually has this problem been brought under control.

3. What is a feasibility study? Why did businesses make use of them in regard to computer installations?

Basically, a feasibility study is nothing more or less than an in-depth inquiry into the organization and structure of a firm to determine whether some planned event will be necessary or effective, or both.

In the case of the computer, businesses had to take a hard look at the organization of their information systems to see whether the computer could be inserted into the system on an economical basis. Would it pay for itself? Would it increase the capacity of the information system to handle business growth? Could the proper people be hired or trained? What would be the relationship of the computer staff to the other personnel in the company?

In the early computer days, computers were not cheap. To bring a computer into the firm meant the expenditure, in rents or purchases, of millions of dollars, and the commitment to a continuing budget expense month after month and year after year. With such large expenditures possible, management demanded proof that the computer could indeed be useful. To provide this information certain basic types of feasibility studies were developed.

Today, such studies are still required if the job is to be done properly. But a good deal of information has been gathered about the elements of a successful system so the feasibility studies can be more swiftly and cheaply done.

4. **Name some of the advantages of making use of an outside computer specialist in determining whether a business truly needed a computer. What were some of the disadvantages of using such an individual?**

One of the advantages of the study by the outside expert was that the business was subjected to an objective study devoid of vested interest. The outsider could poke and probe the organization as an assignment, knowing it would not affect his or her personal career. And the outside specialist does this sort of thing for a living and is, therefore, more practiced at what needs to be dug out and what can be done with the information once it is at hand. The outside specialist also might have developed his or her own team of experts, which can probe the business in an orderly way without disrupting the day-to-day operations of the firm.

The disadvantages inherent in outside consultation include the fact that the outsider does not have the deep interest and commitment to the success of the enterprise that in-house people naturally feel. And, of course, the outsider is a stranger who has to poke and probe a good deal even to gather the most fundamental information about the business. Much can be missed in the short time allowed for the probe. What is said about the enterprise is not always what is actually going on in the enterprise. Of course, the outsider costs a good deal of money. And since the money is paid by the firm, the outsider might be reluctant to offend those who will write the check. These are a few of the disadvantages.

5. **What is meant by the term "data processing family?" What are some of the new members of that family that you might know which are not mentioned in the chapter?**

When we use the term *data processing family* we have reference to all those people who work directly with computers and computer installations—the programmers, center manager, librarians, keypunch operators, and the like.

With the advent of computer terminals we find that many operational personnel in the business become inadvertent members of the family. There is something enchanting about computing equipment—it often draws involvement and interest of a high degree. So it would be perfectly natural if operating personnel would gradually grow more and more interested in most matters related to computing and computer operations.

With smart terminals and the possibility of tailoring them to the business enterprise, we may get a new group of system/machine designers. That is, we might find a marriage between knowledges about systems themselves and the kinds of equipment that can be designed and built to serve the purpose. In the past, systems analysts have had to be familiar with the kind of equipment available, but they did not have to have an intimate part in the premanufacturing development of such equipment—at least not to the sharp degree they do today.

Massed data files present their own class of special problems. As data banks grow in size and in number, we are apt to have a new kind of individual in the organization—the mass data specialist. This has elements of the librarian in it, but is inclined to make a number of special demands which have not yet developed or been sensed.

6. What is "record dependency?"

Record dependency is a form of fear or timidity. Basically, it is a refusal to make a decision without documented and complete information, since to do otherwise would be to take a risk. As we get more and more familiar with masses of data on paper, we tend to rely more and more on documentation before daring to act. And, of course, there is the feeling that if a vast quantity of paperwork is in support of a decision which turns out to be wrong, the buck then can be passed to those who compiled the report—and blame does not fall on oneself.

Computers can produce a veritable sea of printed "information." The tendency, then, is to demand a number of computer printouts before actually attempting to act. The hidden assumption is that anything produced by a computer is more real and more accurate than anything produced by observation or fractional notation. Also, there is a tendency to believe that the more "information" one has the more accurate the information is. The is the "mass makes truth" principle. It is a fantasy.

7. What is "defensive documentation?"

Defensive documentation is a subelement of record dependency. It boils down to doing absolutely nothing unless there are physical records which would cover you in case of failure. Or worse, it is the principle that you never act unless there is a collection of paper somewhere which explains why you acted and what that action was.

Where record dependency permits the individual to refuse to decide because "there is not enough information on which to base a decision," defensive documentation says, "I will only decide those things that I can clearly document."

8. Just how are record dependency and defensive documentation related? What are some of the dangers involved in these activities for the business?

Record dependency is the broader of the two terms. It includes the more specific matter of defensive documentation.

The dangers of these activities are that they preclude action when action is needed. And if action is decided upon, they tend to limit the kind of action to only that which can be documented —on which one can put the best possible face.

Since both record dependency and defensive documentation are acts of fear, we can assume fear of that acute nature could well distort the ability of an individual to make a judgment.

Businesses that severely punish managers to make wrong decisions tend to guarantee both defensive documentation and record dependency as a way of life.

9. What exactly is the "ultimate test" that a naive manager can apply to determine whether a computer center is effective?

If the period is shortening between the time that data needs to be gathered and a decision is made, this is the *ultimate test* of success of any information system, including the computer systems we have been discussing.

Computers are installed to gather information faster and more efficiently than could be done otherwise. Computers are installed because they can perform arithmetic and logic faster than could be done otherwise. Computers have been installed to make decisions more quickly and easily. If the time between data gathering and action point is expanding rather than shrinking, the computer (or other information system) is a public failure!

10. What is the "mass data problem" from the point of view of the business enterprise?

Unfortunately, the computer has been a primary instrument in preparing and presenting ever-increasing amounts of paper to management. If the computer is the arithmetic and logic machine it is supposed to be, the computer should receive the burden of reducing the actual amount of paper that has to be presented to managers. This is the heart of the "mass data problem." Managers are getting more "information" than they can possibly read and summarize mentally.

There is another element in the mass data problem. It is simply that the more information you have, the harder to find exactly what you need, and the more expensive such a search becomes.

11. Name a few of the problems involved in data accessibility.

Data accessibility is a subset problem of the mass data problem mentioned earlier. Basically, the more information we have on file, the harder it is to find applicable information, and the more expensive the search is. Also, along with the problem of access is the problem of filing. Under how many different cross-indexed topics will we file information so that we can find it? We do not always know precisely the title of the information we seek. Cross-indexing, then, is very important.

Also, we must realize that the more information we demand, gather, and store, the more expensive that information becomes. Storage costs are being reduced every day, but storage is still not cheap. What we really want is to be able to decide, before storage is necessary, just exactly what needs to be stored.

Data accessibility also involves a time factor. The more information we have on hand, the longer it may take to dig out the information we need. This could, in industries demanding high-speed decisions, turn out to be a fatal flaw. When it is too late to make a judgment, the amount of information we have on hand to make the judgment is of no use at all.

12. Why are we concerned, in this chapter, with who structures the business job?

Traditionally, management people carried the task of deciding what jobs were needed in the business and what the qualifications were for the job. But the computer tends to make demands of its own upon the operating personnel of a business and also intrude upon their time. In a serious way, this proved to be part of the definition of the job. The demands of the computer for documentation and other items eats into management's definition of what should be done with the time available. This business of job definition, auditing, and control is still the primary responsibility of management.

Indirectly, the demands of the computer for information for problem solution also tends to intrude upon management's decision about what should operating personnel be doing. Both sides of the coin, then, tend to be job defining in unexpected ways.

13. What are some of the problems inherent in a company data processing committee?

A data processing committee, like any other, tends to get tasks done in inverse proportion to the number of members on the committee.

Often data processing committees do not contain a member or members from top management, with the result that any decision made by the committee is subjected to yet further review. In this latter review, much that has been explained and decided has to be done all over again. And the senior people involved do not have the advantage of familiarity with the problem as it developed during the committee deliberations.

Often the data processing committee elects (or management appoints) the head of the computer center to chair the committee. This immediately sets up a bias, no matter how accidental, toward the computer problems of the center and not toward the general information problems of the firm.

The broader the constituency of the data processing committee, the more likely the goals and needs of the whole enterprise will be considered. It is not necessary that the members of the data processing committee be computer experts—although a fair amount of knowledge of the limitations of computers and computer personnel would go a long way toward helping solve company-wide problems.

14. Name some of the things you believe should be included in any management EDP report.

The cost of the data processing operation itself is very important. We need to know how much has been spent for what in the computer center. We need to know how many dollars assigned to other departments are fed back into the computer center for services performed. We need to know what the communication costs of the enterprise are. We need to know whether the service provided is the service asked for and expected by the operating personnel. We need to determine whether the current mode of operation is the cheapest mode possible. We need to know whether the center works for the enterprise or the enterprise is working for the computer center.

Certainly any proper EDP report will look to the future communication and problem solving needs of the enterprise and lay early plans for meeting these problems in the cheapest possible way. This means keeping a very keen eye out in regard to technological developments and to the customary reductions in cost which such developments can bring.

Also, an EDP report should contain information in regard to the expected expansion of the business as a whole, and just what demands this will place upon the communication facilities and equipment of the computer center and upon the computer center personnel.

15. Name at least one method of determining whether a consistently prepared business report is really needed.

Probably the most effective method is to prepare the expected report but to fail to send it to those who have received it in the past. If the report is not missed, it was certainly not seriously needed. If inquiries about the missing report come in suddenly and in good number, then one knows that the report is important, is needed, and should be continued. There is no need to make the matter any more complex than that.

We have now completed our answers to the highlight questions to chapters 7 through 11. Again, we have tried to couch our answers in such a way as to trigger further inquiry and further discussions.

STUDENT SELF-TEST

There are two ways in which the self-test might prove useful. You might wish to take the test without any reference to the chapters in the book or to the answers which follow the test. If you achieve a grade of 70 percent or more, you can assume you understand a good deal of what you have read. If you take the test as an open-book test (referring to the chapters themselves on a "look-up" basis) you should achieve a grade of 90 percent or higher to feel sure you have understood the material presented.

Take a separate sheet of paper and list the appropriate terms for the blanks below:

1. A ________________ ________________ is most often a private or quasi-private corporation which is, in fact, a monopoly for a given

type of service, and is therefore regulated by the state and federal governments.

2. A public utility must build and provide facilities which can handle ____________ loads of activity in spite of the fact that this capacity will not be needed often and will not be used regularly.
3. Where the public utility will often have a ____________ ratio of average use to the total capacity of the system, the private utility can see to it that the ratio of average use is very close to maximum capacity of the system.
4. Utilities have, in the past, been classified into four general headings: ____________ carriers, ____________ utilities, ____________ or ____________ facilities, and ____________ facilities.
5. When several programs are available in internal storage, ready to be executed, we call the function ____________.
6. If there are to be large data banks at computer sites, methods have to be worked out to keep this type of information reasonably ____________.
7. The ordinary telephone lines, so familiar in the United States, were not originally designed for ____________ transmission of information.
8. We would expect a computer public utility to provide a number of ____________ programs to perform normal mathematical functions, certain types of household chores, and the general accounting requirements of families.
9. When a computer can talk back to the terminal operator and ask questions to clarify communications, we say that the computer is in ____________ mode.
10. Programs designed by other computer terminal operators who are willing to let the programs become available to anyone who wishes to use them are called ____________ programs.
11. Programs designed by the terminal user for a specific and confidential purpose are called ____________ programs.
12. Security systems need to include some method of ____________ the terminal user to be sure the right person is asking for the right information.
13. When a customer's expenditures could be posted directly to the bank concerned by a computer, we are talking about ____________ ____________ transfer.
14. Today there is a small "black cloud" on the horizon of the computer utility—it is the ____________.
15. The personal computer does not normally require extensive ____________ ____________ measures since only the person who purchased the machine is likely to have access to its memory.

16. When we transmit millions or tens of millions of digits per second, we are working in what is called ______ ______ .

17. In a public computer utility we would expect a mathematical language, a business language, and quite probably a ______ language.

18. Computer programmers like to think in boxes, wherein each box represents a procedure made up of several computer statements. We call this process, when it is put on paper, ______ ______ .

19. Cultural uniformity is very dangerous since it can turn the common response into the preferred response and the preferred response into the only ______ response.

20. Civilization—elegance combined with technological support—has a major sin, a sort of built-in booby trap. We call this sin ______ .

21. An adequate data base could be called the ______ memory of the business.

22. ______ storage has the quality that any datum stored therein can be found as quickly as any other.

23. The compromise between random searching ability and mass storage is a feature of most ______ memories.

24. A magnetic tape is read ______ .

25. A magnetic ______ band is wrapped around each data cartridge.

26. When information is moved from one kind of storage medium (like a cartridge) to another kind of storage medium (like disks) before entering the computer, we say such information is ______ .

27. Probably the largest labeled storage unit in the computer, from a programming point of view, is the ______ .

28. A million bytes of information is called a ______ .

29. When like items must be grouped together before they can be handled by the computer or by the storage medium that the computer is using, we call the handling ______ ______ .

30. When we can directly inquire of the computer about any given item which arrives at the desk chronologically, we have a case of ______ ______ data processing.

31. A tape from which information may be abstracted, but upon which we cannot write, is called a ______ tape.

32. The grandfather, father, son system of tape storage is an example of an ______ protection.

33. An arrangement of vertical tracks on a set of disks, though conceptual, is an example of a ______ of information.

34. The most common methods for arranging files are ______ sequence or ______ sequence.

35. The identifier of a volume of computer information is called a volume ______________ .

36. There are three methods of sharing data bases: device sharing, channel sharing, and ______________ sharing.

37. Almost any data base has some kind of basic minimum information unit. We most often call that unit of information (collection of bytes) a ______________ .

38. In the case of a national data base with credit files on each and every citizen, those who have received poor ratings are apt to find themselves outside the ______________ .

39. We will probably see ______________ computer utilities established before we see the establishment of ______________ computer utilities.

40. By far the cheapest, but not always the most effective, method of large-scale data storage is the ______________ ______________ .

41. In this text we have called the sales people, the clerks, the production people, the direct supervisors, and most of the managers of a business firm ______________ personnel.

42. When the regular employees of a firm are constantly feeding information, on demand, to the computer system, we refer to them as ______________ slaves of the system.

43. Computer terminals with considerable calculating and memory power in their own right are called ______________ terminals.

44. A rather common rule in the computer field, which attempts to define the centers of usage of information, is called the ______________ data processing rule.

45. ______________ ______________ is the amount of time it would normally take to get an item online to the computer center, get it processed, and get the answer returned.

46. Distributed data processing takes a ______________ view of the enterprise.

47. Those places where activity actually takes place—where customers are contacted, where sales are closed, and so on—are called ______________ nodes.

48. Unusual material infrequently needed and which can be stored in some central location is usually called ______________ data.

49. In the ______________ pattern of distributed data processing we do not have a centralized computer system but rather have a series of fairly sophisticated mini computers linked to one another.

50. In the ______________ configuration of data processing, we are apt to find a central computer hooked directly to a series of simple or smart terminals.

51. In the ______________ linkage one might see a large-scale central computer connected to several mini computers, each of

which in turn is connected to an appropriate number of smart terminals.

52. The act of measurement gives an importance of an artificial kind. Equally, the act of translation into computer language and the acts of ________________ and storage can give a datum a sanctity which it could never otherwise maintain.
53. In the ________________ configuration we might find several mini computers, each with its own data base. And each of the minis would be hooked up with an appropriate number of smart terminals.
54. In the early computer days, it was imagined that a highly centralized computer system would eliminate most of ________________ management.
55. One can only generate real interest in an activity to the degree one has control over that activity. This should be a compelling argument in favor of ________________ of management processes.
56. Computers, properly distributed throughout the firm, properly supported by data bases no larger than they need to be, ought to be able to reduce the enormous amount of ________________, which is one of the great expenses of modern business.
57. Distributed data processing is apt to be slowed down considerably by its natural conflict with already well-established ________________ data processing configurations.
58. The larger the data base, the more difficult is the business of ________________ information.
59. In the old days, there was a joke that about 60 percent of the benefit to be gained from installing a computer came from a company's preliminary ________________.
60. Distributed data processing will present management with the opportunity to ________________ the computer terminals, and the minis, with which they may be connected, to the particular tasks at hand.
61. The art of ________________ (linking the terminals, computers, and special equipment) has grown mightily in the last decade.
62. Information is said to be the ________________ of the enterprise.
63. Three decades ago, Del Harder of the Ford Motor Company used the term ________________ to describe the mechanical handling of automobile parts between some of the assembly processes at the Ford manufacturing plant.
64. The original ________________ ________________ has been nothing less than a long series of decades, each one of which saw some machinery take over some of the previous muscle jobs performed either by animals or human beings.
65. ________________ ________________ is simply information which is fed back into a work process so we can adjust, while working.
66. Possibly the oldest and the simplest example of ________________

________ is the fly-ball governor attached to the old-fashioned steam engine.

67. Motors, or other equipment, whose job it is to adjust the operations of an automated system to meet preestablished criteria after it has been determined a variation from the norm has occurred, are called ________ ________.

68. A human being might well be called a class A ________.

69. A petroleum cracking plant or a chemical plant would be an excellent example of a ________ industry.

70. A small plant making sections of the undercarriage of a particular model of aircraft on a small-lot order basis would be a good example of a firm using ________ ________ production techniques.

71. The application of energy and machinery to replace human or animal muscle is called ________.

72. A system is ________ when human intervention is not necessary from the start to the finish of operation.

73. The term ________ ________ is frequently and erroneously used to describe the interjection of the computer into the paper-handling activities of modern business offices.

74. Major changes have been taking place in service industries during the last decade or two. Properly these changes would better be called ________ than automation.

75. Small independent businesses are disappearing and small ________ businesses are taking their place at what seems to be an increasing rate.

76. While it can realistically be said that automation will actually require less ________ per item manufactured, this may not be quite the problem we face in the future.

77. The Aswan Dam in Egypt is a classic picture of the ________ problem.

78. It has been said that everything which was a sin during the medieval period became a ________ during the Renaissance and vice versa.

79. One of the important necessities of a truly automated plant is the need of a ________ market for that plant's product.

80. Large-scale product manufacturing centers, representing concentrations of energy, talent, and capital, are likely to become ________ centers.

81. Originally, the computer was assumed to be a complex ________ instrument primarily for the use of engineers and scientists in the business enterprise.

82. In early computer days, business problems presented at the computer center for solution were generally given ________ priorities than the scientific problems.

83. Studies to determine the condition of an enterprise, and whether or not it truly needs a computer, are called ____________ studies.

84. As business grew more experienced with computers the need for ____________ consultants tended to decline.

85. ____________ ____________ is the gentle art of never making a decision without large quantities of facts and paper to support it.

86. ____________ ____________ means that often managers will not consider it necessary to make a decision because the reports they have received are inadequate.

87. The ultimate test of computer effectiveness is that the date when data must be gathered is moving ____________ to the date when the data must be used.

88. An indication that all is not well in the data processing center is the situation where the operational personnel of the enterprise are in a state of ____________ relative to the computer.

89. Since the computer is both a logic and an arithmetic machine, there is no inherent reason for great masses of ____________ output from the computer.

90. It is possible these days to forgo computer ____________ entirely by producing appropriate diagrammatic images on cathode ray tubes for terminals in the manager's office.

91. Another test of the effectiveness of a computer center from the point of view of the general manager is whether or not the data asked for is received in time in the proper ____________ .

92. There are many computer installations in the country wherein requests for data are ____________ longer than they were prior to the installation of the computer.

93. An additional test the general manager, sans knowledge of the details of computer operations, can apply is the question, "Who demands problem ____________?"

94. The demands from the computer center for information and the type of printouts sent out to different operational personnel by the center have a tendency, on their own, to ____________ the job that is to be done.

95. In many businesses the data processing manager is required from time to time to present to higher management a summary of the month's or year's activities. This constitutes what is called the management ____________ report.

96. A ____________ ____________ section of a good EDP report is nothing more or less than an honest evaluation of parts of the computer operation which are no longer of valuable economic service to the enterprise.

97. A ____________ report is a computer report which has a mailing list, which was established some time ago, and which is sent to interested managers or other personnel on a regular basis.

98. The third generation of computers was best suited to large-scale ______________ operations.
99. An information net of sufficient thoroughness that decisions at any level can be based on facts, and that the facts upon which judgment will be based will be as good in one part of the enterprise as another, is an example of the achievement of the ______________ to manage.
100. One of the primary effects of computers on management, initially, was a certain serious loss of ______________ over the affairs of the enterprise.

This test was put together to give you the opportunity to see how well you could remember and understand the meaning of a number of terms which were introduced in the last five chapters. In checking the answers you may have given perfectly acceptable synonyms for the words given. Count these as points earned.

ANSWERS TO TEST QUESTIONS

---

1. public utility
2. peak
3. low
4. common, power, community or regional, communications
5. multiprogramming
6. secure
7. high-density
8. standard
9. conversational
10. shared
11. proprietory
12. identifying
13. electronic funds
14. minicomputer
15. security
16. burst mode
17. domestic
18. block diagramming
19. approved
20. bureaucracy
21. organized
22. random
23. auxiliary
24. serially
25. tape
26. staged
27. volume
28. megabyte
29. batch processing
30. real-time
31. read-only
32. organizational
33. cylinder
34. ascending, descending
35. label
36. memory
37. field
38. system
39. private, public
40. magnetic tape
41. operational
42. functional
43. smart
44. 80/20
45. lag time
46. network
47. activity
48. exception
49. ring
50. star
51. step-star

52. classification
53. ring-star
54. middle
55. decentralization
56. cross-talk
57. centralized
58. cross-indexing
59. self-analysis
60. tailor
61. interfacing
62. heart (or mind)
63. automatization
64. Industrial Revolution
65. negative feedback
66. negative feedback
67. servomechanisms
68. servomechanism
69. process
70. job order
71. mechanization
72. automated
73. office automation
74. mechanization
75. franchised
76. energy
77. energy-net
78. virtue
79. guaranteed
80. control
81. scientific
82. lower
83. feasibility
84. outside
85. defensive documentation
86. record dependency
87. closer
88. slavery
89. paper (or detailed report)
90. printouts
91. format
92. delayed
93. solution
94. define
95. EDP
96. phase out
97. scheduled
98. centralized
99. facilities
100. control

CHAPTER 13

THE NEW OFFICE

PURPOSE OF THE CHAPTER In this chapter we are going to take a broad look at the possibilities for the "new office."

For over 30 years the arrival of the totally electronic office has been a consistent prediction. Such an office is on the way—eventually. But, as in the case of automation, the progress has been much slower and more expensive than expected. And, too, we must not forget that many of the modern office machines require a new way of thinking about old problems. This sort of effort is usually slower in coming because it requires the breakdown of old habits of performance and the creation of new ones.

We know that the productivity of American industry has risen over 80 percent during the last few decades. No such comparable increase has occurred in the office. Estimates are the productivity there has risen but 5 percent at best. We know that the cost of office labor, like all labor in the nation, has risen about 6 percent annually. We know that automated techniques have brought cost factors under control so that there is an annual drop nearing 10 percent in such expenses.

Most important, we know that office forces make up about one fourth of all the labor force in America. Is this because the demands for information have grown so large? Or is this because office efficiency cannot keep pace with industrial efficiency and staffs have grown accordingly? We will explore some of these issues in this chapter.

TERMS AND CONCEPTS

- primary office functions
- clerk
- control
- job boredom
- lost records
- filing and finding
- duplication and mailing
- hard copy
- storage costs
- storage
- offline storage
- calculation
- memory typewriter
- reformatting
- copy preparation
- indexing
- verbal networks
- visual networks
- smart desk computers
- cathode ray display
- conference networks
- symbiotic systems
- micrographics
- automatic routing
- office automation
- business memory
- cleric
- barracks organization
- personnel turnover
- turnover rates
- transportation
- interoffice communications
- bottlenecks in the office
- microfilming
- magnetic media
- item searching
- editing
- updating functions
- desk terminals
- transmission
- document by-products
- intercom
- digital plotters
- facsimile transmitters
- visual terminals
- satellite nets
- microfiche
- altering film records
- office mechanization

Again, we are going to encounter many familiar terms in new settings. The computer, after all, is a universal sort of machine—it can be used to solve a great variety of different problems in different ways. Somehow it works out that the office is not so very different from the factory. The business is the production of information, not artifacts; but many organizational techniques will be common to both. We will be considering ideas as well as machines. It is the set of ideas that is important.

WHAT OFFICES DO

Offices, in the past, have performed two primary functions. First, their personnel read, sort, classify, calculate, duplicate, file, and respond to various types of communication to the firm. Oral contacts are usually committed to some written form at the time the contact occurs. Letters, invoices, purchase orders, and the like coming to the organization by mail are often recast in format and then dealt with in an orderly fashion. Thus, an office used to be defined as a place where paperwork was done for an organization.

The second primary function the office has performed, in the past, is that of memory. Memory as here used would involve the storage of tangible records (usually paper documents of various sorts) and the arrangement of these records in readily available files. It used to be said with some accuracy that a fire which caused serious property loss to a business was not as serious as one which caused the destruction of the records. For without the records, the firm has no accurate and indisputable memory of its past acts and commitments. In short, the firm has lost control of its own destiny until such time as these records can be recreated.

Early in our history offices were staffed by clerks. *Clerk* is a descriptive term derived from the word *cleric*. As those of us who remember history lessons know, clerics (churchmen) wound up doing the office work in the medieval period because they were about the only people who could read and write and deal with such information. Earlier still, the Babylonians and the Egyptians used religious institutions to maintain their records. Again, the scribes (in those days they were not known as clerics or clerks) were members of various religious orders and it was the order which trained the scribe.

Why all this expensive attention in ancient times to libraries, scribes, and records? Even the early Babylonian and Egyptian royalty knew that he or she who controlled the records, kept the library, took the census, knew the produce of the kingdom, and set the taxes had firm control. In fact, the ancient palace cultures depended very seriously on accurate records. Control, then, is the benefit that the office brought, and control is one side of the power coin. It is really a question of accurate memory. Orders cannot be issued to either armies or tax collectors unless one knows who they are, where they are, and what they have done in the past. Rumor and gossip won't do as sources of information for this type of large-scale activity, and this became clear very early in the history of civilized man.

PAST PROBLEMS

Ancent and modern offices consistently have had to face a series of special problems. Let us explore a few of them.

Barracks organization. When a functioning organization, be it church, army, or business, gets very large the office forces grow large, too. And observation reveals that the office can grow faster than the overall organization itself. This should not be very surprising since the amount of cross-communication between people goes up geometrically as the number of people involved goes up arithmetically.

Large offices generally have made use of the barracks form of organization. We are speaking of central areas filled with row upon row of desks and individuals working at those desks. We find typists, bookkeepers, checkers, order-fillers and what have you, all in a large room or a collection of large rooms. Such an arrangement was made to enhance communication among the office people who needed to communicate. Even more important, such an arrangement made it possible to design specific routes for special kinds of papers, such as invoices, purchase orders, and the like. Through the office would flow a river of paper. The channels had to be carefully planned. And, of course, the large central office lends itself to economical supervision—at least on the surface.

Job boredom. These mass offices, with paper functions broken down into small, easily understood, and repetitive tasks, did the work reasonably well, but had a sad type of human cost—boredom. So in many places the modern office is faced with error problems—that kind of carelessness which comes to the work one does when the mind is on some other thing. We call it daydreaming. Boredom can also come when one is not certain whether or not whatever one does has any real significance to the organization for which one works. Why worry about details when no one has ever explained why the detailed work is important, what the detail is used for, and where the information goes when it leaves the office?

Personnel turnover. The fractioning of jobs and the boredom which results has a corollary development—rapid job turnover. This in turn results in a higher office cost because of the necessity of at least minimal training on a repetitive basis. Again, we have a feedback loop to deal with. When the job is broken down into small segments to make training easier, the job can become dull, causing turnover, which in turn causes the need for the training of more people more often. We are reminded of the hamster in his habitat—a great deal of running goes on, but the actual amount of travel is insignificant. Oddly enough, there is some evidence to show that in large centrally organized offices the turnover rate tends to stay reasonably consistent through both good and bad economic times. This would lead us to wonder if the problem is not inherent in the way the office is organized, rather than on economic impingements from outside. At least it is a problem which is worth looking into very seriously when offices are redesigned in the future.

Even though office salaries are lower (on the average) than many other skilled-occupation salaries, the cost of training can become significant when turnover is rapid. It is not so much how little we spend as how often we spend what we do.

Lost records. Very large offices have enormous quantities of paper to handle. The results is that files can grow large and complex. The size and complexity alone will cause records to become lost. It is not even necessary that the records be misfiled—only that the person searching for the record is not aware of all the possible classifications under which the record could have been filed. The more people performing the filing function, the more likely these natural differences are to occur. New employees in the office who are not familiar with the records systems of the office can further complicate the matter of filing and finding. Again, the rate of turnover can materially affect the result. The higher the turnover the more often the errors are likely to occur, and the more difficult the task of clearing up filing problems on the part of the long-term regular personnel. In some offices it has been said the new trainees can disorganize the files at a rate faster than the trained employees can solve these ever-present but rather artificially created problems. This may not be common, but it surely is possible.

Transportation costs. Since large offices are assemblages of equipment, paper, and people, we know the latter, wherever they may actually live, must somehow assemble on Monday morning and each day of the week through Friday. This mass movement of people involves an enormous economic cost. We cannot say that organizations do not share these costs, since many large organizations pay considerable taxes. These taxes in turn go to support various forms of public transportation. And it would be an unwise office employee who drives daily to work who does not weigh the cost of the automobile and the cost of driving as a significant part of the cost of employment.

More important than cost, however, is the time commitment made by the employee. In the larger cities, from 45 to 90 minutes may be spent going to work and also coming home from work. This is, often, genuinely unproductive time if the person is required to drive an automobile through heavy city traffic. And we are not measuring the physical or psychological strain of such alertness, and what it might do to the general condition of the employee when he or she does safely reach the job, or does safely reach home at night. Tension and strain can interfere with work and can also, we have learned during the last few decades, take a significant toll of human health. Poor health or poor work, or both, also are significant economic costs for both the business organization and the working individual. This should not be treated lightly when we go about the matter of weighing what the "new" office should be.

Duplication and mailing. Most offices today still have a major commitment to paperwork in spite of the host of electronic aids which have been invented since World War II. Particularly, the duplication and mailing costs of offices can be considerable. When an original document arrives at the office, or when an original document is created at the office due to verbal contact, the process of duplication begins. There are many staff members who must have a record of the transaction in order that the business may perform the service required.

Even where there are central files in the organization, duplication may take place because many of the staff want documents on hand so that retrieval time for the record will be very short. And it has become a habit, in many offices, to send copies of any particular document to all those who might be concerned, one way or another, with what is going on. All this duplication and distribution costs money and also time.

Mailing costs are both external and internal. Moving documents around by interdepartmental mail, though it requires no postage, does have significant costs. The in-house mail organization hires employees and pays them salaries. There must be some kind of clearing station for the distribution of interoffice communications. Often this type of operation makes up the bulk of the actual mailing costs of an organization. And things "interoffice" do not always go well. There is an old joke about putting into the interoffice mail anything you wish to get rid of permanently and never hear about again. Regrettably, this is often more of a fact than a fancy for large organizations with complex intercommunication systems.

Expensive communications. Paper is so common and each single sheet so cheap that we tend to discount the cost of preparing records and letters. It always comes to executives as something of a shock to discover that each letter they dictate and mail can actually cost several dollars. The work itself looks simple, the cost of paper low. But employee time is seriously involved. First, a letter is dictated, then it is typed, then it is proofread, then it is delivered to the executive. He or she may wish to make further alterations or corrections, so the process is repeated. After a final check has been made, the letter is handled by several additional people before it is actually confined to the U. S. mails. Throughout this process employee time is being spent and the dollar cost tally grows. Letters do indeed cost several dollars each. Phone calls actually are a good deal cheaper. Why do letters continue, then? Because businessmen and women traditionally want "hard" copies of what they have done and what they have agreed to. Oral communication too often can turn out badly, with misunderstandings of all types cropping up. And human memory is a notoriously bad filing system when one wants cold facts unaltered by emotional or perceptual variations. There is no doubt about it, hard copies of transactions provide a good deal of safety for the business enterprise. The new office needs a more reliable, cheaper, more widespread, and more effective form of communication than the letter, the written memo, or the host of other interoffice and outer-office written com-

Office problems

munications. We will discuss some of the alternatives, in due course. Here we merely are roughing out the problems which every large office faces.

Bottlenecks. Every office of any size runs into the problems of bottlenecks in the communication lines. Someone puts a memo in an "in" basket somewhere, and there it lies as the hours tick by and the days march along to months. No action takes place because the important document slumbers alone and unattended. There is no automatic monitoring system to do a follow-up and a check on precisely where the document is and whether someone is doing something about it. The larger the office, the greater the number of documents involved, the greater the variety in the type of document, and the more staff involved in processing the document, the more likely there are to be bottlenecks where the work stops and time and money lie wasting.

Bottlenecks may be either accidental or deliberate. In any group of people there are bound to be difficulties, from time to time, in the matter of interpersonal relations. And it is not rare that someone sitting at a control position in a paper network (that single point where a document must pass before it is spread out through the organization) can sabotage anyone who has become an "enemy," real or imaginary. The deliberate bottleneck is the harder of the two to deal with, but fortunately makes up the smaller amount of the problem. The inadvertent bottleneck, once discovered, can be reasonably and quickly cured. The most typical cause, of course, is work overload—when a critical person at a desk is receiving more actual work than can be properly dealt with. In such a case, a backlog piles up and an automatic and continually increasing delay system is set up. The cure is to divide the work properly after determining just how much of a load each critical-point desk can actually handle.

Record storage costs. Paper records have to be filed and kept, usually for a fairly long time—from three to seven years. Stored paper usually occupies files, and files take up physical space. Physical space, in turn, in any business, must be maintained and this means the involvement of continual expense. In many large organizations whole warehouses are kept for the storage of records from the past and, even though these records may seldom if ever be referred to, they are necessary under the law. Worse, though it is true that records could be culled from time to time to reduce storage costs, the culling operation itself can involve more money than the actual idle storage. This means the amount of storage space assigned to old or obsolete records may continue to grow steadily.

Microfilming techniques have been applied to the problem of permanent record storage, with significant reductions in the expense of such storage. More important, at the time of the microfilming a certain amount of automatic culling may take place. So, not only are the records reduced in size, but the number of records being reduced may be cut down. Also, microfilm records tend to be filed in a more orderly way than paper records, and this means a record can be retrieved more quickly and with greater ease than would otherwise be the case. But even microfilmed records take up space, and the microfilming process is not cheap when a large number of records are involved. So businesses still face expensive files and expensive file maintenance problems. When we deal with the "new" office we will see if there are any satisfactory solutions to this problem when we combine the forces of word processing and the computer. *Word processing* is a general term which has to do with the application of scientific and management techniques that are so familiar in the factory to the business of office records, their creation, maintenance, and disposal.

We have now explored some of the principal problems which cause difficulties and expense for businesses attempting to keep accurate track of their current situation by consistent and regular reference to the past. Let us see what improvements the "new" office can bring.

THE COMPUTER IN THE OFFICE

The computer can, if properly programmed and installed, take care of several important matters for the modern office: storage, calculation, updating, editing, and reformatting. In the past, computers primarily have been used for computation, but in recent years a greater recognition has been given to their logic abilities, and this latter area can turn the computer into a competent and efficient copy producer and editor for the office.

Storage. The modern office may take advantage of the enormous storage capacities of the modern computer. Magnetic cards, magnetic tapes of various kinds, and magnetic disks can all hold very densely packed information, as we have discovered in earlier chapters. Of the magnetic media, tapes are quite likely the cheapest storage devices. Disk packs, as packs, are considerably more expensive. The offline type of storage (tapes and disks which have been removed from the drives) is actually the most important. We must gradually come to grips with the fact that an electronic record, though invisible to the eye, is nonetheless a permanent type of record which is, in fact, considerably easier to store and to protect than vast files of paper records. More important, if the tapes or disks are properly filed, great quantities of data can be scanned very quickly when the devices are mounted on their respective drives and the computer is given the task of doing the searching.

The problem facing the modern office is to decide what quantity of internal computer storage is necessary for operations, what amount of offline storage is required, and the particular devices which represent the most economical form of storage given the simple gross fact that we do not file to file, but rather file to *find* quickly and cheaply. Some offices in the past were always certain to transfer information from their disk packs to magnetic tapes. This was because the tapes had a greater storage density (number of characters which could be written per inch of tape) than disk packs, were considerably cheaper, and the transfer of the data from one medium to the other could be done at the rate of millions of digits per second. The transfer of such data was linear and did not require item-by-item searching. Admittedly, it took time to find the appropriate tape, to mount that tape on a tape reading device, and to transfer the information to a disk pack (for later item-by-item or data-group-by-data-group searching). But storage costs were indeed reduced, and careful planning could take care of leaving on mounted disk packs the most frequently needed information.

Electronic office storage can be arranged much like a modern library. The greater the call for an item the more likely it is to be separated into a special kind of storage where it can be readily available.

Furthermore, as in libraries, statistics can be kept on the amount of usage for any particular type of datum, and the appropriate storage medium selected. It is a matter of common-sense organization integrated with modern equipment. Many of the techniques useful in the past are no less useful now that we are in the process of modernizing the office to meet the electronic needs of today.

Calculation. We need not dwell too long on the fact that the computer is an enormously more rapid and versatile calculator than any of the mechanical devices of the past. More important, computer programs can be generalized to routinely handle calculations of a similar nature by merely stating the size of the numbers being fed into the machine and the particular sequences of calculations which are required. The sequences are subroutines or subprogram units which can be assembled in a tailor-made way to accomplish what we want. Over the years since the late 1940s, hundreds of thousands of standard routines have been programmed and are available to any modern computer center. The amount of special programming has been reduced and the cost of calculation has dropped a hundredfold. From a cost point of view, the advantage is that we can substitute readily available and reliable programs for both clerical skill and special training. If one understands which calculation to use and when, he or she does not require the skills of the mathematician. It is possible to listen to good music, and understand it, without personally possessing the ability to create it. Mathematics is much the same.

Editing. In the area of copy editing, the computer, particularly the combination of mini computer and smart terminal, is coming to the rescue of overburdened office staffs. Beginning with the simple memory typewriter and moving upward through the smart terminal to the mini computer, the office can bring the power of the computer (or some of its important elements) to bear on the problem of producing letters, reports, accounting statements, and the like with speed and accuracy. Editing is part of the complex of language-manipulating activity which we have chosen to call "word processing."

Typically, a secretary, making use of a memory typewriter, can generate a letter and make corrections on the rough draft in such a way that a correct copy is rapidly and automatically produced. And since the correct letter or report copy is stored inside the typewriter itself, one can produce more than one copy rapidly and on demand. Or one can go further and rearrange lines, sentences, or paragraphs to suit other purposes.

Ideally, a memory typewriter would have the capacity to contain hundreds or thousands of standard paragraphs that could be used to construct letters of a tailored type on demand. This is because the situations which come before a business office are frequently of a predictable nature. More important, the best kind of psychological and literary reply could be created for each type of situation. Again, this would reduce the amount of training and the educational level demand on office help.

If the memory typewriter is replaced by a smart terminal with the facilities of the memory typewriter and the cathode ray tube, and with the ability to do most straightforward calculations, we have an extremely powerful editing device.

We can go yet one step further. In turn, hook the smart terminal to a mini computer and take advantage of the enormous increase in available computer memory and the greater programming flexibility of the computer. In this event, many types of copy editing can be done directly on the cathode ray tube by means of a light pen or a typewriter keyboard input. The operator can see the changes as they are being made and can read the final form of the copy, which will be stored without the necessity of preparing a hard copy at the same time.

If the smart terminal is a part of a network of interlinked devices, copies can be reproduced, at will, at different points in the enterprise where they are needed.

Updating. Computers, by means of their extremely rapid search abilities, can be used to good advantage to update accounts, forms, and other stored materials. Since the storage is electronic, corrections can be made quickly and updated copies produced. Too, there are a number of standard "library" routines available, with most computers, to automatically handle the business of updating accounts and the like when the new information is fed into the system. A well-planned computer center usually can take care of the process of updating during quieter moments in the computing day.

Updating in the past generally has been confined to quantitative material; but there is no reason the same pattern could not be applied to the task of bringing master copies of legal contracts, paragraph units of letters, and advertising copy up to date. Such updating could be done on a sentence-by-sentence or a paragraph-by-paragraph basis as desired. Again, the end result would be ability to call up the document quickly and in the best possible final form.

Reformatting. Reformatting is a more complete activity than updating or simple editing. Here we are talking about taking information and completely rearranging it to suit a purpose other than the one for which it was originally compiled. We might want to take all of the accounts receivable, which were originally grouped by customer name, and rearrange them into a document that related the accounts receivable to geographic marketing areas. This would provide geographic distribution of debt, rather than a customer-by-customer list of accounts due.

One of the great advantages of the computer is that once a basic

Things the computer can do

data set has been stored, there are programs which can be written to rearrange the material in any number of formats suitable to the particular needs of different sections of the enterprise, and which, in the new format, are more easily read and more useful to those asking for the information.

DESK TERMINALS

Desk terminals (usually a typewriter keyboard and printer in conjunction with a cathode ray display tube) bring the computer to the office desk and replace the limited calculator. Desk terminals then can be used in the matter of copy preparation, editing, storage, transmission, and indexing. Now let us deal with each of these in turn.

Copy preparation. When a typist or secretary sits at a desk and prepares a letter or contract, or some other office form, on the desk terminal, a number of new powers are available. First, as the rough draft is typed, it is simultaneously being stored. Since the storage is electronic, a backspace followed by a strikeover (correction) results in a clean copy in storage, since the principle of destructive read-in and nondestructive read-out applies. When a final correct copy is achieved, the appropriate letter or other document can be produced quickly. In a well-ordered system, much more can take place. The stored document could quickly and electronically be fed into a computer and from there be transferred to an appropriate file. At the same time, the letter, if it is important to other offices in the enterprise, could be either reproduced at those stations (they, too, would have appropriate desk terminals) or, more likely, an index notice of some kind could be produced on the other terminals. An alert signal could be given that a particular type of document important to those stations had been produced. When the stations involved want to examine the material, it could be called up by a simple request to the central mini computer holding the files for the several desk terminals.

It is not necessary, of course, to interrupt the work at any of the active desk terminals. When those machines are idle the computer could monitor the lines and produce the appropriate index. Or the computer could signal the desk terminal operator, during any idle time, that an index list of important material is coming. Or the system could be set so the material list of indexed items could be produced at the end of the day just before the terminals are shut down. However one wants to arrange the matter, one is involved in a communication net wherein any material produced at any desk terminal that would be of concern to any other department in the business will be made available on demand to that department.

Editing. A desk terminal could have the same general editing abilities as we have discussed earlier. If the desk terminal has its own memory, the job can be done there; or if the desk terminal is connected to a mini computer, the full abilities of the mini computer can be called in to assist with the editing job. Any final material produced can be indexed, stored, and communicated to anyone else concerned who has similar facilities available.

Storage. Storage, with the smart terminal, may be local, temporary, or permanent. That is, the material simply could be stored for a few days in the memory of the smart terminal, or it can be sent temporarily to the mini computer with instructions to destruct after a certain passage of time. If the material is important, the mini computer can be instructed to arrange matters for permanent storage. At the time of the permanent storage, various other terminal locations can again be sent an indexed listing of what is stored and how it can be called up when needed. Once more we see the advantages of a desk terminal and computer mated to form a computer net.

Transmission. One of the reasons offices were created was to make possible the movement of information (usually on sheets of paper) from one desk to another quickly and efficiently. Since desk terminals and their related mini computers are electronic, the transmission of data can be instantaneous. There is no need for the physical transmission of actual objects. Communication lines merely have to be opened and the material can be transmitted at electronic speeds with far greater accuracy controls than have been available in the past. With this electronic transmission ability, we have the disappearance of one of the major reasons for the barracks-type of office which we discussed earlier. Individual office workers could be closer to the point of action where the information itself is created. One of the age-old conflicts (between staff and line people) might thus begin to disappear. What applies between desk terminals and between mini computers may also apply between communication stations in buildings, in cities, in states, and even (with certain improvements in satellite communications) in countries. An office might well require to be redefined from a group of people in a common location to individuals arranged in a common communication network.

Indexing. We have mentioned indexing earlier in this discussion. What we refer to is the business of creating a single line of copy, or less, which reveals to anyone concerned the nature and general content of some larger document. This index line (or sentence) is all that need be transmitted to other stations. Since all stations are on the same communication line, or have access to shared lines, the information can be called up electronically when it is needed. Libraries have had much experience in classifying and indexing books, magazines, and papers. Many of these techniques could be applied to the business of identifying the materials created at any desk terminal, and to the making of appropriate lists available to others needing to know what was done, when, why, and with whom.

It is indexing which can make or break the success of any communicative network. The index system must reveal information in an indisputable way to those who are searching. If one cannot find out what one needs to know, it is of no consequence whether the file is made up of paper, part of a network, a sophisticated electronic system, or not. The matter of concern has vanished as surely as though never recorded. So while the desk terminal operator may now require less of certain skills than the old-fashioned secretary, in certain areas, the desk terminal operator should be well trained in the matter of indexing the material created. This is the key to success or failure. This key is dependent not so much upon electronics or computers but on the well-trained, fully functioning human brain. There doesn't seem to be any final substitute for alertness, skill, and intelligence.

A by-product of all this creating of documents, using desk terminals, should not be overlooked. Because the information is electronically stored at one store or another, it is *already* in computer-usable form. This is very important since it means the elimination of the conversion of paper document to computer-readable form. The old-fashioned keypunch or magnetic tape typewriter can vanish. The material to be used by the computer is automatically created as a by-product of the creation of the original document at the desk terminal. We have what is called "dual document preparation." A complex term is here used for a simple and useful idea.

VERBAL NETWORKS

Offices for many decades (since the common use of the telephone) have been verbal networks. A great deal of time is spent talking over the telephone in almost any modern office. Again, were it not for the old-fashioned paper with which the offices of the past were forced to deal, the telephone itself should have led to the general dispersal of office forces. But the paper was there, and the telephone merely helped clarify what was written—or permitted communication about what to do with what was written, or permitted some avoidance of the writing in the first place.

The ordinary office intercom (either independently or in conjunction with the telephone system) is another common form of verbal network used in offices. The use of the intercom usually has been confined to groups of people who have a need for frequent daily contact and who do not wish to be inconvenienced by dialing long telephone numbers. So one form of intercom system has been the simple buzzer combined with the telephone. One merely presses the intercom button on the telephone, dials a single digit, and the buzzer sounds in the appropriate office. The conversation then takes place over the telephone. In another form, the offices are equipped with desk devices which are much like small push-button radios. One merely has to hold down the appropriate button to talk, and release the button to listen. For all of that, we are still saddled with the necessity of being in the near vicinity of one another, because the paper we use dictates its own conditions.

VISUAL NETWORKS

Visual networks, which are electronically possible, have not been exploited to the same degree as oral networks. This has been due to the fact that the oral communication lines have not had the capacity (in the past) to carry the detail required in the creation of pictures and diagrams at high speed. But with the advent of the smart terminal, certain kinds of facsimile transmitters (electronic devices which can scan and transmit drawings and pictures), and many types of digital plotters, the carrying capacities of communication lines have been upgraded.

Smart desk computer terminals can now be equipped with digital or graphic plotters similar to the one shown in Figure 13–1. Information of a complex type can be transmitted between terminals using this device. Clearly, this type of visual material can reduce the amount of verbal transmission necessary. The old Chinese saying, "A picture is worth a thousand words," is not an idle one.

FIGURE 13–1. Hewlett-Packard 7200 series graphic plotter

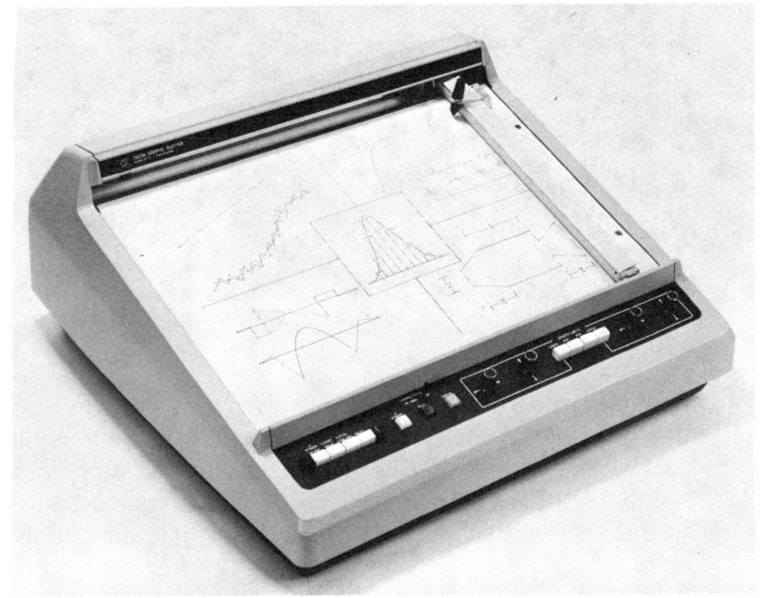

Courtesy of Hewlett-Packard Corporation

Plotters produce what we call "hard copy." Cathode ray tubes can present "soft" copy, such as that shown in Figure 13–2. Or photographic techniques can be employed to make hard copies from the picture on the cathode ray tube. There also are certain kinds of plotting devices which can duplicate on paper what appears on the cathode ray tube at the same time the picture is presented.

If documents as well as oral information can be transmitted from one point to another at near the speed of light, many of the former reasons for physical groups of people disappear. We could have an "office" made up of 20 people in 20 different geographic locations who could correspond with one another both verbally and visually in fractions of a second. If the communication facilities were in the employee home rather than a centralized office, and if the information is on call from a computerized central file, what then is the necessity or the advantage of driving to work each day to sit at a desk in a barracks room? The answer is clear enough—none! What would

FIGURE 13–2. Cathode ray tube display

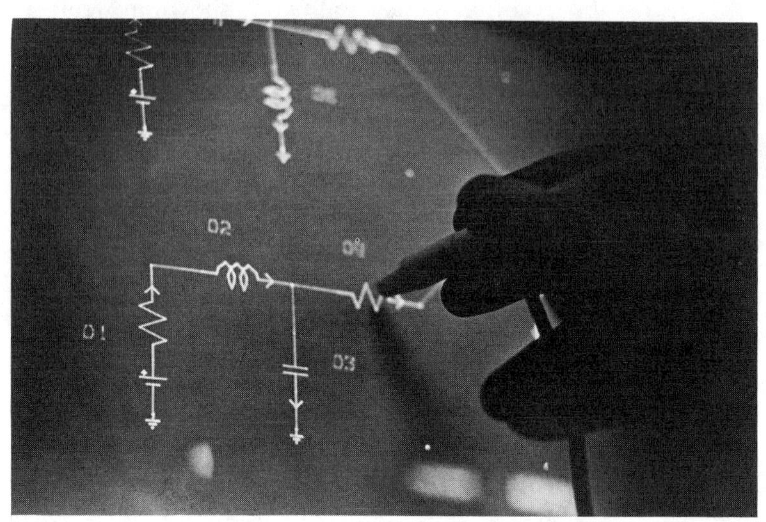

Courtesy of International Business Machines Corporation

be the monthly economic savings to employees who no longer had to spend money for cars (at least extra cars), or money for gasoline each week, or lose time in transit? Enormous! Why has this not instantly happened? First, the networks are going to cost money. We would require lines to be strung, in the way telephone lines have been strung, to most homes (or buried, as they are today). And these lines would need to be of a carrying capacity in excess by far of the current abilities of the telephone wires. And old habits are hard to break. We are used to supervising people, and not just the work they do. In all of us there is just a touch of the will to dominate. It would be very hard to dominate 20 or 30 people scattered over an area of a hundred-mile radius. All we would be able to do would be evaluate the usefulness and the quantity of the work they actually do.

In due course the networks will come, if they prove to be economically profitable. In slower course, our habits will change. The increase in leisure, the increase in productivity, the decrease in wasted resources, are too obvious to be held at bay too long. The limiting factor will be the recovery of the cost of stringing the more complex communication lines and in upgrading the quality of the lines which are to carry the messages.

Visual terminals, such as the one shown in Figure 13–3, have the advantages we have already listed; but notice that correction can be by keyboard or light pen (depending on the sophistication of the computer and the program which is driving the arrangement). In better programs, the light pen can be used to mark off a figure or

FIGURE 13–3. Profit statement on display

Courtesy of International Business Machines Corporation

category to generate a detailed analysis of the particular item appearing on the display. And if these terminals are properly linked to other office personnel in other quarters, a sort of electronic committee meeting can be held—the result of which is a jointly modified document.

CONFERENCE NETWORKS

Ideally, we should move from memory typewriters through smart terminals, through mini computers, to complete conference networks. The networks would include all of the communication devices (earlier mentioned) at each station plus simultaneous audio/television transmission. We would require for this type of electronic conference a grid of television screens—say a unit with five or more small individual cathode ray tubes set in some kind of grid. This would mean we could see a number of different individuals on the screen segments at any given time. We then could have almost all of the advantages of a full conference meeting. And if each of the sub-pictures were equipped with audio output, we actually could have a situation where people could debate and interrupt one another at will—much as they do in our ordinary workaday conferences where we all actually meet in the same room.

Participants in the electronic conference could, using either digital plotters or facsimile transmitters, literally pass papers back and forth to one another as they talked, argued, and debated the important points of the conference. More important, all these transmissions and debates could be recorded in their entirety and stored to be recalled when needed—pictures, facsimiles, comments, and all. Surely this would give the business a far more accurate memory than it has had in earlier circumstances. The argument that people will be less frank, were they to know their remarks are going to be stored and possibly reviewed at a later time, would seem, at least in formal institutions, to be spurious. Perhaps it would be good to have to measure one's words more carefully than in casual conversation. Perhaps the end result would be an elegance and economy of expression we would otherwise not achieve—although we must admit the Watergate tapes tend to refute such an assumption. Still, for all of that, the more accurate and realistic the memories of an institution, the more likely it can accomplish the tasks for which it was put together.

We must be careful at this point. The American society is moving to a near-paranoic level in regard to the amount of personal information which may be revealed. The categories *Mr., Mrs.,* or *Miss* are now forbidden on certain forms in the state of California—that is, the general counsel has advised that they are not legally proper (whatever that may be construed to mean). We are referring to certain forms used to collect information for employment. Presumably it is not legitimate to know the marital status of the individuals one intends to hire. Of course, it can be argued that government and private institutions ought not to hire on the basis of maleness or femaleness or marital status, but rather solely on abilities. Undoubtedly in the past there have been prejudices expressed about sex and marital status.

And yet, and yet! If employers become so careful they are afraid to express their needs as they see them, and if we become so sensitive to having opinions, right or wrong, recorded, how then are we distinguishable from the most fearful of dictatorships? Putting it another way, if in America we cannot move out of fear of law suits, and in a dictatorship we cannot move out of fear of prison, are we not in a very similar unhappy circumstance?

These are social problems of a subtle nature. Their resolution will come slowly and with some pain. And let us not think that computers, smart terminals, networks, electronic storage, et al. are not all imbedded in this problem. They are. Many times we will see what we believe to be sensible progress delayed, not for technical or financial reasons but for social reasons—or social fears. This is why it is never really comfortable to say that an achievement of technology will bring such clear improvements as to be soon enacted.

SATELLITE NETS

From time to time in the newspapers we can read about communication nets being set up intercompany and intracompany by making use of satellites. The satellite is a cheaper form of communication than millions of miles of wire. It is the satellite which will make the intracompany or intercompany conference economically possible in the next decade or so. The initial expense is high, but the carrying capacity of such devices is enormous. And if the traffic load is sufficient, the cost of individual messages will be very low. We must not forget the average business letter is estimated to cost $8.25 or more (when overhead and other expenses are taken into account). We might like to believe a telephone call costs only a quarter. But again, when we calculate executive time, overhead, and the myriad other expenses backstopping the telephone call, we find it costs at least $4 and possibly more. The satellite, then, if it can send messages (and it can) at rates lower than the ones specified (after suitable calculations for overhead and personnel time), has full economic justification. Since the satellite will have easily expandable capacity, it will have a lead advantage in the future that our current grounded communication lines may not.

Again, the fear of losing privacy, the reluctance to have our reactions permanently recorded, the possibility of message interception and misuse—all these may slow down the progress of the application of technology, economically feasible or no.

Satellites have certain additional advantages which we must mention. Information may be sent in bursts (high-density swift transmissions, taking only fractions of a second). The information could, we believe, also be coded (scrambled) in such a way as to maintain company and governmental secrets as required. And satellites might bring to an end the day-by-day business of executive travel. Will the airlines, heavily dependent upon business travel, be injured? Quite possibly. Will company competitive positions improve? Quite possibly.

SYMBIOTIC SYSTEMS

The "new" office may make use of what we call *symbiotic* computer or terminal systems. By the term we have reference to a cooperative effort between the computer and an operator or between the smart terminal and the operator. The computer or terminal may contain computer programs whose function is to assist the clerk, or typist, or secretary, or bookkeeper in the business of performing his or her work. For example, if a particular and common type of error is made, it is possible for the computer to advise the operator at the instant of the occurrence that an error has been made. It also is quite possible for a properly programmed computer to suggest the correct step or steps which should be taken to accomplish the task.

Theoretically, we could put into a computer of large storage capacity many of the standard operating formats of the business. When one of the personnel makes an error in judgment in regard to any of these standard procedures, the computer could intervene and ask appropriate questions or suggest appropriate answers. We mentioned, in an earlier chapter, that in its most primitive form the IBM System/32 could recognize misspelled words when it had been issued the call codes for certain routine procedures. These misspellings would cause the computer to intervene or to make corrections depending upon the program involved.

Any terminal system in the new office also would make use of some kind of data support system. Here we would be combining the normal type of computer memory with new techniques in micrographics. *Microfiche* is the name of a system of reducing images of documents onto indexed cards or sheets in such a way that they can be retrieved quickly. It is not uncommon to get between 200 and 300 images of documents on the equivalent of half a sheet of 8½-by-11 paper. Not only can individual items from a microfiche file be viewed on a screen, but an 8½-by-11 copy can be made when

"WE ARE IN THIS THING TOGETHER—
I CAN BE A LOT OF HELP."

Symbiosis

needed. More important, the computer itself can be tied into this kind of data storage in such a way that the terminal operator, the computer, and the microfiche file can all work together. Here we have what we call "data provision support." Each station in the office can get all the information necessary, through the computer and micrographics, to respond to any inquiries, to copy any necessary documents, and to transmit this information to others in the organization.

More recent techniques being developed permit the alteration of these microfiche files. That is, the film becomes a viable medium on which changes and alternatives can be recorded and the material then refiled for later use. The film approaches the flexibility of the magnetic type of storage.

Automatic routing is the final element in a truly symbiotic data handling system. By this we mean merely that any information gathered at any station in the new office can be routed quickly to any other station anywhere in the new office (or the company, for that matter) by means of electronic communication devices. No need to make copies. No need to rely on the old-fashioned mails. The information can be relayed to other points in the enterprise as quickly as it is generated.

IMPLICATIONS

Let us turn our attention to the implications of what we have discussed so far in this chapter.

First, a truly electronic office could as well be in one place as another. That is, the reasons for gathering people together in barracks room arrangements would be gone. The communication between stations would be electronic, and this communication would include papers, pictures, live conferences—any of the normal means of communication available to people meeting together. There is no technical reason why the office worker could not stay in the home to do the work if the home were properly equipped.

Once the barracks room arrangement vanishes, we also might be able to consider the possibility of keeping offices staffed 24 hours a day. The work load could be so arranged that the flow of communicative office work was never interrupted. The argument that this will not work very well, because most people won't work at night, would be acceptable except for the long experience of industries operating three eight-hour shifts per day. Some small bonuses might be required, as they are in industry, but the idle time would vanish and the gains might be considerable.

If the office is in the home, the physical costs of the industry could move from buildings to equipment. That is, the money which would normally be invested in the construction, maintenance, and operation of large barracks offices could be assigned to the provision of appropriate equipment in the home.

Second, we have been discussing, in many ways, the mechanization of the office rather than its automation. For, if we remember, automation implies the elimination of the human being from the process (with the possible exception of certain types of general supervisors). The very nature of the office—as an information agency dealing, often, with unique problems—would preclude total automation of services for quite some time. But there are many routine elements in the office which could be truly automated. If we are mechanizing offices, and we are, then certain types of rigidities are bound to follow. There will be a constant pressure to make communications more standard in nature, to reduce the content of the files to that which is frequently called for, and in general to bring the "office product" to the types of uniformity already familiar in industry.

Third, since one fourth of the labor market is actually working in offices, we might well conjur the reduction in automobile traffic and general physical movement, which would occur if we could truly put the office in the home—or at least disperse the offices around the city, the state, or the nation, to reduce the actual amount of travel required. This might well be an intermediate step—to plan one's organization to have ten or fifteen small offices near the workers, instead of one big one in the central city. The computer is peculiarly adept at solving these kinds of linear flow problems.

Now let us look at some of the unhappier sides of the coins we have just presented. The human being is a social animal. The long evolutionary development involved people cooperating in near physical proximity to one another. What would it be like to be isolated, surrounded by electronic equipment, in the home? Would the electronic communication be sufficient to give the feeling of social contact? Or would office workers resent not meeting one another face to face on a daily basis?

Would the isolation, via equipment, make the office worker even less sympathetic to the customer and less interested in the primary purpose of the enterprise? Much can be learned by the simple process of walking down a hall. Much can be learned about the feelings and attitudes of manufacturing workers just by meeting them in the corporate parking lot. Much of the esprit de corps so necessary to the successful organization is made up of inadvertencies of contact—the communication, in a casual way, of enthusiasm—the aura of a firm clicking along happily doing its job. Could this be lost if the people involved in communication are isolated, save as they use the communicative devices we have mentioned? There is no certain way to tell until it is tried. But we do know that some office workers resent the intrusion of electronic equipment and resent the cubbyhole isolation they currently face because some of the machinery is sufficiently noisy to require isolation.

If the electronic equipment we have been discussing, combined with the computer, acts symbiotically to raise the performance level of people—or conversely, allows people with more limited abilities to perform office work successfully, might we not create a group of illiterate outsiders—isolated from the main threads of the enterprise—dogmatically dealing with the problems only as the machinery they use permits them to understand the problems? We mention, again, the difficulty one faces of dropping a book from a book club, or bailing out from under a record club, or getting any kind of special treatment as needed from these large merchandising operations that have been computerized. Perhaps the lower prices will keep most people from bitter complaint. But the heart of the enterprise it its office function, its information center. The whole point of the office is the quick response to information needs. We can ill afford the "book club syndrome" there.

HIGHLIGHT QUESTIONS

1. What are the two primary functions that offices, in the past, have been known to perform?
2. Where did the word *clerk* originate?
3. Define the term *barracks organization*.
4. Relate boredom and fractioning of jobs.
5. Why is it said that the use of paper is an expensive form of communication?
6. Name one or two types of bottlenecks that you believe might occur in a large office.
7. See if you can give a definition of the term *word processing*.
8. Name a pair of problems facing the modern office in terms of computer applications.
9. How can the computer help in copy editing?
10. Describe some features of which an ideal memory typewriter could boast.
11. Name some of the uses to which a desk terminal could be put, from the point of view of the secretary doing the work.
12. What is the primary by-product of using desk terminals and mini computers to produce information in the first instance?
13. Define a verbal network.
14. What is a conference network?
15. What are some of the advantages of satellite communication systems?

READINGS

Clarke, Arthur C. *Profiles of the Future*. New York: Popular Library, 1977.

Arthur Clarke will take you into a speculative future, which is a delightful trip whether correct or no. Particularly, you will want to read chapter 16, "Voices from the Sky."

Diebold Group, eds. *Automatic Data Processing Handbook*. New York: McGraw-Hill, 1977.

You may want to review the contents of part 3 on computer peripherals, part 5 on communications technology, and section 8 on the computer and society.

Elliott, C. Orville, and Wasley, Robert S. *Business Information Processing Systems*. Homewood, Ill.: Richard D. Irwin, 1975.

Covers most of the information you might need to understand the basics of information processing systems and the computer. Chapter 10, on communication techniques and devices, is particularly useful.

Martin, James, and Norman, Adrian R. D. *The Computerized Society*. Englewood Cliffs, N.J.: Prentice-Hall, 1970.

A little out of date now, but still good reading. You will particularly want to read chapter 3, on the symbiotic ages, and possibly chapter 4, on the disappearance of money as an exchange medium.

MAGAZINES

Fortune, October 1977.

Beginning on page 41, you will find a series of advertisements about office equipment. But much more important, you will find an excellent, lengthy, and up-to-the-minute essay on information processing and the office of tomorrow.

Time, 14 November 1977.

Beginning on page 57 and extending for a number of pages, you will find a number of office equipment advertisements intermixed with an excellent essay on the office of tomorrow. Dr. Vincent E. Giuliano is the author of the textual material, and it is well worth the reading.

CHAPTER 14

THE SOCIAL BENEFITS

PURPOSE OF THE CHAPTER We are going to attempt to summarize the various social benefits which can arise with the proper application of the computer to the solution of human problems in a social setting. In some areas we will be reviewing what has gone before, but in a more general way. In other areas we will add new material—again, somewhat more general in nature.

Now, then, in order to tie the book together as a unit and to make it possible for you to link the terms in chapter 1 with the discussions in chapters 14 and 15, we are going to use the *same* headings for these last two chapters that we used for the first one. Whenever you are in doubt about the meaning of one of the terms, such as *culture* or *civilization,* you can flip back to chapter 1 and refresh your memory.

We have kept the benefits in one chapter and the hazards in another, so you could consider them as *totalities.* It is difficult to try to weigh the benefits in one case against the hazards in that case alone. Actually, in the long run it will be the total benefits and the total hazards which will compete with one another in determining the fate of computers, automation, and our civilization.

We will risk a few simple predictions, though we are fully aware only fools and madmen dare to do so. We will never know, until they actually arrive, what great human dramas (plagues and wars) might interrupt what we think to be the normal progress of our budding civilization. Still, it is good to try to look ahead—some problems that we think about may well appear, and it is better to have thought a little than not at all. The totally unexpected future event will have to be dealt with as best we can when we need to.

TERMS AND CONCEPTS

Some of these terms have appeared in earlier chapters but not quite in the conceptual way that we can now treat them. We have, after all, explored the computer somewhat, and automation a little, and can put this knowledge to work.

- self-definition
- credit society
- computer as tradition
- leadership practice
- capital equipment
- point of action
- intellectual enhancement
- verbal and symbolic communication
- global village
- domestic servant
- democratic process
- free social good
- cosmic question
- perception enhancement
- simulating the future
- unifying processes
- semiautomatic offices
- uses of power
- dynamic symbol of representation
- focus of information
- household management
- new worship
- definitions of success
- inherent constraints
- sense extension
- computer dependencies
- fallacious logic
- purchasing power
- informational center
- accurate representations
- time compression
- generational continuity
- social order
- economic power
- economic pace
- technological difficulties
- problem discovery
- reality orientation
- labor outlets
- spans of control
- computer access
- flow of events
- sensory boosts
- realistic assessment
- inventive enterprise

SOCIETY

Since societies are collections of people who have banded together to achieve some common ends, usually definitive and economic, we are entitled to inquire what computers and computing might do to this process of banding.

The computer is a very sophisticated communication device. It can bring both arithmetic and logic to bear upon problems. And it can bring the same arithmetic and logic to the matter of communication. In such an event, our communications should become more efficient. That is, the computer should be able to assist us in the matter of being understood. Understanding usually comes from an exchange—an opinion is expressed, questions follow, answers are given, further questions are triggered. This two-way communication should ultimately result in greater understanding. In fact, to be human is to be able to handle just such exchanges and just such common communications. The computer, then, can be thought of as a high-powered communication device which we will put to work in the matter of social exchange.

More important, the computer in combination with various electronic communication networks means that we can extend the boundaries of our banding—to create ever larger social groups. We have gone from families to clans, to tribes, to city states, to nations, to empires. There does not seem to be any rational reason why, with the aid of computer networks, we could not create the "one world" of which we often speak.

There is one basic underlying assumption to this prediction. We assume that it is possible to make computer communications clearer and simpler and less exotic than they currently are. That is, we depend for such an achievement upon our ability to make the computer speak a language more closely attuned to our natural languages. Progress is being made in this area, but it is slow, and there is always the tendency of the expert to refine matters to the point where they can no longer be understood by the layman. This would be the fatal disease that could prevent the greater social cooperation and banding which the computer and its related fields (communications and libraries) make a genuine possibility.

CULTURE

Culture, as we have said earlier, includes at least a collection of traditions, a set of survival techniques and artifacts, a collection of artistic artifacts, a collection of mores (methods of behavior which are defined as acceptable or unacceptable), a defined set of interrelationships among its members, and a cosmic view (how the society fits into the world or universe at large).

The computer itself could well become one of the traditional artifacts of the modern world. We must not, to keep perspective, think of the computer as either a being or an intelligence, however sophisticated the computer may become. It is primarily an artifact, a tool, an extension of the human race. But what a tool it can be! At last we can triumph over the matter of space and time—at least from the point of view of the small globe on which we live. We can, via the satellites and the electronic nets of which the computer is a natural part, keep in constant touch with one another. We can trade definitions of our humanity with the closest and the farthest cultures. We can use the computer to probe and to inquire, to ask and to answer, to seek and to find, to summarize and to categorize. We cannot yet make the computer think, but we can make the computer help us

think better than ever before. The computer, then, is an artifact of the Western world of the 20th century. It is part and parcel of our self-definition. It is the ultimate expression of the triumph of science and information theory. Without the computer our present culture would dramatically change and perhaps decline. Our current dependency is too intimate and too thorough. The computer has so reduced the price of information that it can almost become a free social good.

Ultimately we must ask: Is it good to know? And since we are human, the answer must be yes. We must not here confuse the action (knowing) with the end use to which it is put. Undoubtedly information can be used for ill purpose—but that does not make knowing, as such, itself an evil. To want to know is irretrievably tied up with the matter of being a person. A tool, then, that leads to greater knowledge for greater numbers should, in the long run, be a tool for the enhancement of humanity.

A culture includes a collection of artistic artifacts, and the computer has started down the artistic road. Recently an article appeared about an artist who used the color-reproducing Xerox machine to make remarkably interesting pictures. The Xerox did not "make" the pictures; the artist, using the Xerox as the brush, did. In the same way the computer could be used by a competent artist to produce a symphony or to write an interesting book. The computer could not conceive the symphony or the book. But the computer, properly programmed by the artist, can generate the end result. The tool does not dictate to the artist—it is the vehicle by which he or she achieves the end in sight. But, caution—the type of brush or tool available sets certain inherent constraints on what can indeed be done. The computer might lead the artist into the exploration of areas never before assailed.

We can expect, then, that artists will more and more turn themselves to modern tools to create modern modes of art suitable, as they view it, to the 20th century and the kind of humanity which the century represents. And we must recall that our art is part of our self-definition. We will move from complex computer art works of various kinds to ever more complex works. In so doing, the artist will help us understand not only our culture but how the artifacts we use in that culture work on our definitions of ourselves.

The computer already has had a serious effect on our cultural mores. It is the computer and the computer net which have made it possible to extend the credit society to ever greater limits and to ever greater numbers of people. It used to be said that "a penny saved is a penny earned," but no more. The cry now is to use the credit, which has been extended, to build and to buy, to extend ourselves into tomorrow. For some people this has meant a great deal of trouble. For others, it has meant a great deal of convenience. For the society as a whole, the use of credit can well be the difference between poverty and prosperity—all the ballots are not yet in on the matter, and the economists do not yet agree. We should note, though, that the natural limits on credit (the lack of information generally available) have been lifted by the computer. Credit is extended when business folk know whether or not the people to whom they extend the credit can stand the strain. The computer provides just such information. This means more and more credit can safely be extended to more and more people. It also means those who do not have credit will tend to be cut out of the mainstream of the credit culture, for good or ill.

To use a credit card is no longer a sign of sloth. To spend before you have the money is no longer a sin. To buy today and pay tomorrow is said to be the anchor of our prosperity. Well, it may be. And we cannot deny the contribution of the computer to this vast credit net. More people can have more things sooner, and the industrial empires grow. Here we are looking at the good side of the coin. In the next chapter we will more properly explore the hazards of such events. But all in all, we cannot deny that the computer has made a significant contribution to the extension of credit and to the pace of the economy.

The computer also has begun to impinge upon what we have called "a defined set of interrelationships among the members of the society." The computer *does* monitor and control the kinds of communication we can do at a distance. In this way the computer sets certain new limits on the interrelationships we would establish with one another. Insofar as the computer has made it possible to reach more people more quickly and more accurately, it has enhanced the communication net on which the culture depends. Insofar as the computer has limited the type of communication which can take place, it has stolen something from the culture. On balance it would

The computer as intermediary

appear that the computer has helped us extend the range and number of our interrelationships. We do not yet know whether this is being done in too narrow a framework and whether some of our inherent humanity has been lost in the process. We suspect that might be the case, but we will also leave that matter to the next chapter.

And what of our cosmic view? Has the computer made any changes here? Oh, yes, perhaps in the long run, the greatest change of all. We now use the computer in conjunction with the radio telescope, the x-ray telescope, and the infrared telescope to extend the range of the human eye to areas in space almost unbelievably distant. We use the computer to run the space vehicles which, at this moment, are probing the planetary neighbors in our own solar system. Surely all this extension of our senses must give us a larger and broader cosmic view. Surely this profound exploration of the universe must make us somewhat more humble and somewhat more curious. We now think the once unthinkable—mankind may not be the only thinking race in the universe. There might be other creatures elsewhere, yet further along than we. It is the computer in conjunction wth other technological developments which may one day provide an answer to this profound cosmic question.

Through the computer we now know a good deal more about our fellow members of the solar system than ever before. Through the computer we have enhanced our view of our own galaxy. And through the computer we learn of strange new things in the universe—black holes, white dwarfs, red giants, quasars, and pulsars, and all manner of strange and wonderous existences. New eyes and new ears for the human race! And with that a new, more fully developed, and perhaps more awe-inspiring cosmic view. It has been a long slow trip from the cave to the moon. There is yet a long way to go. The computer provides one or two rungs in the long ladder we would yet climb.

Let us sum up by saying the computer has become a tradition—one associated with the Western scientific world. Let us say that the computer is being used as a survival artifact and is helping us develop sophisticated survival techniques. Let us say that the computer is defining, for good or ill, our interrelationships in a more rigorous way. Let us finally admit that the computer is a very useful tool in the broadening of our cosmic view. All this is quite a contribution for even a complex artifact.

CIVILIZATION

We have defined civilization in this book as a "touch of elegance." We related civilization to a certain richness of spirit which generates tolerance and curiosity. Has the computer made any significant contribution in this direction? Is the computer part and parcel of our civilization? Yes, it is. Ours is a civilization of high technology, and the computer is one of our newest and best triumphs in the field of high technology. So, we are clear in supposing that our civilization has developed a number of dependencies on the computer and its further development.

We have said, earlier in the text, that technology is one of the main support systems of a civilization. We can expect the computer, as a tool, to lead our own civilization to ever greater technological triumphs. We are not here going to argue whether technological triumphs are good or bad—only that civilization has, in the past, defined them as good. We do know that some of our technologies have caused us difficulty (automobiles generate smog, for example). But on the whole of it, we have become dependent on our technologies and would be loathe to retreat to the somewhat simpler life of the countryside. Hopefully, we will use our technologies to solve the problems our technologies have created, and this need not necessarily be an endless squirrel run.

The computer will further enhance our civilization by helping us refine the techniques by which we think. That is, we can test our logic against the logic of the computer. And insofar as logic is useful in human intercourse, we can enhance our perceptions.

Also, via the computer, as we deal with more and more problems both scientific and human, we ought to develop better methods for the preservation of the race. The computer is the one instrument that currently makes it possible for us to deal with the enormous complexities of ecology. It is the only device capable of handling all the variables required. And let us not forget that the computer is as agile in helping us discover problems as it is in their solution. Many of the new pollutions we now face could not have been uncovered but for the wonderful ability of the computer to sniff through thousands of variables and highlight those that might contain a possible danger in their variation.

BUREAUCRACY

The computer is a tool of the bureaucracy. Or put it another way: Without the large-scale bureaucratic organizations, the computer could not exist—it is a complex device and demands large-scale and complex structures to create it. But the computer is one of the few new devices which makes it possible, if we have the will, to tame the bureaucracy—to bring control of large and complex structures and events into fruition. So the child is not only the child but could well become the master.

The computer can help the bureaucracy define its tasks more accurately. The computer can move through myriads of jobs and myriads of individuals and put the proper pair together. The computer can become an integral operating part of vast communication nets—and we need those nets to keep track of what our bureaucracies are doing. And the computer is a necessary tool for those who would monitor the bureaucracy and define the responsibilities of individuals within such a complex network.

The computer and mechanisms related to it can get on with the matter of the development of the vast, immediately accessible libraries, which a bureaucracy needs to keep fantasy and confusion under control. And properly used, the computer can bring humanity into the large-scale organization. This facet of computer power has not yet been properly explored or properly applied. But the computer can deal with individual events and can treat such events in an individualistic way—that is one of its great powers. What we need to do is understand that the computer is not a slave to uniformity but its master. We can have a variety of products just because the computer can plan them. We can have a variety of individualistic communications just because the computer can handle so much information at such a high rate of speed.

MANAGEMENT

If the computer is to have value for management, the value sought is to free management from the ordinary, the daily, and the routine so that those who manage can give full attention to the unique, the individual, and the odd development. In short, the computer can assume a number of ordinary burdens so that management can practice leadership. The computer, in other words, can administer, and management can at last find the time to think and plan and manage.

Also, the computer can assist management to plan new directions. The computer, as a tool, has enormous power in gathering the variables and calculating with them, to generate different scenarios of the future. These scenarios may be large in number, based on slight variations in the information fed into the computer. We can, then, plan out a number of futures. And using the computer we can see down which road we move and then develop yet further scenarios to accommodate the changes we discover along the way. Ultimately, we should be able to refine matters down to a few possible situations, work out solutions for each, and not succumb to the inertia of surprise.

This ability of the computer to simulate the future may be particularly useful for managers in their constant attempt to determine where their current goals will lead them. It is possible to develop programs which carry the plans to their logical conclusion. The advantage is that the computer is not an emotional being and does not have emotional commitments. It can, and it will, uncover fallacious logic. It can, and it will, develop the paths—no matter how thorny they might become, no matter how much we wish to deny the result of our own plans. In this sense the computer can keep the manager "reality oriented"—a powerful gift for those who know how to use it.

MECHANIZATION

In the first chapter of the book we noted that mechanization had to do with the application of physical devices to productive tasks. The computer, as we have discovered, has the ability to mechanize certain intellectual tasks—those that are complete, consistent, and clearly defined. The computer can be used, of course, to increase the scope of mechanization in the sense that more and more processes can be unified and monitored by the computer in conjunction with mechanization. This will not necessarily bring about automation, but this surely will extend mechanization itself to more and more industrial and service industries. The computer, then, takes up the planned informational connections between machines. The combination of machines can act, by means of this computer-monitored intercommunication, as a system. The system need not yet be considered automated because human intervention need not necessarily be entirely removed. But, of course, as mechanization is extended through greater and greater amounts of a process, the amount of human physical effort and human intellectual interference should decline. The decline in physical and intellectual effort should, in the long run, reduce the costs of manufacture. Direct labor would no longer be a significant element in the process. This means that the closer the mechanized (or automated) system runs to maximum capacity the lower the cost per unit of product, since the major element in the process is not labor, is not materials, but is capital equipment.

Naturally, a highly mechanized or automated system, running at near maximum capacity, requires the guarantee of a market for the product produced. This requirement comes into direct conflict with the fact that machines do not consume, people do. So, as the mechanization and automation continue, the payments to direct labor will decrease. This would lead to a drying up of the purchasing power of ever increasing numbers of people unless some exit from this problem is deliberately planned. Since the cost of extending the range of mechanization via the computer is considerable, and the investments will be made slowly, we do have some time to look ahead and do some careful planning. As farms mechanized and the proportion of those involved in agriculture fell to about 5 percent of the population, a vast host of jobs opened up for people in the burgeoning cities. Is there some comparable labor outlet currently in the wind? No, frankly, there is not. The service industries which were supposed to soak up the labor slack have themselves been very busy mechanizing—so there is no refuge there.

We are then faced with the possibility that the positive virtues of extended mechanization may come against a stone wall—idle people do not have the means to buy the products, however efficiently made and however cheaply priced. Still, the benefits of extended mechanization (uniformity of product, reliability, lower cost, efficient uses of resources) all will tend to keep the process in a state of expansion and growth. Until such time as the labor demands are seriously shrunk, there will be general prosperity for people.

No money, no sales

Informational mechanization, primarily applied to the handling of paperwork, is the next big step before automation. Word processing, semiautomatic offices, the generation of records at the point of action—all will continue to grow. Mechanization of this type, via the computer, is likely to develop, and true automation is not. It is the peculiar aspect of informational work that human intervention is constantly required—not physically, but mentally. And we must not underrate the necessity, in a social context, of human to human contact. Mechanization will not be successful in the informational areas if it is accompanied by indifference and rigidity. It is the peculiar nature of machines (from the human point of view) that they are indifferent to human puzzles and human emotions. The office, then, is both an informational center and a point of social relationships.

We must be somewhat wary in applying mechanization too rapidly and too rigidly there. But again, if the office can be mechanized to the point that response time is seriously cut down, and people find out what they need to know quickly and efficiently, then the computer will bring great benefits to the office. The costs of intellectual work are rising; the computer and only the computer can successfully cut them down to size. Too, as our wood supplies decrease and our demands for paper supply rise, we must seek another medium of storage. The computer has the answer to this—high-density magnetic storage.

Finally, we must note that mechanization brought about an enormous increase in human strength, singly and collectively. Many lifting, hauling, and moving tasks are performed today which would have been nearly impossible in earlier times. Or, if they were possible, they would have required masses of people and long years of effort (the pyramids are a good example). We suspect that the computer, properly applied to problems, has and will continue to increase the strength of our intellectual effort. Again, fewer people will require fewer hours to solve ever more complex problems. It was once said that every mathematician had, in his or her desk drawer, the secret plans for a bridge across the Atlantic Ocean. But the calculations would have taken several lifetimes. Today we could, if we would, plan such a bridge and in a matter of hours check all of the calculations for stress and endurance. By such means the human race extends the span of its control through time—a not inconsiderable contribution from the computer.

INTELLECTUAL POWER

In our early treatment of intellectual power we understood it to mean the ability to investigate, to understand, to quantify, to predict, and to simulate. The computer has made this kind of activity possible on a greater scale than ever before. But what is more important, the computer has been able to extend this power to ordinary people —who could not before, alone, have given successful attention to such matters. In this sense the computer is an intellectual enhancer. We call such an intellectual relationship between the person and the computer "intellectual symbiosis." The machine depends upon the human for direction, the human depends upon the machine for intellectual power in terms of both capacity and speed.

Again, we would repeat that information is the vehicle of organization, and that organization is the precursor to the effective use and dispersal of power. To the degree the computer brings greater rationality and capacity to intellectual tasks, the computer enhances our ability to organize. Our ability to organize provides greater control over events (another label for power), and permits the dispersal of the benefits of power to more and more people. Or, because of its enormous ability to keep track of events, and to integrate them into accurate representations, the computer tends to preclude the inadvertent misuse of power. We must be careful to remember, however, that even the computer cannot stop the abuse of power or the abusive uses to which information could be put by people with evil intent. The safeguard here would be a matter of being certain that only authorized people have access to the computer or to the information, and that some kind of thorough and consistent auditing procedures are designed and enforced.

The computer can deal with the matter of verbal communication very well. That is, the computer can produce information stored in its memory in about any orderly fashion we wish. The computer also can make large contributions in the area of symbolic communication, since the computer, via the cathode ray tube and other pictorial means, can summarize in an elegant fashion all the statistics the computer contains. Still more important, a properly equipped computer with properly prepared programs can produce dynamic symbol representation—it can make living pictures on the cathode ray tube that provide the maximum kind of information and additionally provide instant information about the flow of events. The computer also has the ability to compress time. That is, the computer can give a picture of the changes in traffic taking place on the streets (by means of black lines, the thickness and direction of which depend upon the actual traffic being measured) over a 24-hour-day in a matter of a few minutes. Thus, the computer can dynamically summarize for us today in a few moments the total pattern of events of the previous 24 hours. The presentation would be rapid. The visual details would be lost due to compression, but the overall event could be portrayed very well. Then the computer could be instructed to slow down the presentation dynamically or to give, say, a minute inspection of any single hour of the previous day. It would be difficult to abstract quickly from actual printed figures what the computer can present visually in a few minutes. And we must remember that the human animal is superbly equipped to handle just this type of informational presentation. We are not naturally equipped to deal with vast pages of numeric information. In fact, we frequently go to great lengths to avoid such presentations.

By its ability to summarize information in either normal printed form or pictorial form, the computer can also contribute to what we call "the focus" of information. That is, the computer can highlight information based on any criteria we might choose to select. This ability of the computer—basically, one of searching through vast amounts of information and selecting what fits the criteria—

has not been used as much as it should be. We still tend to ask the computer to give us all the information, when what we really need is *pertinent* information. Properly used, the computer can provide us with the kind of information that we need in quantities which we can handle with ease. This is basically what we mean by "the focus" of information.

HIGH TECHNOLOGY

The computer, in conjunction with other technological developments (or as the goad to further technological developments), has much to contribute in the area of high technology. For example, we can expect in the near future worldwide information nets of such power and complexity that anyone willing to pay a reasonable fee can be in touch with any other individual willing to pay that fee on a worldwide basis. At first these world information nets will be used by governments and large industries, for the initial costs will be high. But, as with the telephone, the telegraph, and the TV cable, these costs eventually will drop to the point where they will be available to the ordinary citizen earning an ordinary wage. At this point we will be approaching what has been called "the global village"—a world in which all the members are intimately in touch with one another. What this will do to the concept of the national state is highly unpredictable. We do know that as roads and information systems improved it became considerably easier for the separate states in America to become the United States. Such an event could, in time, occur worldwide.

Some of our high technology has already moved "out of this world" in terms of the exploration of the space immediately surrounding this planet. Men have gone to the moon in machines. Machines with many of the capabilities of men have gone to Mars. Currently, there are rockets on the way to Jupiter and Saturn. It is, in large measure, the computer which has made this type of adventure worthwhile and possible. More important, it is a host of small mechanisms with computer ability which have made it unnecessary to send persons on the trip. People are much more delicate than machines. It is this delicacy which would preclude a casual human exploration of Venus, Mars, Jupiter, or Saturn. Machines can be constructed to endure almost unimaginable heat. Machines also can function in a cold which would destroy living tissue. What is important is that while these machines are not living tissue they can behave, intellectually, as though they were. They can investigate by motion or by visual means, and they can transmit this information back to human viewers in safer climes. The robot machines of which we are speaking are very close examples of total automation. They still receive directions, from time to time, but only to accomplish special tasks, adjust for unpredictable error, or mend a maladjustment. In the main they operate according to plan, pretty much out of reach and pretty much on their own.

We need not, however, go to the planets or to the stars to take advantage of the fact that the computer, combined with mechanisms, can become the super eyes, ears, and fingers of a newly enhanced mankind. It is the enhancement which is important. We can expand, through robotlike devices, the visual spectrum of the human animal to include the infrared and the ultraviolet. We can keen the ears of mankind through devices so sensitive they can pick up murmurs miles away. We can enormously enhance the strength of human fingers, or increase their sensitivity through computerized mechanisms. And we can go one step further. Given these sensory boosts, we can pass the burden of their gross interpretation to the machinery itself and bother ourselves only with the refined result. Here lies much of the power of high technology—it is man beyond himself, or, to be fair, woman beyond herself.

Will computerized mechanisms lead us to the stars? No! For a certainty they will precede us to the stars, for machines can endure long years of slow journey and patient years of waiting. Machines can slumber and then be aroused to do the job they were designed to do. There are strange elements to deal with, though. The machines may leave during one generation, send their messages back to another, and then finally return to a third. We may live to see the day our computerized machines bring a new kind of continuity from one generation to the next. The grandparents ask the questions, the parents receive the answers, the children reap the benefits.

AUTOMATION

It does not seem likely that we could ever achieve true automation without the computer. The computer is the natural brain of any automated system. The evaluation, in detail, of feedback requires an evaluating mechanism. And the more complicated or variable the feedback, the more complicated the evaluating machinery requires to be. So the computer can move us further and further down the road to complete automation as the computers themselves grow more sophisticated. We should be able to design systems which can conduct themselves without human interference for months or years at a time. Ultimately, they may not even require human supervision. We would then have achieved the perfect slave—both intelligent and muscular.

And with the newer computers we can now give attention to automating complex systems which we never before thought could be so treated. There is no reason to assume (save in matters of economic cost) that the process should not continue at an increasing rate.

COMPUTERS

We can expect these continuing trends in the computer field:

1. Bigger memories.
2. Higher speed.
3. Lesser size.
4. Less power consumption.
5. Increased portability.
6. Simpler languages.
7. Greater flexibility.
8. Wider application.
9. Lower cost.

All these trends have been going on for two decades or more. Now they are happening at an increasing rate. There is no known reason, yet, why they cannot continue for another decade or two. We cannot predict that any shattering new concepts will come about in any given time period. But based on past experience we can surely say that some such concepts will come, and they may send the computers off in entirely new and unexpected directions. There are social benefits yet to occur which we cannot imagine. However, the general trend will be toward making it possible for human beings to increase their humanity in ways never before possible—to unburden themselves of yet more tiresome tasks, to avoid the dull and the routine, to abjure the tedious and the tiresome. We cannot claim that a newfound leisure is dangerous to the race—for the race is ingenious and adaptive.

INSTITUTIONS OF CIVILIZATION

How will the computer and its partner, automation, affect the main institutions of civilization? Let us explore a little.

We have selected the family unit as one of the undergirding structures of civilization. While we will assume, here, that we are talking about the ordinary family (two adults, some children), we need not necessarily be bound by that. The family unit could be broadly defined as any group of adults or children, living together for their common good. In any event, in the computer the family can find a new domestic servant. If the computer is attached to robotlike devices to perform many of the tedious tasks of family life, perhaps family life will become less of a burden. And with that burden removed, the ideas about marriage and commitment may change back to earlier notions. It may once more be fun to be married, to have children, to work with a happy unit. More time may become available to improve interpersonal relationships, to the degree that divorce and disaster become less common. Children may be able to learn more in the

"NOW THEN, OUR LESSON FOR TODAY WILL CONCERN THE FUNDAMENTALS OF DIVISION!"

The computer as teacher in the home

home through computer teachers and computer entertainment. Parents may be able to avoid boredom with each other. All this could happen just because many of the "duties" of household management and operation are removed from the hands of busy parents. There will be less fatigue and with that, hopefully, less aggravation. A child is always worth more attention than parents feel they can honestly afford. Perhaps that, too, will change. And we must not forget that the computer itself may provide new economic tools and new training techniques (disguised as games) which members of the family may rely upon in their search for that employment that is both attractive and economically productive.

We said earlier in the book that the government was one of the mainstays of civilization, particularly in the matter of keeping order and providing for defense. We would expect the computer to be able to provide the kind of information (about crime, for example) which would aid in keeping a society in good order without unnecessary oppression. We will have to assume, at the outset, that many of the oppressions are due to ignorance and error and not to malice. And, of course, defense could be affected in two ways. First, as the world becomes more the global village, there ought to be less cause for misunderstandings and less cause, therefore, for war. Second, such defense as would be required could be more realistic and hence less expensive. Right now, defense budgets are very large, particularly because it is so difficult to know just where the money ought to go, what machinery ought to be built. So, ever cautious, the military people generally ask for the best on all possible fronts. This, of course, they cannot always have. So the computer can help in the matter of a realistic assessment of the problems, the dangers, and the future. That is the best the computer can do. In fact, that is the best the human being can do. We must hope, but we must not let hope triumph over experience. And the computer can build experience through simulation—a far less dangerous and expensive process than the actual fighting of real battles and the winning or losing of real wars. Yes, it is fantasy in some ways; but it is the kind of fantasy that can lead to reality, and a kind of reality that can lead to genuine hope.

There can be no doubt about it. We would rather not have any defense costs at all. But in the long long meantime, we would rather have the efficient and inexpensive defense than the costly and erroneously one. The former can often provide safety, the latter only disaster.

How can the computer possibly affect religion—one of the former mainstays of the civilized life? Well, one supposes that it, by the development and assistance of the human intellect, can provide us with an image of a more subtle God. Or the computer can be used to muster its strength to examine the contradictions in our religious views and perhaps help us remove them. It is a sad thing to see one people kill another in the name of a benign religion. It is a sad thing to experience a narrow and a punitive religion. Religion was intended to broaden the human view and those unique qualities in the human being which we call kindness and love. Perhaps as it enhances our intellect the computer can free us for greater humanity. As the computer puts us in touch with the world, perhaps we will become less provincial and more internationally friendly in our views. We are, after all, one species.

There is always the danger that new devices can lead to new kinds of worship, or to the search for flying saucers, or whatever. We will deal with that problem when we turn our attention to the dangers of the computer, rather than its benefits.

We have said that enterprise (economic problems and their means of solution) is one of the mainstays of civilization, and so it is. Without economic prosperity, a civilization is not really possible. It is hard to be a philosopher when you require to hunt a rabbit for a dinner and when the pangs of hunger ceaselessly gnaw at your innards. No, civilization requires a certain amount of leisure for at least a small number of the members of the civilization. The more comfort and leisure we can provide to the many (as against the few) the more likely we will be able to build a civilization that is satisfactory and, hence, a civilization which can last.

The computer and the mechanism combined into automation can free the human race from problems of poverty and of want as never before. And to that degree the computer can free the race for the contemplation of art and music and the happier emotions. We have experienced the enormous productivity of the mechanized farm. We have seen the wonders of production of modern industry. We know for a fact that Western ways have provided more good things for more people than ever before recorded in history. We want to continue those processes in such a way as not to so deplete our resources that our future generations are put into poverty and terror. The intelligent use of industry and technology can do this—it is contribution enough.

There are those who say that democracy depends, for its survival, upon a certain basic prosperity of the people. Automation, properly governed, can bring about great prosperity to more people. In so doing it can directly enhance the democratic processes. Enterprise, we have learned, does not necessarily go along with democracy. The one does not automatically cause the other. But one can, from experience, come to believe that inventive enterprise leans heavily on democracy. It is, we think, inventive enterprise which we need.

AMERICAN CIVILIZATION

American civilization is said to be founded on the concepts of democracy and free enterprise. The first is a political form, the second an economic form. In general, it is still safe to say that the two seem to have brought about a remarkable country. The computer, because it can provide more information to more people, should serve to reinforce democracy. The founding fathers believed a democracy depended upon an educated people. The computer can be a formidable educational tool—sophisticated and untiring. It is said that democracy depends on prosperity, and that the free enterprise system (recognizing all its imperfections) certainly has brought more prosperity to more people than any other political form known to man either in the past or currently existing. The figures are indisputable, and there is no reason to assume the figures lie. Or putting it another way, any nation that must guard its borders to keep its people in, and build walls to keep itself isolated, is not likely to be able to provide any compelling argument for its long existence—in contrast to those nations which do not require walls and do not require the use of barbed wire and internal visas. The greatest testimony to the reality of both freedom and prosperity is the mobility of the people. It is no accident, then, that the Western world and now Japan are known as places where people are extremely mobile. Mobility is not commonly associated with political freedom, but one thinks perhaps it ought to be.

The computer—because it can through automation provide relief from hard work and yet increase productivity, and because it can combine with mechanisms to bring about both physical and intellectual automation—may well provide us with new definitions of success. For good or ill, the American's evaluation of his or her fellows has been one of economic success. If economic matters fall more into the hands of machinery and less into the hands of individuals, we may well have to redefine our terms. To be a success might no longer mean just prosperity. It might come to mean contributions to the betterment of the race in terms of love or kindness or understanding. At least this is what the philosophers say, and who are we to deny them?

Consumption has been one mark of American success. If we can really produce more than we could possibly consume, we may be forced to a new definition. It will do us no harm to be in such a position.

The computer and mechanization already have brought new kinds of economic power. The newspapers are full of such events. We do not require to flog the concept to death with detail here. We should only note and try to long remember that information is now a commodity and also a means to economic power as never before in history. The computer is primarily an information machine. An automated plant is a plant which uses information in its own guidance. These are concepts which we can sit back and conjure at leisure. We have the leisure, by the way, just because computers and mechanization have already provided us with a good deal of economic power.

Can the computer help us in the pursuit of happiness? Probably not. Happiness is a human thing. And because happiness is a human thing, it is an individualized production. There does not seem to be any way we can automate or compute happiness, or necessarily even agree on what we mean by the term. So let us not assign to the poor old computer things it cannot handle. Such contributions as the computer can make in these directions will at best be indirect. We do not wish to slaughter the mechanism with the sword of expectation.

IMPLICATIONS

This has been a chapter of implications. We do not require to give the implications of the implications—this would be to go too far. Let us steal quietly into our summary and be done with the happier side of the computer and its potential.

SUMMARY

In these last two chapters ("Social Benefits" and "Social Hazards") and before "Final Recapitulation," we have painted our pictures with a broad brush—we have not bothered with detail, nor should we. If we cannot be general at the end of a text, where can we be? What we have sought in this chapter and will in the next is possibility—the trigger of further thought.

We have seen that our societies might broaden, via the computer and the communication network, to include more and more people. We also have hoped that these binding communications will be more specific and hence more truthful. We have seen that the computer is a tool—an artifact of culture. And as an artifact of culture it will take part in our cultural definitions. We notice the computer will not do art work, but could well be the vehicle by which new art work is done. We know the computer will push our systems of credit cards and credit utilization further along the road. We noted the computer could affect the way we define our interrelationships. It can make them better or it can make them rigid. We noticed the computer can be used, in conjunction with other mechanisms, to explore the solar system and perhaps, one day, the nearby stars.

Since the computer can become one of the instruments of prosperity and of leisure, it can become one of the further support structures to hold up our civilization. We noted that productivity and prosperity are somehow closely tied to what we have, in the past, called successful civilizations. We should also have noted that the computer as a communicative device can help bring about the cohesion which is also required if a civilization is not to perish in its own sloth or inertia. We have observed that the computer can help relieve many of the bureaucratic problems created by large-scale organizations. Again, the cure lies in the fact that the computer is a superb communication device as well as an excellent calculator.

Does a civilization rest on knowledge? Yes, it does. Can the computer contribute in this area? Yes, particularly in the generation of vast libraries whose contents will be easily accessible to those who need or want the information therein—or better yet, accurate summaries of the information therein. We noted the computer might buy the manager time, and time is what the manager needs to consider the course he or she has set for himself or herself, the employees, and the firm. The manager who can only stay with the day-to-day activities of the firm is not managing but administering. New directions are seldom set by the latter. We have seen that the computer can be of particular help to the manager in the matter of simulation, which makes possible better prediction not only of what will result from choices currently made but of choices that ought to be made.

Once again we attempted to make clear the difference between mechanization and automation and the role that the computer plays in turning the former into the latter. Automation, of course, will raise our productivity and perhaps present us with new problems, such as the need for a guaranteed income and a guaranteed market for the products so generously produced. These could be said to be social problems brought about by economic achievements. We also noted that information handling could be mechanized, and we owe the debt of that possibility to the computer. And we must not underrate the contribution of machines to relieving the strains of human muscle.

We have explored the potentialities of increased intellectual power, not for the few but for the many, not by brain alone but by computer and brain in combination. And let us not forget that information is the vehicle of organization and that organization the means to power. We could conjur a book on that subject alone.

We gave some attention to the unique possibilities of the computer as a presenter of dynamic rather than static information. And we noted the human animal likes dynamic presentations better than static presentations.

We also took a look at some of the future possibilities for what we have called high technology—the global village, the exploration of space, the boost to our senses. We saw, in passing, certain continuing improvement in the computers themselves, and we can go further, then, with all these predictions—at least as far as the improvements will carry what we now know.

Finally, we explored the institutions of civilization and some of the effects the computer might have on these. Any statement about effect in these areas is bound to be as speculative as it is bold—perhaps even foolish. But we took the plunge, anyway.

The computer will probably carry the American civilization a little further down its former road before any significant changes occur. The most likely change would be in our definition of success.

HIGHLIGHT QUESTIONS

1. How would you define society? What contributions do you think the computer could make in the area of social communication?
2. Name some of the supporting mechanisms of what we call culture, and tell how the computer might contribute to one or two of those.
3. How can the computer help us refine our thinking processes in a way which is supportive of what we have called civilization?
4. Why is the computer a "tool of bureaucracy?"
5. What single major and significant item can the computer "buy" for management?

6. How does the computer mix with mechanization to generate automation?
7. How can the computer help contribute to the building of intellectual power?
8. What kind of information is pertinent to intellectual power?
9. Is the computer an example of high technology?
10. In what ways can the computer contribute to the exploration of space?
11. Give the best definition you can of automation.
12. Name four or five trends that you think the computer will follow, in the way of development, in the next decade or so.
13. Do you believe the computer will have much effect on the family structure in our society?
14. Name some of the uses the computer might find in the fight against crime in America.
15. What primary change might the computer make in the American civilization?

READINGS

Kleinberg, Harry. *How You Can Learn to Live with Computers.* Philadelphia: J. B. Lippincott, 1977.

As personable an introduction to the world of computing as you could possibly find. The good things computers can do come peeping out through the pages. There is a good deal of wisdom in this small book.

Rothman, Stanley, and Mosman, Charles. *Computers and Society.* Chicago: Science Research Associate, 1972.

A popular book in the computers and society field. Here you will find a good bit of introductory material and an exploration of both the good and the bad effects of the computer. Chapter 10, "Social Issues," is of particular interest.

Sanders, Norman. *The Corporate Computer.* London: McGraw-Hill, 1973.

The subtitle of the book, "How to Live with an Ecological Intrusion," pretty well sums up the gist of the book. Again, the main benefits can be derived from the readings, and Mr. Sanders is not too hard on the computer difficulties.

Schneider, Benn Ross, Jr. *Travels in Computerland.* Reading, Mass.: Addison-Wesley, 1974.

A literary trip and gentle spoof on some of the difficulties—and a good bit of warmth and hope for the terrible task—of putting the computer to work.

CHAPTER 15

THE SOCIAL HAZARDS

PURPOSE OF THE CHAPTER

In this chapter we will summarize some of the actual and some of the expected social hazards which will be accentuated by the computer's arrival on the scene. Again, we will use the general terms and structures which we developed and defined in chapter 1. This will make the contents of chapter 15 comparable to the contents of both chapters 1 and 14. Having absorbed the main contents of the central part of the book you should be able to read chapters 1, 14, and 15 and develop a rather interesting point of view for future questions and discussion.

The potential hazards of the computer in business, in law, in art, and in literature have received a great deal of publicity of the newspaper type in recent years. There naturally will be a temptation to write of the hazards at great length. We will attempt to keep the contents of this chapter equal to those of the previous chapter, even though we might, guiltily, have to skip a few of the more exotic headline presentations of the last few years.

We will try to deal with the hazards in a broad way because the narrower our predictions, the more likely they are to be dead wrong. If we are reasonably broad in what we consider, we are not likely to be quite so wrong or quite so at a loss when actual surprises present themselves on the horizon.

TERMS AND CONCEPTS

The terms and concepts we list here should, in the main, be rather familiar. We are introducing them again with their negative connotations. This is a good check method for you to determine whether you remember the main points of the chapter. If you can say something about each of the concepts or each of the words, you will know you have pondered the situation and the terms and concepts are less likely to slip away.

You might wish to go one step further. Take the social advantages of any given segment, compare these to what we have called the social hazards, and see if you can combine the two to create some new kind of compromise which leads in a new direction. This used to be called "the thesis, antithesis, synthesis system."

logic machine
halos of correctness
to "know"
pursuit of power
process ties
intellectual power
energy conservation
collusion
public sector
the computer artifact
machine culture
medieval sin, modern virtue
passion versus ignorance
control as a goal
concentrated industries
large-scale centralization
intellectual product
surface variation
public sector
defining American civilization
extending artifacts
caste systems
world civilization
social conscience
monopolistic control
primitive myth
those in power
private sector
computer in the household
computer influence on art
ultimate computer
democratic incommensurables
achievements of bureaucracy
profit versus persons
dehabilitation
intellectual centralization
antitechnology
laws and punishments
double-bladed axes

SOCIETY

What, we might ask, that is negative, will the computer do to the collections of people who have banded together to achieve some common ends—usually definitive and economic, which we call "society."

First, the computer probably will make it possible, as we have said in the previous chapter, to bring ever larger numbers of people together through an extensive communication net. At first blush this might appear to be a good thing and not present too many difficulties.

In that we would probably be wrong. The larger the group we gather, the more likely there is to be serious dissension, and the more likely the dissensions are to be incommensurable. We like to believe that if we can only explain our point of view with sufficient fullness to anyone else they will naturally agree with us. It is usually difficult for us to believe, out of hand, that anyone could be so diametrically opposed to what we believe that no possibilities of reconciliation exist. It matters not what we believe—the agonies of past history and potential war will always be present to remind us of the unhappy truth.

Now, the computer, by virtue of the fact that it must standardize the communication forms and often actually limit them, will give us the false notion that standardization means agreement. We might come to believe that since we agree with all the members of a group on these peculiarly machine-oriented points and languages, that universal agreement is both likely and possible. Thus, the first major social hazard includes the notion that the computer will, not by intent but by action, deceive us.

The fact that we have large groups banded together does not guarantee that any particular kind of security or happiness will develop for the individual. The ant colony, by virtue of organization and hierarchy, functions very well. But we find little of an appealing nature in the life and times of the individual ant. So, while the computer might help us create very sturdy bands of people who can survive, as a group, almost any strain, we might also find the general loss of happiness which comes to human beings when they no longer feel they are in control of events or even of their own individual destinies. This is one of the main objections to bureaucracy, no matter what the manufacturing achievements.

Since the computer is largely a logic machine (if we think of mathematics as a subset of the broader logical universe), we might come to believe that the human emotions are somehow second-class and not worthy of our attention or our approval. Or putting the matter in a slightly different way, if we cannot quantify or do logic with the emotions, we might tend to discount them at just those times and places where their recognition would be most important. Rare indeed is the individual who is motivated by the cold clarity of logic and the immutable argument of rationality. To be so, in fact, may mean a certain kind of inhumanity.

CULTURE

The computer is currently an artifact. As an artifact it will influence our culture. If it is a pervading artifact (and it is rapidly becoming so), then the influence is bound to be major. We have said that a culture includes a collection of traditions, artistic artifacts, survival techniques, and mores. We also add a set of interrelationships among members of the culture and some kind of cosmic view.

In a culture we can only achieve what we can achieve as human beings, and can only achieve what can be added to our skills by the tools we have. We say the early proto-men were limited because their tools were relatively simple. Or, we used to say, that to be human was to have invented tools. Recent research and discovery say otherwise. We are now relatively safe in this statement, "the tool invented man." If one kind of tool can invent one kind of human, it follows as surely as the day the night that another kind of tool can invent another type of man. We have an example of this—the difference between hunting man, on the one hand, and agricultural man, on the other. It is said that it is agriculture (and the subsequent importance of land as property) that has led us down the path to civilization and to war. We define war as the concerted effort of an entire society and all of its members against another society and all of its members—not the casual collisions which might occur between hunting parties.

Now we have a new tool, the computer, with both the ability to do certain types of "thinking" for us, and the unique ability to drive our machines. Surely this will permit yet another definition of man (we use man here to include both the female and the male of the species —a literary convenience we hope you will allow). First, the computer will give us a notion of intellectual power which we have never had before. And it will give us a time extension, in the sense that complex problem solutions may be compressed into short periods of time never before permitted. Hence, the ability of man to solve problems will be dramatically extended for any given life-span, however short that span may actually be. We are likely, then, to see our culture in longer terms than ever before. We may deliberately plan to extend the artifacts of our culture further and further into the future. And we may not be able to think of any particular type of future which does not include these artifacts (the computer, communication nets, and servomechanisms). Perhaps the Romans could not think of any future which did not involve the institution of slavery. It may have been a fatal flaw. Our fatal flaw may be that we cannot define a future in which the complexities of thinking given us by the computer cannot continue to exist. And in the event of some major disaster (the exhaustion of the resources of the planet being a case in point), we might find ourselves unable to sustain what we have come to call civilization. This is a serious hazard—the kind that can chill a soul on a cold clear night when a good walk in the snow generates thinking.

Certainly the computer may influence our art. The "painter" may use the computer to create dynamic images, and these dynamic images on the cathode tube could be called art. They could be photographed on movie film and preserved for galleries and display. If this

The computer as artist

is the case, they will also be severely limited by the capabilities of the computing machinery we assemble. Or they may be limited to the ingenious abilities of people who are both artists and computer experts to adapt to the physical limitations of the machinery. This is not new in the history of art. It need not be evil. But the machine is, for all of that, a machine. And as a complex machine it will take away from the muscles and the mind of the human race certain delicacies which we cannot mechanically duplicate. It could, then, quite clearly, narrow our abilities to express ourselves through art forms. More dangerous than the limitations are definitions of "good" and "bad" which might follow. "This is good art because it is machine art. This is bad art because it is human art." Well we may shudder. But if the computer, because of its ability to do much intellectual work, becomes itself a unique definition of what is good and true, then the shudder may be shortly over the horizon. Here, then, is the danger. The computer is complex. We admire complexity. We credit the machine with greater abilities than it may actually have. These "halos" of correctness and virtue are expansible to all things that fall under the control of the computer. So the machine culture sets its standards of value not to suit its unique humanity but to suit its unique machines.

Our cosmic views are almost always affected by our technology. After Sir Isaac Newton, we found a God who made a clockwork universe that ticked happily away. After Einstein, we found a more subtle God, one given to fields and exotica. After the computer, we may find a ruthless logician God who will serve justice, but without the touch of humanity we have expected of God in the past. Whether God exists is not the point. The human race defines God in terms of its own ability to understand and its own ability to define the meaning of faith. So our cosmic view could become more ruthless and more mechanical—more directed to logic than to love. There is a hoary old joke in the computer field which contains a warning. There was once a brilliant scientist who had built the ultimate computer. For months he thought of the most difficult question he could give the machine. Having done so, he presented the machine with this query, "Is there a God?" The computer purred a while and then, chattering through its output mechanisms, answered, "There is now!" It is a joke, to be sure. It is also a clear warning of possibilities. We would do reasonably well to heed the potential in the warning.

Our cultural mores change with time. We all know that. We know we live in a "credit" society. We know also that in another earlier day to owe money was to flirt with prison. To loan money and charge interest was to sin. Or we might say that it is interesting that our modern world defines everything that used to be a medieval sin as a modern virtue. We have said earlier that those with "bad credit" may become social outcasts (if they are not already). But worse, we noted there might be (because of the vast communication net we are abuilding) no escape from such a status. This is to make something of a permanent caste system. And a caste system is incommensurable with democracy.

To "know," in the past, has always involved a great deal of mental effort on the part of the knower. With the help of the computer, to know might merely come to mean "to know how to get available information." Are the two different? Yes, they certainly are. What is in the mind can be conjured with. What is in the machine can be called up and only then conjured with. We think the former is more important for creativity and invention. We think the latter is more important for defending the position one has already taken. While many a good theory has been destroyed by a fact, we also might note that many a good theory has been prevented by a misunderstanding of the facts at hand. The more facts we have at hand the more limited our speculations will be. There are those that hold this a good thing. There are many of us who do not!

So we believe our culture will be profoundly affected by the computer as one of our main artifacts. We believe it will influence, enormously, our other artifacts, our survival techniques, our art and music, our mores, and ultimately our cosmic view. There is no necessary or guaranteed evil, save as we pretend it is not possible or likely. Ultimately, the greatest evil is not passion but ignorance.

CIVILIZATION

If the computer develops the reach and scope we expect it will, then it is possible we may ultimately have a world civilization. And if this civilization is achieved, the computer and the communication net are likely to make it standardized. A good thing? Not necessarily. There has been a variability in cultures and civilizations which has, when they collide, forced upon the human race a host of inventions and developments. Rome once ruled the world—save for its outer boundaries. Lo; The outer boundaries are what changed Rome. If we get a truly global civilization, where then are the boundaries? Where are those gnatting fringes which will eat away at the status quo and cause change? Outer space? Well, that could be a long and dreary wait. No, a worldwide civilization might prove peaceful, but it might also prove dull. It might be a safe world in the sense that solitary confinement is safe. But we do not think that is quite the hope we have for the world and for ourselves. If civilization is an attitude—that touch of elegance that sees good in barbaric art and in strange new things—what then if there is no barbaric art and no new things? No one seems to be certain why the Maya one day gave up their culture and their cities and vanished into the jungle. Was it quick? Was it slow? We do not know. But there is always the intriguing possibility that one day the Maya had had quite enough of a rigid civilization, shrugged their collective shoulders, and walked off into the jungle, leaving the rigid priests and administrators to communicate only with themselves in splendid loneliness. Is it not true that such a concept makes you smile a little? Is it not true this seed of desertion rests within us all? Bureaucracy has many virtues, and one most dreadful sin—it is usually irretrievably dull. A world bureaucracy would be the ultimate frustration. So much, then, for the final goad—driving man or woman out of the cities into the hills for a gentle respite of a century or two of convivial barbarism. Could it happen? We do not know. Should we think about it? Certainly!

BUREAUCRACY

Mass production and overall well-being can be listed as the general achievements of our bureaucracies. Uniformity, limitation, and dullness are also achievements of our bureaucracies. We endure the latter because the benefits of the former once seemed so clear and evident. But the computer has the unique ability to expand the bureaucracy, to define it more clearly, to control its input and output forms, to monitor what is done and what is to be done—to weave a complex and ever-tighter net toward those achievements which the collective bureaucracy define as achievements. More people may be better tended and better fed. More people might become sheep to the mechanical shepherd. The danger is that we are likely to overlook a simple and unusual fact. Creativity is an individual human act. Committees do not create—they deal with individual creations and bring them into a general focus. Bureaucracies at best manage and at worst administer. But what do they manage and what do they administer? That which has been created by individuals, modified by committees, and deemed worthy by the larger whole. This is the double-bladed axe of bureaucracy. Those without access to bureaucracy's tools—to wit, the communication net and the computers—may be unable to influence the bureaucracy into new modes and new ways. Ultimately, human survival may be at stake. We are all familiar with the 3,000-year-long history of the Egyptian civilization. We also are familiar with its famous rigidities in government and in art. We are all, from our historic studies, familiar with the inability of the Romans to imagine in the fashion of the Greeks. The peace of Rome was the death of the Greek élan. Rome could only borrow, in the main; it could not create. And Rome, for all of that, was, for the time, the greatest bureaucracy the human race had yet put together—certainly it was the largest. It also, ultimately, became one of the most corrupt because form dominated over substance. We are probably no more astute than the Romans, though we like to think we are. We do seem to have the same general ambitions and goals—a single world of uniformity and peace.

MANAGEMENT

There can be no doubt the computer is a boon to management. Never before in history has management had a better opportunity to genuinely control events, plan for future events, and establish refined measures of performance. And never before has management had such unmitigated opportunity to power. It is said that power is the only human appetite which has no satiation point. And a management steeped in the pursuit of power for its own sake can be dangerous. The computer requires large expenditures of money and careful organization, and these two "virtues" are precisely what the managers of large organizations can bring into play. It is then likely that managers will more and more have the facilities of power, and that the single citizen less and less such mechanical assists.

Will management use the computer to increase the opportunities for dispute and variance, or will management use the computer to decrease heretical ideas and opportunities to keep the firm on its "chosen path?" This is the fundamental question. Historical experience does not bode well for what managers might do. We have many records of the search for power and its resultant rigidities. We have many records of the blindness to move and of lost flexibility in world leadership. We should, then, remain keenly alert to the *first* signs of the establishment of control for its own sake. We must actively and intellectually push management in the direction of using the computer to carry the ordinary burdens, to the end that there is opportunity for genuine creativity and planning. This is no easy task and one

Computer assignments

that should not be taken lightly. But as consumers, as business folk, and members of organizations, we can only keep the computer in perspective. We can quarrel and query as necessary to place the burden of proof on "convenience" and "computer output." We can be reluctant to turn over to the computer that which properly we should do ourselves.

Managements in the past have not been famous for the early development of social responsibility. Nor does history show any deference on the part of management to the condition of the worker. No, management has usually come to these "new ways of thinking" only on the basis of naked confrontation, either with the employees or with the government itself. We must then be about the business of staying wary and using such governmental forces as are at our command to be certain managers stay within the constraint limits set by the broader social needs of the population. Sometimes this will mean pitting profit against persons—an age-old conflict. But we dare not go overboard. History shows that private enterprise has been the greatest generator of benefits for the individual in the history of man—all of its sins recognized and tallied. And materialistic though businesses may be, either by intention or inadvertency, they have provided individuals with a greater leisure than ever before in history. It is this very leisure which gives us the opportunity to question, watch, and governmentally guide businesses in other directions. So, while we wish to give managements every opportunity to be more realistic, more efficient, and more productive, we can still recognize the need for watchdogging and the need for limitations.

We want skilled management with a social conscience. The computer can provide managers with just the type of information and structure to permit this to be possible as never before. The routes to these doses of preventive medicine are two: governmental computers, which can do the social and legal job of monitoring highly concentrated industries, and the general availability of computer power to the ordinary citizen in a fashion similar to the telephone or the television set. This dispersal of intellectual power is central to what we call democratic government and a fully informed population. Ironically, if businessmen see the potential of profit in providing this kind of service to the ordinary citizen, it is they who will set upon themselves their own limitations. And this is as it should be.

MECHANIZATION

We are likely, in the future, to see mechanization continue apace, particularly in those industries where it has not previously been applied (service industries of various kinds come to mind). We are likely to see the computer linked directly to many mechanisms to preclude the necessity of human intervention (and this on an increasing scale). The danger, of course, is simply that of unemployment. What of those who can only compete with the machine in the performance of tasks which the machine can do cheaper and better? Well, they will be doomed to the same slave status—little reward, long hours, and dehabilitation. So, clearly, mechanization continues to present hazards to each generation in terms of the work which the generation habitually does. In the long run, the machinery brings benefits in terms of efficiency, better product, and new kinds of tasks. But each generation is particularly concerned with its own immediate employment at useful tasks, and with the amount of pay the execution of these tasks will bring. This is the bad side of the coin. What we need, then, is careful job planning in terms of the application of machinery to tasks now performed by human beings. It is to our own self-interest to do so, for, in the final analysis, machines do not buy products which are made by industry, nor do they purchase concert tickets or admire works of art.

The processes of mechanization should be tied to the processes of finding new and different and useful tasks for those the machinery will replace—this on a national and not a local scale. Here, then, is a good task for government and, perhaps, one of the primary tasks of government (after safety and order).

We need, then, in partnership with mechanization, the planned technological development of people. This is largely a matter of education, and it is in education that state governments have long claimed inherent duty.

Mechanization carries a second equally serious hazard. With large-scale mechanization has come large-scale centralization of activities. We have the agribusiness of America in mind. Now, large-scale centralization makes possible the seizure of control by the few. And as in agriculture, we can become shockingly aware that the price of the product can fall to a minor fraction of the cost of packaging, processing, and delivery of the product. A case in point: Dried cereal products are not particularly affected by the price of wheat, or bran, or rice, or corn. Why? Because, generally, the foodstuff itself makes up less than 10 percent of the product cost. Packaging, processing, advertising, and delivery are the major cost items. More important, only a few industries are involved in these processes. Many farmers! Few processors! A natural potential for monopolistic or at least oligopolistic control. With such control we often get administered prices rather than prices of the marketplace. So we find ourselves in the unique situation that, while the farmers are losing money, the prices of foodstuffs in their delivered state increase. This is one of the possible disasters which can come from mechanization and subsequent centralization. We have not, in the past, been too successful at preventing this kind of situation from arising. And subsidies to farmers do not really constitute anything but a short-term solution, no matter how long we have carried such a solution in the past. No, something major has to be done to reduce the delivery costs of many products and to increase the original producer's share of the final price.

We face, then, the continuing spread of this anomoly throughout our industries, whatever their nature.

INTELLECTUAL POWER

If we can apply what we have just said about mechanization qua mechanization to the matter of intellectual power, we can see an enormous hazard over the horizon. What will happen to intellectual employment if we can fully mechanize intellectuality? Precisely what has happened to mechanized industries in the past—centralization. Such intellectual power, highly centralized, is incommensurable with democracy. Debate and argue the matter as long as you like. Invent the various alternatives you can think of. Still, you will find the incommensurability is there—it will not go away. The only solution we can think of is centralization with restraint; but we are hard pressed to define what those restraints may be, and how much the restraints in the second instance will merely accentuate the natural restraints put down by intellectual mechanization in the first instance. We have here a genuine paradox and one about which we ought to do more thinking than we generally do.

Information is a commodity, we have said. And, as with all commodities, information can then be bargained and sold. Information, then, can be held and marketed by the few for the profit of the few to the many. The end result would be that those with the machinery at their beck and call can centralize the inventive and intellectual powers of the society. Having centralized them, they can control them. Perhaps this is the greatest of all the dangers we have considered so far in this chapter. Perhaps it is the one about which we should be the most alert. And more important, it is the one type of power which seems to form an almost incontestable possibility for an elite, a caste, a privileged few.

The solution that occurs to us is the general one—we must make computer power available to the largest number of people at the cheapest possible cost. Again, and in short, we must turn the genius of American industry into spreading the intellectual product throughout the culture. We use the sword to control the sword. It would appear to be the only way. Further, we are going to have to be certain that there are competing intellectual commodity sellers. We want as many different firms in this market as we possibly can get, without making the entire operation inefficient. We must have alternative sources of intellectual power—each to control and offset the other.

HIGH TECHNOLOGY

There is a general movement in the Western world (that part which is most heavily industrialized) which could only be called antitechnology. It is a sort of special nostalgia for a simpler life—one uncomplicated by automobiles or smog or crowded subways and stores. And it is dangerous because it is a myth. The more primitive life has been described, quite accurately, as being fearsome, brutal, and short. Life expectancies of 30 to 35 do not constitute what we now call the rich and full life. Industrial countries can push those limits into the high sixties or seventies. And, the broadcasted stresses of industrial life notwithstanding, it is in technological civilizations that the life-span of man has dramatically expanded. So let us be done with nonsense. We want a long and colorful life. We need such a life-span to deal with the problems of technology. To abjure it is to reduce its problems and also reduce our comfort, our health, and our life-span. We require something else as a solution to the problem.

Can we then develop a technology which is energy conservative and does not pollute? Of course we can. We have already taken enormous steps in that direction in the computer field. Year by year, decade by decade, the power of the computer has increased and the energy required to run the computer has decreased—one of the benefits of micro-miniaturization. Will such trends continue? Yes, they will. Will such trends move over to other industries? Yes, they will. We are now faced with wristwatches of incredible accuracy that can run on quantities of power so minute as to fairly boggle the mind.

The trend, then, is very clear. We will use technology to conquer the problems generated by technology. It is a spiral, to be sure. But it is a spiral which can move ever upward in achievement and ever downward in the pollution of the planet and in the consumption of energy. We could not now begin to solve ecological problems had we not had to develop an artificial world inside our rockets ere they left for the moon. We could not now do the subtle probing of forest balance and air-pollution control had we not developed the computers in the first instance. So we need no whimpering retreat to the primitive farm and no great flight from the cities. We do need to turn our computers, our communication nets, our servomechanisms to the tasks at hand to make the environment suitable for habitation.

There is little need to speculate too much about whether people will leave the planet and what they will find when they do depart. We can assume, we think, that the departure will take place. But, since we can only dream of the technological achievements required to succeed, we had better turn our immediate attention to our present survival so we, or our ancestors, may live to see that latter and glorious day.

First we will develop our machines and send them out into a space less hostile than we had previously imagined. And then, one day, we will pack our own kit bags and follow our machinery into the future —one we cannot yet really imagine as well as we would like. We can genuinely believe, though, that such achievements will indeed rest on civilization, technology, communication, and the computer.

AUTOMATION

The danger of automation is obvious—what do we do with all the people we have replaced with self-directing machines? How much can we stand and how fast can we stand it? We do not currently want to face the realistic economic solutions such achievements will bring. But face them we must or we surely will invent a world we cannot handle. We have mentioned the guaranteed market and the guaranteed income. They may prove necessary. We also have mentioned the invention of new tasks—humanizing benefits. These may prove necessary.

Secondary dangers of automation include centralization, standardization, and allocation. Let us deal with them one at a time.

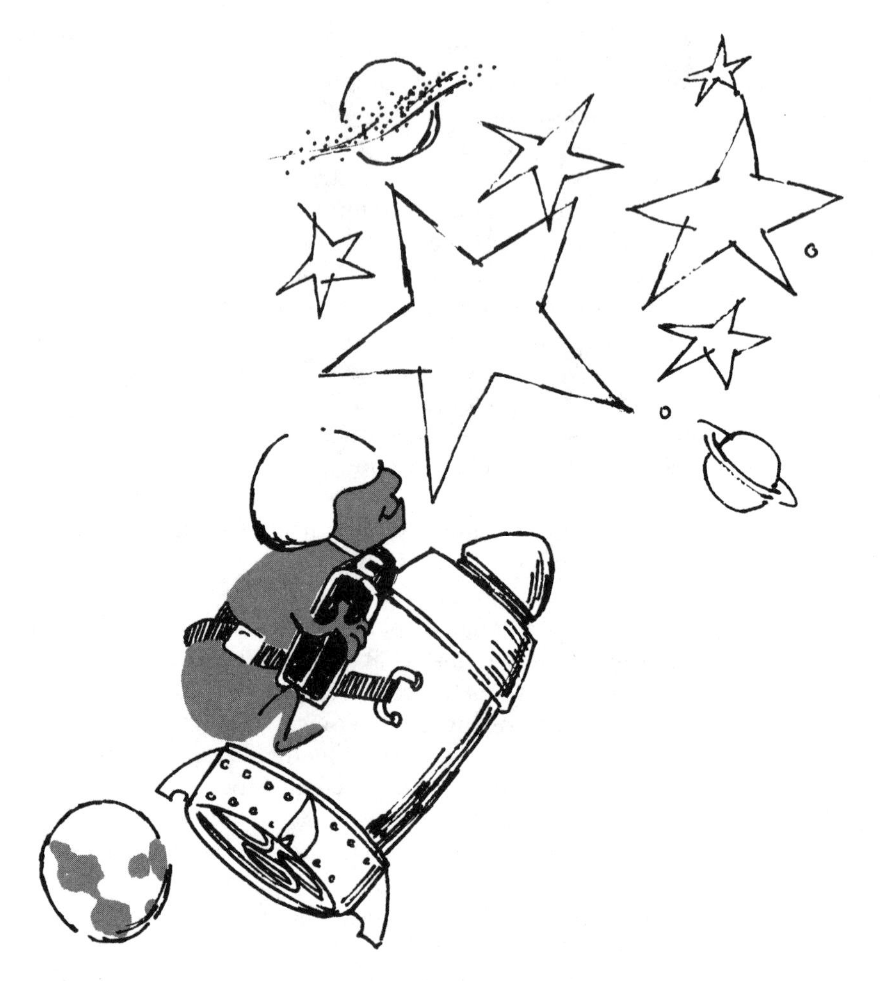

Some distant day

We have mentioned elsewhere in the text that automation requires enormous capital investment, among other things. This means those who can afford to automate are those who are already large industries with great financial power. The tendency of automation, then, will be to continue to centralize processes begun by mechanization, and it will continue them at an ever-increasing rate as the benefits become clearer to industry. We would expect fewer industries to exist, in the long run, in terms of type of product made. Where there are seven car manufacturers, there might be only two or three. Where there are a dozen major meat-packing plants, there might be one or two—and so it would go. Only those with the wherewithal now could begin to play the expensive game we are talking about.

Barring some stunning invention or interference from the government, we can assume that those currently in power will remain in power, and that they will inadvertently or intentionally continue the centralization processes which have been going on for three centuries in the Western experience. While this may not be inherently evil, our past experiences give us pause.

Standardization seems to follow fair at the heels of centralization. There is no doubt it is generally more economical to make one model than ten. There is no doubt that it is more efficient to stick with the simple and the straightforward. A variety of products cause businessmen a variety of headaches—some items sell well, some don't. There is always a thinning out process from the single industry point of view. The variety of things generally seem to arise because outsiders attempt to invade a field of endeavor which has turned profitable, and by doing so, force industries to variegate beyond their natural inclinations. But the greater the capital investment required for such adventurers, the fewer the participants. We do not have many failures really in the car business anymore, because there are so few firms to fail. We have many and splendid failures in the small retail store area just because there are so many. It is the ease of entry which makes the large number of failures possible.

The computer can give us a surface variation—but not an abidingly deep one. So automobile manufacturers can make "many" models and "many" trimmings. Or can they? Do not most of our automobiles look somewhat alike? Is not there a uniformity running throughout all? Yes, there is. Much that is not really different appears different—and appearance is not reality. Does not the uniformity of the automobile seem at times to preclude the genuinely new? Did not foreign marketing firms have to drive Detroit into certain of its current reforms, however reluctantly? Yes, it is so.

COMPUTERS

We have said, in the previous chapter, that computers will continue to develop—with bigger memories, higher speed, lesser size, lower power consumption, increased portability, simpler languages, greater flexibility, wider application, and lower overall cost. These are positive things since they will bring the computer into more and more hands. But the drawback is next. What are the hands doing into which the computer will fall? Some hands are criminal hands, we know that. Some hands would turn the computer to purposes of gathering power where power has not been voted. These are the hazards of any tool. The axe can cut wood, it can kill. The gun can shoot game, but it, too, can kill. The butcher knife cuts the roast and can also, in wrong hands, be used to murder the cook. We can expect from the computer no more and certainly no less than we can from any other tool. So we must be about thinking of the several ways the computer can be turned to crime. We must anticipate the kinds of criminal cases which will come our way. And we must devise laws and punishments suitable to the scope and dimension of the crime. The most likely area (based on previous example) where the computer can shine in errant hands is in the area of embezzlement and grand larcency. The ability to conjur up artificial records, to steal tiddle-bits from hundreds of different accounts, to mask massive thefts of funds—all lie within the range of a good computer and a skilled but evil computer operator. Again, the secret of control lies in the division of duty along the lines similarly taken for such simple jobs as bank cashiers and store clerks who operate cash registers. We do not let the people who handle the cash account for the cash. While we cannot completely prevent collusion we can, by the division of duties, at least make it more difficult than otherwise would be the case. The same type of ordinary management judgment is all that is really required. But it should be obvious that the more managers understand computers the more realistic the constraints will be. So at least some knowledge on the part of management of the true operating techniques of the computer and its enormous power is fundamental to control. It, the control, cannot be passed on willy-nilly to others. It is an inherent management responsibility.

INSTITUTIONS OF CIVILIZATION

Can the computer bring dangers to the institutions of civilization we have reviewed in the previous chapter: to the family, to the government (all levels), and to business. Yes, it can.

For example, in many ways the family has been bound together not only by love but by necessity. That is, the adults in the family have had to carry, during the early years of raising children, a great deal of the logical and intellectual burdens of the family. Because, in yesteryear, the father had to be out and doing as the breadwinner, much of this early intellectual effort rested on the female and helped define both her role anud her contribution to the family. But what of the female role if the computer can take over many of these tasks? Either the female will be free, in the true sense of the word, to seek fulfillment in her own way, or she may conversely find herself without a major intellectual role to play in the family. Some complaints filed today are that, among other things, parents have passed much of the intellectual burden to the family television set, which is the seat of information and the seat of entertainment in many families. If we add the computer to the television set, we could carry this process of parental displacement to its logical extremes. And if we convert the computer to the efficient and handy robot, we go the last major step toward freeing the adult of the burdens of the past. We will also, almost automatically, free the family adults from any real influence on the children in the family, and will pass on to schools and government the responsibilities and the judgments formerly made in the smaller and more intimate unit.

We do not believe the computer will be a primary force in the dissolution of the family unit; but we do believe it can be a significant contributory force to the degree that it tempts adults out of responsibility in the name of freedom. So there is danger here in the accentuation of a trend already observed and commented about today.

The government, of course, has both the money and the desire to put computers to work in the name of law and order and control. There is little of encouragement in this process, because the government has been both notorious for its interference of late in private lives and equally notorious for a certain kind of blind and stubborn bureaucratic stupidity which turns simple and inexpensive jobs into horrors of economic waste and bureaucratic nonsense. The only hope would be that the computer would force efficient and logical operations on an unsuspecting and unaware government through its agencies. This is not likely—or at least our past experiences say this is only a one-in-ten possibility. Yet, if we expect management to take advantage of the computer to increase its ability to plan and think, can we expect less of the government? At least in a democracy we can, from time to time, replace those in government who do not behave in such a fashion. This is a form of indirect and sometimes slow control, but one the importance of which we should not ignore. Such balance of power as we can probably generate would be between the private sector of the economy (business) and the public sector (government). If business can maintain a near equivalent, in computing power and know-how, to that of the government, we might, at best, be able to strike a balance—to let each institution of our civilization stand off the other and serve as watchdog and countervailing force.

Our third institution of civilization, business (the direct economic activity), is already well launched in the computer field, not so much on the ground of virtue but more on the grounds of economic necessity in a highly competitive environment. We can expect business (those already well established and endowed) to continue to expand the uses and facilities of the computer to their private (economic gain) ends. The major evil here is the fact that, if computing facilities and communication facilities continue to be expensive, the entrance of new business into the fold is likely to become increasingly difficult. This would tend to allow competition to weed enterprises down to a significant few. It would then be possible for the producers to dictate to the consumers, instead of the other way around. There are those who claim this is currently true for many of our product classes.

So business can be made more adaptive and efficient by means of the proper use of the computer. It can also be made more obdurate and dominant. That old double-bladed axe is with us once more. If we ask of government that it monitor business, let us also ask of business that it monitor government.

AMERICAN CIVILIZATION

The American civilization, with its concepts of democracy and free enterprise, will be influenced by the computer since, whether invented here or not, the computer has had a prolific growth in the American business environment.

First of all, though the computer is an enormous potential educational tool, it can be the wrong kind of educational tool. It can give us logic. It can give us arithmetic. It can give us information. But it cannot, and perhaps will not, make us human. Children learning from the faceless, tireless, ever-tolerant, academically accurate but indifferent computer might well get a most perverse notion of what it means to be informed, to be alive, to be thinking, to be human. We could fancy a highly developed and intelligent breed of the human race totally devoid of all those wonderful little human aberrations of kindness, love, and stupidity, which make us the colorful species we are.

Not long ago there was an attempt to blame the TV set and its programming for the murderous misconduct of one of our youth. How much easier it might be to blame the teacher when the teacher is the computer and its attendant equipment. The case was thrown out of court, or at least the contention of the defense was disbelieved by the jury. But while a single swallow does not announce the summer, it does say something about the spring which might be coming. Learning may involve more and more than just knowledge. It may involve the intellectual rub of one human being against an other. It may be less a matter of correctness and more a matter of the clash of biases. We really do not know what makes for a successful and useful education. If we did, schools would be less inefficient, less colorful, less expensive—and enormously more productive.

At first the computer, as a consumable item, will soon invade the ordinary American household. In fact, the home computer is already on the way. This could mean the computer will be subject to the same general nonsense of model style-and-trimmings change so common to the American automobile. The computer, popular in the American home market, could become more the symbol of prosperity than the needed tool of the family. Again, this is the American way—status and success measured by the size or number of computers in the home. Eventually, though, the computer could become a necessity rather than a luxury—a needed tool rather than a demonstration of economic well-being. And those who cannot afford the computer (though the prices will continue to decrease) will find themselves somewhat out of the mainstream of American life—as, in some of our more populous states with weak public transportation, as do those without one or two cars in the garage.

Eventually, we believe, the American civilization will be defined in terms of the computer as much as it has been defined during the last three or four decades in terms of the automobile. And if the past is any harbinger of the future, the computer as a home item will spread from this culture to others and, ultimately, be worldwide.

So we will see the computer as an integral part of our definition of the American civilization. Later history books may describe and discuss first the Industrial Revolution and secondly the Intellectual Revolution. On the one hand we replaced slavery with physical machines, and on the other we will have replaced the laboring brain with an intellectual mechanism.

IMPLICATIONS

We have, again, been discussing implications throughout the whole chapter. It would be fun to develop the implications of the implications if we had the time, But we do not wish to be like fleas who have fleas on their backs to bite them—and so ad infinitum. Enough is definitely enough!

SUMMARY

In this chapter we have had a look at some of the potential hazards of the computer in terms of the various titles of the first chapter in the book. We did this so you could review chapter 1, read chapter 14, and do some of your own speculating. If you have understood most of what has been written, you may find many quarrels with the author, and that is as it should be. Each of us is limited by his generation, his experience, and his own perception of events. Conflict and disagreement are not only good, then, but absolutely necessary.

In the main, we have pointed out in this chapter that though the computer may increase and expand societal bonds, this does not necessarily guarantee a good. We have noted the computer is well into being a regular artifact of our culture and hence may help us redefine ourselves in ways that can bode good or ill—we get no guarantee. We are certain the computer will affect our self-perceptions, at least as much as experience has taught us our other tools have done.

We noted the negative possibilities of the computer for civilization as we have defined it. A global civilization might not turn out quite as we hope and expect. We noted the computer can increase the range and scope of the bureaucracy. Properly handled this might be a good.

Badly handled, the computer will merely accentuate the bureaucratic evils already in existence. Management can use the computer to truly manage. Or management may use the computer to design administrations which are as dull as they are ineffective. Again, the choice remains largely a human one based on the ability of the human thinker to transcend the known limits of the computers we use and make.

We noted the unhappier side of mechanization, particularly in terms of potential unemployment. We also noted the need to start thinking now about the kinds of jobs the future will bring. We commented briefly on the problems of future monopolies and oligopolies. They could lie hidden over the immediate horizon.

Intellectual power has always carried certain hazards. Probably concentration of intellectual power is the most dangerous. We do not want a world divided into the few who know and the many who do not. But the natural tendency of business to merchandise a product, of any kind, to the masses, contains the ultimate hope that the intellectual power of the computer will be well distributed throughout the land.

High technology is a treacherous beast—always leaping into new frontiers based on single inventions which, at the time, never really warn us about the grand cataracts that are coming. The transistor and the diode are such devices, and they have taken the computer down in size and expense to the point where almost anyone may soon be able to afford a computer and put it to his or her own uses.

Automation, we have said, will continue, however slowly. And with automation will come the singular task of finding ways to keep unemployment under control. This may be the greatest single challenge to the democratic system and to the capitalistic system. All we can promise for the future is change and adventure. Our final hope is the knowledge that the human animal is a bad-weather animal. Just when we think the game is up and that despair is the only answer, clever individuals find solutions and create new guides for the race.

Computers are prospering and will continue to spread—their uses are just too great to ignore. Our institutions of civilization will be affected, as they have been in the past, by most of our tools. Some influences will be to the good, some to the bad. We hope the former will outweigh the latter. Or, at least, to be astute enough to heed the warnings in good time and take action soon enough to prevent disaster.

The American civilization will use the computer as it has used the automobile—as a useful artifact, as a status symbol, and as a product to be purchased and used to add to leisure or to make work easier in the home, office, or factory.

HIGHLIGHT QUESTIONS

1. Name a few specific ways in which you think the computer will increase the "banding tendency" in our own society.
2. What is unusual about the computer as a cultural artifact? Is this strangeness common to other artifacts?
3. When we say that the computer can "drive our machines," what is meant?
4. Name a difficulty or two in dealing with the kind of *future* that the computer may bring.
5. Name a difficulty or two dealing with the kind of *computer* that the future may bring.
6. What are some of the hazards in a fully developed "credit" society?
7. What is different about the kind of "knowing" the computer may bring, as against the kind of "knowing" we have had in the past?
8. Name some ways the computer might increase the range and scope of a bureaucracy.
9. Why is creativity less likely in a bureaucracy than in the general culture?
10. What is the difference between administration and management? What can the computer do to turn administration into management?
11. Name the single greatest potential hazard inherent in mechanization.
12. What is the single greatest hazard that true automation might bring?
13. What kind of planning can we do to prevent the primary hazard of automation from causing serious difficulty?
14. Why is high technology so hard to predict?
15. What kinds of crime seem best suited to the misuse of the computer?

READINGS

Baer, Robert M. *The Digital Villain*. Menlo Park, Cal.: Addison-Wesley, 1972.

A wise and witty book. You will be taken through some of the language and history of the computer and then plunged into adventures in literature where the computer comes out the villain. Good fun, and several well-made points will be at your disposal.

Drucker, Peter F. *The Future of Industrial Man*. New York: New American Library, 1965.

You will find good sections on the mercantile society and the industrial realities of the 20th century. There is an excellent chapter on free society and free government. Many of the problems presented here in general may be mapped specifically onto the computer.

Galbraith, John Kenneth. *The New Industrial State*. Boston: Houghton Mifflin, 1967.

A very provocative book about the influences of technology and our large corporate structure. While all of the ideas may not be correct, they certainly are worth pondering. Again, this material provides excellent reading and background for the puzzlements about the computer and our future. Pay particular attention to the chapters on the technostructure.

Mowshowitz, Abbe. *Inside Information: Computers in Fiction.* Menlo Park, Cal.: Addison-Wesley, 1977.

You know the computer has arrived as a serious artifact when it appears for both good and evil in the fiction of a society. Many good stories here—all interesting, well written, and designed to make one think.

Schneider, Ben Ross, Jr. *Travels in Computerland.* Reading, Mass.: Addison-Wesley, 1974.

Here you will find a complete story of the arrival and influence of a computer. The hazards and the benefits are dealt with in wit and clarity. It is a story, but a good one.

Wessel, Milton R. *Freedom's Edge: The Computer Threat to Society.* Reading, Mass.: Addison-Wesley, 1974.

Here we come face to face with a whole book of hazards—many more than we could do in our own short chapter. There is a particularly good chapter on data banks, and another on marketing and free competition. The final section on controlling the computer is well done.

CHAPTER 16

FINAL RECAPITULATION

PURPOSE OF THE CHAPTER

We have now completed the text of *Computers, Automation, and Society*. We will first deal with the discussion questions from chapters 13, 14, and 15 and then present a complete test of the major points of the book. And, as before, we will answer the test questions for you.

HIGHLIGHT QUESTIONS, CHAPTER 13

1. **What are the two primary functions offices have, in the past, been known to perform?**

   First, their personnel read, sort, classify, calculate, duplicate, file, and respond to various types of communication to the firm.

   The second primary function the office has performed in the past is that of memory. Memory as here used would involve the storage of tangible records (usually paper documents of various sorts) and the arrangement of these records in readily available files.

   In the well-run office, the personnel not only perform the functions first listed, but they do them in a very personal way. That is, they interpret and adjust in a nonmechanical manner and constantly keep in front of them the goal of personal service. This is something that the computer, alone, cannot do.

   Again, the individual who is shrewd enough to file with special human purposes in mind is far ahead of even the best programmed computer. Logic is useful in filing, but logic combined with a knowledge of the limitations of those who will need to look up information is even better.

2. **Where did the word "clerk" originate?**

   Clerk is a descriptive term derived from the word *cleric*. Clerics (churchmen) often were the only people in a given medieval community who could read and write. Accordingly, dukes and kings and other persons in power often had to depend on the clerks to keep the records of the kingdom and do many of the basic chores of calculation. Later, the term was applied to all those who formed special combinations in order to perform the paperwork duties normally assigned to business and government.

3. **Define the term "barracks organization."**

   Large offices have generally made use of the barracks form of organization. These are central areas filled with row upon row of desks and individuals working at those desks. We find typists, bookkeepers, checkers, order-fillers, all in a single large room or a collection of large rooms. Such an arrangement was made to enhance communications among the office people who needed to communicate and, more important, to design a flow of work through the office that would allow clear pathways for the performance of the several specialized tasks each type of paper document might require.

Barracks organizations are relatively easy to analyze in terms of the amount of paper and the type of paper flowing through the room. One can find and plot out the various activity stations where the actual work is performed. And one actually can measure the amount of traffic (in terms of the number of papers going through the system) and also the amount of time it takes a particular type of document to travel through the room or rooms to completion.

4. **Relate boredom and fractioning of jobs.**

While it is true that the smaller the job the easier it is to learn, it is also true that the smaller the job the more likely it is to be repeated endlessly and the more boring such a small activity is likely to become.

There is no doubt that it is efficient in terms of both training and performance to break jobs into the smallest possible segments. The training period is shortened and the particular task can be developed to a high degree of skill. But in general, the human being is a more complex creature than a machine and does not (given a normal intelligence) react well to monotony. The tendency is to daydream and grow careless.

Recently, "work enrichment programs" have attempted to broaden the number and variety of duties the individual worker can perform. In the main, the result has been less absenteeism, better general work, and higher élan. We can expect such work enrichment or job enrichment programs will continue. We must be careful, though, to be sure that it is not merely the attention being paid to the worker that brings the good result or the improvement, rather than the actual redesign of the job. The ultimate test is whether boredom and carelessness set in again after some reasonable length of time.

5. **Why is it said that the use of paper is an expensive form of communication?**

If we were to very carefully work out all the costs involved in the creation of any given paper record we would get something of a serious shock. For instance, we must include in the cost of the preparation of any document the expense involved in maintaining the space where the work is done (heat, light, janitorial service, paint and repair, air-conditioning, and so on), the cost of the transportation of the workers to the point where the work is performed (these expenses may be met by the employee, but they are thereby likely to force upward the salaries paid to the employees and ultimately become, from the business point of view, a true cost of the production), and all those special benefits (medical contributions, retirement contributions, and other fringe benefits) which are required to be maintained for employee health, efficient work, and welfare. Given, then, the general slowness with which paper records are created, and all of the costs we have listed, we find a single sheet of paper with information on it is an extraordinarily expensive item.

6. **Name one or two types of bottlenecks that you believe might occur in a large office.**

   A lost record, which is required for the posting of information on a number of other documents, constitutes one of the most common forms of office bottleneck. All the while the lost record is being traced and sought, the other work lies waiting. Often one or two very important documents can, if not immediately available, delay the work on dozens of others.

   If one or two key employees in an office are ill or absent for other reasons, serious bottlenecks can develop. Substituting other, inexperienced, personnel does not always solve the problem.

   And if the office is not well-laid out and personnel are wrongly assigned, the coffee break itself (for those occupying key check positions) can backlog all manner of work. This, actually, is one of the most common types of unrecognized bottlenecks which develops in the very large office.

7. **See if you can give a definition of the term "word processing."**

   Word processing is a general term which has to do with the application of scientific and management techniques, so familiar in the factory, to the business of office records, their creation, maintenance, and disposal.

   In somewhat narrower terms the concept has been applied to a combination of special electronic equipment and office personnel to produce, calculate, disperse, and file basic office records. More narrowly yet, it also has come to mean the electronic equipment and techniques which can be used by secretaries to enhance the work they do in the matter of the preparation of paper records or their equivalent.

   It is to be admitted, at the outset, that the modern office is seldom very modern and often uses techniques which are left over from an earlier nonelectronic area. Offices traditionally have been viewed, by many manufacturers, as only a necessary evil where cost-cutting should be exacted as often as possible. Word processing, then, requires a somewhat different philosophy of the office and the work done there if it is to be effectively applied.

8. **Name a pair of problems facing the modern office in terms of computer applications.**

One of the problems facing the modern office is to decide what quantity of internal computer storage is necessary for operations, what amount of offline storage is required, and the particular devices which represent the most economical form of storage, given the simple gross fact that we do not file to file, but rather file to find quickly and cheaply and accurately. Here, by accurate finding, we mean the correct document containing the needed information and, preferably, one which does not require either major interpretation or invention to be useful.

Another common office problem, and one which consumes a great deal of expensive office help, is the matter of editing materials that are to leave the office either for distribution throughout the firm or for distribution to other businesses and government agencies. Much valuable secretarial time is spent in the function of hand-editing and rewriting of original materials. This is an area where a well-designed word processing system can be particularly useful.

A third common office problem, and one which involves, or could involve, a great deal of tedium, is the matter of updating records already on file. The hand-hunt, hand-modify, and hand-file system can be very expensive. If the records are electronically stored, and electronic means of updating have been designed and developed, the expense can be cut down considerably and so can the amount of time spent in the updating process.

Finally, the business of reformatting information cast in one form into an appropriate alternative form is expensive in the old-fashioned office, involving, as it often does, the complete retyping and reproduction of the material. Here again, the computer can contribute enormous power if it is a part of the word processing cycle.

9. **How can the computer help in copy editing?**

Beginning with the simple memory typewriter and moving upward through the smart terminal to the mini computer, the office can bring the power of the computer (or some of its important elements) to bear on the problem of producing letters, reports, accounting statements, and the like with speed and accuracy. Editing is part of the complex of language-manipulating activity which we have chosen to call word processing.

Typically, a secretary making use of a memory typewriter can generate a letter and make corrections on the rough draft in such a way that a correct copy is rapidly and automatically produced. If, however, the memory typewriter is replaced by a smart terminal—with the facilities of the memory typewriter and the cathode ray tube and the ability to do most calculations—we have a much more powerful editing device. We must not forget the enormous memory capacity of the computer. This means the secretary may call up for review and alteration all manner of computer-stored documents. Here is the major contribution of the computer to the processes of editing.

But since we are involved with the computer, it would be possible to write a number of standardized copy-editing programs which the secretary might merely have to activate.

10. Describe some features of which an ideal memory typewriter could boast.

Ideally, a memory typewriter would have the capacity to contain hundreds or thousands of standard paragraphs which could be used to construct letters of a tailored type on demand. The best type of psychological and literary reply could then be created for each type of situation or each kind of inquiry. This should reduce the amount of training and the educational level demand on office help.

Of course, any memory typewriter with the kind of capacity here described would need to be supported by a subject index of the paragraphs available and a short description of the content. This index might include a set of standard letters to which individualizing paragraphs could be added at the beginning and at the end. These paragraphs could be selected from a topical list or generated by the secretary.

Notice, though, that when we eliminate the need for one kind of ability we generally manage to create a need for another. In this case, we would remove certain basic literary requirements, but we would need personnel who were quick at scanning lists and making appropriate judgments and selections.

11. Name some of the uses to which a desk terminal could be put, from the point of view of the secretary doing the work.

If the memory typewriter is replaced by a smart terminal with the facilities of the memory typewriter and the cathode ray tube and the ability to do most straightforward calculations, we would have an extremely powerful editing device. We would expect the person using the smart terminal to be able to do updating, reformatting, calculating, general editing, and original document preparation. Documents could then, if the smart terminal is hooked to a mini computer, be filed and subsequently be readily available.

12. What is the primary by-product of using desk terminals and mini computers to produce information in the first instance?

The primary by-product of using desk terminals is the production of information *already* in computer-usable form. This means no further preparation of the material is required before it can be filed in the computer system. Think of all the keypunching and other such activities which would be eliminated.

13. Define a verbal network.

Offices have, for many decades, been verbal networks. A great deal of time is spent talking over the telephone in almost any modern office. If it were not for the old-fashioned paper with which the offices of the past were forced to deal, the telephone itself should have led to the general dispersal of office forces. The ordinary intercom is another common form of verbal network used in offices.

14. What is a conference network?

A conference network would include all of the communication devices (telephones, intercoms and the like) at each station plus simultaneous audio/television transmission. We would require for this type of electronic conference a grid of television screens —say a unit with five or more small individual cathode ray tubes set in some kind of pattern. This would mean we could see a number of different individuals on the screen segments at any given time. We could then have almost all of the advantages of a full conference meeting. And if each of the subpictures were equipped with audio output, we could actually have a situation where people could debate and interrupt one another at will—much as they do in our ordinary workaday conferences where we all actually meet in the same room.

15. What are some of the advantages of satellite communication systems?

The satellite communication system would make the intracompany or intercompany conference economically possible in the next decade. The initial expense is high but the carrying capacity of such devices is enormous. We expect the cost of transmitting individual messages would be greatly below that of the telegram or the common letter. Satellites also have capacities which can be easily and economically expanded. It is possible with satellite transmissions to use burst mode or to send scrambled messages. This type of activity should provide greater company security than ever available before. And we might expect the satellite and its resulting conference abilities to substantially reduce the amount of executive travel currently required. This, too, would bring special economies to many companies where air fare has been a substantial cost.

HIGHLIGHT QUESTIONS, CHAPTER 14

1. How would you define society? What contributions do you think the computer could make in the area of social communication?

We have, in chapter 1 and elsewhere, defined societies as collections of people who have banded together to achieve common ends—definitive and economic.

Since the computer is a sophisticated communication device, and societies are held together by communication, we would expect that the computer could contribute to more careful and widespread banding. This would mean our communities could share common purposes more fully, and that our communities could be larger than they currently are. The advantage of the computer over the television set is that the TV is largely a one-way communicator, and the computer, combined with an appropriate electronic communication net, can be a two-way communicator. The advantages in the latter case are those that we commonly associate with the ability to converse with an individual face to face.

We also, for our society, might develop (as TV has begun) a more common language with fewer regional variations.

2. Name some of the supporting mechanisms of what we call "culture" and tell how the computer might contribute to one or two of those.

Cultures include a collection of traditions, a set of survival techniques and artifacts, collections of artistic artifacts, collections of mores, a defined set of interrelationships among their members and a cosmic view.

Since the computer is an artifact of our Western culture, we can expect it to be used in the development of survival techniques, further artifacts, arts forms, definitions of good and bad behavior, the enhancement of interrelationships among the members of the society, and even our cosmic view.

Specifically, the computer might help us in matters of law (which would be included in the broader class of mores). The computer libraries and search techniques should make it possible to bring a greater depth and consistency into court judgments. Well-informed juries can reason better than those without appropriate information. Judges who know precedents can make more consistent rulings. Computers actually are being used in law in precisely this way. Also, the computer could be programmed to examine vast numbers of laws and determine contradictions and inconsistencies. This would be of material help to legislators.

The computer might, via the artist, develop into the kind of tool that could produce new and dynamic (moving) picture forms. We are already familiar with the strobe light and the kind of art it can generate. Recently, sound lights have been very popular among the younger people. They find the constant movement and changes of color attractive. A computer-programmed set of such lights could develop a host of interesting patterns and temporary pictures of great attraction and complexity. One wonders if a society may not ultimately be judged by the complexity rather than the simplicity of its art forms.

If the computer comes to represent the society's memory, and if the computer is linked with communication devices to become the society's mode of interaction, we can see that the computer has an enormous potential for either good or bad. The uniformity of the computer could be construed to be a *good* or a *bad* depending upon the point of view of the individual involved with it. But such enormous banding power is not likely to be overlooked in the future.

3. How can the computer help us refine our thinking processes in a way which is supportive of what we have called "civilization?"

Since the computer is both a logic machine and a calculator, it can, in the hands of competent individuals, further refine the sciences of the culture—provide better definitions and more accurate measurements. This should enhance what we call civilization—that touch of elegance we mentioned in the text.

Also, we must not forget that the computer can recognize a greater range of senses than people. That is, the computer can be programmed to deal with "visual" matters in the infrared spectrum (where humans cannot "see"). This dramatic increase in the range of our senses would permit ever more refined judgments, and the refined judgments, in turn, could contribute to greater elegance and sensitivity. This need not be, but it could be.

And, of course, since the computer is a logic machine, it can quickly uncover fallacious logic which is fed into it. This ought to allow a civilization to avoid certan basic kinds of errors in thinking that have, in the past, sometimes led to self-destruction.

4. Why is the computer a "tool of bureaucracy?"

Without the large-scale bureaucratic organizations the computer could not exist. It is a complex device and demands large-scale and complex structures to create and support it. More important, though it is not often recognized these days, a bureaucracy is a rational form of organization, in comparison with other historical organization forms. It attempts to define tasks, determine methods of control, and fill positions on the basis of talent rather than blood relationships or some other extraneous factor. The computer is a logical machine with enormous calculating power. The computer, then, can fit well (definitively) into the bureaucracy and extend its power. For a rational organization to ignore a rational tool would be something of an inherent contradiction.

Again, though, we want to be a little careful. We want to be sure we know the difference between rationality, on the one hand, and rationalization, on the other. The former has to do with good solid thinking, the latter with self-justification.

5. What single major and significant item can the computer "buy" for management?

Properly handled, the computer can provide *time* for managers —time to deal with long-term plans, unusual problems, escape from the daily and routine and ordinary. A thinking management with an eye to the long run can be a good deal more effective than a management harassed by the need to make vast numbers of trivial but daily decisions which could better be made on the basis of policies previously established and adhered to. The computer is a unique kind of tool that can follow policies on a day-to-day basis and leave the management with the opportunity to deal with that which is truly unique and which, then, requires unique handling.

The computer buys time for management in a slightly different way, also. A manager or group of managers using a computer can vastly extend the range and power of problem-solving ability. This is, in one way of thinking, an extension of the natural life-span of any manager. More problems can be handled in the same length of time than ever before and in a more thorough and thoughtful way. This is a slight modification of the increase in life-span which we spoke of earlier.

6. **How does the computer mix with mechanization to generate automation?**

Mechanization is the application of muscle-saving devices to tasks at hand. The computer is the application of intellect-saving devices to problems at hand. The combination of the two systems should bring about what we call automation—self-directing mechanisms capable of meeting problems and dealing with them.

In the past, people invented machines and then found themselves bound to the machines in order to keep them operating in the way they were intended to operate. In short, people traded physical slavery for intellectual slavery of a sort. Now the computer takes us down the next step on the road. We can put computers (our intellectual slaves) to work guiding our physical slaves (the machines). People, then, for the first time since the Industrial Revolution have a chance to be truly free of grinding daily productive tasks.

7. **How can the computer help contribute to the building of intellectual power?**

Computer programs involving thinking processes can be put together by the best minds of the society. These programs could then be used to guide ordinary people on the correct paths toward problem solutions. We know, since Aristotle, that there are certain ways of thinking which are more effective than others. With the computers we have a chance to use those rules in the solution of problems in a cooperative and consistent way. The computer, then can be not only the servant of the thinking person but can also the be guide of the thinking person. The computer can deal with the minute parts of the problem, however complex, and at the same time provide the thinker with the general rules of performance required to solve the particular problem at hand. This is the symbiotic relationship we have mentioned in this book.

If the computer can deal with the intellectual tedium and also point out the generally accepted rules of thought, individuals using the machines will find themselves with a better grasp of the generalities at hand and also with the time and opportunity to see to the development of new and better generalities.

8. **What kind of information is pertinent to intellectual power?**

The most useful information pertinent to intellectual power is *measured* or *quantified* information which can reveal something of its nature thereby. We usually call such information "facts."

And facts are particularly helpful when one is trying to figure out what is going on or what has happened.

Also, information which points out the direction for further information is pertinent to the development of intellectual power. By this we mean that some facts do not fit into our theories, so this sends us on the track of yet further facts and may ultimately lead to the complete revision or refinement of the theory.

Perhaps most important, we are terribly interested in how facts relate to each other—sometimes this is called cause and effect and sometimes it is a matter of correlation. We want to know if fact *A* is the cause of fact *B* each and every time, and if not, why not. We want to know that *A* and *B* always appear together, even if they are not each the cause of the other. Sometimes this leads us to find facts *C* or *D*, which are the actual causes. All of this means a consistent and continuous form of intellectual growth. The computer, with its high speed and ability to deal with many variables, has enormously enhanced our abilities in these areas of thinking.

We might mention, as a caution, that in the main the computer has not yet been effectively applied in the emotional area of human relations. This is largely due to the fact that we find great difficulty in the matter of quantifying or measuring emotions. We know they exist and we know they exist in different degrees. But we are a far cry from the kind of specific measurement we normally accord to true sciences.

9. Is the computer an example of high technology?

Yes, the computer, with all its complexities and inventions, is a superb example of what we mean by high technology. It has had a spectacular development, to be sure, but one which rested on decades and generations of careful scientific work in the fields of mathematics, logic, and physics, just to name a few.

10. In what ways can the computer contribute to the exploration of space?

The contributions of the computer to the exploration of space have already been several. Probably the most important is the ability to send an intellectual machine where it is generally unsafe for people to go.

Second, the computer can oversee the operation of the many complex mechanisms aboard the spacecraft with a greater sensory range and a much faster reaction time than any human could possibly muster. Such refined spacecraft management makes any trip that much safer either for the machines or any people in them.

The computer-monitored spacecraft, then, can actually be a more sophisticated explorer than man himself. The spacecraft can range further and hear, taste, sense, touch, and see much more than any human agent.

But if it should fall upon us to wish to physically travel in outer space, the computer could well be so integrated into the spaceship that the two mechanisms could be thought of as constituting a single active and advisory organism with the soul purpose of enhancing the work of the occupants of the system. This is the general theme (ignoring, for the moment, the possibilities of berserk mechanisms) of movies such as *2001*.

11. Give the best definition you can of automation.

The term *automation* may be applied to any self-directing mechanism or system. By self-directing we mean the ability of the machine or combination of machines to set performance criteria, to measure the result of the effort, and to make adjustments to correct for errors and meet the performance criteria—all this without human intervention of the direct kind.

Another way of thinking about automation is that it represents the combination of both physical and intellectual mechanisms into a coherent self-directing arrangement.

12. Name four or five trends which you think the computer will follow, in the way of development, in the next decade or so.

We can expect continuing trends in the computer field as follows:

1. Bigger memories.
2. Higher speeds.
3. Lesser size.
4. Less power consumption.
5. Increased portability.
6. Simpler languages.
7. Greater flexibility.
8. Wider application.
9. Lower cost.

13. Do you believe the computer will have much effect on the family structure in our society?

No, though the computer might enhance some of the trends which develop. Actually, philosophic changes are more likely to affect the family structure. Women's liberation may continue to affect the internal roles and definitions of the family. We also can expect the state of the economy (whether or not inflation continues or grows more serious) to affect whether or not women continue in the job market, and this continuation might force further family changes. The computer might take on some of the intellectual roles in the family and thus free the woman in the family to turn her intellectual efforts outward.

14. Name some of the uses the computer might find in the fight against crime in America.

A centralized crime computer could keep track of every known criminal in the United States, types of crimes favored, mode of operation, previous arrests and convictions, geographical preferences, present location (if known). Such information would be invaluable—but we must remember the courts have precluded the use of much of this information in actual trials.

The "ideal" arrangement envisioned by some law-enforcement officers is a complete rundown on each citizen of a community linked to his or her driver's license in such a way that a single call to a centralized computer would reveal all the pertinent social and economic data needed on any person. There are those who view this kind of file as a serious breach of individual rights and liberties, so we may be a long way from that kind of information until full legal safeguards have been worked out.

15. What primary change might the computer make in the American civilization?

Since the computer is a remarkable educational instrument, and since the concept of participative democracy leans heavily on general education of the population, the computer could make its greatest contribution by enhancing the education of the ordinary citizen. The better informed the public, the better are the chances for the survival of the democratic form of government. Certainly a nationwide computer net could bring about a situation where information could be fed to government agencies about public needs and opinions at a rate far in access of that currently available and in a condition of far greater accuracy than has ever before been possible.

HIGHLIGHT QUESTIONS, CHAPTER 15

1. Name a few specific ways in which you think the computer will increase the "banding tendency" in our society.

Probably the most specific push toward further banding in the society would be the development of regional or national communication nets. And if these are combined in any way with the television set, we could develop a "national village" where interests in common could be accentuated and differences, over time, be erased.

Also, the common use of the computer would tend to make for a truly common (though perhaps limited) language in which many terms had a common national definition.

And, because we have to deal with computers and their related equipment in rather limited and specific ways, we might find a tendency on a regional or national scale to approach problems in a similar way.

All of these things are both "good" and "bad." There are those who would seriously object to the notion of a nation with such universal commonalities. There is a general feeling that variation in a land as large as the United States is, of itself, a good thing. But if these trends tend to reduce conflict in the country they could, overall, be construed as good.

2. **What is unusual about the computer as a cultural artifact? Is this strangeness common to other artifacts?**

Since the computer is an intellectual artifact, and since man (or woman) is often defined in terms of the tools used, we could expect the computer to have a major impact on concepts such as "self" and "place in society." On the surface, it would appear that an intellectual artifact would be more persuasive and more pervasive than an ordinary "inert" type of artifact.

And finally, because the computer is an intellectual tool, it can invade such areas as art and have an even more profound influence than a simple industrial tool might otherwise have. In short, the computer can be applied to any task which involves the thinking processes of human beings, and this means it is not only a unique artifact but one which will be broadly used.

The intellectual qualities of the computer are not common to most of the other artifacts (with the possible exception of adding machines, calculators, and certain other similar devices) of the human race. The former is an intellectual device and the latter largely devices to accentuate or replace human muscular effort.

3. **When we say the computer can "drive our machines," what do we mean by that?**

Basically, what we mean is that the computer can direct the activities of a number of servomechanisms (usually electric motors) which can move various parts of the machine system to achieve preset goals or make corrections in performance. Perhaps it would be better to say that the computer can "steer" our machines and the servomechanisms can drive them in that direction.

4. Name a difficulty or two in dealing with the kind of future the computer may bring.

Any prediction of the future based on the experiences of the past is likely to be in error, because the past does not reveal to us that "chance events and inventions" which might occur. No one in the 1930s could have necessarily predicted the transitor or the diode or the enormous effect those would have on the future of computers and their general distribution, in economical terms, through the society. So the primary difficulty about the future is that certain chance inventions or events might throw the culture or the civilization into totally unexpected directions.

A second difficulty which would prevent accurate forecasts of the future would be the chance of war or energy shortages of a particular or peculiar kind. We might be able to make some predictions about future wars based on past international injustices, but this too is chancy. A war can either enhance an economy or destroy it, and there is little reason to feel that predictions in this direction will be accurate.

Finally, we do not know just what new computer developments themselves may occur which would profoundly enhance the area of influence of the computer. If certain new types of biological-mechanical memories are built, we might make some kind of unexpected quantum jump in computer abilities which would make former predictions both too primitive and too inexact. We cannot always predict human reactions to such dramatic jumps, either. Sometimes it seems there is a violent human reaction against mechanization, whether it be physical or mental. While a revolt of this type is not common it cannot be totally discounted in the future.

5. Name a difficulty or two in dealing with the kind of computer the future may bring.

As we mentioned briefly in the previous question, the computer might change from a simple mechanical (and electronic) type of device to some kind of mixture of both biology and machine. This is the kind of computer the future might bring. Or we might be able to give the computer certain kinds of enhanced sensory abilities, which cast it not only quantitatively beyond the current human experience but qualitatively as well—so far beyond our own understandings that we invent some kind of godlike machine on which we might place a whole set of foolish dependencies.

And the future might bring a kind of computer so totally integrated into a national region that the whole region might behave in some kind of systematic and organic way—as though the region were some kind of integrated living organism with qualities and actions totally beyond our current predictions. We have something of that nature in the ant nest and the beehive.

6. **What are some of the hazards in a fully developed "credit" society?**

Probably the greatest single hazard to an individual in a totally developed credit society is that, if he or she loses the good credit rating, isolation from the main community might result. Worse, in such an integrated society there would be no place of refuge where a fresh and anonymous start might be made.

Also, without a handy means of currency we might become so dependent on the interlinked credit system itself that a temporary breakdown would result in total chaos and throw us immediately and fatally back into a simple kind of barter system.

The loss of individuality in a fully integrated society could be a serious problem, whether the basis of the integration were credit ratings or some other interesting idea. To be fully integrated may, like the busy ant, destroy the reality of individuality and the sense of individuality itself. If we integrate so well with a society as to destroy the individual boundaries of our own minds, from birth on, we may not truly know what it is to be an individual.

Finally, a credit-oriented society is largely a business society—not necessarily an artistic or social society, in the more human meanings of these terms. There are those who see the business influence in the U.S. as too large and pervasive already, and who do not wish to see a further extension of this allegedly harsh and economic way of life. Businesses are supposed to suppress the emotional aspects of humanity and work in a consistent and logical way. This may be good for business, but we are not certain it is good for humanity.

7. **What is different about the kind of "knowing" the computer may bring as against the kind of "knowing" we have had in the past?**

When we say a computer "knows," we really mean the computer has "on file" certain information. Or we might mean that the computer contains some kind of sophisticated procedure which can be called up to be of assistance in solving a problem.

When we speak of human "knowing," we tend to mean that the mind contains similar information. But, and this is important, that mind does not inactively hold such information—the brain is a dynamic and constantly working mechanism (even in dreams). Therefore, very suddenly, certain unconnected bits of information might fall into place and result in a new idea, a new philosophy, or a new invention. Human knowing, then, is more dynamic and unpredictable than computer knowing.

Perhaps one day in the distant future a more dynamic type of computer memory and "thinking" system may be developed, which would result in the kind of knowing we talk about when we refer to human beings. In that event the differences would be erased, and we would be in a whole new and surprising world—one not necessarily dominated by the human race. In the meantime, it is wise to keep the two different types of knowing—the dynamic versus the file—in mind.

8. **Name some ways the computer might increase the range and scope of a bureaucracy.**

The computer is supposed to be a rational mechanism. The bureaucracy is supposed to be a rational organization. The two systems, then, are natural bedfellows and should get along well together.

Bureaucracies require accurate memories, detailed performance plans, measures of success and failure, and the like. The computer can enhance such memories, keep very detailed performance records, and manipulate the measure of success and failure to achieve some kind of documented result. We would expect that the computer would be used in the bureaucracy to speed up the processes and to extend the range of control. Depending on your view of bureaucracy and its members, this could be construed to be either good or bad for the general population.

Properly used, the computer should make the bureaucratic structure more responsive and dynamic—but there is no guarantee that this will actually be the case. Hopefully, the computer would free bureaucrats to the degree they could spend their time concentrating on the process of management (including dynamic leadership) and spend less time on the simpler matters of day-to-day administration. We recall that administration is more of a paper-shuffling activity than management and certainly has less opportunity for new inspiration and new direction of the enterprise, the educational system, or the government.

9. **Why is creativity less likely in a bureauracy than in the general culture?**

The very formalisms which are the nature of bureaucracy tend to preclude creativity. That is, since jobs are well defined and the criteria for filling those jobs are also thoroughly defined, the combination of the two inclines to keep job occupants working only on those duties which are clearly within their scope. In fact, the more carefully the jobs are worked out, the less likely there is for clashes of authority between different elements in the system—this gives peace but it does not encourage new kinds of thinking about old tasks. And since performance of duties, as defined, tends to be the measure of success in the organization, there is no full-fledged encouragement of variation.

The very size of the bureaucracy, and the need for careful monitoring of performance and careful restriction of tasks at hand, also preclude any surprises in the organization which would lead to some special kind of inventive or creative activity.

The philosophy and intentions of the bureauracy are rigid in nature and largely dominated by the inertia of size. This, too, tends to hinder any genuinely different set of directions, goals, or effort.

10. What is the difference between administration and management? What can the computer do to turn administration into management?

We have, in this text, thought of administration as the performance of assigned duties according to the rules prescribed. So administration tends to be a self-centered, positionally oriented, paper work sort of activity. Management has some of these elements, to be sure, but adds genuine leadership activities (interrelationships between the manager and the personnel) and a certain amount of foresightedness, with the intention of planning for the future. We could say that administration is generally "now" oriented and management is generally "future" oriented.

The computer can contribute toward management by taking upon itself all of those ordinary administrative decisions which require no thought but merely execution. This could free administrators so they could actually begin to give serious thought to the structure in which they reside, and how it might be changed, and to the future of the enterprise or institution. It is the future orientation which would act as a goad to genuinely new thinking or new activity on the part of the manager.

A final difference between the administrator and the manager is the amount of responsibility assigned to each. In general, a manager must be totally in charge of her or his unit and its personnel. The manager must have the power to act on his or her own. The administrator tends to be less responsible and to be more the slave of a set of general regulations which have been rigidly prescribed.

11. Name the single greatest potential hazard inherent in mechanization.

The process of mechanization replaces human muscle with machinery. This is done because the machinery can do more work more cheaply than people can. The hazard, then, is unemployment for those unskilled people the machinery will replace. The old saying that those who would compete with the machine must act like the machine is a true one—this means hard work and an almost slavelike competition for low pay and hard hours.

12. What is the single greatest hazard that true automation might bring?

The single greatest hazard that true automation might bring would be the same hazard (unemployment) that mechanization can bring, only on a scale far more thorough and pervasive than in the past. True automation would so thoroughly enhance the manufacturing power of a few individuals that mass unemployment could result—at least in terms of particular industries. So, automation should come slowly and with a careful eye to the effect it has on employment in whole industries and in large areas of the nation. Fortunately, the very cost of automation tends to mean that the processes will, in fact, be slow.

13. What kind of planning can we do to prevent the primary hazard of automation from causing serious difficulty?

Given the fact that automation could replace people in many of the more tiresome and tedious jobs that we currently require, careful planning for new types of jobs should help to prevent serious difficulty. This would mean a careful examination of all the kinds of services we feel people in the culture should have and which they are not now getting. We may have to redefine what we mean by "service" and what we mean by "education." This work would be toward making it possible for every type of individual to feel more keenly a part of his or her society and be more actively represented in it.

Planning should be on a local, regional, and national basis. And the federal government should be about the business of making it possible for labor to move from an automation-depressed area to one where hand labor is still required. Or if the labor force cannot be moved, perhaps the government could underwrite the movement of the industry itself. This would be considered a normal social cost to ultimately be repaid by the success of the automated enterprises.

14. Why is high technology so hard to predict?

High technology has a heavy dependency on intellectual insight and invention, and because these matters are largely human in their origin they are unpredictable. We just don't know when a genius will arrive on the scene and what he or she will accomplish when present. Nor can we tell, in high technology, what apparently trivial invention will do in the future when that invention has been adapted to new circumstances. Again, we have in mind what the transistor has done to the field of electronics and micro-miniaturization, and what this in turn has done to reduce the costs of calculators, radios, and other electronic devices. Finally, certain types of already extant inventions are sometimes combined to bring about entirely unexpected results. The newer energy cells, combined with devices which use minute amounts of electrical current, come to mind as they combine in the miniature calculator field. Also, the invention of printed circuits has had a profound effect when combined with micro-miniaturization. The combination of such processes and inventions often can bring qualitative changes to our products as well as quantitative changes.

15. What kinds of crime seem best suited to the misuse of the computer?

In the main, paper work crime is best suited to the misuse of the computer. That is, embezzlement and fraud of various kinds which could, in the past, be linked to office work, are now still potentially the more dangerous because the computer can make the changes more rapidly and with greater scope. The type of fraud is old; the mechanism to use in the fraudulent procedure is new and powerful.

And, of course, the very kind of expertise (not commonly held by most citizens) which makes it possible to use a computer in a fraudulent scheme makes it difficult for the ordinary person to detect the fraud until it is dangerous or too late.

STUDENT SELF-TEST

We will now move to the matter of taking a general examination on the entire textbook. Again, if you take the exam on your own, you should be able to achieve a score of 70 percent to be totally satisfied with your understanding of the work. If you take the examination as an open-book one, you should achieve a score of 90 percent or more before you feel comfortably informed.

The last two tests were largely vocabulary tests making use of the "fill-in of blanks" principle. This larger examination will be largely multiple choice so that memorization is not major but understanding is.

When you have completed the examination you should turn to the answers section and make any corrections on missed questions. In this way you will get something of a complete review of what the author feels are the major points in the text.

Multiple Choice Questions:

1. The computer is
   a. not likely to influence our modern culture.
   b. already obsolete as a cultural artifact.
   c. being gradually removed from industry.
   d. an achievement of high technology.
   e. inherently an anti-intellectual mechanism.
2. A good description of the computer would be
   a. an intellectual map follower.
   b. an independent intellectual mechanism.
   c. a mechanical brain.
   d. a simple mechanical artifact.
   e. an extension of man's muscles.
3. The wheel culture has taught us that
   a. the automobile is no good as a substitute for the train.
   b. technology often has side effects we do not expect.
   c. there is no long-run solution to the smog problem.
   d. centralized cities depend on the automobile for their continuation.
   e. suburban sprawl is not related to the automobile.
4. Definitions
   a. must always be supported by measurable facts.
   b. are always premises of a logical syllogism.
   c. never depend upon any type of judgment.
   d. are neither true nor false as we normally use the term.
   e. always refer to concrete, visible objects.
5. A set of survival techniques, a collection of traditions, a collection of artistic artifacts, a set of mores, a defined set of interrelationships of persons, and a cosmic view are some of the elements contained in the definition of
   a. individuals.
   b. families.
   c. cultures.
   d. civilizations exclusively.
   e. any friendly gathering.
6. If one single term were required to describe a civilization, it would most likely be
   a. power.

b. force.
c. size.
d. complexity.
e. elegance.

7. The formal organization through which the government, the church, or the enterprise achieves its goals is called
   a. partnership.
   b. organizational strata.
   c. bureaucracy.
   d. company.
   e. corporation.
8. A manager is distinguished from an administrator by virtue of the addition of
   a. formal work habits.
   b. leadership.
   c. the nature inherent in the task.
   d. the size of the organization.
   e. the layer or strata achieved in the organization.
9. The application of physical devices to productive tasks is called
   a. automation.
   b. intellectualization.
   c. computerization.
   d. mechanization.
   e. powerization.
10. The ability to investigate, to understand, to quantify, to predict, and to simulate is called
    a. intellectual power.
    b. mechanical power.
    c. introspective power.
    d. talent power.
    e. organizational power.
11. Matching stones or sticks to people is an example of
    a. counting.
    b. enumeration.
    c. calculation.
    d. one-to-one correspondence.
    e. integration.
12. The Indian invention of the concept *zero* was a great achievement because
    a. it made mathematical formulas more attractive.
    b. it replaced the old-fashioned *X* of the Romans.
    c. it eliminated the need to add and subtract.
    d. it created an entirely new method of addition.
    e. it made it possible for ordinary people to calculate.
13. Blaise Pascal invented a machine which could
    a. add and subtract.
    b. multiply and divide.

c. handle all four mathematical processes.
d. had a large mechanical memory.
e. could do differential equations.

14. Gottfried Wilhelm Leibniz invented a machine which could
    a. add and subtract.
    b. multiply and divide.
    c. handle all four mathematical processes.
    d. had a large mechanical memory.
    e. could do differential equations.

15. While Joseph Marie Jacquard did not contribute directly to the computing world, we do credit him with the concept of control through
    a. a fully automated loom.
    b. the metallic punched-card pack.
    c. new design in warp and woof length.
    d. the process of engraving.
    e. a totally independent automated system.

16. Charles Babbage is known as
    a. the inventor of the submarine as a concept.
    b. contributor to astronomy.
    c. "the father of the computer."
    d. a developer of operations research.
    e. all of the above.

17. The difference engine was conceived and developed by
    a. Leibniz.
    b. Jacquard.
    c. Babbage.
    d. Pascal.
    e. Aiken.

18. Herman Hollerith invented the first
    a. full scale electronic computer.
    b. differential analyzer.
    c. automatic weaving machine.
    d. punched-card sorter.
    e. transistor.

19. The first commercially available computer in the U.S. was
    a. ENIAC.
    b. the IBM 650.
    c. the IBM 701.
    d. UNIVAC I.
    e. Mark III.

20. We make some note of the IBM 650 because
    a. it was the first widely manufactured and distributed computer.
    b. it could do more things than any other computer then, or since.
    c. it was the first computer ever marketed to business.
    d. it was the first computer to make use of "core" storage.
    e. it was the first totally transistorized computer.

21. Most second-generation computers were
    a. of the "stand-alone" variety.
    b. parts of large and complete communication systems.
    c. designed to make use of satellite communication nets.
    d. involved in "total systems."
    e. gifted with a perfect operational record.
22. The MIS systems often failed during early "third-generation" computer days because
    a. computer experts wrongly felt their machines could replace management.
    b. management includes a human element not easily put into computer terms.
    c. complex system design was itself new and in an experimental state.
    d. all of the above.
    e. none of the above.
23. One of the following elements in not commonly part of the basic IBM S/32 computer:
    a. processing unit.
    b. display screen.
    c. printer.
    d. magnetic disk storage.
    e. magnetic tape storage bank.
24. One of the following could not properly be considered a computer output device of the IBM S/32:
    a. display screen.
    b. keyboard.
    c. printer.
    d. diskette drive.
    e. magnetic disk storage
25. One of the following could not properly be considered a computer input device of the IBM S/32:
    a. display screen.
    b. keyboard.
    c. diskette drive.
    d. magnetic disk storage.
    e. none of the above could be considered input.
26. The diskette drive and disk system would properly be an example of ________ for the IBM S/32.
    a. arithmetic/logic unit.
    b. primary input.
    c. primary output.
    d. main storage.
    e. auxiliary storage.
27. One of the following is an example of offline storage when it has been removed from the drive unit:
    a. cathode ray tube.

b. input keyboard.
c. diskette.
d. printer.
e. magnetic disk storage.

28. From a simplistic point of view, we could say that each addressable storage unit (or cell) of the IBM S/32 can contain
    a. a digit of information.
    b. a word of information.
    c. a paragraph of information.
    d. a page of information.
    e. none of the above.

29. A *register,* as we have developed the concept in the text, would most likely be associated with
    a. typewriter keyboard input.
    b. magnetic disk storage unit.
    c. magnetic diskette storage unit.
    d. arithmetic unit.
    e. none of the above.

30. The ability to erase items in storage by writing over them is known as
    a. nondestructive read-out.
    b. destructive read-out.
    c. nondestructive read-in.
    d. destructive read-in.
    e. none of the above.

31. As a concept, *program modification* would likely involve
    a. changing the wiring of the computer from time to time.
    b. altering instructions in computer storage.
    c. altering the kind of information read into the computer.
    d. changing the elements of a data pack.
    e. none of the above.

32. A computer system of an elementary kind would involve the computer hardware and at least
    a. a national communication net.
    b. a regional communication net.
    c. appropriate computer software.
    d. one or two "slave" computers to the one under discussion.
    e. none of the above.

33. An assembler
    a. will convert a symbolic program to a numeric program.
    b. compile a full program from symbolic data.
    c. convert a numeric program into a symbolic program.
    d. is an executable computer program.
    e. none of the above.

34. Machine-language instructions (executable by the computer) are in
    a. decimal code.
    b. binary code.
    c. alphabetic code.

d. alphanumeric code.
e. FORTRAN.

35. A mnemonic aid, such as ADD or SUB, would be translated into
    a. a computer operation code.
    b. two or more storage locations in the computer.
    c. any spare assembler term available.
    d. the specific location of the instruction containing the mnemonic.
    e. none of the above.

36. In general, an assembler program has a ________ with each pseudo-English statement—this in terms of translation from one form to the other.
    a. one-to-one correspondence.
    b. two-to-one correspondence.
    c. three-to-one correspondence.
    d. four-to-one correspondence.
    e. many-to-one correspondence.

37. A master operating program could be generally assumed to be synonymous with
    a. a machine-language problem program.
    b. a problem program in assembler language.
    c. a control program.
    d. a user library program.
    e. a user data file.

38. A "management program" can be controlled by specific statements in
    a. FORTRAN.
    b. COBOL.
    c. Assembler.
    d. Job Control Language.
    e. none of the above.

39. A collection of job statements is called a
    a. user program.
    b. user data deck.
    c. articulated program.
    d. procedure.
    e. none of the above.

40. We would expect to find, in a computer library,
    a. the supervisory program.
    b. assemblers and compilers.
    c. utility programs.
    d. user programs.
    e. all of the above.

41. The supervisory root program of a computer is usually located
    a. in the user's data library.
    b. in the user's program library.
    c. general computer storage.
    d. a reserved section of computer storage.
    e. in special registers in the computer.

42. Utility programs are synonymous with
    a. user data programs.
    b. user data.
    c. general storage areas.
    d. assemblers.
    e. housekeeping programs.

43. An overlay area makes use of the
    a. auxiliary memories in terms of primary storage.
    b. principle of destructive read-in.
    c. principle of destructive read-out.
    d. principle of nondestructive read-in.
    e. none of the above.

44. A debugged program is one which
    a. won't run.
    b. is guaranteed to give an assembler program.
    c. has errors in construction removed.
    d. has been tested and found wanting.
    e. guarantees to give correct answers to problems.

45. The Hollerith card
    a. is a magnetic card.
    b. has 8 columns and 120 rows.
    c. has 80 columns and 120 rows.
    d. has 80 columns and 12 rows.
    e. is no longer used in any computer installation.

46. The IBM 96-column card makes use of
    a. pure binary coding.
    b. BA8421 coding.
    c. 12,11,0123456789 coding.
    d. ABCXYZ coding.
    e. none of the above.

47. A computer *word* (in terms of the text) is made up of
    a. one byte.
    b. two bytes.
    c. four bytes.
    d. six bytes.
    e. eight bytes.

48. The Transaction Telephone is an example of
    a. a complex computer.
    b. a small stand-alone computer.
    c. auxiliary computer storage.
    d. a computer terminal.
    e. an independent calculator.

49. The light pen is commonly used in conjunction with
    a. a typewriter terminal.
    b. a telephone digit terminal.

- c. a cathode ray tube.
- d. a diskette
- e. magnetic disk storage.

50. An inquiry/display station would usually have an input keyboard and
    - a. an offline printer.
    - b. a cathode ray tube.
    - c. a digital plotter.
    - d. a magnetic drum attachment.
    - e. none of the above.
51. Universal product code symbols are read by
    - a. a light pen.
    - b. a special "desk" scanner.
    - c. only one of the above.
    - d. both *a* and *b* above.
    - e. none of the above.
52. Special printing type fonts are usually used with
    - a. visual scanners.
    - b. cathode ray displays.
    - c. light-pen identifiers.
    - d. computer input punched cards.
    - e. none of the above.
53. A digital plotter is an example of
    - a. a letterpress output device.
    - b. a magnetic-coded dot output device.
    - c. a graphic display device.
    - d. a direct computer-to-photograph output device.
    - e. none of the above.
54. A public utility may be
    - a. quasi-private.
    - b. under no competition
    - c. a monopoly.
    - d. government regulated.
    - e. all of the above.
55. Private utilities
    - a. are not permitted under current law in the United States.
    - b. may have a better ratio of use to facilities than a public utility.
    - c. are always available to compete with any public utility.
    - d. are forbidden to tie one or more private companies together.
    - e. none of the above.
56. Of great value to the public or private computer utility is the concept of
    - a. multiprogramming.
    - b. the stand-alone small computer.
    - c. the development of in-house communication systems.
    - d. total government regulation of utility personnel.
    - e. the vast variations in computer languages and equipment.

57. Voice-grade transmission systems are
    a. all we currently need for effective computer nets.
    b. likely to be replaced by even lower-grade lines for economy.
    c. one of the handicaps to an integrated telephone-computer net.
    d. quite adequate to transmit any of our current data requirements.
    e. none of the above.
58. A "royalty program" is an example of
    a. any available computer program.
    b. a proprietory program.
    c. a program used by high government officials.
    d. something which should be fought by businesses.
    e. none of the above.
59. EFT stands for
    a. energy-free transmission.
    b. electric follow-through transmission.
    c. electronic finding tasks.
    d. electronic funds transfer.
    e. none of the above.
60. A collection of logically interrelated boxes that each signify some set of computer instructions or procedures is called
    a. a computer language.
    b. an assembler language.
    c. a relational language diagram.
    d. a block diagram.
    e. none of the above.
61. The text describes the *sin of civilization* and links the concept to
    a. democracy.
    b. autocracy.
    c. bureaucracy.
    d. meritocracy.
    e. none of the above.
62. One of the great dangers of centralization is
    a. the enormous variation which can develop thereby.
    b. the possibility of seizure and control.
    c. it is so widely scattered and difficult to get together.
    d. it can only be accomplished in a democracy.
    e. none of the above.
63. A national computer utility would involve
    a. information depositories.
    b. a large number of terminals.
    c. a national computer net.
    d. much common-language programming.
    e. all of the above.
64. An intelligent computer terminal
    a. has some computing capacity of its own.
    b. is an example of a stand-alone computer.

c. generally has large-scale computer capacity.
d. cannot function inline with a large-scale computer.
e. is a computer with a dynamic, self-directing memory.

65. A home computer terminal would most likely operate
 a. with an elegant and complex compiler language.
 b. in conversational mode.
 c. only in conjunction with a national network.
 d. with only binary input and output.
 e. only at the hands of highly trained programmers.

66. A "royalty program" is an example of
 a. an assembler language.
 b. a compiler language.
 c. a nonproprietory program.
 d. a shared program.
 e. none of the above.

67. A data base is
 a. not a very useful concept.
 b. the organized memory of the business.
 c. a miscellaneous electronic file.
 d. requires only a small amount of storage.
 e. none of the above.

68. Internal computer storage is usually
 a. random.
 b. used as a blackboard.
 c. rather expensive.
 d. all of the above.
 e. none of the above.

69. Each internal storage unit in the computer is usually
 a. addressable.
 b. unavailable to programmers.
 c. locked out of daily use.
 d. addressable only by page.
 e. addressable only by some two-digit number.

70. We would usually expect to find tracks on
 a. diskettes.
 b. magnetic disk storage.
 c. magnetic tapes.
 d. magnetic drums.
 e. all of the above.

71. Magnetic tapes are usually examples of
 a. auxiliary storage.
 b. single-track coded information media.
 c. a very expensive type of storage, as compared to other magnetic media.
 d. random access storage.
 e. none of the above.

72. Disk banks are usually defined as
    a. internal memory storage devices.
    b. small-scale memory units.
    c. mass online storage.
    d. all of the above.
    e. none of the above.

73. A data cartridge
    a. is not removable from the basic drive unit.
    b. is an example of greater storage than disk packs or drums.
    c. is an example of lesser storage than disk packs or drums.
    d. does not make use of track recording.
    e. none of the above.

74. The "spool effect" is related closest to
    a. magnetic diskettes.
    b. magnetic drums.
    c. magnetic tapes.
    d. magnetic data cartridges.
    e. none of the above.

75. Moving quantities of information from cartridges to disks is part of a process called.
    a. degeneration.
    b. debugging.
    c. debasing.
    d. segmenting.
    e. staging.

76. A "cylinder of information" is often associated with
    a. magnetic disk storage.
    b. magnetic disk packs.
    c. magnetic cartridge storage.
    d. all of the above.
    e. none of the above.

77. Volumes are
    a. always equivalent of cylinders.
    b. always equivalent of tracks.
    c. merely labeled gross storage units.
    d. all of the above.
    e. none of the above.

78. The earliest form of online mass storage was
    a. magnetic tape.
    b. magnetic disk fixed units.
    c. magnetic diskettes.
    d. magnetic disk packs.
    e. none of the above.

79. Tapes usually work best with
    a. inline real-time data processing.
    b. batch data processing.
    c. *a* and *b* above.

  d. individual item select processing.
  e. none of the above.

80. The "grandfather, father, son" principle is
  a. the relationship between programming families.
  b. the relationship between types of programs.
  c. a daily transaction updating technique.
  d. a record security system of file protection.
  e. none of the above.

81. Data base sharing can include
  a. input/output device sharing.
  b. channel sharing.
  c. internal memory sharing.
  d. all of the above.
  e. only *a* and *b* above.

82. Information is
  a. not really as important as it used to be.
  b. power.
  c. always subject to error.
  d. always error free.
  e. none of the above.

83. Sales people, clerks, and production people fit into the class we call
  a. computer personnel.
  b. unnecessary personnel.
  c. operating personnel.
  d. male personnel.
  e. female personnel.

84. Operating personnel frequently face the problem of
  a. being cut off from data processing information sources.
  b. a time lag between the need for information and its availability.
  c. meeting deadlines set by the computer center.
  d. having attention drawn to computer operations rather than their own.
  e. all of the above.

85. Smart terminals are very nearly
  a. mini computers.
  b. useless for operating personnel.
  c. useless for secretarial operations.
  d. always used in auditor's offices.
  e. always inclined to error due to lack of training of personnel.

86. The 80/20 data processing rule
  a. has to do with the storage capacity of computers.
  b. refers to the amount of work done at different locations in the computer net.
  c. refers to the age-benefits clauses drawn up for programmers by the Federal Personnel Board.
  d. refers to the actual amount of work different types of tape units can handle.

e. has to do with the amount of filing and file retention necessary in certain computer installations.

87. A powerful data force at work at the point of customer contact is called
    a. catch-as-catch-can.
    b. let the computer people do it.
    c. reality value.
    d. keypunch contact.
    e. none of the above.

88. The amount of time it would normally take to get an item online to the computer center, get it processed, and get the answer returned is called
    a. turn-down time.
    b. drop time.
    c. artificial time.
    d. lag time.
    e. none of the above.

89. When we have a series of fairly sophisticated mini computers linked to one another but no centralized computer system we have
    a. the ring.
    b. the star.
    c. the step-star.
    d. the ring-star.
    e. none of the above.

90. Where we find a central computer hooked directly to a series of simple or smart terminals we have
    a. the ring.
    b. the star.
    c. the step-star.
    d. the ring-star.
    e. none of the above.

91. When we have a central computer linked directly to a number of mini computers and these, in turn, are linked to smart terminals we have
    a. the ring.
    b. the star.
    c. the step-star.
    d. the ring-star.
    e. none of the above.

92. When we have several mini computers each with its own data base and these are then linked to terminals, we have
    a. the ring.
    b. the star.
    c. the step-star.
    d. the ring-star.
    e. none of the above.

93. "One can only generate real interest in an activity to the degree one has control over that activity," is a good argument for
    a. centralization.
    b. decentralization.
    c. tight high management control.
    d. loose low management control.
    e. all of the above.

94. It is claimed that two out of three workers in the nation are
    a. currently employed in manufacturing.
    b. currently unemployed.
    c. information workers.
    d. computer programmers, librarians, or service personnel.
    e. farmers.

95. The focus of the enterprise should be on activities
    a. involved in accurate record keeping.
    b. which are properly called auditing.
    c. which are called point-of-sale or point-of-contact.
    d. which bring a profit each and every time.
    e. which accent the control of management.

96. When a computer terminal has been designed for a specific type of task, we call it
    a. a basic terminal.
    b. a standard terminal.
    c. a blocked terminal.
    d. a tailored terminal.
    e. none of the above.

97. The business-oriented computer-compiler language is called
    a. FORTRAN.
    b. BASIC.
    c. Super Basic.
    d. Assembler.
    e. COBOL.

98. One of the major problems in dealing with the computer is that
    a. it never gets anything right.
    b. it has an enormous appetite for data.
    c. it cannot output nearly as much information as we can read.
    d. it does not open up any job opportunities.
    e. anyone can operate and run a large-scale computer center.

99. Once you begin to place computer terminals or small computers at the point of maximum use in a business, you have entered into
    a. centralized data processing.
    b. distributed data processing.
    c. counter-planning activities.
    d. irrelevant data processing.
    e. pass-back processing.

100. The term *automatization* was first used in relation to activities at
  a. the Government Census Bureau.
  b. the Federal Trade Commission.
  c. International Business Machines Corporation.
  d. International Harvester Corporation.
  e. the Ford Motor Company.

101. Information which is fed back into a work process so we can adjust, while working, to better meet the standard we have set is called
  a. negative feedback.
  b. positive feedback.
  c. auditing alteration control.
  d. systematic sensing.
  e. change-alter-change routine.

102. A simple mechanical example of feedback is the
  a. way a file drawer closes with a simple push.
  b. the response we get from a telephone inquiry.
  c. the fly-ball governor of a steam engine.
  d. the fan switch on a furnace when manually operated.
  e. none of the above.

103. Machines which adjust the settings of other machines upon receiving signals are called.
  a. computers.
  b. section alterers.
  c. servomechanisms.
  d. steel rolling mills.
  e. none of the above.

104. The human being is an example of
  a. a mechanical type of computer.
  b. an automatic type of calculator.
  c. a neo-feedback altering mechanism.
  d. a class A servomechanism.
  e. a preset standard.

105. A necessary element of automation is
  a. some preset performance standard.
  b. a measuring device to detect variations from a standard.
  c. servo-mechanisms to make, upon signal, necessary adjustments.
  d. all of the above.
  e. none of the above.

106. A petroleum cracking plant is a good example of
  a. job-shop industry.
  b. a cottage industry.
  c. a continuous process industry.
  d. all of the above.
  e. none of the above.

107. One of the interesting things about automation is the tendency to
  a. eliminate direct labor costs.
  b. eliminate indirect labor costs

c. eliminate raw material costs.
d. reduce capital investment required.
e. none of the above.

108. One of the things which a fully automated system must have to be economically feasible is
a. a wide range of nonstandard products to make.
b. some kind of guaranteed minimum market for products made.
c. a ready supply of direct labor forces.
d. no capital equipment older than one year.
e. no initial major capital investment.

109. A collection of general-purpose machines which can produce small lots of product on order is called
a. an automated plant.
b. a cracking plant.
c. a job-order plant.
d. a continuous process industry.
e. none of the above.

110. A term used to describe the complex movements required in a job-order shop is
a. function in/function out.
b. rough terrain.
c. rolling hills.
d. process movement.
e. catalytical conversion.

111. The changes in delivery systems in regard to fast food chains is a good example of
a. automation.
b. extended mechanization.
c. the failure of machine analysis.
d. the elimination of personnel from a process.
e. the failure of the American enterprise system.

112. Rather than *office automation,* we ought to use the term
a. labor mechanization.
b. paper mechanization.
c. intellectual mechanization.
d. computerization.
e. artificial mechanization.

113. Service industries
a. have continued pretty much the way they have always been.
b. are growing at a far lower rate than manufacturing.
c. are being totally replaced by computers.
d. are now undergoing processes akin to mechanization.
e. are, and have been for some time, stagnant.

114. Automation
a. is likely to require concentrated amounts of energy.
b. will completely reduce the energy demands of the U.S. in a decade.

c. requires far fewer raw materials than general manufacturing.
d. will never develop at all, anywhere, in the U.S.
e. is gradually being replaced by mechanization.

115. The Aswan Dam in Egypt is a classic picture of
a. the miracle of energy conservation.
b. computerized power sources.
c. the energy-net problem.
d. American foreign aid that has been wasted.
e. the brilliant application of automation.

116. The current "American ethic" is inclined to come in conflict with the principle of
a. guaranteed income.
b. guaranteed market.
c. federal job creation.
d. all of the above.
e. none of the above.

117. If automation brings about centralization it can also *concentrate* the problem of
a. control positions.
b. decentralization.
c. unemployment.
d. all of the above.
e. none of the above.

118. The characteristic which would make an automated plant work most efficiently might be
a. availability and concentration of highly trained personnel.
b. a certain guarantee of sameness of product.
c. a common agreement on standards of value.
d. a certain guarantee of stable markets.
e. all of the above.

119. Early computer installations were primarily
a. problem-oriented and scientifically oriented.
b. applied to general business problems.
c. concerned with the development of accounting ledgers.
d. all of the above.
e. none of the above.

120. An in-depth study of the needs of the firm prior to a computer installation was called
a. a potentials study.
b. a computer study.
c. a feasibility study.
d. a functional study.
e. none of the above.

Take a separate sheet of paper and list the appropriate terms for the blanks:

121. As businesses grew more experienced with computers, the need for ____________ consultants declined.

122. Over the decades managers have frequently complained of an inability to bring ____________ ____________ to the task of communicating successfully with the hosts of ordinary folk who work in the businesses they run.

123. ____________ ____________ is a rather rare form of disease uncommon to former centuries of man. It means that often managers will not consider it necessary to make a decision because the reports they have received are inadequate.

124. ____________ ____________ is the gentle art of never making a decision without large quantities of facts and paper to support it.

125. If the data collection date is moving ____________ the date when the data for decisions are actually used, the senior manager can feel confident that the external signs from the computer center indicate excellent internal management.

126. A very important indication that all is not well in the data processing center is the typical situation where the operational personnel of the enterprise are in a state of ____________ relative to the computer.

127. One excellent method of avoiding unwarranted management timidity is to have in clear perspective the functions and ____________ of the enterprise.

128. More often than not, the data center ____________ becomes the chairman of the company data processing committee.

129. In many businesses the data processing manager is required from time to time to present to higher management a summary of the year's activities. This constitutes what is called the management ____________ report.

130. The third generation of computers were best suited to ____________ centralized operation.

131. The first primary office function had to do with reading, sorting, classifying, calculating, duplicating, filing, and responding to various types of communication to the firm. The second had to do with ____________.

132. ____________ is a descriptive term derived from the title carried by churchmen of the Middle Ages.

133. Large offices have generally made use of the ____________ form of organization.

134. The fractioning of jobs and the boredom which results has a corollary development, rapid job ____________.

135. Most offices today still have a major commitment to ____________ in spite of the host of electronic aids which have been invented since World War II.

True/False Questions:

136. Paper is so common and each single sheet so cheap, we tend to discount the cost of preparing records and letters.
137. Every office of any size runs into the problems of bottlenecks in the communication lines.
138. Bottlenecks are always deliberate.
139. On the whole, paper records and other storage costs have been rather insignificant to the modern office.
140. When microfilming techniques were applied to office records, they were reported out as a total failure.
141. Offices have, for many decades, been verbal networks.
142. Smart desk computer terminals can now be equipped with digital or graphic plotters.
143. Plotters cannot produce what we call hard copy.
144. If documents as well as oral information can be transmitted from one point to another at nearly the speed of light, many of the former reasons for physical groups become even more important. Here we refer to collections of people.
145. Ideally, we should move from memory typewriters through smart terminals, through mini computers, to complete conference networks.
146. It is the satellite which will make the intracompany or intercompany conference economically possible in the next decade or so.
147. Automatic routing is not an important element in a truly symbiotic data handling system.
148. The computer is not really a very sophisticated communicative device.
149. Culture includes a collection of traditions, survival techniques and artifacts, artistic artifacts, mores, set of interrelationships, but does not include any kind of cosmic view.
150. We are safe in assuming the computer has had no effect at all on our cultural mores.
151. To use a credit card is still, to most businessmen, a sign of sloth and irresponsibility.
152. It is not likely that the computer will have any effect on what we have called "a defined set of interrelationships among the members of a society."
153. We have defined civilization, in the text, as "a touch of elegance."
154. According to the text, the computer is a tool of bureaucracy.
155. Properly used, the computer can bring humanity into the large-scale organization.
156. The ability of the computer to simulate the future is not of particular use to managers.

157. A highly mechanized or automated system, running at near maximum capacity, requires the guarantee of a market for the product produced.
158. Word processing, semi-automatic offices, the generation of records at the point of action—all have grown about as much as they are going to.
159. By intellectual power we mean the ability to investigate, to understand, to quantify, to predict, and to simulate.
160. Information is the vehicle of organization, and organization is the precursor of effective use and dispersal of power.
161. The computer can easily stop the abuse of power or the abusive uses to which information could be put by people with evil intent.
162. The computer cannot deal with the matter of verbal communication very well.
163. The computer, in conjunction with other technological developments, or as the goad to further technological developments, has pretty much exhausted the range and depth of its contribution.
164. It does not seem likely that we could ever achieve true automation without the computer.
165. There is never any danger that new devices can lead to new kinds of worship, or the search for flying saucers, or whatever.
166. Democracy is a political form and free enterprise is an economic form.
167. Consumption has never been considered as a mark of American success.
168. The computer will probably make it possible to bring ever-larger numbers of people together through an extensive communication net.
169. The computer is currently an artifact, and as an artifact it will influence our culture.
170. We can define a future in which the complexities of thinking provided by the computer cannot exist, but which, in other respects, will be pretty much like what we have always known.
171. Our cosmic views are almost always affected by our technology.
172. One important aspect of cultural mores is that they never change.
173. If the computer develops the reach and scope we expect it will, then it is possible we may ultimately have a world civilization.
174. The processes of mechanization should be tied to the processes of finding new and different and useful tasks for those the machinery will replace.
175. Information is a commodity.

ANSWERS TO TEST QUESTIONS

The answers to the test questions are given below with the following qualification: If you have good and sound arguments for calling a true question false or a false question true, you should do so. But, of course, if you have *added* words to the sentence whose truth or falsity you are weighing, you are being just a touch unfair. Take the question naked and pure as it stands and judge it only thus.

And it might also be said that one has to measure the truth or falsity of these last questions in terms of the point of view of the book itself. This is the best approach, since what you are trying to do is to determine how much of what you read you have both remembered and understood.

In the case of the questions that ask you to fill in the blanks, you might not have chosen exactly the same word. Here you will have to determine whether the word you chose means pretty much the same thing as the word the author selected. If it does, count the question correct. Multiple choice questions are less likely to cause this kind of difficulty, since you are asked to choose from a field of possible answers rather than make up one of your own.

---

1. d
2. a
3. b
4. d
5. c
6. e
7. c
8. b
9. d
10. a
11. d
12. e
13. a
14. c
15. b
16. e
17. c
18. d
19. d
20. a
21. a
22. d
23. e
24. b
25. a
26. e
27. c
28. a
29. d
30. d
31. b
32. c
33. a
34. b
35. a
36. a
37. c
38. d
39. d
40. e
41. d
42. e
43. b
44. c
45. d
46. b
47. c
48. d
49. c
50. b
51. d
52. a
53. c
54. e
55. b
56. a
57. c
58. b
59. d
60. d
61. c
62. b
63. e
64. a
65. b
66. d
67. b
68. d
69. a
70. e
71. a
72. c
73. b
74. d
75. e
76. d
77. c
78. a
79. b
80. d
81. d
82. b
83. c
84. e
85. a
86. b
87. c
88. d
89. a
90. b

91. *c*
92. *d*
93. *b*
94. *c*
95. *c*
96. *d*
97. *e*
98. *b*
99. *b*
100. *e*
101. *a*
102. *c*
103. *c*
104. *d*
105. *d*
106. *c*
107. *a*
108. *b*
109. *c*
110. *b*
111. *b*
112. *c*
113. *d*
114. *a*
115. *c*
116. *d*
117. *d*
118. *e*
119. *a*
120. *c*
121. outside
122. computer specialists
123. record dependency
124. defensive documentation
125. toward
126. slavery
127. purposes
128. manager
129. EDP
130. large-scale
131. memory
132. clerk
133. barracks
134. turnover
135. paperwork
136. true
137. true
138. false
139. false
140. false
141. true
142. true
143. false
144. false
145. true
146. true
147. false
148. false
149. false
150. false
151. false
152. false
153. true
154. true
155. true
156. false
157. true
158. false
159. true
160. true
161. false
162. true
163. false
164. true
165. false
166. true
167. false
168. true
169. true
170. false
171. true
172. false
173. true
174. true
175. true

EPILOGUE

If you have reached this point in the book by traveling straight through the many pages, you have come a fair distance, have learned a number of things, and have had an opportunity, three times, to test that knowledge.

This was intended to be a book that was informative, reasonably disciplined in its approach, and hopefully, pleasant to read. You should, by reading, have developed a special vocabulary which will, in the future, permit you to talk about the computer with others more expert than yourself.

If, now, you can carry on an intelligent discussion with a computer-using friend, the book has served its basic purpose. If you have ended the book with the disquieting feeling that there is much that has been omitted and that you yet have much to learn, you are in an even better position. There is much more to learn!

Some fairly strong opinions have been expressed in this book. Other computer people you may talk with may sharply disagree with what has been said and the conclusions drawn. This is as it should be—we do not all see and hear and think alike. Out of these differences progress is made.

Your best next step is to attempt to use BASIC or some other computer language directly at a terminal, construct your own simple programs, test your understandings and your skills by *doing*. There is no substitute for the experience of working with the computer itself.

EJL

APPENDIX A

BASIC

The BASIC language is somewhat like the FORTRAN language we have talked about earlier in the text, with the important exception that it is a language designed to be used with terminals—that is, by people, on a keyboard of one kind or another, directly in contact with the computer.

There are many different types of terminals and many different ways to initiate contact with the computer when you are ready to use the BASIC language to tell a computer about the problem you wish to solve. We will use, for our purposes, the Type 35 Teletype unit with the ASR keyboard. This is merely so we can show you one of the typical methods of contacting the computer. Typically, the contact steps would be:

1. Press the ORIG button. Notice, in Figure A–1, that the ORIG button is the first one in the lowest, rightmost segment of the illustration.
2. The ORIG button pressed, simply dial the telephone number of the particular computer system you are going to use.

FIGURE A–1. The Type 35 Teletype unit with the ASR keyboard

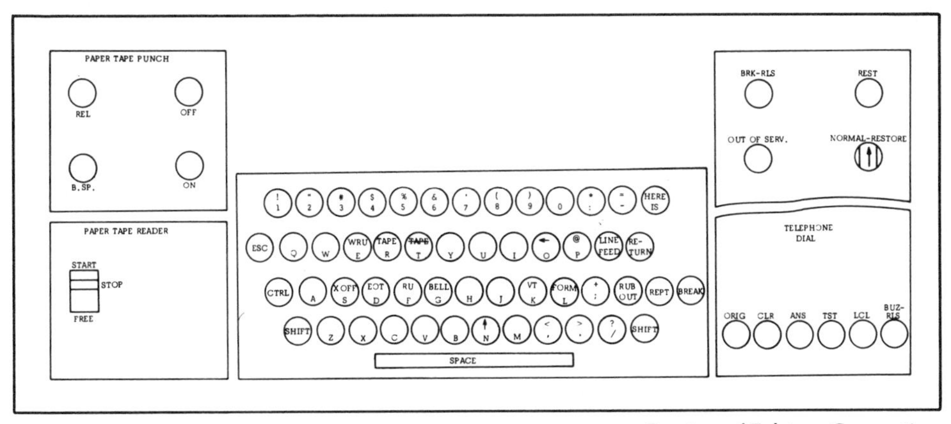

Courtesy of Teletype Corporation

3. The telephoned computer will probably type "USER NUMBER" and "PASSWORD" at your terminal. You must, in order to be able to use the system, give both the control number you have been issued and the correct password—these are parts of the security system of any well-run computer utility.

We won't go into more detail on the terminal operation, since it will vary from installation to installation. We should mention, though, that when you are all through with your program it is customary in many installations to simply type the word "OFF." That will end your contact. Do be courteous to the computer and others and get off the line as quickly as you are through. The telephone lines and the computers are busy these days.

BASIC STATEMENTS

A BASIC statement is a single line typed on the terminal. The line must be numbered. Statements are of two types—those that ask the computer to perform some function, such as an executable statement, or those that provide information necessary for some other statement execution.

An example of an executable BASIC statement would be:

11 LET D = 50.0 + 60.0 + 70.0

The "11" is the statement number. In BASIC, statements are executed by number, *not* by their order in the collection of statements called the program. So if we had statements 7, 9, and 11, they would be executed in that order even if they appeared in the program in the order 9, 7, 11.

"LET" is information to the computer about the kind of statement being used. The computer, with the LET statement, is informed that we intend to do arithmetic. The general form of the LET statement is:

[LET] v=x

"v" means variable—some quantity which will change.

"x" means expression—some collection of numbers and operators such as + or −.

Basically, what the computer gets in the way of results by manipulating the quantities in *x*, the expression, is put away at the storage location represented by *v*.

In our statement, "11 LET D = 50.0 + 60.0 + 70.0," the "D" is actually the name of the location (our "v" in the general form of the LET statement) where the results of 50.0 + 60.0 + 70.0 will be stored. The computer has actually picked a real place in storage and named it "D"—at least that's how it is as far as we, the users of the terminal, are concerned.

Since 50.0 and 60.0 and 70.0 are actual numbers (and not the names of locations in storage), they are called constants. Since these numbers have fixed decimals in them, they are called fixed-decimal constants.

PROGRAMS

We have now seen an example of a BASIC statement. Let us look at a sample BASIC program:

```
ON AT 11:00        6/20/78        IMD        SJ
USER NUMBER, PASSWORD—EJL20, SPARTAN
READY

11  LET D = 50.0 + 60.0 + 70.0
15  LET C = D/3.
20  PRINT "MEAN IS", C
30  END
RUN

          11:01        6/20/78        IMD        SJ

MEAN IS 60.0
TIME          0 MINS        0 SECS
CLEAR
READY
```

The first three lines of printed material in the program are the result of the contact and communication with the computer, including the identification number (EJL20) and the password required (SPARTAN). The computer tells the terminal operator when it is ready with the word READY.

The statements beginning with number 11 and moving down to the word RUN are the program. The word RUN is a *direct* command to the computer to execute the program prepared on the terminal—more on that later.

Below the program proper is the computer's printout of some of the basic identification material and the results of the program itself. The words "MEAN IS" are what we call a literal constant or a character string. The fact that, in our program, these words are inside quotes means they are to come out the same way they went in. So, when we say "MEAN IS", C—we will get the words MEAN IS followed by whatever the calculated value of C turns out to be.

With these preliminaries we are ready to lay out the rules and regulations of the BASIC language in a formal way. When we have explored all that, we will look at another program. Hopefully, you will have gleaned enough information to take a stab at the construction of a program of your own.

RULES FOR STATEMENTS

Each and every BASIC program statement must be given a number. Numbers may be from one through five digits long. Examples would be 2, 44, 404, 55555.

There are two types of statements used in BASIC. The principal kinds are executable and nonexecutable. The executable type of statement is an action statement like LET. The nonexecutable statement is of the type that gives the computer information it needs to be able to deal with an executable statement.

RULES FOR PROGRAMS

Any BASIC program consists of a group of statement lines. The rules are:

1. A line can be made up of one statement and one statement only.
2. Executable and nonexecutable statements may occur in the program in any order you wish.
3. No statement to be typed may be longer than the print line.
4. Statements are always executed in the order of their numbering. The order of entry in the terminal, or the order physically in the program, does not affect order of execution.
5. END *must* be the last statement in any program. No other position in your program is possible for END since it is the conclusion signal for the work you have done.

THE CHARACTER SET

A "character set" is made up of all the admissable symbols that can be used in the particular language. The BASIC character set is made up of 29 "letters" as follows: A through Z, and @, #, and $. What this means is that whenever the rules of BASIC call for "letters," you may use A through Z *and* @, #, $. The digits permitted are: 0 through 9. The special characters we can use are: + (plus), − (minus), * (asterisk), / (slash), ↑ (up arrow), ((left parenthesis),) (right parenthesis), ' (single quote), " (double quote), . (period), : (colon), < (less than), ≤ (less than or equal to), > (greater than), ≥ (greater than or equal to), = (equal to), ≠ (not equal to), ! (exclamation mark), & (ampersand), (comma), ; (semicolon), (blank).

VARIABLE AND CONSTANTS

BASIC provides for both short-form and long-form constants and variables. An integer in the short form is up to eight decimal digits. The value may not exceed 16777215. A fixed-decimal constant may contain a sign, a decimal point, and no more than six digits. (Rules for various versions of BASIC may vary.

Below are examples of fixed-decimal numbers:

12315
22

Examples of the fixed-decimal constant are:

35.
578.12

Floating-point constants make use of the E (standing for exponent) and a signed characteristic to tell how many places to move the decimal to the right (+) or to the left (−). Examples are:

57.8E+1
35.0E+0

The special BASIC statements PRINT or PRINT USING permit us to use the long form of constants or variables. In such a form the integer constant may be up to 15 digits if less than 10^{15}. The F format confines us to 16 digits with a decimal and a sign. (F format refers to fixed-decimal format.) And the E (exponent) format may use up to 10 digits in the mantissa (the number part of the constant preceding the E).

So, then, constants are the actual numeric quantities we might wish to write in our actual statements. These quantities refer to themselves, not to locations in storage where they are ultimately put. They can have any of the three forms just described, and we have two choices of length—long or short.

Some constants are so commonly used that BASIC provides a name for them (and the name refers to the particular constant stored by BASIC at some fixed location in memory). The first is represented by the symbols &PI (refers to mathematical pi). There may be two forms: 3.141593 (short) or 3.141592653589793 (long).

For any of you who are mathematical folk, we have &E, which refers to the "e." Short e is 2.718282 and long e is 2.718281828459045.

And finally, we have the &SQR2 (square root of 2). This will have the form 1.414214 (short) or 1.414213562373095 (long). In other words, we can use &PI, &E, and &SQR2 instead of bothering to type out these actual values. Saves us typing and saves us from errors.

A literal constant is nothing more than a string of characters enclosed in either single or double quotes. It is our intention that these strings should be printed out as labels (without the quotes in the output). Typical would be:

"AVERAGE VALUE IS"
'TITLE OF ITEM IS'

With our literal constants we may use no more than 18 characters. If we are using a quote mark itself in our character string, we must use the alternative type of quote to mark off the character string. That is, if ' is used inside the string, we will use " to mark either end of the string. Or we can do the reverse.

Time to consider variables. These are quantities which will change during our program operations. So we use storage place-names to refer to them, regardless of what these locations contain (since by definition they will change). We can have numeric, alphameric (alphabetic and numeric), or array variables. A variable name is made up of a letter (remember our 29), or a letter *followed* by a number. Place-names like B2, #3, or $ will do for numeric variables. If our variable is alphameric, we will use a letter followed by a $ sign so BASIC will know we have a mixed bag. Examples would be B$ or @$.

If we are dealing with arrays, we use a letter of our alphabet of 29 followed by appropriate dimensions. For instance, B(L) means an array named B with a specified number of elements (L). If we want the sixth item in the array B, we would call it by the name B(6). Two dimensional arrays have the form B(K,I). If we want the fourth row and the fifth column, we would write B(4,5) to find the particular item.

Should we have a mixed array (alphameric), we would indicate such by a name made up of a letter followed by a dollar sign. These *must* be one-dimensional arrays. An array named B that is to be alphameric must be of the form B$(K).

The computer must, when it is setting an array, assume some initial values in these rows or rows and columns. For numeric material, the initial value assumed for each element is zero. For alphameric arrays, the initial value is always 18 blank characters. So when the computer has built an array for you in storage, it is your task to input the values for the array before it can be used in your computations.

BASIC ARITHMETIC

To perform basic arithmetic operations with BASIC we make use of both the LET statement and the DEF statement. The LET statement sets up the [LET] v=x situation, wherein the arithmetic results created by the expression (x) are placed in the storage location signified by the name given to (v). Let us give formal definition for the LET statement and also for the DEF statement and then we can explain the operators used in them.

[LET] v=x

v is a variable.
x is an expression, an alphameric variable, or a literal constant.

During the execution of the LET statement the variable represented by *v* will assume the value of the results of the expression on the right.

So, in a sense, *v* (when named) is the location where the results of the operations of *x* (the expression) are stored. *X* and *v* must have the same mode. That is, when *v* is to be an alphameric variable, then *x* must be an alphameric variable or a literal constant. Or if *v* is a numeric variable, then *x* must be an expression.

If we have a literal constant shorter than 18 characters, the constant will be "padded" with blanks to the right. If the constant is longer than 18 characters, figures are loped off to the right.

Typical LET statements would have the form:

```
 11  LET B=C2–C3*C4
101  LET B=C/3.2
 20  Y= Y2*Y3
```

In the last example, the LET is not present. Actually, as long as we have the "=" sign, the LET itself is implied to the computer doing BASIC. But it is perhaps wise to keep the statement name in the statement so anyone scanning the program, who knows BASIC, will know what we had in mind.

In the general form of the LET statement, we wrote: [LET] v=x. The fact that LET is in brackets means it is optional in the statement as far as the computer is concerned.

Also, when we are writing the general form of a statement (as versus a specific example), lowercase letters such as "x" and "v" would indicate the programmer is to supply the specific information. Uppercase letters such as "V" or "X" must appear in the statement exactly as shown. Remember, we are referring to *general* forms.

DEF FNz(v) = x

DEF identifies the kind of statement for BASIC.

z is a letter.

v is a numeric variable.

x is an expression.

FNz represents the function which we are defining by means of the expression.

Let us take a simple example of how the DEF statement would be used in conjunction with the now familiar LET statement:

```
50  DEF FNR (X) = X*3.0 + (X/X+4)
```

We would call *X* our dummy variable in the function we have just outlined with the DEF statement. Suppose we have a variable called *M* (that is, it is the location of the actual variable). We could then use the LET statement as follows:

```
55 LET Z = FNR(M)
```

In this case, the LET statement will make use of the function FNR, which we have previously laid out. Our *M* variable will be substituted in the function for the *X* (which was what we called a dummy variable). The function will be performed and the results of the function will be stored at *Z*. We could, then, later in the program, use *Z* in some other statement.

Actually, it doesn't matter where in the program we define the function since functions are worked out first in BASIC. So our statement 55 could appear, in the program, before our DEF statement and it wouldn't make any difference to the proper execution of the program. But our *Z* calculation would naturally have to be made before we used *Z* in some other statement.

ARITHMETIC DETAILS

Now that we have briefly explored two of our arithmetic statements, the LET and the DEF, let us turn our attention to further mathematical matters, particularly what we call operators and the hierarchy of operational performance.

Unary operators. Unary operators are what we call *prefix* operators, and we have only two:

+ value of
− negative of

Arithmetic operators. Arithmetic operators are called *infix* operators. This is because they appear between two items (variables or constants) and ask for something to be done with the two elements. They are:

+ addition
− subtraction
* multiplication
/ division
↑ exponentiation

Relational operators. Relational operators are also used in arithmetic, and we have six of these:

< less than
≤ less than or equal to
> greater than
≥ greater than or equal to
= equal to
≠ not equal to

Hierarchy of operations. There used to be an old saying in the grammar schools: "*P*lease *E*xcuse *M*y *D*ear *A*unt *S*ally." This was to give the student a clue as to the hierarchy of mathematical operations: (1) remove *P*arentheses, (2) do *E*xponentiations, (3) *M*ultiply, (4) *D*ivide, (5) *A*dd, and (6) *S*ubtract. We have a similar order in BASIC. Any of the parenthesized operations will be performed from the innermost parentheses to the outermost parentheses. When operators are of the same level, they will be performed from the left to the right. And the hierarchy is generally as expressed above, with emphasis (for us) that multiplication and division are done across the expression before any addition or subtraction is done, unless such items are in parentheses.

With our variables, our constants, and our operators we can construct just about any mathematical expression we wish and be certain of the order of the execution of the elements therein.

SAMPLE PROGRAM

Let us, in the light of our newfound knowledge, look again at the sample program we introduced earlier:

```
ON AT 11:00        6/20/78        IMD       SJ
USER NUMBER, PASSWORD—EJL20, SPARTAN
READY

11  LET D = 50.0 + 60.0 + 70.0
15  LET C = D/3.
20  PRINT "MEAN IS", C
30  END
RUN

           11:00        5/20/78        IMD       SJ

MEAN IS 60.0

TIME        0 MINS        ISECS
CLEAR
READY
```

We will break down the elements and discuss each in detail. First we have:

```
ON AT 11:00        5/20/78        IMD       SJ
USER NUMBER, PASSWORD—EJL20, SPARTAN
```

We have logged on to the computer and completed the required password and user number requests. When the computer has cleared this information successfully, the connection to the computer is properly made. The computer then advises:

```
READY
```

We now have the signal that the computer is ready to receive our program information, and we can begin our actual use of the computer to present the program and data.

```
11   LET D = 50.0 + 60.0 + 70.0
15   LET C = D/3.
```

We will now give the full formal treatment to the LET statement in general form:

[LET] v = x

[ ] indicates that the word LET itself is optional.

v is a variable.

x is an expression, literal constant, or alphameric variable.

The variable left of the equal sign takes on the value of the result of the expression to the right. If *V*, as a variable, is numeric, then *x* must be an expression. If *v* is an alphameric variable, then *x* must be a literal constant or an alphameric variable. We cannot mix modes.

Any literal constant shorter than 18 characters has blanks padded in on the right. When a literal constant is over 18 characters, truncation takes place on the right.

When a constant has no characters, the computer will assume it to be made up of blank characters.

[LET] $v_1, v_2, v_3, \ldots, v_n = x$

Above is the general form of the multiple LET statement.

v is a variable.

x is either an expression, alphameric variable, or literal constant.

The variables to the left of the equal sign take on the value of *x* to the right.

```
20   PRINT "MEAN IS", C
```

Let us now review the full formal rules for the use of PRINT. We will start with the general form:

PRINT $f_1t_1f_2t_2 \ldots f_nt_n$

f may be an alphameric variable, an expression, a literal constant, or it may be null.

t will be blank, a comma, a semicolon, or null.

The print field is "f." This will be put in output format as selected and then printed. Carriage position is determined by "t" (the terminator).

Print lines are divided into zones. Zones are either packed or full. A packed zone has the following variations:

Expression: The print field length in characters determines zone length in characters as follows:

Field Length	Zone Length
2–4	6
5–7	9
8–10	12
11–13	15
14–16	18

Accordingly, a full print zone is 18 characters in length.

We can output expressions, literal constants, and alphameric variables. There are printing rules for these. We will take them in order:

Expressions

Printing starts at the current carriage position unless the line being printed is longer than the space available. In such a latter case, printing will begin on the next line.

Literal constants and alphameric variables

If the terminator character "t" isn't a comma, printing commences at the present carriage position; and if the end of the line comes before the entire field has been printed, the field continues on the next line.

If the terminator character "t" *is* a comma but fewer than 18 places remain in the line, printing will automatically start on the next print line. If the new line is longer than a full print line (will take more than one line), the remainder will be put on a second line.

If the terminator character "t" is a comma and at least 18 places remain in the line, printing begins at the current carriage position. If there is an overflow, it will be continued on the next line.

What happens to the typewriter or printer carriage when a field has been printed? This depends upon the "t" that follows the printed field, and also upon the type of field itself. Let us consider the different fields—again, they would be for a literal constant, alphameric variable or expression, or a null (empty) field.

Literal constant

If "t" is a comma: the carriage will skip the remaining places in the full print zone. If the end of the line is encountered, the carriage spaces to a new line.

If "t" is a semicolon: the carriage will not move unless the end of line is met. If the end of the line is encountered, a new line begins.

If "t" is blank (or null): If the print field happens to be the last field in the statement, a new line is started. If the print field isn't the last field in the statement, the carriage will *not* be moved.

Alphameric variable or expression

If "t" is a comma: the carriage is moved past remaining spaces in the full print zone. If this takes the carriage to the end of the line, a new line is begun.

If "t" is a semicolon: the carriage moves past the remaining spaces in the packed print line and, if the end of the line is encountered, a new line is begun.

If "t" is blank (or null): If what follows is a literal constant, the terminator is interpreted as a semicolon and the rules for semicolon apply. If the print field is the last in the line, the carriage moves to a new line.

Print field is null

If "t" is a comma: the carriage moves 18 spaces unless the end of the line is encountered, in which event a new line is begun.

If "t" is a semicolon: the carriage moves three spaces. If the end of the line occurs, a new line is begun.

If "t" is blank or null: the carriage moves to begin a new line.

These last three sets of rules tell us what happens to the carriage of the printer *after* a field has been printed. The rules that came before had to do with how the field being printed was treated. Its treatment was based on the terminator which preceded it!

---

30 END

The general form of the END statement is:

END [c . . .]

We may simply put END to indicate the completion of our program as we did in the example. Or we can use any character we choose to identify the particular END statement—that is what the "c" in brackets represents.

The END statement causes the compilation of the program (not its execution) to end.

RUN

RUN is a system command (conversation with the computer about what is to be done with the program).

The RUN statement will cause the execution of the actual program currently in the work area of the computer. The computer will print the following: (1) the program's name, (2) the date, (3) the time, and (4) the results of the program in the printing format specified.

Since we don't want to swamp you with too many details too rapidly, let us give thought to yet another program which will permit the introduction of the READ statement, the DATA statement, and the PRINT USING statement.

Our sample program is:

```
CLEAR
READY
10  READ W, X, Y, Z
20  DATA 100, 200, 300, 400
30  LET U = W + X - Y * Z
40  PRINT USING 50, U
50  :THE ANSWER IS ####.##
60  END
RUN
```

CLEAR

This is a system command which orders the computer to clear the work area. The work area refers to those parts of computer storage which are currently being used for this programmer and this program.

In our statement 10 (the READ statement), we have identified our variables as *W, X, Y,* and *Z*. The DATA statement, number 20, gives the values, in order, for the items listed in the READ statement. So in this particular case, *W* is 100, *X* is 200, *Y* is 300, and *Z* is 400. Using the same variable names in the READ statement, we could at some later time substitute a different DATA statement with different values, and these would be assigned, in order.

The logic of the situation is as follows:

1. The READ statement gives the number of variables to be used and

names them for the computer. The computer will assign storage locations to the names so we can, in the future, refer to them by name without bothering to know the details of their storage.

2. The DATA statement provides the values for the variables in the order in which they are listed. That is, the order of names in the READ statement matches the order we intend with the DATA statement.
3. The LET statement uses these variables in its calculations and stores the final result at a place we have named U.

READ $v_1, v_2, v_3, \ldots, v_n$

v is a variable name.

Each named variable is assigned, in order, the values in the data list of the DATA statement.

The mode of the name of the variable, and the mode of the values to be stored in those locations, should be the same.

DATA $c_1, c_2, c_3, \ldots, c_n$

c is a numeric constant or a literal constant.

While the program is being compiled, a data table will be compiled by BASIC. This table takes the values of the DATA statement in the order of their appearance in the DATA statement. The READ statement assumes these values and matches them to the variable names.

Any literal constant we have which contains no characters is assumed to be made up of 18 blanks.

Any literal constant with less than 18 characters is padded by blanks on the right.

Any literal constant with more than 18 characters is truncated (chopped off) on the right.

Our PRINT USING statement means exactly what it says. We are going to print using the image or format control of a special statement identified by the colon. You will note that statement 50 in our sample program is just such an image or format statement. In it we plan out how we want the output data to look when the computer has completed its calculations.

PRINT USING n [$,f_1, f_2, f_3, \ldots, f_n$]

n represents the number of the image statement in the program that is to be used as a guide for the PRINT USING statement.

f may be an expression, a literal constant, or an alphameric variable.

Each field of the PRINT USING statement is going to be edited to fit the image we lay out in the ":" statement. Again, the two items (those in the PRINT USING and those in the image statement) are matched, in order.

When we have more print fields than images (that is, wish to use the same image for all of our output fields), the carriage is returned and the images are reused. If we have more images than fields, the print line is ended when the first unneeded format specification occurs.

The printer carriage is always automatically returned before any edited line is printed.

There are conversion rules:

The data are edited *into* the PRINT line replacing the special signals in the image statement.

If the edited data are briefer than the image, blanks are inserted on the right.

If the edited data are longer than the image, items on the right are chopped off to fit.

If the data are positive and the image has a plus sign, such a sign will appear in the print line. If the data are negative and the image has a negative sign, such a sign will appear in the print line. If the data are positive and the image has a negative sign, a blank will appear in the print line in place of the negative sign in the image. If the data are negative and the image has no sign, a minus sign will be added to the print line. (In this latter case, one would lose a digit chopped off on the right to make room for the negative sign on the left.)

"I" format will convert any decimal fraction to an integer by lopping off the fraction part (beyond the decimal) regardless of fraction part value.

"F" format will cause any value to be in fixed-point mode. A fraction would be rounded or filled in with zeros, depending upon field size specifications.

"E" format converts items to floating-point, one decimal digit to the left of decimal point, rounding the fraction or filling to the right with zeros, depending upon the image in the image statement.

If the field to be printed out is larger (in terms of positions) than the image, asterisks are placed in the output line instead of the data.

: $C_1S_1C_2S_2 \ldots C_nS_n$

This is the general form of the image statement.

: identifies the type of statement it is.

c is a character string.

s is a conversion specification.

The image statement may describe a single line of print, though the statement may be reused.

A character string ("c" in the general form) may include any available character with the exception of "#" which has other uses.

"I" format is made up of optional sign followed by one or more # symbols. (This is the "s" in the general form of the : statement.)

"F" format is made up of optional sign followed by one or more # symbols, *and* a decimal point, and one or more additional # characters.

"E" format is made up of optional sign, one or more # symbols, and four ! (exclamation points). The ! symbols represent places for the E (indicating exponent), a sign, and the exponent itself.

SAMPLE PROGRAM

We will now try to understand the basic functions of the FOR statement and of the NEXT statement. To assist in the matter, we will use another small program as follows:

```
CLEAR
READY
10  READ W, X, Y, Z
20  DATA 100, 200, 300, 400
30  FOR N = 1 TO 5
40  LET E = W + X + Y * N + Z
50  PRINT USING 60, N, E
60  : IF N # THEN E IS ####
70  NEXT N
80  END
RUN
```

If the above program is run, the effective printout should be:

```
12:15        11/21/78        IMD        SJ

IF N 1 THEN E IS 1000
IF N 2 THEN E IS 1600
IF N 3 THEN E IS 2800
```

IF N 4 THEN E IS 2800
IF N 5 THEN E IS 3400

FOR v = x_1 TO x_2 [STEP x_3]

v is a numeric variable.

x is an expression.

x_1 is the initial value of the variable "v."

x_2 is the limit of the range of the variable "v." This cannot be exceeded.

As *v* is altering it may be used as a subscript (as in an array reference).

One may construct a branching instruction to leave a FOR loop before the maximum count is reached. This should be done only by experienced programmers and, even then, carefully.

If we wish to increase the value of x_1 by one each time in the program repetition (loop), we may omit STEP x_3.

Now that we've explored some of the basic rules for the FOR statement, let us apply it to statement 30 in our small program above. The general form was "FOR v= x_1 TO x_2 [STEP x_3]. We converted that to:

30 FOR N = 1 TO 5

So, our "v" is the variable *N*. We have started *N* with an initial value of 1 (our x_1 in the general statement). We have set a limit of 5, which is not to be exceeded (the x_2) in our general statement. We have decided to increment from one to five by ones so we could skip STEP x_3. But if we want to go up by twos (make the "1" trip through the loop, the "3" trip through the loop, and the "5" trip through the loop —three times through), we would have had to specify the STEP thus: 30 FOR N = 1 TO 5 STEP 2. Using the increment of 2, we would only be able to go through the loop three times before the 5 (test value) was reached or not permitted to be exceeded.

NEXT v

The NEXT statement marks the end of the sequence of instructions that are to be repeated.

v represents the variable that is the counter in the associated FOR statement.

The associated FOR statement is the FOR statement that is *numbered* in such a way that it precedes the NEXT statement in terms of the actual execution of the program. (At least, beginners should believe that.) And the associated FOR statement is the one that contains the indexed quantity being altered.

In our next sample program we want to introduce you to the DIM (dimension) statement, which is used to handle arrays. This will give us a chance to explore a pair of additional FOR statements and their use. And it will give us an opportunity to make use of what we call subscripted variables—B(L) as an example.

SAMPLE PROGRAM

```
CLEAR
READY
 10  DIM B(10)
 20  DATA 2, 4, 6, 8, 10, 1, 3, 5, 7, 9
 30  FOR L = 1 TO 10
 40  READ B(L)
 50  LET B(L) = B(L)↑2
 60  NEXT L
 70  FOR L = 1 TO 10 STEP 2
 80  PRINT USING 90, L, B(L)
 90  :B(#) SQUARED IS ###
100  NEXT L
110  END
RUN
```

Let us imagine, in this case, that we are the computer following, step by step, the instructions which are given above.

CLEAR: The computer clears the work area.

READY: The computer informs the programmer it is ready to receive a BASIC program.

10 DIM B(10): The computer is asked to set aside space for an array named B, which is to have ten elements in it.

20 DATA 2, 4, 6, 8, 10, 1, 3, 5, 7, 9: The computer is advised of ten data items which are to be put away, in order as advised by a subsequent READ statement.

30 FOR L = 1 TO 10: The computer is advised there is an integer variable which is to range in value from a starting value of one to an ending value of ten. The increment each time is to be one. So the changing values will be 1, 2, 3, and so on.

40 READ B(L): Since L is currently 1 because of the FOR statement above, the computer will read in item B(1).

50 LET B(L) = B(L)↑12: The computer is told to square the value it finds at B(1) and to store this new value at B(1). (Remember destructive read-in from the main text?)

60 NEXT L: The computer is effectively told to go back to the READ statement where the variable (L) first appears to repeat the steps of reading, calculating, and storing for item B(2). And a full circle is run for that item. So it will go for the full ten items in the array.

Actually, the computer instructions will not be put together inside the computer in quite this way, but we, as programmers, only need to understand the *logical* steps of the program we have written, not the necessary peculiarities of the actual computer language.

When L has reached the value of ten and the tenth squared item has been put away in the array, the work of the loop is completed and the computer would drop down to the next instruction below statement 60. Here it would find:

70 FOR L = 1 TO 10 STEP 2: The computer is told to set an initial value of L to one (it was ten when the computer dropped out of the first loop). And the computer is advised that the increment in the value of L is now to be by twos (not one). This means L will become 1, 3, and so on until 10 is reached or exceeded (which would mean an exit from the loop when L is actually done with the 9 sequence).

80 PRINT USING 90,L,B(L): The second instruction following the FOR is to print out an L and a B(L) according to the format image statement number 90.

90 :B(#) SQUARED IS ###: The image statement says print B and then the particular L value (which in the first instance would be 1), and then the B(1) value (which has been squared and would be 4).

100 NEXT L: Having done one item, the computer is required to go back in the loop and do the same printing for another item (it would not be B(2), however, but B(3)

because the increment in the controlling FOR statement (the STEP) is 2, not 1.

110 END: When the computer has completed the job of printing the five items called for (1, 3, 5, 7, 9), the program ends.

RUN: The RUN statement will cause the computer to begin execution of the program as the programmer finishes at the teletype.

The result of the computer's effort in the execution of this particular BASIC program should be something like the following:

```
13:50        11/21/78        IMD        SJ

B(1) SQUARED IS   4
B(3) SQUARED IS  36
B(5) SQUARED IS 100
B(7) SQUARED IS   9
B(9) SQUARED IS  49
```

Now that we have traveled through the program in a pattern similar to that which the computer could be said to follow, we can have a look at the general form of the DIM statement.

DIM a_1 (d_{11}[,d_{12}]),a_2(,d_{21}[,d_{22}]), . . . ,a_n(d_{n1}[,d_{n2}])

a is an array name.

d is a positive integer.

The DIM statement will allocate storage space for the named array. This statement is a compound statement, in that we may name several arrays and give the size statement for each in turn. d_{11} represents the first dimension. If one array were named, as in our example, and it had only one dimension, the DIM a_1 (d_{11}[d_{12}]) would be simply B(10). The second item [,d_{12}] is optional and may be left out, which is logical. But suppose our array happened to be a ten by ten array. Then we would have B(10,10).

If we have a subscripted variable name (say C(2)) in a program and didn't make a DIM statement, then the computer assumes, by implication, that such a one-dimensional array exists and that it *automatically* will be assumed to have ten members.

If an array name has been implicitly declared, it *cannot* appear in a DIM statement.

If the program contained an implicit array because of a subscripted variable of the form C(2,4), then the computer assumes an array named C with two dimensions (of 10 each) and would reserve space for 100 items automatically. Again, this two-dimensional implicit array could not appear in a DIM statement.

GETTING OUT OF SEQUENCE

We can use four related statements in BASIC to leave the normal program execution sequence. Normal sequence, of course, is moving from one numbered statement to the next higher numbered statement in order. But there are times when we would like to leave such a sequence—for instance, when a test of some kind is made and the condition of the test is met.

Now that we are somewhat familiar with generalized BASIC statements and how to interpret them, we will give the rules for each of the generalized statement forms in turn.

GOTO s

s is a statement number.

This is an unconditional branch instruction. That is, the computer has no choice when it encounters this statement but to go to the statement number represented by *s*. No tests of any kind are made.

GOTO $S_1, s_2, \ldots, s_n$ ON x

s is a statement number. Normally, if there is more than one such number, the numbers would be separated by commas.

x is an expression of some kind. That is, *x* represents some arithmetic maneuver, such as adding, subtracting, multiplying, dividing, and similar quantities to get an arithmetic result.

x can take on any value from 1 to *n*, where *n* is construed to be the maximum number *of* (not the statement number itself) statements following the GOTO word. So if we had listed five statement numbers (separated by commas) after the GOTO, we would know that the result of the expression the program is manipulating should be either 1, 2, 3, 4, or 5.

We can see this computed GOTO (as this type of GOTO is called) permits many different choice paths out of the normal programming sequence.

IF x_1 r x_2 THEN s

x is an expression, alphameric variable, or literal constant.

r is a relational operator ($<, \leqslant, >, \geqslant, = \neq$).

x_2 is a literal constant, alphameric variable, or expression.

s is a statement number in the program.

A typical IF statement might be: 77 IF X < Y THEN 85. The IF statement itself is number 77. *X* is some value. If *X* is less than the value *Y* (remember that *X* and/or *Y* may be a complex expression, such as

A−B*C), then the computer goes to statement 85 for its next instruction. If X is not less than Y, the computer goes on in the program to the statement immediately following the IF statement. (Assuming the next statement in the program is, in fact, the next highest *numbered* statement.)

The BASIC word GOTO could be substituted for the word THEN in the IF statement without causing any change in the performance of the statement.

If x_1 is an expression, x_2 must also be an expression (we don't permit mode mixing). And if x_1 is a literal constant so must x_2 be. And if x_1 is an alphameric variable then x_2 must be one, too.

GOSUB and RETURN are two related BASIC statements which will permit the program to construct a program that may leave a sequence and proceed to a specific statement elsewhere and then return to one of the program statements in a list of statements. Let us give the rules and then use an abstract example of what we have in mind.

GOSUB s

s is a statement number.

RETURN [c]

c is an optional character which we may use in order to identify the particular RETURN statement.

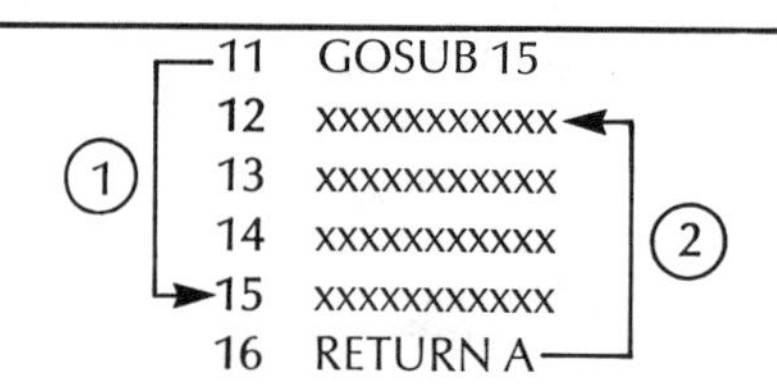

The computer moves to statement 11 and discovers a GOSUB statement, which causes the computer to do two things: (1) to save, in a special list, the instruction number which followed the GOSUB (there may be other statement numbers), and (2) to branch out of sequence to statement 15. When statement 15 has been executed, the RETURN A statement is encountered. This sends the computer back to statement 12, and this statement number is removed from the list of GOSUBs. The computer continues in the program.

This has to be a short appendix, or one could explore a number of different GOSUB and RETURN combinations of great complexity. Perhaps the best thing to do is to construct a few sample programs of your own at the terminal and experiment for results.

INPUT STATEMENTS

We have met READ and DATA as input statements earlier in this appendix. We now need to recognize that there are other input statements: GET, INPUT, RESTORE, and RESET.

INPUT $v_1, v_2, \ldots, v_n$

v is a variable.

An INPUT statement, when it is encountered, will cause a question mark to appear at the terminal (during the program run). You, as the terminal operator, must type in the variables listed in the order you wish them to be identified by the variable names you have given them in the INPUT statement.

Naturally, the number of values you type must match the number of variables you have named. And the type of data must match the mode of the variable (remember to check on the construction of variable names earlier).

Literal constants, in the case of the INPUT statement, do not require quote marks unless the literal itself contains a comma. (We don't want to confuse BASIC.)

RESTORE [c]

c is any character we wish.

The RESTORE statement will see to it that the computer will read in the first element in a DATA statement in the program by executing the next READ statement.

RESET [c]

c is any character.

RESET has the same effect as RESTORE, but a file is used rather than a DATA statement.

When a GET statement follows a RESET statement, information is gathered beginning with the first item in an input file.

GET $v_1, v_2, \ldots, v_n$

v is a variable.

However many variables are called for, they are retrieved from the input file. Again, the names of the variables must match the types of data in the file (modes must match).

The program will stop if there are not enough values in the file to fill out the list of variable names given.

The file from which the GET statement will retrieve information is usually about 858 (or our standard size) per block. We need the name of the file and the number of blocks the file contains when such a file is created by a PUT statement. And we must issue a system command about how to create the file in the first place.

Let us immediately deal with the matter of output statements so we can consider this business of the files.

OUTPUT STATEMENTS

Our output statements are PRINT, PRINT USING, and PUT. We are already familiar with PRINT and PRINT USING (which are terminal operations when we are providing, through the terminal, the data for the program). We can, then, turn our attention to PUT.

PUT $v_1, v_2, \ldots, v_n$

Again, *v* is a variable.

A PUT statement must be used with an OUTFILE (a system command, not a program instruction) statement that names the file and declares the number of blocks in the file. Typically, we might write: OUTFILE BO,1. This would mean we want a file named BO created, which had a single block in it of 858 items (for Call 360 BASIC—one of the BASIC systems).

Later, when we want to use the file BO in a program, we would require another system command called INFILE. It would take the form of: INFILE BO. We could then proceed as described in our GET statement.

We will deal with all of the system commands at the end of this appendix in an orderly way.

For various reasons you might wish, as a programmer, to stop your program midway in execution. There are two BASIC instructions which can serve this purpose:

PAUSE [c . . .]

c is any character (which you might wish to use to identify the particular PAUSE statement).

The terminal will print out a message, at the time of the pause, "PAUSE" at line *n* (where *n* is the statement number of the PAUSE statement itself (remember all *instructions* in BASIC must be numbered).

If the terminal carriage is returned following the PAUSE (an action of the programmer), the program will continue.

STOP [c . . .]

c is any character.

The program execution is *terminated* when the STOP command is encountered in the program.

MATRIX ARITHMETIC

BASIC permits matrix arithmetic. We define a matrix as a two-dimensional array. The DIM statement is used to define any matrices we intend to use in our program. When writing a DIM statement, you should make the matrix or matrices the largest sizes you will need. Later, you may make them smaller by putting a size limit in subscript forms attached to the matrix name. Only the CON, IDN, ZER, MAT GET, and MAT READ statements allow this *redimensioning* of the original stated sizes of matrices.

Let us now take our matrix statements one at a time and define what they can do:

MAT $m_1 = m_2 + m_3$

Matrix m_2 is added to m_3 and the result of the addition (for each and every matching item in the matrices will be stored in matrix order in m_1.

Matrices must obviously match or the arithmetic cannot be performed. That is, they should have the same dimensions.

MAT $m_1 = m_2 * m_3$

m is a matrix (name).

The elements in m_2 and m_3 are multiplied item by item (that is, each item in the same relative position) and the results are stored in m_1.

MAT $m_1 = (x) * m_2$

m is a matrix.

x is an expression.

Matrices must be conformable; that is, they must match in size and shape.

In the case above, each element in the m_1 matrix would be replaced by the result of the arithmetic expression times the equivalent element in m_2.

MAT $m_1 = m_2 - m_3$

m is a matrix.

The equivalent item in m_3 is subtracted from the equivalent element in m_2 and the result is stored in the equivalent matrix position in m_1.

MAT m = ZER[(d_1,d_2)]

m is a matrix.

d is a subscript. (In some cases, *d* may be an expression which results in a value which is a subscript).

In general, this instruction will zero a matrix.

MAT m_1 = TRN(m_2)

m is a matrix.

m_1 cannot be the same matrix as m_2.

m_2 is transposed into m_1.

MAT m = CON [(d_1,d_2)]

m is a matrix.

d is an expression (result of which is a subscript).

The elements of the matrix are turned to the value of 1.

MAT m = IDN [(d_1,d_2)]

m is a matrix.

m assumes the form of an identity matrix.

MAT READ m_1[(d_{11},d_{12})], m_2 [(d_{21},d_{22})], . . . , m_n [(d_{n1},d_{n2})]

or

MAT GET m_1 [(d_{11},d_{12})], m_2 [(d_{21},d_{22})], . . . , m_n [(d_{n1},d_{n2})]

In both these statements (the one with input data, the other from a file), we can get all of the matrix elements read in by *rows* from either the DATA statement (the READ) or a file (the GET).

If the DATA statement or the file is emptied before the matrix is filled, the program terminates.

MAT PRINT $m_1t_1m_2t_2 \ldots m_n[t_n]$

or

MAT PUT $m_1, m_2, \ldots, m_n$

m is a matrix.

t is a comma or semicolon terminator.

The terminator takes care of carriage position as described in PRINT.

Literal strings are not allowed.

A terminating blank will be treated as a comma.

In the case of PRINT, we are bringing a matrix out at the terminal. The elements will be printed out in order *by row.* If the row exceeds the line length, a second line will be printed out, or as many additional lines as are required.

The PUT statement, of course, puts the matrix away in a file.

REM c . . .

We can make remarks all through our programs by using the REM statement. *c* represents any character or set of characters.

Typically, we might use something like:

```
11 REM   THIS STATEMENT IS A  REMARK STATEMENT
```

SYSTEM COMMANDS

Earlier we mentioned that the programmer could talk to BASIC and the computer through a collection of system commands, as distinguished from program statements (the elements of the program we are writing that we want the computer to follow).

Program statements are always numbered and executed in the number order. System commands, on the other hand, are not numbered and are issued when we want the computer to perform a specific kind of duty.

ALLOW *program name*

Program name is the name of the program which was saved and protected, hence the command allows the removal of the program protection in a library.

Program names must be eight characters or less and must begin with a letter of the extended alphabet.

When this command is executed, the particular program may now be generally listed as available to inquirers of library contents.

CATALOG

A list of the user's library programs will be printed.

When libraries are classified as one-star (*) (a library to be shared on a limited basis) or two-star (**) (a library submitted by the terminal user but available to all terminal users), or three-star library (***) (the computer center library available to all users) we can indicate the classification thus:

CATALOG*
CATALOG**
CATALOG***

CATALOG ALL

A list of user programs will be printed. Included in the list will be the program name, the type of file, the program language used, the size of the program, the days since the program was last used, and the number of storage units required.

CLEAR

The work area will be cleared by the execution of this system command.

DELETE *statement number, . . . , statement number*

Type the statement numbers in ascending order and they will be deleted from the program under construction.

If you wish to delete a complete series use the form:

DELETE statement number THRU statement number

The computer will reply READY when deletions have been made.

ECHO (some sequence of characters, letters, or numbers)

The computer will enter the characters being typed at the terminal and then type them out. You may check up to 76 characters.

ENTER *language name*

Choices for language name are BASIC (short-form arithmetic) or BASICL (long-form arithmetic).

The system command will remain effective until another ENTER system command is given in the program.

EXTRACT *statement number, . . . , statement number*

The statements specified above by number will be put in a work area. All the other statements in the program will be deleted.

Alternate form:

EXTRACT statement number THRU statement number

INFILE *file name*

A file previously put away becomes the input for the current program.

File names must be no more than eight characters and must begin with an alphabetic term *A* through *Z* (the limited alphabet). The rest of the name may consist of digits or the extended alphabet.

An infile cannot be an outfile in the same program.

KEY

When a paper tape command TAPE (for loading a program has been given) and one now wants to return to the terminal for input, the system command KEY is used.

LIST (or LIST *statement number*)

All of the program in the work area will be listed if the simple LIST command is used.

If LIST *statement number* is used, this will cause all of the program following the statement number given to be listed from the work area.

LIST-NO-HEADER

A list will be produced but with no headings.

LOAD *program name*

The name is in the user's program library.

The program is placed in the work area of the computer.

You may use the forms:

LOAD* *program name*
LOAD** *program name . .*
LOAD*** *program name*

The star forms would properly indicate the type of program sought.

Any associated data file will also be loaded into the work area.

LOCK *program name*
LOCK *file name*

Prevents destruction of library programs—puts them under protection.

The program cannot be deleted accidentally.

LOGON

Permits the use of another identity number. Computer prints OFF and you may now issue a new identity number and password and proceed.

These changes are made without disconnecting the terminal from the computer. (Some terminal users have more than one identity number and password, since they are authorized to work on different jobs.)

MERGE *main program, subprogram* 1, *statement number* before insertion . . . , *subprogram* 8, *statement number* before insertion

Eight or fewer subprograms can be merged into a main program.

Total size of all programs combined cannot be larger than 452 statements in some BASIC systems.

All programs named must already be in the user's library.

Insertion of subprograms comes after the typed statement number into the main program. If no statement number is given as a guide, the subprogram will appear at the end of the main program.

At the completion of the merge, all statements will be renumbered starting at 100 and raised statement by statement by 10.

NAME *program name*

A name (as given) will be assigned to the program in the work area.

Names must start with an alphabetic letter.

OFF

The terminal is disconnected from the computer.

The amount of processing time and total terminal time will be printed out.

On some terminals an OFF switch also must be flipped.

OUTFILE *file name, length*

This system command will create an outfile in a program.

The PUT statement is required to assign data to the file.

File name must begin with an alphabetic letter.

A PUT statement is a program that will require an OUTFILE command also in the program.

There will be special rules for each type of BASIC and of computer system in the matter of the size of files and file items.

PASSWORD

This system command is used to establish a password.

Passwords generally may be up to eight characters and may be constructed of any combination of numbers, letters, and special characters, including blanks.

POOL* *program name*

This command will cause a named one-star program to be stored in such a way as to permit sharing with other terminal users.

The program must be a program already stored in the user's library.

POOL** *program name*

This command will cause a named two-star program to be stored in such a way as to permit sharing with other terminal users.

The program must be a program already stored in the user's library.

PROTECT *program name*

This command bars any other terminal user from listing or saving this program, which is in the library.

The program must have been a previously saved program.

PULL* *program name*

The one-star program is removed from the library.

Only the terminal user who pooled the program in the first place can pull it.

PULL** *program name*

The two-star program is removed from the library.

Only the terminal user who pooled the program in the first place can pull it.

PURGE *program name*

The named program is deleted from the user's library unless it is a locked program.

The program name must be a valid one—in the user's library.

RENUMBER *new statement number, old statement number, increment*

A new number is given to an old statement as listed, and later statements are numbered according to the amount of increment specified.

RUN *program name*

The named program is loaded, compiled, and executed from the user's library of programs.

Files attached to the program will be brought up also when the RUN system command is executed.

Shared library forms are:

RUN* *program name*
RUN** *program name*
RUN*** *program name*

System will respond "PROGRAM NOT SAVED" if the program is not in the specified library.

RUN

The RUN command alone (without a named program) will cause the program currently in the work area to be executed.

Program name, time, date, and results are printed.

SAVE

The program in which the SAVE occurs will be placed in the user's library.

STATUS

Information will be printed about the program in the work area.

Terminal time and processing time consumed will be specified.
Order of information provided is usually: Terminal Number, User Number, Program Name, Program Length, Language Name, Infile Name, Outfile Name, Terminal Time, Processor Time.

TAPE

Program to be loaded is read from the punched paper tape unit of the teletype.
The command KEY must be given to return the terminal to normal usage.

UNLOCK *program name*

Protection is removed from the program.
Program must be in the library.

UNLOCK *file name*

Protection is removed from the file item.
Program must be in the file.

WIDTH *number of print positions*

The width of a print line is established. Limits are from about 18 through 255 for most systems.
The teletype *actually* has a 72 position line.

ERRORS

When you are initially using a terminal, or if you are experienced but inattentive, you will often receive such error messages from the terminal as:

"INVALID LITERAL CONSTANT"
"OBJECT PROGRAM TOO LARGE"
"TOO MANY IMAGE STATEMENTS"

In other words, BASIC is going to talk to you about the programs you have constructed—so you can make such corrections as required. In many cases you will be given the statement number in which the error occurs.

You should find a catalog of error messages and their full explanations near the terminal where you are working. Also, you usually will find a list of all the standard or special library programs available—by name and what they do.

The following is one final sample program. The programmer is going to establish an outfile for use at some later time. The program is so constructed that the computer will ask the terminal operator to type in the requested values. These will then be put away, in order, in the file named.

Notice that in the program the IF statement is used to determine whether 500 items have been put away. If so, the program will stop. If not, the terminal user will receive requests for more values.

```
CLEAR
READY
100 INPUT U, V, W, X, Y, Z
200 PUT U, V, W, X, Y, Z
300 IF U+V+W+X+Y < 500 THEN 100
400 END
OUTFILE BOSH
READY
RUN
?
```

The question mark at the terminal indicates that the computer is in the process of executing the program and requires the items of data for the file BOSH.

SUMMARY

It simply isn't possible for most people to read an appendix like this one and then proceed to a terminal and successfully construct and run a program in BASIC. Because of space limitations, *that* simply could not be the purpose of this appendix. Actually, all that has been attempted is to give you enough information to pique your curiosity and make you either find a suitable full book on BASIC or go to a terminal and, with the assistance of one of the laboratory people, attempt a simple program or two. If you do this, you may get enchanted with the usefulness of the computer. And you will gain something from the kind of interrelationship between computer and user that no amount of words can actually describe.

The two texts listed under "Readings" should help you get started properly. Or your own nearby installation may have a preferred, but shorter, work which you could use.

READINGS

Diehr, George. *Business Programming with BASIC*. New York: John Wiley and Sons, 1972. A Wiley–Becker and Hayes Publication.

This is a programmed learning type of book that will take you step by step through many of the fundamentals of BASIC. It is an almost painless way to learn.

Hare, van Court, Jr. *Introduction to Programming: A Basic Approach*. New York: Harcourt, Brace & World, 1970.

This is a more complete work about BASIC, which will give you a short history of the computer, the fundamentals, and a full treatment of programming in BASIC.

APPENDIX B

GLOSSARY

This is not intended to be a complete, precise, and technical glossary of the many terms in the computer field. Rather, we have selected those common words used in the field and have tried to give them simple and understandable definitions. In our definitions we seek understanding with as much precision as we can muster. It would be a pleasant world if precision guaranteed understanding, but alas, that is not always the case.

We used words like *culture* and *civilization* in the text. While these terms were necessary in the book, they are not computer terms and hence will not appear in this glossary. Many complete glossaries of a technical nature are available from computer manufacturers and also from the American Standards Association. If you are interested in these, you will probably find them at your local school library.

abacus: a mechanism made up of beads, wires, and a wooden frame designed to perform calculations by moving the beads along the rods and using them as counters and memory aids

access arm: a physical device on a storage unit (such as a magnetic disk pack) which moves the reading and writing unit above an appropriate track (or tracks)

access method: the technique (or techniques) used to transfer data from main storage to input/output devices

access time: the time it takes to move data from storage to some other point, such as registers (internally) or output devices (externally) and the reverse

accumulator: a section of storage or a register in which the results of arithmetic or logic operations are built up

address: the reference location of a datum or a register in storage; a numeric or symbolic reference to some storage location or set of storage locations

address modification: the act or process of altering the address part of a computer instruction by means of other computer instructions

ADP: Automatic Data Processing

algorith: a collection of rules used to solve a problem in some finite number of operations

alphameric: a term used to describe any symbol set, which may include letters, numerical digits, and special characters

arithmetic operation: generally refers to the binary operations of addition, subtraction, multiplication, and division, and also the operations of negation and absolute value

arithmetic unit: the section of a computer or set of circuits in which the arithmetic operations are performed

assemble: to prepare a machine-language program from a symbolic-language program

automatic computer: a machine which performs operations under the direction of an internal program

automation: a systematic combination of mechanical and intellectual devices to make some machine complex self-activating and self-controlling

batch processing: a method of dealing with data in which a number of similar input items are collected for processing during a single computer run

binary: two-state

binary code: any code which uses two characters (0 and 1)

binary coded decimal: the binary number system represented in some special coded form

binary number system: a system using the equivalent of the decimal integer two as a base

bit: a computer colloquial which means "binary digit"

block: any unit made up of characters or words

block diagram: a diagrammatic representation of a computer program

branch: to leave any normal sequence of instructions based on a specific command or the result of some particular test condition

buffer: any device which acts as an intermediary between any two other devices, particularly when the devices operate at different internal speeds.

byte: any collection of binary bits which are treated as a datum

card code: those combinations of holes which represent characters in a punched card (on magnetic cards, the combination of small magnetic fields rather than holes)

card column: a vertical line of punching positions on a punched card

card field: a set number of card columns which have been assigned to a datum

card punch: any device to record information in cards by punching holes in the card to represent some character

card reader: any device which can sense and translate the card code into internal computer code or external printable copy

card row: one of the horizontal lines of punching positions on a punched card

cathrode ray tube: a vacuum tube which is used for some form of visual display

cell: a location (usually inside the computer or one of its storage media)

central processing unit: the collection of mechanisms in the computer which control the execution of instructions

channel: any path along which signals can be sent from one device to one or more other devices, or the reverse

character: any one of a set of elementary signals or symbols (alphabetic character, number, special symbol)

character density: the number of characters which can be recorded in any given space (per inch, and the like)

character reader: a device which reads printed characters directly from a document

character set: a list of the characters which can be coded for a specific computer or similar device

clear: to convert the contents of any storing units to zeros or blanks

closed routine: a routine which acts as an independent unit and can be entered by some basic linkage instructions from a main routine or program

COBOL: *CO*mmon *B*usiness *O*riented *L*anguage; a business-oriented compiler language

code: a meanful representation of any character or group of characters

collate: to merge two uniformly ordered sets of data into a single data unit

command: an instruction related to a channel operation or to a macro computer instruction

common carrier: a company which has been recognized by a regulatory agency as furnishing communication services

common language: any language which can be used by a group of computers or computer equipment

compile: to prepare a machine-language program from a program written in some symbolic forms, usually not on a one-to-one translation basis

computer program: a set of instructions linked in such a way as to describe completely the operations required to solve a particular problem or subproblem

conditional transfer: a branch that occurs upon a certain condition which is tested before the transfer is made

console: the equipment which makes possible direct contact between the computer operator and the computer

constant: a fixed datum

control program: usually any program which manages the resources of the computer in an internal and semiautomatic way

control volume: a volume which contains the indexes of information stored in other volumes or media

CPU: Central *P*rocessing *U*nit

cybernetics: the study of communication and control among various combinations of machines and people

data processing: any manipulation of data by programmed or planned means

data processing system: usually any combination of machines and techniques used to manipulate data in an orderly way

data set: any major block or collection of data in storage which is accessible by means of some key or identifier

data-phone: an AT&T designation of a group of devices which can transmit data over telephone channels

debug: to remove mistakes from a program or routine or to eliminate mechanical or electronic computer malfunctions

deck: a set of punched cards

destructive reading: any reading procedure which destroys that which has been read

digit: a single character; usually 0–9, A–Z, and any special symbols, such as $, #, and the like

digital computer: a computer capable of solving problems by working with discrete data

direct access: retrieval or storage of data by its specific location in a volume (or on a storage device)

disk storage: a storage device making use of magnetic recording on flat, high-speed, rotating disks

display: any representation of graphic data

display tube: cathode ray tube on which information is represented

downtime: usually that portion of operation-assigned time wherein the computer is not functioning due to mechanical failure

dump: a massive output of data, usually the contents of an entire storage unit or a large segment of same

edp: electronic *d*ata *p*rocessing

electronic data processing: the manipulation of data by electronic means

event: an occurrence, usually one which is of importance to some activity

executive routine: a supervisory program which controls the operations of other programs

external storage: any storage device outside the physical confines of the computer as such

feedback: usually, feeding into the system itself information regarding the effectiveness of the system's operation as against some preset standard

field: usually refers to a complete datum in storage or column(s) on cards representing a single datum (e.g., social security number)

file: any collection of records the items of which are ordered and labeled

flowchart: a representation in graphic form of the definition, or analysis, or methods of solution of a problem in which symbols are used to stand for data, operations, direction, and particular equipment

FORTRAN: *FOR*mula *TRAN*slating system; a scientific compiler language

garbage: meaningless information or meaningless computer output

gulp: a group of bytes

hard copy: usually printed copy or photographic copy of computer output

hardware: the physical mechanisms which make up a computer system

heuristic: any process or program which presents the opportunity for a variety of solutions

hierarchy: some specified rank order

housekeeping: any operations in a program which are oriented to putting the program back into operating shape for the next sequence of operations

index: usually a table in some catalog arrangement

inline processing: the handling of data in the order of arrival rather than by grouping at the conclusion of some time period

input area: an area in internal computer storage into which data are initially transmitted from some reading (or other external) device

instruction: a single element of a program; usually some single mathematic or logical operation

instruction format: the structure of an instruction in terms of the allocation of bits or characters to some specific function (such as operation code, address, and so on)

internal storage: storage within the computer proper; usually high-speed, random access computer storage

I/O: *I*nput/*O*utput

iterate: to repeat any sequence of instructions

job: usually any set of activities or instructions which permit the completion of performance unit, such as payroll, or updating a library of information, and the like

job control statement: any statement which identifies a job to be done by the computer or which defines the requirements for the job to be done

key: that part of a word, record, or file which is the word, record, or file identifier (label)

label: a code name for a document, such as a complete computer file or record

leased-line network: any network reserved for the exclusive use of a customer

librarian: usually a program for creating, maintaining, and finding items in a large data collection on file in the computer system

library routine: a debugged routine housed in a computer library which may be worked into any larger routine at will

literal: any symbol which names itself

location: an addressable storage position

loop: a series of instructions that constitute a circular program part from which an exit can be made only upon some testable condition

machine instruction: an instruction in numerical form which can be executed by the computer

macro: an acronym for macro instruction

macro instruction: a term used for a macro instruction statement, which is a statement the translation of which results in several machine-language instructions; a representation of several computer-executable instructions

magnetic ink: ink imbedded with particles of magnetic substance which can be detected by automatic reading devices

main frame: the main part of the computer (sometimes synonymous with cpu)

main storage: usually, addressable internal computer storage

mark-sense: to mark positions on a card or paper with an electrically conductive pencil lead so that it can be read by an appropriate sensing machine

mass storage: usually any large collection of information recorded on an auxiliary online storage medium, such as drum or disk pack

master file: a major reference file of information

memory: generally, this term is used to mean internal computer storage

merge: to combine; to convert two ordered files of information to a single ordered file

MICR: *M*agnetic *I*nk *C*haracter *R*ecognition

microprogramming: the act of putting together a computer program in actual machine-language instruction form

microsecond: one millionth of a second

object language: the term usually means an executable computer language

offline: not connected directly to the computer

offline storage: computer storage devices not electronically connected to the computer

one-for-one: usually, a term referring to the fact that an assembler will translate assembler-language instructions into machine-language instructions item by item

online: subject to control by the computer

online storage: those devices directly connected to the computer and subject to the computer's control

operating system: any combination of software and hardware which, when combined, turn the computer system into a working unit

operation code: a symbolic or numeric representation of a computer operation

optical scanning: a technique for mechanically recognizing characters by their actual images

output: a data moved from internal storage of the computer to other media

overlay: a technique of repeatedly using some area of storage for reading-in information

parallel processing: concurrent execution of more than one program

pass: a run through the computer

peripheral equipment: auxiliary equipment in the computer room usually not directly connected to the computer in any way

primary storage: the main internal storage of the computer

printer: any device which produces hard copy

processor: the program or the equipment which converts a program from some symbolic language to machine language

program: a set of computer instructions which constitutes the plan for the solution of some problem; a sequential set of computer instructions

programmer: a person who prepares programs for a computer

programming: the art of reducing a plan or solution of a problem into a series of instructions for a computer, either symbolic or numeric

programming language: any group of special languages used to prepare computer programs

protected locations: usually areas in storage which can only be entered by a "key" (some special identifier)

punched card: a card of heavy paper stock in which holes may be punched in special code which is sensible to a machine

radix: the base of a number system

random access: the ability to read into or from any storage cell or group of cells in the internal storage by virtue of an identifier called an address

read: to transcribe information from an input device into an internal or some auxiliary storage

reader: any device capable of converting information from one form into another form

real time: the actual time during which a physical activity or process transpires

record: usually, a general term for any data unit which is different and identifiable as a unit

region: usually a group of machine addresses

register: any device which can store data, such as an instruction

report generation: producing complete reports from a set of rules which describe the input file and the format and content of the output report

rerun: to repeat a computer or machine run

routine: any sequence of machine instructions which will perform a function

row: usually refers to a horizontal configuration

scan: examination element by element, usually from high to low or low to high in a series of elements

seek: usually, the activity of a mechanism connected to cartridges or disks to find a track or datum

sequencing: ordering in a series of some kind

serial access: access to a datum by moving through some ordered data collection

service program: standard routine that will assist the computer system in some way

simplex channel: a channel which permits data movement in one direction

software: the support programs provided by the manufacturer to be used with the hardware of the computer to create a system capable of performing computing activities of various sorts

source language: any language that is an input to an assembler or compiler to produce a machine-language translation

special character: any recognizable character which is neither a digit nor an alphabetic character (for example, @, #)

statement: usually, a single instruction in symbolic form

step: usually, one instruction in a computer program

storage cell: the minimum unit of internal storage space in the computer or the minimum unit in any auxiliary storage device

string: any connected sequence of words, characters, or symbols

supervisor: usually, a control program which assists the computer with its operations and which controls such functions as scheduling and the like inside the computer

symbolic address: an address written in characters which must be translated before it can refer to an actual computer location

system library: usually, all the cataloged information at a computer installation that is in computer-usable form

tape: a linear medium used for storing information

telecommunication: usually, communication by electromagnetic systems

teletype: trademark of Teletype Corporation used to denote its communication systems which have keyboards or tapes for sending and receiving information

throughput: a term used to describe the amount of information moved through a computer system

transfer: generally, it means leaving a routine or a program; same as branch

translator: any routine (or program) which can change information from one form to another

turn-around time: the amount of time it takes to get a job done at the computer center

unit record: usually, a punched or magnetic card

visual scanner: an optical scanning device that can deal with printed or written data

voice-grade channel: a channel with sufficient refinement to permit transmission of the human voice

word: usually, a set of characters which have a single addressable location and which will be treated as a single information unit

zone: usually, refers to the 12, 11, or 0 rows in the IBM or Hollerith card

INDEX

This book has been set in 10 and 9 point Optima, leaded 2 points. Chapter numbers are 12 and 30 point Optima and chapter titles are 24 point (small) Optima. The size of the type area is 26 by 46½ picas.

cost

- invasion of privacy
- takeover of human activities (intellectual + physical)

benefits

advanced info (problem solving)